The Fall of the
Athenian Empire

BY THE SAME AUTHOR

A New History of the Peloponnesian War
  The Outbreak of the Peloponnesian War
  The Archidamian War
  The Peace of Nicias and the Sicilian Expedition
  The Fall of the Athenian Empire

*The Great Dialogue: A History of Greek Political Thought from
  Homer to Polybius*
Great Issues in Western Civilization, editor with Brian Tierney
  and L. Pearce Williams
Problems in Ancient History, editor
Hellenic History, with G. W. Botsford and C. A. Robinson, Jr.
The End of the Roman Empire, editor
The Western Heritage, with Steven Ozment and Frank M.
  Turner
The Heritage of World Civilization, with Albert M. Craig,
  William A. Graham, Steven Ozment, and Frank M. Turner

The Fall of the Athenian Empire

DONALD KAGAN

Cornell University Press

ITHACA AND LONDON

Copyright © 1987 by Cornell University Press

First published 1987 by Cornell University Press.
First printing, Cornell Paperbacks, 1991.

International Standard Book Number 0-8014-1935-2 (cloth)
International Standard Book Number 0-8014-9984-4 (paper)
Library of Congress Catalog Card Number 86-32946

Printed in the United States of America

*Librarians: Library of Congress cataloging information
appears on the last page of the book.*

⊗ The paper in this book meets the minimum requirements
of the American National Standard for Information Sciences—
Permanence of Paper for Printed Library Materials, ANSI Z39.48-1984.

Cloth printing   10   9   8   7   6   5   4   3
Paperback printing   10   9   8   7   6   5   4

For Bob and Fred, the best of sons

Preface

This is the last volume of a history of the Peloponnesian War. It treats the period from the destruction of Athens' Sicilian expedition in September of 413 to the Athenian surrender in the spring of 404. Thucydides' history of the war is incomplete, and the eighth book, which breaks off abruptly in the year 411/10, is thought to be unfinished, and unpolished as well. In spite of the incompleteness of his account, his description and interpretation of the war inspire and shape this volume, as they have my earlier ones. The first volume attempted to evaluate his view of the causes and origins of the war as he expresses it in 1.23 and 1.88. The second one examined his assessment of Pericles' strategy in 2.65. The third one addressed his judgment of the Sicilian expedition set forth in the same passage and his estimate of the career of Nicias presented in 7.86.

Thucydides' judgment of the last part of the war appears in 2.65.12–13, at the end of his long eulogy of Pericles and his policies:

Yet after their defeat in Sicily, where they lost most of their fleet as well as the rest of their force, and faction had already broken out in Athens, they nevertheless held out for ten more years,[1] not only against their previous enemies and the Sicilians who joined them and most of their allies, who

[1] The figure given in the MSS is three years. For a defense of the emendation to ten, see *Thucydide, La guerre du peloponnèse*, II, ed. and trans. J. de Romilly (Paris, 1962), 101. A. W. Gomme (*HCT* II, 196–197) reviews the various other suggestions that have been put forth, which include keeping the three or emending it to five or eight, the last of which Gomme prefers. For our purposes here, the correct reading is not important, for no one doubts that Thucydides marvels at the Athenians' ability to hold out so long or that he attributes their defeat, in part at least, to internal strife.

rebelled against them, but also later against Cyrus, son of the Great King, who provided money to the Peloponnesians for a navy. Nor did they give in until they destroyed themselves by falling upon one another because of private quarrels.

This passage implies that even after the disaster in Sicily and the new problems it caused, Athens might still have avoided defeat but for internal dissension. A study of the last decade of the war enables us to evaluate Thucydides' interpretation of the reasons for Athens' defeat and the destruction of the Athenian Empire. It also makes possible an examination and evaluation of the performance of the Athenian democracy as it faced its most serious challenge.

For the course of the war, after Thucydides' account breaks off in 411, we rely directly on several ancient writers, only one of whom was contemporary with the events he described, and none of whom approached the genius of Thucydides. Modern historians of the classical period like to follow, when they can, the narrative historical account that they judge to be the most reliable, and they tend to prefer it to other evidence from sources that they consider less trustworthy. Whatever its merits in general, this practice is unwise for the period between 411 and 404 B.C. Of the extant writers of narrative accounts, Xenophon alone was a contemporary, and his *Hellenica* presents a continuous description of the events of that time. It is natural, therefore, that modern historians should at first have preferred his *Hellenica* to the abbreviated, derivative, and much later account of Diodorus and to the brief, selective biographies of Plutarch, which were aimed at providing moral lessons and were written even later.

The discovery of the papyrus containing the *Hellenica Oxyrhynchia* in 1906, however, changed the situation drastically. Although its author is unknown, the work seems to have been a detailed and careful continuation of Thucydides' history. As G. L. Barber notes, "the papyrus indicates a strict chronological arrangement by summers and winters, competent criticism and analysis of motives, a first-hand knowledge of the topography of Asia Minor, and certain details found in no other work on the period."[2] Several studies have found the superiority of the Oxyrhynchus historian's work over Xenophon's *Hellenica* to be most striking in the accounts of naval battles, but there has been a growing tendency to prefer the papyrus version to that of

[2]G. L. Barber, "Oxyrhynchus, The Historian from," *Oxford Classical Dictionary*, 2d ed. (Oxford, 1970), 766.

Xenophon.³ Since it is clear that the Oxyrhynchus historian was used by Ephorus, the most important source for Diodorus in our period, the credibility of Diodorus' account has grown at the expense of Xenophon's.⁴ That does not mean, however, that we should merely reverse the traditional practice and always follow the Diodoran account when it disagrees with Xenophon. Neither source is full enough or reliable enough to deserve preference prima facie.

Nor can we ignore the contributions of Plutarch in trying to construct a reliable account of what happened. Although he lived half a millennium after the war, Plutarch had a splendid library of works, many of them lost to us, capable of illuminating the course of events. He knew comedies by lost poets of the fifth century such as Telecleides, Phrynichus, Eupolis, Archippus, and Plato Comicus, histories by Thucydides' contemporaries Philistus and Hellanicus as well as his continuators Ephorus and Theopompus. He had access to contemporary inscribed documents; he could see with his own eyes many paintings and sculptures of the fifth century. We may derive a reasonable idea of his value from one of his own accounts of his method: "Those deeds which Thucydides and Philistus have set forth . . . I have run over briefly, and with no unnecessary detail, in order to escape the reputation of utter carelessness and sloth; but those details which have escaped most writers, and which others have mentioned casually, or which are found on ancient votive offerings or in public decrees, these I have tried to collect, not massing together useless material of research, but handing on such as furthers the appreciation of character and temperament."⁵ In pursuing his own purposes he has provided us with precious and authentic information available nowhere else; we ignore him at our peril.

These three authors—Xenophon, Diodorus, and Plutarch—are all important, but none is dominant. Where their accounts disagree, we have no way, a priori, to know whom to follow. In each case, we must keep an open mind and resolve discrepancies by using all the evidence and the best judgment we can muster. Wherever possible, I have explained the reasons for my preference in the notes, but sometimes my judgments rest on nothing more solid than my best understanding

---

³For references and discussion, see P. A. Rahe, "Lysander and the Spartan Settlement, 407–403 B.C." (Ph.D. diss., Yale University, 1977), vi–ix.
⁴I. A. F. Bruce, *An Historical Commentary on the* Hellenica Oxyrhynchia (Cambridge, 1967), 20–22.
⁵*Nic.*, 1.5, translated by B. Perrin.

of each situation. Inevitably, that will seem arbitrary in some cases, but the nature of the evidence about the quality of the sources permits no greater consistency. Introducing and following any general rule would surely lead to more errors than the application of independent judgment in each case.

One further question of method deserves attention. More than one able and sympathetic critic of my earlier volumes has been troubled by my practice of comparing what took place with what might have happened had individuals or peoples taken different actions and by my penchant for the subjunctive mood, or what is sometimes called "counterfactual history." To my mind, no one who aims to write a history rather than a chronicle can avoid discussing what might have happened; the only question is how explicitly one reveals what one is doing. A major difference between historians and chroniclers is that historians interpret what they recount, that is, they make judgments about it. There is no way that the historian can judge that one action or policy was wise or foolish without saying, or implying, that it was better or worse than some other that might have been employed, which is, after all, "counterfactual history." No doubt my method has been influenced by the great historian whom I have been studying for three decades, who engages in this practice very frequently and more openly than most. Let two examples suffice. In his explanation of the great length of the Greeks' siege of Troy, Thucydides says: "But if they had taken with them an abundant supply of food, and . . . had carried on the war continuously, *they would easily have prevailed in battle and taken the city.*"[6] Again, in the conclusion to his summation and judgment of Pericles' career, he says: "Such abundant grounds had Pericles at that time for his own forecast that *Athens might quite easily have triumphed* in this war over the Peloponnesians alone."[7] I believe that there are important advantages in such explicitness: it puts the reader on notice that the statement in question is a judgment, an interpretation, rather than a fact, and it helps avoid the excessive power of the fait accompli, making clear that what really occurred was not the inevitable outcome of superhuman forces but the result of decisions by human beings and suggesting that both the decisions and their outcomes could well have

---

[6]1.11.2. To avoid prejudicing the question, I have not used my own translation but that of C. F. Smith in the Loeb edition, which is reliable and attempts to stay closer to the text than most. The Greek in the emphasized portion reads: ῥᾳδίως ἂν μάχῃ κρατοῦντες εἶλον.

[7]2.65.13: πάνυ ἂν ῥᾳδίως περιγενέσθαι τὴν πόλιν.

been different. In this volume of my history of the war, I shall continue to be explicit in making such judgments.

The reader will easily see my continued debt to many scholars living and dead. Among the latter I must again single out the brilliant George Grote, father of the study of ancient Greek history as we know it today, and Georg Busolt, whose history is a model of learning, thoroughness, care, and dispassionate judgment. Among my contemporaries I must pay tribute to Antony Andrewes, whose magnificent final volume is a fitting capstone to the great monument that his collaborators on *A Historical Commentary on Thucydides*, A. W. Gomme and K. J. Dover, have created. I have also been aided greatly by P. J. Rhodes' impressive *Commentary on the Aristotelian* Athenaion Politeia, and I have learned much about Persia from D. M. Lewis' *Sparta and Persia*.

I am grateful to George Goold, John R. Hale, Paul A. Rahe, and Barry S. Strauss for criticizing all or part of my manuscript. Thanks are also due to the National Endowment for the Humanities and to Yale University for supporting my research.

DONALD KAGAN

New Haven, Connecticut

Contents

Maps

Abbreviations and Short Titles

AJP	*American Journal of Philology*
ATL	B. D. Meritt, H. T. Wade-Gery, and M. F. McGregor, *The Athenian Tribute Lists*
Beloch, *AP*	K. J. Beloch, *Die Attische Politik seit Perikles*
Beloch, *GG*	K. J. Beloch, *Griechische Geschichte*, 2d ed.
Bloedow, *Alcibiades*	E. F. Bloedow, *Alcibiades Reexamined*
BSA	*Proceedings of the British School at Athens*
Busolt, *GG*	G. Busolt, *Griechische Geschichte*
CAH	*Cambridge Ancient History*
CP	*Classical Philology*
CQ	*Classical Quarterly*
CR	*Classical Review*
Davies, *APF*	J. K. Davies, *Athenian Propertied Families*
FGrH	F. Jacoby, *Die Fragmente der griechischen Historiker*
Fornara, *Generals*	C. Fornara, *The Athenian Board of Generals*
GHI	R. Meiggs and D. Lewis, *A Selection of Greek Historical Inscriptions*
Glotz and Cohen, *HG*	G. Glotz and R. Cohen, *Histoire grecque*
Grote	George Grote, *A History of Greece*
Hatzfeld, *Alcibiade*	J. Hatzfeld, *Alcibiade, Etude sur l'histoire d'Athènes à la fin du Ve siècle*
HCT	A. W. Gomme, A. Andrewes, and K. J. Dover, *A Historical Commentary on Thucydides*
Henderson, *Great War*	B. W. Henderson, *The Great War between Athens and Sparta*
Hignett, *HAC*	C. Hignett, *A History of the Athenian Constitution*

IG	*Inscriptiones Graecae*
JHS	*Journal of Hellenic Studies*
Kagan, *Archidamian War*	D. Kagan, *The Archidamian War*
Kagan, *Outbreak*	D. Kagan, *The Outbreak of the Peloponnesian War*
Kagan, *Peace of Nicias*	D. Kagan, *The Peace of Nicias and the Sicilian Expedition*
LAC	*L'Antiquité Classique*
Lewis, *Sparta and Persia*	D. M. Lewis, *Sparta and Persia*
Meiggs, *Athenian Empire*	R. Meiggs, *The Athenian Empire*
Meyer, *Forsch.*	E. Meyer, *Forschungen zur alten Geschichte*
Meyer, *GdA*	E. Meyer, *Geschichte des Altertums*
PCPS	*Proceedings of the Cambridge Philological Society*
PW	A. Pauly, G. Wissowa, and W. Kroll, *Realenzyklopädie der klassischen Altertumswissenschaft*
REA	*Revue des études anciennes*
REG	*Revue des études grecques*
RH	*Revue Historique*
Rhodes, *Commentary*	P. J. Rhodes, *A Commentary on the Aristotelian* Athenaion Politeia
Riv. fil.	*Rivista di filologia e d'istruzione classica*
SCI	*Scripta Classica Israelica*
Ste. Croix, *Origins*	G. E. M. de Ste. Croix, *The Origins of the Peloponnesian War*
TAPA	*Transactions of the American Philological Association*
YCS	*Yale Classical Studies*
ZPE	*Zeitschrift für Papyrologie und Epigraphik*

The Fall of the
Athenian Empire

1. After the Sicilian Disaster

The Athenian attack on Sicily, launched with such great expectations, ended in total failure. Nicias surrendered the pitiful remnants of his army to the Syracusans in mid-September of 413, so news of the defeat could not have reached Athens much before the end of the month.[1] An ancient story says that the first report came from a foreigner who arrived at a barber shop in the Piraeus. Assuming that the Athenians had already heard of the disaster, he began talking about the details. The barber ran to Athens with the news, but no one would believe him. He was thought to be a fabricator and trouble-maker and was put to the rack before witnesses arrived to confirm the story.[2] We need not believe such tales, but the picture they paint of general incredulity is surely right. Thucydides tells us that even when the very soldiers who had managed to escape from Sicily reported the extent of the disaster, they were for a long time disbelieved.[3]

When finally the truth could not be denied, the Athenians responded first in anger and then in fear. First, they lashed out at the politicians who had proposed and argued for the Sicilian expedition (Thucydides bitterly remarks, "as if they had not voted for it themselves"); they

[1] For the chronology, see Busolt, *GG* III:2, 684.

[2] Plut. *Nic.* 30; Athenaeus (9.407) tells the tale of the comic parodist Hegemon whose play so delighted the Athenians that they laughed even on the day when the news of the Sicilian disaster came to them in the theater. "No one left the theater, even though almost everyone had lost relatives. So they wept secretly and did not get up to leave so that their grief at the calamity might not be revealed to the spectators from other cities."

[3] 8.1.1. All references are to Thucydides unless otherwise indicated.

were furious with the seers who had predicted success. Next, they grieved over the men lost in Sicily. Finally, they feared for their own safety when they calculated their own losses and the enemy's gains. They expected that the Peloponnesians, joined by their new allies in Sicily, would sail directly for the Piraeus and attack Athens by land and sea, joined by Athens' allies, who would now surely rebel.[4]

In the panic of the moment, they exaggerated the enemy's capacity to take effective action, but they had good reason for concern over the condition of Athens and its ability to carry on the war. The most obvious problem was manpower.[5] At the start of the war, the Athenians had 13,000 citizen hoplites of fighting age and another 16,000 for garrison duty, of whom about 8,000 were citizens above and below the age for battle and 8,000 were metics. There were 1,200 cavalrymen and 1,600 bowmen; the number of thetes available for service as rowers and marines was between 20,000 and 25,000.[6] The plague appears to have killed about a third of the population and to have crippled and disabled still others.[7] These losses could have been only partially replaced by the time of the Sicilian disaster, which probably killed at least 3,000 hoplites and 9,000 thetes as well as thousands of metics.[8] When account is taken of other casualties suffered between 431 and the autumn of 413, it is reasonable to believe that in 413 the Athenians may have been reduced to no more than 9,000 adult male citizens of the hoplite class of all ages; perhaps 11,000 thetes; and 3,000 metics,— a stunning reduction in the number of men available to fight the war.[9]

At least 216 triremes, of which 160 were Athenian, had been lost in Sicily, and no more than about 100, in different stages of disrepair, were still in the docks at Piraeus.[10] They would be hard-pressed to

[4] 8.1.2
[5] The following discussion of manpower and population owes much to the excellent analysis of Barry S. Strauss in his "Division and Conquest, Athens, 403–386 B.C." (Ph.D. diss., Yale University, 1979), Chap. 2. Other useful accounts are those of Busolt (*GG* III:2, 1400, with n. 5), Meyer (*Forsch.* II, 149–195), A. W. Gomme (*The Population of Athens in the Fifth and Fourth Centuries B.C.* [Chicago, 1967], K. J. Beloch (*Die Bevölkerung der griechisch-römischen Welt* [Leipzig, 1885]), and A. H. M. Jones (*Athenian Democracy* [Oxford, 1969], 161–180).
[6] 2.13.8; for the numbers of metics and thetes, see Strauss, "Division and Conquest."
[7] 3.87.3; 2.49.7–8; Kagan, *Archidamian War*, 71.
[8] Such are the very plausible estimates of Busolt (*GG* III:2, 1400).
[9] These estimates derive from the figures given above and from the arguments in Strauss, "Division and Conquest," 72–91.
[10] Busolt, *GG* III:2, 1400–1401; 1401, n. 1.

find crews, even unskilled and inexperienced ones, from the available thetes. Perhaps as serious a problem was the lack of money to repair the ships, build new ones, and pay their crews. Thucydides' statement that the Athenians "saw no money in the treasury" is probably rhetorical.[11] But from the approximately 5,000 talents available in the public treasury in 431 (excluding the 1,000 talents set aside for extreme emergency "in case the enemy should attack the city with a fleet"[12]), surely fewer than 500 talents remained in 413.[13] Nor could Athens hope to replenish its funds with increased income from the empire. The defeat in Sicily would likely cause rebellions that would reduce tribute payments and increase expenses by requiring expeditions to subdue the uprisings.

At the same time, the domestic economy of Athens was badly hurt. The Spartan fort at Decelea wore the Athenians down financially as well as physically and psychologically. They lost more than 20,000 slaves, they were prevented from working their silver mines, their capacity to use any of their farmland was reduced, and their houses in the country were stripped and stolen by the Boeotians along with any cattle and pack animals that could not be removed to Euboea for safekeeping. They had to import what they needed by a longer route, which increased its cost, and they had to support an armed force needed to guard the walls night and day.[14] Deprived of their means of livelihood, more citizens were compelled to crowd into the city. The increased demand for and the higher cost of importing food and other necessities could not fail to drive up prices. This put a further strain on the public treasury, for the state somehow had to support the needy widows and orphans created by the war.[15]

The propertied classes also suffered from the misfortunes of war. They, too, were compelled to abandon the farms that provided their income, and their houses were vandalized by the marauding Boeotians. We have some clues to the strain they felt. The trierarchy, a public service that the wealthier Athenians performed in turn, required the

[11] 8.1.2.
[12] 2.24.1.
[13] The authors of *ATL* (III, 358) say: "It is evident that in 414 the reserve fund in the treasury of Athena and of the Other Gods must have been once more reduced to the low figure of 422." The figure they give for the year 422 is 444 talents (III, 344, n. 94).
[14] 7.27.3–28.2; Kagan, *Peace of Nicias*, 291–292.
[15] The best discussion of Athens' economic difficulties at this time is that of Busolt, *GG* III:2, 1404–1408.

men appointed trierarchs not only to command a warship but also to fit it out and even to supplement the pay of its rowers. Until the Sicilian expedition, one trierarch had always been appointed for each ship, but soon after the disaster the syntrierarchy was introduced, allowing two men to share the expense.[16] By the end of the war, and perhaps as early as 413, a similar sharing was introduced for the liturgy that provided choruses for dramatic performances.[17] Men of sufficient wealth to perform basic military and religious services for the state were clearly in short supply, so there was little help to be expected from the imposition of the direct war tax, the *eisphora*. We can be sure of only one such levy, in 428, which raised 200 talents, apparently as much as could be collected.[18] The *eisphora* may have been levied again in the years before 425 and, perhaps, also to send reinforcements to Sicily.[19] After the fortification of Decelea, the thorough devastation of Attica, and the Sicilian disaster, the imposition of a direct tax on the reduced fortunes of the Athenian middle and upper classes would have paid for few costs of the war at great expense to morale. The Athenians appear not to have resorted to it again until the very last years of the war, after the emergency reserve fund had been exhausted.[20]

Apart from the shortage of men, ships, and money, Athens also lacked leadership, both military and political. The Sicilian expedition had carried off Athens' most experienced and ablest generals: Demosthenes, Lamachus, Nicias, and Eurymedon. None of the other four generals in 413/12 whose names we know appears to have held a previous command. Alcibiades was in exile in Sparta, the men on whom Athens had relied to command its forces on land and sea were gone, and no one of comparable experience and demonstrated ability was at hand.

The vacuum in political leadership was just as great. Athens' leading politician, Nicias, was dead; Alcibiades and Hyperbolus were in exile; and the demagogues who had supported the Sicilian venture were in

---

[16]For the responsibilities and expenses of the trierarchy, see 6.31.3; Lysias 32.24; M. Amit, *Athens and the Sea* (Brussels, 1965), 103–115; and J. S. Morrison and R. T. Williams, *Greek Oared Ships, 900–322 B.C.* (Cambridge, 1968), 260–263. For the date of the introduction of the syntrierarchy, see B. Jordan, *The Athenian Navy in the Classical Period* (Berkeley, 1975), 70–72.

[17]Scholion to Aristoph., *Frogs* 404; Busolt, *GG* III:2, 1405, n. 1.

[18]3.19.1; Kagan, *Archidamian War*, 144–145.

[19]Such are the suggestions of R. Thomsen, *Eisphora* (Copenhagen, 1964), 172–175.

[20]I accept the argument of Beloch, *AP*, 66 endorsed by Busolt, *GG* III:2, 1407, n. 1. Cf., however, Thomsen, *Eisphora*, 175.

disrepute. In these circumstances, the Athenians invented a new device to provide guidance and stability to their government. They voted "to elect a board of older men to serve as *probouloi*, offering advice and proposing legislation, concerning current problems as the situation may require."[21] There were ten *probouloi*, one from each tribe, and their minimum age was probably forty.[22] Their powers and responsibilities are unclear and were probably never precisely defined. If Thucydides' language is taken most literally and legalistically, they apparently had the power to present a bill to the assembly, thereby replacing the council in this primary function. Some scholars have taken this view of the *probouloi* controlling or replacing the council.[23] But another idea is that the *probouloi* worked together with the council and were really "a sub-committee of the larger body."[24] Others would give them even greater powers, including those of the Prytanies to call meetings of the council and to set its agenda and control the administration of funds, especially in regard to the preparation of the fleet.[25] Belief in these broader powers is not securely based, resting on interpretations of passages in Aristophanes.[26] No one doubts, however, that their unique status, the unusually high minimum age for the office, the fact of their election, their unlimited term of office, and the very vagueness and generality of their commission gave the *probouloi* unprecedented influence and power.

The election of *probouloi* changed the character and function of Athens' normal democratic constitution. Aristotle, moreover, regarded the institution of *probouloi* as an oligarchic element in any constitution.[27] Some scholars, therefore, influenced also by the knowledge that the *probouloi* played a role in the introduction of the oligarchic constitution of the Four Hundred in 411, believe that their election in 413 was already a movement toward oligarchy.[28] There is, however, no reason

[21]This is my translation and interpretation of 8.1.3: καὶ ἀρχήν τινα πρεσβυτέρων ἀνδρῶν ἑλέσθαι, οἵτινες περὶ τῶν παρόντων ὡς ἂν καιρὸς ᾖ προβουλεύσουσιν.

[22]For ancient sources, see Busolt, *GG* III:2, 1409, n. 1. Modern discussions of the *probouloi* are F. D. Smith, *Athenian Political Commissions* (Chicago, 1920), 32–41; and H. Schaefer, *PW* XLV (1957), 1222–1231.

[23]P. Cloché speaks of control (*REG* XXXV [1922], 279) and G. Glotz of replacement (*HG* II, 708).

[24]R. A. De Laix, *Probouleusis at Athens* (Berkeley, Calif., 1973), 32.

[25]Busolt, *GG* III:2, 1409–1410.

[26]*Lysis.* 410–610, 980–1012.

[27]*Pol.* 1298b, 1299b, 1322b, 1323a.

[28]Busolt, *GG* III:2, 1410–1412; Beloch, *AP*, 65; Hignett, *HAC*, 169.

to believe that the *probouloi* were in any way favorable to oligarchy in 413. The commission was created in a thoroughly democratic way, no doubt by a vote of the assembly, as many special commissions had been created in the past. Because the members were chosen during a great emergency and given unusually great powers, they were not simply appointed by a decree of the assembly but had to stand for election, one per tribe, like magistrates and generals. Unlike the introduction of the oligarchy of 411, no violence or procedural irregularities accompanied the creation of the board of *probouloi*. Unlike the true oligarchs of 411, the *probouloi* faithfully and effectively carried on the war against Sparta. They never took a step hostile to the democracy until the coup of 411. Their acquiescence then by no means impugns their fundamental loyalty to democracy, as we shall see.[29]

We know the names of only two *probouloi*: Hagnon, son of Nicias, and Sophocles, of the deme Colonus, the great tragic poet.[30] But those two *probouloi* give us an idea of the political color of the commission and of the political climate at Athens when they were appointed. Hagnon was born no later than 470, for he was a general alongside Pericles during the Samian campaign of 440; thus he was probably more than sixty years old when he was elected *proboulos* in 413. In 438/37 he played an important role in defending Pericles against his political enemies and in the next year was sent to found the colony of Amphipolis. He led campaigns in the Chalcidice in 430 and 429. He was still active as late as 421 as a signer of the Peace of Nicias and then the Athenian treaty with Sparta.[31]

Sophocles was probably born in 497/96, so he was well into his eighties when elected *proboulos*. He was *Hellenotamias* in 443/42 and general in 441/40. By 413 he had been winning prizes for tragedy for more than half a century and was one of the most famous and revered men in Greece.[32] Like Hagnon, he had been associated and worked with Pericles.[33] Both *probouloi* were wealthy, experienced, aged, and

---

[29]See Chapter Six.

[30]Hagnon is established as *proboulos* and father of Theramenes by the evidence of Lysias (12.65) and Xenophon (2.3.30). All references to Xenophon are to the *Hellenica* unless otherwise indicated.

[31]Davies, *APF*, 227–228.

[32]For the date of his birth, see *Marmor Parium* 56 and 54 (*FGrH*, II, 239, 1000–1001). For his place as *Hellenotamias*, see *ATL* II, List 12, line 36. For the generalship, see Androtion *FGrH* III, 324, Fr. 38.

[33]V. Ehrenberg, *Sophocles and Pericles* (Oxford, 1954), 117–140; Kagan, *Outbreak*, 149–153, 175–177.

certainly, in the context of 413, conservative. But their association with Pericles guaranteed that they were neither oligarchs nor enemies of the democracy. After Sicily there was no Pericles, no Nicias, to provide the prudent, cautious, moderate leadership that now was wanted, so, in effect, Periclean moderation was put into commission. It is revealing of the state of Athenian politics that the Athenians believed they must seek such qualities in an earlier generation, that men in their prime could not be found or trusted to provide it. The coming years would show that reckless demagogy had not been permanently eclipsed, that oligarchic plots were not creations of the Athenian imagination, so the attempt to find moderate democratic leadership was both poignant and prudent.

Thucydides approved of the Athenian behavior in this crisis, although not without an epigrammatic slap at the ways of democracy: "In the terror of the moment, as is the way of the *demos*, they were ready to do everything with discipline."[34] In fact, the behavior of the Athenian democracy in this crisis seems remarkably Periclean. Pericles, when he feared that passion would interfere with policy in the first year of the war, had used his unmatched personal authority to limit the democracy temporarily by preventing the meeting of assemblies.[35] Now the Athenian assembly, acting in a thoroughly Periclean spirit—determined, practical, restrained, prudent, and economical— voluntarily placed a limit on itself by giving unprecedented powers to a board of respected and trusted moderates in his tradition. "They decided, so far as the situation permitted, not to give in but instead to prepare a fleet, obtaining timber and money wherever they could, to see to the security of their alliance, especially Euboea, and to reduce public expenditures."[36]

The *probouloi* acted quickly to put this spirit into effect. They gathered timber to build ships, and this was possible because they were once again on good terms with the king of Macedonia, their main source of naval timber.[37] They built a fort at Sunium to help protect

---

[34] 8.1.4.
[35] 2.22.1; Kagan, *Archidamian War*, 55–56.
[36] 8.1.3.
[37] For Macedon as a source of Athenian naval timber, see *IG* I² 71 (with Kagan, *Archidamian War*, 314, n. 28); *IG* I² 105 = *GHI*, 91, And. 2.11; and Xen., 6.1.11. King Perdiccas, whose relations with Athens had been unstable, was once again allied with the Athenians in 414 (7.9) and died some time between then and 410 when his successor Archelaus is recorded as fighting alongside them at Pydna (Diod. 13.49.1). In 413/12, therefore, Athens could readily get timber from Macedon.

the grain ships that had to pass by while the Spartan garrison at Decelea blocked the normal route from Euboea. They abandoned the fort in Laconia, which had produced disappointing results and was a drain on the treasury, for as Thucydides remarks, "if they judged any expenditure useless they curtailed it in the interests of economy." Most especially, the Athenians in the time of the *probouloi* kept a close watch over their allies "so that they might not revolt from them."[38]

At the same time, they introduced a major change in the manner of collecting revenue from the empire. They abandoned the collection of tribute on the basis of assessments imposed by the Athenians on each allied city; instead, they imposed on the allies a 5 percent duty on all goods imported or exported by sea.[39] One reason for the change was the hope of increasing revenue. The tribute from 418 to 414 has been estimated at 900 talents annually. To equal that figure with the new tax would require an annual value of the seaborne traffic in the empire of 18,000 talents.[40] We cannot tell whether such a figure would be easily achieved, but we may view the problem in another way. The Athenians may have made the change not in the hope of collecting more money than they were already getting but more than they might expect to get from the old system under the new circumstances. After all, they were fearing and expecting defections, some, presumably, from those allies most heavily assessed. The shift in the nature of the tax could mean a shift in how heavily each state was taxed and also which citizens within each state bore the burden. We do not know how the several subject states raised the money to pay their tribute; probably practices varied. Very likely, real property was the basis for internal taxation to provide funds for paying the tribute, at least to some degree. The new tax would shift the burden to those engaged in commerce, who may have been burdened less, or not at all, in the past. Thus new sources of revenue might be tapped. Perhaps, also, subjects engaged in commerce, who benefited so greatly from the advantages of the empire, might be less reluctant to pay taxes and better disposed to Athens. Tax relief for the landed citizens, presumably more restive, might reduce the pressures for rebellion as well as increase Athenian revenue.

In the absence of better evidence, all of this is only speculation, but

[38] 8.4.

[39] 7.28.4. The change was probably made in the autumn of 413 (*HCT* IV, 402), just when the *probouloi* were elected (Smith, *Athenian Political Commissions*, 39).

[40] *HCT* IV, 408.

we have reason to believe that at least some Athenians in these years were thinking of novel and daring ways to bind the allies more closely to Athens. Early in 411 Aristophanes presented the comedy *Lysistrata*, and in one scene he portrays an argument between the heroine and one of the *probouloi*.[41] Pressed to explain her plan for ending the war and untangling Greece's troubles, she offers a skein of wool as a metaphor for Athens.

Consider the City as fleece, recently shorn. The first step is Cleansing: Scrub it in a public bath, and remove all corruption, offal and sheepdip.

Next, to the couch for scutching and Plucking: Cudgel the leeches and similar vermin loose with a club, then pick the prickles and cockleburs out. As for the clots—those lumps that clump and cluster in knots and snarls to snag important posts—you comb these out, twist off their heads, and discard.

Next, to raise the City's nap, you card the citizens together in a single basket of common weal and general welfare. Fold in our loyal Resident Aliens, all Foreigners of proven and tested friendship, and any Disenfranchised Debtors. Combine these closely with the rest. Lastly, cull the colonies settled by our own people: these are nothing but flocks of wool from the city's fleece, scattered throughout the world. So gather home these far-flung flocks, amalgamate them with the others.

Then, drawing this blend of stable fibers into one fine staple, you spin a mighty bobbin of yarn—and weave, without bias or seam, a cloak to clothe the City of Athens.[42]

Although it is always difficult to see through the humor of Aristophanes to any factual historical references that may lie behind them, we may agree with those scholars who believe that there is at least a kernel of fact in the comedy of this passage.[43] The joke, at least in part, lies in the extended metaphor that compares the wool fleece with

[41]For the date, see B. B. Rogers, *Lysistrata* (London, 1911), x. Whether the play was performed at the Lenaea or the City Dionysia is not known.

[42]*Lys.* 573–586. I have used the lively and effective translation of Douglass Parker (*Lysistrata*, Ann Arbor, Mich., 1964, 44–45), who identifies the "clumps" as the oligarchic political clubs (91). For the same interpretation see also J. van Leeuwen, *Lysistrata* (Leyden, 1903), 86–87; and Rogers, *Lysistrata*, 72. Andrewes (*HCT* V, 189) believes that the reference is not to oligarchical clubs but more generally to "the professional politicians who monopolize office and evade military service." The clumps, or as Andrewes calls them, tangles, "represents men who bind themselves together for the sake of office," not necessarily oligarchs or conspirators.

[43]Probably the strongest attack on the use of Aristophanes as a source of historical information is a well-known article by A. W. Gomme (*CR* LII [1938], 97–109). For a vigorous statement of the other view as well as a cautionary argument as to how the comedies should be used, see Ste. Croix, *Origins*, 231–244, 355–376.

Athenian policy. But the humor is both timely and enhanced if we assume that there really were contemporary Athenians who advocated a generous policy of extending Athenian citizenship to many heretofore excluded. Busolt suggested: "In the necessity of the time there were also voices audible that recommended reinforcing the citizenry not merely by the admission of resident aliens and well-disposed foreigners [presumably non-Ionian members of the Athenian alliance] but also to unite into a commonwealth the cities considered to be Athenian colonies, *i.e.*, the Ionians and the islanders of Ionian speech, by conferring on them citizen rights with Athens."[44]

Perhaps the replacement of the hated tribute by customs duties within the empire was a step in such a direction.[45] But even if that were so, no proposal to share Athenian citizenship was passed, if any was formally proposed. The Greek city-state was too traditional an institution, too closely tied to ideas of common descent and blood relationships, to extend citizenship readily outside its own ranks. Solon, Peisistratus, and Cleisthenes had enrolled new citizens far in the past, but the trend in the fifth century was away from such generosity. Pericles' law of 451 had narrowed the definition of Athenian citizenship to include only those with two citizen parents.[46] The material and psychological benefits that come with imperial power had not made the Athenians more eager to share their advantages since that time. In any case, the year 413 was not the time to try the experiment. The gesture of offering such unusual concessions immediately after the disaster in Sicily, when the Greek world expected the imminent downfall of Athens, would have appeared to be a sign of weakness and would have encouraged rebellion.[47]

Whatever the attitude of Athens' subjects and allies may have been before the Sicilian disaster, however, there can be little doubt of their attitude by 413.[48] "The subjects of the Athenians were ready to rebel against them even beyond their power."[49] Within a year major places

[44]Busolt, *GG* III:2, 1414. Meyer (*GdA* IV, 12) and Beloch (*AP*, 67) hold the same view.

[45]Such is Beloch's suggestion (*AP*, 67).

[46]See Kagan, *Outbreak*, 103–104.

[47]Busolt, *GG* III:2, 1414.

[48]Even Thucydides' harshest critic says "that the mass of the citizens in the allied or subject states were loyal to Athens throughout the whole period of the empire, *until the final collapse of the Ionian War* . . ." (G. E. M. de Ste. Croix, *Historia* III [1954–1955], 16, emphasis added).

[49]8.2.2.

such as Euboea, Chios, Lesbos, Rhodes, Miletus, and Ephesus had revolted. The success of these rebellions and the encouragement of others, however, required effective support from outside the empire, and its chief source must be the Spartan alliance and especially its hegemonal city.

Thucydides tells us that immediately after the Athenian defeat in Sicily, the Spartans were full of hope and eager to pursue the war to a successful conclusion. He also reveals that Spartan war aims were no longer what they had been. The Spartans calculated that after the overthrow of Athens "they themselves would safely hold the hegemony of all Greece."[50] It is often true that in war the appetite grows with the eating, and in 413 there must have been Spartans whose goals had changed from freeing the Greeks to dominating them. There had been a core of men holding such ambitions at least as early as 475.[51] More-over, we may believe that Sparta's victory at Mantinea, the establish-ment of a permanent fort at Decelea, and the Athenian defeat in Sicily had swollen the number of Spartans who hoped that "they would enjoy great wealth, Sparta would become greater and more powerful, and the houses of the private citizens would receive a great increase in their prosperity."[52]

The growth of this aggressive and ambitious faction in Sparta re-sulted not only from military success but also from the war's accel-eration of trends that were changing the character of Spartan society. The most visible evidence of these trends was the continuing decline in the number of full Spartan citizens. There were some 5,000 Spartan hoplites at Plataea but only about 1,000 a little more than a century later at Leuctra, this in a land that, according to Aristotle, was able to support 1,500 cavalrymen and 30,000 hoplites.[53] This decrease, in part, must reflect a declining birthrate, for the Spartan social and economic system encouraged its citizens to limit the size of their fam-ilies. Full Spartan citizenship and the honor that went with it depended on the citizen's capacity to provide his share to the common mess. For this purpose each Spartiate was given a public grant of land, but some of the time, at least, this public land did not produce enough to provide the needed portion for the common meals. The more children a Spartan had, the more intense the problem, and the Spartans employed a wide

[50]8.2.4.
[51]Diod. 11.50; Kagan, *Outbreak*, 51–52; Ste. Croix, *Origins*, 170.
[52]Diod. 11.50.
[53]*Pol.* 1270a 29–32.

variety of devices to reduce family size including late marriage, polyandry, and pederasty.[54] The Spartan state passed a variety of laws to reverse the population trend, for its interest was to have the largest number of citizen-hoplites possible.[55] But the attempt failed. Spartiates continued to limit the number of their offspring and to seek to acquire as much private land as possible to supplement the public grant. The Spartan constitution had been created to produce a warrior class of equals (homoioi) adequate to defend its land and people, to fix the devotion of that class to the goal of achieving military glory and honor in the service of the state, and to be free from economic need and economic interests. Ironically, it led to a shortage of manpower, a continuing hunger for wealth, and a growing inequality.

Even as the number of Spartiates decreased, however, the proportion of free men in Laconia who were not Spartiates increased. As early as 421 there were 1,000 neodamodeis, helots who fought in the Spartan army and were given their freedom and a piece of land as a reward; by 396 there were at least 2,000.[56] It seems possible that they and their offspring could hope to achieve Spartiate status, for the title implies some kind of citizen status.[57] Another such group were the hypomeiones, or "inferiors." The hypomeiones are mentioned in only one ancient source early in the fourth century.[58] But there is no reason to doubt that they existed during the Peloponnesian War. They seem chiefly to have been men born to the Spartiate class, brought up through the Spartan system of education, and otherwise eligible for Spartan citizenship but whose poverty prevented them from contributing their share to the common meals. As a result, they were excluded from citizenship, respect and honor.[59] Still other free men outside the body of Spartiates were called mothakes. Some of them seem to have been the illegitimate sons of Spartiate men and helot women, but it is likely that others were Spartan-born on both sides but too poor to contribute to the common meals, that is, hypomeiones. They would, however, have gone through the

---

[54]A. Toynbee, *Some Problems of Greek History* (London, 1969), 305–306; P. Cartledge, *PCPS* XXVII (1981), 17–38.

[55]For a summary of Sparta's attempts to stimulate procreation, see P. Cartledge, *Sparta and Lakonia* (London, 1979), 309–311.

[56]5.49.1; Xen. 4.3.2.

[57]U. Kahrstedt, *Griechisches Staatsrecht* (Göttingen, 1922), vol. 1, 46ff. See also the discussion by P. Oliva, *Sparta and Her Social Problems* (Amsterdam and Prague, 1971), 166–170.

[58]Xen. 3.3.6.

[59]Oliva, *Sparta*, 177–178; Cartledge, *Sparta and Lakonia*, 313–315.

Spartan training and would have been elected to a common mess, their portion contributed by a wealthier Spartan patron.[60] Among those *mothakes* known to us are three men who played a significant role in the Peloponnesian War, the military commanders Gylippus, Callicratidas, and Lysander. That these men of inferior origins could reach positions of such honor and eminence meant that others could hope to do the same, if only they could acquire enough wealth to gain the economic basis for admission to a mess and to full citizenship. The best hope for that was through military conquest. The destruction of the Athenian Empire in the Aegean offered the opportunity for the acquisition of wealth for the victorious Spartans and honor for their leaders. Men who lacked the means for citizenship could hope to gain it through warfare. Men like Gylippus and Lysander, who already held citizenship but whose position of honor and respect was clouded by inferior origins, could hope to improve their status by victory in war. All of these men would provide powerful pressure for a more forward and aggressive policy than was normal for Sparta.

Nor did the drive for "the hegemony of all Greece" lack support in higher Spartan circles. The faction that had been eager to break the Peace of Nicias since 421, that had favored sending help to the Syracusans and fortifying Decelea, must have been riding high after the defeat of the Athenians in Sicily. Agis, still bearing the glory and influence given him by his victory at Mantinea, was at Decelea, enjoying powers unusual even for a Spartan king and eager to increase his reputation and power by pursuing the expected collapse of the Athenian Empire under his leadership.[61]

Those Spartans who traditionally had opposed adventures outside the Peloponnesus, had favored the Peace of Nicias, and had resisted sending help to Sicily and setting up a fort in Attica were certainly less prominent in 413. The pacific King Pleistoanax found his already weak position further undermined by the condemnation and exile of his brother for cowardice at the battle of Mantinea.[62] So he was in no position to provide effective leadership with the cautious policy he favored, especially after Mantinea and Sicily. Yet he and those who agreed with him, normally the dominant element in Sparta, had even

---

[60]The most important contribution to the above account is the article of D. Lotze, (*Historia* XI [1962], 427–435). Other useful discussions are Oliva, *Sparta*, 174–177; and Toynbee, *Problems*, 345, n. 3.

[61]For the powers and influence of Agis at this time, see 8.5.1–4 and *HCT* V, 12.

[62]5.72.1; Kagan, *Peace of Nicias*, 126–128.

more reason than ever to oppose an aggressive resumption of the war. Athens still held Pylos and Cythera, from which the Athenians could foment trouble among the helots. The presence of growing numbers of *neodamodeis* and *hypomeiones*, although armed to fight in the Spartan cause, must have been the source of great disquiet. Early in the fourth century, Xenophon describes such men as unable to conceal their eagerness "to eat the Spartans raw."[63] No more than fifteen years earlier the danger they presented would not have escaped any Spartan who cared to look. The rise in the influence of Agis and the aggressive men around him would have provided even more reason to fear an undertaking that would move Spartan and Peloponnesian armies far from home and whose success would strengthen their power even more. Although not in a position to prevent vigorous prosecution of the war in 413, the friends of a cautious and peaceful policy could be expected to cause trouble if the expected easy victory did not come quickly.

The aggressive group faced practical problems at once. Building ships would require money, but manning them would cost even more. Raising rebellions in the Aegean and the Hellespont, supporting them against the Athenians, and facing the Athenians in naval battles would require large fleets that might need to stay at sea for long periods, and their sailors would have to be paid. Sparta itself was in no position to provide the necessary forces. The Spartans had few ships and little or no money. They had relied in the past on their allies for both, but the war had done terrible things to the economic strength of the most important allies. Thucydides tells us that Sparta's allies were "jointly enthusiastic" to be rid of the great hardships of the war, "even more than they had been before."[64] But some at least seem to have been less eager than others. The Corinthians stalled when the Spartans proposed to sail from the Isthmus to help the Chians launch their rebellion, asking for a delay until after the Isthmian games.[65]

Even when Sparta's allies from the Greek mainland were zealous, moreover, they were not able to provide the amount of naval power needed to defeat Athens. When the Spartans prepared for the war in the Aegean, they established a quota of ships to be built by each of their allies: 25 for themselves and the same number for the Boeotians; 15 for the Corinthians and the same number for the Locrians and

[63] 3.3.6.
[64] 8.2.1.
[65] 8.9.

Phocians together; 10 for the consortium of Arcadia, Pellene, and Sicyon; and another 10 for the team of Megara, Troezen, Epidaurus, and Hermione.[66] The total aimed at was 100 triremes, a number not adequate to achieve supremacy over the Athenians. But there is reason to doubt that even that quota was achieved. In the spring of 412, only 39 ships were ready to begin the campaign.[67] For the rest of the war at sea there were apparently very few ships sent from Sparta's mainland allies and, even then, only rarely.[68]

The Spartans also put great hope in their Sicilian allies, thinking "they would probably come at the beginning of spring with the great naval force they had already been forced to acquire."[69] In this respect, too, the Spartan hopes proved to be excessive. Thucydides tells us of only 20 ships from Syracuse and 2 from Selinus that joined the Spartan fleet in 412.[70] Xenophon reports that these 22 ships were joined by 5 more from Syracuse, which arrived in 409 in time to help in the defense of Ephesus.[71] The paucity of the Sicilian contribution to Sparta's campaigns in the Aegean and Hellespont may well have been related to troubles at home. A democratic revolution at Syracuse undercut the position of Hermocrates, the greatest champion of Spartan interests and of a forward policy.[72] He was exiled and killed in an attempt to return to power, and his democratic opponents were clearly not interested in vigorous support for a Spartan war far from home after the threat from Athens was gone. In 409, moreover, Carthage launched a major campaign to conquer Greek Sicily, which fully occupied the Sicilians for the rest of the century.[73] The Spartans could not have

---

[66]8.3.2.

[67]8.7; of them only twenty-one were hauled over the causeway from the Corinthian to the Saronic Gulf whence they could sail into the Aegean (8.8.4, 10.2).

[68]Thucydides mentions five Corinthian, one Megarian, and one Hermionian ship that Astyochus took to Miletus (8.33.1); he tells of five from Corinth, two from Ambracia, and one each from Leucas and Pellene captured by the Athenians at Cynossema (8.106.3). Xenophon tells of a naval expedition to the Hellespont in 410 led by Clearchus consisting of fifteen ships manned by "Megarians and other allies" (1.1.36). Diodorus mentions the Boeotians as holding the left wing at the battle of Arginusae in 406, but he gives no figures. These seem to be the only references to the participation of Sparta's mainland allies in the naval war after 413.

[69]8.2.3.

[70]8.26.1. Diodorus (13.34.4 and 63.1) puts the number of Syracusan ships at 35, making no mention of Selinuntians, but Xenophon (Xen. 1.2.8) confirms the Syracusan figure at twenty. Presumably, they were the same forces that fought at Cynossema and Cyzicus (8.104–106; Xen. 1.2.8).

[71]1.2.8.

[72]Diod. 13.34.6, 39.4, 63, 75.2–9; Xen. 1.1.27–31, 3.13.

foreseen these events, but their experience in the Archidamian War might have made them wary. In 431 they had asked their allies in Sicily and Italy for 500 ships and received none.[74] To expect a vast reinforcement, far from Sicily and after the Athenian assault had been shattered and there was no more danger, would, in any case, have been unrealistic.

The Spartans and their allies thus had no prospect of acquiring sufficient ships or funds from their own resources. Realistic hopes of defeating Athens, even after the Sicilian disaster, depended on the possibility of obtaining support from the only source rich enough to produce success, the treasury of the Persian Empire. To gain Persian support, however, the Spartans would have to come to terms with the Great King, and that promised to be no easy task. They took great pride in their reputation as leaders of the Greek resistance to Persia, which dated from the sixth century.[75] In fact, they had entered the war proclaiming the slogan "Freedom for the Greeks."[76] The Persians, however, would certainly demand at least the recovery of their dominion over the Greeks of Asia Minor in return for support of the Spartan war against Athens. It would be difficult for most Spartans to accept the abandonment of the Asiatic Greeks as the price of a Persian alliance. The conservative faction was sure to attack such a bargain as dishonorable, but even aggressive Spartans might be reluctant to undo the glory obtained by the Greeks under Spartan leadership by freeing their fellow Greeks from Persian rule. Moreover, the more rapacious among them wanted revenues from the Greek cities diverted from Athens not to Persia but to Sparta. Negotiations for the necessary Persian aid would be delicate, and success was by no means certain.

In 413 there was good reason to think that the Persians might be willing to join in the war against Athens. The growth of the Athenian Empire had come at Persia's expense, driving the Persians from the Aegean Sea and the Hellespontine waterways and depriving the Great King of the Greek cities of Asia Minor and the revenues they produced. Probably more serious than the financial loss was the blow to the pride of the Achaemenid monarchs, each of whom styled himself "Great

[73]Diod. 13.54.
[74]2.7.2.
[75]Lewis, *Sparta and Persia*, 62–63.
[76]1.124.3; 1.139.3; 2.8.4; 3.32.2, 63.3; 4.85.1, 86.1.

King, King of Kings, King of peoples with many kinds of men, King on this great earth far and wide, etc."[77]

Even after the Peace of Callias had put a formal end to the war between Athens and Persia at mid-century, hostilities continued, sporadically and at a lower level, in what one scholar has called a "Cold War."[78] The Persians appear to have violated the peace by supporting rebellions against Athens in Caria, Lycia, Mysia, and the Hellespontine area, and the Athenian penetration beyond the treaty line into the Black Sea appears to have been a counterviolation.

In any case, the behavior of the Persian satrap Pissuthnes in 440 was certainly an act of hostility toward Athens. He made an alliance with the Samian rebels and held an Athenian garrison hostage on their behalf.[79] No doubt Pissuthnes was an especially powerful and independent satrap, as his later rebellion would show.[80] But there is no reason to think he was acting against the royal will. The report that a Phoenician fleet was moving against the Athenians on Samos was convincing enough to make Pericles take sixty ships from the blockading force and sail toward Caria to head it off. Although it never appeared in the Aegean, it may have been intended merely to draw Athenian attention and weaken the effort at Samos.[81] The movement of the fleet would clearly indicate official approval of the satrap's action. In any case, Pissuthnes' behavior was neither disowned nor punished.

It was probably soon after the suppression of the Samian rebellion,

---

[77]For this form of the royal title, see Lewis (*Sparta and Persia*, 78). The Persian kings may even have felt a religious injunction to regain the coastal regions of their empire in Asia Minor; for S. K. Eddy (*CP* LXVIII [1973], 247) the Persian king's "right to rule all Asia rested on no less a sanction than the will of Ahura Mazda himself."

[78]Eddy, *CP* LXVIII (1973), 241–258; Lewis (*Sparta and Persia*, 59–61) challenges some of Eddy's interpretations, arguing, in general, that the evidence for Atheno–Persian conflict is pushed too hard, but he does not deny the reality of some such conflict.

[79]1.115.4–5. Diodorus says that the 700 mercenaries the Samian rebels raised were a gift from Pissuthnes (12.27.3), and there is no reason to doubt, at least, that they were raised with the satrap's permission, with due respect to Lewis (*Sparta and Persia*, 59, n. 65).

[80]Ctesias 52. He was also of royal blood, the grandson of Darius I (Lewis, *Sparta and Persia*, 55 and 80).

[81]Such is the suggestion of Eddy (*CP* LXVIII [1973], 250). Lewis (*Sparta and Persia*, 59–60) believes there was no Persian fleet, but Diodorus (12.27.5) and Plutarch (Per. 26.1) flatly state otherwise. Even if these later sources are unreliable, the undoubted fact that Pericles believed in the fleet's reality should weigh more heavily than Lewis' doubts about a "tight" timetable for mobilizing the Phoenician navy. If there was such a fleet, we can, in Lewis' words, "hardly acquit the King of complicity."

perhaps in 437, that Pericles led his famous expedition into the Black Sea to demonstrate Athenian power in the region and, perhaps, to warn the Persians not to repeat the indiscretion of Pissuthnes.[82] Probably no such warning was needed in the 430s, for the failure of the Spartan alliance to support the Samians and the Athenian victory were enough to indicate that the power of Athens in the Aegean was still too strong to challenge in peacetime. Nor should we forget that the coast of Asia Minor was a very small part of the concerns of the Great King, who had troubles and responsibilities all over a vast empire. The perspective in Susa or Persepolis was very different from that in Athens, Sparta, or even Sardis and Dascylium, where Persia's westernmost satraps had their palaces.

The outbreak of a major war in Greece in 431, however, presented the Persians with another occasion to annoy the Athenians. In the spring of 430 factional strife at Colophon gave Pissuthnes the opportunity to intervene again. He sent a subordinate, Itamenes, with some non-Greek troops from the vicinity; Itamenes took the city, driving the friends of Athens into exile at Notium. There, factional quarrels broke out again, one side obtaining mercenary soliders from Pissuthnes. At last the Athenian general Paches arrived, defeated the mercenary army and the pro-Persian faction, established an Athenian colony at Notium, and restored the friends of Athens to control of Colophon.[83] The behavior of the Persian satrap persuaded anti-Athenian exiles from Ionia and Lesbos that Pissuthnes was ready to join the Spartans in the war against Athens, but they were unable to convince the timid Spartan admiral Alcidas to seize a coastal town as a base for a general Ionian revolt.[84] Pissuthnes appears also to have supported rebellions against Athens in Caria some time between 430 and 425, and the Athenians may have retaliated by levying tribute from towns under Persian control on the Black Sea.[85]

Late in 425 the Athenians received striking evidence of the danger to them posed by Persia. One of their generals intercepted Artaphernes, a Persian envoy from the Great King of Sparta. At Athens his letters were translated and read, clearly revealing diplomatic negotiations. The Great king did not know what the Spartans wanted.

---

[82]For the date and purpose of the expedition, see Kagan, *Outbreak*, 387–389; cf., however, Lewis, *Sparta and Persia*, 60, n. 70.

[83]3.34.

[84]3.31.

[85]Eddy, *CP* LXVIII (1973), 255–256.

"Though many envoys had come to him, they did not say the same things. If they wanted to say anything that was clear they should send men to him in the company of the Persian messenger."[86] Whatever the problems of communication may have been, there can be no doubt of what the Spartans wanted. As early as 430 they had sent a mission to the Great King to see if "they might persuade him to provide them money and join with them in the war."[87] There were evidently more missions in the interim, but what must have alarmed the Athenians in 425 was the discovery that the Persian king now took the initiative.

We can only speculate about the Persian motives. Perhaps the news of the totally unforeseen Athenian success at Pylos and Sphacteria was responsible. We should remember that all of the Greeks expected Athens to yield after a few years of resistance at most. Little that happened before 425 would have brought that assumption into question, so there was no reason for the Persians to intervene. They could hope that the Spartans would do their work for them, that in due course the Greek cities of Asia Minor would be conquered without much effort. The Spartan surrender at Sphacteria changed all that. The shock destroyed Spartan confidence, allowed the Athenians to raise the tribute and solve their financial problems, and encouraged expectations of a helot rebellion, defections from the Spartan alliance, and an Athenian victory.[88] Darius might fear not only the reaffirmation of Persian exclusion from the Aegean and the Hellespont but even more attacks from a victorious, strengthened, and emboldened Athens.

For the Athenians, the new Persian initiative was alarming. All that had been accomplished by their miraculous success at Sphacteria could be undone if Persia placed its wealth and naval power at the disposal of the Spartans. They therefore sent Artaphernes back to Ephesus on a trireme in the company of some Athenian envoys to the Great King. We are not told the intent of their mission, but it seems likely that they at least meant to improve relations with Persia and prevent an agreement between Persia and the Spartan alliance. Whatever their purpose, it was not achieved, for at Ephesus they learned that King Artaxerxes had died, so they returned to Athens.[89]

Thucydides mentions no further negotiations, but in 391 the orator Andocides spoke of a treaty negotiated by his uncle Epilycus "estab-

[86] 4.50.2.
[87] 2.67.1.
[88] 4.40–41; Kagan, *Archidamian War*, 248–251.
[89] 4.50.3.

lishing friendship forever" with the king of Persia.[90] Athenian orators
are notorious for their distortion and even invention of historical information to suit their needs, and Andocides is equally guilty.[91] The
evidence of inscriptions, however, lends considerable support to the
historicity of the treaty of Epilycus. A fourth-century copy of a fifth-
century decree honors a certain Heracleides for his role in helping to
negotiate a treaty with the Persian king. Although establishing the
probable date and content of the treaty requires an ingenious combination of epigraphical restoration and interpretation, one distinguished
epigrapher and historian is confident enough to say: "Few things are
more certain in fifth-century history than that the decree honours
Heraclides of Clazomenae for helping an Athenian embassy on which
Andocides' uncle Epilycus, a member of the Boule, served to negotiate
a treaty with King Darius in 424–423."[92]

There need be no surprise that the Athenians moved as swiftly as
possible to prevent Persian assistance to Sparta. By the end of 424,
Brasidas had taken Amphipolis and was threatening to disrupt the
entire Thracian-Macedonian region of the Athenian Empire. Persian
support in ships and money would liberate Brasidas from reliance on
the untrustworthy king of Macedonia and unleash him for further
conquests, perhaps even for a march eastwards to the Hellespont. Such
a terrifying prospect easily explains why the Athenians rushed to make
terms even with the newly enthroned and very insecure king of Persia,
Darius II.

The confusion resulting from the death of Artaxerxes I has led one
scholar to speak of the ensuing period as the "Year of the Four Em-

[90]And. 3.29.
[91]Andrewes, *Historia* X (1961), 2–3.
[92]Meiggs, *Athenian Empire*, 135. The most important inscription is *IG* II² 8 = *GHI*,
70. Since the inscription mentions τὰσπονδάς and βασιλέως, the topic is clearly a
treaty with the Great King of Persia, who alone is called "the king," without further
description. The date 424/23 is established by a set of linkages with officials listed on
inscriptions datable to that year set out by H. T. Wade-Gery (*Essays in Greek History*
[Oxford, 1958], 201–232). D. L. Stockton's vigorous assault on the major aspects of
this interpretation (*Historia* VIII [1959], 61–79) is met successfully by Andrewes (*Historia* X [1961], 3, n. 6) and Meiggs-Lewis (*GHI*, 202–203). There have been several
suggestions for different dates ranging from 422/21 to a little before 415. Lewis has
evaluated them and has also made good use of evidence from the Persian Empire,
including a new tablet from Babylon. He concludes: "I do not think that the current
dating of the treaty is obviously wrong, and the new tablet, by advancing the date at
which Darius may seem likely to come out on top, usefully relaxes the rightness of
the timetable" (*Sparta and Persia*, 77).

perors" in analogy with the chaotic year of civil war following the death of the Roman Emperor Nero.[93] Artaxerxes was succeeded by his only legitimate son, the offspring of his Persian wife, who took the throne as Xerxes II. But Artaxerxes had also sired 17 bastard sons by various concubines, and one of them, Sogdianus, was able to seize the throne and kill Xerxes only forty-five days after his accession. His position was soon challenged by another of Artaxerxes' bastard sons, Ochus, satrap of Hyrcania. Ochus' rebellion was successful, and he took the throne as Darius II, being recognized as king as early as August 16, 424.[94] But 16 bastard sons of Artaxerxes remained, as well as others whose pure Persian blood and descent from the royal family might make them think they had a better claim to the throne than Darius. In fact, he was soon faced with a rebellion, the first of several, led by his full brother Arsites.[95]

In these circumstances, Darius must have been no less eager than the Athenians to come to an agreement. Far from having any interest in helping the Spartans, Darius needed protection against Athenian intervention on the side of his enemies, for Arsites was already employing Greek mercenaries against him.[96] These considerations help explain the treaty of Epilycus and may even lend support to Andocides' version of its terms. The usual view is that the new treaty was merely a renewal of the terms of the Peace of Callias, and so it may have been.[97] However, in the special circumstances of 424/23, both sides may have wanted stronger assurances of friendly relations and noninterference.[98]

From the Persian point of view, at least, the treaty proved opportune. Some time, probably not long, after the defeat of Arsites, Darius faced

[93]Lewis, *Sparta and Persia*, 73.
[94]Our knowledge of these events comes chiefly from Ctesias (43–51), briefly and generally supported by Diodorus (12.64.1 and 71.1). For an excellent discussion of the difficult chronological problems, see Lewis, *Sparta and Persia*, 70–77.
[95]Ctesias 50–51. Andrewes (*Historia* X [1961], 4) is right to conclude that the rebellion must have occurred "right at the beginning of the reign." Not only is it the first event mentioned by Ctesias after Darius' accession, but "the last sentence of this section joins executions of Xerxes' murderers with the execution of Arsites."
[96]Ctesias 50.
[97]Wade-Gery, *Essays*, 211; Andrewes, *Historia* X (1961), 5; Meiggs, *Athenian Empire*, 135.
[98]A. Blamire's perception of the situation seems to me to represent the best understanding of the motives of both Athenians and Persians. See his article in *Phoenix* XXIX (1975), 21–26.

another uprising, this time by Pissuthnes, the satrap at Sardis.[99] This rebellion was even more dangerous, for Pissuthnes was the legitimate grandson of Darius I, the experienced and well-entrenched satrap of an important province, and his army included a force of Greek mercenaries.[100] Darius sent a force against him under the three generals, the chief one being Tissaphernes. They bribed the mercenaries away from the satrap, paying off their chief with lands and cities. Pissuthnes was killed and his satrapy given to Tissaphernes. Darius was forced to beat off still another, apparently lesser, threat to his throne some time after 418.[101]

During these troubles Darius must have been glad he had come to terms with Athens, especially between 421 and 415, when Athens was formally at peace and in practice regaining its strength and ambition. After the defeat of his enemies, however, and the establishment of his rule on a firm basis, Darius might look westward in the hope of regaining Persia's lost provinces. But with Athens at peace, Sparta occupied in the Peloponnesus, the Athenian navy in control of the sea, and the Athenian treasury being filled by the increased tribute payments while not being drained by military expenditures, the Persian king could take no action. He must wait for a better opportunity. As one scholar has put it, "had it not been for the Athenian expedition to Sicily, he might have had to wait for a very long time."[102]

An objective and well-informed observer of the scene in 413 might have drawn some surprising conclusions. In spite of the Sicilian disaster, the damage it had done to Athens, and the great enthusiasm of its enemies, the outcome of the war was not much more predictable than it had been at its start in 431. If the Athenians could keep their nerve, limit expenditures, and keep control of their allies, they need not give in, even though the defeat in Sicily provided an invitation for Persian involvement. Unless the Persians were willing to make a considerable investment, the Athenians could not be defeated at sea, and Persia's willingness to pay the price had yet to be demonstrated. No

---

[99]Ctesias 52. The date can be any time between 423 and 415; H. D. Westlake's arguments for a date early in the reign, in *Phoenix* XXXI (1977), 321–322, are persuasive.

[100]For Pissuthnes' lineage, see Lewis, *Sparta and Persia*, 55. The commander of the mercenaries was an Athenian named Lycon, but as Andrewes (*Historia* X [1961], 4, n. 10) and Westlake (*Phoenix* XXXI [1977], 321, n. 8) point out, his origin is no indication of the policy or actions of his native state.

[101]Ctesias 53. For the date, see Lewis, *Sparta and Persia*, 81.

[102]Lewis, *Sparta and Persia*, 82.

one could be sure that the Great King might not again be distracted by problems in his vast empire. Even if he were not, there still remained the question of whether his goals were compatible with those of the Spartans. As in 431, no Athenian strategy could guarantee a victory over the Peloponnesians, but even with its reduced resources, a Periclean stand-off was still possible. What was different in 413 was that the possibility of victory was available to Sparta if it could find a way to engage Persian power on its side and use it effectively. That possibility existed, but it would not be easy to realize. In 413 the issue was still very much in doubt, and the key to its resolution lay not in Athens but in Sparta and in Persia.

2. The War in the Aegean

The last phase of the Peloponnesian War, Thucydides tells us, started with both sides making preparations for it as if it were just beginning.[1] Once again the initiative lay with Sparta while Athens stayed on the defensive, guarded her treasury, and watched over her allies. This time, however, there was no offensive element, not even a measured and limited one. After Sicily, the Athens of the *probouloi* had to be even more cautious than Pericles had been.

Sparta, on the other hand, needed to be more aggressive and inventive, and under the leadership of Agis the Spartans were ready to try. Archidamus had warned that if they went to war in 431 they would pass that war on to their sons, and in 427/26 the old king, at least, had done so.[2] His son, who commanded the Spartans at Decelea in 413, was a more appropriate leader for the kind of war that was now necessary than his cautious and reluctant father would have been. Agis' career before the battle at Mantinea had been marked by misfortune, bad judgment, failure, and even disgrace. He had entered that battle accompanied by ten *xymbouloi*, advisers sent to watch over him, having avoided serious punishment only by promising to redeem his previous blunders by brave deeds in battle.[3] His leadership at Mantinea amounted to a comedy of errors that would have produced tragedy for Sparta had not Agis benefited from the timely restraint of an adviser, disobedience to his absurd orders, and an important tactical

---

[1] 8.5.1.
[2] 1.81.6 (Archidamus' prediction); 3.89.1 (Agis' first command).
[3] Kagan, *Peace of Nicias*, 105–109.

error by the enemy.[4] But victory has magical powers to erase the memory of previous error, especially a victory of the magnitude and significance of Mantinea. Agis emerged from that battle a hero, and the disobedient captains were punished, putting the official seal of approval on Agis' strategic genius.

In 413 the Spartans sent him to command their permanent garrison at Decelea, where he enjoyed extraordinary powers. He had full authority "to send the army wherever he liked, to gather troops and collect money. And during this period the allies obeyed him more than those in the city of Sparta, one might say, for having an army under his own control, he could swiftly appear anywhere and inspire fear."[5] Agis, moreover, appears to have been eager to use this unusual power aggressively to extend Sparta's hegemony over the Greeks. Even before Mantinea, there are clues that may indicate his association with the aggressive faction in Sparta, and his behavior at that battle was that of a man given to rash aggressiveness in an attempt to achieve military distinction.[6] In any case, his actions in 413 made clear his energy and determination to advance Spartan hegemony.

Late in the autumn of 413, Agis took part of his army from Decelea and marched northward into Central Greece to the region of the Gulf of Malis (see Map 1). There, he carried off many cattle as well as a sum of money extorted from the Oeteans in payment and revenge for a standing grudge. The Oeteans had attacked and oppressed both the neighboring Trachinians and Doris, the traditional ancestral home of the Dorians, leading the Spartans to establish a colony at Heraclea in Trachis in 426. Heraclea was troubled immediately by misrule on the part of its Spartan governors and by attacks from its neighbors.[7] In the winter of 420/19 Heraclea received such treatment from its local enemies that the Boeotians dismissed the Spartan governor and took control of the city themselves, ostensibly to prevent it from falling into Athenian hands, but the Spartans were angered.[8] It seems clear that Agis' purpose was more than revenge and included the recovery of Heraclea, for that colony was back under Spartan control by 409,

[4] Ibid., 109–132.
[5] 8.5.3.
[6] For Agis' association with the aggressive faction, see Kagan, *Peace of Nicias*, 84–86, 90; for his behavior at Mantinea, see ibid., 105–132.
[7] 3.92–93.
[8] 5.51–52.1.

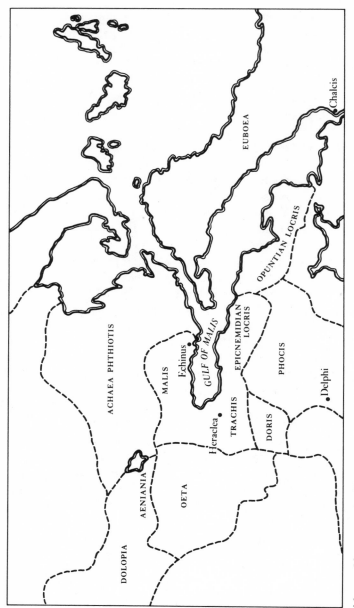

MAP 1. HERACLEA AND ENVIRONS

Chalcis

EUBOEA

OPUNTIAN LOCRIS

EPICNEMIDIAN LOCRIS

PHOCIS

Delphi

ACHAEA PHTHIOTIS

MALIS

Echinus

GULF OF MALIS

Heraclea

TRACHIS

DORIS

OETA

AENIANIA

DOLOPIA

26

when its Spartan harmost, or governor, was dying in battle against the Oeteans.[9]

The Spartans had been eager to found the colony, Thucydides tells us, because of its strategic location, "for a fleet could be equipped there against Euboea in such a way as to have only a short crossing."[10] In light of Sparta's plans for fomenting rebellion in the Aegean, the recovery of Heraclea might seem reason enough for Agis' expedition, but he clearly had larger plans in mind. He forced the Achaeans of Phthiotis and other allies of the Thessalians, probably the Aenianians, Dolopians, and Malians, to pay him money and to give hostages. He placed the hostages at Corinth for safekeeping and used them to try to force their people into the Spartan alliance. The Thessalians objected but could do nothing to prevent the Spartans' actions.[11] Moreover, there is some evidence that Agis may also have gained control of Echinus and the borders of the Gulf of Malis at this time.[12] These actions go far beyond the Spartans' establishment of a colony at Heraclea in 426 and point to the policy of expanding their alliance and power into Central Greece, a policy they would follow early into the next century.[13] The actions also show that in 412 Agis was willing to

[9]Xen. 1.2.18. Andrewes (*HCT* V, 9) suggests that the Spartans regained Heraclea before Agis' expedition, "for if it has remained in Boeotian hands till now Thucydides' silence about this would be hard to explain." But Thucydides never mentions Sparta's recovery of its colony anywhere, so his silence about it, whenever it occurred, remains hard to explain, as are so many of his silences. It is better to believe, with H. D. Westlake, that "the activities of Agis in this area must have included the reestablishment of Spartan control over the important outpost at Heraclea" (*JHS* LVIII [1938], 35). Xenophon says explicitly that the Spartan governor in 409 was called "harmost." H. W. Parke's suggestion that the Spartan governors of Heraclea were harmosts from its founding in 426 is persuasive (*JHS* L [1930], 39).

[10]3.92.4.

[11]8.3.1. Thucydides mentions only the Achaeans among the Thessalian allies. The others, as Andrewes points out (*HCT* V, 9), must be the same peoples who assailed Heraclea in 420 (5.51.1).

[12]The Athenian speaker in Aristophanes' *Lysistrata* (1169–1170), when asked to make a counterdemand to the Spartans' request for the restoration of Pylos, mentions Echinus and the Gulf of Malis, as well as the long walls of Megara. All of these names are grist for the comedian's mill, for they provide splendid opportunities for obscene double meanings. It is precisely the genius of Aristophanes to provide real contemporary allusions as the basis for his jokes. We know that Pylos and Megara, each of which allows obscene interpretation, were real places subject to bargaining. There is no reason to doubt that the other two references were equally relevant. As Andrewes points out, "it can hardly be coincidence that Agis had been active here little, if at all, more than twelve months before" (*HCT* V, 9).

[13]*HCT* V, 10.

pursue vigorous and aggressive action that went beyond traditional bounds.[14]

Upon his return to Decelea from the Gulf of Malis, Agis received visits from two sets of envoys to discuss rebellion from the Athenian Empire. First came the Euboeans, encouraged, no doubt, by Agis' recent campaign near Heraclea. Agis received them warmly and sent word to Sparta for Alcamenes and Melanthus to lead 300 *neodamodeis* to Euboea. As they were preparing to cross over to the island, another embassy arrived, this one from Lesbos. The Lesbians were accompanied and supported by the Boeotians and were able to persuade Agis to delay the Euboean expedition and support a rebellion on Lesbos instead. The Boeotians promised to provide ten ships; Agis would provide an equal number, along with Alcamenes as harmost, or commander, and his corps of *neodamodeis*.[15] Agis may have been persuaded by the offer of ten ships or by some strategic consideration not mentioned by the ancient sources, but we also suspect that he was much influenced by the Boeotians, whose growing power and strategic location gave them considerable importance in the new situation.

Agis made these decisions at Decelea by virtue of his special powers, but his was not the last word. Two other delegations came to seek Spartan support for rebellions from Athens, but they went not to Agis at Decelea but to Sparta itself. One came from Chios and Erythrae, and, most striking, it was accompanied and supported by an envoy from Tissaphernes, the Persian satrap of Sardis.[16] The other one was composed of two Greeks, Calligeitus of Megara and Athenagoras of Cyzicus, exiles from their home cities, speaking in behalf of Pharnabazus, satrap of the Hellespontine province with his capital at Dascylium. They urged the Spartans to support the rebellions of Greek cities in the Hellespontine region.[17] The most remarkable part of these

---

[14]Westlake (*JHS* LVIII [1938], 35–36) has suggested an even more ambitious purpose for Agis' actions: "to reopen the land-route to Thrace." This would allow the Spartans to cause defections from Athens in the Chalcidice, to prevent the Athenians from obtaining timber for ship-building in Macedon, and to put more pressure on Thessaly. Since execution of this "northern plan" never went beyond these actions around the Gulf of Malis, we cannot be sure of these grander goals. Nor is there evidence to support Westlake's suggestion that Alcibiades, collaborating with Agis, was the inventor of the scheme (see Hatzfeld, *Alcibiade*, 214).

[15]8.5.1–2. For a discussion of the role of harmosts, see H. W. Parke, *JHS* L (1930), 37–39; and G. Bokisch, *Klio* XLVI (1965), 129–239.

[16]8.5.4.

[17]8.5.4–5, 6.1.

developments was that two Persian satraps, each acting under the urging of the Great King, offered to cooperate with Sparta in the war against Athens.

What led Darius to abandon his recent treaty with Athens, not a dozen years old, and the older Persian policy of maintaining peace with Athens that dated from mid-century? Thucydides tells us that both satraps had lately been pressed by the Great King once again to collect tribute from the Greek cities in their provinces. The king plainly was also holding his satraps responsible for the payment of arrears of tribute, which they had been unable to collect from the Greek cities because of the Athenians.[18] Both, therefore, hoped to weaken the Athenian power and remove Athens' hold over the cities, and both sought an alliance with the Spartans for that purpose. Tissaphernes had a special reason for wanting an alliance with Sparta. Amorges, bastard son of Pissuthnes, was in rebellion against the Great King in Caria, and Tissaphernes had been ordered to bring in Amorges, dead or alive.[19] Thucydides later makes it clear that soon after the Persian negotiations with Sparta, the Athenians were allied with Amorges, and the orator Andocides says that the Athenian decision to make an alliance with Amorges was the cause of Persia's decision to join with Sparta.[20]

Andocides considered the alliance with Amorges an example of Athens' "customary mischief," the abandonment of powerful allies in favor of weaker ones.[21] Modern scholars, assuming that the alliance with Amorges was concluded before the Persian negotiations with Sparta, regard the alliance as a foolish and frivolous gamble that was respon-

---

[18] 8.5.5. In theory these cities could be thought of as owing payment ever since their liberation in the Persian War of 480/79, but Herodotus tells of a law whereby arrears in tribute were forgiven upon the accession of a new king (6.59), so the arrears demanded could date no earlier than 424. O. Murray (*Historia* XV [1966], 148–149) makes a persuasive argument, however, that Darius demanded only the arrears for the period since each satrap took over his province, in Tissaphernes' case "some time after 420 and before 412—a maximum of eight years, and probably less than four." Andrewes (*HCT* V, 16) rightly points out that Thucydides' language, especially his use of the word νεωστί, "lately," for the timing of the king's demand, suggests something new that had recently changed the situation and suggests that "the obvious new factor is Athens' support of Amorges and breach with Darius." But the date of that support and breach is not known and is not the only possible "new factor," as will be argued below.

[19] 8.5.5.

[20] 8.28.2–5, 54.3; And. 3.29.

[21] 3.29.

sible for the change in Persian policy.[22] But apart from the assertion of Andocides, there is no evidence for the date of Athens' alliance with Amorges. Some scholars have tried to use an inscription that seems to place an Athenian general in Ephesus in March of 414 as evidence for Athens' support of the revolt of Amorges at that time.[23] They suggest that the general was there in connection with the alliance with Amorges "to prevent Tissaphernes collecting tribute," or "presumably operating in support of Pissuthnes and Amorges," or on the assumption that "Athenian support for Amorges would be a reason for a general being there in 414."[24] But this is mere fantasy. There are many reasons why an Athenian general might have been in Ephesus in the spring of 414, and support of a rebellion of Amorges is one of the least likely. Later events would show that the loyalty of Ephesus was very much in question, so a general might have been needed to keep an eye on the Ephesians. Another possibility might be the desire on the part of the Athenians to collect arrears in tribute by a show of force, as they had done elsewhere. On the other hand, Ephesus was by no means the likeliest place for an Athenian force sent to help Amorges, for Miletus was closer to his base at Iasus.[25] The inscription is simply of no use in dating Athens' alliance with Amorges.

We are left with the claim of Andocides, and that orator "is at all times a bad witness."[26] In his speech *On the Peace*, Andocides supports his thesis with three examples showing Athens supporting weak allies in preference to strong ones. The first is the alliance with Amorges. The second alleges an offer from the Syracusans, before the Sicilian expedition, of an alliance with Athens. The third is Athens' decision to launch an attack on Laconia in 414 at the behest of its Argive allies.[27] The last of these examples is factually correct, although incomplete and tendentious. The second is certainly an invention without factual

---

[22]Opinions are cited by H. D. Westlake, *Phoenix* XXXI (1977), 319, n. 2.

[23]The inscription (*IG* I² = *GHI*, 77, 1.79) reads στρατεγὸι ἐν Ἐφ[έσοι . . . , and the restoration of Ephesus is plausible.

[24]The quotations are from H. T. Wade-Gery (*Essays in Greek History* [Oxford, 1958], 223), R. Meiggs and D. Lewis (*GHI*, 236), and A. Andrewes (*Historia* X [1961], 5), in that order.

[25]These and other likely suggestions are made by Westlake (*Phoenix* XXXI [1977], 323).

[26]Andrewes (*Historia* X [1961], 2). Westlake (*Phoenix* XXXI [1977], 325) adds that "the speech of Andocides *On the Peace* is conspicuous, even among those of Attic orators, for its inaccuracies."

[27]3.29–31.

basis.[28] The first example, the alliance with Amorges, however, falls into a separate category, neither entirely true nor completely false. The basic facts are correct: there was a treaty of Epilycus, an alliance with Amorges, Persian support for Sparta, and Athenian misfortune as a result. But the "conclusions derived from these facts are by no means above suspicion, and there is reason to believe that [Andocides] is guilty of trying to deceive his audience."[29] If Andocides is correct and the Athenians made their treaty with Amorges before the Persian negotiations with Sparta, we should have expected Thucydides to have made note of that fact. Although his omissions are not infrequent and sometimes are inexplicable, this one appears especially unlikely. Not only would it be important for the reader to know the correct order of events to comprehend cause and effect, but in this case, reporting the events as Andocides does would forcibly support one of Thucydides' chief interpretative themes, the reckless foolishness of the Athenian democracy.[30] It seems more likely, therefore, that Andocides has distorted the chronology to make his point, a common practice among Athenian orators.[31] If that is so, the Athenians would have joined with Amorges only after they knew of the Persians' overtures to Sparta "in the following spring, . . . when the Athenians knew that Tissaphernes was plotting against them."[32] At such a time, Athens would have little to lose and something to gain by joining with a rebel against the Persians.

But what, if not the news of an Athenian treaty with Amorges, persuaded the Persians to approach Sparta with offers of help? The most obvious and likeliest answer is that other news set events in

---

[28]Andrewes (*Historia* X [1961], 3) says that this assertion "must be imaginary, a reckless heightening of the dramatic decision taken by Athens in 415." Westlake points out that the story is not mentioned elsewhere, and he thinks it was "probably a fabrication of his [Andocides'] own designed to strengthen his plea for peace" (*Phoenix* XXXI [1977], 325).

[29]Westlake, *Phoenix* XXXI (1977), 325–326.

[30]Westlake's statement of the matter deserves quotation: "One aspect of relations between the Athenians and Amorges might have been expected to have aroused the interest of Thucydides if indeed, when already engaged on a major offensive in Sicily, they chose to sacrifice the advantages of their treaty with Persia by supporting a rebel and thereby provoking Persian reprisals. Thucydides would surely have ranked this decision among the errors in judgment whereby, in his opinion, through abandoning the advice of Pericles, they brought upon themselves their ultimate defeat (2.65.7–13)" (ibid., 327).

[31]Ibid., 326.

[32]Ibid., 328–329.

motion—news of the Athenian disaster in Sicily. There is no chronological barrier to such an interpretation, which seems far more attractive than an unsupported reliance on Andocides. The Sicilian defeat came in September, and the Persian mission to Sparta could have come as late as March in the following year, a period of at least five months, which was plenty of time for the Great King to get the news, to decide on a change of policy, to communicate it to his satraps, and for them to send embassies to Sparta.[33] If we accept the significance of the Sicilian disaster in the Persian decision, the date of the Athenian treaty with Amorges in relation to the Persian negotiations with Sparta becomes less important, and we can better understand Thucydides' lack of interest in precision on this point. After the news of Sicily reached Persia, the Great King could be expected to seek the recovery of his lost domain from a badly wounded Athens and to join with Sparta to achieve those ends. If Amorges sought Athenian help in the autumn or winter of 413/12, the Athenians would not have been reckless or foolish to accept. "It was their best chance of keeping the Persians busy and giving them no opportunity to assist Sparta in 'liberating' the cities of Ionia."[34] Whether the Persians had already begun discussions with Sparta, as the silence of Thucydides powerfully argues, or would do so soon, as acceptance of the chronology of Andocides indicates, makes little difference. Reality required a positive response. "In the desperate situation in which the Athenians found themselves their decision to cooperate with Amorges was not foolhardy but perfectly reasonable."[35]

That the envoys from the Persian satraps went not to Agis but directly to Sparta was, no doubt, both normal and natural, although they may also have learned of Agis' negotiations with the Euboeans and Lesbians. They were not, in any case, acting in concert but as rivals, each trying to win Spartan support for a rebellion against Athens in his own province. Each wanted to bring back the Greek cities under

[33]Lewis (Sparta and Persia, 87, n. 25) says of the chronology proposed here that "it is likely to be a tight fit" and leans toward the theory of the Athenian treaty with Amorges as a cause of the Persian volte face. He concedes that the other interpretation "is perhaps possible," but his arguments against it are limited to the following assertion: "it seems unlikely that the King can have had reliable news of it until well on in November." On the contrary, such astonishing and important news would probably have traveled faster than most. In any case, a November date for the king's reception of the information in no way excludes the chronology suggested here.
[34]A. G. Woodhead, Thucydides on the Nature of Power (Cambridge, Mass., 1970), 147.
[35]Westlake, Phoenix XXXI (1977), 329.

his jurisdiction and to make them pay tribute to Persia, and each wanted the credit for bringing the Spartans into alliance with the Great King.[36] The Spartans were also divided in counsel, even more so than the Persians. First, there was a division between opinion in Sparta and the plans of Agis at Decelea. The king had decided on support for the Lesbians, but in Sparta there was no thought of such an action. The suggestion has been made that the rejection of Agis' plan in Sparta was evidence of the continuing rivalry between kings and ephors,[37] but there is little reason to think so. The political situation at Sparta in 413/12 is far from clear, but it was more complex than a struggle between ephors and kings. We must assume that Pleistoanax remained hostile to all adventurous policies that required expeditions outside the Peloponnesus, and naval ones at that, but Pleistoanax and those of his view were out of favor. Agis was working with the Boeotians, and we may guess that he was supported by the friends of Xenares and Cleobulus, the aggressive ephors of 420/19 whom Plutarch called "the Boeotian party."[38] But Xenares was dead, Cleobulus had returned to obscurity, and other men were influential in Sparta.

In Sparta itself, Thucydides makes clear, "there was great conflict, so that some tried to persuade the assembly to send an army and navy to Ionia and Chios first, while others argued for the Hellespont."[39] We do not know who supported the proposal of Pharnabazus, but we do know that the proposal of the Chians and of Tissaphernes was supported by the ephor Endius, urged on by his hereditary family friend Alcibiades. Sound arguments could be made in support of any of the four proposals. The loss of Euboea would be a terrible blow to Athens. The Athenians had moved their flocks to that island early in the war, and they counted on it for provisions. When it finally revolted in 411, they were more frightened than after the Sicilian disaster, for "they got more benefit from it than from Attica."[40] If the Spartans could acquire control of Lesbos, they would gain a large, rich, and populous island. Even more important was its strategic location, for it was well situated to serve as a base for a campaign to cut off Athens' lifeline

---

[36]8.6.1.

[37]Hatzfeld, *Alcibiade*, 216.

[38]*Nic.* 10.7.

[39]8.6.2. Although the assembly is not specifically mentioned, the language of Thucydides makes it plain that the discussion and decision took place in the Spartan assembly. See Lewis, *Sparta and Persia*, 89.

[40]Flocks: 2.14; provisions: 7.28.1; revolt in 411: 8.96.1–2.

through the Hellespont, the quickest and surest way to end the war. Pharnabazus' offer had a similar appeal, with the additional attraction of Persian financial support.

The Spartans, however, were much more attracted to the proposal from the Chians and Tissaphernes. The offers from Euboea and Lesbos were less tempting because they carried with them neither a Greek fleet nor the promise of Persian support. At first, the proposal of Pharnabazus might seem the best, for success in the Hellespont promised the quickest victory, and his envoys brought with them 25 talents in hard cash.[41] Pharnabazus, though independent of Tissaphernes, appears to have had less power than the satrap of Sardis, who may have held a "superior command in the west for the war against Athens."[42] Nor could he offer a significant fleet, as the Chians could, and the Spartans may have been embarrassed to prefer alliance with a satrap to an opportunity to come to the rescue of a Greek state seeking freedom.[43] All of these things were reasons enough for the Spartans to choose to aid Chios, supported by Tissaphernes, but Thucydides offers a different reason for their decision. He clearly implies that the fact that Alcibiades, working through the ephor Endius, supported the Chians and Tissaphernes was what decided the issue.[44]

Here, as elsewhere, Thucydides appears to exaggerate the influence of Alcibiades, but we should not doubt that the Athenian renegade advocated the course described or that his advice had some effect on his friend and, through him, on the Spartan decision. That advice in

[41]8.8.1.

[42]Such is Andrewes' plausible interpretation of Thucydides' account of Tissaphernes' title: βασιλεῖ Δαρείῳ τῷ Ἀρταξέρξου στρατηγὸς ἦν τῶν κάτω (8.5.4) (HCT V, 13–16). Lewis (Sparta and Persia, 86) is cautious about Tissaphernes' powers and especially about his relationship with Pharnabazus, but he says of the phrase that "the implication should be that he holds a position different in kind and probably wider in extent than the simple satrapy of Sardis."

[43]This last suggestion is made by Lewis, Sparta and Persia, 89.

[44]The relevant passage is 8.6.2–3, where Thucydides first speaks of the division of opinion at Sparta; then tells us that the Spartans, nevertheless, inclined toward the Chians and Tissaphernes; and next says: ξυνέπρασσε γὰρ αὐτοῖς καὶ Ἀλκιβιάδης. ... The γὰρ seems clearly to have a causal force here, as Andrewes' refutation (HCT V, 19) rightly assumes. That Endius was cooperating with Alcibiades after being tricked by him in 420 (see Kagan, Peace of Nicias, 66–70) is surprising, and not enough is known of the affair in 420 to permit a confident explanation. On the assumption that Endius and Alcibiades were not confederates on the earlier occasion and that the Spartan was really tricked, Andrewes' explanation will serve better than most: "In these different circumstances they could be useful to one another, and the quarrel of eight years ago forgotten."

part, must have come from his intelligent appraisal of the military and diplomatic situation, but Alcibiades was always in a precarious situation in Sparta. He needed to prove his value to his ever-suspicious hosts, and the campaign in Ionia implied by the support of a Chian revolt offered him a unique opportunity. He had important friends at Miletus, Ephesus, and Chios in the Ionian region, where he might hope to present himself to the Spartans as an "indispensable man."[45]

The Spartans, though inclined toward the view of Alcibiades and Endius, proceeded with caution. They sent a *perioikos* (a non-Spartan Laconian) named Phrynis to Chios to see if the Chian navy was as large and the city's power as great as the Chians claimed. When he returned with affirmative answers, the Spartans voted to take the Chians and the Erythraeans, who lived across the bay from them, into their alliance. They decided to send forty triremes of which ten should sail immediately under their admiral, or navarch, Melanchridas to join the Chian fleet of sixty ships. Before they could leave, however, toward the end of the winter, perhaps in late February of 413, an earthquake occurred. Taking this as a bad omen, they reduced the preliminary mission to five ships and appointed Chalcideus to its command.[46] Even then, they acted with characteristic deliberateness, for well into the spring of 412 they had launched no fleet and had taken no other action. The Chians, in fear that the Athenians would learn of the secret negotiations and take steps to prevent the rebellion, pressed the Spartans to send out a fleet at once.[47]

---

[45] The term is used by Hatzfeld, *Alcibiade*, 217. For Alcibiades' influence at Miletus, see 8.17.2. Andocides (*Against Alcibiades* 30) and Plutarch (*Alc.* 12.1) mention the honor shown to Alcibiades by the Chians and Ephesians at the Olympic games. They also mention the Lesbians in this connection. Satyrus (*apud* Ath. 12. 534d), a biographer of the third century A.D., includes Cyzicus in the list of those paying tribute to Alcibiades on this occasion. Lesbos is irrelevant to the choice before Alcibiades. Even if Satyrus is right to include Cyzicus among the places where Alcibiades was influential (*pace* Hatzfeld, *Alcibiade*, 217, n. 2), his influence there could not be as important as his many connections in Ionia, especially Chios.

[46] 8.6.4–5. Andrewes points out that earthquakes were taken seriously at Sparta and normally would be enough to postpone an expedition entirely. He suggests that this time "the omen was interpreted as showing divine displeasure with Melanchridas personally, not with the enterprise as such" (*HCT* V, 19–20). Very likely that is the interpretation that won out, but Spartan history is full of evidence indicating that the interpretation of omens and other divine signs depended on the reigning political climate. The determination to proceed with the expedition even in the face of so serious an evil omen powerfully reveals the strength of the militant forces in Sparta and the weakness of Pleistoanax and the conservative forces.

[47] 8.7. MS B offers the reading, ἅμα δὲ τῷ ἦρι τοῦ ἐπιγιγνομένου θέρους, which

The ships Agis was collecting for the expedition he had planned, as well as other Peloponnesian warships, were gathered off the western side of the Isthmus in the Gulf of Corinth, presumably at the Corinthian port of Lechaeum. The Spartans sent three envoys to ask that the entire fleet (there were thirty-nine ships at the time) be hauled across the Isthmus and sent to Chios at once. Most, if not all, of the ships belonged to the allies, so a meeting of the Peloponnesian League was a practical necessity before any action could be taken.[48]

Thucydides' account of its deliberations is far from complete, but he shows clearly enough that the meeting was not a mere formality and a ratification of orders from Sparta. The assembly at Sparta had decided simply to accept the proposal of the Chians and Tissaphernes, and the orders conveyed by the envoys were meant to carry out that decision, nothing more. What came out of the meeting of the Peloponnesian League was something different and more complicated, a compromise plan that clearly revealed the continuing division of opinion among the Spartans. When the news came to Agis that his own strategy had been rejected in favor of the Chian project, he must have been disappointed, but experience had made him more cautious and politically clever. The decision of the Spartan assembly could not be overthrown, but the meeting of the Peloponnesian League provided an opportunity to salvage something of his own policy. Outwardly, he did not object to the change of strategy, but what came out of that meeting was a decision not only to send a fleet at once to Chios under the command of Chalcideus but also to send ships to Lesbos, as Agis had planned, under the command of Alcamenes, "the same man whom Agis had in mind."[49] There can be no doubt that this supplementary mission was voted because of the influence of the Spartan king.

A third and more surprising mission was added to complicate further the originally simple plan. After the campaign at Lesbos, still a third

---

suggests that the Chian pressure and the Spartan response took place immediately at the beginning of spring, in March, and that reading is accepted by both Steup and Weil-Romilly. But the other MSS read τοῦ δ᾽ ἐπιγιγνομένου θέρους, and I agree with Andrewes (*HCT* V, 20) in preferring their version. The meeting of the Spartan alliance at Corinth discussed in 8.8 must have followed soon after the Chian communications, and it was followed immediately by the Isthmian games in June. The first Spartan action, the sending of envoys to Corinth asking for ship movements, probably came in April or even in May.

[48]8.7. As Lewis (*Sparta and Persia*, 89, n. 34) rightly points out, "the need to consult the allies arises from the fact that it is their ships which are going to be used."

[49]8.8.2.

commander, Clearchus the son of Ramphias, was to take the force to the Hellespont. Now the ambassadors from Pharnabazus quickly withdrew after the decision at Sparta had gone against them, taking their money with them, and they took no further part in the planned expedition.[50] This provides evidence that the faction favoring a Hellespontine strategy, though once defeated, had not given up and still commanded enough influence to gain some recognition, although at a low priority, for its own program. The assignment of a different commander for each phase of the projected campaign indicates the degree of division and distrust among the factions and the absence of commanders sufficiently distinguished and respected to overcome such divisions.

The Peloponnesian League voted to move immediately. Thucydides tells us that they planned to sail to Chios boldly and openly, "for they were contemptuous of the impotence of the Athenians, since no large Athenian fleet was yet in evidence."[51] But some part of the timidity and caution that the Peloponnesians had displayed in naval matters from the first still remained. After all, they had gathered their own fleet on the western side of the Isthmus from where it must be dragged across over the causeway to the Saronic Gulf, where they might be exposed to attack from Athens. Even then, when a force of almost forty ships had been gathered, they chose to make the trip in two separate detachments, twenty-one ships crossing the Isthmus first and sailing toward Chios at once and the remaining ships following later. According to Thucydides, this was done to prevent the Athenians from attacking either contingent lest they leave themselves open to attack by the other.[52] These were strange tactics to produce a greater degree of safety. The more normal course would have been to seek safety in numbers and send the entire force together, thus overawing the depleted Athenian navy, which had not yet dared show itself. Nor does such cautious and ill-advised behavior accord well with the alleged contempt of the Athenian navy. For all of their bravado, the Peloponnesians seem still to have been nervous and poorly led when they went to sea.

In spite of the eagerness of the allies to set sail, the expedition was delayed by the arrival of the time for the Isthmian games and the

[50] 8.8.1.
[51] 8.8.3–4.
[52] This is my understanding of the puzzling passage in 8.8.3.

Corinthian refusal to sail until they were completed. Here Agis intervened, offering to allow the Corinthians to maintain their truce while he "made the expedition his own business," that is, took command, leaving the Corinthians behind. From the Corinthian point of view, this was entirely unacceptable, for it would mean that the war would continue during the games, making the sacred truce a sham. Combatants from both sides would be distracted by and involved in the war, and others would be deterred from coming to the Isthmus. The games, which brought not only honor but also profit to the host city, would be a failure.[53] The Corinthians, therefore, refused and, presumably, gained enough allied support to prevent Agis from having his way.

The delay had serious consequences, as the Chians had feared when they had urged haste on the Spartans. The Athenians learned that a plot was brewing and sent the general Aristocrates to confront the Chians with the charge. When it was denied, he demanded that they contribute some ships to the allied navy as a sign of good faith (and, perhaps, as hostages for their good behavior). The plotters were cautious men and had to be confronted before they were ready to act. They were oligarchs who feared that the common people would be hostile to their plans if they were revealed prematurely. There was also a faction among the upper classes that was friendly to Athens. Finally, and most important, the delay of the Peloponnesians in answering their call had convinced them that they would not come at all. For these reasons the Chians obeyed Aristocrates' demand and sent seven ships to the imperial fleet.[54]

Only after the Isthmian games, in July of 412, did the first detachment of the Peloponnesian fleet sail out of Corinth's eastern port at Cenchreae under the command of Alcamenes (see Map 2).[55] It was soon challenged by an Athenian fleet of the same size as its twenty-one ships, for the Athenians had taken advantage of the truce to attend the Isthmian games, where they learned more about the Chian plot and the Peloponnesian plans for aiding it. On their return to Athens, they set up a watch on Cenchreae and prepared a fleet to meet the

[53] This is how I interpret Agis' offer reported on 8.9.1, following a suggestion of Hatzfeld's (*Alcibiade*, 219). He goes so far as to say that Agis secretly favored the delay, for it gave him the chance to gain the command of the expedition.
[54] 8.9.2–3. For the pro-Athenian faction at Chios, see 8.38.3; and Andrewes, *HCT* V, 22–23.
[55] 8.10.2. For the date, see Andrewes, *HCT* V, 23–24.

ships they expected to sail from it. When Alcamenes' fleet came out of harbor, the Athenians tried to draw him out to the open sea for a battle, but the Spartan admiral turned back to his harbor. The Athenians did not pursue, for they did not trust the seven Chian ships that made up a third of their force. They withdrew to the Piraeus, where they added ships to bring their fleet up to a total of thirty-seven. Then they renewed the chase, pursuing the enemy fleet as it was making its way southward along the coast. At the sight of the Athenians, Alcamenes hastened to seek safety in the deserted port of Spiraeum, just north of the Epidaurian border.[56] The Athenians caught one Peloponnesian ship before it could reach safety, but the others reached the harbor. The Athenians then attacked them by land and sea, destroying most of their ships on the beach and killing Alcamenes.

The next day the Corinthians came with naval reinforcements, and other allies in the neighborhood sent help too. But the Athenians were not satisfied with the victory they had already achieved. They sent a fleet to keep watch on the enemy and established their main camp on a small island near by, sending to Athens for reinforcements. They were determined to let no Peloponnesian fleet sail into the Aegean and to seize whatever opportunity offered to destroy the enemy's forces. The Peloponnesians were greatly daunted by what had taken place. They found themselves needing to guard their ships in a deserted place that offered neither supplies nor protection. They were so baffled that their first thought was to burn the ships to prevent their falling into Athenian hands. On reflection, they decided instead to draw the ships up and shore and guard them with their soldiers until a chance of escape should occur. Agis at Decelea learned of their situation before the news got to Sparta, and he sent Thermon, a Spartan, to replace the fallen Alcamenes as commander.

The news came to Sparta as a great shock. The first report the Spartans received came by prearranged signal from a courier on horseback. The ephors had ordered Alcamenes to dispatch such a messenger as soon as his ships set sail so that they could send the five ships under Chalcideus to join him. Spirits were high, and the men were eager to sail. Then came the news of the defeat, the death of Alcamenes, and the blockade at Spiraeum. The mood changed at once from excitement to discouragement and gloom. "Having failed in their first

---

[56] 8.10.3. For the name and location of the port of refuge, see Andrewes, *HCT* V, 24–25.

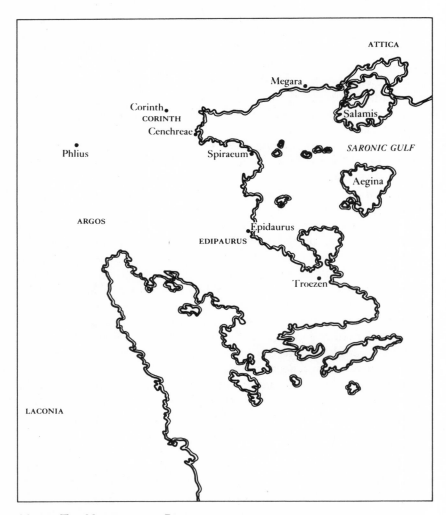

ATTICA

Megara

Corinth
CORINTH
Cenchreae

Phlius

Spiraeum

Salamis

SARONIC GULF

Aegina

ARGOS

Epidaurus
EDIPAURUS

Troezen

LACONIA

MAP 2. THE NORTHEASTERN PELOPONNESUS

undertaking in the Ionian war they no longer thought of sending out their ships but even wanted to recall those that had already put out to sea."[57]

This sharp change of mood would have passed in time, and the Spartans could not have failed to make another attempt at spreading and supporting rebellion in the Aegean. Any other policy would have meant conceding victory to Athens at a time when the chances for defeating the Athenians were greater than ever. We may assume that Agis, hearing of the discouragement of his countrymen, would have used his considerable influence to restore their purpose and determination. But that would take time and probably lose the opportunity of gaining Chios as a solid base of operations and its fleet as a large nucleus of the force needed to overthrow Athens. Thucydides, therefore, is probably right to emphasize the important role played by Alcibiades in moving Sparta to action again. He went to the ephors (more easily since his friend Endius was one of them) and urged them to send out the five ships under Chalcideus not, as originally planned, to join the other Peloponnesian ships coming from Corinth but to sail directly to Ionia with himself on board. He argued that if this fleet sailed at once, it would arrive before the news of the defeat suffered by the Peloponnesian fleet. Alcibiades would tell the Ionians of Athens' weakness and Spartan eagerness, and he would be believed more than others because of his uniquely intimate knowledge of both Athens and Sparta and because of his influence with leading Ionians.[58]

To Endius he privately indicated a more personal motive: "It would be good (*kalon*), through the agency of Alcibiades, for him to cause Ionia to revolt and to make the King an ally of the Spartans and not to allow this to become an exploit (*agonisma*) of Agis."[59] He did not

---

[57]8.11.3. This is the only place where Thucydides speaks of an "Ionian War," a name some scholars have given to the entire period between 413 and 404. That is an inappropriate usage, as H. D. Westlake makes admirably clear: "Thucydides uses τοῦ Ἰωνικοῦ πολέμου (8.11.3) but only in a local sense for 'the war in Ionia' and not distinguishing it from other wars. The less appropriate 'Decelean war' soon established itself as the conventional term, presumably representing the viewpoint of contemporaries resident in Athens" (*CQ* N.S. XXIX [1979], 9).

[58]8.12.1; Andrewes, *HCT* V, 25–26.

[59]8.12.2. Thucydides is widely and plausibly thought to have used Alcibiades as a source of information. If so, this may be a quotation of Alcibiades' argument to Endius. The language, in any case, is interesting. It is the language of aristocratic contest, whether in Homeric military combat or Pindaric athletic competition. The words used to translate *kalon* and *agonisma* are inadequate to represent the full range of meaning they evoke. *Kalon* connotes beautiful, good, right, noble; *agonisma*'s most basic meaning

mention that his own position of honor and influence would likewise gain from such an achievement. That would be motive enough for Alcibiades to press his case, but an even stronger motive seems to have impelled him. Thucydides explains his actions with this observation: "for he happened himself to be at odds with Agis."[60] That simple and chaste remark almost certainly refers to a great scandal at Sparta that became notorious in antiquity. In a quarrel over the succession to the Spartan throne early in the fourth century, Agesilaus accused his rival of being illegitimate, offering as evidence a reference to an occasion when an earthquake drove an unnamed adulterer from the chamber of Timaea, Agis' wife, into public view. Plutarch provides the name of the adulterer: Alcibiades.[61] It is reasonable to identify this earthquake with the one mentioned by Thucydides in late February of 412. By July the news would certainly have reached Agis and caused his displeasure with Alcibiades. It was only a matter of time now before Agis would move against him. Alcibiades' best hopes lay in bringing off so great an achievement as to make him invulnerable even to the hostility of the Spartan king. Failing that, his only salvation lay in escape to the last possible refuge, the Persian Empire. The expedition to Ionia offered both possibilities. From the Spartan point of view, Alcibiades' proposal was doubly attractive. With little risk or expense to Sparta, Alcibiades might achieve what he promised. If not, the Spartans would be rid of an increasingly troublesome visitor.[62]

---

is contest, from which comes the secondary sense of a prize for winning a contest, and by extension it comes to mean an achievement or exploit. If Alcibiades used these words, they reveal either his own aristocratic, self-centered attitude toward the goals of war; his belief that they would appeal to such an attitude in the Spartan Endius; or both. If the words were invented by Thucydides, they may reveal his understanding of Alcibiades' character.

[60]8.12.2.

[61]Xen. 3.3.1–2; Plut. *Alc.* 23.7; *Ages.* 3.1–2. One of Plutarch's sources was Duris of Samos, a writer of the late fourth and early third century, who claimed descent from Alcibiades. Another may have been Theopompus of Chios, who was born about 378 B.C. (Andrewes, *HCT* V, 26.) Both the bastardy of Leotychidas, Timaea's son, and the paternity of Alcibiades have been challenged by M. Luria (*Klio* XXI [1927], 404–419). His arguments are answered by J. Hatzfeld (*REA* XXV [1933], 387–395; and *Alcibiade*, 217–219). Andrewes (*HCT* V, 26) points out the chronological difficulties in believing Leotychidas to be the son of Alcibiades, concluding that "none of this is quite impossible, but cumulatively it is not very probable." That is a reasonable conclusion, but even if the fact of Alcibiades' paternity is denied, we need not doubt the adultery or the reality of the rumors that existed and were widely believed in Sparta. They would be enough to account for Thucydides' description of Alcibiades as Agis' "personal enemy," ἐχθρός (8.45.1).

[62]Hatzfeld, *Alcibiade*, 220.

The little fleet under Chalcideus needed speed, luck, and secrecy to reach its destination safely, undetected by the Athenians. Its leaders achieved secrecy by seizing everyone they encountered on the crossing, not releasing their prisoners until they reached the harbor of Corycus on the mainland, some forty miles from the capital city of Chios.[63] There they met with some of their Chian confederates and took their advice to sail to Chios immediately and to arrive suddenly, without advance notice.[64] Their arrival, as the oligarchs had arranged, took place just at the moment when a council was assembling. It generally has been believed that in 412 the Chian constitution was oligarchic and that the body convened was the oligarchical council.[65] But as early as the sixth century, Chios had a popular council (boule demosie) as well as an aristocratic one, and its failure to be mentioned by name in the one relevant fifth-century decree we have from Chios does not argue against its continuation as late as 412.[66] By that time, it may well have included members from all classes, noble as well as common, and may have been the only important council in the state. Such a situation would readily justify Thucydides' praise of the prudence and security with which the Chians governed their city, particularly when we re-member his praise of the Athenian government of the Five Thousand as "a moderate blending of the few and the many."[67] Most probably, the Chian constitution in 412 was mixed, or a moderate oligarchy, and its council likely contained a cross-section of the population.[68]

Such a conclusion best explains the events surrounding the arrival of Chalcideus and Alcibiades in Chios. The oligarchs were keeping their plot a secret from the people at large, but if the constitution were

[63]See Map 3.

[64]8.14.1.

[65]For references, see T. J. Quinn, Historia XVIII (1969), 24; see also W. G. Forrest, BSA LV (1960), 180; and Andrewes, HCT V, 22–23.

[66]For the inscription naming the popular council, see GHI, 8. W. G. Forrest (BSA LV [1960], 180) uses the fact that "the only surviving prescript of a state decree from the fifth century reads only βουλῆς γνώμη" as part of an argument to show the constitution of fifth-century Chios was oligarchic. Not only is the argument from silence based on a single inscription too slender to support such an interpretation but it might support the opposite conclusion equally well. The only boule directly attested at Chios is the one called demosie; it is possible to believe that over time the modifier became otiose and was dropped, so that the only council at Chios in the fifth century may have been the one called "popular" in the previous century.

[67]Thucydides' praise of the Chian goverment: 8.24.4; of the Five Thousand: 8.97.2.

[68]In reaching these conclusions, I have benefited most from the views of T. J. Quinn (Historia XVIII [1969], 22–30).

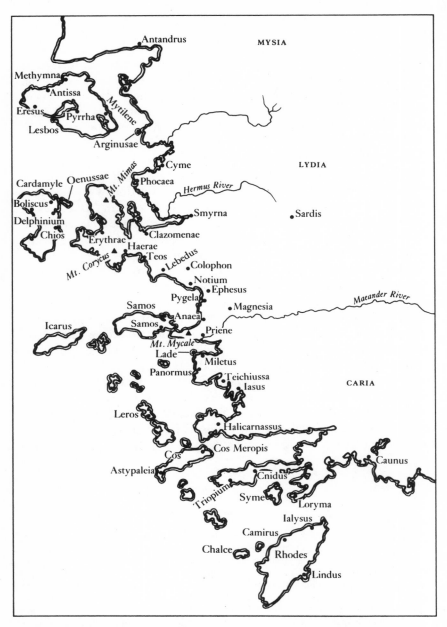

MAP 3. IONIA AND CARIA. Adapted from A. W. Gomme, A. Andrewes, and K. J. Dover, *A Historical Commentary on Thucydides*, V (Oxford, Oxford University Press, 1981), xii, by permission of the publisher.

oligarchic and the council under the control of the few, there was no need for the careful timing of its meeting. In that case, the Spartans could have been brought in and won support at any time, but a popular or mixed council, most of whose members knew nothing of the planned rebellion, needed to be taken by surprise even to allow so dangerous an action as to admit representatives of Sparta to their deliberations. Thucydides tells us that "the many *(hoi polloi)* were in a state of amazement and panic," and presumably, he refers to the majority in the council. But the oligarchs, who had arranged the affair with the aim of producing such shock and fear, quickly introduced Chalcideus and Alcibiades.[69] We may well believe that the presence of Spartan ships and soldiers played a larger role than the eloquence of the speakers in changing the allegiance of the Chians. Still, Alcibiades' careful presentation must have played a part. He suppressed the news of the Peloponnesian defeat and the fact that their fleet was currently shut in by an Athenian blockade at Spiraeum. He told them that a large, additional fleet was on its way, and this caused the Chians to embark on rebellion, bringing Erythrae with them.[70]

This remarkable coup clearly bears the stamp of Alcibiades' approach to war. It aimed at, and in this case achieved, great results at small risk. A tiny fleet and brilliant chicanery had brought to the Spartan cause sixty warships to help challenge Athenian naval supremacy, a safe base of operations, and the first crucial defections from the Athenian Empire. Like his earlier undertakings, the one at Chios relied less on force and power than on persuasion and deception and less on fighting ability than on diplomatic skill. In these efforts, among his last on behalf of Sparta, Alcibiades appears to have done his native city more harm than ever before. His advice to send a force to save Sicily and to fortify Decelea were not acted upon fully or quickly, and he took no part in the execution of either mission.[71] In bringing about the rebellion of Chios, however, his role was crucial in conception,

[69] 8.14.2.

[70] 8.14.3. Some scholars have seen in this incident evidence for the general theory that the lower classes in the Athenian Empire welcomed Athenian rule and resisted rebellion. There is nothing in what we know about the events at Chios in 412 that compels such a conclusion. The facts as we have them are consistent with Quinn's evaluation: "As regarding pro-Athenian feeling, this seems to have amounted to little more than fear of Athens, and there is certainly no justification for claims that most Chians welcomed Athenian domination" (*Historia* XVIII [1969], 30).

[71] See Kagan, *Peace of Nicias*, 257–259.

design, and execution. As he had promised, he had shown the Athenians that he was still alive.[72]

Alcibiades and Chalcideus wasted no time before exploiting their victory. They took three ships to Clazomenae and brought it into the rebellion. Next they moved against Teos, Chalcideus with twenty-three ships from the sea and a force from Erythrae and Clazomenae marching overland. The fleet encountered an Athenian fleet at sea and pursued it to Samos when the Athenian commander Strombichides fled before superior numbers. The land force came to Teos and was received in a way that reveals much about the problems faced by the Ionian cities. Before Strombichides had been forced to flee to Samos, he had come to Teos and had asked the Teians not to rebel. When the army from Erythrae and Clazomenae arrived at their gates, they at first refused them admission. But when the Teians realized that the Athenians would not return, they allowed the army to enter. The soldiers from the rebel cities tore down the wall facing inland to keep the city open to their control, receiving help from a force sent by Tissaphernes.[73] The Teians appear to have acted not on the basis of internal divisions, class divisions, or preferences for one constitution over another but merely out of a prudent concern for their safety. As long as Athenian power was present, they remained loyal. When it was absent, and hostile forces arrived, they accommodated to the new reality. Not much later the Chians and their local allies brought about the rebellion of Lebedos and Haerae, two small towns near Teos, and then withdrew. Then Tissaphernes personally brought an army to finish demolishing the walls of Teos, and he also departed. The appearance of the Persians and their evident interest in resuming control when the situation permitted must have made the protection of Athens seem more attractive. But without their walls, the Teians were in no position to resume the alliance with Athens. When the Athenians' admiral Diomedon arrived with ten ships, the best agreement he could make was that the Teians henceforth would admit the Athenians *as well as* their enemies.[74] Throughout the rest of the war, they pursued this unheroic but prudent policy and avoided the disasters suffered by others.[75]

Before long, the movement Alcibiades and Chalcideus had set in

[72]Plut. *Alc.* 22.2.
[73]8.16.
[74]8.19.3–4; 20.2.
[75]My account is based on H. D. Westlake's article (*CQ* N. S. XXIX [1979], 12–14).

motion at Chios brought about defections in most of the mainland area opposite that island: Erythrae, Clazomenae, Haerae, and Lebedus were in rebellion, and Teos was an open city. Farther to the south, the great city of Ephesus had joined the revolt.[76] Also defecting was Anaea, a small city but strategically located opposite Samos and close to Miletus.[77] Now Alcibiades was ready to bring over Miletus, the jewel of Ionia. Arming the men from the Peloponnesian ships, he left them behind at Chios and replaced them on the ships with Chian crews. The exchange of crews was intended in part, no doubt, to reassure the Chians of a continuing Peloponnesian commitment and, perhaps, to deter opposition to the change of sides. Thucydides, however, tells us the main reason: "Alcibiades, since he was on very close terms with the leading men of Miletus, wanted to win the Milesians over before the arrival of the Peloponnesian ships and, upon the Chians and himself and the Chalcidians and, as he had promised, upon Endius who had sent them out, to confer the prize for having, along with the Chian forces and Chalcideus, caused the rebellion of the greatest number of cities possible."[78]

Once again Alcibiades and Chalcideus moved swiftly, taking care to avoid Athenian ships coming to the rescue, and arrived barely in time to bring Miletus into revolt before the Athenians could prevent it. The rebellion of Miletus was important in itself, but it also provided a base for the spread of rebellion into southern Ionia and Caria and the islands offshore. It was also well situated for launching an attack on Amorges' base at Iasus.[79] Alcibiades had carried out the first part of his pledge, and the defection of Miletus made it possible to achieve the second part. No sooner did the city rebel than Tissaphernes came to negotiate an alliance between the Spartans and the Great King.

The result was a remarkably one-sided document. The Great King should have "whatever territory and cities" he or his ancestors held,

---

[76]Lewis, *Sparta and Persia*, 90, n. 39.

[77]8.19.

[78]8.17.2. Some scholars have seen in the exchange of crews a desire to weaken the democratic forces at Chios and to overawe a possible popular uprising. I have emphasized the explanation offered by Quinn (*Historia* 18 [1969], 27–28), although the two do not necessarily contradict one another. Alcibiades and Chalcideus would have wanted Chians in his fleet to encourage and reward those who rebelled, but he could have done that without exhange crews. Later events would show that Chios contained friends of Athens (8.38.3), so leaving a Peloponnesian force on the island would be prudent.

[79]8.17.3–4; Andrewes, *HCT* V, 40.

and the Persians and Spartans together would work to stop payments to Athens from those cities. If any subjects should rebel against the Great King, the Spartans should aid the king against them, and if there should be any rebellion against the Spartans, the king would aid his new allies. Both allies should fight together against Athens and make no separate peace.[80] The antirebel clause was entirely in favor of Persia, for the Spartans faced no trouble from their allies, whereas the Persians were at war with Amorges and might well consider all Greek cities lost since 480 still to be in a state of rebellion. Nothing was said of financial arrangements or of the level of support, financial and other, that the Persians would provide to Sparta. The territorial clause, taken literally, would return to the Persians all Greek lands they held before Salamis. Later, a distinguished Spartan would proclaim his outrage at its full implications: "It was dreadful," he said, "that the King should even now claim to rule the lands that he and his ancestors had previously held, for that involved the enslavement again of all the islands and Thessaly and Locris and everything as far as Boeotia; instead of freedom the Spartans would be imposing Persian domination upon the Greeks."[81] Small wonder that the Spartans kept this agreement, with its "monstrous concessions," secret.[82]

The conclusion of so cynical, yet disadvantageous, an agreement requires explanation. The treaty negotiated by Chalcideus was never ratified by the Spartans, so the suggestion has been made that it was never more than a draft, "an outline or sketch of preliminaries of a treaty of alliance and that it represents essentially, or perhaps uniquely, the point of view of Tissaphernes that he has put in the hands of the Spartan commander Chalcideus."[83] Presumably, Chalcideus accepted

[80] 8.18.
[81] 8.43.3; the speaker was Lichas.
[82] The quotation is from Busolt, GG III:2, 1426–1427. Grote likewise calls the territorial clause "this monstrous stipulaton" (VII, 376). Busolt (GG III:2, 1427, n. 1) rejects the secrecy of the treaty on the basis of 8.36.2, where "the Peloponnesians," just before a second agreement with Persia is made, are said to be dissatisfied with the earlier one. But these unspecified Peloponnesians were probably few, especially well informed, and in on the secret. Hatzfeld (Alcibiade, 222, n. 4) presents persuasive arguments in favor of secrecy, and Will, although he does not discuss the issue, makes a statement that seems to argue strongly for the need for secrecy: "These Spartan concessions were too scandalous not to frighten those very people who had already 'medized' and who were at present ranged in the camp of the Spartans against the Athenians" (Le monde grec et l'orient, vol. 1, Le Ve siècle (510–403) [Paris, 1972], 364, my translation).
[83] G. De Sanctis, in Studi di storia della storiografia greca (Florence, 1951), 86–87.

it without demur because of his incompetence.[84] But whatever its legal status, the agreement was effective, for almost immediately the Spartans put their forces at the service of Tissaphernes in his campaign against the rebel Amorges, just as they promised in the treaty.[85] Another approach is to emphasize the vague, imprecise, incomplete nature of the agreement: "this is a very simple-minded document. . . . No one seems to be thinking the first clause through to the point of determining, for example, whether Sparta is going to have to go back on her new treaty with Erythrae." In this view Sparta's motives are inexplicable: "Since Chalkideus, the negotiator of the treaty, soon got killed (24.1), no one was in a position to ask him what he was playing at."[86] Other scholars speak of the necessities of war and Sparta's great hatred for Athens, which blotted out all thought of the future.[87]

There is considerable merit in this view, but it still leaves open the question why the Spartans should make a treaty with so few advantages to them, one that they would soon reject and renegotiate. Chalcideus may have been a diplomatic neophyte, easy for an experienced Persian like Tissaphernes to gull, but at his side stood Alcibiades, a veteran of many negotiations and far from innocent of the diplomatic arts. It is not hard to believe that Alcibiades helped persuade his inexperienced commander to act quickly. No doubt he argued that quick action was needed if Chalcideus were to get the credit for bringing about the great achievement, an alliance with Persia. Details were unimportant, he might well say, and could be changed later. The main thing was to get a commitment from the Persians before some other Spartan, perhaps a member of Agis' faction, could arrive and win the prize. All of this is conjecture, for no ancient source speaks of Alcibiades' role. But if Alcibiades did not make such arguments to Chalcideus, they were at least relevant to his own circumstances. His time was running out, as the enmity of Agis threatened his position and his safety. He needed striking achievements, and he needed them at once. The treaty of Chalcideus might be criticized, but for the moment it was a great

[84]Hatzfeld (*Alcibiade*, 222) speaks of "the inexperience of Chalcideus, badly informed in diplomatic formulas and oriental tricks."
[85]8.28.2–4. The point is well made by Hatzfeld, *Alcibiade*, 222, n. 5.
[86]Lewis, *Sparta and Persia*, 90–91.
[87]Busolt, *GG* III:2, 1427, n. 1. In the same vein J. B. Bury (*History of Greece*, rev. R. Meiggs, 4th ed. [New York, 1975], 307) says: "In the hope of humbling to the dust her detested rival, the city of Leonidas now sold to the barbarian the freedom of her fellow-Greeks of Asia."

success, and the Athenian exile who was thought to have cuckolded a Spartan king was living from moment to moment. With the risings in Ionia and the treaty with the Great King, Alcibiades could claim to have kept his promises to Endius, the ephors, and Sparta. Time would show that these successes were flawed, but Alcibiades had turned the tide, shaken Sparta from its timidity and lethargy, and set it on the path to ultimate victory.[88]

[88]In analyzing the role of Alcibiades, I have followed the persuasive suggestion of Hatzfeld (*Alcibiade*, 222–223).

3. Athens Responds

News of the Chian rebellion moved the Athenians to quick action, for they recognized the greatness of the danger threatening them: "the remaining allies would not want to remain quiet when the greatest state was in rebellion."[1] In this emergency they took the serious step of turning to the reserve fund that they had put aside at the beginning of the war. One thousand talents had been placed on the Acropolis, not to be used unless an enemy fleet was attacking by sea, and the death penalty threatened any man proposing to use the fund for any other purpose.[2] In the summer of 412, however, the Athenians concluded that they should wait no longer. They removed the penalties against putting the question and voted to use the reserve fund to meet the immediate danger.[3] But building new ships would take time, and immediate action was needed. At the same meeting they ordered the generals Strombichides and Thrasycles to abandon the blockade of the Peloponnesians at Spiraeum and to sail swiftly to Chios, and they recalled the seven Chian ships, now obviously unreliable, from the same blockade. To replace all of these ships, they quickly manned others to maintain the blockade and were planning to put thirty more out to sea. "Their zeal was great, and there was nothing petty in their effort to send aid against Chios."[4]

[1] 8.15.1.
[2] 2.24.1. One hundred of the best ships and their captains were also set aside for the same purpose, but Thucydides makes no further mention of them. They must have been used for some other purpose well before the Chian revolt.
[3] For the date, see Philochorus (*FGrH* III, 328, Fr. 138); Busolt, *GG* III:2, 1422, n. 3; and Andrewes, *HCT* V, 23–24, 37.
[4] 8.15.2.

The Athenians had great need for such enthusiasm and were right to tap their emergency reserve fund at this time. Unless the rebellion at Chios was checked at once, it would soon spread to the entire empire, depriving the Athenians of income and placing greater demands on such money as they had. Each day that passed with the rebellion not suppressed was a day that the Athenians could not collect commercial taxes from some of their allies but must never the less pay their own rowers to try to end the rebellion. The Peloponnesians, moreover, could not be kept from Ionia forever. The longer the rebellion lasted, the greater the likelihood of Persian support for the Peloponnesian fleets. The longer the enemy fleet was at sea, the smaller the tactical advantage for the more experienced Athenian rowers and officers. The Athenians were entirely right to treat the crisis as if an enemy fleet threatened the Piraeus and the safety of Athens. Every moment counted, and the Athenian commanders needed to take the swift, bold, decisive actions that would promise quick success, even at some risk. A cautious policy that might contain the rebellion without snuffing it out would be at least as risky as a bold one, for Athens' slender resources were unlikely to bring success in an extended war.

The generals who took command of the Athenian forces in July of 412 had been elected early in the spring, when the Athenians were probably in very much the same sober mood that had led them to introduce the *probouloi*. Very likely, their political views would have ranged from moderate to conservative, but all would have been seen as respectable, patriotic men who could be trusted in this moment of need. Nineteenth-century scholars divided the generals during 412/11 into democrats and oligarchs or moderates and oligarchs, depending largely on their later behavior during the oligarchic coup of 411.[5] But their responses to the coup were not necessarily predictable, and any political views that lay behind them, particularly among the oligarchs, would not likely have been paraded before the people. Strombichides, Diomedon, and Leon would prove to be staunch democrats, whereas Phrynichus, Onomacles, and possibly Scironides would become supporters of the oligarchic movement,[6] but all would have come forward

[5]Beloch, *AP*, 66; Busolt, *GG* III:2, 1412; Meyer, *GdA* IV:2, 267.
[6]About the political inclinations of other generals—Thrasycles, Euctemon, Charminus, and Eucrates—there is no good evidence. For the list of generals, see Fornara, *Generals*, 66. For brief discussions of nine of them, see *HCT* V, 37, 43, 59–60, 72. The tenth, Eucrates, is not mentioned by Thucydides but is called a general by a scholiast to Aristophanes (*Wasps* 103).

as moderates in the election of March of 412. Even Phrynichus, who later would be a leader of the oligarchic coup, was condemned afterward as a poor man, a sycophant, and a turncoat democrat.[7] As one shrewd commentator has put it, "all that we can certainly say is that Phrynichus was a man with a long public career, who could be labelled as a democratic leader and inspired enough trust to be appointed general in 411 at an advanced age, presumably on the basis of his past record in office."[8] His colleagues must have fit into the same general category and no doubt were chosen for a variety of reasons arising from their personalities, careers, and connections.

More important than their political associations at the moment were their experience and talent. None of the new generals is known to have held that post before.[9] Perhaps some of them had served as trierarchs, although most of these captains of triremes would have been lost at Syracuse. Events would soon show that the Athenians still had officers and crews capable of distinguished naval service worthy of their predecessors, but in the summer of 412, no one had that combination of daring, skill, experience, and personal authority needed to produce success.

Strombichides' tiny fleet of eight triremes could do little to resist Chalcideus' Peloponnesian force, almost three times the size of his, and he was forced to flee to the Athenian base on Samos, where he was soon joined by Thrasycles' fleet of twenty ships.[10] Nineteen ships of the combined fleet pursued the Peloponnesians on their way to bring about the revolt of Miletus, but the Athenians arrived too late to prevent its fall. All they could do was take up a position at the island of Lade, just offshore, to keep watch on and blockade Miletus. In spite of the Peloponnesians' striking success, their position was far from secure. The arrival of further Athenian reinforcements might reverse the situation swiftly and change the entire course of events.[11]

[7]Lys. 20.11–12, 25.9.

[8]Andrewes, *HCT* V, 59–60.

[9]The lists for the previous years are far from complete, so we cannot be absolutely sure each was a neophyte. We can be confident, however, that none played a role of enough importance to deserve mention in the sources, which are good for the preceeding years. Fornara (*Generals*, 66) lists Strombichides among the generals for the previous year, but his reasoning is not convincing. Neither Beloch nor Busolt includes him in the list for 413/12, and Andrewes (*HCT* V, 37) makes no mention of an earlier generalship.

[10]8.16.

[11]8.17.3. Busolt (*GG* III:2, 1426) points out the precariousness of the Peloponnesians' position.

Chalcideus and Alcibiades had reason to fear the imminent arrival
of Athenian reinforcements, although they could not know when they
might come or how many there might be. Since they outnumbered
the enemy twenty-five to nineteen, the argument for a preemptive
attack was strong, but they took no action. Chalcideus' next decision
was still more surprising. The Chians, who were curious to know the
state of the blockade and how their fellow citizens were faring and
were eager to bring about further rebellions in the region, sailed to
Anaea, the port closest to Miletus, where it was safe for them to land.[12]
Instead of urging them to join him and using his increased force to
attack the Athenians at Lade, he sent a message to the Chians to sail
back home. Thucydides gives either no explanation of Chalcideus'
command or one that is unsatisfactory, depending on how his text is
read.[13] The suggestion has been made that Alcibiades was behind
Chalcideus' failure to take action and that he restrained the Spartan
commander because he was already in the service of Tissaphernes,
"the only man who could protect him against the vengeance of Agis."[14]
But even if suspicion of Alcibiades was already rife among the Peloponnesians in Ionia, and even if Alcibiades was already trying to ingratiate himself with the Persian satrap, there is no reason why
Tissaphernes should object to a Spartan attack on the Athenian fleet

---

[12]8.19.1; *HCT* V, 42.

[13]The MSS read: ἀποπλεῖν πάλιν, καὶ ὅτι Ἀμόργης παρέσται κατὰ γῆν στρατιᾷ.
Some editors connect the report of Amorges' anticipated arrival over land with the
order to the Chians, seeing it as an explanation of that order. Others make the casual
relationship clearer by deleting καὶ. There is, however, no reason to alter the MSS or
to accept the expected arrival of Amorges as an explanation of the order to the Chians.
As Andrewes (*HCT* V, 42) points out, Amorges must come from south of Miletus and
could pose no threat to the Chians at Anaea. Nor, one might add, could he pose a
threat to the Chian ships if they chose to sail to Miletus. If the statement about Amorges,
therefore, was intended to explain Chalcideus' order to the Chians, it fails because it
is irrelevant. Andrewes rightly concludes that the order to the Chians and the statement
about Amorges should be dissociated. He suggests that the latter was meant to answer
the Chian question "What is the situation at Miletus?" His own suggestion about the
motive for Chalcideus' order is less persuasive and properly tentative: "probably that
the Chians were too close to the main Athenian fleet—though Chalkideus could hardly
know yet of the approach of Diomedon." Before Diomedon's arrival with sixteen ships
(8.19.2), we know of no Athenian forces at Samos. Even after he came there were only
three Athenian ships at Samos at the time of its civil war (8.21). There was no hindrance
of which we know to the movement of the ten Chian triremes from Anaea to Miletus,
nor does Thucydides' account provide us with any reason for Chalcideus' order, which
remains enigmatic.

[14]S. Van de Maele, *Phoenix* XXV (1971), 37.

blockading Miletus at Lade.[15] His immediate goal was the defeat of Amorges. The decision to bring the ten Chian ships south to Miletus to strengthen Spartan forces there and then attacking and defeating the Athenians at Lade, thereby making it easier to attack and defeat their ally Amorges, should have pleased the satrap greatly. If Alcibiades were working to win his favor, the Athenian renegade should have urged an attack on his countrymen at Lade.

The most obvious explanation for Chalcideus' inaction is also the likeliest. Like most Spartan commanders before and after him, he was cautious, slow to take the initiative, and particularly reluctant to risk a fight at sea with an Athenian fleet, even one significantly inferior to his own in numbers. The Chians, exposed to Athenian attacks since their own revolt, were now eager to spread the rebellion, share the danger with others, and relieve the pressure on themselves. If Chalcideus had allowed the Chians to join him, they would surely have pressed him to attack the Athenians at Lade. With thirty-five ships to nineteen, he would have found it difficult, if not impossible, to refuse an encounter he did not want to fight. Nor was his attitude foolish or cowardly. The Athenians had lost most of their ships and many rowers and officers at Sicily. Their navy was not what it once had been. But the Spartans and their Peloponnesian allies had not acquired any greater naval skills than the pitifully inadequate ones they had dis-

---

[15] Thucydides seems to date the beginning of the suspicion against Alcibiades after the death of Chalcideus (8.24.1) and the battle of Miletus (8.25–26): Ἀλκιβιάδης μετὰ τὸν Χαλκιδέως καὶ τὴν ἐν Μιλήτῳ μάχην τοῖς Πελοποννησίοις ὕποπτος ὤν, καὶ ἀπ' αὐτῶν ἀφικομένης ἐπιστολῆς πρὸς Ἀστύοχον ἐκ Λακεδαίμονος ὥστ' ἀποκτεῖναι. . . . "After the death of Chalcideus and the battle at Miletus Alcibiades, being an object of suspicion to the Peloponnesians and a letter having come to Astyochus from Sparta as a result of this ordering him to be killed, . . . he withdrew to Tissaphernes" (8.45.1). Hatzfeld (*Alcibiade*, 225, n. 7) believes that the letter to Astyochus was instigated by the Peloponnesian allies serving with the Spartans in Asia Minor, Van de Maele (*Phoenix* XXV [1971], 37, n. 21) agrees with him but believes the suspicion arose after the death of Chalcideus and before the battle of Miletus, thus explaining why Alcibiades might have been working in behalf of Tissaphernes earlier than is generally thought. Andrewes (*HCT* V, 95), although not unsympathetic to such interpretations of ἀπ' αὐτῶν, shows that they are neither inevitable nor easy. Another approach, as Andrewes points out, is to take "αὐτῶν as neuter, 'as a result of this,' " that is, to take the passage to mean that the letter condemning Alcibiades came from Sparta as a result of suspicions of him arising among the Peloponnesians, location unspecified. In that case, the passage would seem better to support a date for the rise of suspicion against Alcibiades after the battle of Miletus. Andrewes sees problems with this reading, too, but does not exclude it. This passage seems too unclear to support Van de Maele's theory that Alcibiades was already working for Tissaphernes because he was already the object of suspicion among the Peloponnesian forces in Ionia.

played in the earlier stages of the war. In the next years the first important naval engagements of the Ionian War at Cynossema and Cyzicus would demonstrate that Athenian tactical superiority at sea continued.[16]

Chalcideus' delay put an end to the Peloponnesians' advantage and the chance of fighting a naval battle quickly against a less numerous enemy fleet, for the Athenians had already sent a reinforcing fleet of sixteen ships under Diomedon. They had left Athens soon after Thrasycles and arrived in time to meet the ten Chian ships sailing north from Anaea. Diomedon was able to capture four Chian triremes, although their crews escaped.[17] Soon Leon brought another squadron of ten ships from Athens, bringing the Athenian fleet in Ionian waters up to a total of forty-six, one ship having sailed to join the blockading fleet at Lade and twenty-six at Athens' main base on Samos.[18]

While the Athenians were establishing Samos as their chief base of operations, an uprising occurred on that island unique in its bitterness, even during the cruel course of the Peloponnesian War. The common people rose up against the aristocrats of the governing oligarchy with the assistance of the crews of three Athenian warships that were docked at the island.[19] They killed 200 of the Samian noblemen and exiled another 400. They seized their lands and houses, distributing them among themselves. The vindictive revolutionaries seem to have deprived the aristocrats of their civic rights and even of the right of intermarriage with the newly dominant lower class.[20] The new democracy on Samos was powerfully dependent upon Athens for support against a countercoup, perhaps supported by a colony of oligarchic exiles long since established at Anaea on the coast just opposite the

---

[16]Cynossema: 8.104–106; Cyzicus: Xen. 1.11–18.

[17]8.19.3–4.

[18]Leon: 8.23.1; twenty ships at Lade: 8.24.1. For a useful discussion of ship numbers in the Aegean, see *HCT* V, 27–32.

[19]I formerly held the view that the Athenian settlement of the Samian rebellion of 440 included the establishment of a democratic government there (Kagan, *Outbreak*, 176, and n. 16). I have since been persuaded by the arguments of E. Will (*REA* LXXI [1969], 305–319) and T. J. Quinn (*Athens and Samos, Lesbos and Chios* [Manchester, 1981], 13–23) that the government of Samos between 439 and 412 was an oligarchy in which the *dynatoi*, or aristocrats, played the leading role. For a careful and objective discussion of the evidence and the issues, see *HCT* V, 44–47, 155–156, 257. The use of the term *aristocrats* is justified by the term δυνατοί.

[20]8.21. I derive the deprivation of civic rights from μετεδίδοσαν οὔτε ἄλλου οὐδενός ....

island.[21] Consequently, the Athenians judged them to be entirely trust-worthy and granted them autonomy.[22] That trust was vindicated, for the Samian democracy remained loyal to the Athenians throughout the war, even after the Athenian navy was destroyed at Aegospotami.[23]

With Samos secure, the Athenians were in a position to challenge the ambitions of the still-zealous men of Chios. Eager to expand the number of rebels, the Chians did not wait for significant Spartan aid to arrive before moving ahead with the program agreed upon the previous spring at Corinth.[24] With thirteen ships under the Laconian *perioikos* Deiniadas, they sailed to Lesbos and immediately brought Methymna into rebellion, leaving four ships there to lend support. The others then sailed on to Mytilene and caused it, too, to rebel. At the same time, a land army of Peloponnesians, the sailors from Chalcideus' ships who had been left at Chios,[25] and the allies from the neighborhood marched northward along the mainland coast under the command of the Spartan Eualas.[26] Starting probably from Erythrae, they passed through Clazomenae, Phocaea, and Cyme, apparently bringing those important cities over to their side.[27]

Meanwhile, the Spartans had broken through the blockade at Spiraeum, with the loss of four ships. The survivors refitted at Cenchreae and sailed for Ionia under the command of Astyochus, the new navarch sent to take command of the entire Peloponnesian fleet.[28] He arrived

---

[21]For Anaea, see *HCT* V, 42, 45–46; Quinn, *Athens and Samos, Lesbos and Chios*, 17–19.

[22]What precisely was implied by this grant is unclear. Perhaps they were given some judicial privilege (G. E. M. de Ste. Croix, *CQ* LV = N. S. II [1961], 272). Possibly, they were given the right to strike coins, as J. P. Barron (*The Silver Coins of Samos* [London, 1966], 100–101) suggests. The gesture was probably of more psychological than practical importance, bespeaking a special relationship of trust and confidence between the two democracies and promising a new relationship after the war. Some scholars connect *IG* I² 101 (see D. M. Lewis, *BSA* XLIX [1954], 29–31) with this grant of autonomy, but the inscription is not dated and is too fragmentary to be useful.

[23]Xen. 2.2.6.

[24]8.8.2.

[25]8.17.1; *HCT* V, 50.

[26]8.22.

[27]*HCT* V, 50.

[28]8.20.1. There has been considerable debate about whether at this time the navarchy was a regular, annual office, undertaken and relinquished at specific times of the year. The most influential affirmative argument was made by Beloch (*GG* II²:2, 269–289). The most recent negative argument is made by R. Sealey (*Klio* LVIII [1976], 335–358), who believes that the navarchy was made a regular magistracy with a fixed term only about 409. Until then, he believes, the navarch was appointed for specific tasks, and his term ended with completion of the task. (For briefer, but useful discussions,

in Chios with four ships to find the Chian fleet at Lesbos. Two days
later, adding a Chian ship to his little fleet, he sailed off to join the
main Chian force at Lesbos and to give what help he could. He landed
at Pyrrha, moving on to Eresus the next day. There, he learned that
an Athenian fleet of twenty-five ships under the generals Leon and
Diomedon had landed on Lesbos earlier on the same day as his own
arrival. The Athenians had escaped detection and had taken the enemy
by surprise at Mytilene. They defeated the Chian ships in the harbor,
won a battle on land, and took the main city of Lesbos on the first
assault. Astyochus brought Eresus into rebellion and set out along the
northern coast of the island to try to save the rebellion at Methymna
and to cause one at Antissa. But these efforts failed. Thucydides says
that "everything on Lesbos was going against him," so he embarked
his troops and sailed back to Miletus. Without the support of a fleet,
the land army did not continue on its way to the Hellespont but
dissolved, each allied contingent returning to its own city.[29] The attempt on Lesbos had failed entirely and with it the plan the Peloponnesians had formed at Corinth to end the war swiftly by taking
Chios and Lesbos and cutting the Athenian lifeline with an expedition
to the Hellespont.[30] Typical Spartan hesitation had given Athens time
to recover, and the arrival of Leon and Diomedon at Lesbos had turned
the tide for the moment in favor of the Athenians.

The Athenian commanders wasted little time putting matters in
order on Lesbos and turned quickly to the offensive. Their main purpose was the recovery of Chios, but first they took Clazomenae, a
coastal town not far from it.[31] After returning to Lesbos, they set sail
for the island that had been first to revolt and was still the most active
in bringing other cities into rebellion. Leon and Diomedon seized the
Oenussae islands, just off the northeast point of Chios, and the fortified
towns of Sidussa and Pteleum on the Erythraean peninsula, on the
mainland just opposite Chios, as nearby bases for conducting a close

---

see Busolt [*GG* III:2, 1429, n. 3] and Andrewes [*HCT* IV, 38; V, 43–44, 454–455]).
Whichever view is correct, we should not expect to find the Spartans behaving with
perfect regularity in sending out new navarchs, for the record shows many
inconsistencies.

[29]8.23.5. The reading ὁ τῶν ξυμ[μάχων] in the papyrus II²⁴, as restored by Powell,
is preferable to the reading of the MSS ἀπὸ τῶν νεῶν. For supporting arguments, see
HCT V, 53; and *Thucydide, La guerre du péloponnèse*, ed. and trans. R. Weil and J. de
Romilly (Paris, 1972), VIII, 17, n. 5.

[30]8.8.2.

[31]8.23.6.

blockade and seaborne assaults.[32] The Athenians easily controlled the
sea with their twenty-five ships against an unknown number of the
Chians, who were, therefore, unable to prevent them from landing.[33]
The Athenians were also superior on land, for they had brought along
hoplites from the catalog of regular heavily armed infantrymen, con-
scripted to serve as marines in place of the thetes who usually served
in that capacity.[34] The Athenians were victorious time after time as
they sailed around the island, and finally, the Chians ceased to come
out to offer battle against them. The Athenians proceeded to ravage
and plunder their rich, well-cultivated, and well-stocked country, untouched by enemies since the Persian War. This desperate situation
naturally caused some Chians to wish that the rebellion had never
taken place, and some of them now plotted to bring their state back
into Athenian hands. The ruling officials became aware of the plot but
moved cautiously. They called Astyochus from Erythrae with his four
ships and asked him to help as they considered "how they might put
an end to the plot most moderately, either by taking hostages or in
some other way."[35] In fact, Astyochus, took hostages, and for the time
being Chios was safe from internal disruption.[36] The Athenians, however, continued to dominate the island by land and sea and to ravage
its wealth. The first Ionian state to rebel was no longer in a position
to spread the uprising and was on the point of defeat and punishment.

[32]8.24.2. For each location of these places, see *HCT* V, 55, and Map 3.

[33]For the number of Athenian ships, see 8.23.1. The Chian ships mentioned up to
this point are seven taken by the Athenians from the blockading fleet at Spiraeum
(8.15.2), four captured without their crews as they sailed from Anaea (19.3), nine
defeated by the Athenians at Mytilene (23.3), and one lost at Methymna (23.4). Twenty
remained blockaded at Miletus. In the spring the Spartans had sent the *perioikos* Phrynis
to check on the Chian claims. He was satisfied of the truth of their claims, but he does
not appear to have seen all of the ships claimed with his own eyes. He reported that
"there were not less than sixty there *from what the Chians said*" (ἀφ' ὧν οἱ Χῖοι ἔλεγον)
(8.6.4). The Chians may or may not have been exaggerating their forces to win Spartan
support. Perhaps they included in the total some ships that were not seaworthy. In
any case, we never hear of more than forty-seven of their ships at any one time. The
ease with which the Athenians controlled the sea around Chios at this time suggests
that they may have been superior numerically as well as tactically.

[34]Andrewes (*HCT* V, 56) suggests that the hoplites were compelled to serve on the
ships because thetes were in short supply after the heavy losses in Sicily. That is likely,
but it is also possible that the generals made a special request for such troops, knowing
that fighting on land would be important on this occasion.

[35]8.24.6.
[36]8.31.1.

Its leaders must have seemed to have made a grave error in choosing to launch an uprising against the still potent Athens.

At this point in his narrative Thucydides makes a remarkable digression, defending the Chians against the charge of recklessness or even foolishness.[37] He ranks them second only to the Spartans in their ability to combine good fortune with self-restraint (*eudaimonia* and *sophrosyne*) and admires them for governing their city more securely even as it grew greater. "And even in regard to this rebellion, if they seem to have acted contrary to their own safety, they did not risk undertaking it until they were sure that they would meet the danger along with many good allies. They also knew that, after the Sicilian disaster, the Athenians themselves did not deny that their situation was very bad. And if they miscalculated among the uncertainties that are part of the human condition in this life, they shared this error with many others who thought the same thing—that the Athenian empire would quickly be destroyed."[38] It is tempting to think that here Thucydides was defending the moderate oligarchy of the Chians, the sort of regime of which he thought so highly, against the accusation that it had behaved with precisely the same dangerous recklessness as the unbridled Athenian democracy that he held responsible for the Sicilian campaign and other foolish acts.[39]

Even before their attack on Chios the Athenians had turned their attention to reducing Miletus, the only other major Ionian city still in rebellion. The blockading squadron at Lade launched a raid on Panormus on the coast to the south of Miletus. They quickly withdrew, but in the fighting they killed the Spartan commander Chalcideus. Later in the year, perhaps in October, they undertook a much more important campaign.[40] The generals Phrynichus, Onomacles, and Scironides had brought a fleet of forty-eight ships, some of them troop carriers, to Samos.[41] Crowded onto these ships were no fewer than 3,500 hoplites—1,000 from Athens, 1,000 from their Aegean allies, and 1,500 from Argos. This was a large force of infantry for Athens to put into the field at any time, but it was truly remarkable so soon

---

[37]H. D. Westlake (*Individuals in Thucydides* [Cambridge, 1968], 236) suggests that such a charge was made at the time, which is highly plausible.

[38]8.24.4–5.

[39]Compare his praise of the Athenian government of the Five Thousand at 8.97.2.

[40]For the date, see Busolt (*GG* III:2, 1432); and *HCT* V, 58.

[41]8.25.1. For discussions of the numbers of triremes and troopships, see Busolt (*GG* III:2, 1433, n. 1); and *HCT* V, 28.

after the Sicilian disaster. Apart from its military purposes, the gathering of so large an army, including so many loyal allies, must have had a considerable effect on the morale of the Athenians who saw it muster and sail off from Piraeus. The effort was proof of Athenian determination to stamp out the rebellion in Ionia before it could become more dangerous.

The generals wasted no time. From Samos they sailed to Miletus, made a landing, and set up camp. The total number of the enemy's forces is unknown, but they consisted of 800 Milesian hoplites; the Peloponnesian marines and, perhaps, some of the sailors that had come with Chalcideus; a corps of mercenaries in the service of the satrap Tissaphernes; Tissaphernes himself, at the head of his cavalry; and, perhaps at his side, Alcibiades, the Athenian renegade, tenuously still in Spartan service.[42] The order of battle set the Argives, who were Dorians, against the Ionian Milesians. Thucydides says that the usual Dorian contempt for Ionian opponents caused the Argives to advance in disorder, far ahead of the rest of their line. Whatever the reason, the Milesians treated their attackers roughly, killing at least 300 and defeating the rest. The Athenians and their Ionian allies were more fortunate. First, they routed the Peloponnesian contingent, and then, they drove off the Persians and their mercenaries. When the Milesians saw what had happened to their allies, they made no attempt to assist them but withdrew into their city. The Athenians made camp before Miletus, having won a great victory, which they formally marked by setting up a trophy. The enemy had been driven from the field, and his remaining forces were huddled in Miletus. All that remained was to wall off the city and wait for it to surrender. The Athenians had no doubt that "if they recovered Miletus the other cities would also readily come over to them."[43]

With the Athenians victorious on land and superior at sea, there was nothing to prevent their success. If only thirty of the newly arrived squadron were triremes, with this number added to the twenty warships already engaged in the blockade, the Athenians would have had an advantage of fifty to twenty-five ships. The Peloponnesians' fear of a sea battle had made them unwilling to fight when they were more numerous, so the Athenians had little to fear at sea under the new

---

[42]8.25.2. For the forces from Chalcideus' fleet, see Busolt (*GG* III:2, 1433; 1426, n. 1); and *HCT* V, 74. For Alcibiades, see 8.26.3.
[43]8.25.5.

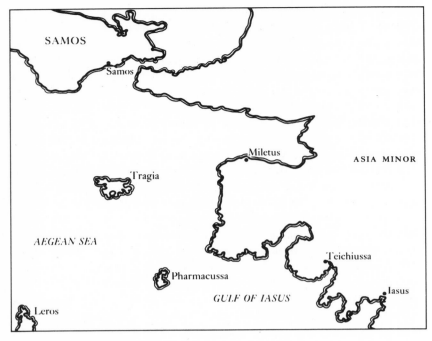

MAP 4. MILETUS AND IASUS

circumstances. But as evening was approaching on the day of the Athenian victory, news arrived that changed the situation significantly. From the nearby island of Leros word came to Phrynichus and his colleagues that a large enemy fleet, fifty-five strong, had arrived and was on its way to Miletus. From Sicily came Hermocrates, nemesis of the Athenians, leading twenty triremes from Syracuse and two from Selinus. With some difficulty, he had persuaded the weary and distracted Syracusans and the Selinuntines, alone among their Sicilian allies, "to take a hand in the final destruction of Athens."[44] The remaining ships were Peloponnesian, and the whole fleet was commanded by the Spartan Therimenes as it sailed across the Aegean. He was under orders to bring it to the navarch Astyochus at the end of the voyage.

Therimenes touched land at Leros, where he learned that the Athenians were at Miletus. Since Leros is some forty miles away, he sailed

[44]8.26.1. For the situation in Sicily, see Busolt (*GG* III:2, 1423). Diodorus (13.34.4, 63.1) gives the number of ships under Hermocrates as thirty-five, but see *HCT* V, 61.

into the Gulf of Iasus to get better information, landing and making camp at Teichiussa.[45] There, he encountered Alcibiades, who had come on horseback from Miletus, and learned the outcome of the battle. Thucydides tells us that Alcibiades was eloquent in urging swift action. "If they did not wish to destroy their position in Ionia and their cause in general, they should go to the aid of Miletus as fast as possible and not stand by while it was walled off."[46]

The Peloponnesians took him seriously and made ready to sail for Miletus at dawn, but Alcibiades' speed and eloquence proved to be irrelevant. Before the Peloponnesians could move, the Athenians had withdrawn and had left Miletus in enemy hands. The news of the approaching Peloponnesian fleet had not daunted Onomacles, Scironides, Strombichides, and Thrasycles, who wanted to stay in place and fight a naval battle to the finish, but the remaining Athenian general, Phrynichus, argued against them.[47] Thucydides reports his speech in indirect discourse:

He said that he would not do it [fight a battle himself], nor would he allow them or anyone else to do so, so far as he was able. For when it was possible to fight at a later time, having more certain knowledge of how many ships the enemy had and how many of their own were available against them, having prepared adequately and at leisure, he would never, giving way to the charge of disgrace, run a desperate risk. It was not shameful for the Athenians at sea to make an opportune strategic withdrawal, but it would be more shameful to be defeated, in any circumstances whatever. For the state did not face disgrace only, but also the greatest danger; after the disasters they had undergone it was hardly justified voluntarily to undertake any offensive action whatever, unless it was absolutely necessary; it was even less justified, without being compelled, to rush into dangers of their own choosing.[48]

He advised the Athenians to collect their wounded and their hoplites and supplies, but not their booty, which would burden the ships too heavily, and return to Samos. "From there, when once they had gathered together all their ships, they could launch attacks whenever the time might be ripe."[49]

Phrynichus' argument carried the day, and the Athenians sailed to Samos at dusk, "their victory incomplete," for Miletus was unconquered and now free from both siege and blockade. A further conse-

[45]See Map 4. For the location of Leros and Teichiussa, see *HCT* V, 62.
[46]8.26.3.
[47]8.27.1. For the names of the generals present, see Busolt (*GG* III:2, 1434); and *HCT* V, 63.
[48]8.27.2–3. For a discussion of the textual difficulties, see *HCT* V, 63–64.
[49]8.27.4.

quence of the Athenian withdrawal was the swift and angry departure of the Argive hoplites.[50] Thereafter, Argos played no part in the war. Caution at Miletus seems to have cost the Athenians the aid of one of their most important allies.[51] The Athenian retreat had still another unhappy consequence. The next morning the reinforcing fleet under Therimenes sailed from Teichiussa to Miletus. Deprived of a battle, they waited a day and collected the twenty-five ships of the late Chalcideus' squadron, now freed from blockade. They would have returned to Teichiussa the next day, since they had left their sails, masts, and rigging, but Tissaphernes arrived with his army and persuaded them to sail against Amorges at Iasus. Amorges had not been told of the Athenian retreat, so his people assumed that the approaching fleet was Athenian and made no effective resistance. The Peloponnesians took Amorges alive and turned him over to Tissaphernes. The mercenaries who made up Amorges' army were mostly Peloponnesians, so they were simply taken into the Peloponnesian force. Iasus was sacked, its people were sold to Tissaphernes for the equivalent of 20 drachmas each, and what was left of the town was turned over to Tissaphernes.[52] The Peloponnesians returned to Miletus and put a Spartan, Philippus, in charge as governor.[53] The Athenians had lost another ally, the Persians were rid of an annoying distraction, and the Spartans and Persians had cooperated to achieve their first victory together.

Although Thucydides characterizes the Athenian victory at Miletus as incomplete, he gives Phrynichus his full approval and unusual praise:

[50]8.27.6. The text reads: πρὸς ὀργὴν τῆς ξυμφορᾶς, and it is usual to take ξυμφορᾶς to refer only to the defeat of the Argives in battle. I prefer to understand it in its primary sense of "event" or "circumstance" and to connect it with the whole event at Miletus, which included a defeat for the Argives accompanied by a victory for the army of which they were part, followed by a disappointing and apparently ignominious retreat. It is hard to see why the Argives, however angry for their defeat, should think it a good and honorable reason to depart. A much better reason, from the point of view of Greek notions of honor, would be anger and chagrin at being deprived of a chance to avenge their defeat by future fighting.

[51]The Argives had fought alongside the Athenians in large numbers at Mantinea, sent a contingent to Sicily, and were present in force at Miletus at this moment of great peril to Athens. The battle of Miletus in 412 is the last time they fought. Busolt (GG III:2, 1435) and Meyer (GdA IV:2, 273, n. 1) suggest that Argos may have made a formal peace with Sparta soon after, but they offer no evidence. Since the Argives offered the Athenians help in 411 (8.86) and associated themselves with the mission to Persia in 408 (Xen. 1.3.13), an Argive–Spartan peace treaty seems unlikely.

[52]8.28. For some interesting suggestions about the fate of Iasus and its people, see M. Amit, SCI II (1975), 57–59.

[53]8.28.5.

"Later on no less than on the present occasion, in this matter but also. in all the others in which he took part, he appears not to have been lacking in intelligence."[54] In the face of such an endorsement by the great contemporary historian, we need not be surprised that most modern historians have accepted Phrynichus' point of view.[55]

A different judgment, however, is possible and was made by Phrynichus' contemporaries. His four fellow generals had strongly disagreed with him before he persuaded at least two of them to vote for withdrawal. In the next year, moreover, he was charged, along with Scironides, who must have been more closely identified with the final decision than the others, with responsibility for the loss of Iasus and Amorges.[56] Peisander was engaged in a plot to overthrow the democracy and may have acted from political or personal motives, but the men who found Phrynichus and Scironides guilty were not part of the plot but were good democrats who voted to replace the deposed generals with sound democrats such as Diomedon and Leon.[57] Their verdict may have been influenced by the intervening events, but that does not make it less honest or correct.[58]

In fact, there is good reason to agree with Phrynichus' judges and to blame him for the misfortunes that followed upon his decision not to fight. Thucydides' account allows us to reconstruct the debate in

[54]Thucydides' word for "intelligence" is *xynesis*, and throughout his work he applies it sparingly. He uses it only for men such as Themistocles, Brasidas, Pisistratus, and Hermocrates of Syracuse, and he associates it with such terms as "excellence" (*arete*), "competence" (*hikanos*), and "courage" (*andreia*). Themistocles 1.138.3; Brasidas 4.81.2 (with *arete*); Pisistratus 6.54.5 (with *arete*); Hermocrates 6.72.2 (with *hikanos* and *andreia*). Further evidence of Thucydides' high regard for this quality is that in speeches he reports Pericles as praising it (1.140.1) and Cleon as condemning it (3.37.4–5).

[55]Most, in fact, who have noticed or discussed the issue. Grote is an exception in blaming Phrynichus for failing to warn Amorges of his withdrawal, but on the main point he follows Thucydides. Busolt (*GG* III:2, 1435) and Meyer (*GdA* IV:2, 272) offer arguments in support of Phrynichus, whereas Ferguson's account in *CAH* (V, 316–317) clearly implies approval.

[56]8.54.3. The charge against Phrynichus and Scironides was Ἴασον προδοῦναι καὶ Ἀμόργην. προδίδωμι often implies betrayal and treason, but it need not. It may simply mean "giving over" or "surrendering." Andrewes' excellent note (*HCT* V, 127) is worth quoting here: "not a matter of treacherous communication with the enemy . . . ; the charge is rather that by persuading his colleages not to fight Therimenes (27) he was responsible for these losses to Athens. προδοῦναι in Greek covers this without difficulty." If the ancient tradition can be trusted, Thucydides himself had been convicted of *prodosia* at Amphipolis in 424 (see Kagan, *Archidamian War*, 299). Perhaps his sympathy for Phrynichus derives, in part, from their common experience.

[57]8.54.3. For the politics of the new generals, see 8.73.4.

[58]For the controversial nature of Thucydides' opinion, see *HCT* V, 66.

the Athenian camp at Miletus with some degree of probability. He says that Phrynichus had clear information about the enemy's ships. Probably, he argued at first that the enemy's numerical superiority made it unwise to fight. The other generals, eager for a battle, must have questioned the report's accuracy. Phrynichus, instead of insisting on the reliability of his facts, shifted his ground and used uncertainty about the enemy's numbers as a reason for not fighting. Apparently, the other generals raised the cry of cowardice, arguing that for the Athenians to refuse battle at sea, the element that they proudly claimed to master, would be shameful. Once again, the artful Phrynichus turned their argument against them, claiming that the real shame was not in strategic withdrawal but in defeat at sea under any circumstances. All of this was mainly sophistry, but he had still another argument. Echoing the language of Pericles, he urged them not "to rush into dangers of their own choosing."[59] After the Sicilian disaster, the Athenians were in no condition to take the offensive. This last point, we may believe, was what won over Phrynichus' colleagues as it also has persuaded modern scholars.

Busolt believes that an attack of uncertain result "would have been highly excessive; a defeat would have had the loss of the land army, too, as its result. In fact, the outcome would have been very uncertain, for the Athenians did not have their previous tactical superiority. . . . The days of Phormio were over."[60] Meyer's view is the same: "The absolute command of the sea, trusting in which Phormio could bravely encounter a more numerous enemy in 429, was gone; at the moment Athens' position in respect to the enemy was scarcely better at sea than for decades past it had been on land."[61] These estimates of Athenian naval prospects in 412 do not accord well with the evidence, being far too pessimistic. To be sure, the days of Phormio were over, but Athens continued to maintain tactical and psychological superiority over its enemies at sea, even after the Sicilian expedition. Earlier in the year the Peloponnesian fleet had been intimidated in Corinthian waters and had been driven to land at a deserted and inconvenient base. Later, nineteen Athenian ships were enough to frighten twenty-five of the enemy into staying in port and enduring a blockade. The

[59]8.27.3. The words αὐθαιρέτους κινδύνους are ones used by Pericles in his speech in 432, on the eve of the war (1.144.1). Whether or not Phrynichus used these words, Thucydides' decision to report or insert them is unlikely to be accidental.
[60]Busolt, *GG* III:2, 1435.
[61]Meyer, *GdA* IV:2, 272.

Athenian fleet under Diomedon and Leon easily swept the seas around Chios and Lesbos clear of enemy ships. In the spring of 411, although the entire Ionian coast was no longer in Athenian hands, the Spartans were so afraid of the Athenian fleet that they sent an army to the Hellespont by land.[62] Only two years after Phrynichus refused battle at Miletus, an Athenian fleet inflicted a defeat on the Peloponnesians at Cynossema in the Hellespont, although it was outnumbered seventy-six to eighty-six.[63]

Alone among modern scholars, Andrewes has correctly described the tactical and strategic situation. The Athenians had lost their best crews in Sicily, but "they had not lost all their skill, nor the Peloponnesians their sense of inferiority." Phrynichus' argument for drawing back from Miletus to fight better another day had this flaw: "that under the conditions he desiderates here Athens could never be sure of forcing a battle." As long as the Spartans had a secure base on land, they could refuse naval battles while sending off armies by land and, by eluding the Athenian navy, even by sea to cause further rebellions from Athens. The Athenians' best hope of getting the enemy to fight a sea battle, in fact, lay in "luring the enemy out against an apparently inferior force." The opportunity Phrynichus refused "offered such a chance in that Therimenes had to take some positive action to save Miletos and Phrynichus' colleagues expected that he would offer battle by sea. If they had been allowed to hang on and fight, the course of the war might have been very different."[64]

Even the modern supporters of Phrynichus concede that a naval victory at Miletus would have been of decisive importance to the Athenians. "If they succeeded in achieving the fall of Miletus," Meyer says, "the attempt of the Peloponnesians would be shattered and the Athenian Empire restored."[65] For Busolt, "the retreat signified the abandonment of the fruits of the siege and of the prospect of recovering Miletus and all Ionia."[66] He goes on to list the further consequences of that retreat: the freeing of the Peloponnesian fleet at Miletus from

---

[62]8.61.1. Amit (*SCI* II [1975], 63) has seen the significance: "The forces moved by foot (πεζῇ) from one theatre of war to another—which shows that the sea route was closed to them. It is unnecessary to stress how difficult and tiresome it was for an army to cover the long distance (200–250 miles) from Ionia to the Hellespont on foot."

[63]8.104–106.

[64]*HCT* V, 66–67.

[65]Meyer, *GdA* IV:2, 271.

[66]Busolt, *GG* III:2, 1435.

blockade, the abandonment of effective fighting against the Chians, "the abandonment of their ally Amorges to his fate, and the departure of the Argives." To that list we may add the loss of Rhodes that would soon follow, the loss of almost all of the coast of Asia Minor, and the freeing of the enemy to carry the war into the Hellespont. The Athenian decision not to fight a naval battle at Miletus was a unique opportunity lost. Its psychological consequences were as serious as its material results. The rebels were given breathing space and new hope. The Spartans and Persians were given an opportunity for successful cooperation. The moderate democracy of the *probouloi* was deprived of the kind of victory that would have given it the prestige to resist oligarchic plots that we know were taking shape. The dangers of a battle against odds were well worth the risks, for the dangers of not fighting were at least as great. Moreover, there is no reason to believe that even a defeat for Athens would have been disastrous. Only in the unique circumstances and confined quarters of Syracuse harbor did a naval defeat need to mean the destruction of a fleet. Even when the Athenians were successful in major battles, they rarely destroyed a majority of the enemy's ships. It was still less likely that the Athenians would suffer major losses in a naval battle at Miletus before breaking off the fighting and retreating to Samos for safety, and as we have argued, the best evidence indicates that Athenian superiority in tactics and morale made any defeat unlikely. In following the advice of Phrynichus, the Athenians made a serious blunder that cost them dearly.[67]

---

[67] Amit (*SCI* II [1975], 56, n. 35) suggests that Phrynichus' advice represented not undue caution but treason. We have no evidence to support that suggestion, and it is hard to think of a motive for treason at this moment.

4. Sparta's Riposte

The withdrawal of Athens' fleet from Miletus presented the Spartans and their allies with the chance to revive the rebellion in the Athenian Empire that had been almost extinguished and to extend it to new regions that were as yet untroubled. It might seem that they should have moved swiftly, using their temporary numerical advantage at sea to rescue Chios, which was the first state to rebel, an important source of support to the rebellion of others, and a key base for spreading the naval war to the vital area of the Hellespont, but a formidable set of problems prevented such action. The Spartans' sense of inferiority at sea, combined with their proverbial caution, usually led them to avoid naval battles, even when their numbers were greater. They also lacked experienced, competent, and trustworthy leaders who were capable of formulating good strategies and tactics and acting on them swiftly and effectively. The short terms and limited naval experience of Spartan commanders were only part of this problem. The last decade of the war shows that, as in the past, Spartan commanders far from home were subject to corruption and often allowed personal and political rivalries to interfere with the conduct of their duties. To all of this must be added the Spartan dependence on Persian support in a war in which the goals of the collaborating powers were far from identical.

The Spartan fleet under Therimenes arrived at Miletus the day after the Athenian withdrawal. Therimenes neither pursued the Athenians to seek a battle nor took his force northward to turn it over to the navarch Astyochus at Chios. Instead, he did a service for Tissaphernes in recovering Iasus from Amorges and withdrew to the safety of Miletus. The Spartans had sent Pedaritus the son of Leon with Therimenes to serve as governor of Chios. Therimenes did not try to deliver him to his post by sea at the risk of a naval encounter with the Athenians but was content to send him overland to Erythrae in command of the mercenary troops taken from Amorges.[1] From Erythrae he could make his way across the strait to Chios.

So the Spartan navarch was still at Chios separated from his navy by the Athenian fleet at Samos when Tissaphernes came to Miletus, probably in early November of 412, to deliver the pay he had promised to the sailors in Sparta's service.[2] Each received a month's pay at the rate of an Attic drachma per day, a figure apparently agreed upon in the discussions at Sparta the previous winter.[3] For the future, however, the satrap said he would pay only half as much unless the king ordered him to pay the full drachma. Therimenes was not navarch and had only the limited mission of delivering the new fleet to Astyochus. He made no complaint at the cut in pay, but Hermocrates, the fiery Syracusan commander, argued effectively enough to win a small concession; each sailor would receive slightly more than a half-drachma each day.[4]

We may wonder about the absence of Alcibiades from these discussions. He had been instrumental in persuading the Spartans to give aid to Chios, as Tissaphernes wanted, rather than support risings in the Hellespont, according to the wishes of the rival satrap Pharnabazus. He was at Chalcideus' elbow when he negotiated the first Spartan treaty with Tissaphernes.[5] He had fought alongside Tissaphernes at the battle of Miletus. He had then proved his devotion to the Spartan cause by riding to the Spartans' fleet at Teichiussa and urging them to sail immediately to save Miletus. He was famous among all of the Greeks for his personal charm and persuasive skill. Surely, he must be the perfect man to argue the Spartan case with the Persian satrap.[6]

But in the month or so between the battle of Miletus and Tissaphernes' return to that city to pay the forces, Alcibiades had changed

[1] 8.28.

[2] 8.29.1. For the date, see Busolt, *GG* III:2, 1436.

[3] 8.5.4–5. See *HCT* V, 70.

[4] 8.29. Thucydides' language does not permit a clear and certain understanding of just how much the concession amounted to. A neat, but by no means conclusive, suggestion is that under the new arrangement each sailor would receive 18 drachmas each month instead of the 15 that a simple half-drachma rate would yield. For a good discussion of the problem, see *HCT* V, 70–72.

[5] 8.17.4.

[6] Aid to Chios: 8.6.3; Miletus and Teichiussa: 8.26.3.

sides again. Recent events had compelled the Athenian renegade to turn his coat once more and to seek safety with the Persian satrap. Some time before the battle of Miletus an Athenian raid on Panormus killed the Spartan commander Chalcideus, depriving Alcibiades of a close colleague.[7] Thucydides says that suspicion against Alcibiades arose among the Peloponnesians "after the death of Chalcideus and the battle of Miletus."[8] These events were probably no more than a few weeks apart, and Thucydides seems to imply that the death of Alcibiades' influential ally allowed suspicions among the Peloponnesian forces to be bruited about publicly until soon after the battle of Miletus, when Alcibiades joined Tissaphernes.

About the same time as the battle of Miletus a new board of ephors took office in Sparta.[9] The departure of Endius from the ephorate deprived Alcibiades of urgently needed support, for as Thucydides emphasizes, "he was a personal enemy of Agis and for other reasons did not inspire confidence."[10] His origins, his personality, and his previous record are perhaps enough to explain why he was the object of distrust in Sparta and needed friends in high places to protect him there. It is less clear why the Peloponnesian soldiers and sailors in Ionia should have come to suspect him of treason, for it was surely at their instigation that a letter was sent from Sparta to Astyochus ordering the navarch to kill Alcibiades.[11]

Thucydides does not give any reasons for the suspicion, apart from the general sense that Alcibiades was untrustworthy, but it is not hard to imagine how such thoughts came to be directed against such a man. Results of the expectations he had raised had been very disappointing. The general rebellion that was expected in the Athenian Empire had been repressed almost as soon as it had begun. Far from serving as a major base of operations and providing important support, Chios was

---

[7]8.24.1.

[8]8.45.1.

[9]Busolt (*GG* III:2, 1437) dates the change of ephors about the beginning of October. Both he (1432) and Andrewes (*HCT* V, 185) date the battle of Miletus in late September or early October.

[10]8.45.1.

[11]Hatzfeld (*Alcibiade*, 225, n. 7) has rightly understood Thucydides to mean that the decision in Sparta was based on complaints from the allied forces in Ionia, although the text is difficult, as Andrewes (*HCT* V, 95) points out. The severity of the sentence makes it clear that Alcibiades was suspected of a capital crime such as treason. Busolt (*GG* III:2, 1437) has no doubt that this was the charge or that Alcibiades was innocent of it.

under siege and was a drain on the Peloponnesians' resources. Athens, far from being exhausted and ready for collapse, had shown itself able to put to sea with a formidable fleet that continued to daunt its enemies. In the month or more between the death of Chalcideus and Tissaphernes' arrival in Miletus, the Peloponnesian soldiers had received none of the pay promised them. Chalcideus, advised and urged on by Alcibiades, had made a treaty with the Persians that was terribly one-sided and would later be denounced as scandalous and as conceding the enslavement of Greeks to the Persian king.[12] This kind of talk must have come to the surface after the death of Chalcideus. After the battle of Miletus, suspicion must have grown even greater. The Peloponnesians had been beaten in a land battle where Tissaphernes' small force of mercenaries had done them little good. The fleet under Therimenes arrived in time to save Miletus, but the numerical superiority it gave them at sea was used for no Spartan purpose. Instead, it was employed to defeat Amorges and turn over Iasus to the satrap. "Where was the financial support, where was the promised war of liberation? When Alcibiades had insisted during the previous winter that the Spartans accept Tissaphernes' offer had he not played Persia's game rather than Sparta's?"[13]

Even before the death of Chalcideus, Alcibiades' situation was becoming more precarious, for he knew of Agis' hostility and of the forthcoming change of ephors, and he saw that events had not gone as well as he had hoped. No doubt he used the occasions when he was with Tissaphernes to establish friendly relations with the satrap, for he might soon need another haven. The change of sides, however, did not take place until after the battle of Miletus, for immediately after the battle he was still active in the Spartan interest.[14] The decisive moment was probably when Alcibiades learned that the letter ordering his death had been sent to Astyochus. The news may well have reached him before it got to the navarch, for we may assume that Endius or some other Spartan friend sent him warning as soon as the decision was made.[15] In any case, he got the news of his condemnation well

[12] 8.43.3.
[13] These are the questions that Hatzfeld (*Alcibiade*, 225) suggests the suspicious Peloponnesian forces were asking.
[14] 8.26.3.
[15] There is a romantic ancient tradition (Justin 5.2.5) that the warning came from Agis' wife, Timaea. Thucydides does not make clear just when Astyochus received the order and Alcibiades the warning. S. Van de Maele (*Phoenix* XXV [1971], 39–40)

before Astyochus' arrival in Miletus, giving him time to offer his services to Tissaphernes and seek asylum with him.

When Tissaphernes appeared in Miletus in his role as paymaster early in November, therefore, Alcibiades had been with him for some weeks.[16] The ancient writers were much impressed by the ease with which Alcibiades won his way into the satrap's favor, the warmth with which he was received, and the highly influential position he so quickly achieved. They emphasize the charm of his appearance, speech, and manner; his successful flattery; and the chameleonlike ability with which he adopted the style and customs of those whose favor he sought. "Therefore," says Plutarch, "though in other respects [Tissaphernes] was the greatest hater of the Greeks among the Persians, he so gave way to the flattery of Alcibiades as to outdo him in counter-flattery." The proof is that Tissaphernes named a most beautiful park in his possession "Alcibiades," and everyone continued to call it by that name.[17] Thucydides says that Alcibiades became the satrap's "adviser in everything" and that Tissaphernes "gave his confidence" to him,[18] but we should not think that the Persian was entirely taken in by the clever Athenian or even that it was guile and instruction that he needed from him.

In the winter of 412/11 Tissaphernes faced several problems with which he might hope Alcibiades could help him. The failure of the Ionian rebellion against Athens to take fire, spread rapidly, and lead to quick Athenian defeat and withdrawal must have surprised him as

---

makes an ingenious and plausible case that the letter from Sparta arrived at Chios while Astyochus was engaged in campaigns on the coast of Asia Minor. Those activities seem to have taken at least two weeks (8.31), so Astyochus would have learned of his orders no sooner than the passage of that time. Alcibiades' friends would have sent the news to him at least as early as the Spartan government sent out the deadly order, so Alcibiades would have gotten the news well before the navarch, probably in mid-October.

[16]This account is based on the belief shared by many scholars (e.g., Busolt [*GG* III:2, 1438, n. 1] and Hatzfeld [*Alcibiade* 226, n. 5]) that 8.29 and 8.45.2 describe the same events. Andrewes (*HCT* V, 95–97) believes otherwise: "I find it more likely that 45.2–3 represents a separate stage of the argument about pay." He points out that there are some differences in detail between the two accounts, but he understands that the incoherence of the two accounts does not allow certainty about which hypothesis is better. To my mind, the differences are so trivial as to argue for identity, and they are easy to explain as deriving from different emphases by the historian writing at different times.

[17]*Alc.* 24.5. Other passages in a similar vein are *Alc.* 23.3–6; Athenaeus XII, 534B, 535E; Nepos, *Alc.* 5.3; Justin 5.2.5–8.

[18]8.45.2; 46.5.

well as the Spartans. We may guess that when he encouraged the Spartans to support the rebellion in Chios, promising to pay their men 1 drachma a day for the purpose, he expected a quick campaign and an easy victory. Instead, the Athenians had quickly recovered the initiative, brought a significant fleet into play, and threatened to snuff out the rebellion. The arrival of a large Peloponnesian fleet and Phrynichus' caution had prevented that outcome, but now he faced the prospect of supporting, at least in part from his own funds, a much larger force than he had expected and, for a period whose end he could not foresee. He did not need Alcibiades to advise him to reduce the promised rate of pay, although he gladly received it. The adherence of Alcibiades offered him a unique individual who knew both Athens and Sparta well, had friends in both camps, and was useful as a source of information and an effective communicator. It was not Alcibiades' plan that he needed.[19] "The real use of the Athenian exile, was to assist the satrap in carrying [his own plan] into execution; and to provide him with those plausible pretences and justifications, which he was to issue as a substitute for effective supplies of men and money."[20] If it pleased Alcibiades to make much of his intimacy with the satrap, to make it obvious that he was Tissaphernes' trusted adviser and confidant, and even to act as the Persian's spokesman on occasion, Tissaphernes did not mind as long as the advice agreed with his own judgment and Alcibiades continued to be useful.

Public display of his intimacy and influence with Tissaphernes pleased Alcibiades greatly; his own plans depended on others, particularly the Athenians, believing that he had the power of influencing, perhaps even controlling the satrap's policy. His safety required that the Spartans should not triumph, for the deadly vengeance of Agis and hostility of the Spartans and Peloponnesians were unlikely to wane with time.[21] To be sure, he was still subject to the death penalty at Athens, but he placed greater hope in the milder and more forgiving nature of the Athenian democracy. Thucydides reveals Alcibiades' purposes in advising Tissaphernes:

Alcibiades gave Tissaphernes and the King the advice he did while under their protection, on the one hand, because he thought it was the best advice for them; at the same time, he was working diligently for his own return to

[19]As Hatzfeld (*Alcibiade*, 228) suggests.
[20]Grote, VIII, 4.
[21]Plut. *Alc.* 25.2.

his native land, for he knew that if he did not destroy it he might some day persuade the Athenians to allow him to return. And he thought that the best way to persuade them was if it appeared that Tissaphernes was on intimate terms with him. And that is exactly what happened."[22]

The first part of Alcibiades' advice was equally suitable to the needs of both the adviser and advisee: to cut the pay given to the Peloponnesians in half and to pay even that irregularly.[23] No doubt it was also equally obvious. Alcibiades' contribution was to provide specious arguments to justify the action and to advise Tissaphernes to bribe the Peloponnesian generals and ship captains to accept those arguments. Tissaphernes, who could probably think of such a plan unaided, succeeded in quieting all of the commanders in this way except for Hermocrates the Syracusan, who alone vigorously argued against the reduction.[24] Alcibiades was probably most effective when he heard that rebellious Ionian cities asked for financial support from the satrap. Flinging in the face of the Chians their own great wealth and reminding the other cities that they had paid money to their Athenian oppressors, he said that they should be willing to use the same money to secure their own liberty.[25]

Alcibiades also suggested that Tissaphernes "not be in too great a hurry to end the war and not to wish to give command of the land and sea to the same power, either by bringing on the Phoenician ships he was preparing or by increasing the number of Greeks to whom he provided pay." Instead, he should allow the two powers each to control its own domain so that the king could always use one side against the other that might trouble him. The wisest, cheapest, and most secure course would be "to wear the Greeks out, one against the other."[26] Alcibiades appeared to believe that the Persians had it in their power to end the war quickly if they chose: Tissaphernes might hire additional Greek forces. But it is far from clear that even significant numbers of additional forces would have helped. Events had shown and would continue to show that victory required a defeat of the Athenian navy, and such defeat depended on well-trained crews of rowers. We have

[22]8.47.1. This passage seems to be one of the strongest in support of the theory that Alcibiades was an important source of information for Thucydides in Book 8. See Brunt, *REG* LXV (1952), 72–81.
[23]8.45.2.
[24]8.29.2; 45.2.
[25]8.45.3–5.
[26]8.46.1–2.

no reason to believe that Greek oarsmen were available who were better than those already in use. The second device named by Alcibiades is surprising: to call in the Phoenician fleet. Thucydides has him speak of "the Phoenician ships that he was preparing," but no previous mention has been made of any such ships. Probably, there had been some talk earlier of bringing them into the Aegean, which Thucydides did not mention. Perhaps the hope of gaining their support may help to account for Chalcideus' acceptance of so one-sided a treaty. However, we must ask whether the promise of a Phoenician fleet had any reality at the moment. Some doubt has been expressed that such a fleet existed.[27] But Thucydides asserts its reality firmly, and we have no reason to doubt him.[28] Whether Tissaphernes ever intended to use it in the Aegean will be discussed below,[29] but in the early winter of 412/11 the Phoenician ships were clearly not ready for use. In the short run, at least, Alcibiades' second suggestion suited the satrap well.

Alcibiades' last proposal was that Tissaphernes should abandon his alliance with Sparta and draw closer to Athens. He argued that the Athenians, as practicing imperialists, would have no hesitation in abandoning the Greek cities on the continent while maintaining control of the sea and the islands in it for themselves. They would be "more suitable partners in empire."[30] The Spartans, on the other hand, had come as liberators of the Greeks, and they would hardly abandon their freedom to the Persians when they were unwilling to leave them in the hands of other Greeks. They would not cease to be a menace until they were removed. Alcibiades' advice, therefore, was that Tissaphernes should "first, wear out both sides, then reduce Athenian power as much as possible, then finally, drive the Peloponnesians from his land."[31]

These arguments should not have been persuasive. They pictured the Spartans as simple idealists, totally committed to the cause of freedom and to their allies, whatever the cost. A glance at Sparta's behavior toward its Peloponnesian allies and its Melian colonists would have served to raise questions about the accuracy of this description of Sparta's character and policy. Nor was this picture of Athens more

[27]E. Delebecque, *Etudes classiques* II (1967); Ann. Fac. Lettres Aix-en-Provence, XLIII, 23, and *Thucydide et Alcibiade* (Aix-en-Provence, 1965), 177.
[28]8.87.2–3.
[29]See Chapter Nine.
[30]8.46.3.
[31]8.46.4.

reliable. The events of the previous seventy years did not reveal a state likely to leave the Greek coastal cities free as long as it retained a powerful navy. Alcibiades was making the best case he could, but we need not think he deceived the Persian satrap. Tissaphernes acted on those parts of Alcibiades' advice that pleased him and ignored the parts that did not. His purposes were best served for the present by maintaining good relations with the Greek renegade, so he made no objection. He continued to show favor to Alcibiades, to keep him close, and to consult him publicly. He provided even the reduced salaries to the Peloponnesians only irregularly, and he restrained them from fighting at sea by promising the imminent arrival of the Phoenician fleet. The result was to damage their general situation and to reduce the quality of the fleet. Alcibiades was free to carry on his private negotiations with the Athenians, his status with Tissaphernes apparently high. Tissaphernes was free to deal with the consequences when and how he chose.[32]

The Peloponnesian fleet lay idle in the harbor of Miletus for three months, from about the beginning of October until the end of December.[33] That delay allowed the Athenians to send reinforcements to Samos, 35 ships under Charminus, Strombichides, and Euctemon.[34] When they recalled their ships from Chios to Samos, in the first half of November, the number there reached a total of 104, and Athens had regained command of the sea lost when Phrynichus refused battle at Miletus.[35] The Athenians divided their fleet, sending 30 ships north to Chios and 74 to resume the blockade of Miletus. The opportunity there, however, once abandoned, did not present itself again. The Athenians no longer threatened the city by land. They had to content themselves with fruitless naval sorties, for the Spartan fleet refused battle, although they outnumbered the enemy 80 to 74.[36]

In the north, however, the Spartan navarch Astyochus was not idle. He was at Chios gathering hostages to prevent a revolution when he

[32]8.46.5.
[33]Busolt, GG III:2, 1440, n. 1.
[34]8.30.1. They replaced Leon and Diomedon, who appear to have returned to Athens, probably with some ships (8.54.3). For discussions of the problems in getting a clear and unambiguous account of the numbers of ships from Thucydides' account, see HCT V, 27–32.
[35]8.30.2: ἐθαλασσοκράτουν. For the date, see Busolt (GG III:2, 1440, n. 4).
[36]8.30.2. Andrewes (HCT V, 73) points out that this "speaks badly for Phrynichus' argument in c. 27." So it does, but we should remember that the reluctance to fight might have owed something to Tissaphernes' tactics.

received word that the fleet under Therimenes had arrived in time to save Miletus, so that "the condition of the [Peloponnesian] alliance had been improved."[37] Encouraged by the news and given an opportunity by the temporary withdrawal of the Athenian fleet from Chios to Samos, he launched attacks against Athenian positions on the coast opposite Chios. Although given some small support by Tamos, Tissaphernes' lieutenant in Ionia, he failed in assaults on Pteleum, near Erythrae, and Clazomenae (see Map 3). Bad weather put an end to the campaign and forced him to take refuge in the friendly ports of Phocaea and Cyme.[38] In these cities, he was approached by envoys from Lesbos who urged him to assist them in a renewal of their revolt. He would have been glad to help, but the Corinthians and other allies, presumably including the Chians who manned ten of his twenty ships, were reluctant because of the previous failure to bring the island over, so he was compelled to return to Chios. There, he was soon joined by Pedaritus, Sparta's designated governor of Chios, who was leading a band of mercenary soldiers. These men had served Amorges and had been taken into Spartan service after his defeat at Iasus. Beginning at Miletus late in October, Pedaritus marched them northward along the shore as far as Erythrae, where he crossed over to Chios.[39]

The Lesbians once again asked Astyochus to support a renewal of their rebellion. The navarch now had his own ships, the troops under Pedaritus, and a force of 500 men who had been armed by Alcibiades and Chalcideus and left on Chios as a garrison.[40] He therefore proposed to Pedaritus and the Chians that they take their forces to Lesbos and cause it to revolt, for in doing so, "either they would gain more allies or, if they failed, do harm to the Athenians."[41] But Pedaritus refused, saying he would not relinquish the Chian ships for that purpose. Our knowledge of the details of the Spartan constitution does not allow certainty about the correct relationship between the governor of an allied city and the navarch. Thucydides' language seems to indicate that Pedaritus, the governor of Chios, thought he had the right to control the actions of the Chian fleet, regardless of the wishes of the navarch Astyochus, whose command of the Peloponnesian vessels Pe-

[37] 8.31.1. See 8.24.6.
[38] 8.31.2–4.
[39] 8.32.1; 8.28.5.
[40] 8.17.1.
[41] 8.32.3.

daritus does not question.[42] Opposed by the Chians, as well as his Spartan colleague, Astyochus had no choice but to abandon his plan to aid the Lesbians, but it was not with good grace. As he left for Miletus, finally to take up the command of his main fleet, he threatened the Chians and swore not to come to their aid if they should need him.[43]

Subsequent events have persuaded some that a fuller understanding of the quarrel requires an attempt to understand Sparta's confusing internal politics. Some scholars have connected Astyochus with the faction of Endius and, therefore, with Alcibiades, but the evidence is too thin for confidence.[44] Nor is it possible to associate Pedaritus with a single Spartan faction, although he certainly had great influence at home. The conflict between the Spartan commanders may have resulted simply from an honest difference of opinion about what course was best, aggravated, perhaps, by the clash of personal ambitions.

As Astyochus sailed southward to take command of the main Spar-

---

[42]It is likely that no such situation had ever occurred before. Astyochus' failure to challenge Pedaritus' authority in making the refusal may have resulted less from constitutional precedent than from the great influence Pedaritus appears to have had in Sparta. He had distinguished forebears (*HCT* V, 69), and his views were taken seriously in Sparta (8.4; 39.2).

[43]8.33.1.

[44]Busolt (*GG* III:2, 1469) says: "He belonged without a doubt to the party of Endius, the friend of Alcibiades," and H. D. Westlake very cautiously endorsed that opinion (*JHS* LXXVI [1956], 99–104). This view seems to be based on the fact that Astyochus was navarch the same year that Endius was ephor, but there are formidable barriers to drawing political conclusions from the coincidence. One crucial assumption is that ephors were chosen for their political views or associations, but P. A. Rahe has shown that "the ephors were not elected in such a way that social eminence, factional struggles, or policy considerations could predominate, but rather were chosen by some process in which chance played a greater role than preferential selection" (*Historia* XXIX [1980], 385–401). P. J. Rhodes' rebuttal (*Historia* XXX [1981], 498–502) does not decrease the persuasiveness of Rahe's views on this point. However that may be, the association of Astyochus with Endius rests on a second assumption: that the navarchy was an annual office, like the ephorate, and that both officials were elected at the same time. However, we do not know when the elections for either office were held, and there is a dispute about whether the navarchy was an annual office in 413/12. If navarchs were chosen for specific assignments and lay down their commands when the job was done, Astyochus could have been designated navarch any time after Chalcideus (who was not navarch) replaced the navarch Melanchridas as commander of the small fleet going to Chios, probably in February of 412. Since Chalcideus was friendly with Alcibiades and Alcibiades with Endius, Endius' faction was clearly influential at the time, so Astyochus' connection with Endius' faction would be plausible if he were appointed then or soon after. If the office was already annual, we have no adequate reason to connect Astyochus with Endius' faction. Van de Maele's apparently unique attempt to associate Astyochus with Agis is even less persuasive (*Phoenix* XXV [1971], 39).

tan fleet at Miletus, he barely missed disaster. An Athenian fleet of thirty ships was sailing northward to Chios from Samos.[45] Their paths would have crossed with dire results for Astyochus, who had only sixteen ships, had not luck intervened. The two fleets anchored one night at Corycus, near Erythrae, separated only by a headland that concealed them from one another. Morning would have revealed their presence, but a false rumor of treason at Erythrae drew Astyochus away and caused him narrowly to escape running into the Athenians, who suffered losses in a storm before making their way to Lesbos.[46]

At Miletus Astyochus found morale good. The troops were still enjoying the booty they had taken from Amorges, the Milesians were cheerfully making their contribution to their maintenance, and "the Peloponnesians still had everything they needed for their camp."[47] Tissaphernes had paid a full month's salary, and the time must not yet have come for a second installment. The satrap, moreover, had caused a rebellion at Cnidus, and a Peloponnesian force under the Spartan Hippocrates had arrived there.[48] Half of this force was put on patrol duty at nearby Triopium to prey on merchant ships coming from Egypt to Athenian ports, and the others remained to defend Cnidus. The Athenians at Samos got word of the newly arrived fleet and its intentions and launched an attack. They destroyed the ships at Triopium, but their attacks on Cnidus failed. Cnidus remained in the hands of Sparta and its allies, strategically situated to cause trouble for Athens.

Even before Astyochus' arrival in Miletus the Spartans had been negotiating a second agreement with Tissaphernes that came to be known as the "treaty of Therimenes."[49] Thucydides tells us that the initiative for negotiating a new agreement came from the Spartans,

[45]8.30.2.
[46]8.33–34.
[47]8.36.1.
[48]8.35.1. With him came a fleet of ten ships from Thurii, which had lately fallen into the hands of the anti-Athenian faction (Plut. *Mor.* 835d–e), of which the Rhodian exile and famous athlete Dorieus was the chief captain. In addition, there was one Laconian ship and one from Syracuse, for a total of twelve.
[49]8.36.2; 43.3; 52. Scholars have had some difficulty with the notion that Therimenes, apparently a subordinate official, should have negotiated a treaty that was then called by his name. But the status of Therimenes does not seem to have been lower than that of Chalcideus, whose role as negotiator of the previous treaty is not in doubt, and the language of Thucydides indicates clearly his belief that Therimenes was responsible for the agreement. There is no evidence that Astyochus or any other Spartan present objected to any part of it.

who thought that the first treaty was inadequate and less in their own interest than in the king's.[50] In fact, Therimenes obtained some changes that might be considered improvements. Gone was the offensive language stating that the Greek cities of Asia "belonged" to the Great King. Instead, the new relevant clause spoke in the traditional language of nonaggression agreements familiar to the Greeks. This time there was no clause requiring each side to assist the other in putting down rebellions by subordinate cities, a clause that required commitment from Sparta, as in the defeat of Amorges, but could not conceivably require action from Persia. Unlike the first agreement, the treaty of Therimenes spoke openly of the Great King's obligation to pay the Greek forces he called upon. This agreement established not merely an alliance *(symmachia)*, as had Chalcideus' agreement, but a treaty and friendship *(spondai kai philia)*.[51] In the earlier agreement the contracting parties agreed to stop the Athenians from collecting tribute, whereas in the new one the Spartans agreed not to collect any themselves. This appears to accept a more respectable status for the Spartans. "In effect, Spartan recognition of Persian control has been exchanged for an undertaking that the Spartans will not attempt to succeed to the Athenian position."[52]

From this point of view, the treaty of Therimenes might be seen as a kindly gesture by Tissaphernes in which he gratified the wishes of the Peloponnesians, perhaps to "show a willingness to oblige after his curtailment of their pay."[53] But the new agreement yielded nothing of substance to the Spartans whereas it met Persian needs in the new circumstances better than the old treaty. The insertion of more tactful language in no way abandoned any of Persia's claims. The clause requiring aid against rebellious allies was no longer needed after the suppression of Amorges. The promise to pay Greek forces was limited to the number the Great King summoned and said nothing about the amount of pay. The most important change in the new agreement is one of mood and attitude and is reflected in the first clause: "Whatever

[50]8.36.2.

[51]8.37. These last words are precisely the ones used by Andocides (3.29) in setting forth the terms of the treaty that his uncle Epilycus negotiated with Darius in 424/23. As Andrewes puts it, "his 'friendship' with Athens ... is now transferred to Sparta" *(HCT* V, 80).

[52]Lewis, *Sparta and Persia,* 93.

[53]Busolt, *GG* III:2, 1443. He goes on to point out that Tissaphernes had other motives as well.

territory and cities belong to King Darius or belonged to his father or their ancestors, against these neither the Spartans nor their allies shall go either for war or to do any harm."[54] Tissaphernes, encouraged by the advice of Alcibiades, had chosen a policy of depriving the Spartans of regular and adequate support, of playing a delicate diplomatic game meant to wear down both Greek sides to his own advantage. What Tissaphernes had to fear in the near future was the Spartans' hostility, attacks on his own territory, and independent Spartan attempts to raise money from cities the Persians regarded as their own. The treaty negotiated with Therimenes would guard against those eventualities. "The security against Spartan designs on the Greek cities in Asia gives the new draft of the treaty its characteristic stamp."[55]

Therimenes and Astyochus, if he played any part in the negotiations, seem not to have had any diplomatic experience, so we should not be surprised if they were taken in by skillful bargainers such as the wily satrap and his brilliant adviser. Still, it is hard to see how the Spartan negotiators could have done better in the circumstances. Therimenes must have been instructed to try to improve the terms of the earlier agreement, for he would hardly have undertaken negotiations without orders from home, but he was given nothing with which to bargain. Tissaphernes had already achieved his immediate goal with the defeat of Amorges and the recovery of Iasus. Since the Athenian withdrawal from Miletus, he faced no immediate threat from Athens. He could readily endure Spartan displeasure, but the Spartans needed his co-operation if they were to pay their forces and carry on the war. Therimenes was not the man to risk breaking off relations with Persia by making unacceptable demands. A stronger Spartan line would require a more forceful, influential, and independent negotiator whose position at home was fully secure, but the Spartans who sent out Therimenes were not yet ready to change the policy established by Endius and Alcibiades of relying on the support of Tissaphernes in the war against Athens.

Soon after the completion of negotiations, Therimenes formally turned over command of his fleet to the navarch and sailed off in a

---

[54]8.37.2. The balancing clause forbidding the Great King and his subjects from attacking the Spartans or their allies is of no significance, for no such prospect was realistic at the time.

[55]Busolt, *GG* III:2, 1444.

small boat, never to be seen again.[56] Astyochus now commanded about ninety ships against the Athenian squadron of seventy-four nearby at Samos,[57] but like his predecessor, he remained on the defensive. The Athenian fleet made several sorties against Miletus, but each time Astyochus kept his ships in port and refused to rise to the bait, conceding the Athenians command of the sea. This was the beginning of a long period of inactivity by the navarch, during which his men came to grumble ever more loudly and openly that this policy was leading to the ruin of the Peloponnesian cause. After a time they came to suspect him of corruption: "he attached himself to Tissaphernes, it was said, for his own gain."[58] Some scholars have believed the accusation and explained his inertia on those grounds,[59] but the evidence is far from compelling.[60] Thucydides himself reports the allegation but does not endorse it.[61] An adequate explanation for Astyochus' behavior does not require theories of corruption and treason. The promises of

[56]8.38.1. Van de Maele (*Phoenix* XXV [1971], 44), who believes that Astyochus was guilty of treason and already working together with Tissaphernes and Alcibiades against Spartan interests, suggests that the conspirators may have "eliminated" him to prevent him from reporting their activities at Sparta. Apart from other considerations, to be discussed below, and the absence of any hint of foul play in Thucydides or any other ancient source, there is no need to be surprised by the drowning of a man attempting to sail across the Aegean in a small boat in November or December.

[57]Andrewes (*HCT* V, 29) places the figure at ninety. Busolt (*GG* III:2, 1445) suggests eighty-eight plus six more at Cnidos.

[58]8.50.3; see also 83.3.

[59]Belief in the charge goes back at least to Grote (VII, 401) and has had more recent champions, including Hatzfeld (*Alcibiade*, 324, 238, n. 1, 253), Delebecque (*Thucydide et Alcibiade*, [1965], 87), and, with a vigorous discussion, Van de Maele, *Phoenix* XXV (1971), 42–43.

[60]Among those rejecting the accusation are Busolt (*GG* III:2, 1445, n. 5) and H. D. Westlake (*Individuals in Thucydides* [Cambridge, 1968], 304—307).

[61]Van de Maele believes that in 8.50.3 Thucydides lends his own authority to the charge against Astyochus, asserting that after the restricting words ὡς ἐλέγετο (it was said), he "makes this accusation his own by connecting to it: 'it was also exactly because of that—διόπερ—that he only mildly resisted the reduction in pay' " (*Phoenix* XXV [1971], 42–43). But there is no better reason to associate Thucydides' own judgment with this latter clause than with the former. The passage reads: προσέθηκέ τε, ὡς ἐλέγετο, ἐπὶ ἰδίοις κέρδεσι Τισσαφέρνει ἑαυτὸν καὶ περὶ τούτων καὶ περὶ τῶν ἄλλων κοινοῦσθαι. διόπερ καὶ περὶ τῆς μισθοφορᾶς οὐκ ἐντελοῦς οὔσης μαλακωτέρως ἀνθήπτετο. As Andrewes says, the qualification ὡς ἐλέγετο "easily covers both clauses" (*HCT* V, 118). His comment on ὡς ἐλέγετο deserves quotation: "Ascriptions of motive and items of backstairs history are often thus qualified. . . . The most strongly worded statement of Astyochus' corrupt submission to Tissaphernes comes at 83.3 in the mouth of discontented Peloponnesian sailors, and the present passage probably comes from a similar source, distrusted by Thucydides and not identical with the source for the main story" (ibid.).

Tissaphernes to bring on the Phoenician fleet and the typical reluctance of a Spartan commander to risk a naval battle with an Athenian fleet not much smaller than his own are enough. Nothing he did in his career as navarch reveals the talent or character needed to launch a bold Spartan policy at sea.

While the southern theater remained quiet, there was action at Chios. The Athenian fleet that had barely missed cutting off Astyochus on his way to Miletus fought its way through stormy seas to Lesbos.[62] Three ships were lost in the storm, but the remaining twenty-seven, carrying a force of hoplites, crossed over to Chios under their generals Strombichides, Onomacles, and Euctemon. They set to work fortifying Delphinium, a strong point with good harbors on the east coast of the island, just north of the city of Chios. The Chians were in no condition to offer serious resistance. Discouraged by their previous defeats, they also suffered from dissension. Pedaritus, in fact, put to death Tydeus the son of Ion, perhaps the famous tragic poet, and his supporters on a charge of sympathy with Athens. He then imposed a narrow oligarchy in place of the by-no-means-democratic mixed constitution that had been in effect.[63] Perhaps there had been some growth of the pro-Athenian forces caused by the dangerous situation. More likely, the people Pedaritus killed were the hostages collected by Astyochus to prevent trouble. Pedaritus plainly took a harsher approach to the problem of Chian security than did the navarch. His measures were effective, for we hear of no further pro-Athenian activity. Indeed, as the pressure became greater, Chios clung to the Peloponnesian cause.[64]

At the moment, however, the Chians were filled with mutual suspicion and fearful, convinced that their own forces and Pedaritus' band of mercenaries were no match for the Athenians. In their despair they sent to Miletus for help, but Astyochus continued to refuse. Pedaritus now wrote a letter back to Sparta complaining of the navarch's behavior. Thucydides' language indicates that the complaint was about something more serious than poor generalship; it suggests at least some breach of law.[65] The authorities at Sparta would take his charges se-

[62]8.30, 34, 38.1.
[63]See above, 43–45.
[64]Quinn, *Historia* XVIII (1969), 29–30.
[65]8.38.4: ἐπιστέλλει περὶ αὐτοῦ ἐς τὴν Λακεδαίμονα ὁ Πεδάριτος ὡς ἀδικοῦντος. ἀδικέω implies wrong-doing rather than poor judgment. See Westlake, *Individuals*, 296.

riously, but meanwhile the situation at Chios grew worse. The Athenian fort at Delphinium had an effect on the Chians similar to that which the Spartan fort at Decelea had on the Athenians.[66] The Chians possessed a vast population of slaves whose very number caused them to be treated harshly.[67] Naturally, they were quick to flee to the safety of the Athenian fort and to assist their liberators with their knowledge of the terrain. Once the fortifications at Delphinium and around the Athenian camp and ships were completed, the position of the Chians would be far worse than that of the Athenians troubled by the Spartans at Decelea, for the Athenians ruled the sea. In these circumstances, the Chians made one more appeal to Astyochus, begging him "not to look on while the greatest of the allied cities in Ionia was shut off from the sea and devastated by raids on land" but to come immediately with his entire fleet before the fortifications were completed, while there was still hope.[68]

Astyochus was still reluctant to comply because of his quarrel with the Chians, according to Thucydides, but for even more sordid motives in the view of others.[69] However, Astyochus had an excellent reason for holding back. To aid the Chians he must not only sail past the 74 Athenian ships at Samos but also sail toward the 27 triremes blockading Chios. Thus his 90 or so ships would need to confront 101 of the enemy's superior ships. In the understated words of a sage historian, "the outcome would have been very doubtful."[70]

But the allied forces with Astyochus were moved by the appeals of the Chians, and he could not ignore the pressure of their eagerness to sail, so "he set out to prepare to give aid."[71] Perhaps he was also moved by the knowledge of Pedaritus' complaints to the Spartans at home and the need at least to seem responsive to the needs of the Chians. Ironically, the response to Pedaritus' letter of complaint provided Astyochus with an excuse for not going to the aid of Chios, for as he was preparing to go, word came that a Spartan fleet of twenty-seven ships under the command of Antisthenes had arrived at Caunus carrying

[66] The similarity is pointed out by Busolt (GG III:2, 1446).

[67] Thucydides says that Chios had a more numerous slave population than any state except Sparta. Andrewes (HCT V, 86–87) is surely right in saying that the Athenians must have had more slaves than the Chians. His suggestion that Thucydides is referring to the proportion of slaves to free is attractive.

[68] 8.40.

[69] Van de Maele, Phoenix XXV (1971), 42–43, attributes Astyochus' refusal to treason.

[70] Busolt, GG III:2, 1447, n. 2.

[71] 8.40.3: ὥρμητο ἐς τὸ ἐβοηθεῖν. I believe my translation is justified by the imperfect of ὥρμητο and by Astyochus' previous and subsequent behavior.

eleven *xymbouloi*, "advisers," with orders "to share in the conduct of affairs in whatever way should be best."[72]

The dispatch of *xymbouloi* to oversee the actions of an unsuccessful general was not unprecedented. Twice the brilliant Brasidas had been sent to bolster disappointing naval commanders, once alone and once with two companions,[73] but the closest parallel is with the ten advisers that were attached to Agis after his failure to fight in the Argive plain in 418 had led to the fall of Orchomenus. Without their consent the king could not lead the army out of the city, and they kept a close watch on him in the field.[74] The leader of the eleven advisers sent to Astyochus was the rich, famous, and influential Lichas, an Olympic victor in the chariot race and a man of important diplomatic experience who was certain to overshadow the navarch.[75] The board's powers were even greater than the usual ones of advice and oversight with which Agis had been threatened. Lichas and the other *xymbouloi* were empowered to depose Astyochus, if they saw fit, and replace him with Antisthenes. All of this may be attributed to the suspicion created by Pedaritus' letter, but there were further orders that must have stemmed from a more fundamental change of opinion in Sparta. The *xymbouloi* were to take as many of the ships with which they came and of the Peloponnesian ships already in Ionia as they chose, place them under the command of Clearchus the son of Ramphias who was with them, and send this force to Pharnabazus in the Hellespont.[76]

These last orders represented a fundamental change in strategy, shifting the focus of the war from Ionia to the Hellespont. The decision to support Chios had been made under the influence of Endius and Alcibiades, but by late November or early December of 412 the former was no longer ephor, the latter had abandoned the Spartan cause for the court of the Persian satrap, and their strategy no longer seemed attractive. Chios was besieged, begging for help, and, apparently, on the verge of surrender. Tissaphernes was proving to be a slippery ally who negotiated humiliating and unsatisfactory treaties, did not meet his financial obligations, used the Spartan forces for his own purposes, and warmly received the double renegade Alcibiades. Those Spartans who had originally favored collaboration with Pharnabazus in the Hel-

[72]Arrival: 8.41.1; orders: 39.2.
[73]To Cnemus in 429 (2.85.1) and to Alcidas in 427 (3.69.1).
[74]5.63.4.
[75]On Lichas, see *HCT* V, 85; and Kagan, *Peace of Nicias*, 75–76, 134–135.
[76]8.39.2.

lespont and those who had not, but opposed Endius and Alcibiades, were ready to turn against what now seemed a failed strategy toward what seemed a better one. The letter from Pedaritus must have supplied the finishing touch to a change of policy already under way.[77]

Antisthenes' fleet set out about the time of the winter solstice, then December 24.[78] At Melos they met ten Athenian ships and captured three of them. They rightly feared that the others that escaped would warn the Athenians at Samos of their approach, so they took a circuitous route to the south, reaching safe anchor at Caunus on the southern coast of Asia Minor, for that city seems to have revolted from Athens about the same time as Cnidus.[79] From there they sent word to Astyochus asking for a convoy to bring them to Miletus, which had now become the main Peloponnesian base in Ionia since the Athenian siege of Chios. Astyochus probably received their message at the very end of December, and Thucydides tells us that he at once gave up any idea of sailing to Chios, "thinking that nothing should come before convoying so great a fleet, so that together they might dominate the sea, and bringing across in safety the Spartans who had come to investigate him."[80] From the point of view of his personal interests and given the danger of facing the Athenian fleet without reinforcements, Astyochus' action is fully comprehensible. We should not forget, however, that as far as he knew it meant the abandonment of Pedaritus and the force with him as well as the Chians. But Astyochus had never wanted to sail to Chios anyway, and the summons from Caunus provided him with an excuse that even the eager allies must accept.

As he hurried south, the navarch found time to sack the town of

---

[77]Busolt (*GG* III:2, 1448) sees the change as the work of Agis' faction, but there is no evidence to support his view. Originally, Agis had wanted to support rebellion in Euboea. Then the Boeotians persuaded him to put that aside in favor of a Lesbian rebellion (8.5). Agis lost out to Endius and Alcibiades but helped force a compromise at the congress of the Spartan alliance at Corinth. There it was decided to go first to Chios, then to Lesbos, with Alcamenes (Agis' designee) in command, and then to the Hellespont under the command of Clearchus (8.8). Clearly, Endius and Alcibiades favored the first plan, Agis the second, and some third faction the third. Astyochus' attempts to take Lesbos had failed, removing that island as a plausible target for Spartan action. Agis presumably must have joined the third faction in advocating a Hellespontine strategy, but it was not his favorite and he was not its author. The failure of the Chian strategy and the failures of Astyochus appear to have forged an alliance between the remaining factions.
[78]8.39.1; *HCT* V, 84.
[79]8.39.3; *HCT* V, 86.
[80]8.41.1.

Cos Meropis on the eastern end of the island of Cos (see Map 3). Its walls had been destroyed by earthquake and its inhabitants had fled, so he lay waste to the countryside. Given the urgency with which he had set out, this detour made little strategic sense. No doubt he was eager to establish a record of aggressive activity, for the very least charge that might have been made against him was lack of initiative. He arrived at Cnidus at night, but the natives did not let him land. The Athenians had learned of the landing of Antisthenes' fleet at Melos and of their arrival at Caunus. They sent Charminus with a fleet of twenty ships south to the coast of Lycia and the neighboring islands of Syme, Chalce, and Rhodes to intercept them. The Cnidians wanted Astyochus to sail on and seek out the Athenian ships.[81]

The behavior of the two sides in these days reveals much about their thinking. The Spartan fleet under Antisthenes lived in constant fear of encountering an Athenian fleet of comparable size. When the Spartans arrived in Caunus, they assumed that the Athenians would send a fleet to challenge them, so they would not proceed until convoyed by a large fleet from Miletus. Astyochus plainly agreed with their caution and hurried to give them the requested protection, taking perhaps sixty-four ships with him and leaving eighteen or so to guard Miletus.[82] No doubt he felt safe in doing this because he knew that the entire Athenian fleet was located to the north at Samos and Chios. Probably he did not know of Charminus' expedition to the south, but if he did, it would not deter him, since his advantage would be better than three to one. All of the Spartan actions speak of great caution when facing the Athenians at sea without an overwhelming numerical advantage.

The Athenian attitude was different. On learning that twenty-seven new Spartan ships had come to Caunus, they had no hesitation in sending a detachment to engage them. This reduced their force at Samos to fifty-four to face perhaps ninety of the enemy at Miletus, but they seem to have had no fear of being attacked at their main base. The fleet of Charminus must sail past Miletus to reach its destination, but he seems to have been unconcerned by the threat of being inter-

---

[81] 8.41.2–3.
[82] These numbers are provided and explained by Busolt (*GG* III:2, 1448 and 1441, n. 3), and they must be approximately correct. Andrewes (*HCT* V, 29–30) rightly emphasizes the difficulty of arriving at precise numbers, but he believes that Astyochus brought the main body of the fleet. As to their number, he says: "Whatever the precise figure, they far outnumbered Charminus' twenty" (87).

cepted by a force from Sparta's main base. Although the Athenians knew that Antisthenes had twenty-seven they thought it was safe to send only twenty ships of their own against him. All of these actions reveal clearly that both sides had accepted that the Athenians were superior at sea unless confronted by overwhelming odds.

Astyochus heeded the appeal of the Cnidians and hurried south to Syme in the hope of meeting Antisthenes' squadron at sea before the Athenians could ambush it. Instead, rain and fog confused and scattered his fleet as it approached the island. In fact, he had stumbled on the Athenian fleet of Charminus. The Athenians were entirely unaware that Astyochus had ever left Miletus. The only Spartan ships they expected were the twenty-seven of Antisthenes. Although caught by surprise and without their full numbers, the Athenians characteristically attacked.[83] Advancing against what turned out to be the left wing of Astyochus' fleet, they sank three ships, damaged others, and were winning the battle until, to their astonishment, the whole fleet appeared, and they were surrounded. Even so, they were able to break through and escape to safety, losing only six ships. Astyochus sailed to Cnidus, where he was soon joined by the fleet from Caunus. Then the entire unified fleet proudly sailed to Syme to set up a trophy of victory over the twenty ships of Charminus.[84]

When the Athenians at Samos heard the news of the battle, presumably from the survivors, they gathered their ships and sailed to Syme. Even with the ships returning with Charminus, they would have had fewer than seventy ships against the ninety or so under Astyochus; yet they sought an encounter. In spite of the odds Charminus had faced, they were embarrassed by his defeat.[85] More attractive than revenue, however, was the prospect of finally meeting the Spartan fleet at sea to fight a decisive battle. But even with a significant numerical advantage and in the presence of the xymbouloi, Astyochus stayed in port at Cnidus and refused battle.[86]

---

[83] 8.41.1–2. Andrewes' suggestion (HCT V, 89) that the ships were absent "perhaps from hurry, or perhaps some had put in elsewhere for the night," is appealing.

[84] 8.42.

[85] In the Thesmophoriazusae, produced probably at the Great Dionysia in the spring of 411, perhaps three or four months after the battle, Aristophanes has the female chorus tease Charminus for losing a naval battle (804). If there is any substance behind the joke, which is at least partially a play on words, the Athenian public, too, may have regarded any naval defeat as disgraceful. For the date of the performance, see HCT V, 184–193, and A. H. Sommerstein, JHS XCVII (1977), 112–126.

[86] 8.43.1.

Astyochus' fleet was now joined with Antisthenes' ships at Cnidus. Since the *xymbouloi* had orders to investigate and evaluate the charges against Astyochus, and since important matters in which the navarch must be involved impended, we may assume that they made their inquiries and held their hearings at once. There can be no doubt that they acquitted Astyochus, because he continued in office and carried out his duties until replaced some time in the summer of 411.[87] Their failure to remove him, although specifically empowered to do so and provided with a potential replacement, should discredit any idea that sending the board of *xymbouloi* was part of a political maneuver on the part of one Spartan faction to remove the representative of another. It would have been easy enough to find a pretext: he had enjoyed little naval success, disappointed the allies, quarreled with Pedaritus, and failed to carry out the order to capture and kill Alcibiades. The inquisitors could not have been determined in advance to dislodge the navarch, and their investigation must have shown him to be innocent of wrong-doing.

With that matter out of the way, the Spartans were prepared to meet Tissaphernes when he came to Cnidus to discuss their grievances with them. Lichas took the leading role in the conference. The earlier draft agreements negotiated by Chalcideus and Therimenes had never been ratified at Sparta, as Lichas' easy dismissal of them shows.[88] The Spartan commanders in Ionia had acted as though the agreements were binding, but even so, the treaty of Therimenes contained a clause permitting further negotiation if either party should be dissatisfied.[89] Lichas, therefore, made assault on the previous agreements. "It was scandalous that the King still claimed to rule all the territory that he and his ancestors ruled in the past, for that would mean that all the islands would again be enslaved by him, as well as Thessaly, Locris, and everything as far as Boeotia; instead of freedom the Spartans would bring the Greeks subjugation to the Persian Empire." If a better treaty were not concluded, "the Spartans would not abide by these, nor did he ask for support on such terms."[90]

Lichas' intentions are not easy to determine. On the surface it might appear that he was expressing his own and Sparta's sincere outrage at the price in Greek freedom that the previous negotiators had paid for

[87] 8.85.1.
[88] 8.43.4.
[89] 8.37.3; 43.2.
[90] 8.43.3–4.

Persian aid. But Lichas was surely one of the Spartans who soon negotiated a third treaty with the Persians in which even Sparta's strongest defender admits "the liberators have conceded Asia to the King."[91] When, after the negotiation of that treaty, the Milesians drove out a Persian garrison with the warm approval of their Greek allies, Lichas was displeased and told them that they "and all the other cities in the King's land should be slaves to him, in a moderate way."[92] It was hardly, therefore, the love for Greek freedom that moved Lichas to speak as he did. Perhaps, in light of the outcome of the conference, it might be thought that the bold and provocative speech was meant to break off the alliance with Persia and allow Sparta to pursue an independent policy in Ionia. But Thucydides tells us that the subject of the conference was not only revision of the earlier agreements but also "how the rest of the war might be fought to the greatest advantage of both sides," and after all, Lichas did conclude his remarks with a demand for the negotiation of a new treaty.[93]

Probably Lichas took a hard line with the intention of establishing a high base from which to negotiate a better treaty. The language of the previous agreements, with their clear abandonment of the Greeks of Asia to the Persians, was embarrassing at the very least, and the lack of a specific provision for Persian payment and support already had proved to be a serious problem. Lichas must have thought that his inexperienced and unimpressive predecessors had simply not been tough enough and that a hard line on lofty moral grounds from a veteran statesman of high personal prestige would have better results. If those were his expectations, they were quickly and rudely disappointed, for Tissaphernes was offended and angered and walked out of the meeting.[94] Without knowing it, Lichas had lent credibility to Alcibiades' advice that the Spartans could not be trusted as allies, for they, unlike the Athenians, seemed wedded to the idea of liberating the Greeks under Persian rule.[95] In any case, it would be unwise for Tissaphernes to negotiate while the Spartans were in such a mood. It would be better to let them stew, without the benefit of Persian sup-

[91] 8.58; Lewis, *Sparta and Persia*, 107.
[92] 8.84.5.
[93] 8.43.2; 43.4.
[94] 8.43.4. Some scholars have suggested that the satrap's reaction was feigned, but there is no reason to think so. Tissaphernes was not accustomed to hearing such language from Spartan negotiators.
[95] 8.52.

port, until they saw the situation in a more favorable light. Policy as well as vanity combined to make the satrap break off the conference.

Antisthenes and the *xymbouloi* had been ordered to move the center of warfare north to the Hellespont, and it may be that Lichas' cavalier tone with Tissaphernes was influenced by the expectation that he soon would be supported by Pharnabazus, the satrap of Hellespontine Asia. An opportunity soon arose, however, that kept the Spartan fleet in southern waters. A group of powerful men from Rhodes approached the Spartans at Cnidus, urging them to sail to the island to bring it over to the Peloponnesian side. The offer was tempting, for the island was large by Greek standards, with a considerable body of men available for military and naval duty and a prosperous economy to lend financial support. Deserted by the Persian satrap of Ionia, the Spartans saw the acquisition of Rhodes as part of an opportunity by which they might be able to support their fleet "from their existing alliance, without asking Tissaphernes for money."[96] With a fleet of ninety-four ships, they sailed to Camirus on the western shore of the island (see Map 3). The three cities of Rhodes were not unified into a single state, and they were democracies. The people of Camirus were taken entirely by surprise, knowing nothing of the coup arranged by the oligarchical conspirators, and fled in fear of this mighty armada.[97] Called together in an assembly of all of the Rhodians, they, along with the people of Lindus and Ialysus, had no choice but to revolt from Athens and go over to the Peloponnesians about mid-January of 411.[98]

The Athenians received reports of the Spartan intentions beforehand, but by the time they got to Rhodes from Samos, they were too late. This, too, was part of the price they paid for failing to take Miletus; without a closer base than Samos, they could not protect southern Ionia, Caria, or the islands of the southern Aegean. Another price was soon revealed, one that sharply contradicts Phrynichus' assertion that if the Athenians refused battle at Miletus they would be able "to fight at a later time . . . having prepared adequately and at leisure." Although the Athenian fleet, numbering only about seventy-five to the Spartans' ninety-four, stood boldly out in the open sea off Rhodes, the Spartans refused battle. Andrewes has shrewdly noticed the defect of Phrynichus' strategy: "When the Peloponnesians felt themselves inferior but

---

[96] 8.44.1.
[97] On the situation at Rhodes, see *HCT* V, 91–92.
[98] 8.44.1–2. For the date, see Busolt, *GG* III:2, 1450.

had a secure base, they could decline battle with safety, while sending off detachments by land or even by sea to stimulate fresh revolts from Athens; and the Athenians could not keep up with this."[99] The Athenians could do nothing for the moment but sail back to Samos, contenting themselves afterwards with making raids from Samos and the closer islands of Cos and Chalce.[100]

The behavior of the Spartans at this point is interesting. New leaders had just arrived from a Sparta that was impatient with previous diplomacy, strategy, and leadership. They had vigorously denounced standing agreements and rejected Persian aid under them. Then they moved swiftly and successfully to win an important ally from Athens. They were free now to carry out their instructions to move the main theater of the war to the north, to abandon the unsatisfactory Tissaphernes, and to cooperate with his rival in the Hellespont. All that stood in their way was an Athenian fleet that was inferior numerically but offered battle nonetheless. This, if ever, was the time to fight, for time was less on the Peloponnesian side now that there would be no more money from the Persians. Yet the Peloponnesian ships stayed in port and refused the chance to fight. Nor was this only a temporary delay. The Spartans pulled their ships onto the Rhodian shore in mid-January and did not put them into the water again until well into the following spring.[101] Why didn't the Spartans fight? The explanations sometimes offered for Astyochus' earlier inactivity at Miletus are even less useful here, for there is no hint that the wealthy Lichas and his colleagues had been corrupted by Persian gold, while Tissaphernes' abrupt and angry departure meant that they could no longer be expecting the imminent arrival of the Phoenician fleet. The likeliest explanation is that in the weeks since their arrival, Antisthenes, Lichas, and his colleagues must have learned what Astyochus already knew—that the Peloponnesian fleet was no match for the Athenians in a fair fight at sea unless its numerical superiority was overwhelming. That opinion must have been widespread among the captains of the Peloponnesian ships and must have been supported by their performance in the raids launched by the Athenians. These things must have persuaded the new leaders to remain inactive at sea even as the enemy

[99] *HCT* V, 66.
[100] 8.44.3.
[101] 8.44.4. Thucydides says that the fleet stayed out of action for eighty days. If this figure is correct, it may present problems for Thucydidean chronology. For an excellent discussion, see *HCT* V, 92–93, 147–149.

continued to blockade Chios close to starvation and to undertake discussions with Tissaphernes.

The events of the rest of the winter further revealed Spartan reluctance. It was at this time that the Athenians deposed Phrynichus and Scironides on the charge of betraying Amorges and losing Iasus and sent out Leon and Diomedon in their place.[102] The new generals were given command of an Athenian force that boldly attacked Rhodes even while the Peloponnesian ships were beached on the island. The Athenians defeated a Rhodian army that came out to meet them and then moved to Chalce, from which they continued to launch raids. Although Thucydides gives us no figures, this could not have been as big a fleet as the Peloponnesians had beached at Rhodes, but its aggressive attitude is clear. The Athenians moved their base from Cos to Chalce "because it was easier for them to keep watch from there in case the Peloponnesian fleet should put out to sea in any direction."[103] Thus an Athenian fleet, certainly smaller than their own, taunted the Peloponnesians by taking up a position close to them and launching raids from it, but the Peloponnesian ships stayed on the beach.

Next a message came to the Spartans at Rhodes from Pedaritus at Chios. The Athenian fortification was complete, and unless the entire Peloponnesian fleet came, the island would be lost. Pedaritus, on the basis of his previous experience, could hardly be confident that his plea would be answered, so he acted in his own behalf. With his full force of mercenaries and Chians, he attacked the part of the Athenian fortification that protected the Athenian ships. Surprise brought limited success. He broke through and captured some ships that had been hauled on shore, but the Athenian counterattack defeated both mercenaries and Chians. Casualties were high and included Pedaritus himself, who was killed in his desperate attempt. Afterward the condition of the Chians was worse than ever: "They were blockaded still more than before by land and sea and there was great famine there."[104]

The Spartans at Rhodes could not easily ignore Pedaritus' plea, and Thucydides tells us that they fully intended to heed it.[105] They were

---

[102]Although the charge was brought by Peisander as part of his plot, and therefore had political motives, the condemnation was made by a free Athenian jury before the overthrow of the democracy. The outcome of his advice and strategy as described above must have predisposed the jury to take a harsh view of his behavior.
[103]8.55.1.
[104]8.55–56.1.
[105]8.55.2.

serious enough to ignore an Euboean invitation to bring that important island into rebellion after the Boeotian capture of Oropus made success more likely. Instead, their navy put to sea from Rhodes on a course for Chios at the end of winter, perhaps some time in March,[106] but it never got there. As they came to the region of Triopium, the Spartans saw the Athenian fleet from Chalce sailing north. This time the Athenians did not seek a fight but continued on to Samos. The Spartans did not pursue them but gave up their plans for rescuing the Chians and put in at Miletus, "seeing that it was no longer possible for them to bring help to Chios without a naval battle."[107]

How can we explain the surprising behavior of both sides? The Spartans, after pulling their ships on to the beach at Rhodes all winter in fear of the Athenian fleet, at last sailed north in the direction from which the Athenians had been challenging them. As Thucydides tells the tale, they should have had every expectation of meeting the Athenians at sea and fighting a battle. Yet at the first sight of the enemy fleet, the Spartans gave up the attempt to rescue Chios and tamely sailed to port. The Athenians, on the other hand, had moved their fleet south to Chalce precisely to challenge the Spartans, to watch their movements, and to force a battle when possible. Yet the Spartan sortie found them away from their station at Chalce, sailing northward toward Samos, and when they saw the Spartans on the open sea, they ignored the long-sought opportunity and kept sailing. Neither Thucydides nor any other ancient source explains this odd behavior.

A clue may lie in the Boeotian capture of Oropus. Its strategic position in the hands of the enemy seriously threatened Euboea's continued possession by the Athenians. The conquest of Oropus immediately encouraged some Eretrians to pursue plans for rebellion of the kind that had already been alive on Euboea the previous year and to seek the support of the Spartan fleet at Rhodes.[108] At this time Euboea was of vital importance to Athens. When it revolted in the summer of 411, Thucydides says "there was greater panic than ever before. For neither the disaster in Sicily, though it seemed great at the time, nor any other event had ever before frightened them so." The fleet at Samos was in revolt, there were no more ships or men to sail them, revolution threatened to break out in Athens itself, and now a terrible

---

[106] 8.60.1–2. For the problem of the date, see *HCT* V, 147–149.
[107] 8.60.3.
[108] 8.5.1.

disaster was added to all of this "in which they had lost not only a fleet, but worst of all, Euboea, which was of more value to them than Attica."[109]

The island was no less important to the Athenians a half-year earlier, so when they heard of the loss of Oropus, they must have reacted swiftly. They need not have learned of the Eretrian mission to Rhodes to assume that some such attempt would be made. There must have been a temptation to sail at once to Euboea to be sure of its security, but such a move would leave the great Spartan fleet at Rhodes free to sail north, to raise new rebellions, to rescue Chios, to threaten Samos and Lesbos, and even to make its way to the Hellespont and the Athenian lifeline. Sober second thoughts would suggest the course the Athenians apparently chose: to withdraw to Samos, await events, and be in a position to move swiftly either to Euboea or elsewhere as necessary. They did not engage the Spartans off Triopium because in the uncertainty of the moment they wanted to reach Samos as soon as possible in case they needed to go on to Euboea at once.

On the other hand, when the Spartans received the Eretrian envoys, they must have realized how great was the threat to Athens caused by the loss of Oropus and anticipated that the Athenians would sail to Euboea at once. That would explain their decision to sail north from Rhodes after months of inaction. They must have expected that the Athenians would sail northwest from Chalce, on the most direct route to Euboea, leaving the way to the north, and the relief of Chios, free. When they saw the Athenians off Triopium, they gave up hope of rescuing Chios and returned to the safety of their main base at Miletus, which the withdrawal of the Athenians to Samos had at last allowed.

Whatever the value of these speculations, the Spartans would probably have been unable even to attempt a voyage to Chios had there not been a change in their relationship with Persia earlier in the winter. While the Spartan fleet was still at Rhodes, Tissaphernes experienced a change of heart and sought to renew friendly relations with Sparta and its allies. He was moved to this decision by several considerations. Under the influence of Alcibiades, he had engaged in discussions with Athenian envoys to consider a change of alliances, but these talks had failed.[110] Whatever his intentions may have been, the outcome left him

[109] 8.96.2.
[110] 8.56.

without Greek allies and with no adequate force to bring about a satisfactory end to the war and the recovery by Persia of its former complete control of Asia Minor. He had turned away from Sparta because he wanted to wear out both sides, and at the beginning of winter, he had thought that the Spartans' numerical superiority at sea made them the stronger power.[111] No doubt Lichas' harsh language and lofty talk about liberation frightened him in the same direction, but the events of the winter proved his calculations wrong. The Athenians, though fewer than the enemy, ruled the sea unchallenged while the Spartan ships were beached.

What Tissaphernes feared now was not Spartan victory but Spartan desperation. Since their renunciation of Persian aid, the Spartans had collected 32 talents from Rhodes. At the rate of 3 obols per man per day that would not maintain the crews of the Peloponnesian ships at Rhodes for a month, much less the eighty days that Thucydides tells us they stayed there.[112] As they ran out of money to sustain them, Tissaphernes was afraid either that the Spartans "would be compelled to fight a naval battle and lose, or that their ships would be emptied by desertions and the Athenians would attain their ends without his aid; but beyond that, what he feared most was that they would ravage the mainland in search of subsistance."[113] Perhaps Tissaphernes thought that his recent conversations with the Athenians, though abortive, would show that he was not permanently bound to the Spartans' cause and make them more reasonable.[114] In any case, he wanted the Spartan fleet under his control at Miletus, where it could defend that strategically important port from Athenian attack and where he could keep a watchful eye on its activities.

Thucydides tells us nothing of the Spartans' reasons for changing their attitude and policy, but they are not hard to understand. The Persian talks with the Athenians must have alarmed them. Their hopes of being able to support their fleet without Persian funds had proved to be illusory. Worst of all, the events of the winter had shown that they could not hope to defeat the Athenians at sea without a great deal of help from the Persians. Money was needed immediately, but the behavior of the Spartan leaders both before and after the conclusion of the third agreement with Persia suggests that they counted on the

[111] 8.52.
[112] 8.44.4; *HCT* V, 92, 137.
[113] 8.57.1.
[114] Such is the suggestion of Lewis, *Sparta and Persia*, 102.

vast numbers of the promised Phoenician fleet for any hope of victory at sea. For these reasons a chastened Spartan leadership met Tissaphernes at Caunus and negotiated the terms of a treaty, probably late in the month of February.[115]

The new agreement resembled the previous one in some ways, containing a nonaggression clause, reference to Persian financial support, and a commitment to wage war and make peace in common, but there were significant differences. The formality and detail of the preamble suggest that this agreement was meant to be the basis of a formal treaty to be ratified by both home governments.[116] This time the signatories, in addition to Tissaphernes, are not "King Darius and his sons" but "Hieramenes and the sons of Pharnaces" who act "concerning the King's affairs." The son of Pharnaces can only be Pharnabazus, satrap of the Hellespontine region of Asia Minor.[117] Pharnabazus may have been included at Spartan insistence.[118] At least the Spartans had taken his money to fit out ships for action in the Hellespont.[119] But King Darius may have wanted him involved, too, since the status of Asia was at issue.[120] Little is known of Hieramenes, but he appears to have been a relative of the Great King. "If so," as Lewis says, "he would not be unsuitable as a visiting representative of the King."[121] His presence emphasizes the degree to which the Great King, although not mentioned in the preamble, was more clearly involved in the shaping of this treaty than its predecessors. He had evidently made a specific agreement about maintenance of the Peloponnesian ships. There is a reference to "the King's ships" and their proposed use, which could not have been made unless he was consulted. The first clause of the treaty, moreover, deals with the definition of his empire and could not have been composed without his direct approval.[122]

That clause reads: "All the territory of the King that is in Asia shall

---

[115] 8.57. The heading of the actual treaty recorded by Thucydides in 8.58.1 says it was made "in the plain of the Maeander," and the divergence between the two passages has provoked comment. Andrewes has an interesting suggestion that this treaty, unlike the first two, was ratified in Sparta, occasioning delay so the negotiations would have taken place in Caunus and the formal signing on the Maeander later, perhaps early in April (HCT V, 138–139).

[116] 8.38.1; HCT V, 143.

[117] HCT V, 139; Lewis, Sparta and Persia, 104.

[118] As Busolt (GG III:2, 1451–1452) suggests.

[119] 8.39.1.

[120] Lewis, Sparta and Persia, 104.

[121] Ibid.

[122] Ibid.

belong to the King; and about his own territory the King may decide whatever he wishes."[123] The first statement is clearly a concession to the Spartans and a concession to the complaints of Lichas. There is no mention of the Great King's father or ancestors and the territory they once held. Darius limits his practical claims to Asia. The second statement has given rise to speculation about possible rejection of clauses limiting the Great King's freedom of action contained in the Peace of Callias, made with Athens at mid-century, or to some Spartan proposals, unknown to us, about the status of the Greek cities in Asia. But once again, Lewis' suggestion seems most persuasive: "it may simply reflect an angry outburst of the King when faced with the difficulty about the definition of his empire. If he is going to accept an explicit limitation to Asia . . . there is to be no quibbling about his rights there."[124]

The most important change is in the plan for waging the war implied in the new agreement. Until now the only forces referred to have been the Peloponnesian ones summoned and maintained by the king. The implicit assumption has been that they will do the fighting and the Great King only the paying. It is only later that there is even a suggestion about bringing in significant royal forces, namely, the Phoenician fleet.[125] The new agreement, however, introduces a complete change of perspective. The Great King's ships are the center of attention and the focal point of expectations for military success. Tissaphernes, who remains in charge of the Persian conduct of the war in spite of the presence of Pharnabazus and Hieramenes in the preamble, will maintain the Peloponnesian forces on the basis of the specific financial agreement only until the Great King's ships come. After that they may stay on at their own expense or receive money from Tissaphernes, not as a grant but as a loan to be repaid at the end of the war, and war is to be waged by both sides in common "when the King's ships shall have come."[126]

We cannot be sure whether the Persians had really decided that the war must and could be won by bringing a large Phoenician fleet into action. The sorry record of Phoenician warships against Greeks, the doubts of Thucydides, and the fact that the fleet never appeared compel

[123]8.58.2.
[124]*Sparta and Persia*, 106.
[125]8.37.4; 46.1.
[126]8.58.5–7.

us to raise the question.[127] What we cannot doubt is that the firm promise of such a reinforcement was the major element in persuading the Spartan leaders, including Lichas, to approve an agreement that was not substantially better than the one he had so vehemently denounced.[128] The Great King may have abandoned his extravagant claims to the conquests of his ancestors, but they were never more than a rhetorical phantom, pleasing to Persian vanity and tradition but having no substance.

The Spartans, on the other hand, formally abandoned the Greeks of Asia and their own role as liberators, whatever their ultimate intentions may have been. That was a difficult and humiliating action, and we may be sure they would not have taken it unless they felt compelled to do so. The events of the winter of 412/11 had clearly shown that they could not carry on the war without Persian support. Even financial support alone, certainly at the level Tissaphernes and the Great King were willing to give it, would not be enough to defeat the astonishing resiliency of the Athenians and their continued superiority in skill, morale, and tactics at sea. Victory over Athens, they must have thought, would require not only money to maintain their own ships but also a vast increase in the size of the fleet opposing the Athenians. Sobering experience had shown them that, except in special circumstances, such as a battle fought in narrow enclosed waters like those of the Syracuse harbor, they could not hope to defeat the Athenians at sea without the overwhelming numerical superiority that only the Phoenician fleet promised by the Persians could provide. Tissaphernes knew perfectly well that Spartan expectations of the imminent arrival of the Persian fleet was the key to the agreement and essential for their cooperation. Thucydides tells us that right after the treaty had been concluded the satrap set about "preparing to bring the Phoenician ships," as he had promised; "at any rate, he wanted to make it conspicuous that he was preparing."[129]

The renewal of friendly relations with Persia and the financial aid it provided gave the Spartans an opportunity to undertake some actions

[127]For the performance of the Phoenician navy, see D. Lateiner, *TAPA* CVI (1976), 281–288; for the doubts of Thucydides, see 8.87.

[128]Busolt (*GG* III:2, 1452) says: "The treaty was no more favorable than the one of Therimenes peremptorily rejected by Lichas." Lewis (*Sparta and Persia*, 103–104) agrees: "If realities alone are considered, the third treaty is rather worse for Sparta than the second."

[129]8.59.

of their own at once, even before the Great King's ships arrived. Almost immediately after their arrival at Miletus, probably early in April, they sent a considerable force on foot to the Hellespont under the command of the Spartan Dercylidas.[130] The plan may have originated with the Milesians, for the first target of the expedition was Abydos, a Milesian colony on the Asiatic shore of the Hellespont, but it appears also to have been concerted with Pharnabazus, the Hellespontine satrap.[131] The new agreement with Persia seems to have encouraged and enabled the Spartans to extend their activities beyond Tissaphernes' province, as their original plan and latest orders required. Since we hear nothing of new troops coming from the Peloponnesus and since Thucydides describes Dercylidas' army as considerable, it seems likely that the Spartans were able to recruit many soldiers from the Greeks of Asia Minor. Persian money and the promise of victory inherent in the expectation of the arrival of the Phoenician fleet appear to have changed the attitude of these Greeks, perhaps another important result of the recent treaty. At the same time, we should notice that the Spartans were compelled to send their army to the Hellespont by land, and it has been pointed out "how difficult and tiresome it was for an army to cover the long distance [200 to 250 miles] from Ionia to the Hellespont on foot."[132] This is a powerful reminder that the Athenians still ruled the sea and that the Spartans were afraid to challenge them directly, but it may be that the march of Dercylidas was meant to deal with that problem, among others.

Thucydides tells us nothing of the intentions behind the expedition, perhaps because they seem obvious. Clearly, it would be desirable to bring about rebellions in parts of the empire as yet untouched by defection and thereby deprive the Athenians of resources. To do so on the Hellespont, moreover, was even more effective because of the threat such rebellions posed to essential Athenian trade and supply lines. It was predictable, therefore, that any success in that region would force the Athenians to react swiftly by using their fleet in the Hellespont, and the nearest Athenian fleet was at Chios. If Dercylidas succeeded on the Hellespont, the opportunity might arise to relieve Chios.

[130]8.61.1. Thucydides says the march began "at the very beginning of spring": ἅμα τῷ ἦρι εὐθὺς ἀρχομένῳ, which Busolt (GG II:2, 1454) places early in April.
[131]Milesian colony: 8.61.1. At 8.62.1 we are told that both Abydos and Lampsacus went over "to Dercylidas and Pharnabazus."
[132]Amit, SCI II (1975), 63.

Dercylidas arrived at Abydos, perhaps in early May, and quickly brought the rebellion not only to that city but also to Lampsacus two days later (see Map 5). The Athenians reacted as might have been expected, sending Strombichides to the Hellespont with twenty-four ships, some of them transports carrying hoplites. He was able to recover Lampsacus but not Abydos. The best he could do was to sail over to Sestus on the European side and establish it as "a fortress and a look-out post for the whole Hellespont."[133] But the Spartans had obtained a foothold on that vital waterway.

Word of Dercylidas' achievement reached Astyochus and the other Spartans at Miletus about the same time that some very good news from Chios arrived. While the Spartans had been at Rhodes, still not daring to sail north to Chios at the risk of a naval battle with the Athenians at Chalce and before the movement of the Athenian fleet from there led them to go to sea, they had made one small effort to help the Chians in another way. They had sent the Spartan officer Leon, who had come to Ionia with Antisthenes' squadron, on a single ship to Miletus. There he collected eleven others that had been left behind to guard the port and sailed for Chios to replace Pedaritus as commander of the island. This was possible only because the main Athenian fleet was not at Samos but still at Chalce. At Chios Leon joined twenty-four Chian triremes. Against this squadron of thirty-six triremes, the Athenians had thirty-two ships; some of them, however, were troop transports and not very effective in a battle of triremes.[134] Leon's contingent included some of the most zealous fighters on the Peloponnesian side: five ships from Thurii, four from Syracuse, and one from Anaea, where the oligarchic exiles from Samos were settled.[135] Perhaps, although Thucydides does not mention them, the extraordinary leaders Dorieus of Thurii and Hermocrates of Syracuse were among their cities' contingents. However that may be, Leon's force gave a good account of itself. In a tough battle, the Peloponnesian ships got the better of the fighting but could not win a decisive victory before darkness came. The men were compelled to withdraw into the city, and the blockade continued.[136] But the Chians and their allies had won the upper hand at sea.[137]

[133] 8.62.2–3.
[134] 8.61.2–3. Troopships: 8.25.1, 30.2, 62.2.
[135] HCT V, 150.
[136] 8.61.3.
[137] 8.62.1.

MAP 5. THE HELLESPONT. Adapted from A. W. Gomme, A. Andrewes, and K. J. Dover, *A Historical Commentary on Thucydides*, V (Oxford, Oxford University Press, 1981), xiv, by permission of the publisher.

Proconnesus

Arctonnesus

Cyzicus

PROPONTIS

Priapus

Harpagium

Parium

Aesepus River

Granicus River

Lampsacus

Cardia

CHERSONNESE
(GALLIPOLI)

Sestos

Abydos

Madytus

Cynossema

Elaeus

Rhoeteum

Scamander River

Sigeum

Tenedos

Imbros

The departure of the Athenian force under Strombichides for the Hellespont, leaving only 8 ships behind, gave the Chians under Leon thorough command of the sea around their island. This gave Astyochus the courage to venture out to sea. Cautiously sailing from Miletus, he slipped past Samos to Chios. He gathered the Chian and allied ships that were there and, in a concerted movement, brought his entire fleet, certainly more than 100 warships, to Samos, challenging the Athenians to fight.[138] This time it was the Athenians who refused to fight. Although the Spartans had clear numerical superiority, it was only marginally greater than what they had enjoyed at Rhodes the previous winter, when the Athenians were the aggressors and the Spartans refused to fight.[139] Thucydides explains the Athenians' restraint simply and briefly: They did not come out against Antyochus because "they were suspicious of one another."[140] The reference is to the civil strife that had recently broken out among the Athenians and divided them into increasingly hostile factions.[141]

The result was a complete reversal in the situation. For the moment, at least, Athens had lost control of the sea and the initiative in the war. The failure to take Miletus when the opportunity was at hand had stopped the Athenians from snuffing out the rebellion of Ionia before it was fairly started and quickly led to the loss of most of the mainland cities and some key islands. Now, with the naval blockade of Chios broken, the Athenian hold on that crucial island became precarious. Worse yet, the Spartans had achieved a base on the Hel-

---

[138]8.63. Thucydides is not as clear about these movements as we would like. Andrewes (*HCT* V, 153) believes Astyochus slipped past Samos with two ships, collected only the twelve ships brought for Miletus by Leon, and brought them back to Miletus, from where he sailed with the whole fleet to Samos. The account given here assumes that Astyochus gathered all ships stationed at Chios and sailed with them directly to Samos, where he met the rest of his fleet coming from Miletus. This would avoid his having to sail past Samos again to Miletus with a fleet whose size would make it noticed but which was too small to risk a battle. The text will not allow certainty. Thucydides gives no numbers for Astyochus' fleet on this occasion, although he specifies its number at 112 later (8.79.1), and Busolt (*GG* III:2, 1455) gives that number for this force. The Spartans had at least 94 ships at Miletus and perhaps as many as 36 at Chios, for a total of 130. Presumably, they would have left at least a few ships at each place, but it seems safe to place the battle fleet that went to Samos at least at 100.

[139]At Rhodes the Spartans had 94 ships to no more than 74 Athenian, although the Athenians probably had left at least a few ships to guard Samos. Perhaps the real ratio was 94 to 64, a difference of 29. This time the Athenians had their 74 ships to face anywhere from 100 to 115 ships, a difference of from 26 to 41.

[140]8.63.2.

[141]See Chapter Five.

lespont that was a deadly threat to the Athenians and would require them to shift a major part of their attention to that newly opened theater of war. In this difficult situation, the Athenians needed the greatest commitment and unity to meet the challenge, but instead they were torn by dissension. The beginning of this negative turn of events can readily be traced to the decision made under the influence of Phrynichus not to fight at Miletus late in the summer of 412.

5. The Revolutionary Movement

In 411 the Athenians entered the hundredth year since the expulsion of tyranny and the establishment of their freedom. For almost that entire period, since the reforms of Cleisthenes in 508/7, they had enjoyed a democratic constitution, moderate at first and more complete since the changes introduced by Ephialtes and Pericles toward the middle of the century. The passage of time and the growth of Athenian power and prosperity under the democracy had dampened almost all interest in trying to destroy it and replace it with oligarchy, the most common form of government among the Greeks. From time to time there were rumors of oligarchic plots, but none even reached the stage of action.[1] Most Athenians of the upper class accepted the democracy, either vying for leadership within it or standing aloof from politics, although almost all leading Athenian politicians until the Peloponnesian War were of noble birth.

Yet hostility to the idea and reality of democracy did not disappear. Greek tradition, after all, was overwhelmingly aristocratic. The epics of Homer, the most widely known and influential works of all Greek literature, presented a world whose values were entirely aristocratic. It was for the nobles to make decisions and give orders and for the commoners to know their place and obey.[2] The poems of Theognis of Megara reflected the bitterness of aristocrats whose world was over-

---

[1] Thucydides (1.107.6) mentions suspicion of a plot to overthrow the democracy before the battle of Tanagra in 457 and suspicion of a conspiracy to establish either an oligarchy or tyranny just before the Sicilian expedition in 415 (6.60.1).

[2] *Iliad* 2.188–278; see M. I. Finley, *The World of Odysseus*, 2d ed. (New York, 1964), 113, 118–119.

thrown by the political and social upheavals of the sixth century, and his words and ideas were remembered and had a powerful influence on enemies of democracy well into the fourth century, when they were quoted with approval by Plato. Theognis divided mankind into two distinct types: the good and noble and the bad and base. The distinction is based on birth and establishes a clear and firm tie between social status and virtue. The noble alone possesses judgment *(gnome)* and reverence *(aidos);* therefore, the noble alone is capable of moderation, restraint, and justice. These are qualities enjoyed by few, and the many who are without them, who lack judgment and reverence, are necessarily shameless and arrogant. The good qualities, moreover, are acquired only by birth; they cannot be taught: "It is easier to beget and rear a man than to put good sense into him. No one has ever discovered a way to make a fool wise or a bad man good. . . . If thought could be made and put into a man, the son of a good man would never become bad since he would obey good counsel. But you will never make the bad man good by teaching."[3]

The Theban poet Pindar, "the Voice of Aristocracy" as Werner Jaeger has called him, must have exercised an even greater influence on the Athenian upper classes. He lived past the middle of the fifth century, and his odes celebrated the athletic triumphs in the games that were so important in aristocratic culture. His message was much the same as that of Theognis: the nobly born were inherently superior to the mass of people intellectually and morally, and the difference could not be erased by education.

> The splendor running in the blood has much weight.
> A man can learn and yet see darkly, blow one way,
> then another, walking ever
> on uncertain feet, his mind unfinished and
> fed with scraps of a thousand virtues.[4]

The capacity for understanding is innate. Only the natively wise can comprehend his poetry and other important things:

> There are many sharp shafts
> in the quiver

[3]Theognis 429–438.
[4]*Nemea* 3.40–42, in *The Odes of Pindar*, trans. Richmond Lattimore (Chicago, 1959), 101.

> under the crook of my arm.
> They speak to the understanding; most men need
>   interpreters.
> The wise man knows many things in his blood; the
>   vulgar are taught.
> They will say anything. They clatter vainly like
>   crows against the sacred bird of Zeus.[5]

The implication of these beliefs is that democracy is, at the very least, unwise. To some, it would have seemed unfair and immoral as well.

In the fourth century, Plato and Aristotle must have been repeating old complaints when they pointed out the unfairness of democracy: "it distributes a sort of equality to equal and unequal alike";[6] democratic justice is "the enjoyment of arithmetical equality, and not the enjoyment of proportionate equality on the basis of merit."[7] These views, appearing in philosophical works of the fourth century, show that the old idea of the natural and permanent separation between the deserving and undeserving classes distinguished by Theognis and Pindar lasted through and beyond the war. The *Athenian Constitution*—a pamphlet found among the works of Xenophon although surely written, probably in the 420s, not by him but by an unknown author often called "The Old Oligarch"—shows clearly that similar feelings existed during the war.[8] The author has been influenced by the dispassionate and objective approach of the Sophists, but passionate discontent is apparent beneath the surface. "As for the constitution of the Athenians, I do not praise them for having chosen it, because in choosing it they have given the better of it to the vulgar people *(poneroi)* rather than to the good *(chrestoi)*." They use the lot for positions that are safe and pay a salary but leave the dangerous jobs of generals and commanders of the cavalry to election and "the best qualified men."[9]

By the 420s time and change had altered the basis of distinguishing the classes. Whereas noble birth had been the criterion for Theognis and Pindar, the importance of money in shaping morality and political competence was emphasized by the author of the *Athenian Constitution*:

---

[5] *Olympia* 2.86–87, trans. Richmond Lattimore, in *ibid.*, 7–8.
[6] Plato, *Republic* 558C.
[7] Arist. *Pol.* 1317b.
[8] For a discussion of this pamphlet and the ideas in it, see Kagan, *Outbreak*, 138–140. For the date, see W.G. Forrest, *Klio* LII [1970], 107–116, and Ste. Croix, *Origins*, 308–310.
[9] Pseudo-Xenophon, *Athenaion Politeia* 1.1, 3.

"In every country the aristocracy is contrasted to the democracy, there being in the best people the least licentiousness and iniquity, but the keenest eyes for morals; in the people, on the other hand, we find a very high degree of ignorance, disorder, and vileness; for poverty more and more leads them in the direction of bad morals, thus also the absence of education and in the case of some persons the ignorance that is due to the want of money."[10] There can be no doubt that the author and men of his class had thought carefully about what a good constitution, in contrast to democracy, would be. What they wanted was *eunomia*, the name Tyrtaeus had given to the Spartan constitution and that Pindar had applied to the oligarchy of Corinth. In such a constitution the best and most qualified men will make the laws. The good men *(chrestoi)* will punish the bad *(poneroi)*; only the *chrestoi* will deliberate about public affairs, "and they will not allow madmen to sit in the council or speak in the assembly. But as a result of these good measures the people would, of course, fall into servitude."[11] The author understands, therefore, that bad government *(kakonomia)*, democracy, that is, is in the interest of the people, and he expects them to act in their own interest to preserve it. "But anybody who without belonging to the people prefers living in a town under democratic rule to living in one oligarchically has prepared himself for being immoral, well knowing that it is easier for a bad person to remain unnoticed in a town under democratic than in one under oligarchic rule."[12] These words leave no doubt that the author and men like him regarded the overthrow of the democracy and its replacement by a better constitution as a moral obligation, but when he wrote, the democracy seemed secure and unshakable.[13]

[10]Ibid. 1.5.

[11]Ibid. 1.9. In 1.8 and 9 *eunomia*, either as a noun or in verbal form, appears three times. H. Frisch *(The Constitution of the Athenians* [Copenhagen, 1942, rpt. New York, 1976], 201) says "in conservative usage the word simply meant the good old oligarchic form of society." Thucydides (1.18.1) applies the term to the Spartan constitution.

[12]Ibid. 2.19.

[13]R. Sealey *(Essays in Greek Politics* [New York, 1967], 111–132) has argued that "differences of opinion on forms of government" (130) played only a minor role in shaping the decisions of the men who made the revolution. If one considers their intellectual and moral training and heritage, along with the evidence of the *Athenaion Politeia*, however, that position seems hard to sustain. To change the constitution was not merely an intellectual game played by earnest students or sophistic political scientists, as W. G. Forrest *(YCS* XXIV [1975], 37–52) seems to imply, nor a function of class conflict in the Marxist sense but a moral necessity. For an arguent against Sealey's view along different lines, see P. J. Rhodes, *JHS* XCII (1972), 115–127.

By 411 the practical problems facing the democracy, its failures, and its blunders intensified discontent with its institutions at the same time that they provided the opportunity to attack them. The removal from the scene of respected leaders such as Cimon, Pericles, and even Nicias and their replacement by the likes of Cleon, Hyperbolus, and even the nobly born but personally disreputable Alcibiades made democratic rule harder for noblemen to accept. The absence of strong, respected political leaders created and intensified divisions among the Athenians. In 411 the vacuum of leadership seems to have been filled increasingly by the *hetairiai*, the clubs that played an ever more important part in Athenian politics, especially among the enemies of democracy.[14]

The members of these clubs, as well as others in the propertied classes, had borne and were still bearing unprecedented financial burdens. The costs of waging the war were higher than in the earlier years because of the existence of a Peloponnesian navy that threatened the Athenians' empire and food supply and required them to keep as large a fleet as possible at sea the year round. Meanwhile, the expenditure from the public treasury to civilians had not diminished but probably had increased.[15] At the same time, public revenue was severely curtailed by rebellions of tribute-paying allies and the reduction of income from customs duties caused by the war's interference with commerce. The problem was made more intense by a reduction in the number of Athenians wealthy enough to assume the financial burden of religious and military services required by the state. On the eve of the war in 431, the number of Athenian men of hoplite census or above, the status required for eligibility to perform these liturgies, may have been as high as 25,000.[16] By 411 the great plague and war casualties, especially the losses in Sicily, seem to have reduced that number to about 9,000.[17] Neither figure is either precise or secure; yet any reasonable adjustment will still reveal a stunning diminution in the number of Athenians available in 411 to pay the state's expenses.

Those expenses must have been very high if the speeches that have come down to us under the name of Lysias are any indication. In one of them, a certain Aristophanes is said to have spent almost 15 talents

---

[14]For a discussion of the *hetairiai*, see Kagan, *Peace of Nicias*, 204–205.
[15]See above, 3.
[16]That is the estimate of R. Thomsen, *Eisphora* (Copenhagen, 1964), 162–163.
[17]See above, 2. This is the figure given by the speaker in Lys. 20.13 as the number of those enrolled as being capable of bearing arms, that is, as hoplites or cavalrymen.

on public services, including payments of the special war taxes, and service as trierarch.[18] In another the speaker recounts his expenditures for the years 411/10 to 404/3, a total of almost 10 talents. His list provides us with evidence of the variety of public obligations imposed upon Athens' wealthier citizens: he produced tragic and comic dramas; paid for choral competitions, dancers, athletic contests, and trireme races; equipped six triremes for battle in seven years; and during that time twice contributed his share of the *eisphora*.[19] To be sure, he boasts that he spent four times what was legally required, so the less generous men of his class might have had to spend no more than 2.5 talents during the same period, but even that was a very high sum. We must remember that a talent consisted of 6,000 drachmas, that a drachma was a very good day's pay in the late fifth century, and that in those years an Athenian citizen rowing in the fleet was expected to get by on half that amount. Another way of understanding the meaning of these sums is to note that Nicias, one of the richest men in Athens, was expected to leave an estate of no more than 100 talents and that his son, not a notorious wastrel, left no more than 14 talents to his heir. There is good reason to think that the fortunes of many Athenian families were seriously reduced by public services during the Peloponnesian War.[20] By 411, and especially in the years since the Sicilian disaster, the unprecedented expense would already have been strongly felt, and it would not take much imagination for the propertied classes to see that there would be similar and even greater demands in the future.

The moral standing of the democratic regime, the alleged foolishness of its policies and incompetence of their execution, the decline in the quality of leadership, and the heavy burden of public financial obligations were all problems of long standing for those Athenians skeptical of the democracy, although all of them were intensified in the years after Sicily. The new element in 411 was the dismal prospect for success or even survival in the war against the Peloponnesians. The dismay after the Sicilian disaster had quickly given way to determination and action. The Athenian response to rebellion in the empire

---

[18]Lys. 19.42–43. The speech is dated to about 388/87, at the end of the Corinthian War, and so the total must include a good deal spent after the Peloponnesian War. One expenditure mentioned, however, is for the Sicilian expedition from 415 to 413, so some considerable portion must have been spent during the earlier war.

[19]Lys. 21.1–5.

[20]Lys. 19.45–48.

had been remarkably successful and seemed to be on the point of stamping it out entirely. Had the Athenian forces been able to recover Miletus and Chios, the Persians might well have decided that the reports of Athens' imminent demise had been greatly exaggerated and withdrawn their support from the Peloponnesians, putting an end to Sparta's Aegean adventure and the threat to the Athenian Empire.

That opportunity, however, had been lost as a result of Phrynichus' decision at Miletus. Instead, the rebellion had spread to the Hellespont and threatened the Athenian lifeline. The emergency reserve fund was gone, and the treasury was empty.[21] Tissaphernes had healed the breach with the Spartans and promised to bring the Phoenician fleet into action against the Athenians.[22] Finally, the Spartans had gained a foothold on the Hellespont and threatened to cut Athens' supply lines and win the war. The installation of *probouloi* in 413 had already changed the democratic constitution to a degree. In the face of these difficulties and dangers, it would not be surprising to find many Athenians in favor of further change in the domestic situation, some curtailment of democratic practices, a more efficient arrangement, and perhaps even a change of regime. History is full of examples of states, even democracies, abandoning their ordinary practices in wartime, especially in times of crisis. Great Britain put aside ordinary political competition in 1940 and formed a national government. The form of the cabinet was changed, placing the administration in the hands of a very few men and almost dictatorial power in the hands of Winston Churchill, who was both prime minister and minister of defence. There was every reason, even for loyal democrats, to favor some limitation on the democracy, and this was even truer for its enemies.

It is evidence of the powerful general support for the traditional full democracy and of the oligarchs' lack of initiative that the movement to alter the constitution did not begin in Athens. The instigator was the renegade Alcibiades, whose sense of self-preservation and undiminished appetite for power and glory led him to seek his restoration to the Athens that had condemned and cursed him only a few years earlier. He was an outlaw to both the Athenians and Spartans, and

---

[21] In June of 411 the democratic leaders of the Athenians at Samos said that the city was no longer supplying money for them: οἵ γε μήτε ἀργύριον εἶχον ἔτι πέμπειν, so that the soldiers had to get their own: αὐτοὶ ἐπορίζοντο (8.76.6). Xenophon confirms this statement by reporting that in the following winter the Athenian generals in the Hellespont had to spend time collecting money: ἀμφότεροι ἠργυρολογηκότες (1.1.12).

[22] See above, 98–99.

his only security lay in the protection offered by Tissaphernes, but his situation was precarious, for the satrap was a wily man, ambitious and keenly aware of his own interests. He was using Alcibiades surely no less than the Athenian was attempting to use him, and it was only a matter of time before the Persian's interests might lead him to abandon his protégé. Alcibiades' plan, therefore, was to take advantage of his influence with Tissaphernes and to gain Persian support, safety, and victory for the Athenians.[23] To this end, he sent communications to "the most important men among them," presumably the generals, trierarchs, and other influential individuals, asking them to mention him—and, no doubt, the great influence he had with Tissaphernes— "to the best people."[24] They were to say that he wanted to return to Athens but only if they established an oligarchy instead of the base democracy that had banished him. In that case, he would come back, bringing the friendship and support of Tissaphernes with him. These messages had the intended effect, "for the Athenian soldiers at Samos perceived that he had influence with Tissaphernes," and envoys from the camp left Samos to discuss the situation with him.[25]

Although Thucydides' narrative makes clear the vital part played by Alcibiades in starting the oligarchic movement, his own judgment places the emphasis elsewhere. "But even more than the influence and promises of Alcibiades, of their own accord, the trierarchs and the most important men among the Athenians at Samos were eager to destroy the democracy."[26] Most scholars have emphasized the initiative taken by Alcibiades without noticing the nuance provided by Thucydides, but the difference should not be overlooked.[27] Here we have not a statement of fact but an interpretation of why the Athenian leaders at Samos, all of them, acted as they did (for Thucydides makes

---

[23] 8.47.

[24] 8.47.2

[25] 8.47.2; 8.48.1.

[26] 8.47.2; τὸ δὲ πλέον καὶ ἀπὸ σφῶν αὐτῶν οἱ ἐν τῇ Σάμῳ τριήραρχοί τε τῶν Ἀθηναίων καὶ δυνατώτατοι ὥρμηντο ἐς τὸ καταλῦσαι τὴν δημοκρατίαν.

[27] The vast majority of scholars have given the greatest prominence to the role of Alcibiades. Perhaps the strongest statements are by Grote (VIII, 7): "Such was the first originating germ of that temporary calamity which so nearly brought Athens to absolute ruin, called the Oligarchy of Four Hundred: a suggestion from the same exile who had already so deeply wounded his country by sending Gylippus to Syracuse . . . ," and M. F. McGregor, who says that Alcibiades "plotted the oligarchic revolution that produced the Four Hundred" (*Phoenix* XIX [1965], 42). E. F. Bloedow, citing the passage quoted above in n. 26, emphasizes the eagerness of the Athenian plotters on Samos (*Alcibiades Reexamined* [Wiesbaden, 1973], 34, n. 213).

no distinction or exception) and what their intentions were. Careful readers of Thucydides have rightly warned of the need to distinguish between his report of facts, which have the highest claim to our belief, and his interpretations, which are open to greater question.[28] In this case, especially, we must be cautious, for in the one specific instance we can check, Thucydides is clearly wrong. Who "the most important men among the Athenians" may have been we can only guess, and we do not know who the trierarchs at Samos were, with one exception, Thrasybulus, the son of Lycus of Steiria.[29] Thucydides tells us that when the Samian people learned of an oligarchic plot to overthrow the democracy in Samos they came to Thrasybulus, among others, "who seemed always to be especially opposed to the conspirators."[30] Thrasybulus and his colleagues then rallied the sailors to the defense of the Samian democracy and put down the oligarchic uprising. Soon after, they compelled all of the soldiers, and especially those who had been involved with the oligarchs, to swear an oath of loyalty to the democracy.[31] The newly sworn, thoroughly democratic army then deposed its generals and elected new, reliably democratic ones in their stead, among them Thrasybulus.[32] He would spend the rest of the war as a loyal democratic general and emerge from it as the hero who resisted

[28]See the perceptive remarks of G. E. M. de Ste. Croix: "Thucydides was such a remarkably objective historian that he himself has provided sufficient material for his own refutation. The news columns in Thucydides, so to speak, contradict the editorial Thucydides, and the editor does not always speak with the same voice" (*Historia* III [1954–1955], 3). P. J. Rhodes' warnings about Thucydides' account of the events of 411 are also apposite: "He was in exile when these events took place, and therefore had the advantage of not being directly implicated and the disadvantage of being dependent on what others told him. He has added to the facts a good deal of interpretation. He was a writer proud of his ability to probe beneath the surface and to discern what was 'really' happening, what the 'real' aims of the men involved were; and though we may well think his judgment shrewd we must follow it with caution. It is of course true that men often have aims which they will not acknowledge in public; but most men act from mixed motives for much of the time, and (though they may have other aims too) are not often wholly insincere in the aims which they do profess in public. Concentration on one motive, to the exclusion of others, is to be suspected as much when indulged in by the best of ancient authorities as when indulged in by modern scholars. Thucydides' statements of what men 'really' wanted are not factual statements of the same kind as his statements of what they publicly said or did; and if we accept only those aims which he claims to have detected beneath the surface we may distort the truth more than if we recognize only those professed aims which he disallows" (*JHS* XCII [1972], 115–116).

[29]On Thrasybulus, see *HCT* V, 264; and Davies, *APF*, 240.

[30]8.73.4.

[31]8.73.58; 75.

[32]8.76.2.

and finally overthrew the oligarchy of the Thirty Tyrants and restored democracy to Athens. No Athenian has a better claim to the title of convinced and loyal democrat than Thrasybulus, and none less deserves the accusation of being "eager to destroy the democracy," yet he is included among the men against whom Thucydides makes that charge. If Thucydides is mistaken or misinformed in this instance, he may be equally wrong in other cases, so we must not simply accept his opinions without question but examine each case on its own merits. Certainly, Thrasybulus was one of those at Samos who received Alcibiades' words warmly and favored bringing him back.[33] For him, at least, Alcibiades' proposal represented something different from a long-awaited opportunity to overthrow Athenian democracy, and there is reason to think that he was not alone.

So we may well believe that the movement to bring back Alcibiades and to alter the form of government in Athens was suggested by the Athenian renegade for his own reasons and accepted by the Athenian leaders at Samos for theirs, but the reasons of that group were clearly not all the same. Within this group at Samos, even at this early stage (perhaps in November of 412),[34] we can discern two very different factions. One was that of Thrasybulus. "He always held to the same opinion," says Thucydides, "that they should recall Alcibiades."[35] This means that at some time, at least, he was willing to accept limitations on the Athenian democracy, for Alcibiades' first messages to the Athenian notables at Samos was to that effect.[36] In fact, if we accept Thucydides' report of Alcibiades' demands as both accurate and precise, we might believe that Thrasybulus was even prepared to overthrow the democracy and replace it with an oligarchy. In light of his later actions, it is hard to believe that of the great democratic hero, and it is possible that Thucydides' informant was wrong in this particular instance. More likely, Alcibiades did use such words, but Thrasybulus and men like him balked at it and forced him to change his language. When a delegation from Samos crossed over to meet with him, at any rate, he no longer used the offensive word *oligarchy* but promised to return and perform his wonders "if the Athenians were

[33]8.76.7; 81.1.
[34]Busolt, *GG* III:2, 1467.
[35]8.81.1.
[36]8.47.2. Here and throughout my discussion of Athenian politics in this volume I am indebted to W. J. McCoy, "Theramenes, Thrasybulus and the Athenian Moderates," Ph.D. diss., Yale University, 1970.

not under a democracy." The subtle shift in language was probably real and a concession to men like Thrasybulus who were prepared to alter the constitution but not to move to oligarchy.[37]

No matter how we interpret the language, however, there is no escaping the fact that as early as November of 412 and in the months following, Thrasybulus was ready to limit and alter the powers of the Athenian democracy. Although he knew Alcibiades' condition for return, he persuaded the Athenian forces at Samos to vote to grant Alcibiades immunity from prosecution, recall him to duty, and elect him general, and it was he who personally sailed across to Tissaphernes and brought Alcibiades back to Samos.[38] Why did this great democratic paladin act in this way? Thucydides' answer is simple and clear: "He brought Alcibiades back to Samos thinking that the only safety for Athens was if he could bring Tissaphernes away from the Peloponnesians and over to their side."[39] Thrasybulus was convinced that without a Persian breach with Sparta, Athens was doomed. Winning the war required winning over Persia, and he believed that only Alcibiades could do that. If salvation meant placing limits on the democracy, Thrasybulus was willing, although he would resist excessive departures from the existing constitution.[40]

We can get a good idea of what limitations Thrasybulus regarded as acceptable from Alcibiades' reply to the mission sent by the Four Hundred at Athens in the summer of 411 to the forces at Samos. By that time, Alcibiades had been rejected as not "suitable" for oligarchy by the Four Hundred at Athens. His future prospects lay with the forces at Samos and especially with their leader Thrasybulus. It is more than unlikely that the flexible renegade would specify conditions that were not in accord with those of Thrasybulus. In fact, it would be surprising if those conditions were not shaped, in part at least, to suit his views. Alcibiades required that the council of Four Hundred, the ruling body of the oligarchy, be disbanded and the old democratic council of Five Hundred be restored. But he approved the curtailment

[37]The first passage says Alcibiades wanted to come home: ἐπ' ὀλιγαρχίᾳ (8.47.2). The second says that he will gain Persian friendship for Athens: εἰ μὴ δημοκρατοῖντο (8.48.1). As McCoy points out, Thucydides does not report Alcibiades as using the term *oligarchy* again ("Theramenes," 24).

[38]8.81.1; 82.1.

[39]8.81.1.

[40]For a good discussion of the importance in Athens and Samos at this time of the idea of safety or salvation of the city, σωτηρία, see E. Lévy, *Athènes devant la défaite de 404, histoire d'une crise idéologique* (Paris, 1976), 16–27.

of pay for public services and the rule of the Five Thousand, the limited group of citizens who exercised privileges formerly open to the full democratic assembly.[41]

Thrasybulus was unwilling to accept oligarchy in the form of the rule of the council of Four Hundred, but he was willing to curtail the rights and privileges of the people to receive pay and to exercise fully their political function to the extent of accepting a fully competent citizen body as small as about Five Thousand. In what political category does such a man belong? He cannot be called an oligarch, as we have seen; no ancient author ever speaks of him in that way, and no contemporary Athenian would have thought such a designation appropriate. Neither was he an uncompromising, or what modern historians have traditionally called a "radical," democrat; else he would have resisted any limit to the people's power. What is left is the traditional designation "moderate," a term that suits Thrasybulus perfectly and, in the sense described above, one that does not have merely loose connotations but clearly denotes a political position.[42]

The other group involved in the discussions with Alcibiades fully deserves Thucydides' description as men who sought to destroy the democracy and to establish an oligarchy of their own accord. Thucydides mentions the names of two of these men who took part in the conspiracy at Samos: Phrynichus and Peisander.[43] Neither man was an oligarch of long standing. Both, in fact, had reputations for being

----

[41]8.86.6. For a discussion of the privileges of the Five Thousand see Chapter 8. The issue is whether that body had exclusive access to all of the rights of citizenship or merely to the right of holding office.

[42]The concept that Athenian politics in 411 is best understood in terms of three factions:—radical democrats (or merely "democrats"), moderates (moderate democrats, moderate oligarchs, or simply "moderates"), and oligarchs—dates from at least nineteenth-century historians such as Beloch, Meyer, and Busolt and has been the usual way of understanding the situation ever since. R. Sealey (*Essays in Greek Politics* [New York, 1967], 110–132, and especially 127–130) has dismissed the importance and even existence of a group such as the "moderates," at least from a constitutional point of view. He rightly dismisses Alcibiades as not deserving such a designation and much less persuasively argues against Theramenes' right to the title. He says nothing, however, about Thrasybulus, which is a serious omission. The evidence makes it clear that some Athenians favored oligarchy unequivocally, others would brook no change whatever, and still others stood between these two rigid positions. This third group was inevitably more varied than the other two, and its members had less in common. Some leaned more to one extreme and some to the other, but all can conveniently, accurately, and significantly be called moderates. If such a category did not already exist, we should need to invent it.

[43]8.48.4; 49.

demagogues; Peisander had played an important role in the prosecutions during the scandals of 415, and Phrynichus was clearly a successful democratic politician.[44] We cannot tell whether these democratic politicians joined the conspiracy to establish an oligarchy in 411 from a sincere change in conviction or for reasons of personal advantage. The speaker in Lysias' speech in "Defense against the Charge of Subverting Democracy," delivered a few years after the war, charges both men with helping establish the oligarchy because they feared punishment for the many offenses they had committed against the Athenian people.[45] The speech is tendentious and the charges vague, but there may have been some truth behind them. Peisander must have made many enemies in his vigorous investigations of the scandals of 415. It was he who helped turn the inquiry into a general reign of terror, and it was he who proposed the decree lifting the ban against torturing Athenian citizens during the inquisition.[46] There would surely be many with charges to bring against him, many to sympathize with them, and much for him to explain. Of Phrynichus' career before 412/11 we know little, but his performance as general in that year must already have been controversial by November of 412. About a year earlier, he had opposed the unanimous opinion of the other Athenian generals and withdrawn from Miletus, avoiding a naval battle that might have crushed the Ionian rebellion at once.[47] The immediate result had been the abandonment of Amorges to the Persians. In the year since, Athenian fortunes had gone from bad to worse. As we shall see, some Athenians were ready to blame Phrynichus.[48]

---

[44]Lysias (25.9) speaks of them as demagogues who later turned to oligarchy. In the case of Peisander the title is clearly justified, for he was a frequent butt of the comic poets (*HCT* V, 116), and Andocides (1.36) describes him, along with Charicles, as being thought of in 415 as the most well disposed to the people: εὐνούστατοι εἶναι τῷ δήμῳ. For his role in the prosecutions of 415, see And. 1.27, 36, 43, and *HCT* IV, 383–388. For a defense of Peisander against the charges of hypocrisy, opportunism, and self-seeking, see A. G. Woodhead, *AJP* LXXV (1954), 132–146. The position of Phrynichus before 411 is more difficult to determine, but there is no good reason to reject Lysias' listing of him alongside Peisander as a well-known democratic politician who later went over to oligarchy. The cautious conclusion of *HCT* (V, 59–60) is justified: "All that we can certainly say is that Phrynichos was a man with a long public career, who could be labelled as a democratic leader and inspired enough trust to be appointed general in 411 at an advanced age, presumably on the basis of his past record in office."
[45]Lys. 25.9.
[46]And. 1.36, 43.
[47]8.27.
[48]8.54.3.

Both men, therefore, may well have had pressing personal reasons to fear the continuation of democracy and so to favor a change.

Whatever their motives, these men, unlike Thrasybulus, did not join the movement to make possible the return of Alcibiades, the reversal of Persian support, and therefore an Athenian victory. Phrynichus resisted the return of Alcibiades from the outset, denied that he could do what he promised, intrigued to prevent his return, and became active in the conspiracy only after Alcibiades and the prospect of Persian help had been excluded from it.[49] Peisander, after he learned that Alcibiades could not or would not deliver Persian support, joined in excluding him from their future plans and then took a leading part in trying to establish oligarchy in Athens.[50] Once they joined the movement, these men were firmly, vigorously, and permanently committed to the oligarchical cause. Thucydides says of Phrynichus that "he showed himself, beyond all others, the most eager for the oligarchy; ... once he set to work he revealed himself as the most reliable."[51] Peisander was the one who put forth the motion to establish the oligarchy of the Four Hundred and, according to Thucydides, was the man in the public arena who played the greatest and most zealous part in the destruction of the democracy. He also took the lead in forming an oligarchic conspiracy on Samos, and when the oligarchy was overthrown at Athens, he went over to the Spartan camp at Decelea.[52] Although Peisander and Phrynichus may have come to the position for purely opportunistic reasons, both clearly and fully deserve the designation "oligarchs." The men on Samos, then, who came together and decided to negotiate with Alcibiades were from the first divided into two distinct types whom we may call "oligarchs" and "moderates."

The response of the "trierarchs and the most important men" at Samos to Alcibiades' messages was to send representatives to hold discussions with Alcibiades. Thucydides does not mention any names, but Peisander and Thrasybulus were probably members of the delegation.[53] There they heard the same promises to bring over to Athens'

[49] 8.48.4–7; 50–51; 68.3.
[50] 8.56; 63.3–4.
[51] 8.63.3.
[52] 8.67; 73.2; 98.1.
[53] 8.48.1. Thucydides merely says that τινές crossed over from Samos. Nepos (*Alc.* 3) names Peisander as one of the intermediaries, calling him a general, which he was not. Perhaps he was a trierarch, although we have no evidence to that effect. In any case, his leading role in the entire affair makes his participation likely (see Busolt, *GG* III:2, 1467, n. 2). The suggestion that Thrasybulus took part derives from his position as trierarch and his continuing close association with Alcibiades.

side not only Tissaphernes but also the Great King of Persia. This time the condition he set, if Thucydides' paraphrase is precise, was that he would do these things "if they did not retain the democracy, for in that way the King would have greater trust in them."[54] We may guess that moderates like Thrasybulus had reacted badly to the word *oligarchy* in Alcibiades' earlier communications and that the alert exile had adjusted his language to reduce unnecessary friction. "Not to retain the democracy" could be understood differently by moderates and oligarchs but "replacing the base democracy with an oligarchy" would not.[55] When they returned to Samos with their report, the important men who had sent them were much encouraged. Thucydides still does not distinguish among them, saying of all of them that they had great hopes of bringing the government into their own hands and also of overcoming the enemy.[56] No doubt, the two factions we have discerned emphasized different aspects of those hopes.

The next step was for the leaders to form "those suitable" into an effective political body by means of an oath.[57] Thucydides calls this political body a *xynomosia*, which often means conspiracy, with all of its nasty connotations, and he may have intended that sense. But the word may also mean merely a group of men united for political purposes and bound by an oath. Thucydides uses the same word to describe the political clubs of long standing in Athens, and when Thrasybulus organized the democratic forces at Samos, he had them swear an oath of loyalty to the democracy.[58] Whatever Thucydides meant, we should not think of this organization as a secret cell limited to a few conspirators. "Those suitable" probably included soldiers from the ranks, for many of the thousand hoplites sent on the Milesian campaign were at Samos.[59] The organization certainly included Thrasybulus and, therefore, could not have been simply an oligarchic conspiracy.

The organization's next step makes it clear that secrecy was not an important part of its character, for it called the men of the Athenian

---

[54] 8.48.1: εἰ μὴ δημοκρατοῖντο (οὕτω γὰρ ἂν πιστεῦσαι μᾶλλον βασιλέα).
[55] This is the suggestion of McCoy, "Theramenes," 24, who seems to have been the first to notice the change in terms.
[56] 8.48.1. This is my understanding of this difficult passage. For a discussion of the textual problems, see *HCT* V, 107–108.
[57] 8.48.2.
[58] 8.54.4; 74.2.
[59] *HCT* V, 106, 108; Busolt, *GG* III:2, 1467, n. 2.

forces at Samos together "and openly told the many that the King would be their friend and provide them with money if they took back Alcibiades and were not governed by a democracy."[60] Thus the soldiers and sailors were told everything that the members of the organization knew. There was no use of the word *oligarchy*, but that word had been abandoned by Alcibiades himself in his private conversations with organization leaders. If the common man did not know that plans to establish a narrow and permanent oligarchy lurked in the hearts of some members, neither did insiders such as Thrasybulus.

"The mob," as Thucydides refers to the assembly of soldiers and sailors, "even if it was somewhat annoyed at the moment by what had been done, subsided into silence because of the hopeful prospect of pay from the King."[61] This account of what must have been a heated and extended discussion is both tendentious and brief. The implication is that the Athenian forces at Samos were prepared to allow the restoration of the traitor Alcibiades and an attenuation of their beloved democracy because of greed.[62] The passage brings to mind Thucydides' explanation of the popular enthusiasm for the Sicilian campaign of 415. "The mass of the people and the soldiers hoped to get money at the moment and to make an addition to their empire from which they would have a never ending source of income."[63] Whatever the reasons the ordinary fighting men of Athens may have had for supporting the Sicilian expedition, they had stronger motives than greed for being willing to consider even unwelcome proposals late in 412 and to think such unthinkable thoughts as were being proposed to them. The salvation of their city was at issue, perhaps their own lives and those of their families, for they could not be sure that a victorious and vengeful enemy would not treat Athens as the Athenians had treated Scione and Melos. No doubt there were outcries at the suggestion of Alcibiades' return and even louder ones at talk of not being governed by a democracy. Probably the intervention of trusted men such as Thrasybulus helped calm the gathering and remind the men that by swallowing such bitter pills they could obtain the financial support that would allow them to carry on the war and win it.[64]

[60] 8.48.2.
[61] 8.48.3.
[62] Meyer (*GdA*, IV, 286) has caught the sense well: "To the crowd of sailors who were told of Alcibiades' demands and promises the prospect of plentiful wages was welcome in the highest degree." See also Hatzfeld, *Alcibiade*, 233.
[63] 6.24.3.
[64] McCoy, "Theramenes," 25–26.

After the meeting with the soldiers and sailors, the leaders of the movement held a session with most of those friendly to it to consider further Alcibiades' proposals. Everyone approved, except Phrynichus, who opposed them totally. His speech appears to have responded, in turn, to each of the arguments that had been made in support of the proposals. He did not believe that the Great King could be brought over to the Athenian side, for his interests pointed in the opposite direction. The Athenians no longer had a monopoly of effective sea power in the Aegean and had lost major cities of their empire to the Peloponnesians, so the Persians had less reason than before to purchase Athenian friendship. They mistrusted the Athenians, from whom they had suffered much over many years, whereas the Peloponnesians had not done them any harm. Someone must have suggested that if the Athenians replaced their democracy with an oligarchy, it would ease their imperial problems; cities that had rebelled, usually under oligarchic leadership, would return to fealty and further uprisings would be prevented. To this Phrynichus replied with a hard-headed analysis of the realities of empire that rejected the primacy of the class struggle. None of these predictions would come true, he said, for none of the allies "will want to be enslaved with either an oligarchy or a democracy rather than to be free under whichever of these happens to exist."[65] The allies took even less comfort in the rule of the Athenian upper classes than in that of the commoners, for the former profited most from the empire and were less careful about due process.[66]

Phrynichus' most important argument, however, was that Alcibiades was not to be trusted. He cared nothing for oligarchy or democracy. He wanted a change in the current constitution merely to make possible his own recall at the request of his partisans. If his plan went forward, Athens would be torn by civil strife, something it could not afford at this dangerous moment. Alcibiades could not deliver Persian support; he could not bring back rebellious allies or prevent future rebellions. At present, therefore, Phrynichus saw no virtue in any of the proposals.[67]

Phrynichus' advice was to reject the advances of Alcibiades and go

<hr />

[65]8.48.5. I agree with D. W. Bradeen (*Historia* IX [1960], 268–269) that this is a correct estimation of the attitude of the Greeks within the Athenian Empire and that Thucydides shared that view as he makes clear in 8.64. For a different view see Ste. Croix, *Historia* III (1954–1955), 1–41.
[66]8.48.4–6. For a valuable discussion of these points see *HCT* V, 110–113.
[67]8.48.4, 7.

on as before, but it was precisely because that path seemed both profitless and dangerous that the movement had taken shape. Accepting Phrynichus' advice would mean an end to the movement, and some scholars have thought that this was his intention, that late in 412 he had not yet turned against democracy.[68] That is difficult to believe, for not only did he appear as a key figure in the conspiracy within a few months, but more to the point, he would not have been invited to this private meeting of friends of the movement if he had been hostile to it. His opposition must be attributed not to constitutional preference but to a more practical motive: dislike and fear of Alcibiades. We are not informed when those feelings arose or what the reasons for them were. A speaker in the law courts refers to Phrynichus as a *sykophantes*, an informer for pay. If there is more than slander in the charge, we might guess that there had been occasion for Phrynichus to annoy a man whose way of life was a standing invitation to informers.[69] A more likely source of conflict might be found in Phrynichus' career as a democratic politician, which almost surely put him in conflict with Alcibiades before his departure for Sicily. All of this is only conjecture, but we should not doubt that Phrynichus already considered Alcibiades a dangerous enemy when he spoke at the meeting of the movement's notables at Samos.[70] Perhaps others knew of his private motives, and that may help explain the absence of any support for him. In any case, he persuaded no one, and the meeting decided to accept Alcibiades' proposals. They appointed an embassy under the leadership of Peisander to go to Athens and work to bring about the return of Alcibiades and to put down the current democracy in order to win over Tissaphernes.[71]

[68]Grote (VIII, 10) says: "Though Phrynichus was afterwards one of the chief organizers of the oligarchical movement, when it became detached from, and hostile to Alkibiades, yet under the actual circumstances he discountenanced it altogether." See also Hatzfeld (*Alcibiade*, 234), who says that Phrynichus was at this time "an active democrat."

[69]Lys. 20.11–12.

[70]That is made clear in Phrynichus' letter to Astyochus sent immediately after the meeting. In it he informed the Spartan admiral of the conspiracy and of Alcibiades' part in it, excusing his own treachery on the grounds that "it was pardonable to plot evil against a man who was his enemy even to the disadvantage of the state": ξυγγνώμην δὲ εἶναι ἑαυτῷ περὶ ἀνδρὸς πολεμίου καὶ μετὰ τοῦ τῆς πόλεως ἀξυμφόρου κακόν τι βουλεύειν (8.50.2). But Phrynichus had no reason to know that Alcibiades had already become his enemy as a result of his speech at Samos. As far as we know, the speech had not yet been reported to Alcibiades, nor had he reacted to it. The evidence seems to support the idea of a preexisting hostility.

[71]8.49.

Phrynichus now found himself in a most dangerous position. The news of his opposition would certainly get to Alcibiades before too long, and the plan to recall the renegade was under way. He needed a scheme to prevent the return of his enemy, and he produced an imaginative and daring one. Phrynichus wrote a letter secretly to Astyochus, the Spartan navarch who was at Miletus, revealing the details of Alcibiades' plot, including the plan to bring Tissaphernes and the Persians over to the Athenian side. His excuse, as we have seen, was the hostility of Alcibiades and the threat it posed to his own safety. Apparently, Phrynichus had not yet learned of Alcibiades' flight from the Peloponnesian camp and assumed that Astyochus could easily lay hands on the Athenian exile.[72] The stratagem, therefore, would have been doomed from the first if Astyochus had merely done the obvious and ignored the letter about which he could do nothing. Instead, he took the initiative and went to Magnesia to see Tissaphernes and Alcibiades. He told them the contents of the letter and established a close relationship with Tissaphernes. It was later rumored that his actions in this affair and in other matters were prompted by bribes from the satrap.[73]

Alcibiades' reaction was to write a letter to those in charge at Samos revealing Phrynichus' treachery and asking that they put him to death. Phrynichus was now in great peril. His mistake about the whereabouts of Alcibiades and his misjudgment of Astyochus had produced a situation in which he might be killed by the leaders at Samos even before the restoration of his enemy. He now concocted an even more imaginative and desperate scheme. He wrote another letter to Astyochus, complaining of his breach of honor, but offering a great opportunity. He was prepared to offer the Peloponnesians a way to destroy the entire Athenian army at Samos, since it was without walls. He explained his action, once again on the grounds of the increased danger to his own life at the hands of his greatest enemy. Once again Astyochus turned the information over to Alcibiades.

Somehow Phrynichus learned that Astyochus had betrayed him and was working against his interests.[74] Alcibiades had again written a letter to Samos, which had all but arrived, telling of Phrynichus' latest

---

[72] This point is well made by H. D. Westlake in *JHS* LXXVI (1956), 101. Although I do not accept some of his conclusions, I have learned much from his close and perceptive reading of Thucydides.

[73] 8.50.3; 83.3.

[74] *HCT* V, 119–120, suggests how he might have done so.

treachery. Once again Phrynichus' strong nerve and quick wit produced a stratagem. Before the accusation could arrive, he told the army at Samos that he had received information of an enemy plan to attack the Athenian camp, just as he had secretly urged. He told the Athenians to be watchful and to build fortifications to defend against the attack, and so they did. When Alcibiades' letter arrived soon after, its effect had already been undermined by Phrynichus' trick. Alcibiades, already suspected by many Athenians, was thought to have given further evidence of his untrustworthiness. The Athenians believed that Alcibiades knew of the Peloponnesians' plans because of his association with them and was acting out of personal enmity in claiming that Phrynichus knew about them too. Instead of doing Phrynichus harm, the letter raised his credibility, for he had warned the Athenians of precisely the danger Alcibiades described.[75]

That is the story, essentially as Thucydides tells it, and it is a difficult one to understand fully. One scholar has gone so far as to deny the reality of the entire incident, to assert that there were no such letters and that the story was created from whole cloth by Alcibiades to destroy his enemy Phrynichus, but there is no reason to go that far.[76] We must believe that the bizarre epistolary exchange took place and try to understand the actions and motives of the participants. Some questions arise at once; how could a man as shrewd as Phrynichus be so foolish as to speak out against the plan to bring back Alcibiades in a company strongly committed to his return? How could he have acted out of fear, as Thucydides says, when everywhere he shows himself to be a bold and brave man? Why did he write Astyochus a second letter, knowing that the Spartan navarch had already betrayed him? If Astyochus had not been bribed and was not acting out of self-interest, how can his actions be explained? One way has been to accept Thucydides' account that fear was the cause of Phrynichus' behavior. But this does not explain his decision to write a second letter to Astyochus as part of a shrewd scheme in which he expected to be betrayed and planned in advance to carry out the trick that undid Alcibiades.[77] However, the idea of a scheme answers too few questions and flatly

[75] 8.51.
[76] The theory is put forth by Hatzfeld (*Alcibiade*, 235–236). It is refuted effectively by Westlake, *JHS* LXXVI (1956), 99–100.
[77] That is the suggestion of Grote, VIII, 12–13, followed by many others.

contradicts Thucydides' account, which indicates that Phrynichus was taken by surprise.[78]

Another explanation likewise assumes that Phrynichus expected his second letter to be betrayed and used that betrayal as part of his scheme but rejects fear as his motive. Instead, "the stratagem of Phrynichos was partly designed to influence the military and political situation in the interests of Athens."[79] Phrynichus' speech at Samos was sincere, wise, and brave. When it failed to persuade, Phrynichus turned from oratory to trickery to save the Athenians from the mistake of bringing back Alcibiades and introducing factional strife at so dangerous a moment. Astyochus was taken in because of his inexperience and general lack of ability. "The narrative of Thucydides certainly suggests that these failures could have been due to the defects of Astyochus in character and intellectual qualities and that there is no need to seek any more sinister explanation of them, as his exasperated troops did."[80] This view, too, contradicts the narrative of Thucydides, and although it improves on the first by considering the behavior of Astyochus, it explains that behavior by incompetence or stupidity. Those qualities surely exist and often explain military and political behavior, but before resorting to such an explanation, a historian prefers to exhaust the other possibilities. Even if the answer lies in the foolishness of a participant, it is desirable to understand what he was thinking when he miscalculated.

Here is a different account of this strange affair. If we accept that Alcibiades and Phrynichus were enemies of long standing, as the text of Thucydides suggests, we can readily understand Phrynichus' willingness, indeed his need, to speak out at the meeting on Samos against his enemy's return.[81] Such an action would be both inspired by fear and rational. One reason for the total failure of his speech may have been the general knowledge of the enmity and the dismissal of the argument on ground of bias. Phrynichus then wrote to Astyochus out of fear for his own safety. In doing so, he made two mistakes: he did

---

[78]See *HCT* V, 119–120.

[79]Westlake, *JHS* LXXVI (1956), 100.

[80]H. D. Westlake, *Individuals in Thucydides* (Cambridge, 1968), 305–306. For a fuller discussion of Astyochus' inadequacies see *JHS* LXXVI (1956), 102.

[81]Westlake asserts that "Thucydides does not state or imply that Phrynichos was at this stage influenced by personal antipathy towards Alcibiades" (*JHS* LXXVI [1956], 99, n. 1). He is correct, but I have argued that his narrative makes it more than likely that such a previous enmity existed.

not know that Alcibiades was no longer in the Spartan camp, and he failed to foresee the reaction of Astyochus.

The Spartan navarch was no longer in a position to lay hands on Alcibiades, even had he wanted to. Nor could he ignore the warning lest the whole plot succeed and the Athenian renegade succeed in bringing Tissaphernes over to the Athenian side. Instead he went to Magnesia. By sharing the contents of the letter, he also revealed that he knew of the plot, a revelation that must have come as a blow to Alcibiades and a shock to Tissaphernes, who probably knew nothing about it. Whatever Tissaphernes' true intentions, he surely had made no commitment, and it must have been acutely embarrassing to Alcibiades to have the satrap learn that he had promised to bring the Persians over to Athens. As Westlake rightly says, "the motives and aims of Astyochos in this episode seem to have been almost wholly unknown to Thucydides."[82] He is also right to say that the navarch did not make the trip just to deliver a message but to discuss it and negotiate as well. We must agree that he had come "to remonstrate with Alcibiades and Tissaphernes . . . and to attempt to deter Tissaphernes from concluding an agreement with the Athenians."[83] Just revealing the plot to Tissaphernes and making clear his own knowledge of it, no doubt, had a deterrent effect, for Alcibiades' relationship with the satrap began to decline almost immediately.[84] Probably Tissaphernes regarded Astyochus' revelation as a friendly act and drew closer to him. Perhaps he rewarded him with a cash gift, as oriental potentates were accustomed to do and as more than one Greek official was accustomed to accept. Perhaps that was the source of the rumor of bribery, a reward for services rendered misconstrued as a bribe for services to be rendered, but it may well be that the friendly relations established at this meeting help account for his less-than-vigorous efforts to secure more pay for the Peloponnesian sailors later.[85]

Alcibiades, embarrassed and angered, at once wrote to his influential friends at Samos telling them of Phrynichus' letter and asking them to put him to death. Phrynichus, desperate and in a panic, wrote again to Astyochus, telling him how he could make a successful attack on the Athenian army at Samos. Thucydides relates this action as being seriously intended to succeed and makes no suggestion that Phrynichus

[82]*JHS* LXXVI (1956), 102.
[83]Ibid.
[84]8.56.2.
[85]8.50.3; 83.3.

expected it to fail. Modern historians, as we have seen, find this impossible. Surely, since Phrynichus knew his first letter had been betrayed, he must have expected the same treatment for the second. The first letter had asked Astyochus to do something that turned out to be impossible and whose consequence would be neither dramatic nor decisive, even if it were possible. In the circumstances, Astyochus' action was not remarkable. The second letter, however, invited the navarch to do something within his power that promised to produce an astonishing victory that might put an end to the war in a single stroke. As Westlake says, "the prospect of destroying the Athenian forces at Samos and thus probably being instrumental in bringing the war to a speedy end was a dazzling one that can hardly have failed to attract him."[86] Phrynichus, in his desperation, might well have hoped that Astyochus would deal with the second letter differently from the first. Presumably, a victorious Astyochus and a grateful Sparta would honor and reward the man responsible for their success. In any case, Phrynichus would avoid the doom surely awaiting him on the return of his bitter enemy. Alcibiades was not the only Athenian politician with remarkable flexibility and grandiose personal ambitions who was ready to betray his city to secure his safety and advance his career.[87]

It is usual to treat Phrynichus' invitation as though it were truly irresistible and to explain Astyochus' unwillingness to accept it either by the alleged bribery on the part of Tissaphernes or by his "lack of initiative and imagination," his "weakness" and lack of "diplomatic finesse," and his "Spartan caution and distrust."[88] But he would have been very stupid indeed had he put any trust in the offer of Phrynichus, of whose treacherous character he had ample proof. It did not require un-Spartan imagination, initiative, and daring, only the usual Spartan "caution and distrust," to fear exactly what Westlake alleges Phryni-

---

[86]*JHS* LXXVI (1956), 101.

[87]To sustain his belief that the second letter was a ruse intended to produce the result that it did, Westlake (*JHS* LXXVI [1956], 101–102) is compelled to make assumptions not justified by the evidence. The first is that Phrynichus gave Astyochus instructions for the attack, which would bring about a Peloponnesian defeat, Thucydides says nothing of this. A second assumption is that from the first, Phrynichus meant to warn the Athenians of the impending attack and urge them to build defensive fortifications. But this directly contradicts Thucydides' account, which makes it clear that he warned of the attack only *after* learning that Astyochus was working against him and that a second letter from Alcibiades was on the way (8.51.1; see *HCT* V, 119–120). Thucydides clearly thought that Phrynichus would have kept silent and allowed the attack had he not been warned of the second betrayal by Astyochus.

[88]Westlake, *JHS* LXXVI (1956), 102–103.

chus had in mind, that is, a trap. No doubt this was a major reason for not accepting the invitation, and the easiest way to deal with it would have been simply to ignore the second letter. The likely result would have been the arrest and execution of Phrynichus, but the conspiracy to bring back Alcibiades and to use him to win over Tissaphernes would go forward and continue to threaten the Spartan cause. Astyochus, instead, revealed the contents of the second letter to Alcibiades and Tissaphernes.[89] This will have had the effect of making it clear that the plot to restore Alcibiades to Athens was still under way. That information could only have the effect of further undermining Alcibiades' influence with the satrap and making it harder to carry out his promises at Sparta's expense.[90]

A further result was that Phrynichus was able to warn the Athenians of the alleged attack and entirely to undermine Alcibiades' letter. Instead of doing Phrynichus harm, it confirmed his warning and strengthened his position for the time being. On the other hand, it increased distrust of Alcibiades in the Athenian camp.[91] The incident clearly had caused a rift between Tissaphernes and Alcibiades, creating an impossible situation for the latter when the conspirators finally sent an embassy to Magnesia to negotiate with the satrap. The collapse of those conversations put an end to the oligarchic conspirators' interest in restoring Alcibiades and led to the achievement of a new treaty between Sparta and Persia.[92] The Spartans could hardly have asked more of their navarch than to achieve such results in dealing with such experienced and wily maneuverers as Alcibiades, Phrynichus, and Tissaphernes. Perhaps he was not so simple after all. The movement against democracy in Athens no longer involved the prospect of having Alcibiades work against Sparta and bring Persian aid to Athens. Either

[89] 8.50.5. Thucydides says that Astyochus gave the letter to Alcibiades, but there is no reason to believe that he did not reveal it to Tissaphernes as well.

[90] Westlake (*JHS* LXXVI [1956], 103) believes that Astyochus showed the second letter because he trusted Alcibiades more than Phrynichus and because he "was convinced that Alkibiades still favoured the Peloponnesian cause and was not intriguing to win the support of Tissaphernes for Athens." Astyochus, however, not only knew of Alcibiades' double betrayal but had himself been ordered by the Spartan government to put the traitor to death. Had he believed in Alcibiades' continued commitment to the Spartan cause after all that, he would have been simpler than even a Spartan has a right to be.

[91] 8.51.3.

[92] For the rift, see 8.56.2; for the embassy and its outcome, 8.56; for the treaty, 8.57–58.

it would bring civil strife that would present Sparta with a new opportunity for victory, or if the most committed oligarchs were successful, it might bring a peace offer that Sparta could accept. In either case Sparta's situation was excellent.

6. The Coup

While Phrynichus, Astyochus, and Alcibiades were exchanging betrayals in Samos and Magnesia, the Athenian antidemocratic movement went forward. The ambassadors from the movement at Samos, led by Peisander, arrived in Athens late in December and probably stayed there during the period in which the correspondence passed between Samos and Magnesia and for some time afterwards.[1] It is important to remember that the members of the embassy knew nothing of the events that raised new suspicions about Alcibiades and alienated the movement from him. Peisander and his colleagues would make their argument keeping Alcibiades and his promises at the center. This meant that moderates like Thrasybulus were still firmly attached to the group and would use their considerable influence to gain support for the proposed changes. It also meant that the true oligarchs involved would need to temper their language to suit those moderates.

At some time after their arrival, the ambassadors addressed the Athenian assembly.[2] The heart of their presentation was that only with Persian help could Athens be saved and prevail over the Peloponnesians, and this could be achieved only by the return of Alcibiades and an alteration of the constitution. If Thucydides' language is precise, it is worth noting that the terms used to describe the change in mode

---

[1] For a good discussion of the chronology, see *HCT* V, 124, 131, 186–187.

[2] Thucydides' language suggests that the assembly took place soon after Peisander's arrival in Athens, although it is not incompatible with a longer interval. Since he arrived in Athens probably late in December and seems to have left it not much earlier than late February of 411, it seems better to assume a slower pace of activity. See *HCT* V, 131.

of government were even less alarming than before: the Athenians could achieve their ends by "adopting a different form of democratic government."³ Such language was expedient in making the case to what would surely be a resistant Athenian assembly, but pressure by moderates within the movement may also have had some influence.

In any case, both proposals met strong resistance. Many spoke against any alteration in the democracy. Alcibiades' political enemies cried out against his return as an outrage against the laws, and the noble clans responsible for the celebration of the mysteries condemned the proposal on religious grounds. Peisander met the challenge masterfully. He began with an advantage that few, if any, other members of the movement possessed: he was still believed to be "a man of the left," a democratic politican, perhaps even a demagogue.⁴ Such a man had a better chance of gaining a hearing for the unwelcome proposals than a more conservative figure, but his rhetorical and parliamentary skills were even more effective than his reputation. Thucydides' description makes it clear that he rose to speak to a wild and tumultuous assembly that interrupted him with contradictions and complaints. His very effective technique was to call on all of his hecklers in turn and ask them if they had any hope for the salvation of the city in the present conditions in which Sparta had as many ships and more allied cities than Athens and the Persians supplied it with money while Athens had none. Had they any other hope than bringing back Alcibiades and, with him, Persian aid? The answer was that there was no other hope, and Peisander drove home the obvious conclusion: they must recall Alcibiades, who was the only man who could bring them Persian support, and they must change the constitution because Alcibiades required it and because it was necessary to win the Great King's trust. The oligarchs in the movement wanted constitutional change for its own sake. The moderates wanted the return of Alcibiades, and he required an alteration in the regime to guarantee a safe return, so they were prepared to accept it. There is no independent

---

³8.53.1: μὴ τὸν αὐτὸν τρόπον δημοκρατουμένοις. I have used the translation of C. F. Smith. For a translation with the same sense and a useful explanatory note, see *Thucydide, La guerre du Péloponnèse*, ed. and trans. R. Weil and J. de Romilly, VIII (Paris, 1972), 43.
⁴Aristophanes treats him as a demagogue of long standing in the *Lysistrata* (490–491), produced at the Lenaean festival in February 411, certainly some time after his speech in the assembly. For the interpretation of Aristophanes and the date, see *HCT* V, 189. See also A. H. Sommerstein, *JHS* XCVII (1977), 112–126.

evidence that the Persian king cared about questions of oligarchy or democracy; no doubt the assertion that he did came from Alcibiades.[5]

The language Peisander used to talk about the proposed change in the constitution was even more careful and moderate than before. The Athenians could not achieve their goals, he said: "Unless we are governed more sensibly and place the offices, to a greater extent, into the hands of a few."[6] The word translated as "more sensibly" is *sophronesteron*, and in addition to having neutral meanings, it had oligarchical implications as well.[7] It would have been inoffensive to many listeners, but the shrewder and better informed would have recognized the ambiguity. The second clause appeared to explain the first in a way that made the project seem even less threatening. The implication was that the democracy would remain the same in all respects, except that there would be a limitation on officeholding. That would still not be popular in some quarters, but it could easily be seen as a sensible, necessary, and modest step. With an exhausted treasury, Athens could not easily afford to pay its officials, so why not limit offices to those who required no subsidy? It was an idea with natural appeal to the moderates and was probably formulated with their cooperation or with them in mind. Peisander concluded by pointing out that in the current crisis they should take less account of constitutional forms and more of the safety of the city. He shrewdly pointed out, moreover, that if they did not like the new constitution, they could always change it back to the old one.[8]

The last point was a telling argument. Thucydides says that the assembly was not pleased by what Peisander had said "about the oligarchy." He must be referring to those listeners who understood what lay behind the ambiguity of "more sensibly" but surely not to the majority, for the assembly as a whole accepted Peisander's arguments. They were persuaded that there was no other salvation and so acted out of fear as well as out of the expectation of the later restoration of full democracy.[9] They voted to send Peisander and ten others to ne-

---

[5]8.53. For an intelligent attempt to understand just what went on in the assembly, see *HCT* V, 124–125. My own interpretation is somewhat different.
[6]8.53.3: εἰ μὴ πολιτεύσομέν τε σωφρονέστερον καὶ ἐς ὀλίγους μᾶλλον τὰς ἀρχὰς ποιήσομεν.
[7]*HCT* V, 159–160.
[8]8.53.3.
[9]8.54.1.

gotiate with Alcibiades and Tissaphernes "in whatever way seemed best to them."

After this major success, Peisander turned to lesser, but important, business in behalf of the movement. Phrynichus, the clever and dangerous enemy of Alcibiades, remained a general at Samos, where he was in a position to cause further trouble. Peisander brought charges against him for betraying Iasus and Amorges. Thucydides says that these accusations were false, and no doubt they were if taken literally. But the Athenians were long accustomed to bringing charges of treason, bribery, and other malversations against generals they held responsible for important reversals. Thucydides himself had been the victim of such a charge. In attacking Phrynichus for his part in the loss of Iasus and the capture of Amorges, Peisander had shrewdly seized on the best way to be rid of Phrynichus. As we have seen, the decision to refuse battle with the Peloponnesian fleet at Miletus, forced by Phrynichus against the unanimous opinion of his colleagues, proved to be a turning point in Athenian fortunes.[10] Not only was the chance lost to take Miletus and crush the rebellion, but Iasus and Amorges were abandoned, and the southwestern and southern coast of Asia Minor and the important island of Rhodes also went. Thereafter, the enemy regained secure control of Chios and was able to move the war into the Hellespont. It was not unreasonable to place a great deal of the blame for all of this on Phrynichus, as the Athenian people plainly did. They voted to remove him and one of his colleagues, Scironides, from the command and to replace them with Diomedon and Leon.[11] Peisander, to be sure, acted out of secret motives meant to aid the cause of the movement, but the Athenian people knew nothing of this, and they were the ones who freely made the decision to remove Phrynichus. The fact that they replaced the two deposed men with staunch democrats such as Leon and Diomedon shows that they were still free agents.[12] The people, therefore, must have been angry with Phrynichus beforehand, and Peisander took advantage of their feelings to achieve his ends.

[10] 8.27.
[11] 8.54.3. They were apparently punished no further, for Phrynichus was free and in Athens when he emerged as a leader in the oligarchical movement of the Four Hundred several months later. See 8.68.3. We have no information about why Scironides was removed.
[12] They played a critical role in resisting the oligarchic coup and saving the democracy at Samos (8.73.4).

But Peisander had still another mission to accomplish before leaving Athens. He went around to the political clubs that had long existed in Athens for the purpose of mutual assistance in the law courts and in competition for office. In a democracy these secret societies of aristocrats, bound together by oaths, were inclined toward oligarchy, although in normal times they could not act upon their prejudices.[13] But the period during February and March of 411 was not a normal time, so when Peisander went among them, urging them to unite their forces and "plan together to overthrow the democracy," we may believe that he was heard with enthusiasm. Peisander apparently made these visits alone, unaccompanied by colleagues from the movement who might have other, more moderate views. He was thus able to speak bluntly and honestly. His later actions reveal him to have been fully committed to an overthrow of the democracy and its replacement by a narrow oligarchy in which he had a prominent position. We should not lose sight of the fact that from the first, the movement to alter the constitution was fundamentally divided between men with very different goals. Having completed his mission in Athens, Peisander collected his ten ambassadorial colleagues and set off to see Tissaphernes.

The envoys arrived at the court of Tissaphernes, probably again in Magnesia.[14] What they saw must have impressed them with the power and influence of Alcibiades, for he sat in the satrap's presence and served as his spokesman. Thucydides gives the impression that Alcibiades did all the talking and negotiating while Tissaphernes was silent. It would have been easy to believe that the brilliant Athenian was in control and the Persian under his spell, but the reality was very different. "Alcibiades' position in respect to Tissaphernes," Thucydides tells us, "was not very secure."[15] Yet from the moment that Alcibiades went over to Tissaphernes, this is apparently the first time that there is any trouble between them; in fact, the picture that emerges from Thucydides' account until now is one of great influence on the part of Alcibiades and great confidence and respect on the part of Tissaphernes: "Alcibiades became his adviser [the word is *didaskalos*, whose primary meaning is teacher or instructor] in all things"; "he gave his confidence to Alcibiades because of his good advice." Alcibiades urged the satrap to go over to the Athenian side, and Tissaphernes "wanted

[13]8.54.4–5. For a good discussion of these clubs, see *HCT* V, 128–131.
[14]For another suggestion of the place of meeting, see Lewis, *Sparta and Persia*, 103, n. 77.
[15]8.56.2.

to be persuaded if it were in any way possible."[16] Until then things had gone remarkably well for Alcibiades. His advice that Tissaphernes should work to wear down both sides had found favor. Emboldened by his success to think of a triumphal return to Athens, Alcibiades had changed his story and urged the satrap to support the Athenians, and again his counsel was well received. When he communicated with his friends at Samos, he must have believed that he could carry out his promise to bring Persian aid. But now, Thucydides tells us, Tissaphernes had gone back to the idea of wearing out both sides, and Alcibiades' relationship with him had become insecure.

What had caused the change? Thucydides' only explanation is that the satrap had become more afraid of the Peloponnesians,[17] but that explanation is puzzling, to say the least. When Tissaphernes had expressed his willingness to follow Alcibiades' advice and go over to the Athenian side "if it were in any way possible," he had done so even though "he feared the Peloponnesians because they were present with more ships than the Athenians." Since that time, the Peloponnesian naval advantage had not grown, and in fact, their general position had deteriorated. They had suffered a defeat at Athenian hands on Rhodes and were blockaded on that island, their ships drawn up on the beach in humiliating fashion to avoid the risk of an attack by the less numerous Athenian force that kept watch over them.[18] They had suffered a serious defeat on Chios, where their general was killed; the Athenians were in control of land and sea; and the situation of the Chians seemed hopeless.[19] Tissaphernes clearly had less to fear from the Peloponnesians than before, so we need a different explanation for his change of heart. The only one available arises from the tricky correspondence between Phrynichus and Astyochus. It is reasonable to assume that Tissaphernes knew nothing of Alcibiades' plot until Astyochus revealed it to him. The news must have shaken his confidence in his brilliant but treacherous adviser. The outcome of the affair, which reduced Alcibiades' influence among the Athenians at Samos, must also have raised doubts about his usefulness in the future. Tissaphernes must have decided to place less confidence in Alcibiades and to pursue a more neutral policy for the time being. Perhaps he could use Alcibiades to win concessions from the Athenians that would make further

[16]8.45.2; 46.5; 52.
[17]8.56.2.
[18]8.55.1.
[19]8.55.2–3, 56.1.

fighting and expense unnecessary. In any case, he would have made his change of attitude and policy clear to Alcibiades before the meeting, since the Athenian exile would serve as his spokesman.

When the meeting began, therefore, Alcibiades knew that he could not deliver what he had promised, that the satrap's demands were such that no Athenian negotiators could accept them. In a desperate situation, all he could hope to salvage was the illusion that he still had as much influence with Tissaphernes as he had led the Athenians to believe.[20] His purpose was to make it seem that the negotiations' inevitable failure was due to the Athenians' unwillingness to accept terms that he thought reasonable and that his failure to bring over Tissaphernes was not due to his inability but to his decision not to bring him over in light of the Athenians' attitude.

The negotiations were not brief, but extended over three sessions.[21] Thucydides tells us that Tissaphernes demanded that the Athenians give up all of Ionia. Presumably, this means all of the cities on the western coast of Asia Minor, an important part of their empire.[22] He also required that they give up "the adjacent islands and other things." This would include many major places and sources of imperial revenue such as Rhodes, Samos, Chios, and Lesbos. In spite of the great loss this meant for Athens, the envoys agreed to these demands. At the third and final session, however, Alcibiades conveyed a demand from the satrap that the Athenians refused. He required that the Athenians allow "the King to build ships and to sail them along his own coasts wherever and in whatever numbers he wished."[23]

[20] This interpretation departs from Thucydides' in one important respect. He believes that Tissaphernes entered the negotiations not wanting to make any agreement διὰ τὸ δέος, "because of fear" (8.56.3), whereas the suggestion here is that the demands he made were seriously intended and would have led to agreement had the Athenians accepted them. The main reason for the suggestion is the extreme implausibility of the motive mentioned by Thucydides, greater fear of the Peloponnesians than before. We must remember that Thucydides had no independent knowledge of Tissaphernes' thinking and was badly placed to make a good estimate. There is no reason to believe that he had ever met the satrap. The likeliest source for the entire affair is Alcibiades (P. A. Brunt, REG LXV [1952], 80), and as usual, he appears to have magnified his own part in events and to have persuaded Thucydides (ibid., 95).
[21] This would appear to be further evidence that Tissaphernes sincerely hoped to reach an agreement on his terms. If he wanted no agreement with the Athenians out of fear of the Peloponnesians, he need not have held the conference. If he saw some value in having the conference and placing the onus of its failure on the Athenians, he could have presented all of the demands at the first session. The extended discussions suggest an attempt to gain an agreement.
[22] 8.56.4; HCT V, 134.
[23] 8.56.4. This translation accords with the reading of all of the MSS: ἑαυτοῦ, except

At first, it might seem that the Athenian envoys were straining at a gnat after having swallowed a camel, for surely the Athenians could not claim the right to prevent the Persian king from doing as he liked in the waters off his own coasts. The fact is, however, that although the Persians had lost control of their Aegean coast in the years since the invasion of 480/79, they retained control at least of Dascylium on the northern shore of Asia Minor, facing the Hellespont, and of ports on the southern shore as well. They might have moved ships into the Aegean or the Hellespont, but since mid-century they had not done so. The likeliest explanation is that they were prevented from doing so by the Peace of Callias, made with the Athenians probably in 449.[24] Whether or not there had been a formal treaty, and the debate continues, the Persians seem to have accepted the terms attributed to it de facto. For four decades, no Persian fleet had threatened Athens' security, but now the Great King wanted a change. Even a victory over the Peloponnesians would not be worth making an agreement that would allow the Persians to bring fleets into the Aegean and Hellespont, where they could cut off Athenian supplies and attack Athens, and whatever allies remained to it, at any time. The envoys could not agree to such terms because no free Athenian assembly would accept them. The Athenians, angry with Alcibiades, refused and broke off negotiations. They believed that he had deceived them and was unwilling to persuade Tissaphernes to propose acceptable terms. At least, Alcibiades had succeeded in maintaining the illusion of his power over Tissaphernes.[25]

The frustrated and angry ambassadors returned to Samos toward the end of March.[26] The fiasco at the court of Tissaphernes put an end to the negotiations with Alcibiades. At a discussion within the movement, it was decided "to let Alcibiades alone, since he refused to join them, and besides, he was not a suitable man to come into an oligarchy."[27] Alcibiades' behavior at the negotiations had plainly convinced most of the conspirators that he had been leading them on and had no intention of bringing Tissaphernes and the Persians over to their side. That belief probably gave vent to what must have been an

---

C, which reads ἑαυτῶν. For a defense of the reading accepted here and good discussions of the issues, see *HCT* V, 134–135, and Lewis, *Sparta and Persia*, 101, n. 74.

[24] Kagan, *Outbreak*, 107.
[25] 8.56.5.
[26] 8.63.3. For the date, see *HCT* V, 154.
[27] 8.63.4.

old and widely held opinion that so ambitious and egoistic a man could never function as one of a limited number of equals, as an oligarchy requires. By casting Alcibiades aside, they also abandoned hope of gaining Persian support for the Athenian war effort, but they did not lay aside the plan for changing the constitution. On the contrary, they believed that since they were in danger because of what they had already done, they must go forward and find ways to succeed.

What was the source of the danger they feared? Athenians both at Samos and Athens knew of the plan to change the constitution, since it had been announced publicly. It ought not to have been unduly dangerous for the members of the movement to say that they had decided to abandon the plan since its object, the return of Alcibiades and the acquisition of Persian aid, could not be achieved. That, in fact, is what the moderate trierarch Thrasybulus must have done, for he would have no part in the further activities of the movement; his next contact with it would be as a leading opponent.[28] It seems likely that other moderates in the original movement may have dropped out as soon as the negotiations with Alcibiades and Tissaphernes failed. But the remaining members of the movement still believed that Athens' safety and their own well-being required a change. We know that some were devoted oligarchs for whom constitutional change was a goal in itself. Others may have thought that without Persian financial assistance there was even greater need to economize and to eliminate or reduce the public payments that were part of the full democracy. We need not imagine that the remaining members of the movement were all extreme and hardened oligarchs to understand why they were unwilling to give up what was left of their plan. But now they were deprived of their most plausible and acceptable reason for making a change. Hereafter, they could expect greater resistance and hostility. The departure of Thrasybulus and perhaps others like him, moreover, increased the danger. He knew who the conspirators were and what they had in mind. He was a person of importance and ability. Since he had broken with the movement, he might lead an attack upon it. Since they were unwilling to abandon the movement, they were right to see danger. They resolved to keep the movement alive, to provide from their own resources money and whatever else was needed, and to hold out in the war.[29]

[28] 8.73.4.
[29] 8.63.4.

The first step was to make their situation secure at Samos. They worked to gain firmer control of the hoplites in the army, a more natural constituency than the propertyless sailors in the fleet.[30] Then they plotted with "the important men" of Samos to establish an oligarchy on that island.[31] Without the support of a friendly government at Samos and the hoplite corps of the Athenian forces there, the movement had no future.

The next part of the plan required bringing Athens itself under the movement's control. To that end Peisander, along with half of the embassy that had accompanied him to the conference with Tissaphernes, sailed for home. Their mission included still a third part of the plan: the establishment of oligarchies in the cities of the empire. This had been part of the scheme from the beginning, and Phrynichus' arguments notwithstanding, the conspirators still believed it would succeed.[32] Peisander and his five companions were to stop in any allied cities on the way to Athens. The other five envoys scattered to different areas of the empire to try to establish oligarchies in each place.[33] The conspirators clearly believed that this policy was the way to save the empire and carry on the war.

Peisander and his group were successful in setting up oligarchies in the imperial cities through which they passed. They were even able to collect some hoplites along the way to help them with their work in Athens.[34] But the only instance of such a constitutional change described in some detail by Thucydides did not work out well. The general Dieitrephes, who was on his way from Chios to a post in Thrace, also was a member of the movement. When he reached Thasos, he put down the democracy and established oligarchic rule. After two months, however, the oligarchs joined forces with their friends who had been driven out by the democracy and had gone into exile in the Peloponnesus. The newly established oligarchs on the island built fortifications against an Athenian attack and their friends brought a fleet under the Corinthian general Timolaus. The oligarchs of Thasos

---

[30]8.63.3: τά τε ἐν αὐτῷ τῷ στρατεύματι ἔτι βεβαιότερον κατέλαβον. We should take τῷ στρατεύματι in its strict sense as "the army," not more loosely as "the military force." We know that there were quite a few hoplites at Samos: 8.24.1; 25.1. See W. J. McCoy, "Theramenes, Thrasybulus and the Athenian Moderates" (Ph.D. diss., Yale University, 1970), 36, n. 141.

[31]8.63.3.

[32]8.48.5.

[33]8.64.1–2.

[34]8.65.1.

no longer needed "aristocracy" in subordination to the Athenians when they could have "freedom" in partnership with the Spartans.[35] The new government appears to have included a council of three hundred that exiled democratic friends of Athens and confiscated their property.[36]

The outcome was a surprise and a disappointment to the Athenian oligarchs and appears to have confirmed Phrynichus' dark predictions about the general ineffectiveness of their plans to maintain the empire by establishing oligarchies in it. Thucydides makes plain his agreement with Phrynichus. He regards the affair at Thasos as typical of what happened in the other subject cities: "After the cities got hold of moderate government and freedom to act as they liked, they went on to absolute liberty, caring nothing for the specious *eunomia* of the Athenians."[37] Thasos was certainly not a proper test of Phrynichus' general theory that the Greeks preferred the independence of their city, regardless of constitutional form or party interest, for the Thasian oligarchs probably distrusted the sincerity of the Athenian oligarchs or, at least, their ability to win out in the long run over the strongly entrenched Athenian democracy.[38] It seems to be better evidence of another point he made: that the upper classes in the imperial cities, far from regarding the Athenian aristocracy as their natural allies and saviors, thought of them as hand in glove with the masses and likely to be even harsher masters if freed from the checks of democracy.[39]

The defection of the Thasian oligarchy from the Athenian alliance took place probably in the second half of July, but in May, as Peisander and his colleagues made their way toward Athens, abolishing democracies and collecting hoplite supporters as they went, the situation still seemed promising.[40] When he arrived in the city, Peisander found that his plans had gone forward swiftly and successfully. His exhortations to the gilded youths of the aristocratic clubs had found an eager and effective response. Bands of young men had carried out a number of assassinations, the most notorious being that of Androcles, the lead-

[35] 8.64.2–4. For the role of Timolaus, see *Hell. Oxy.* 7(2).4; and *HCT* V, 158. For the possibly ironic sense of the word *aristocracy*, see *HCT* V, 158.
[36] For a discussion and interpretation of the inscriptions on which these statements are based, see H. W. Pleket, *Historia* XII (1963), 70–77, especially 75–76.
[37] 8.64.5.
[38] See Pleket, *Historia* XII (1963), 74–75.
[39] 8.48.6.
[40] 8.65.1. For the dates, see *HCT* V, 157–158.

ing popular politician of the day.[41] Thucydides offers two reasons for his murder: because he was a demagogue and they wanted to please Alcibiades, who was expected to return and bring the friendship of Tissaphernes with him. This reveals that Peisander and his colleagues had not told their associates of the failure of the negotiations at the court of Tissaphernes or of the breach with Alcibiades. We may be certain that the omission was intentional. There were far fewer devoted oligarchs and political opportunists in Athens than there were men willing to work for a limit on the democracy, however severe and however long in duration, in order to gain Persian support in the war. Revealing that the movement had broken with Alcibiades, had given up hope of Persian help, and was aiming at oligarchy for its own sake would certainly alienate the moderates in the movement in Athens, just as it would those on Samos.

Since the conspirators in Athens did not know of the change in the movement's direction, we can readily understand the rest of their activity. They had openly proposed the cessation of pay for all but military duties and the limitation of the number who could take part in public affairs to no more than 5,000 consisting of those able to serve the state with both property and person, that is, those of hoplite status and higher.[42] Thucydides regards this talk as merely a facade to deceive the masses and hide the real aims of the conspirators, which was to gain all of the political power for themselves.[43] But once again, that ignores the significant difference between the true oligarchs and their opportunistic collaborators, on the one hand, and the moderates, on the other hand. We have seen that such a difference existed, and we shall see further evidence of it throughout 411.[44] The public proclamation of these moderate proposals by the young conspirators in Athens, who seem to have been among the most extreme members of the movement, are better understood as something other than camouflage. We should remember that when the conspirators at Athens received

---

[41] 8.65.1–2. On Androcles, see *HCT* V, 161.

[42] 8.65.2–3.

[43] 8.66.1.

[44] Andrewes has seen the problem clearly. His comment on 8.66.1 deserves quotation: "This sentence amounts to a statement that there were no 'moderate oligarchs' who actually believed in the programme set out in 65.3, which is improbable in itself (cf. 67.2n) and inconsistent with what is described at 97.1 and highly praised at 97.2. . . . Thucydides seems to treat the Four Hundred as a monolithic group of extremists" (*HCT* V, 163). He explains this view of Thucydides' as deriving from his sources (252–253).

their instructions in February and early March, before Alcibiades' departure for the meeting with Tissaphernes, the plan of the movement was to bring him back, and it had the support of moderates such as Thrasybulus. The whole program bore the stamp of the moderates, so it is not surprising that their political ideas should have been the ones proclaimed during the absence of Peisander. To the oligarchs, this may have been only window dressing, but the moderates must have been sincere. The movement in Athens had not been informed of the change in the plan and its shift away from the moderates' goals, so its members continued to propose the moderate program, whatever their private views.

Thucydides mentions two motives for the murder of Androcles, but his account suggests a third as well. We should not forget that the assassination was only one of several, that the murderers "killed some others who were inconvenient in the same way, secretly."[45] These killings seem to have been part of a calculated policy of terror that would weaken the opposition and open the way for the overthrow of the democracy. Thucydides presents a vivid picture of how effective that policy was. The popular assembly and council still met but were managed and dominated by members of the movement who were the only ones to speak and who completely controlled the agenda. The lack of opposition came from a sense that the conspiracy had a broad base and from simple physical fear: "If anyone should speak in opposition, he was immediately killed in some convenient way."[46] No search was made for the criminals, nor were trials held of any one suspected. No one spoke up, and so great was the fear that merely escaping harm was thought good fortune. The great size of the city, which led to a degree of anonymity rare in Greek life, further increased fear, for it was easy to believe that strangers were conspirators and that the conspiracy was widespread, and it was hard to get at the truth. Even members of the democratic faction approached one another with suspicion, for the most unexpected people were clearly involved in the movement, including well-known demagogues such as Peisander and Phrynichus, whose involvement in an oligarchy seemed inconceivable. "These men created the greatest distrust among the mass of the people and contributed the most toward the security of the oligarchs by al-

[45] 8.65.2.
[46] 8.66.2.

lowing them to count on the mistrust of the people toward themselves."[47]

This was the situation in Athens when Peisander and his colleagues arrived in Athens and undertook the decisive actions to overthrow the democracy. The climate of fear was essential, for the conspirators did not mean to seize power by means of naked force or by trickery combined with force, as was usual in other coups d'etat. Their plan was to gain control with the greatest show of legality and due constitutional process possible, a wise scheme in a state with a century-old tradition of democracy and due process. They called a meeting of the assembly to take the preliminary steps needed to produce a change in the constitution by legal means. Thucydides tells us that they proposed the selection of ten men to be a commission for drafting proposals *(syngrapheis)* for the best management of the state. They were to have "full powers" for this purpose (presumably, whatever they proposed, the council would be required to put before the people).[48] Also, they were to present their proposals to the assembly on a fixed day.[49] Thucydides' narrative plainly indicates that the Athenian people accepted these proposals out of fear.

Aristotle tells essentially the same story, providing some additional details but differing from Thucydides about one important fact and providing an entirely different picture of the mood and motive of the people. He tells us that the motion to establish the commission was introduced by a speech on the part of Melobius and formally moved by Pythodorus of Anaphlystus.[50] In his version, the commission is to be made up of thirty men, the ten *probouloi* already in place and twenty others, all to be more than forty years of age. These thirty *syngrapheis* were to swear an oath to propose such measures as they thought best for the state and to put into writing their proposals "for its salvation."[51] The proposal also provided that others, apart from the commissioners, should be free to propose whatever they thought best so that the people

[47]8.66.5. My translation here is based on the Budé edition by Weil and de Romilly.
[48]*HCT* V, 165.
[49]8.67.1.
[50]Arist. *Ath. Pol.* 29.1. Both men were probably members of the oligarchic Thirty who ruled Athens in 404/3 (*HCT* V, 212–213; Rhodes, *Commentary*, 370–371). Rhodes points out that a speech by someone other than the proposer of a bill is unparalleled in Athenian practice and suggests that the reason here may be that Pythodorus, the formal mover, was a member of the council and that Melobius, the true author, was not.
[51]29.2.

could choose the best suggestion of all put before them. To this motion Cleitophon tacked on an addition requiring the *syngrapheis* to investigate the traditional laws *(patrious nomous)* established by Cleisthenes when he founded the democracy to help them with their deliberations, on the grounds, according to Aristotle, that "Cleisthenes' constitution was not democratic, but similar to that of Solon."[52] Ever since the discovery of the papyri bearing the work called the *Athenian Constitution*, attributed to Aristotle or to a member of his school, scholars have sought ways to decide between its account of the events of 411 and that of Thucydides or to reconcile them, but the latter appears impossible.[53]

There can be little doubt that Thucydides' picture of a constitutional change brought about by a coup by means of terror, force, and deceit is more believable than Aristotle's account of a leisurely and legal transition. The murders, intimidation, and other irregularities that Thucydides reports were unquestionably real, although omitted by Aristotle, and they account for the people's submission much more persuasively than Aristotle's assertion that "what chiefly persuaded the many was the belief that the King would fight on their side if they made their state an oligarchy."[54] On one point of fact, however, Aristotle is undoubtedly right: the board of *syngrapheis* was made up not of ten but thirty men.[55] Of them, ten were the *probouloi*. This is evidence of shrewd political judgment on the part of the leaders of the movement. The only *probouloi* we know about are Hagnon and Sophocles.[56] They were venerable and respected men, as, no doubt, were the others, who could provide a comforting sense of legitimacy and continuity. The appointment of a special drafting committee was not

---

[52] 29.3.

[53] The papyri bearing the work were published in 1880 and 1891. For a fine discussion of the history of the text and many of the problems arising from it, see the introduction to Rhodes' excellent *Commentary* (1–63). For useful discussions of the scholarly debate on the events of 411, see *HCT* V, 240–256; and Rhodes, *Commentary*, 362–368. In spite of the ingenious attempts of some scholars, the two accounts cannot be perfectly reconciled. Most scholars prefer the general picture and mood provided by Thucydides but are prepared to correct and supplement his version with material from Aristotle when necessary. That seems a sound strategy and is followed here. There continues to be considerable disagreement in judging particular details and events, as the discussion below will reveal.

[54] 29.1.

[55] Two ancient writers of Athenian history, Androtion and Philochorus, confirm the figure of thirty. See *FGrH*, III, 324, Fr. 43, and *HCT* V, 164–165, as well as Rhodes, *Commentary*, 372–373.

[56] See Chapter One.

unusual. It could be argued that just as the establishment of the board of *probouloi* had been an emergency war measure that somewhat limited the democracy without altering it fundamentally, so, too, would the modifications in the new regime be moderate and unthreatening. The *syngrapheis* who would plan it would include those same trusted elders whose loyalty and inoffensiveness had been demonstrated already. Both Hagnon and Sophocles were old Pericleans, "neither likely to prove an enthusiastic oligarch."[57] However, they would be outnumbered and overawed by the other twenty, appointed by and probably including the extremists, perhaps Peisander himself.[58]

Aristotle reports an anecdote that reveals the mood in which the *probouloi* may have undertaken their new responsibility. It describes an exchange in which Peisander asks whether Sophocles had voted to install the Four Hundred, along with the other *probouloi;* Sophocles admitted that he had. "What?" Peisander asked, "Didn't that seem a wicked thing to do?" "Yes," he replied. "So you yourself did this wicked thing?" "Yes," said Sophocles, "for there was nothing else to do that was better."[59] The encounter probably took place after the overthrow of the Four Hundred, perhaps in the months immediately afterward.[60] Sophocles, no doubt, had reason to suggest his lack of enthusiasm for the role he had played after the fall and disgrace of the government he had helped to install. Still, it is easy to believe he spoke the truth. Nothing in his career before or after 411 suggests that he was an oligarch. In spite of the events of 411, he lived out his years as a respected, even revered, figure under the fully restored democracy, which did not fail to punish those whom it blamed for the oligarchic coup. Sophocles, we may presume, like his fellow *probouloi* and the other Athenian moderates, saw no way out of the present danger other than to recall Alcibiades and hope that he could bring Persian aid with him. His words suggest that he knew that some of the men involved had other purposes of which he did not approve, but he thought that he must take the risk of cooperating with them in the absence of any alternative that promised safety for the city.[61]

---

[57] *HCT* V, 165.

[58] Ibid.

[59] *Rhet.* 1419a, 25–30.

[60] For an interesting and plausible discussion of the possible time and circumstances of this incident, see M. H. Jameson, *Historia* XX (1971), 541–568.

[61] Jameson's shrewd analysis deserves quotation: "Sophocles admits to having been fully aware of the nature of the 400 when he voted for them. They were an unpleasant

On the appointed day, the assembly met again but not in the usual place on the Pnyx beside the Acropolis. Instead, the session took place on the hill called "Colonus Hippius," somewhat more than a mile from the city, where there were shrines to Poseidon, the Eumenides, and Prometheus and possibly an enclosure convenient for an assembly of not too great a size.[62] We are not told why the meeting was moved or why this place in particular was chosen. Although the assembly sometimes met away from the Pnyx, it rarely seems to have done so in the fifth century and never at Colonus. Modern scholars have guessed that with the site outside the walls and with the Spartans freely roaming Attica from the fort at Decelea, Athenians without armor, that is, the poor, would have been afraid to come or that a force of armed men, justified by the danger, could have been used to intimidate the Athenians.[63] This might have played some part in the thinking of the conspirators, but just moving from familiar and comfortable surroundings to an unusual and unfamiliar place would have been unsettling to the ordinary Athenian and the politicians not involved in the conspiracy and would make it easier for Peisander and his collaborators to dominate the scene. We are not told what pretext was used for the change of venue, but with the support of the *probouloi*, the leaders of the movement could easily persuade the prytanies to do as they were told.

Whether the board of *syngrapheis* studied the "ancestral laws of Cleisthenes," we do not know, but it turned out that they had little need to do so. They made no proposals "for the best management of the state" or "for its salvation" but limited themselves to a single motion: "to allow any Athenian to make any proposal he liked without penalty." The standing constitutional prohibition against illegal proposals, the *graphe paranomon*, was suspended, with heavy penalties imposed on

---

necessity. The *probouloi* were much concerned with the financial problems of the state after the Sicilian disaster. They would not have been elected in the first place had they shown any strong inclination towards peace with Sparta, and Aristophanes depicts his *proboulos* as an unreconstructed nationalist (*Lysis.* 421ff.). The necessity they saw must have been for Persian money held out by Peisander as available only through Alcibiades and an oligarchic government. They may also have been sympathetic to recall of the victims of the hysteria of 415 B.C., and especially the relatively competent Alcibiades, impossible so long as the current democratic leaders were in control. They were motivated by realism rather than dogma" (ibid., 560).

[62]8.67.2; *HCT* V, 165–166.

[63]For a discussion, and rejection, of the importance of the military element, see Busolt, *GG* III:2, 1478, n 2. See also *HCT* V, 165–167.

anyone trying to make use of it.[64] Thucydides is firm in saying that
the commission proposed nothing else.[65] Perhaps the *syngrapheis* could
not agree, some wanting to propose a narrow oligarchy, others preferring a moderate reform, and still others opposing any change at
all.[66] More probably, the conspirators wanted nothing more than a
removal of the legal barriers to revolutionary proposals and got exactly
what they wanted from the commissioners—zealous, resigned, or intimidated as each might be.

The provision inviting any Athenian to make any proposal he liked
suggests an atmosphere of freedom of speech totally at odds with the
menacing and tightly controlled mood at Colonus. The only speaker
was Peisander, who now openly revealed the program of the conspirators.[67] For the duration of the war, pay for public service not connected with the war was abolished, except for the nine archons and
the prytanies, that is, the nominal and effective heads of state, who
would be paid only 3 obols a day.[68] The core of the program, however,
was the establishment of a council of Four Hundred "to rule in whatever way they thought best, with full powers."[69] The Four Hundred
were to be chosen in a most unusual way. The assembly would select
a board of five called "presidents" (*proedroi*) who in turn would select
a hundred men who then would each choose three more to make up
the council of Four Hundred. In the threatening circumstances, the

[64] 8.67.2; *Ath. Pol.* 29.4.
[65] 8.67.2.
[66] Such is the suggestion of *HCT* V, 167.
[67] 8.67.3; 68.1. It is possible that Peisander was a member of the board of *syngrapheis*
and that his proposal was formally on their behalf, but I prefer to think he acted
independently of that group. Thucydides' account fits that more closely. Aristotle's
account can be understood either way. He begins his description of the program
proposed at Colonus in this way: μετὰ δὲ ταῦτα τὴν πολιτείαν διέταξαν τόνδε τὸν
τρόπον. The subject of διέταξαν may be the *syngrapheis* (as Rhodes [*Commentary*, 381]
believes) or the Athenian people (as *HCT* V, 217, argues). After the fall of the Four
Hundred, everyone involved would have wanted to shift the responsibility for the
introduction of that regime to someone else or at least to share the guilt. Aristotle's
account provides a greater sense of due process and legality; the commission, including
the *probouloi*, produces the program that will do away with the democracy; it is not
the work only of Peisander and his collaborators. This accords perfectly with the
general, and entirely misleading, picture he provides of a legal and gentle transition.
For a shrewd analysis of the reasons for the differences in the accounts, see E. Will,
Le monde grec et l'orient, vol. 1, *Le V*ᵉ *siècle (510–403)* (Paris, 1972), 377–378.
[68] *Ath. Pol.* 29.5; Rhodes, *Commentary*, 382. Thucydides' compressed account of this
measure is that "no one should hold office any longer under the present constitution
nor receive pay" (8.67.3). For the reasons for this compression, see *HCT* V, 168.
[69] 8.67.3: ἄρχειν ὅπῃ ἂν ἄριστα γιγνώσκωσιν αὐτοκράτορας.

assembly would choose the *proedroi* designated by the conspirators. The Five Thousand, publicly mentioned in previous discussions,[70] consisting of the men of the hoplite census and above, were also to be drawn up, and the Four Hundred were empowered to call them together whenever they saw fit.[71] The assembly passed these measures without dissent and dissolved. The democracy that had reigned for almost a century would be replaced by a regime that excluded the lower classes from political life and turned the present management of the state over to a narrow oligarchy.

Thucydides, writing long after the event and fully aware of the outcome, treats this occasion as the plain and simple establishment of the oligarchy of the Four Hundred and dismisses all talk of the Five Thousand as a smokescreen. But to the participants, without the benefit of hindsight, the program must have seemed consistent with the plans of the moderates that had already been the basis of public discussion. The elimination of payment for almost all public services except those related to the war and the establishment of an active citizen body of about five thousand men limited to those of the hoplite census or higher were the elements of their program. The introduction of a smaller body of Four Hundred, temporarily charged with the conduct of affairs until the Five Thousand could be brought into being, was an entirely reasonable addition. None of this should have caused any anxiety for the moderates in the movement. The only question

[70] 8.65.3.

[71] 8.67.3; *Ath. Pol.* 29.5. The divergence between Thucydides and Aristotle is very stark at this point. Thucydides does not mention the appointment of the Five Thousand, since he regards their existence as theoretical and inconsequential at this time. Aristotle does not mention the Four Hundred here. Instead, he describes the plan as turning the state over to "those of the Athenians most capable of serving the state with their persons and their property, to the number of not less than five thousand" (29.5). He pictures the Four Hundred as coming into being only later. In his version, the Five Thousand met and elected a committee of 100 to draw up a permanent constitution for the future and another for the present. This latter, temporary constitution established the rule of the Four Hundred in a perfectly legal way. The proposal was made by the commission of 100 and ratified by the assembly of the Five Thousand. Although they contain some complementary elements, there is no way to reconcile these accounts, and Thucydides' version is clearly superior. In fact, Aristotle contradicts himself, for after describing the activities of the Five Thousand related above, he says that after the establishment of the Four Hundred, the Five Thousand were selected "in name only." It is plain that Aristotle is following two sources, one of them Thucydides, and has not resolved the differences between them. The result is a not fully coherent account that is far inferior to the terse but consistent narrative of Thucydides. The simplest and most attractive explanation for the divergence at this point is that "Aristotle was deceived by a single deceitful document" (*HCT* V, 255).

concerns the project for the return of Alcibiades and the winning of Persian support. Peisander and his friends knew that this was no longer part of the plan. Did the moderates in Athens know it as well? We can not be sure, for we do not know whether word of the failure of the negotiations with Tissaphernes had yet come from Samos. If it had not, Peisander was perfectly capable of concealing the truth from the moderates in the movement, as he concealed it from the public. In that case, the continued collaboration requires no explanation. It is possible, however, that they had learned the truth. If so, their cooperation with Peisander and the oligarchs might be explained as Thucydides explains the decision by the members of the movement at Samos who chose to continue after negotiations had failed, "because they were already in danger" and it was safer to go forward.[72] Still another possible explanation, not incompatible with that offered by Thucydides, is that the moderates, although they would have liked to obtain the return of Alcibiades and Persian help, still preferred an end to the waste of money on payment for nonmilitary services and the limitation of active citizenship to the propertied classes as devices to help Athens survive the crisis and win the war.

Thucydides chooses this moment to describe the men who led the movement to overthrow the democracy: Peisander, Phrynichus, Antiphon, and Theramenes.[73] In a later passage, he pictures most of the members of the Four Hundred who helped to overthrow it as merely self-seeking opportunists acting out of personal ambition.[74] There is no reason to think that he held a different opinion about Phrynichus and Peisander. Phrynichus, as we have seen, had been a democratic politician, who joined the antidemocratic movement in 411.[75] By now he had become the most zealous for oligarchy because "he was afraid that Alcibiades was aware of his treasonous exchange with Astyochus at Samos and believed that no oligarchy would ever restore him."[76] That is as clear an explanation of a selfish motive as Thucydides offers for any of the conspirators, and nothing we know contradicts it.

---

[72] 8.63.4.
[73] 8.68. Aristotle (*Ath. Pol.* 32.3) lists all except Phrynichus as the men most responsible for the establishment of the oligarchy. Since he appears to be following Thucydides here, it seems possible that a copyist inadvertently allowed the last name to be omitted (Rhodes, *Commentary*, 408).
[74] 8.89.3.
[75] See above, Chapter 5.
[76] 8.68.3.

About Peisander's motives Thucydides says nothing, pointing out only that he was the most publicly visible of the conspirators, "in all respects openly the most zealous in the plot to destroy the democracy."[77] His reputation as a demagogue dates from the 420s, and his extravagantly zealous behavior in the witch hunts surrounding the scandals of 415 is consistent with that reputation. He may have become a sincere convert to oligarchy after the Sicilian disaster, or he may have seen the oligarchic movement as a rare opportunity for personal advancement. Certainly, there is nothing in his career before 411 to suggest a commitment to constitutional change, and his actions are consistent with the charge of opportunism.[78]

Antiphon was a different sort of person. Whereas Phrynichus and Peisander had been active and highly visible politicians well before the coup, Antiphon worked behind the scenes. He seems to have been the first professional speech writer in Athens. Thucydides calls him "the one man most able to help someone contesting both in the law courts and in the assembly." Presumably, this talent was used chiefly on behalf of the upper classes, for we are told that he became "an object of suspicion to the masses because of his reputation for dangerous cleverness."[79] Perhaps because of this suspicion he himself did not take part in the tumult of political life in the Athenian democracy or in the arena of the law courts. He had spent much time in planning ways to overthrow the democracy, and he "had devised the whole affair and had established the way in which it had been brought to this point." The picture that emerges is that of the mastermind behind the plot for whom men like Peisander were tools to be manipulated. What we know of him is entirely consistent with the view that he was sincerely devoted to the overthrow of democracy and its replacement by a true, narrow oligarchy; prepared to wait long and work hard for the day of vindication; and ready to act ruthlessly when that day came. Thucydides expresses extraordinary admiration for him as a man "inferior to no one in his own time in *arete* and the very best both in conceiving

---

[77] 8.68.1.

[78] For useful discussions of Peisander, see *HCT* V, 116; Rhodes, *Commentary*, 407–408; and A. G. Woodhead, *AJP* LXXV (1954), 131–146.

[79] 8.68.1. I have translated the word δεινότης as "dangerous cleverness." I think the suspicion he aroused was of the same kind as that which arose against Socrates who was thought to be δεινὸς λέγειν, a dangerously clever speaker (Plato, *Apology* 17b). For the suggestion that the people's suspicion arose from Antiphon's oligarchic views, see G. Gilbert, *Beiträge zur inneren geschichte Athens im zeitalter des peloponnesischen Krieges* (Leipzig, 1877), 309.

an idea and expressing it in speech." *Arete* has many meanings, but to Thucydides' readers, it would have conveyed many aspects of excellence: courage, nobility, and moral worth. Although Antiphon was later convicted and executed for treason, and Thucydides praises the constitution that succeeded the overthrow of Antiphon's oligarchy, the historian praises him in terms reserved for the likes of Themistocles and Pericles. All of this suggests that he was no mere opportunist.[80]

Of the four leaders, Theramenes, whom Thucydides describes as "a man of great ability in speech and judgment," turned out to be the most important and the most controversial. Within a year of the coup, Phrynichus and Antiphon were dead and Peisander in exile, never to return. Theramenes, however, was to play an important and highly visible role in Athenian public affairs until his death in 403. Having helped to establish the oligarchy of the Four Hundred, he also played a major role in overthrowing it in favor of a more moderate regime. When that regime was overthrown, he served as general and trierarch under the restored democracy, negotiated the peace with Sparta at the end of the war, took part in the rule of the Thirty Tyrants that followed the peace, and died a martyr's death protesting its excesses. For these accommodations to different regimes and for his skill in surviving dangers, he earned the reputation in some quarters as a shifty and adroit politician who would always maneuver so as to secure his own position.[81] Critias, the leader of the extreme wing of the Thirty Tyrants, called him *kothornos*, the buskin or theatrical boot that could be worn on either foot, "for as the buskin fits both feet he faces both ways."[82] Lysias savagely assaults him as a self-seeking hypocrite, uninterested in any particular constitution or principle, prepared to sacrifice all of them and the men who had been his friends and collaborators to his own selfish interests.[83]

Aristophanes' jibes are meant to provoke laughter, or at least smiles, and are not sound evidence for Theramenes' overall reputation or for its justice. We must remember, moreover, that the play was performed soon after the affair at Arginusae, where Theramenes and his fellow trierarch Thrasybulus had escaped punishment while their superiors had been condemned to death. Critias made his remark in the midst of a speech leading to the condemnation and execution of Theramenes,

[80]*HCT* V, 170–177; Rhodes, *Commentary*, 408.
[81]Aristoph. *Frogs*, 534–541, 967–970.
[82]Xen. 2.3.31.
[83]Lys. 12.62–78.

and Lysias needed to blacken Theramenes' reputation to make his case
against the defendant Eratosthenes. He needed to do so because Eratosthenes was expected to plead in his own defense that he had acted
as a member of the faction of Theramenes, sure evidence that after
his martyrdom Theramenes' reputation stood high enough in the estimation of the restored democracy to shield his supporters. These
charges are badly tainted by the men who made them and the circumstances in which they were made.

On the other hand, there was an ancient tradition that held Theramenes in the highest esteem. Diodorus, probably following the fourth-
century historian Ephorus, gives him credit for the dissolution of the
oligarchy and the institution of a constitution "from the citizens." He
gives him sole credit for advising the restoration of Alcibiades, and
"because he was the introducer of many things for the good of his
country he received extraordinary approval." He calls him "a man
who, in the orderliness of his life and in prudent judgment (phronesis),
seemed to surpass all others."[84] The most impressive praise comes from
Aristotle. He reports him to have been the leader of the group that,
in the turmoil after the defeat of 404, "did not belong to any political
club and in other respects seemed second to none in their zeal for the
ancestral constitution (patrios politeia)."[85] Beyond that, he includes
Theramenes, along with Nicias and Thucydides, the son of Melesias,
among the three best politicians in recent Athenian history. The other
two, he says, were not controversial, but because Theramenes lived
in a period of political turmoil, there is a difference of opinion about
him. "Nevertheless, for those who do not judge superficially it seems
clear that he did not destroy all constitutions, as those who slander
him say, but carried them all forward so long as they did not break
the fundamental law; he was able to participate in all kinds of constitutions, which is the job of a good citizen, but refused his consent to
illegal regimes and was hated for it."[86] The objectivity of these eulogies
is also suspect. Men who took part in the oligarchies of 411 or 404 had
powerful reasons to put the best face on the career of Theramenes and

[84] 13.38.2.
[85] Ath. Pol. 34.3.
[86] Ath. Pol. 28.5. Rhodes (Commentary, 360) believes that this evaluation is not Aristotle's but was found "in one of his more sober sources." I am inclined to agree with
P. E. Harding (Phoenix XXVIII [1974], 110–111) that the judgment is Aristotle's own,
but his argument that there was no defense of Theramenes as a moderate before Aristotle
is not persuasive.

to associate themselves with the man whose reputation they embel-
lished. Aristotle, the political theorist who championed the virtues of
the middle class and the moderate constitution, had every reason to
praise Theramenes, whom he saw as its standard-bearer.[87] The document commonly called the "Theramenes Papyrus" suggests that debate surrounded Theramenes even during his lifetime.[88] As a result of
this ancient controversy, it is small wonder that modern scholars have
ranged in their judgments from the uncompromising condemnation of
Grote to the warm and sympathetic appreciation of Beloch.[89]

Since the ancient evaluations are either partisan or ambiguous, our
own judgment must be based on the facts of his career, as best we can
determine and understand them. One collection of facts, usually ignored or given insufficient weight, is the close connection between
Theramenes and Thrasybulus. We must emphasize that the two men
were agreed in their willingness to limit the democracy in order to
bring back Alcibiades and gain Persian support for the conduct of the
war. Thrasybulus on Samos resisted the Four Hundred while Theramenes in Athens cooperated in their rule, but Theramenes took the
lead in overthrowing the oligarchy and establishing the moderate rule
of the Five Thousand that recalled Alcibiades to Athens, these later
actions constituting a policy entirely in accord with the wishes of
Thrasybulus. The two men served as generals together in the Hellespont and, together with Alcibiades, collaborated effectively to win the
battle of Cyzicus.[90] That victory permitted the restoration of the full
democracy under which the two men continued to serve, working with
Alcibiades to clear the enemy from the Hellespont.[91] Both returned

---

[87]Harding, *Phoenix* XXVIII (1974), 111; Arist. *Pol.* 1295a–1296b.

[88]See R. Merkelbach and H. C. Youtie, *ZPE* II (1968), 161–169; A. Henrichs, *ZPE*
III (1969), 101–108; A. Andrewes, *ZPE* VI (1970), 35–38; and R. Sealey, *ZPE* XI
(1975), 279–288.

[89]Modern evaluations of Theramenes seem to have been influenced by contemporary
political concerns no less than the ancient ones. Grote, the unwavering champion of
democracy, had nothing but contempt for the man who was willing to attenuate it:
"He was a selfish, cunning and faithless man—ready to enter into conspiracies, yet
never foreseeing their consequences and breaking faith to the ruin of colleagues whom
he had first encouraged, when he found them more consistent and thoroughgoing in
crime than himself" (VIII, 55). Beloch's prejudice is even more obvious: "We who are
involved in the same struggle today against a covetous proletariate and against an equally
covetous aristocracy (*Junkertum*) will not deny our sympathy to the ancient champion
(*Vorkämpfer*) of our cause" (GG II:2, 392). Here we have the voice of a nineteenth-
century German liberal.

[90]Xen. 1.1.12–22.

[91]Diod. 13.66.

to Athens with Alcibiades in 407.[92] In 406 the two men served together as trierarchs at the battle of Arginusae, both were assigned by the generals to help the men on the disabled vessels, and both stood side by side during the trial.[93] After the war the two men took different paths in response to the defeat. Thrasybulus, exiled by the Thirty, organized an army of liberation against the government of the Thirty installed by the Spartans. Theramenes stayed in Athens, became a member of the Thirty, and worked consistently and bravely, ultimately at the cost of his life, to turn it into a moderate regime. In his speech defending himself against the assault of Critias, he named Thrasybulus among the "capable leaders" the Thirty had foolishly banished.[94] It is noteworthy that after his death the Thirty thought it reasonable to invite Thrasybulus to take his place among their number.[95]

However, the two did not hold identical views. It may be that Thrasybulus was willing to limit democracy only temporarily and for purely practical reasons. Theramenes seems to have preferred a limited democracy to the full one favored by most Athenians. Thrasybulus seems to have mistrusted the oligarchs entirely after his experience with the conspiracy of 411. Theramenes, to the end, expected to be able to guide the oligarchic movement toward a moderate constitution not too far from democracy. But from 411 to the end of the war, they worked together closely and effectively, pursuing the same policies and holding the same offices under different regimes. Nobody, in antiquity or in modern times, thought to charge Thrasybulus with inconstancy or self-seeking. He built an army in exile and restored a democracy considerably more moderate than the one destroyed by the Spartan victory.[96] On the other hand, rather than endure the true, narrow, oligarchy imposed by Critias, Theramenes protested, at the cost of his life, against the exile of worthy men and the narrowing of the franchise beyond moderation. The difference between Theramenes and Thrasybulus appears to have been one of emphasis, personal style, and temperament more than of basic political ideas and personal integrity.

To be sure, in each regime Theramenes sought office and influence

---

[92]Diod. 13.18.2–64.3; Nepos *Alc.* 5.4–6.

[93]Xen. 1.6.35–7.35.

[94]Xen. 2.3.42.

[95]Diod. 14.32.5.

[96]A. H. M. Jones, *Athenian Democracy* (Oxford, 1969), 23–58, 79–96; McCoy, "Theramenes," 194.

consistent with his high ambitions and talents. To that extent he acted in pursuit of his personal ambitions, as Thucydides says. But a man who risked his life to resist an illegal and brutal rule in which he could have not only survived but prospered does not deserve a reputation as a mere slippery self-seeker. He deserves instead to be believed when he defends himself against the charge that he is an opportunist who changes sides when it benefits him:

I, Critias, am always at war with those who think that there will never be a democracy until the slaves and those who would sell out the state for lack of a drachma shared in the government and, at the same time, I am also opposed to those who think that no good oligarchy can exist until the state is ruled tyrannically by the few. But to manage the state along with those who are able to serve it with their horses and shields, that is the constitution I have thought best in the past, and I do not change my opinion now.[97]

It took men of the caliber of this extraordinary quartet to overthrow a democracy so firmly established and "to deprive of their freedom a people who not only had not been subjects but for half of the century of their freedom had been accustomed to rule over others."[98] Under such shrewd and determined leadership, the conspirators moved swiftly to take control of the city. The first step was to get rid of the democratic institutions that were still in place and functioning. The constitutional change had been imposed on a terrified, confused, and leaderless assembly. Each day that passed posed the threat that the democrats would recover and undo the decision at Colonus. Peisander appears not to have named a date for the transition of power from the old democracy to the new regime, and many Athenians must have expected a delay until the conciliar year came to an end in about a

---

[97]Xen. 2.3.47. It is interesting to compare Theramenes with George Savile, Marquis of Halifax, the seventeenth-century politician who earned a reputation as "the Trimmer of Trimmers." He wrote an essay in his own defense called "The Character of a Trimmer" in which he defended the many shifts he had taken during his career: "This innocent word *Trimmer* signifieth no more than this, That if Men are together in a boat, and one part of the company would weigh it down on one side, another would make it lean as much to the contrary; it happeneth there is a third Opinion of those, who conceive it would do as well, if the Boat went even, without endangering the passengers." Quoted in J. Hamburger, *Macaulay and the Whig Tradition* (Chicago, 1976), 90. The emphasis on safety is a common bond. Theramenes, however, appears to have been more firmly committed to a particular form of government—the limited democracy governed by the hoplites and cavalry—than was the more pragmatic Halifax.
[98]8.68.4.

month.[99] The conspirators could not wait that long. On the fourteenth day of the Attic month Thargelion, June 9, 411, a few days after the meeting on Colonus, they seized the reality of power.[100] Waiting for the Athenians to go to their military posts at the walls and the training fields, the conspirators stayed back, not far from where their weapons were stacked. They had orders to prevent anyone not in the plot from taking up arms and interfering with the proceedings. They were assisted by armed men from Tenos, Andros, Carystus, and Aegina, perhaps as many as 400 or 500, who had been gathered for the coup. With these men preventing resistance, the Four Hundred, armed with daggers under their cloaks and supported by the 120 young bravos who had terrorized Athens, burst into the council-house. They had brought along money with which to pay the members of the democratic council for the remainder of their term and then ordered them out.

The coup was a complete success. The councillors took their money and left without trouble. The other citizens made no move to interfere. The Four Hundred appointed the prytanies and presiding officers by lot, as in the old council, and performed the customary prayers and sacrifices upon taking office. Every effort was made to preserve a sense of continuity, normality, and legality, but few could have been deceived. For the first time since the expulsion of the tyrants, the state had been captured by a faction by means of threats and force.

[99]HCT V, 179–180; Rhodes, *Commentary*, 405–406.
[100]The date is provided by *Ath. Pol.* 32.1, its modern equivalent by B. D. Meritt, *Proceedings of the American Philolosophical Society* CXV (1971), 114, with Rhodes, *Commentary*, 405–407. Aristotle gives this as the date the old council was dissolved and has the Four Hundred take power peacefully and legally, with the approval of the people under the aegis of the Five Thousand, eight days later. Even those who try to save Aristotle's account or parts of it do not believe in such a delay (e.g., Rhodes, *Commentary*, 406). Some scholars believe that 14 Thargelion was the date of the assembly at Colonus and that the seizure of power took place on the same day. I accept Andrewes' arguments for rejecting that view and believing that the seizure of power took place a few days after the meeting at Colonus (A. Andrewes, *PCPS* XXII [1976], 14–25).

7. The Four Hundred in Power

The coup was a complete success. The councillors took their money and left without trouble. The other citizens remained quiet and made no move to interfere. The Four Hundred appointed their presiding officers by lot, as in the old democratic council. They seem to have allowed the archon and the treasurers elected by the democracy to remain in office.[1] Every effort was made to preserve a sense of continuity, normality, and legality. No doubt this was meant to calm the people, to make the transition smoother, and to reduce the chance of violent resistance, but also it must have reflected the influence of the moderates, who were still part of the movement in Athens.

Even after the coup, the support of the moderates remained vital, so the conspirators found it desirable to temper their brutal seizure of power and their establishment of a relatively narrow governing council by making promises of a more moderate future. At the meeting on Colonus hill, a board of registrars *(katalogeis)* had been appointed to draw up the list of the Five Thousand and had begun its work, although the list was never completed or published.[2] The same assembly appointed a committee of *anagrapheis* to draft a permanent constitution for the future.[3] Both measures reflect the influence of the moderates,

---

[1] *HCT* V, 194–195.

[2] That the registrars were appointed and set to work follows from 8.67.3 and Lys. 20.13. See *HCT* V, 203–204, and Rhodes, *Commentary*, 386.

[3] Aristotle (*Ath. Pol.* 30.1) says that the Five Thousand selected a hundred men from their own number "to draft a consitution," and modern scholars refer to them as the *anagrapheis*. In 30–31 he describes the proposals they produced, and in 32.1 he claims they were approved by the Five Thousand. Since the Five Thousand never came into

who expected the rule of the Four Hundred to be temporary and to give way to a new constitution of the Five Thousand when the immediate crisis was over.

In the days after the seizure of power by the Four Hundred, the committee for drafting a constitution must have begun its deliberations. No doubt the moderates put forward a plan giving power to the Five Thousand and establishing a broad oligarchy to take effect immediately or at least quite soon. The extremists, however, had something different in mind. They intended to keep the Four Hundred in control for the time being and to maintain a narrow oligarchy for the future. They would certainly insist on the continued rule of the Four Hundred, but they could not yet afford a rift with the moderates. They also faced the problem of persuading the fleet at Samos to accept their new regime, a task that would be much easier if the new constitution could be portrayed as more moderate and less oligarchic.[4]

The result of the discussions was a compromise: the committee proposed two new constitutions, one for immediate use and the other for the future. The immediate constitution officially established the government of the council of Four Hundred, lending its foundation an air of legitimacy by styling it "in accordance with the ancestral tradition" and granting its members the power "to act in whatever way they thought expedient."[5] The Athenians, moreover, were to obey whatever laws they might enact in the matter of the constitution, not to change any, and not to introduce any new ones.[6] These provisions gave the Four Hundred all of the powers they needed and rendered their supposedly transitional regime permanent. To this extent they represented the wishes of the extremists.

In return, the Four Hundred agreed to the promulgation, at the same time, of a draft constitution for the still unspecified future. Its details need not detain us long, for it was never put into effect and

---

existence, this cannot be true. No explanation is without problems, but the one offered by Rhodes (*Commentary*, 387) is persuasive: "The Colonus assembly will have decided in principle that the constitution should be based on a powerful boule of Four Hundred and a residual assembly of 'Five Thousand,' and as it appointed the *katalogeis* to register the Five Thousand it appointed the *anagrapheis* to work out the details of the new constitution."

[4]8.72.

[5]κατὰ τὰ πάτρια (*Ath. Pol.* 31.1). The reference is to Solon's council of 400 (*Ath. Pol.* 8.4). For a defense of that council's historicity, see Rhodes, *Commentary*, 153–154.

[6]*Ath. Pol.* 31.1–2. For the meaning of this passage and, especially, for τοὺς Ἀθηναίους as the subject of χρῆσθαι, see Rhodes, *Commentary*, 401.

was incomplete, omitting any reference to the judiciary, for instance. It appears to have been influenced by the federal constitution of Boeotia and smacks of theoretical discussion with the Sophists. The state was to be managed by a council of unspecified number drawn from members of the Five Thousand over the age of thirty who would serve without pay. Unexcused absences from meetings of the council would be punished by a fine. The council itself was to be divided into four sections, each section serving, in rotation, on behalf of the full council for one year. Since the generals and other major officials must be chosen from the council in office at the time, they could serve only one year in four, just one of many inconveniences in this draft constitution that reveal it to be the work of impractical theorists.[7] The extremists cared little about such details, since they had no intention of giving way to a new regime. They were willing to assent to any scheme for the future as long as they kept a firm grip on power in the present. Shrewder moderates no doubt recognized the weaknesses of the draft constitution but were glad to get any promise of a change to a broader regime in the future. Details could be worked out when the situation permitted.

It was probably on the twenty-second of Thargelion (June 17, 411), eight days after seizing power, that the Four Hundred formally inaugurated their rule with the customary prayers and sacrifices. At the same time, no doubt, the *anagrapheis* published their two new constitutions, one for the present and one for the future, claiming the two had been voted by the Five Thousand.[8] But the vote of approval was entirely a fiction, for the body of the Five Thousand had not been designated and, therefore, could not assemble. The Four Hundred probably presented the constitutions in the form of a decree of the Five Thousand, complete with the name of the president of the meeting and the date of enactment, to lend verisimilitude to the fraud.[9] Although this would not have fooled the moderates or those outside the Four Hundred who were well connected and alert to events, most Athenians were frightened, confused, and ignorant. Both before and well after this public event, most Athenians believed that the Five

---

[7]*Ath. Pol.* 30 describes the constitution for the future. For valuable discussions of its provisions and of previous scholarship, see *HCT* V; and Rhodes, *Commentary*, ad loc.

[8]Such is the very plausible reconstruction of events by Rhodes (*Commentary*, 406). He follows the general approach of Meyer (*Forsch*, II, 425–435) and Hignett (*HAC*, 359–360, 373).

[9]Andrewes, *PCPS* XXII (1976), 22.

Thousand might already exist. In any case, a main target of this propaganda was the Athenian force at Samos, and the soldiers and sailors there could be persuaded even more easily.[10] By their formal and ceremonial assumption of power, their publication of the constitutions, and the implicit evidence they seemed to give that the Five Thousand both existed and functioned, the Four Hundred hoped to gain internal harmony and the external legitimacy to allow them to cope with the serious problems they faced.

Several difficulties preclude a satisfactory understanding of the regime of the Four Hundred during the brief period of fewer than four months during which it ruled.[11] The first is the very brevity of the regime; in so short a period there was little time for plans and intentions to reveal themselves. Our major sources, moreover, were not in Athens at the time and were dependent on highly biased reports at a time when partisan feeling ran unusually high. Some of the important actors were executed on the collapse of the regime, and others fled into exile. Membership in the Four Hundred was not something of which anyone in Athens would later boast, so any information available from survivors within the ruling group would probably have been selective and tendentious. The evidence we receive from contemporary orations suffers from the same disabilities. A great deal of what the Four Hundred planned and set in motion lies buried in the silence of those participants who did not survive the regime and the silence and distortions of those who did. Still another difficulty arises from the division within the ruling group that appears to have existed from the start, although its public manifestations did not occur until later. Thus it is often hard to tell whether an action of the Four Hundred represents the views of one or another faction or a compromise between the two.

Still, it is both important and possible to examine the work of the Four Hundred, although we are often forced to resort to conjecture in attempting to understand it. The regime was born in crisis, and its leaders at once confronted problems they could not avoid. Their most immediate and pressing need was to establish themselves securely in Athens. They must also find a way to win over the Athenian forces

---

[10] Ibid., with n. 20.

[11] *Ath. Pol.* 33.1 says that they ruled for "about four months" (Μῆνας μὲν οὖν ἴσως τέτταρας) and that their archon the next year (411/10) held office only for two months. Since they took power on the fourteenth or twenty-second day of the penultimate month of the previous year (412/11), their regime will have lasted at least two to three weeks less than four months.

at Samos and so unite the Athenian people under their rule. They further must decide on a policy toward the empire. They must determine what their policy should be toward their enemies, the Peloponnesians and the Persians. Should they continue the war or seek peace? If they chose war, what should be the strategy? If not, what terms of peace should they accept? However they decided these questions during the immediate crisis, what should be the character and goals of Athens in the long run? Toward the end of June of 411 the Four Hundred set out to answer the questions.

The first actions of the Four Hundred, as we have seen, were cautious, aiming at the impression of moderation, legality, and continuity. The council's presidents were chosen by lot, as in the democracy. Callias, the democratically chosen archon for the year 412/11, and the treasurers as well appear to have continued in office until the end of their terms.[12] There was no hurry about replacing these officials, but the new government needed to be sure of the loyalty of the armed forces in Athens, so they acted swiftly to appoint a new board of generals, a cavalry commander, and ten tribal commanders. They may have made those appointments in the week between their seizure of power and the formal inauguration. They did not even follow the procedure prescribed in the constitution for the immediate, provisional regime, which required a preliminary muster of all hoplites after the formal establishment of the council. It seems highly unlikely that they ever chose a second set of officers following the new process.[13] This was a departure from legality and normality, but in matters involving military force and, therefore, the immediate security of the regime, the conspirators could not afford such niceties.

We know the names of six of the new generals and possibly a seventh.[14] Alexicles, Aristarchus, Aristoteles, and Melanthius were from

[12]*HCT* V, 194–195.
[13]*Ath. Pol.* 31.2 gives the description of these appointments and of the procedure provided. For a discussion of some of the problems in this account, see *HCT* V, 230–231. Rhodes' view (*Commentary*, 401) that the leaders of the Four Hundred acted swiftly and without regard to legalities in choosing new officers seems to explain the evidence best.
[14]Busolt (*GG* III:2, 1490, n. 3) provides the evidence for the sixth. To their number Fornara (*Generals*, 66) adds Dieitrephes, citing 8.64.1–2. There we are told that Dieitrephes, who was general-elect for 411/10, anticipated events by joining the oligarchs, assuming his command in the Thraceward region and seizing Thasos on behalf of the oligarchy. This would have occurred some months before the appointments in June. The Four Hundred may well have chosen him as one of their generals at that time, as Fornara assumes, but the assumption is not necessary. After all, Dieitrephes had

the extreme wing, and Theramenes and probably Thymochares were moderates. This proportion on the board of generals seems to be an accurate representation of the distribution of power within the ruling group. The extremists held the upper hand, but they must make some concessions to the others. The treatment of potential dissidents and enemies within Athens may have reflected the same division and compromise. The new regime put some men to death and exiled or imprisoned others, but the numbers were not large.[15] Whether everyone wanted to move cautiously or the moderates restrained the others we cannot know.

Some of the Four Hundred, presumably the extremists, wanted to institute a general recall of men exiled under the democratic regime. We do not know how many were in exile or precisely who they were, but they will have included generals elected by the democracy such as Pythodorus, Sophocles, and the historian Thucydides.[16] These men, presumably, would have lost whatever admiration they may have had for untrammeled democracy as a result of their treatment at its hands, if Thucydides is at all typical.[17] Most of the exiles were probably those men who had fled or were expelled in connection with the sacrileges of 415. Some of them were undoubtedly inveterate enemies of democracy, and those who were not may well have been embittered by their experience. After the war, the exiles were clearly oligarchs friendly to Sparta, and the Spartans made their recall a condition for peace.[18] There is good reason to believe that many of the exiles of 411 were enemies of democracy to some extent. Thucydides' language makes that clear, for he says that the failure to recall the exiles was an exception to the "great departures from the rule of the *demos*" in which the Four Hundred otherwise engaged.[19] Their reason for holding back, he tells us, was Alcibiades. A general recall and amnesty would have allowed him to return, something the extremists would not welcome at all. However, they could have recalled the exiles and specifically

been elected under the democracy and, in spite of his deeds, might not have seemed as reliable as the conspirators would have liked.

[15] Thucydides (8.70.2) says that the victims were not many. The specific reference is to those put to death, but there is no reason to think that the exiles and imprisonments were widespread.

[16] 4.65.3; 5.26.5.

[17] For Thucydides' political opinions, see M. F. McGregor, *Phoenix* X (1956), 93–102.

[18] *Ath. Pol.* 34.3; Xen. 2.2.20; Plut. *Lys.* 14.4; And. 3.11.

[19] 8.70.1.

excluded the traitorous renegade on any number of grounds,[20] but "this would have advertised the loss of their hope of Persian aid to be negotiated through Alcibiades, the bait originally held out to the people."[21] It would also have widened the rift between the extremists, hostile to Alcibiades, and the moderates, closely associated with him. The decision not to recall any exiles appears to have been another compromise.

From the beginning, some members of the movement had expected the establishment of a new regime in Athens to help in the management of the empire. They had expected that news of the government of the "better" people *(kaloi k'agathoi)* in Athens and the offer of a similar change of government in the allied states would bring rebellious allies back into the fold and prevent future uprisings.[22] About the middle of May, the conspirators sent the general Dieitrephes to put down the democracy in Thasos.[23] At the same time, on their way from Samos to complete the coup at Athens, Peisander and his colleagues did the same thing in several other cities, perhaps Paros, Naxos, Andros, Tenos, and Carystus.[24] The experiment badly disappointed the hopes of the Athenian oligarchs. In Thasos the newly installed, pro-Athenian oligarchy lasted no more than two months. A band of exiles who earlier had been driven from Thasos by the Athenians were working with the Peloponnesians to bring their native state into rebellion, and they found support inside it. As part of a well-coordinated plan, the aristocrats in the city built walls to defend against an Athenian attack at the same time that their friends in the Peloponnesian camp were able to bring in a small fleet under the Corinthian commander Timolaus, which effected the rebellion. Far from making Thasos a more reliable ally, the establishment of oligarchy there had only made its defection easier by abolishing the democracy that would have opposed it.[25] We have specific information only about Thasos, but the experience there seems to have been typical. Thucydides expresses the firm opinion that "in Thasos events contradicted the expectations of those Athenians

[20]Andrewes (*HCT* V, 182) suggests that he might have been singled out for exclusion because of the curse he incurred through the alleged profanation of the mysteries, but that would have involved many others as well.
[21]Andrewes, *HCT* V, 182.
[22]These hopes can be deduced from their caustic refutation by Phrynichus in 8.48.5.
[23]8.64.2. For Dieitrephes, see *HCT* V, 156–157; for the date, 157–158.
[24]8.64.3; *HCT* V, 161.
[25]8.64.5. *Hell. Oxy.* 7.4 provides the evidence for Timolaus. See also *HCT* V, 158–159.

who were establishing an oligarchy, and I think it was the same in many other subject states." We have no reason to doubt that he was right.[26]

The revolt at Thasos occurred in mid-July by which time it was only one of several indications of the failed hopes and expectations of the Four Hundred in Athens. Well before that event, their plans for bringing the war to a satisfactory conclusion had run into trouble. From the beginning of the movement, the conspirators had asserted their determination to carry the war through to victory; in fact, that goal had been the main attraction of the movement for many partici-pants.[27] The conspirators later reaffirmed the same purpose vehe-mently, even after they learned that Alcibiades could not keep his promise to deliver Persian aid.[28] We know of nothing that should have changed their purpose; yet no sooner were the Four Hundred in power than they sent an embassy to Agis to negotiate a peace.[29] Thucydides gives no explanation for the reversal in policy, but it is impossible that all members of the movement had been insincere from the first, es-pecially in light of their resolution "to hold on in the war and eagerly contribute money and whatever else was necessary from their own private resources."[30] Some of them, however, whom we have called the extremists, seem to have used the promises of Alcibiades to bring victory as a cloak for their true purpose, the establishment of a narrow oligarchy in Athens under their own control.

A shrewd observer of the scene in Athens would have realized that the establishment of oligarchy and the continuation of the war were incompatible. The fight against Sparta and her Persian ally required a dominant role for the fleet, that is, for the lower classes and their leaders. As long as the salvation of the city lay in the hands of the masses, there could never be an oligarchy. Only peace gave any hope

---

[26] 8.64.5. The rest of his statement—"for once the cities had acquired a sensible regime and immunity for their actions they proceeded to complete freedom, having no pref-erence for the specious 'good government' (*eunomia*) of the Athenians"—has provoked disagreement. It seems clearly to be an endorsement of the opinion of Phrynichus that the people of the empire were less influenced by class and factional interests than by a common desire for freedom and autonomy. For a useful discussion of the events at Thasos and how they bear on the debate, see H. W. Pleket, *Historia* XII (1963), 70–77.

[27] 8.48.2.
[28] 8.63.4.
[29] 8.70.2.
[30] 8.63.4.

166 THE FALL OF THE ATHENIAN EMPIRE

of taming popular power, for with the fleet at home and its crews disbanded, the oligarchs might hope to rule by terror and ultimately by the acquiescence of the hoplites. The extremists, therefore, must have planned to seek peace from the beginning but concealed their intentions until the right time. Once the city was cowed by terror, the Four Hundred were in power, and the extremists held the upper hand within it, they could pursue negotiations.

Even then, however, they could not ignore the moderates, who might be intimidated or persuaded into joining in peace negotiations but would insist on honorable terms that would allow Athens to retain its power and empire. The extremists, on the other hand, although they preferred to keep the empire, were prepared, in the last resort, to make peace "on any terms tolerable," even those requiring them to bring in the enemy and to give up Athens' walls and fleet and, with them, its autonomy.[31] Theramenes and his moderate supporters, on the contrary, always found such terms intolerable. It was precisely to prevent such a betrayal that Theramenes led the effort that overthrew the Four Hundred.[32] He had joined the movement against the democracy in order to wage the war more effectively; he worked for the overthrow of the oligarchy when he suspected it of preparing to sell out to the Spartans; under the restored democracy, he played a leading part in the fighting until, in 405, the battle at Aegospotami put an end to all hope. In 411 he and his moderate associates were unwilling to make major concessions to the Spartans.

That is not to say that Theramenes and his associates were unwilling to discuss terms of peace with Sparta. They may have hoped that the Spartans' failure to win the expected easy victories in the Aegean and Ionia, combined with the inadequate and unreliable support provided by Tissaphernes, might have made them ready to agree to a reasonable peace, especially with an Athenian regime that was no longer a radical democracy. If the enemy was prepared to make peace on the basis of the status quo, well and good. If not, the war would continue. The extremists, although they were ultimately ready to make far greater concessions, preferred the status quo. On these terms, both factions within the Four Hundred could agree, so the Athenian ambassadors offered the terms to King Agis at Decelea.[33] He rejected their proposal

[31] 8.90.2; 91.3. See also *HCT* V, 307–308.
[32] 8.90–91.
[33] 8.70.2. Thucydides does not mention the terms. Aristotle (*Ath. Pol.* 32.3) cites them as ἑκάτεροι τυγχάνουσιν ἔχοντες. Busolt (*GG* III:2, 1490, n. 1) suggests that the

out of hand: there would be no peace "unless they surrendered their maritime empire."[34]

Perhaps there were some in Sparta who might have been willing to negotiate further, but Agis gave them no opportunity. He still retained the extraordinary influence he had gained at Mantinea and had increased with his command at Decelea.[35] He wanted no negotiated peace but victory and the glory that went with it. Because he did not believe that the long-established Athenian democracy would tolerate the newly installed oligarchy for long, he did not think that the internal struggle in the city was over. For him, the embassy was evidence of Athenian weakness, which he meant to exploit with swift action. He believed that if he brought a force of sufficient size to the walls of Athens at this moment, when it was torn by civil strife, he could take the city. He expected either that they, distracted by their internal quarrels, would surrender on his terms or that he could easily storm some part of the city walls, which were undefended because of the civil war. He therefore called a large army from the Peloponnesus and took his own force from Decelea to meet it before the city.[36]

But Agis had miscalculated. For the moment, the Athenians in the city were at one in their determination to resist. The guardians of the walls stood firmly at their posts. A variety of forces representing all classes in Athenian society—cavalrymen, hoplites, light-armed warriors, and archers—launched an attack when the enemy came too near the walls. Agis was forced to retreat. He sent back the army he had summoned from the Peloponnesus and withdrew his own force to the fort at Decelea.[37] Agis' action did not turn the Four Hundred from their search for peace, but they continued to send embassies to him. The embarrassment of defeat had chastened Agis, who had painful memories of what might happen to a Spartan king who conducted a private policy that failed.[38] Not only did he greet the Athenian ambassadors more politely but he also urged them to send embassies to Sparta. The vigorous Athenian reaction showed that a quick and easy

---

peace terms and the response of King Agis (see n. 29, above) reported by Aristotle are merely inferred from Thucydides' account. There is no reason, however, to doubt the independence and authenticity of the evidence in *Ath. Pol.* 32.2.

[34] *Ath. Pol.* 32.3.
[35] 8.5.
[36] 8.71.1.
[37] 8.71.2–3.
[38] 5.63.4; Kagan, *Peace of Nicias*, 91–106.

victory at Athens was not at hand and that serious negotiations might
be desirable, but any hope that the Four Hundred could easily make
peace depended on the unlikely possibility that the government at
Sparta would be willing to accept the terms so swiftly rejected by
Agis.

Not long after the skirmish with Agis' army, the Four Hundred
turned to the problem of relations with the Athenian forces on Samos.[39]
The plot to overthrow the Athenian democracy had originated there
and included a design to establish an oligarchy on Samos as well, but
things had not gone according to plan. Even before the coup in Athens,
perhaps in March of 411, Peisander had persuaded some of the leading
men on Samos to try to set up an oligarchy on the island.[40] These men
had taken part in the democratic revolution of the previous year, but
now Peisander was able to convince them to change sides. They formed
themselves into a conspiracy of Three Hundred, took a common oath,
and planned an attack on their former collaborators in the democratic
faction that ruled Samos. It would be interesting to know why they
were willing to turn against the new Samian democracy so soon after
they had taken part in its establishment, but neither Thucydides nor
any other ancient writer tells us. Perhaps they merely sought to increase their own power and advantage within the Samian ruling group,
or perhaps they judged that the future of Athens lay with the oligarchs
and wanted to gain favor and advantage by joining them.[41] In any
case, they proceeded in the same way as the oligarchic conspirators at
Athens: by means of terror. Acting in concert with the general Charminus and other Athenian oligarchs on Samos, they murdered Hyperbolus, who had lived on the island since his ostracism in 416. The
infamous Athenian demagogue must have had some prominent place
in the democratic movement on Samos, because Thucydides says that
the Samian Three Hundred regarded their role in the assassination as
"giving a pledge of good faith" to the Athenian oligarchs.[42]

This was only one of several similar acts, but instead of paralyzing
their opponents with fear, these acts of terror alerted them to the danger
and moved them to defend themselves. The Samian democrats went
for help to those Athenians whom they trusted above all others to be

[39]8.72.1–2. For the timing of their action, see 86.3; and *HCT* V, 184, 285.
[40]8.63.3; 73.2–3. For the date, see *HCT* V, 154.
[41]For a discussion of the motives of the Samian Three Hundred, see R. P. Legon,
Historia XXI (1972), 156.
[42]8.73.3.

friends of democracy and enemies of oligarchic conspiracy: to the generals Leon and Diomedon, "for these men bore the oligarchy unwillingly because they were honored by the people"; to the trierarch Thrasybulus; and to Thrasyllus, although he was only a hoplite in the ranks. The Samians sought out these men because they were among those "who always seemed to be most opposed to the conspirators."[43]

Thucydides' language here reveals important information about the state of affairs at Samos that points in a different direction from his general account. Instead of a monolithic conspiracy of oligarchs working to overthrow the democracies in Athens and Samos, we see a more nuanced picture. Staunch democrats such as Leon and Diomedon had accepted the idea of bringing back Alcibiades and altering the democratic constitution at Athens, however unhappily they viewed this plan. Were they among those whom Thucydides has characterized as part of "the mob," who, "even if they were somewhat annoyed for the moment by what was being done, kept quiet by the pleasant prospect of pay from the King?" Or were they among those "conspiring to install oligarchy" who went off privately to consider their detailed plan of action after making their general intentions known to the Athenian forces on Samos?[44] It is hard to imagine that any two Athenian generals, almost always chosen from men of the upper classes, could deserve the former designation but no less difficult to believe that staunch democrats such as Leon and Diomedon proved themselves to be could have been thought of as instigators of oligarchy. Evidently, they fit in neither group and require some other designation. Because of their rank they could not have been excluded from the private deliberations once it was publicly announced what was afoot. Thus that inner circle must have included true oligarchs like Peisander but also thoroughgoing democrats like Leon and Diomedon, who reluctantly tolerated the course of events. To an outsider, they may have seemed part of the leading group and therefore friendly to oligarchy, at least to some degree. That would explain the otherwise incomprehensible decision later taken by the Athenian democrats on Samos to dismiss them along with the other generals and those trierarchs thought to be unreliable.[45]

Even more striking is the democrats' confidence in the trierarch

---

[43] 8.73.4.

[44] 8.48.3.

[45] 8.76.2. See *HCT* V, 268, which includes the perceptive observation that "no exception is made for Leon and Diomedon, who disliked the oligarchy (73.4) but may have been thought to have acquiesced in it too easily."

Thrasybulus, one of the original authors of the plan.[46] His inclusion in the very small number of those foremost in their opposition to the conspirators is hard to understand, unless the Samian democrats saw important differences among the men who had started the movement. We must assume, although Thucydides does not say so, that Thrasybulus publicly renounced his membership after the inner circle turned away from Alcibiades and that he quickly became known as an enemy to those who plotted to establish an oligarchy without offering Alcibiades, Persian support, and victory over the Peloponnesians in return. To the people on Samos, natives and Athenians, the members of the movement to alter the democracy in Athens and Samos were not all the same. Some were true oligarchs; others were friends of democracy who grudgingly went along with events; at least one had publicly denounced the movement and had become its notorious enemy.

The Samian democrats pleaded with the Athenians they trusted to help save them and preserve for Athens the island crucial for the survival of its empire, and their faith was justified. The chosen Athenians went individually to spread the word to reliable Athenian soldiers and especially to the crew of Athens' messenger ship *Paralus*, whose crew was well known for its adherence to the democracy and its hatred for oligarchy.[47] For their part, Leon and Diomedon were always careful to leave some ships to guard Samos when they sailed off on any mission, apparently being sure to leave the *Paralus* among them. Their care and vigilance was soon rewarded. When the oligarchic Samian Three Hundred launched their coup, the Athenian sailors, and especially the crew of the *Paralus*, were on the scene to stiffen resistance. The victorious Samian democrats showed considerable restraint, executing thirty of the ringleaders, sending three others into exile, and declaring an amnesty for the others.[48]

The democratic countercoup on Samos must have taken place toward the middle of June, about the same time or shortly after the oligarchic coup in Athens, for when the *Paralus* left for Athens to announce their victory, the Samian and Athenian democrats did not yet know that the Four Hundred were in power there.[49] When the *Paralus* arrived, its crew was arrested. Two or three of them were imprisoned; the rest were placed on a troopship and sent to keep watch on Euboea. Cha-

[46] 8.47.2.
[47] 8.73.5.
[48] 8.73.6.
[49] 8.74.1.

ereas, a zealous democrat who had taken an active part in the resistance to the oligarchs on Samos, managed to escape and return to the island.[50] There, he gave a lurid and exaggerated account of the oligarchic rule in Athens: he said that people were being punished with the whip, that no criticism of the government was permitted, that outrages were being committed against women and children, that the oligarchs intended to imprison relatives of the men on Samos who were not friendly to their cause, and that they threatened to kill these relatives if the men on Samos did not yield to them; according to Thucydides, "he told many other lies, as well."[51]

Chareas' speech infuriated the soldiers. Their first thought was to do violence to those they held responsible, whom Thucydides describes as "the principal authors of the oligarchy," and "those of the others who took part in it." But they were restrained by "the men of moderate views."[52] Who belonged to these groups? Peisander, who certainly took a leading part in establishing oligarchy among the Athenians on Samos, was in Athens, and Phrynichus probably was too, but Charminus and others unnamed were still on the island.[53] The second group must have included even proven friends of democracy such as Leon and Diomedon, for in the passion of the moment, they were deposed from their generalships, presumably because they had been among "those others who took part," however reluctantly, in the movement that brought in oligarchy. The third group certainly included Thrasybulus and Thrasyllus, for they played the leading roles in the events that were now taking place. Also, they must have taken the lead in preventing violence and in bringing about what amounted to an amnesty for those who had taken part in the oligarchic movement in its

[50]8.74.2–3; *HCT* V, 266.

[51]8.74.3.

[52]Thucydides (8.75.1) describes the three designated groups as follows: (1) τοὺς τὴν ὀλιγαρχίαν μάλιστα ποιήσαντας, (2) τῶν ἄλλων τοὺς μετασχόντας, (3) τῶν διὰ μέσου. There is no problem about the translation of the first two, but the third is more difficult. C. F. Smith calls this third group "those who took a neutral position," and other editors have adopted a similar interpretation, but Andrewes is right to cast doubt on it. As he points out, there is no parallel for this form in Thucydides, and "one may doubt if many Athenians were genuinely indifferent between democracy and oligarchy" (*HCT* V, 267). Busolt called them "die Gemässigte" (*GG* III:2, 1493); Rex Warner, "the more moderate party"; Weil and Romilly, "les modérés." I have adopted Crawley's version, but all of the versions that use the concept of moderation are preferable to those implying neutrality.

[53]*HCT* V, 267. We may deduce Charminus' role as a leader of the oligarchs from his complicity in the attempt to overthrow the Samian democracy (8.73.3).

Samian phase, since they included those who had taken part in the oligarchy in the new oath to which they swore the Athenian and Samian armed forces: "to be governed by democracy and to live in harmony, to pursue the war against the Peloponnesians vigorously, to be enemies to the Four Hundred and not to enter into negotiations with them."[54] Hereafter, Athenians and Samians would stand together against the Four Hundred in Athens as well as the Peloponnesian enemy. But Thucydides also tells us that these men were the leaders of the movement that had restored democracy to the Athenian forces on Samos and to the Samians themselves, a goal they now proclaimed openly.[55] We must not forget, however, that Thrasybulus was one of the trierarchs who had played a part in the movement that brought about the oligarchy. Clearly, his actions in the interim must have led the Samian and Athenian democrats on the island to forgive and forget his participation. Our analysis of Thucydides' account, however, reveals that Thrasybulus had been a member of the movement to alter the democracy, later became a most trusted and respected democratic leader, and was at the same time a moderate. For the rest of his career he remained an unwavering democrat, opposed to involvement with any kind of oligarchy. Had it been otherwise, he too like his fellow demesman Theramenes, might have been called by his enemies an opportunist seeking only to advance his personal ambitions. His performance in 411, however, reveals that he was a patriot, comfortable with democracy but prepared to curtail it somewhat, at least temporarily, to enhance Athens' chances of victory in the war. When the oligarchic movement promised to recall Alcibiades and gain the expected aid from Persia, Thrasybulus joined it, along with others who shared his views. When the more extreme elements took control and excluded Alcibiades from the plan, Thrasybulus quickly and effectively disassociated himself from the movement. Thereafter, he opposed the oligarchs, whom he no longer trusted, and put his hopes for victory in a plan to persuade the democratic forces on Samos to bring back Alcibiades. He prevented violence against his former colleagues in the movement and supported an amnesty similar to the one observed in 403 with which he is so gloriously associated.[56] In short, he revealed himself to be a moderate.

[54]8.75.2.
[55]8.75.2.
[56]*Ath. Pol.* 40.2–3.

The soldiers demonstrated their regard for Thrasybulus and Thrasyllus by electing them generals, along with others whose names we
do not know, to replace those deposed in the same assembly.[57] The
convening of an assembly that took to itself the right to remove officers
chosen at Athens was in itself a kind of declaration of sovereignty in
which the Athenian forces on Samos claimed legitimacy for themselves
instead of the oligarchic government at home. The speeches with which
their new leaders encouraged the assembly made that clear.[58] They,
not the oligarchs in Athens, were the majority; they had the greater
resources, and they alone could retain control of the empire and the
tribute that flowed from it; the city had revolted from them, not they
from the city. With a strong base at Samos they could hold off the
enemy and force the oligarchs to restore democracy to Athens. Even
if these hopes were too optimistic, they could always find a safe place
to settle elsewhere, as long as they retained their great fleet. These
and similar assertions encouraged the men, but at least one speaker,
almost surely Thrasybulus, made an argument that implied a specific
action: If they recalled Alcibiades and granted him immunity, he would
bring them an alliance with the Persians. The assembly, however, did
not respond to that suggestion. Thrasybulus' influence was too new
and the hostility to Alcibiades too great to permit such an action as
yet.[59]

Even as the Athenians on Samos were putting an end to divisions
among them, discord arose within the Spartan forces, not many miles
away in Miletus. Angry soldiers, especially the Syracusans, complained loudly about their situation. During the previous winter, the
fleet had lain idle for months at a time. In the spring, at last, they had
fought and achieved some success at Chios, but they had failed to press
their advantage and allowed the Athenians to remain safely in port on

---

[57] For suggestions as to who the other new generals may have been, see *HCT* V, 268.

[58] Thucydides (8.76.3) tells us that the soldiers at the assembly rose to make speeches
offering advice and encouragement, reporting their gist in direct statement. At most
Athenian assemblies the speakers tended to be the generals and other elected officials
as well as leading politicians. Probably the same was true on this occasion. Andrewes
(*HCT* V, 268) is reminded of a commander's speech to his troops. Grote (VIII, 48)
assumes the speakers were Thrasyllus and Thrasybulus, and he is probably right. The
reference to the return of Alcibiades in 8.76.7, moreover, strongly points to Thrasybulus, who "always held to the same opinion . . . that they should recall Alcibiades"
(8.81.1).

[59] 8.76.7.

Samos.[60] The soldiers were outraged at the missed opportunity to force a battle while the Athenians were torn by internal discord and their fleet divided between Samos and the Hellespont. They blamed the navarch Astyochus for his unwillingness to fight and for his credulity in believing that Tissaphernes was really planning to bring on the promised Phoenician fleet. They were bitter, too, against the Persian satrap himself for failing to pay their wages fully and regularly, and they accused him of deliberately trying to wear down their strength by delay.[61]

The complaints grew so serious that Astyochus was compelled finally to call together a council, where the decision was made to force a major battle. When they received word of the democratic counterattack on the Samian oligarchs, they launched their fleet in the hope of catching the Samians and Athenians in the midst of a civil war.[62] About the middle of June, therefore, they put to sea with their whole fleet of 112 ships, having sent the Milesians over land to meet them at Mycale, just off the eastern tip of Samos (see Map 3). The Athenians had been forewarned of the enemy's intentions and had sent word to Strombichides in the Hellespont to return his fleet to Samos, for they were badly outnumbered with only 82 ships. They had taken up a position at Glauce on the Mycale promontory, and when they saw the Peloponnesian fleet sailing over from Miletus, they withdrew to Samos to wait for Strombichides. A numerical advantage of over 36 percent was more than the Athenians cared to challenge, especially when reinforcements were on the way. The Peloponnesians made camp at Mycale, where they added the Milesians and local troops to their hoplite force and prepared to sail against Samos the next day. But before they could do so they received the news that Strombichides had arrived at Samos with ships that brought the Athenian total to 108. Faced with so small a numerical advantage, Astyochus lost his taste for battle and retreated to his base at Miletus. It was now the Athenians who sought a decisive encounter, but when they sailed to challenge the enemy at his home base, Astyochus refused to come out to meet them. The situation was restored to what it had been the previous winter: the Athenian fleet, although slightly inferior in numbers, commanded the sea.[63]

[60] 8.61–63.2.
[61] 8.78.
[62] 8.79.1. For the timing, see *HCT* V, 272.
[63] 8.79.

Later naval encounters would show that Astyochus' caution was wise, and for some time the Peloponnesian fleet stayed at Miletus, unwilling to risk a battle, but Astyochus could not fail to take some action.[64] His men, already restless and angry, became even more rebellious after the most recent failure to engage the enemy. Since Tissaphernes was not meeting his financial obligations, moreover, the Spartan navarch would not long be able to maintain his ships and crews. At the same time, Pharnabazus, the satrap of northern Anatolia, kept inviting him to bring his forces into the Hellespont and promised to provide support for them. The attractiveness of his appeal was strengthened by messages from Byzantium asking the Peloponnesians to come and support their proposed defection from Athens. For some time, moreover, Astyochus had been under orders from Sparta to send a force to assist Pharnabazus, and its designated commander Clearchus was on the spot, waiting to go.[65] For months Astyochus had failed to carry out those orders and continued to cooperate with Tissaphernes, but as the days of summer passed, he could delay no longer. Soon he would need to return to Sparta, where he was sure to face complaints against his inaction and lack of accomplishment.[66]

Late in July, Clearchus set sail with forty ships. His goal was the Hellespont, but it was not safe to take the direct route that would bring him past the Athenian fleet at Samos, so he set out toward the west and the more open sea. This course avoided the Athenians, but it took him into one of those sudden Aegean storms so deadly to triremes. He was forced to take shelter with most of his fleet at Delos, from which he crept back to Miletus when the seas were calm. But

[64] 8.80.1. For a defense of the imperfect ἀντανήγοντο against the aorist proposed by Classen and Steup, see HCT V, 274. For an endorsement of Astyochus' caution, see Busolt, GG III:2, 1495.

[65] 8.80.1–3. For Clearchus and the orders, see 8.8.2 and 39.2. Busolt very plausibly places the date of the Byzantine revolt in early August (GG III:2, 1496), so the fleet probably sailed late in the previous month.

[66] Mindarus arrived to relieve Astyochus not much after this moment, although Thucydides is vague about when. Busolt's estimate, some time in August, makes good sense. Andrewes (HCT IV, 38; and V, 280–281), following Beloch, believes the navarchs took office "near the autumn equinox," that is, late September. He recognizes, however, that Astyochus seems to have been relieved somewhat earlier and suggests the explanation may be irregularities in the Spartan calendar. R. Sealey (Klio LVIII [1976], 335–358) believes that the navarchy was not yet a regular, annual office. Even if he is right, Astyochus had no reason to be comfortable. He obviously had satisfied the board sent to investigate him earlier (8.39.2), but he could not expect to last much longer without some success.

ten ships, under the bolder or luckier Megarian general Helixus, made their way to the Hellespont and brought about the revolt of Byzantium. Soon Chalcedon, on the other side of the Bosporus, Cyzicus, and Selymbria, joined the uprising.[67] This was an important achievement, for it seriously threatened the Athenian grain supply and would require some response that might change the situation in Sparta's favor.

The new Spartan initiative appears to have had an important effect on the Athenians on Samos. Ever since the restoration of democracy in mid-June, Thrasybulus had continued to argue for the restoration of Alcibiades without success, but now his case seemed irresistible. The main check on the Peloponnesians until now, it must have seemed, had been the unreliable and inadequate support provided by Tissaphernes. Now they had gained the support of Pharnabazus, who might prove a more reliable paymaster and whose province, in any case, included Athens' vital supply line. It was imperative to act quickly to challenge the Spartan position in the Hellespont. The Spartans' co-operation with Pharnabazus, moreover, seemed to endorse Alcibiades' claims that Tissaphernes was not firmly committed to them and might be persuaded to change sides. In those circumstances, Thrasybulus was able to gain the support of a majority of the soldiers for a decree recalling him and granting him immunity from prosecution. Thrasybulus himself sailed off to bring Alcibiades to Samos, "thinking that the only salvation lay in bringing Tissaphernes over from the Peloponnesian side to their own."[68]

The first meetings between Alcibiades and the Athenians must have been uncomfortable on both sides. For many who received him, he was still an accursed defiler of the city's religion, a renegade, a traitor, and the instigator of oligarchic revolution against the democracy. For Alcibiades, the return was not precisely the one he had planned. He did not come back to an Athens purged of the democracy that had exiled him or, in fact, to Athens itself but only to Samos. His immunity protected him against his condemnation and the outlawry that went with it, but from Samos he could do nothing about the curses pronounced on him in Athens.[69] Still, some of his worst enemies—Androcles, Phrynichus, and Hyperbolus—were gone, and he had always known how to operate in the world of democratic politics. He must

[67]8.80.3; Busolt, *GG* III:2, 1496, n. 4.
[68]8.81.1.
[69]Plut. *Alc.* 22.5, 33.3; *HCT* V, 275.

have sensed the hostility that some of the democrats still felt, but most were ready to forget the past if Alcibiades could help them win the war.[70]

In still another way, Alcibiades' position was weaker than what he had planned. Instead of returning to Athens as the focal point of a broad coalition in which he was the indispensable central figure, he had been brought back to a Samos divorced from the city, as the protégé of one faction, the moderates, and especially of a single powerful leader, Thrasybulus. Rejected by the oligarchs in Athens and suspected by the democrats on Samos, Alcibiades knew that his prospects, indeed his safety, depended on maintaining good relations with Thrasybulus and his colleagues. But however great his admiration for Alcibiades' abilities and no matter how old and close their friendship may have been, Thrasybulus was nobody's puppet.[71] His long and brilliant career over a quarter-century would show him to be an independent figure of great military and political talents and clear ideas of his own, with a strong will and powerful determination. When he brought Alcibiades to Samos, we may be sure that he did so to pursue a policy and to achieve goals of which he approved. We may be certain also that he used the trip back to Samos to discuss that policy and those goals with Alcibiades. Alcibiades could hardly fail to follow his lead in those early days in the Athenian camp.

In his speech to the Athenian assembly on Samos, Alcibiades could not avoid saying something about his embarrassing past. Apparently, he chose to be brief on this subject, complaining emotionally about his misfortune at being exiled, presumably unjustly, but making no attempt at a formal defense and naming no villains.[72] This was not the time to speak at length of the past and his private grievances or to make enemies; it was a time to fix the minds of his listeners on the future and the wonders he could perform for them. For his ultimate success, he needed not only to win over the Athenian forces on Samos but also to change the situation in Athens to allow his return there and thus unify Athens' forces. Finally, he must defeat the Peloponne-

[70]Hatzfeld, *Alcibiade*, 246.

[71]C. Pöhlig (*Jahrbücher für Klassische Philologie*, Suppl. IX [1877–1878], 233–234 and n. 6) makes a plausible case for the old and close association of the three contemporaries, Alcibiades and the two fellow demesmen, Theramenes and Thrasybulus. Note 6 traces the evidence for their long and close association in public affairs.

[72]Thucydides (8.81.2) tells us only that "he wailed loudly about the personal misfortune he had suffered because of his exile."

sians. He therefore directed his remarks not only to the men who could hear him but also to two other audiences: the oligarchic leaders in Athens and the Peloponnesians. His purpose, according to Thucydides, was threefold: to gain the respect of the army on Samos and restore their self-confidence, to increase the Peloponnesians' suspicion of Tissaphernes and thereby make them lose hope of victory, and to bring fear of Alcibiades into the hearts of those controlling the oligarchy in Athens, thereby breaking the hold of the extremist oligarchic clubs.[73] He devoted the major part of his speech, therefore, to his influence with Tissaphernes, which he greatly exaggerated, and the satrap's eagerness to help the Athenians if only he could trust them. He would bring the Phoenician fleet, already gathered and waiting at Aspendus, to them, not to the Peloponnesians. They would never be at a loss for financial support while Tissaphernes had any money of his own; "in the last resort he would even sell his own bed,"[74] but he would do so only if Alcibiades was returned safely to the Athenians and could serve as a guarantee of their good behavior.[75]

Alcibiades' rhetorical power had not faded in his extended absence from Athenian assemblies. His words had their intended effect and more. The soldiers immediately elected him general "and gave over to him control of all their affairs."[76] Not only had he succeeded in filling his listeners with new confidence, but they were already contemptuous of the Peloponnesian enemy and ready to sail to the Piraeus and seek revenge against the Four Hundred. That was not Alcibiades' intention, and he argued against sailing to Athens and leaving the undefeated enemy behind. Many still wanted to sail, but Alcibiades seems to have carried the day with the argument that the first business at hand was for him to go to Tissaphernes and work out the details of their association. Alcibiades was eager to get to the satrap as soon as possible. His standing with the Athenians depended on their belief

---

[73]8.81.2. The last clause is my interpretation of ἵνα οἵ τε οἴκοι τὴν ὀλιγαρχίαν ἔχοντες φοϐοῖντο αὐτὸν καὶ ᾗαλλον αἱ ξυνωμοσίαι διαλυθεῖεν, which Thucydides mentions first. For a useful comment, see HCT V, 276.

[74]8.81.3. The young prince Cyrus would later make a similar promise to Lysander: if the Great King's funds and his own money ran out, he would break up his gold and silver throne on his behalf (Xen 1.5.3). As Andrewes says (HCT V, 276), "either Persian satraps were addicted to expressions of this type, or it had become a standard Greek rendering of Oriental phraseology."

[75]8.81.3; HCT V, 277.

[76]8.82.1. He was given no formal extraordinary powers but merely exercised leadership de facto. See HCT V, 277.

in his relationship with Tissaphernes, and only he knew how shaky was his influence over the satrap. When last at Tissaphernes' side, Alcibiades had been a man without a country whose safety depended on the goodwill of the Persian, a mere tool of the satrap's. Now he wanted to show Tissaphernes that he was once again an Athenian general in control of a powerful fleet and "able to do him good or ill." Alcibiades, according to Thucydides, "was using the Athenians to frighten Tissaphernes and Tissaphernes to frighten the Athenians."[77] Although we know that events proved him overconfident, we need not doubt that Alcibiades expected that the new circumstances would allow him to bring Tissaphernes over to the Athenians.

We do not know if Alcibiades knew of conditions in the Peloponnesian camp at Miletus, but the situation there certainly made his hopes seem plausible. The soldiers grumbled ever more loudly against the iniquities of Tissaphernes, and now their officers joined in the dissatisfaction. The satrap had used their failure to go out and fight the Athenians at sea as an excuse for being even more remiss in paying their salaries, and the officers feared that unless they fought a decisive battle or went somewhere else to get support, the crews would desert. They focused their resentment, naturally enough, on the navarch Astyochus. He had always been reluctant to fight the Athenians, and they thought he was not tough enough with Tissaphernes; now they suspected him of having been bribed by the satrap to act in that way. Finally, the contingents from Thurii and Syracuse confronted Astyochus and demanded their pay. He answered with the tactlessness that usually marked the behavior of Spartans to foreigners and even raised his swagger-stick to threaten Dorieus, the great athlete and commander of the Thurian force. In a rage, his crews were about to stone the navarch, who escaped only by fleeing to an altar.[78]

The Milesians were quick to take advantage of the discomfiture of Astyochus and of the soldiers' anger at Tissaphernes. They captured the fort the satrap had built in their city and drove his garrison from it to the approval of the allies and the Syracusans in particular.[79] In

---

[77] 8.82.2.

[78] 8.84.1–3. I have translated βακτηρίαν as "swagger-stick" to convey in modern terms what I take to be its significance in Sparta. See *HCT* V, 279.

[79] 8.84.4. It is noteworthy that Lichas, the ξύμβουλος who protested so bitterly against the second draft-treaty between Sparta and the Persians, chided the Milesians and told them that they and the other Greeks of Asia Minor should submit quietly to the Great King's rule until the war had been won. The Milesians were so irked that they later

the midst of the tumult, the new navarch, Mindarus, came to relieve Astyochus. It was only August, but we cannot be sure he was replaced because of the complaints against them, although in this case that is surely possible.[80] Astyochus sailed for home, and we get some idea of the tenseness and complication of the political situation at Miletus from the passenger lists of various ships sailing from there to Sparta at that time. The Milesians were on their way to complain against the behavior of Tissaphernes, thinking, no doubt, that a good offense was the best defense against the charges he would certainly bring against them for their attack on his garrison. With them went Hermocrates, the Syracusan, the hero of Sicily, and for some time the harshest critic of Tissaphernes. His purpose was to complain against the satrap and his collaborator Alcibiades, who were deliberately ruining the Peloponnesians with their duplicitous policy.[81] Along with Astyochus sailed Gaulites, a Carian who could speak both Greek and Persian and Tissaphernes' envoy. The satrap, too, intended to take the offensive by complaining of the Milesian attack on his fort, but his spokesman was also instructed to defend his master against the charges his enemies would bring against him.[82]

All of this turmoil must have delighted Alcibiades, who was at the side of Tissaphernes during at least part of it.[83] Soon after his return to Samos, the ambassadors from the Four Hundred at Athens also arrived from Delos, where they had stopped on hearing of the democratic revolution on the island.[84] Their attempt to speak before the assembly was shouted down by the angry soldiers, who wanted to kill the men who had destroyed the democracy. Finally, the ambassadors

refused Lichas burial in their territory (84.5). We are not told the reason for Lichas' action. Perhaps it was merely practical, meant to avoid any greater breach with Tissaphernes, in which case we need not deduce anything from this passage about his or Sparta's attitude toward the legalities of the third treaty, which Lichas had helped negotiate, nor about his or Sparta's ultimate intentions. For discussion of these points, see Ste. Croix, *Origins*, 154–155, 313–314; Lewis, *Sparta and Persia*, 104–105; *HCT* V, 279–280.

[80] See above, n. 66.

[81] Hermocrates had a special motive for going to Sparta with his complaints at this time. He had lately been relieved of his command by the restored democracy at Syracuse. (For a defense of this date for his dismissal against Xenophon's statement that it happened in 410 [1.1.27–31], see *HCT* V, 281–285.) Tissaphernes took advantage of his exposed situation as an exile without a command to attack him (8.85.3).

[82] 8.85.

[83] Thucydides (8.85.4) tells us that Alcibiades had already left Tissaphernes and returned to Samos when Astyochus and the others set sail for Sparta.

[84] 8.72.1; 77.

were allowed to speak, and they delivered their message according to instructions.[85] They insisted that the revolution had been made not to destroy the city but to save it. There was no intention of betraying it to the enemy, for the Four Hundred could easily have done so when Agis made his attack on the walls.[86] They asserted that the new regime would not be a narrow oligarchy of the Four Hundred but that the Five Thousand would govern.[87] They also denounced Chaereas' charges as lies, assuring their audience that their relatives were safe.

[85] Instructions: 8.72.

[86] *HCT* V, 285.

[87] My understanding of this assertion derives from a combination of 8.72.1 and 8.86.3. In the former passage, the oligarchic leaders at Athens instruct their ambassadors to tell the army at Samos "that not only Four Hundred but Five Thousand were taking part in the government, although, because of military service and activities outside Attica, no matter had ever yet arisen so important to bring the Five Thousand together for deliberation." πεντακισχίλιοί τε ὅτι εἶεν καὶ οὐ τετρακόσιοι μόνον οἱ πράσσοντες καίτοι οὐ πώποτε Ἀθηναίους διὰ τὰς στρατείας καὶ τὴν ὑπερόριον ἀσχολίαν ἐς οὐδὲν πρᾶγμα οὕτω μέγα ἐλθεῖν βουλεύσοντας ἐν ᾧ πεντακισχιλίους ξυνελθεῖν. In the latter the ambassadors tell the assembly on Samos "that all of the Five Thousand will take part in the government in turn." τῶν τε πεντακισχιλίων ὅτι πάντες ἐν τῷ μέρει μεθέξουσιν. Both passages have caused editors and commentators considerable trouble.

As far as I can determine, all have taken the first statement to claim that no assembly of 5,000 or more had gathered in Athens either since the start of the war or in its later phase and have found that hard to believe, since several acts of the assembly required a quorum of 6,000. But a likelier reading of the passage is that it refers only to the period since the establishment of the oligarchy. After all, that is the period at issue. What the Four Hundred want to say to the men on Samos is something like this: "The government at Athens is not by Four Hundred but by Five Thousand. You have not heard of any meetings of the Five Thousand because in the brief time we have been in power our military commitments in defending the walls and guarding against attacks and our missions overseas have prevented that. We would have made special efforts to have such a meeting, nonetheless, but nothing has come up important enough to justify extraordinary measures." οὐ πώποτε is emphatic, as Andrewes says (*HCT* V, 183), but not specific.

The problems with the second passage include its translation. Some understand it as I have above, but others think it means that "all citizens will be members of the 5,000 in their turn." This reading makes no sense as a practical matter, but the other makes difficult, if not impossible, Greek. Andrewes (*HCT* V, 285–286) suggests the clause is corrupt on the grounds that "the envoys are not likely to sandwich anything of great constitutional subtlety between statements that they are not surrendering to the Spartans and not maltreating the sailors' families." In my view, however, the subtleties, if they exist, do not matter. What the envoys are trying to communicate is that the government will not be a narrow oligarchy and that the 5,000 will be the real rulers. Since that is a lie, we need not be unduly concerned with what subsidiary lies they were prepared to tell and whether Thucydides' account has them precisely right. If it is at all correct, the envoys have already told a different story from the one in their instructions, and they were surely capable of inventing whatever corroborative detail might be necessary.

Whatever truth there may have been in these arguments, they failed in their purpose. The Athenian forces continued to be angry, and a suggestion that they sail immediately to the Piraeus and attack the Athenian oligarchs soon gained strong support. So strong was the sentiment for such an action that Thucydides says "no one else could have restrained the mob at that moment," but Alcibiades did so.[88] If Thucydides is right in this judgment it would indicate that the fear and anger of the Athenian soldiers and sailors on Samos had grown since the last meeting and that the envoys' attempts to calm them may only have inflamed their emotions. It would also show how swiftly Alcibiades' influence had grown, overshadowing that of his colleagues, even Thrasybulus.[89] But Thucydides goes even further: "It seems that for the first time at that moment, and more than anyone, Alcibiades rendered a service to his city, for when the Athenians at Samos were determined to sail against their fellow citizens—and if they had done so the enemy would most certainly have gained control of Ionia and the Hellespont—he was the one who prevented it."[90]

[88]8.86.5. The passage implies that his intervention at a previous assembly to prevent a similar expedition (8.82) was less crucial and that the other leaders would also have been successful. The suggestion made by Holzapfel in the nineteenth century that the two reports represent a doublet of the same event has been generally rejected. See Meyer, Forsch., II, 410; Busolt, GG III:2, 1497, n. 2; HCT V, 287.

[89]We must read Thucydides' judgment here with some caution, however. Plutarch provides the detail omitted by Thucydides: that collaborating with Alcibiades was Thrasybulus, "who was said to have the loudest voice of all the Athenians" (Alc. 26.6), and there is no reason to doubt him. P. A. Brunt (REG LXV [1952], 59–96) believes that "Alcibiades was probably an informant of Thucydides for certain incidents recorded in Books V, VI and VIII" and that "Thucydides was inclined to magnify Alcibiades' influence on the course of events" (95). His argument is most persuasive. For a discussion of his importance in shaping Spartan policy and Thucydides' account of it, see Kagan, Peace of Nicias, 252–259.

[90]I have accepted the reading of B: καὶ δοκεῖ Ἀλκιβιάδης πρῶτον τότε καὶ οὐδενὸς ἔλασσον τὴν πόλιν ὠφελῆσαι. The other MSS have πρῶτος instead of πρῶτον, which would yield a translation something like C. F. Smith's: "Alcibiades seems then in an eminent degree, and more than anyone else, to have benefited the state" (Loeb edition, vol. 4, 343). The main objection to B's version has been well and succinctly stated by Brunt: "If this is accepted, Thucydides here asserts that Alcibiades had never previously rendered any service to Athens. . . . But it is quite incredible that Thucydides should have denied that Alcibiades had even *seems* to have rendered any service to Athens before 411, and the reading of the majority of manuscripts should unquestionably be accepted" (REG LXV [1952], 61, n. 1). But I think Brunt is placing too much weight on the word *seems* and not interpreting it correctly. It is not a question of how Alcibiades' earlier career seemed to some uninstructed person or collectivity but how it seemed to Thucydides: that is, what was his own interpretation of it? Crawley's translation, "Now it was that Alcibiades for the first time did the state a service," and Warner's, "It was at this point, it seems, that Alcibiades did his first

Most scholars have agreed with this judgment, but it deserves scrutiny.[91] Without a doubt, the policy of restraint served Athens well. The Spartans were not able to conquer the parts of Ionia and the Hellespont still in Athenian hands, as they surely could have done had the Athenian fleet sailed for Piraeus. Within a month or so, moreover, the oligarchy in Athens collapsed, and the fleet and the city united to pursue the war against the Peloponnesians. The first result was predictable, but the second was not. When the Athenians decided not to leave Samos, they had every reason to think that the oligarchy would remain in force, posing a threat to the security of their relatives and their property. Besides, the possibility always existed that the Four Hundred would betray the city to the enemy as, in fact, they seem to have tried to do. The loss of Athens would surely have been a disaster of greater proportions and one harder to retrieve than the loss of Ionia and the Hellespont. An attack on the Piraeus, on the other hand, given the serious division within the Four Hundred, might have been quickly successful. A united Athenian force could then have sailed to the Hellespont and fought a naval battle. Subsequent events suggest that they would have won such a battle and retrieved control of the lost territories. Such counterfactual conjectures can never be verified, but at least, they serve to indicate the thinking that might have moved those who opposed Alcibiades and Thrasybulus and to balance the overwhelming power of the fait accompli in shaping our judgment. In Grote's view, "the impulse of the armament was not merely natural, but even founded on a more prudent estimate of the actual chances, and that Alcibiades was nothing more than fortunate in a sanguine venture."[92] That judgment seems at least as plausible as Thucydides'.

---

great act of service to his country," appear to me to catch the meaning well. The question then is not whether Alcibiades' previous actions *seemed* to be useful to Athens but whether they were.

I do not find it hard to believe that Thucydides might have regarded Alcibiades' efforts to subvert the Peace of Nicias, undertake a Peloponnesian policy that led to a Spartan victory at Mantinea, and launch the Sicilian expedition as being at best of no use to Athens. Andrewes shows clearly (*HCT* V, 286) that this judgment is Thucydides' personal opinion. He also provides persuasive linguistic arguments in favor of πρῶτον. For our present purposes either reading will do, for both reveal that Thucydides strongly endorsed Alcibiades' resistance to an attack on the Piraeus at this moment.

[91]For some examples, see E. F. Bloedow, *Alcibiades Reexamined* (Wiesbaden, 1973), 38–40.

[92]Grote, VIII, 56. The argument offered here is little more than a paraphrase of Grote's. As far as I know, no one has taken the trouble to refute it; Busolt (*GG* III:2, 1499, n. 2) merely takes note of it without comment. Bloedow (*Alcibiades Reexamined*,

After order was restored, the expedition to Athens having been prevented, Alcibiades responded to the envoys from the Four Hundred. Thucydides tells us that "Alcibiades himself answered the ambassadors and sent them on their way,"[93] but his charge to them was very much the program of Thrasybulus and the moderates. "He was not opposed to the rule of the Five Thousand, but he demanded that they depose the Four Hundred and restore the Council of Five Hundred." He was thoroughly in favor of any economies they might have made to provide better for the armed forces, and he admonished them to hold out and not yield to the enemy. As long as the city was safe in Athenian hands, there was great hope for reconciliation.[94] No doubt the majority of his audience would have preferred a restoration of the full democracy, but its chosen leaders still aimed at the moderate regime they had sought from the start. We may assume that Alcibiades preferred a less fully democratic government to the restoration of the rule of the demagogues that had been his undoing, so he agreed with the views of his sponsor Thrasybulus.

The main purpose of Alcibiades' speech, however, was to influence the men who ruled Athens. He could hardly expect that the extremists would allow a dissolution of the Four Hundred and the end of oligarchy, but he could hope that the report of his words would encourage the moderates to resist any excesses planned by the extremists, perhaps even to take control themselves. Such a development would be of the greatest value to Alcibiades, for the extremists were opposed to his return, and some, like Phrynichus, would resist it at any cost. Still another aim of his words, perhaps the most important, was to dissuade

---

38–41) seems to be the only scholar generally sympathetic, but he carries the argument much farther than Grote. He believes that the fleet's departure from Samos and the consequent loss of Ionia and the Hellespont would have upset the balance of power that Tissaphernes was trying to maintain and forced the satrap to come over to the Athenian side. He, therefore, would have brought up the Phoenician fleet, and the Athenians wou'd easily have regained the lost regions. Once the Athenians had gained Tissaphernes' active support, they might well have retained it. I find it hard to believe that Tissaphernes could ever have lent active support to the Athenians against a Spartan force that was supported by Pharnabazus. In 411, neither Tissaphernes nor the Great King had reason to believe that an Athenian victory would be in his interest. No matter how independent Tissaphernes may have been, moreover, he was still subject to the Great King, and I cannot accept that the latter would allow one of his satraps to support one Greek army in a war against another Greek army supported by a different satrap.

[93] 8.86.6. Busolt (*GG* III:2, 1499) accurately captures the mood conveyed by Thucydides' description: "He dismissed the ambassadors like a sovereign."

[94] 8.88.6–7.

the Four Hundred from making a separate peace with the enemy. In the circumstances, that must mean surrendering command of the city, for the Spartans could not afford to make peace leaving the city in the hands of unguarded Athenians when the main Athenian force was still at war and beyond their control.

In fact, there was real danger of such a peace. To Samos came an Argive delegation offering their assistance to the Athenian people on the island, a demonstration that the Argive democracy recognized the forces at Samos as the true Athenian state and the Four Hundred as usurpers. With them they brought the crew of the *Paralus;* they had been captured by the Four Hundred and then sent in a troopship to guard Euboea.[95] Showing remarkably bad judgment, the Four Hundred later ordered them to carry a delegation to Sparta consisting of Laespodias, Aristophon, and Melesias, the last perhaps the son of Pericles' old opponent Thucydides. Their purpose must have been to try again to negotiate peace, but we are not told what terms they were authorized to offer or consider. When they reached the territory of Argos, the crew turned on them and delivered them to the Argives, "since they were among those who were chiefly responsible for overturning the democracy."[96] Since Thucydides did not name them in the company of those he regarded as the leaders of the revolution, the implication may simply be that these men belonged to the extremist group. However that may be, the delegation never reached Sparta. It is possible that they might have reached an agreement if they had, but good fortune, or the bad judgment of the Four Hundred, played into the hands of the men on Samos.

As the summer of 411 came to an end, the Four Hundred, and especially the extremists who hoped to establish a permanent oligarchy, had failed in all of their major undertakings Instead of making the empire more secure by installing oligarchical regimes in the subject states, they had brought about further rebellions. They had not been able to make peace with the enemy. They had failed to establish a friendly oligarchy on Samos; instead, they saw the crushing of the oligarchic movement within the Athenian force on that island and its replacement by an angry democracy that was barely restrained from sailing to attack them. They had alienated Thrasybulus, one of the founders of the movement, and had seen him become a very effective

---

[95] 8.74.2.
[96] 8.86.8–9. For Melesias, see Davies, *APF*, 232–233.

leader of their enemies. No less serious, they had seen Alcibiades, once a major part of their hope for success, join the hostile force on Samos and pledge himself to their destruction. His insistence and that of Thrasybulus on the dissolution of the Four Hundred was certain to encourage defections on the part of their moderate friends in Athens. Their prospects for survival were grim. The question was whether they could bring in the Spartans to save them before it was too late.

8. The Establishment of the Five Thousand

Alcibiades' message did not reach Athens in its original form. The ambassadors returning from Samos must have reported first to the oligarchic leaders who sent them, and those leaders must have edited their report, for their account differed significantly from what Alcibiades had said.[1] They told of his urging the men in Athens to hold out in the war and to make no concessions to the Spartans and of his hopes of reconciliation and victory, but they said nothing about his friendliness to the idea of the Five Thousand, his hostility to the rule of the Four Hundred, and his call for a restoration of the old Council of Five Hundred. To reveal those points would have been too dangerous, for dissension within the Four Hundred was already rife. A full and accurate report of Alcibiades' remarks would have been inflammatory, but even the edited version heartened the dissidents. Thucydides tells us that they "were the majority of those taking part in the oligarchy who were even before this discontented and would gladly rid themselves of the affair in any way if they could do so safely."[2] They had already begun to meet in groups and to complain of the course of events.

The leaders of the dissidents were two men who were important figures and officeholders in the Four Hundred, Theramenes the son of Hagnon and Aristocrates the son of Scelias. We have already dis-

---

[1] As far as I know, only W. J. McCoy ("Theramenes, Thrasybulus and the Athenian Moderates" [Ph.D. diss., Yale University, 1970], 81–82) has noticed the difference and its meaning.

[2] 8.89.1; 86.6–7.

cussed Theramenes (in chapter 6), whose later career and dramatic death made him famous, but Aristocrates, too, was a considerable figure. He played an important part in Athenian public life as early as 421, when he seems to be the same man who signed the Peace of Nicias and the alliance with Sparta. He was important enough to be the butt of a joke by Aristophanes in 414 and should be identified with the general whom the Athenians sent to Chios in 412. He was active in establishing the oligarchy and was a regimental commander in the army under the Four Hundred. Some later writers give him the chief credit for overthrowing the Four Hundred and establishing the government of the Five Thousand. He was elected general by the restored democracy in 410/9 and again as a colleague of Alcibiades in 407/6.[3] Andrewes says: "he could hold office under all kinds of regime and we could take him as a trusted soldier with no strong political feelings, drawn into the Four Hundred by the hope of Persian help in the war."[4] That is fair enough, but we should remember that Thucydides plainly includes Aristocrates in his general condemnation of the men who brought down the Four Hundred in pursuit of their own personal ambitions. We should remember also that if we knew nothing of the careers of Theramenes and Thrasybulus after 407, they would seem remarkably similar to that of Aristocrates. All supported the movement to overthrow the Athenian democracy; all turned against the oligarchy of the Four Hundred; all did well under the restored democracy; and all were associates of Alcibiades. There is no reason to doubt that Aristocrates had political opinions and that they were much the same as those of his collaborator Theramenes: both men were moderates.[5]

Characteristically, Theramenes and Aristrocrates took a moderate position in the discussions. They announced that they feared not only

[3] I agree with Andrewes (*HCT* V, 295) that although Aristocrates' patronymic does not appear in every passage, all references are to the same man.

[4] *HCT* V, 295, where the evidence for Aristocrates' career is collected.

[5] Andrewes' understanding of Theramenes, scattered throughout his commentary, seems fundamentally correct. It is summed up in *HCT* V, 300: "nothing in Theramenes' record contradicts the programmatic statement given to him in X[en]. II. 3.48, that he was opposed to the extremes of both democracy and oligarchy.... The formula of *Ath. Pol.* 28.5, that he encouraged various regimes ἕως μηδὲν παρανομοῖν but opposed them when they got out of hand, would allow him to be sincere in his promotion of both oligarchies, and in his subsequent opposition.... The modern opinion ... may yet be correct, that Theramenes from the start and consistently favoured a 'moderate constitution.' " Although Aristocrates' career seems to have ended before the episode of the oligarchy of the Thirty at Athens in 404/3, I see no reason why he should not be credited with a similar outlook.

Alcibiades and his army on Samos but also "those who had been sending embassies to Sparta, lest they do some harm to the city without consulting the majority."[6] They did not urge the discontented to take up arms and launch a counterrevolution. Given the uncertainty and suspicion of the times and the capacity for murder and terror still controlled by the extremists, that would be too dangerous. If such an action failed, moreover, it would increase the danger of the betrayal of the city at which their words hinted. They did not even use the perilous language of opposing the movement toward extreme oligarchy. Instead, they spoke of constitutional reform by which the Four Hundred would be asked merely to carry out promises they had already made: "to appoint the Five Thousand in fact and not in name and [thereby] to establish a more equal polity."[7] Privately, no doubt, they feared a betrayal of the city far more than an attack from Samos. In fact, they were stirred to action by the news that Alcibiades had acquired a position of leadership on Samos, which persuaded them that the days of the oligarchy were numbered.

Thucydides goes out of his way to assert that the call for the Five Thousand was only a political slogan behind which the dissident leaders concealed their envy of the other members of the Four Hundred, who had gained dominant positions at their expense, and their personal ambitions. Although we have suggested that other forces were at work, we need not doubt that such thoughts and feelings played some part. These men were Athenian politicians and, therefore, had been raised in a highly competitive culture in which ambition to achieve a position of leadership and respect in the state was natural and nothing of which to be ashamed; still, we should not overestimate such motives. More pressing than jealousy and ambition were two other motives: fear and patriotism. If the oppressively narrow oligarchy was left to its own devices, it might turn under pressure against suspected dissidents of whom Aristocrates and Theramenes would be obvious examples. If the Samian democrats took control of Athens from a still united and narrow oligarchy, none of its founders could expect much mercy from the victors. On the other hand, as the danger to the government grew, so did the incentive for the extremists to seek shelter in a Spartan occupation. Everything we know about the moderate leaders tells us that they opposed yielding Athenian independence. The honors they

[6]8.89.2.
[7]Ibid.

received from the restored democracy are ample evidence that their fellow citizens never doubted the sincerity of their patriotism or the goodness of their motives, nor should we.

As much as the news from Samos encouraged the moderates, so did it alarm the extremists, whose leaders Thucydides names as Phrynichus, Peisander, Antiphon, and, for the first time, Aristarchus, probably a member of the cavalry.[8] Since the extremists had received the news of the restoration of democracy to Samos their fears had grown. As a result of that news they had sent the ill-fated second embassy that never reached Sparta.[9] They had also begun to build a fort on the harbor at Piraeus on Eëtioneia at the same time. Eëtioneia was the name of a promontory extending south for some distance across the mouth of the harbor and dominating traffic in and out (see Map 6). On the north and west a wall defended it from attack by land. On its western, seaward side the wall ran to the southern tip of the peninsula, ending at a strong tower. Phrynichus and his colleagues were now adding two new walls to these fortifications: one along the eastern end of the peninsula toward the harbor and the other running south from the northern wall to the eastern end of the harbor, enclosing a stoa in which they required everyone to store such grain as was already on hand and whatever new shipments arrived. The port had already been well fortified against attack from outside by land or sea. The new arrangements would allow a small force to control the harbor against assaults from within, as well. Their pretext was the need to defend the port against attack by the forces on Samos, but Theramenes and the moderates quickly saw through it. Its true purpose, they said (and Thucydides endorses their opinion), was "so that they could admit the enemy by land and sea whenever they wished."[10]

The extremists, therefore, had been preparing to betray the city,

---

[8]8.90.1. Aristarchus is mentioned in 92.6 as going to the Piraeus with some "young cavalrymen," presumably as their leader. He may be the same man who was a choregus in 442/41 (Davies, *APF*, 1663).

[9]8.86.9.

[10]8.90.3. For a discussion of Thucydides' account of the topography and the problems it presents, see *HCT* V, 303–6. At least some of those problems seem not to be serious. Andrewes says "it is hard to see the urgency of completing or preventing a wall on the harbor shore." On the contrary, for a small group of men plotting to betray their city, the need for a truly secure refuge would have seemed urgent, and a base that could be attacked by boat from the harbor would not be adequate. Although I agree that a wall to protect the base on the landward side was even more urgent, the wall facing the harbor was also necessary.

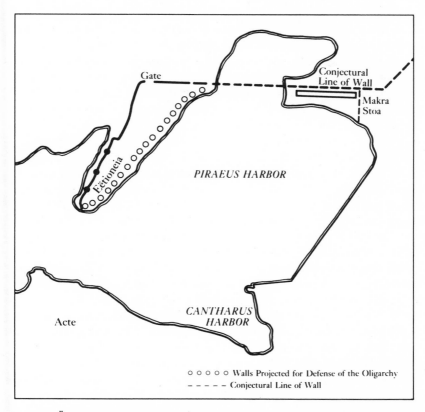

MAP 6. EĒTONEIA. Adapted from A. W. Gomme, A. Andrewes, and K. J. Dover, *A Historical Commentary on Thucydides*, V (Oxford, Oxford University Press, 1981), xv, by permission of the publisher.

should it become necessary, even before their ambassadors returned from Samos, and the moderates had already been suspicious, alarmed, and hostile to their designs. After they learned of the return of Alcibiades to Samos, however, the extremists were driven to even greater efforts. Alcibiades' hopes of causing dissension within Athens had been fulfilled: the extremists "saw that both the majority of the citizens and some of their own group whom previously they had believed trustworthy were changing their minds." The extremists were now desperate and prepared to betray the city. Thucydides tells us that they would have preferred to establish oligarchic government and maintain Athenian rule over the empire; failing that they would have liked to keep their ships, walls, and Athenian autonomy, but rather than fall victim to a restored democracy "they would bring in the enemy and, abandoning ships and walls, make any terms at all on behalf of their city if only they could save their own lives."[11] So they increased the pace of construction of the new walls at Eëtioneia and also sent an embassy of a dozen men, including Antiphon and Phrynichus, to try to make peace with the Spartans "on terms that were in any way tolerable."[12] Thucydides' comments make it clear that such terms would allow any settlement that left the extremist leaders alive.

Typically, Thucydides does not directly give us the details of the negotiation, but evidence scattered throughout his account permits some reasonable conjecture. Presumably, Phrynichus, Antiphon, and the others began the bidding with a request for a peace based on the status quo, which the Spartans quickly rejected. Next, they might have offered to settle for abandoning the empire while keeping walls, ships, and autonomy; that was certainly the farthest they could hope to get the moderates and the other Athenians to go. The Spartans, however, were well aware of the split between Athens and the fleet at Samos, and they probably also knew of the tension within Athens itself. They had no need to make even that concession, for civil strife might soon hand them an easy and total victory. The embassy returned from Sparta, therefore, "having made no agreement for everyone."[13] The language plainly implies that they had, however, negotiated an agreement for *someone:* themselves and their fellow extremists. For some time the Spartans had been planning with the Euboeans to help them revolt against the Athenians. The Spartan commander Agesandridas had gathered a fleet of forty-two ships for that purpose, and at that very moment they were at Las in Laconia waiting to sail. Theramenes charged that the ships were not on their way to Euboea but to Eëtioneia and a sneak attack on the Piraeus. Later events and Thucydides' own

---

[11]8.91.3.

[12]8.90.2. Plutarch (*Mor.* 833e–f) names Onomacles and Archeptolemus son of Hippodamus as members of the embassy.

[13]8.91.1.: οὐδὲν πράξαντες ἀνεχώρησαν τοῖς ξύμπασι ξυμβατικόν. Most editors and translators take τοῖς ξύμπασι to refer to the entire Athenian people, but Andrewes (*HCT* V, 307) thinks it refers to the other members of the Four Hundred, apart from the extremists. I see no reason to reject the more obvious reading, but either will do for our present purposes, which is to notice that the passage says that the ambassadors had failed to bring back a general agreement but clearly implies a secret one on behalf of the extremists. Andrewes sees that point but attributes it to Theramenes. The words cited above, however, belong to Thucydides, and the implication is his.

judgment endorse his opinion.[14] Failing to negotiate an acceptable peace, Phrynichus, Antiphon, and their colleagues had arranged to betray their city in exchange for their own safety.

As the extremists hurried to complete the new walls, suspicion increased among more patriotic Athenians. For some time Theramenes had been complaining about the new construction, possibly even outside the confines of the Four Hundred's council chamber.[15] Those complaints required considerable courage in an atmosphere of treachery and political assassination. Anyone to whom he spoke his mind might betray him, but he took the lead nevertheless. That atmosphere had been created in the previous spring with the murder of Androcles.[16] Perhaps it was no coincidence that the counterrevolution gained impetus from another assassination. As Phrynichus was leaving the council-chamber before noon, when the *agora* was crowded, he was stabbed to death. Thucydides tells us that the assassin was one of the garrison-troops who had escaped, but the plot included others, both Athenians and foreigners, some of whom were later honored and rewarded for the deed by the restored democracy.[17] An Argive accompanying the killer was caught and tortured, but he revealed no names, and no one was punished. The Four Hundred's inaction encouraged the opposition, and a new development filled them with an even greater sense of urgency: news arrived that the Peloponnesian fleet had left Las, put into port at Epidaurus, and ravaged Aegina. The dissidents—Theramenes, Aristocrates, men from both inside and outside the Four Hundred—held a meeting. Theramenes pointed out that Epidaurus and Aegina were not on the route to Euboea from Las (see Map 7). The intention was clearly to attack the Piraeus, as he had warned, "so it was no longer possible to remain quiet."[18] Many speeches followed, full of suspicion and rebellious sentiment, but at last they determined a course of action.

How much of what followed was concerted and how much improvised cannot be determined, but there certainly was a considerable

---

[14]Thucydides: 8.91.3.

[15]8.91.1: Ταῦτ' οὖν ἐκ πλέονός τε ὁ Θηραμένης διεθρόει suggests that Theramenes' complaints were at least somewhat open and public. They may, as Andrewes says (*HCT* V, 309), have been addressed only to members of the Four Hundred, but the information that previous discussions were in small groups in secret κατ' ὀλίγους τε καὶ κρύφα (92.2) does not preclude the involvement of some men outside that circle.

[16]8.65.2.

[17]8.92.2. Busolt, *GG* III:2, 1503, n. 5; *HCT* V, 309–311.

[18]8.92.3.

MAP 7. LAS TO EUBOEA

element of planning and significant communication between the dissidents at Athens and the hoplites who were working on the walls at Piraeus. Theramenes' chief collaborator, Aristocrates, was one of the taxiarchs, the regimental commander of his own tribal contingent among the soldiers at Piraeus. He took the first step by having the hoplites arrest the general Alexicles and place him in custody. Thucydides describes Alexicles as "a general from the oligarchical faction and especially inclined to the members of the clubs."[19] He was what we have called an "extremist." Hermon, commander of the garrison

---

[19]8.92.4, reading τοὺς ἑταίρους τετραμμένον with most manuscripts. See *HCT* V, 311–312.

at Munichia, took part, but Thucydides emphasizes that the corps of hoplites was thoroughly in favor. The army as a whole, instigated no doubt by the moderate leaders, had unseated their extremist general, itself a revolutionary act, and had threatened the base that the extremists must control if they were to admit the Spartans and save themselves.

News of the uprising in the Piraeus came to the Four Hundred as they were meeting in the council-chamber. The extremists were immediately ready to take up arms and began to threaten Theramenes and his fellow moderates, whom they suspected of being responsible. Theramenes, however, could not fail to have anticipated the moment, and he was ready with a response. He defended himself against the accusations and declared himself ready to join in the rescue of Alexicles. The extremists were taken by surprise and allowed him to take along another general who shared his views. In spite of Theramenes' open and frequent criticisms of their policies, the extremists were not yet sure of his disloyalty or, perhaps, not confident enough of their own strength within the Four Hundred to resist his boldness. The best they could do was to send Aristarchus and a corps of young cavalrymen to the Piraeus.

So an army marched from Athens toward another army at the Piraeus, and a serious civil war seemed to threaten. By this time, however, the force at the Piraeus had imprisoned its oligarchic general and was commanded by moderates, and two of the three generals of the army coming from Athens were moderates as well. What followed was not a battle but a charade. Aristarchus expressed his anger to the hoplites, and Theramenes, too, pretended to scold them. Most of the hoplites held fast, however, and asked Theramenes the leading question "did he think that the fortification was being built to any good purpose or would it be better to destroy it?" He answered that if they thought it best to destroy it, he agreed with them. On hearing that, the hoplites and many of the civilians in the Piraeus began to tear down the fortification accompanied by the exhortation, "whoever wants the Five Thousand to rule instead of the Four Hundred, let him get to work."

Thucydides tells us that this slogan was addressed "to the crowd" but by whom?[20] Surely it came from the moderate leaders who must have choreographed the performance to achieve their chief goals: the

[20] 8.92.10–11.

destruction of the fortifications that could permit the betrayal of the city to Sparta and the beginning of a movement toward the constitution they had sought from the beginning, the rule of the Five Thousand.[21] Thucydides says that those chanting the slogan were concealing behind it their true desire, a return to the full democracy. But they were afraid to reveal their true desire, fearing that the Five Thousand might already exist and that demanding the full democracy might expose each man to danger, since his neighbor might be a member of the ruling group. However, such reasoning could not apply to the moderate leaders or to any other members of the moderate faction within the Four Hundred, for they knew with certainty that the Five Thousand did not exist, but even when applied to the ordinary soldiers, Thucydides' assertion raises doubts. Why should men who had arrested their general, had been prepared to fight a battle, and were beginning to tear down a fortification ordered by the reigning government shrink from joining in a general shout in favor of restoring democracy? What significant additional danger would they incur by such an act? No doubt many, if not most, of the hoplites would have preferred a restoration of the democracy, had they thought about it. However, it seems better to believe that they were not shouting out of fear but were simply joining a chorus instigated by the moderates.[22]

Shouting, however, would not bring down the oligarchy and replace it with a moderate government. What was needed was a way to exert pressure on the extremists without starting a civil war. The moderates were aware that the Spartans had been counting on open civil strife among the Athenians to give them an easy victory. We may well believe that the men who had calmed the people when the news of the arrest of Alexicles had filled the city with fear by reminding them that the enemy was near had been inspired by the moderate leaders.[23] On the next day, therefore, they followed a moderate course meant to force the extremists to yield but not to fight. The army in the Piraeus completed the destruction of the fortifications and released the oli-

---

[21]Andrewes (*HCT* V, 314) thinks that the slogan was shouted by the hoplites to the citizens of the Piraeus. So it may have been, but I believe that the first shouts came from those in on the plan, instructed by the moderate leaders.

[22]Caution is always advisable in rejecting what Thucydides tells us. In this case, however, he is revealing to us the *thoughts* of a large body of men. We might wonder how he could know them even if he were present, but he was not. We are thus dependent on an opinion about so difficult a subject by an unknown informant. In such circumstances, an independent judgment seems permissible.

[23]8.92.8.

garchic general Alexicles. Then they held an assembly and voted to march on Athens, but they did not seek out the enemy to force a battle. Instead, they stopped at the parade ground at the Anaceium, the precinct of the temple of the Dioscuri. There, delegates from among the Four Hundred came to calm the soldiers and reason with them. They promised to publish the list of the Five Thousand and to allow the council of Four Hundred to be chosen from that body in any way it should decide. They urged the men to be calm and not to endanger the state and everyone in it. The appeal was effective, and it was agreed to hold an assembly in the theater of Dionysus on a stated day to discuss the restoration of harmony.[24]

We do not know whom these spokesmen were or whom they represented. Did the extremists approve? Presumably they consented; otherwise they would surely have fled to save their lives, as they did later.[25] But was their offer sincere? It probably was not, for they thought that allowing as many as five thousand men to share in the government amounted to outright democracy.[26] More likely, they were playing a delaying game in the hope that the Spartans would yet save them. On the day set for the meeting to restore harmony among them, presumably only a few days later, the Athenians were gathering at the theater when the news came that the Spartan fleet, having moved from Epidaurus to Megara, had left that city and was sailing toward Salamis. The obvious target was the Piraeus, and all the Athenians regarded this as the fulfillment of Theramenes' prophecy: the ships were coming to occupy the fortification that the extremists had been building but which the people had fortunately destroyed. Thucydides thinks it is possible that the voyage was the result of a plan arranged in advance while the Spartan fleet was at Epidaurus, but it is more likely that they, knowing of the dissension among the Athenians, hoped to arrive at an opportune time and take advantage of a civil war to seize the port. We cannot know the intentions or instructions of the Spartan commanders, but Thucydides supported the charge that the extremists were building the fort in order to let the enemy in.[27] In light of that, it is easy to believe that the fleet was on its way to carry out a plan concerted in advance, perhaps as early as the last unsuccessful peace mission or, at the latest, during its stay in Epidaurus or Megara. The

[24] 8.93.
[25] 8.98.1.
[26] 8.92.11.
[27] 8.91.2–92.1.

commanders could easily have been given orders to cover all contingencies. They should sail to the Piraeus and land at Eëtioneia if the extremists held it; from there they could take the port or, if that was not possible, block its entrance. In either case, they could then starve the Athenians into submission. A second possibility was that the extremists would not hold Eëtioneia but that the Athenians would be so diverted by civil war that the Spartans would find the harbor unguarded and achieve the same result. If both of these hopes failed, they could simply sail on by and aim for Euboea.

In fact, the actions of Theramenes, Aristocrates, and the other moderates had made those hopes vain. They had destroyed the fortifications that would have allowed the extremists to hold Eëtioneia, and they had prevented fighting between the factions. When the Athenians heard of the approach of the enemy fleet, they ran to the Piraeus at once with their entire army and manned the ships and fortifications to defend the harbor. Seeing that the plan had failed, Agesandridas and his forty-two ships sailed past the city, heading south toward Sunium. The city had been saved.[28]

The fleet's destination was clearly Euboea, the place that, since the Spartan establishment of the fort at Decelea had shut them off from the rest of Attica, "was everything" to the people enclosed within the city of Athens, the Piraeus, and the walled space between them.[29] There were already a few ships guarding the island, some manned by the crew of the *Paralus* and possibly under the command of Polystratus, but not enough to meet the threat.[30] The Athenians, therefore, hurried to the rescue, forced to use crews that had not trained together. The commander was Thymochares, a moderate general, possibly the one who had accompanied Theramenes on his march to the Piraeus.[31] We

---

[28]8.94–95.1.
[29]8.95.2: Εὔβοια γὰρ αὐτοῖς ἀποκεκλημένης τῆς Ἀττικῆς πάντα ἦν.
[30]For the crews, see 8.74.1; for Polystratus, *Lys.* 20.6, 14; and *HCT* V, 202, 318.
[31]8.95.2. We may deduce Thymochares' allegiance from the following: if he was already a general, as seems likely, he would have been appointed by the Four Hundred and so could not be a democrat. In the immediate circumstances, however, the frightened and angry Athenians would certainly not trust anyone tainted by extremist associations. That leaves only a moderate or someone totally apolitical. In the heated climate of September of 411, the latter possibility seems most unlikely. Andrewes (*HCT* V, 317–318) suggests that he might not have been a general under the Four Hundred but appointed to that post for the first time by the assembly at the theater of Dionysus, which voted for the expedition. If so, the same arguments point to his being a moderate.

do not know how many ships he took with him, but when he arrived at Eretria, the Athenian fleet reached a total of thirty-six.

Waiting for him some seven miles away across the strait at Oropus were Agesandridas and the Peloponnesian fleet. Agesandridas had the advantage not only of numbers and more experienced crews but also of good preparation, a rehearsed plan of battle, the element of surprise, and the collaboration of the Eretrians. The Athenians arrived and went at once to seek a meal in Eretria. They could not obtain food in the marketplace, as they had expected, but had to seek it in private houses at some distance from the shore. This was part of the plan concocted by the Eretrians and the Spartans: when the Athenians were scattered and away from their ships, the Eretrians raised a signal, and Agesandridas attacked at once. The Athenians were forced to race for their ships and put to sea immediately, as soon as they were manned, without having time to arrange an effective formation. Even so, they fought well for a time but after a while were routed and driven to shore. Still unaware of the Eretrian treachery, many sought safety in the city but were killed by the citizens. Some escaped to safety in Chalcis and some to an Athenian fort in Eretrian territory. The Athenians lost twenty-two ships and their crews, and the Peloponnesians set up a trophy of victory.[32] Soon the entire island joined in the rebellion, except for Histiaea at the northern end, which had been held by Athenian colonists since the Euboean rebellion of 446.[33]

The news from Euboea frightened the Athenians even more than the news of the Sicilian disaster, for their situation was considerably worse than it had been in 413. Their treasury was about empty, and of their fleet, only the twenty ships that had escaped from Euboea remained. Since the defeat in Sicily, they had lost access to most of Attica, and now they had lost Euboea, which had been a substitute for it. Beyond that, they were divided among themselves, with dissension at Athens and the entire city separated from the fleet at Samos. At any time, open warfare might break out in the city, or the force on Samos might attack the people in Athens. In a rare demonstration of sympathetic understanding, Thucydides asks, "was it not natural

---

[32]Diodorus tells the story of the battle differently (13.34.2–3, 36.3–4). His version provides the Athenians with forty ships under two unnamed generals who quarrel with one another and lose the battle. There is no reason to prefer him to Thucydides here.

[33]8.95.3–7. Thucydides refers to Histiaea as Oreus here (95.4). Presumably, the Athenians who colonized the area in the form of a cleruchy changed its name. See *HCT* V, 320.

that they were dismayed?"[34] But what terrified them most was the proximity of the enemy fleet at a time when the Piraeus could not be defended at sea. Even if all twenty surviving ships of the battle at Euboea had made it safely home, they were no match for the victorious fleet of Agesandridas.[35] They were sure that the Spartans must already be on their way to attack the harbor, and Thucydides expresses his own opinion of what the result would have been. Had the Spartans been bold enough they could either have blockaded the port, intensifying the factional strife, or set up a siege, which would have led the force on Samos to come to the rescue of their relatives and their city, thereby losing the entire empire from the Hellespont to Euboea. The Spartans, however, were "the most convenient of all people for the Athenians to fight," as they proved on this occasion, among many others. They missed their opportunity, revealing the difference between their national character and that of the Athenians. They were slow and timid, while the Athenians were quick and enterprising, and the latter qualities were the ones needed for ruling the sea. The Syracusans showed those qualities, fighting against Athens better than other peoples because they had the same characteristics.[36]

These observations by Thucydides once again endorse the judgment of Alcibiades in restraining the troops on Samos and also the analysis made by the Corinthians at the congress in Sparta in 432, but they are puzzling in some respects and not entirely persuasive.[37] The Spartans' character had at least saved them from events such as the Sicilian disaster: from their point of view the Athenians' characteristics might make them seem in some ways "the most convenient of opponents," for it is hard to imagine how Athens could have lost the war had it not risked so much in Sicily. Nor had the Syracusans shown much swiftness, daring, or enterprise until the arrival of the Spartan general Gylippus.[38] It is interesting, too, to consider the wisdom of a Spartan naval blockade of the Piraeus or a siege, which would have required an associated blockade. Events suggest that the result internally would have been not an increase in dissension but the expulsion of the extrem-

[34]8.96.1–2.
[35]Thucydides says that the Athenians had no ships to defend Piraeus (8.96.3: σφῶν ἐπὶ τὸν Πειραιᾶ ἐρῆμον ὄντα νεῶν). He either believes the ships had not returned or is speaking loosely.
[36]8.96.4–5.
[37]Alcibiades, 8.86.4; Corinthians, 1.70.
[38]See *HCT* V, 322–323.

ists and the unification of the state under the moderates. The former had lost their support and their confidence, and the latter were on their way to full control. A Spartan attack could be expected to hasten both developments. News of a Spartan blockade or siege would almost surely provoke an attack by the Athenian forces on Samos, but we need not be greatly surprised that the Spartans chose to try. A fleet of the size and quality of the one at Samos could easily have destroyed the much smaller force under Agesandridas. The victorious Athenian fleet under Thrasybulus and Alcibiades could then happily unite with an Athens led by Theramenes and Aristocrates. With no further threat at home, the reunited military and naval forces of Athens could sail out to meet the Peloponnesian fleet with good hopes of victory and the recovery of lost territories. Events would soon show that such hopes were entirely realistic. The Spartans, moreover, were still on bad terms with Tissaphernes and were badly paid and supplied, and they had not yet made an agreement with Pharnabazus. They had good reason, therefore, to doubt the wisdom of provoking an attack on the relatively small naval force that was available for an assault on the Piraeus. Any prudent general, not only a sluggish and unenter-prising Spartan, might be reluctant to make such an attack.

In fact, the Spartans did not attack, but the actions taken by the Athenians in expecting an attack show clearly how they would have met the challenge. They at once manned twenty ships, presumably all available, to defend the harbor as best they could. Then they held an assembly, the first of several, on the Pnyx, and the location was significant. The assembly that overthrew the democracy had carefully been moved away from the Pnyx, the usual place of assembly under the democracy, to Colonus; the meeting intended to produce harmony between the extreme oligarchs and the other Athenians was held in the theater of Dionysus. The return to the Pnyx must have been the result of a deliberate choice meant to indicate a return to a situation before the establishment of oligarchy. The very first meeting deposed the Four Hundred, but it did not restore the full democracy. Instead, "it turned affairs over to the Five Thousand," defined as those who could furnish themselves with arms, and it forbade payment for hold-ing any public office. This was the moderate program, and we should not be surprised that it, and not the full democracy, was introduced, for almost all of those attending the assembly were of hoplite status or higher. At the same time, we should not lose sight of the symbolic meaning of the choice of the Pnyx: to those deliberating in the assembly

held there that day, chiefly hoplites, its actions were compatible with
movement toward some greater degree of democracy.

The Athenians who took part in shaping the new regime in the days
that followed had reason to feel relief and pride. Their moderate leaders
had helped them sail safely between the Scylla of betrayal to the
Spartans and the Charybdis of civil war. The city was free and united;
the way was clear to unification with the forces on Samos. This happy
result was not inevitable. Indeed, escape from disaster had been a very
close thing. Had Theramenes and Aristocrates been slower to recognize
the danger and allowed the fortification of Eëtioneia to reach completion, the extremists could have betrayed the city to Sparta. Had they
been less skillful in managing the countercoup, the two sides might
have engaged in open civil war, with the likely result being a successful
Spartan intervention. For their actions at this time, Theramenes and
Aristocrates, perhaps more than the glamorous renegade on Samos,
deserve to have it said that they, "more than any other, were useful
to the state."[39]

The regime of the Five Thousand lasted for fewer than ten months.[40]
We know little about its constitution, and the meaning of the few facts
on which our understanding is based is much disputed. In addition to
saying that the assembly at the Pnyx voted to turn the government
over to the Five Thousand, that is, to those who could equip themselves
as hoplites, Thucydides tells us that it forbade payment for public
service.[41] Aristotle uses almost the same words: "they turned affairs
over to the Five Thousand who provided their own hoplite equipment,
voting that no office should be paid,"[42] but he adds important information about the end of the regime, which occurred after Thucydides'
narrative breaks off: "the people quickly took away their control of the
state."[43] Thucydides characterizes the new regime as "a moderate mixture in regard to the few and the many."[44] Aristotle praises it as appropriate to the occasion, for "a war was in progress and the state was

[39]8.86.4.

[40]It was installed some time in September of 411 (Busolt, GG III:2, 1508, n. 3) and
was replaced by the democracy by June or July of 410 (Rhodes, *Commentary*, 414–
415).

[41]8.97.1: τοῖς πεντακισχιλίοις ἐψηφίσαντο τὰ πράγματα παραδοῦναι (εἶναι δὲ
αὐτῶν ὁπόσοι καὶ ὅπλα παρέχονται) καὶ μισθὸν μηδένα φέρειν μηδεμιᾷ ἀρχῇ.

[42]*Ath. Pol.* 33.1: τὰ πράγματα παρέδωκαν τοῖς πεντακισχιλίοις τοῖς ἐκ τῶν ὅπλων,
ψηφισάμενοι μηδεμίαν ἀρχὴν εἶναι μισθοφόρον.

[43]*Ath. Pol.* 34.1: Τούτους μὲν οὖν ἀφείλετο τὴν πολιτείαν ὁ δῆμος διὰ τάχους.

[44]8.97.2: μετρία γὰρ ἥ τε ἐς τοὺς ὀλίγους καὶ τοὺς πολλοὺς ξύγκρασις ἐγένετο.

in the hands of those bearing arms."[45] We should accept the obvious implication of the evidence and believe that political rights, that is, the right to vote in the assembly, serve on juries, and hold public office, were restricted to those of the hoplite census and higher, excluding the thetes.[46] As we have seen, this should be no surprise, for most of those voting at the assemblies were hoplites, and most of the thetes were on Samos.

One of the great changes effected by the counterrevolution was the transfer of the seat of power from the council of Four Hundred to an assembly that was many times larger.[47] But how large was that assembly? Whatever its original meaning may have been, the figure of 5,000 was by now purely conventional. The important idea was that all who could provide themselves with hoplite equipment or serve in the cavalry should participate, and in September of 411, their number may have been about 10,000.[48] The participation of some such number in the conduct of affairs would well justify the concept of a moderate mixture or blend of the few and the many, for it was neither the

[45]*Ath. Pol.* 33.2: πολέμου τε καθεστῶτος καὶ ἐκ τῶν ὅπλων τῆς πολιτείας οὔσης.

[46]The case would be even stronger if we accepted Krueger's emendation of a passage in Diodorus (13.38.1) that reads: "and they established the constitution of the state from among the hoplites" (καί τὸ σύστημα τῆς πολιτείας ἐκ τῶν ὁπλιτῶν) as does G. Vlastos ("*Isonomia politikê*," in J. May and E. G. Schmidt, eds., *Isonomia* [Berlin, 1964], 20, n. 6). I think he is right to call the manuscript reading πολιτῶν "senseless" and to accept the emendation, but it is safer not to rely on it. The paucity of evidence has given rise to considerable dispute about the nature of the new regime introduced in September of 411. Some scholars, e.g., W. S. Ferguson (*CP* XXI [1926], 72–75; *CAH* V [1927], 312–347, especially 338–341) and G. Vlastos (*AJP* LXXIII [1952], 189–198) believe that the new constitution was the "constitution for the future" described in *Ath. Pol.* 30, but Hignett (*HAC*, 376–378) has convincingly argued against that view. Grote (VIII, 77–80), without the benefit of the *Ath. Pol.*, denied that there was a constitution of the Five Thousand, considering it as a restoration of the old democracy with only minor modifications. A version of that view was revived by G. E. M. de Ste. Croix (*Historia* V [1956], 1–23) and somewhat extended by R. Sealey (*Essays in Greek Politics* [New York, 1967], 11–32). They argue that the new constitution deprived those below the hoplite census not of all political rights but merely of the right to hold office. That opinion seems to have been refuted satisfactorily by P. J. Rhodes (*JHS* XCII [1972], 115–127) and Andrewes (*HCT* V, 323–328).

[47]Rhodes (*JHS* XCII [1972], 122–123) emphasizes this shift and sees it as an important aspect of the meaning of Thucydides' term ξύγκρασις.

[48]That is the guess made by Andewes (*HCT* V, 329), who rightly emphasizes the uncertainty of any estimate. The figure of 9,000 is often adopted, because that is the number mentioned in *Pro Polystrato* (Lys. 20.13). But the reliability of the facts asserted in that speech is limited, and even if we take the speaker's assertion seriously, that Polystratus enrolled this number in his work as *katalogeus*, that work would have taken place under the aegis of the Four Hundred, not at the time of the Five Thousand.

narrow oligarchy of the Four Hundred nor the full democracy that
allowed all citizens to take part in political life.

There was also a council, and what little evidence we have suggests
that it may have consisted of 500 members but that it was elected, not
chosen by lot like the old democratic council.[49] It also appears to have
had greater power and discretion.[50] The function of the *nomothetai*
mentioned by Thucydides is unclear; perhaps they were established
at an early meeting of the new assembly of the Five Thousand to
evaluate the constitutional proposals still to be brought before them,
or they may have been a commission to revise the legal code.[51] A new
board of *katalogeis*, no doubt, will have been appointed to compile the
official list of those eligible to sit in the assembly. In other respects,
the constitution seems to have been the same as in the old democracy.
Some elections must have been held, for we know that the eponymous
archon chosen by the Four Hundred, Mnasilochus, was replaced by
Theopompus after having served only two months.[52] Perhaps the other
archons were replaced as well. The generals chosen by the fleet at
Samos continued to serve, along with some of the moderates who had
been chosen by the Four Hundred. Perhaps there was an election to
confirm these men in office and to elect new men to substitute for the
oligarchic generals.[53] The court system seems to have functioned in
the old way, although the juries will have excluded the thetes.[54] The
limited evidence we have, then, seems to show that the government

---

[49]Alcibiades had told the embassy from the oligarchs at Athens to replace the council
of Four Hundred with the old council of Five Hundred (8.86.6), but that does not
prove that they did so. A decree of the newly restored democracy in 410 (And. *De
Myst.* 96) tells us that a "council of five hundred chosen by lot" (ἡ βουλὴ οἱ πεντακόσιοι
λαχόντες τῷ κυάμῳ) existed at that time, and some have thought that the language
emphasizes the practice of allotment. From this, historians conclude that there was a
previous council of Five Hundred under the constitution of the Five Thousand, which
was not allotted but elected (Meyer, *GdA*, IV, 303 and n. 2; Hignett, *HAC*, 279, 372,
378; Rhodes, *Commentary*, 412). M. Jameson (*Historia* XX [1971], 566) is in general
agreement but does not accept the special emphasis the others see. The evidence is not
conclusive, but an elected council of Five Hundred is consistent with it and entirely
plausible.

[50]Jameson, *Historia* XX (1971), 564–566; Rhodes, *Commentary*, 412.

[51]Andrewes (*HCT* V, 330) makes the former suggestion; Hignett (*HAC*, 375), the
latter.

[52]*Ath. Pol.* 33.1.

[53]Busolt, *GG* III:2, 1510 and n. 2.

[54]See the decree moved by Andron ordering the arrest of Archeptolemus, Onomacles,
and Antiphon during the rule of the Five Thousand in Plut. *Mor.* 833e–f. See also
Rhodes, *Commentary*, 412.

of the Five Thousand functioned in a manner similar to that of the full democracy, with the important exception that the thetes did not take part.

Thucydides awards the constitution of the Five Thousand high praise, perhaps calling it the best government Athens had in his life-time.[55] Aristotle, as we have seen, also rated it highly, saying that the Athenians "seem to have been governed well at that time, for a war was in progress, and the state was in the hands of those bearing arms." That praise no doubt expressed the sentiments of its author more accurately than the realities of the situation, for the main weakness of the new constitution was that it did not meet the needs of Athens precisely in respect to its military forces. The moderates who intro-duced it were determined to wage war against the enemy, but to do so successfully, they must unite the hoplites and cavalrymen in the city with the even more important force on Samos. But that force was made up chiefly of thetes whose service in the fleet was vital for victory but who would be excluded from active participation in the new con-stitution. With the advantage of hindsight, we can see that such an arrangement could not last long. It was only a matter of time until the men who rowed the ships would insist on the restoration of their full political rights. The irony confronting the moderates was that their

---

[55]8.97.2: καὶ οὐχ ἥκιστα δὴ τὸν πρῶτον χρόνον ἐπί γε ἐμοῦ Ἀθηναῖοι φαίνονται εὖ πολιτεύσαντες. The meaning of this sentence has been much disputed. It is not certain whether the praise is intended for the entire period in which the Five Thousand ruled or only its first part; whether οὐχ ἥκιστα is a superlative and, if so, a strong or a weak one; or if εὖ πολιτεύσαντες means that the Athenians at that time had a good constitution or only that they managed their affairs well. For a full discussion of the problems, see G. Donini, *La posizione di Tucidide verso il governo dei cinquemila* (Turin, 1969). Andrewes (*HCT* V, 331–339) also offers a valuable discussion, placing the passage in the context of Thucydides' political ideas. He translates it: "The initial period (of this regime) was one of the periods when the affairs of Athens were conducted best, at least in my time" (330). I find it hard to believe that Thucydides would distinguish between the quality of the constitution or government in the first period of the regime's existence, as opposed to a later one, when it lasted only nine or ten months. The softer superlative rather than a stricter one is possible but not necessary. What I find hardest to accept is the suggestion that Thucydides refers not to constitutional arrangements but only to the management of affairs. The words that follow—"for it was a moderate blend in respect to the few and the many, and it was this that first allowed the state to recover from its wretched circumstances," καὶ ἐκ πονηρῶν τῶν πραγμάτων γενομένων τοῦτο πρῶτον ἀνήνεγκε τὴν πόλιν—seem to indicate that Thucydides refers to both constitutional and political matters but makes the latter subordinate to the former. I prefer to translate the passage as follows: "For the first time, at least in my own time, the Athenians seem to have been well governed." But Andrewes' version is closer to the consensus.

future and that of their city depended on achieving a union with the fleet at Samos, but if they achieved it, the constitution they favored must collapse.

Theramenes and his associates, however, moved forward hopefully to deal with their problems. The first step was to unite the city with the fleet at Samos, and to this end they voted the recall of Alcibiades and other exiles who were with him.[56] The action was the work of Theramenes, and it finally accomplished the aims that had moved the moderates to collaborate with the oligarchs in the spring of 411.[57] Athens was governed by what they considered a sensible, prudent, and economical government and had at its disposal again what they judged to be the incomparable diplomatic and military talents of Alcibiades. As he had almost ruined the state as its enemy, he might save it when restored to it.

We do not know just what the decree said, but Alcibiades' actions suggest that it did provide for a complete exculpation or pardon. Since it confirmed the fleet's election of Alcibiades as general, it must have abolished his outlawry and the threat of penalty that went with it,[58] but it may have left him in the same situation as in the autumn of 415, after his accusation but before any trial: "he was not offered rehabilitation but the possibility of returning to rehabilitate himself."[59] Certainly, he did not come back to Athens at once but waited almost four years until the summer of 407. Although his chief enemies were dead or out of power and his friends in control, he seems to have been unwilling to return to face the Athenian people and a possible trial in his present circumstances. Plutarch's account of his state of mind is persuasive: "he thought that he should not come back with empty

[56]8.97.3. The other exiles were presumably associates of Alcibiades condemned with him in the sacrilege scandals of 415.

[57]Diodorus (13.38.2) gives him sole credit for the restoration, and Cornelius Nepos (*Alc.* 5.4) names him alone as supporting the return. In reference to the restoration of Alcibiades after the fall of the Four Hundred in 411, Plutarch mentions no names but attributes it to the friends of Alcibiades, now cooperating with the people (*Alc.* 27.1). He later mentions a decree for his recall in 407 moved by Critias "previously" (*proteron*). Most scholars place Critias' motion in 411, but I agree with Andrewes (*JHS* LXXIII [1953], 3, n. 7) in thinking that *proteron* means an earlier meeting of the assembly in 408.

[58]Nepos (*Alc.* 5.4) tells us that the decree gave him equal power with Thrasybulus and Theramenes: "suffragante Theramene, populi scito restituitur parique absens imperio praeficitur simul cum Thrasybulo et Theramene."

[59]Hatzfeld, *Alcibiade*, 257.

hands and without achievements, because of the pity and the grace of the masses, but full of glory."[60]

Thucydides tells us that immediately after the change of regime, Peisander, Alexicles, and other leading oligarchs stole away to the Spartan fort at Decelea. According to a speech delivered early in the fourth century, the flight of the members of the Four Hundred began even earlier, "after the death of Phrynichus."[61] To be sure, some may have fled immediately, and Aristarchus certainly must have moved quickly. He hurried to the Athenian fort at Oenoe on the Boeotian border and, in his capacity as general, persuaded the besieged garrison there to surrender the fort to the enemy before they could learn of events at Athens.[62] But there is considerable evidence that in the days and weeks after the fall of the Four Hundred the situation in Athens was unclear.[63] Even some of those most deeply implicated in the oligarchy did not flee immediately but, in spite of Thucydides, Alexicles, Aristarchus, and perhaps Peisander, too, stayed long enough to take part in some memorable public events.

In those early days of the regime of the Five Thousand, Theramenes and his moderate associates needed to walk a fine line. The memory of the oligarchy was fresh, and no less fresh was the recollection of its misdeeds, including suspected treason. Although the moderates had led the overthrow of the Four Hundred, many of them had been members. On the one hand, they needed to guard against any attempt by the extremists to restore the oligarchy or betray the state. On the other hand, they needed to take some steps to separate themselves in the public mind from those same extremists who had been their colleagues in the Four Hundred. At the same time, they could not move too quickly or too boldly lest they encourage a popular outrage against *anyone* who had taken part in the Four Hundred. One of their first actions, therefore, seems to have been a decree of the assembly moved by Critias the son of Callaeschrus against the corpse of Phrynichus.[64] The decree ordered that the dead man be brought to trial on a charge

[60]*Alc.* 27.1.
[61]8.98.1. Thucydides seems to emphasize the suddenness of the escape: Ἐν δὲ τῇ μεταβολῇ ταύτῃ εὐθὺς, κ.τ.λ. Lysias (13.73) says οἱ πολλοὶ τῶν τετρακοσίων ἔφυγον, which, as Busolt (*GG* III:2, 1510) says, is greatly exaggerated.
[62]8.98.
[63]My understanding of the situation immediately after the installation of the Five Thousand owes much to Jameson (*Historia* XX [1971], 541–568).
[64]Lycurgus, *Against Leocrates*, 113.

of treason, and when he was convicted, his bones were exhumed and removed beyond the borders of Attica, his house destroyed, his property confiscated, and the verdict and penalties inscribed on a bronze stele.[65] An ancient commentator connects this charge with Phrynichus' activities as general on Samos,[66] but it probably referred to his more recent activities on behalf of the Four Hundred, perhaps his negotiation with the Spartans.[67] Critias was probably a member of the Four Hundred, and in spite of his later activities as leader of the extreme oligarchs after the war, this motion shows him to have been one of the moderates in 411.[68] The strange case may have arisen as a response to an attempt by Phrynichus' supporters to punish his assassins;[69] if so, that would be evidence of an atmosphere in which the extremists still felt comfortable enough to take the offensive in the law courts. More likely, the moderates took the lead, testing the waters with an attack on a man who had many enemies and was safely dead. The honor of the turncoat extremist did not go undefended, for both Aristarchus and Alexicles spoke on his behalf.[70] Obviously, both extremists at first felt safe enough not only to stay in Athens but even to defend their associate. The outcome of the trial, however, was probably a sufficient sign of the new mood in Athens. We may guess that they fled to join the enemy soon after.

The moderates were soon encouraged to move against living extremists, some of whom were bold enough to stay in Athens to stand trial. It is possible that Peisander remained long enough to answer the charges brought against him but escaped before his sentence could be imposed.[71] We can be certain, in any case, that they brought an action

[65]Craterus, *FGrH* III, 342 Fr. 17; Plut. *Mor.* 834b; Lycurgus, *Against Leocrates*, 113.

[66]Scholiast to Aristoph. *Lys.* 313 = Craterus *FGrH* III, 342, Fr. 17. The scholiast may be confusing this charge with the one made earlier by Peisander that brought about his deposition (8.54.2) on the grounds that he had betrayed Amorges. He may also have been thinking of Phrynichus' communications with the Spartan admiral Astyochus.

[67]8.90.2. Those negotiations were carried on at the same time as the work on the fort at Eëtioneia, and the negotiators, no doubt, were thought to have planned treason.

[68]On Critias as a moderate member of the Four Hundred, see Busolt, *GG* III:2, 1462 and n. 3; and G. Adeleye, *TAPA* CIV (1974), 1–9. Against that view, see H. C. Avery, *CP* LVIII (1963), 165–167.

[69]That is the suggestion of Jameson, *Historia* XX (1971), 552.

[70]Lycurgus, *Against Leocrates*, 115.

[71]Jameson, *Historia* XX (1971), 555. Jameson has constructed an ingenious argument that places the exchange between Sophocles and Peisander in the context of a trial in which the poet is bringing charges against the politician on behalf of a dead man.

against three of the leading oligarchs, Archeptolemus, Onomacles, and Antiphon. It is dated to the twenty-first day of the prytany, so the moderates had waited at least three weeks after the collapse of the Four Hundred before attacking the ablest of the extremists. The generals brought charges of treason against the three men for their role as ambassadors who negotiated with the Spartans "to the detriment of the state." Andron, who had been a member of the Four Hundred and was now a member of the new council, proposed a decree ordering the generals and ten councillors whom they would choose to arrest the accused and bring them to trial.[72] Lysias later placed the chief responsibility for this action on Theramenes, who was one of the generals: he accused these men and had them put to death, "wishing to appear trustworthy to you, the people."[73] Although these remarks are part of a tendentious and hostile attack on Theramenes, they contain a considerable measure of truth. Like the other moderates, Theramenes was eager to separate himself from his former colleagues, and this trial allowed him to do so. At the same time, we need not doubt that he and the moderates, no less than the other Athenians, were eager to rid the Athenians of traitors, actual and potential.

Onomacles seems to have fled, but Archeptolemus and Antiphon stayed to defend themselves, the latter making the finest defense of any Thucydides ever heard.[74] Even after the conviction of Phrynichus, there was evidently reason for Archeptolemus and Antiphon to hope for a favorable verdict. Polystratus, a member of the Four Hundred and one of their *katalogeis*, had gotten off with a fine, and many others appear to have been acquitted.[75] But the two oligarchs did not escape. They were sentenced to death and executed. Their property was confiscated, their houses torn down, their bodies denied burial in Attica or any land under Athenian control, and they and their descendants and any one who might adopt their descendants deprived of the rights of citizenship. Their condemnation and punishment were to be in-

---

Although the evidence is inadequate to allow confidence, the reconstruction is at least plausible.

[72][Plut.] *Mor.* 833e–f. For Andron's membership in the Four Hundred, see *FGrH* III, 342 Fr. 5a.

[73]Lys. 12.67: βουλόμενος δὲ τῷ ὑμετέρῳ πλήθει δοκεῖν πιστὸς εἶναι.

[74]8.68.2. Thucydides says that the charge was taking part in establishing the Four Hundred. That could not have been the formal charge, which was the one made in the motion of Andron, but it was widely believed to be the underlying complaint. See *HCT* V, 176, 198–201.

[75]Lys. 20.14; Jameson, *Historia* XX (1971), 553–555.

scribed on a bronze stele to be placed near the ones bearing the decrees concerning Phrynichus, and stones were to be placed on the former sites of their houses bearing the legend "Land of Archeptolemus and Antiphon the two traitors."[76]

The fate of Archeptolemus and Antiphon should have been enough to drive any remaining extremists into flight and to end any further threat of betrayal of the city to the enemy. It probably also succeeded in gaining the moderates greater confidence from the masses who still may have been suspicious about their role in the Four Hundred. Certainly, Thymochares retained his naval command, and Theramenes sailed to the Hellespont, where he served in close collaboration with Thrasybulus and Alcibiades.[77] It seems likely that the moderates now thought the new regime sufficiently secure and could turn their attention to prosecuting the war.

[76][Plut.] *Mor.* 834.
[77]Thymochares: Xen 1.1.1; Theramenes; Andrewes, *JHS* LXXIII (1953), 2–3.

9. The War in the Hellespont

The moderate regime had moved to defend its position in Athens from betrayal by oligarchic extremists and from suspicions that its leaders were too closely associated with them. Before long, however, it faced a new external challenge to Athens' control of the Hellespont, its grain supply, and the very survival of the city. In August of 411, a small but effective Peloponnesian fleet had made its way to Byzantium and caused a rebellion there and in some neighboring towns.[1] The Spartans were unable to exploit the opportunity fully because of quarrels within the Peloponnesian forces and the hopes some of them still had that Tissaphernes would bring on the Phoenician fleet.

We may be sure that the new navarch Mindarus received instructions before he left, and it is more than likely that the orders reflected a growing disenchantment with Tissaphernes. The satrap was not meeting his financial commitments; was oppressing Greeks in Ionia, at least in the eyes of many Peloponnesians on the spot; and seemed to be flirting with the enemy now that Alcibiades was back in the Athenian camp at Samos.[2] The political situation in Sparta had also changed. The original decision to move into Ionia in collaboration with Tissaphernes had been strongly influenced by Alcibiades and his friend Endius.[3] Since that time Alcibiades had turned his coat twice and had returned to the Athenian camp, Endius was no longer an ephor, and Tissaphernes had become an object of suspicion. Mindarus, therefore,

[1]See above, 8.80.3–4.
[2]For a useful discussion of possible Spartan thinking at this moment, see Lewis, *Sparta and Persia*, 110–114.
[3]8.5–6.

must have been given greater discretion than his predecessor to reassess the situation and to move the major effort from the Aegean to the Hellespont if he saw fit.

Still, he could not abandon Tissaphernes too soon. Although the satrap was paying badly, he had once paid well and might be persuaded to do so again. Besides, he had promised to bring the Phoenician fleet to Sparta's aid, and although he had not yet carried out that promise, the ships had arrived at Aspendus in June.[4] It would be rash to break off with him while there was still a chance he might deliver them. Finally, there was the treaty the Spartans had sworn with Persia that required them to work with Tissaphernes. Although they had much reason to complain of the Persians' failures to carry out their part of the bargain, those failures had to do chiefly with disagreements about amounts and schedules of payments and were not clear-cut. Mindarus may well have received orders telling him to ascertain once and for all whether the Phoenician fleet was coming. If he judged that it was not, that could be taken as a clear breach of the treaty and adequate grounds for the Spartans to ignore it.

Thucydides is certain that the Phoenician ships—147 of them—really had come to Aspendus.[5] They never sailed into the Aegean, however, and Thucydides is not entirely certain why. He reports three contemporary opinions and then gives his own: "To me it seems as clear as it can be that he did not bring on the fleet in order to wear out and paralyze the Greek forces, to let them decay while he was making the voyage to Aspendus and delaying there, and to create an equilibrium by joining neither side so as to make it stronger."[6] Modern scholars, however, have proposed another explanation, suggested by a passage in Diodorus: Tissaphernes defends his actions to the Spartans, explaining that he had sent the fleet back because he had learned that the kings of Arabia and Egypt were plotting against Phoenicia.[7] Moreover, Aramaic documents of the Persian Empire speak of revolts

---

[4]8.87.3. For the date, see D. M. Lewis, *Historia* VII (1958), 392.
[5]8.87.3. For different numbers given by other ancient writers, see *HCT* V, 290.
[6]8.87.4.
[7]13.46.6. Throughout book thirteen Diodorus confuses Tissaphernes with Pharnabazus, attributing the acts of both to Pharnabazus and never mentioning Tissaphernes. As Lewis (*Historia* VII [1958], 393) points out, the man doing the fighting described here must be Pharnabazus, but the explanation can only have been given by Tissaphernes. In spite of the confusion, we seem to have an explanation offered after the fact by Tissaphernes to the Spartans. Whether it was true or false, there is no reason to doubt that it was put forward.

in Egypt that might belong to this period. Some scholars believe that the danger was so great "that the fleet was removed from Tissaphernes' command and returned to Phoenicia, where it might be needed in operations against the rebels."[8] But it would be surprising, though not impossible, if such an important rebellion with such a significant outcome took place and Thucydides knew nothing about it.[9] The new evidence, moreover, says nothing about any Arabian activity and little about the extent and importance of the Egyptian movements, which, in any case, cannot be dated with precision or certainty. There may have been some truth in all of the motives of Tissaphernes reported by Thucydides: to exhaust the Peloponnesian forces, to defend himself before the Spartans against charges of treachery, and perhaps even to blackmail the Phoenician sailors into paying him money for releasing them from service, but the best explanation seems to be his own. Tissaphernes never intended to use the fleet but meant to wear down and equalize both sides so that he would be in control. We need not doubt that the satrap explained his behavior to the Spartans as caused by a major threat to Phoenicia, but that was only a pretext.[10]

Mindarus stayed at Miletus for over a month in the hope that the Phoenician ships would appear.[11] The delay must have been most annoying, for the lieutenants Tissaphernes had left behind at Miletus, principally the Egyptian Tamos, provided no support at all.[12] But the Phoenician ships did not come. The strain was even greater because

[8]Lewis, *Historia* VII (1958), 396, endorsed by Andrewes, *HCT* V, 290, 445–456.

[9]D. Lateiner (*TAPA* CVI [1976], 267–290), argues strongly against the likelihood that such an event could have escaped the historian's notice and narrative and supports Thucydides' own interpretation. He emphasizes the poor record of the Phoenician fleet against the Greeks and believes, therefore, that Tissaphernes never intended to use it because, among other reasons, it could not have been the decisive force Thucydides expected it to be.

[10]Lewis (*Historia* VII [1958], 396) says: "Alternately [to the theory of a real and serious revolt in Egypt], but perhaps less probably, Tissaphernes decided that he did not want the fleet, but used the Egyptian revolt as a plausible excuse for the Spartans." Not only would I reverse the order of probability, I would also point out that the passage in Diodorus (13.46.6) does not speak of a revolt in Egypt but of a plot against Phoenicia. There is no reason why Diodorus' source should have gotten Tissaphernes' excuse wrong; the reference, therefore, does not support the conclusions Lewis draws from the Aramaic documents.

[11]Diod. 13.38.4. Mindarus arrived early in August; Thucydides places Mindarus' decision to leave Miletus "about the same time" (ὑπὸ δὲ τοὺς αὐτοὺς χρόνους, 8.99.1) as the flight of the oligarchs from Athens and the betrayal of Oenoe (8.98), which Andrewes (*HCT* V, 341) persuasively puts late in September or even early in October. Those dates would have Mindarus waiting at Miletus between six and eight weeks.

[12]8.99; Tamos: 8.32.1, 87.3; *HCT* V, 74.

Pharnabazus continued to urge the Spartan admiral to bring his fleet into the Hellespont and cause rebellions in the cities of the Athenian Empire on their shores. Finally, Mindarus received the word that set him free. When Tissaphernes sailed to Aspendus, the Spartans sent one of their officers, Philippus, with him. Now Mindarus received letters from Philippus and from another Spartan, Hippocrates, who was stationed at Phaselis near by, telling him that Tissaphernes was deceiving the Spartans, that the ships would never come because they had set sail and were on the way back to Phoenicia.[13] This gave Mindarus hard proof that Tissaphernes would not keep his promise, and he released the Spartans from their obligations to the deceptive satrap. They were now free to go to the Hellespont, join his rival Pharnabazus, and try to end the war quickly by cutting off Athens' main source of food.

The Peloponnesian fleet under Astyochus at Mycale had numbered 112 ships. Since that time 10 of their ships had gotten through the Hellespont to raise rebellions at Byzantium and in neighboring cities; either Astyochus or Mindarus had sent another 16 ships to reinforce them.[14] These 16 ships had gained control of part of the Chersonnesus on the European side of the straits. Now Mindarus sent a squadron of 13 ships under the Thurian commander Dorieus to cope with a rebellion that threatened Spartan control of Rhodes.[15] Although he was shifting the main theater of operations to the Hellespont, Mindarus could not ignore the threat in the south, especially since Alcibiades had taken a fleet of 13 ships in that direction when he heard of Tissaphernes' voyage to Aspendus.[16]

The Spartan admiral faced no easy task, for between the remaining 73 ships at Miletus and his goal to the north lay the Athenian naval base at Samos. When last encountered there, the Athenians had disposed of 108 triremes, which the Spartans had been unwilling to engage

[13] Thucydides does not say that the ships had sailed eastward, but Diodorus (13.38.5) flatly reports that Tissaphernes "sent the fleet back to Phoenicia" ἀπέστειλε τὸν στόλον εἰς Φοινίκην, and there is no reason to doubt him. At this point, he clearly knows some facts omitted by Thucydides. In the same passage, for instance, he tells us that Mindarus sent Dorieus to Rhodes with a small fleet, a fact confirmed by Xenophon (1.1.2).

[14] Mycale: 8.79.1; ten to the Hellespont: 8.80.3–4. Thucydides mentions the sixteen reinforcing ships in 8.99 as having been sent "earlier in the same summer," but he does not say just when or who sent them.

[15] Diod. 13.38.5.

[16] 8.88.

with 112 ships. Since then the Athenians had sent 20 ships to meet the Spartan challenge in the Hellespont and 13 with Alcibiades, leaving 75.[17] Mindarus did not want to risk a battle at such odds if he could help it. Although a naval battle at some time was inevitable, the Spartans would prefer to fight it in the confined waters of the Hellespont, always near land, where they could enjoy the support of the Persian army of Pharnabazus, rather than to face the more experienced and skillful Athenians on the open sea in the familiar waters around Samos. Mindarus, therefore, planned to sneak past the Athenians. Acting swiftly and secretly, he put his fleet into good order and suddenly headed westward out to sea in the hope of slipping past Samos before the Athenians knew he was gone. A storm came up, however, forcing him to take shelter at Icarus for five or six days (see Map 3), but his luck was not entirely bad, for he was able to make his way to Chios without being intercepted.[18]

Alcibiades was away in the south, and Thrasybulus had been sent ahead to deal with a revolt at Eresus on Lesbos,[19] so Thrasyllus, not an experienced commander, was in charge on Samos. He had been raised from the rank of mere hoplite to the office of general, although he appears never to have commanded a regiment or a ship. His important role in checking the oligarchic rebellion on Samos seems to have been the chief reason for his popularity and his election,[20] but his inexperience would soon prove costly.

The escape of the Spartan fleet was not the only problem facing the new commander of the Athenian forces on Samos. A rebellion had once again broken out on the important and troublesome island of Lesbos. The city of Methymna on the northern shore of the island (see Map 3) had been one of Athens' staunchest allies. The Methymnaeans were the only loyal Lesbians during the great Mytilenian rebellion of 428/27 and, along with the Chians, were the only autonomous allies still providing ships instead of tribute at the time of the Sicilian campaign.[21] The Sicilian disaster, however, shook even its

[17]See HCT V, 31, 344. Thrasybulus took five ships to deal with a rebellion at Eresus (8.100.4–5), but we cannot be sure just when.
[18]8.99.
[19]8.100.1, 4–5.
[20]For the career of Thrasyllus, see the fine article of W. J. McCoy, AJP XCVIII (1977), 264–289. For his early career and rise to influence, see 265–266.
[21]3.2, 5, 18, 50; 6.85; 7.57. At 6.85.2 the Athenian Euphemus refers to the Chians and Methymnians as both being autonomous and providing ships: νεῶν παροκωχῇ αὐτόνομους. At 7.57.5, speaking in his own voice, Thucydides describes the Chians

solidarity. The arrival of a Spartan fleet in 412 brought it into rebellion, but the Athenians were quickly able to recover the town, along with the rest of the island.[22] The rebellion had been led by the aristocrats in the city, and the restoration had driven them into exile. The aristocrats had recruited about 300 mercenaries from the mainland under a Theban commander named Anaxarchus and had attacked their city. Driven off with the help of an Athenian garrison from Mytilene, they refused to give up, marched to Eresus in the southwestern portion of the island, and brought it into rebellion.[23]

The problem presented by the defection of Eresus was not especially serious. The other cities on the island were secure, there was a garrison at least at Mytilene, and Thrasybulus had already sailed to Eresus with five ships, a force that arrived too late to prevent the fall of the city but was adequate to keep the situation in hand.[24] With the knowledge that the Spartans were at Chios in force and on their way to the Hellespont, Thrasyllus should have sailed to Chios at once to force a battle, if possible, but at least to guarantee that Mindarus would not get through. Instead, he hurried to Lesbos with fifty-five ships, leaving the rest to guard his base on Samos. At Lesbos he added the small Methymnaean navy and two Athenian ships returning from the Hellespont, bringing his fleet up to sixty-five triremes. With the soldiers from this force, he was determined to recover Eresus by assault or by whatever means might be necessary. At the same time, he was sure that he could keep Mindarus at Chios by placing lookouts at both ends of the island and on the mainland opposite its eastern end.[25] In full

---

as autonomous and providing ships but the Methymnians as being "subjects" who supply "ships and not tribute": Μηθυμναῖοι μὲν ναυσὶ καὶ οὐ φόρῳ ὑπήκοοι. For a discussion of the difference in terminology, see *HCT* IV, 434–435.

[22]8.22–23.

[23]8.100.3.

[24]Thucydides tells us (8.100.4–5) that Thrasybulus sailed from Samos only after hearing that the exiles were crossing over from Methymna to Eresus. That suggests that he was not unduly alarmed by events on Lesbos. He rightly relied on the garrison and the loyal citizens to save Methymna and thought that a small force was adequate to deal with Eresus. Presumably, the Spartans had not yet left harbor at Miletus or, at least, the Athenians did not know they had.

[25]That is my understanding of 8.100.2: σκοποὺς μὲν κατεστήσατο καὶ ἐν τῇ Λέσβῳ καὶ ἐν τῇ ἀντιπέρας ἠπείρῳ. Andrewes (*HCT* V, 344–345) believes that the lookouts were located on the Erythrae peninsula opposite Chios and on the south coast of Lesbos, from which they might see ships coming from Chios in any direction. Perhaps that is where Thrasyllus should have placed them, but we must remember that he had no experience in such matters and that the lookouts failed to detect the Spartan ships. Thucydides' language, moreover, seems to suit the interpretation offered here.

confidence he sailed along the coast to Methymna and ordered food to be prepared for a long stay during which he would use Lesbos as a base for attacking the Spartans at Chios.[26]

In his inexperience and his eagerness to accomplish everything at once, Thrasyllus failed to carry out his major responsibility. As the Athenians attacked the walls of Eresus in leisurely fashion, never thinking that the Spartans could pass them unnoticed, Mindarus used his opportunity.[27] He stayed at Chios for only two days, just long enough to take on food and some money for the dash northward. Well before dawn on the third day, he sailed not in a westerly direction toward the open sea, where the Athenians at Eresus would be more likely to detect him, but eastward, toward the narrow waters between Lesbos and the mainland.[28] By noon he was safely at the Phocaean coast; he had his evening meal opposite Mytilene, stopped again briefly in the dark opposite Methymna, and about midnight dropped anchor safely at Rhoeteum and Sigeum, at the mouth of the Hellespont. He had traveled some 110 miles in about twenty hours, eluded the Athenians, changed the theater of operations, and altered the course and nature of the war. His was a daring and imaginative achievement worthy of the highest praise. The Athenians' failure to prevent it was a serious error that endangered the very existence of their city.

The eighteen Athenian ships stationed at Sestos received the news of the Spartan fleet's arrival by fire signals from their lookouts on the heights of Gallipoli, and the blaze of the Peloponnesian campfires on the Asian shore opposite them confirmed it (see Map 8).[29] Confronted by overwhelming numerical superiority, they had no choice but to try to escape as quickly as possible before their path was blocked. They set out at once under cover of darkness, keeping close to the European shore of the straits, in the direction of Elaeus and the open sea. They succeeded in escaping the notice of the sixteen Peloponnesian ships on guard at Abydos, even though these ships had been alerted in advance by a messenger ship sent by Mindarus to keep watch and prevent their

---

[26]8.100. Diodorus (13.38.7–39.1) offers a different explanation for the Athenians' action. He says they went to Lesbos with only sixty ships and waited there for reinforcements to arrive from their allies. Only three had arrived when they learned that Mindarus had passed them, so they pursued him to the Hellespont. Thucydides' account here is detailed and informed, and we should prefer it.

[27]8.103.2.

[28]We must accept Haacke's emendation ‹οὐ› πελάγιαι (8.101.1) with most editors and against Grote. See Busolt, *GG* III:2, 1516, n. 2.

[29]8.102.2.

escape.[30] At dawn the Athenians encountered Mindarus, who gave chase but was able to capture only four ships; the others made their way safely to the islands of Lemnos and Imbros. After a vain attempt to take the Athenian base at Elaeus, Mindarus took his fleet back to the main Spartan base at Abydos. Two stragglers who had pursued too far and had been late in getting back fell into the hands of the Athenian fleet, only now arriving at the Hellespont from Lesbos, too late to prevent the union of Mindarus with the Peloponnesian fleet at Abydos. The next day the Athenians arrived at Elaeus and brought back the ships that had taken refuge at Imbros. For the next five days they prepared their ships, planned strategy, and practiced their technique under the watchful eye of the commander-in-chief, Thrasybulus.[31]

When he was ready, he sent the Athenian fleet, 76 strong, into the Hellespont toward Sestos in a single column close to the Gallipoli shore.[32] Grote is very critical of the Athenian strategy: "The description of the battle tells us how much Athenian manoeuvring had fallen off since the glories of Phormion at the beginning of the Peloponnesian war; nor would that eminent seaman have selected for the scene of a naval battle the narrow waters of the Hellespont."[33] But this judgment ignores the serious limitations within which Thrasybulus had to work. Once Thrasyllus had allowed the Peloponnesians to get past him and into the Hellespont, the Athenians had no choice but to follow. Not to challenge Mindarus' control of the straits would have been to allow

[30] 8.102.2: προειρημένης φυλακῆς τῷ φιλίῳ ἐπίπλῳ, ὅπως αὐτῶν ἀνακῶς ἕξουσιν, ἤν ἐκπλέωσιν is very difficult to interpret and has been understood differently by various editors. The meaning accepted here is based on the suggestion of a scholiast. Andrewes (HCT V, 349–350) also prefers that interpretation and provides a valuable discussion of alternatives. He ignores, however, Grote's very different interpretation (VIII, 106, n. 1), which argues that Mindarus' message to the fleet at Sestos was to keep watch for his main Peloponnesian fleet sailing into the straits so that it could come to his rescue if he were being pursued by the fleet of Thrasyllus. This is not without its own difficulties but might be right.

[31] 8.102.2–103. Thucydides tells us only that "they prepared for the battle for five days." Neither he nor Diodorus (13.39–40) tells us who was in command, although both mention Thrasybulus and Thrasyllus, and Thucydides speaks of "other generals." I deduce that Thrasybulus was in general command from the fact that he was an experienced trierarch and Thrasyllus was not; from the fact that he commanded the right wing, which was both the place of honor and, in this battle, the crucial location; and from the fact that it was he who set up the trophy of victory (Diod. 13.40.6).

[32] 8.104.1–2. For the number, see HCT V, 351. The description of the battle of Cynossema that follows is based on 8.104–106 and Diod. 13.39–40.

[33] VIII, 110.

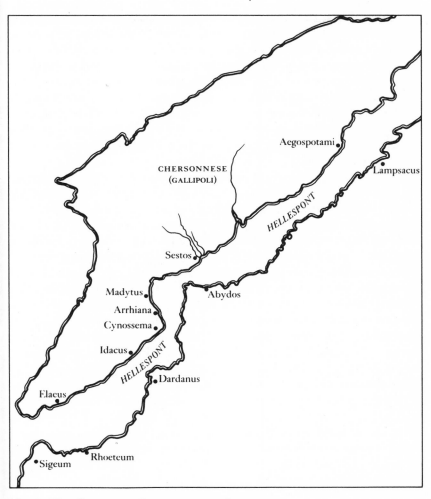

MAP 8. THE BATTLES OF CYNOSSEMA AND ABYDOS

the Spartans to cut off the grain route. Unless the Spartan admiral were foolish enough to come out and challenge them in more open waters, and he was not that foolish, they must fight him within its narrow confines. Perhaps Thrasybulus exercised his crews for as long as five days in the hope that Mindarus would make the mistake of seeking them out, but when it was clear he would not, there was no point in further delay. Once they had made the decision to enter the Hellespont, moreover, the Athenians' only reasonable plan was to move forward in single column, so as to be able to turn most swiftly and simply to meet any enemy attack. By staying close to the European shore, they remained closer to the safety of their bases, should they be needed, and they gave themselves the fullest possible time to react to an enemy assault.

Circumstances, therefore, had given the Spartans almost every advantage in the battle to come. With eighty-six ships they had a significant numerical superiority.[34] They were able to fight with their base near by at their backs, and they could choose the place and moment of attack that suited them best. Mindarus' plan of battle made good use of all of these advantages. He positioned his ships between Abydos and Dardanus, a distance of some seven and one-half miles.[35] Placing the Syracusans on the right, the farthest up into the Hellespont, he himself took command of the left wing, nearest its mouth.[36] He allowed the Athenian column to move forward until its left wing had passed the promontory called "Bitch's Tomb" (Cynossema), so called because the tomb of Hecuba, changed into a dog according to legend, sat on its heights. The Athenian line stretched from Arrhiana on the left to Idacus on the right.[37] When the center was just in front of Cynossema, where the strait was at its narrowest, he launched the first attack, hoping to use surprise, speed, and the weight of numbers to drive the enemy center toward the crowded waters near the shore, where the superior fighting ability of his marines would be most effective.[38] His own assignment was likely to be the most difficult: to outflank the enemy and cut off his escape, for Mindarus intended to

---

[34]For the number, see 8.103.1 and *HCT* V, 350–351.

[35]8.104.2.

[36]Diodorus (13.39.4) says that Hermocrates was in command, but he must be wrong, for Thucydides has told us that the Syracusan commander had already been relieved and had sailed off to Sparta (8.85).

[37]8.104.2. These locations are not known.

[38]For the superiority of the Peloponnesian marines, see Diod. 13.40.1.

use this very favorable opportunity to destroy the Athenian fleet entirely.[39] The center should have little trouble carrying out its part of the strategy; if it succeeded, the resulting weakness in the Athenian center might lure the right to hurry to its aid, thereby allowing Mindarus to cut them off. Should that occur, it would be relatively easy to catch the Athenian right between the victorious Peloponnesian center and the ships of Mindarus. After that it would not be difficult to destroy the isolated Athenian left at leisure.

Thrasybulus placed Thrasyllus at the head of the column, on the left wing opposite the Syracusans. He himself commanded the right, opposite Mindarus.[40] We cannot be confident of what strategy he may have planned in advance. Since the initiative lay with the enemy, he must be prepared to react swiftly to whatever occurred, but it was possible, at least, to try to anticipate Mindarus' strategy and to make contingent plans. Thrasybulus either anticipated the strategy very well, or he reacted with a shrewd and sure instinct when he saw the course of events.[41] Mindarus allowed the Athenian left under Thrasyllus to move beyond the narrows in front of the Cynossema promontory. When it had passed by, around the sharp bend that cut off the sight of the rest of the Athenian fleet, and when the center had come to the narrowest part of the strait, the Peloponnesian center launched its attack with excellent results. The left under Thrasyllus had its hands full with the ships in its waters and, in any case, could not could not see what was happening to the center because of the promontory that cut off vision down the strait.

The outcome of the battle hung on the action of the Athenian right under Thrasybulus. Had he tried to assist the center, he would have failed, because he would have been badly outnumbered by the combination of the enemy's center and left and would have been trapped between them. His ships and the entire Athenian fleet would have been annihilated. Thrasybulus, however, did not fall into the trap. When he saw Mindarus moving toward the mouth of the strait to cut off escape, he employed the greater speed of the Athenians to defeat

[39]For the most useful account of the battle, see Busolt, *GG* III:2, 1517–1519.
[40]Diodorus (13.39.4) erroneously reverses the position of Thrasyllus and Thrasybulus.
[41]Thucydides' language seems to me compatible with either possibility. After describing the Peloponnesian intentions he says: οἱ Ἀθηναῖοι γνόντες (8.104.4). γνόντες could mean "knowing the enemy's intentions" or "perceiving what the enemy was doing."

the maneuver and extend his line beyond that of the enemy. The price of this necessary tactic, however, was to weaken the line, most seriously in the center, which was under the most intense pressure. The Peloponnesians easily defeated the outnumbered and isolated Athenian center, drove many ships aground, and even landed troops to follow up their success. At this critical moment the Peloponnesians' inexperience and lack of discipline cost them the victory. Had they reorganized their line and joined the left wing of Mindarus in pursuit of the ships of Thrasybulus, they probably would have sunk or captured many of them. At the least, they would have been able to destroy the forces under Thrasyllus, win a great victory, and establish firm control of the Hellespont. Instead, emboldened by their victory, individual ships began to pursue single Athenian triremes, some pursuing one, others another, until their own line was in disorder. At just the right moment, Thrasybulus struck. He stopped extending the line away from the center, turned to face the ships of Mindarus that were coming at him, and routed them. Then he turned on the disordered Peloponnesian center and wrought havoc. With their discipline already broken, the Peloponnesian ships fled without a fight. Moving in the direction of Sestos, they came around the bend of Cynossema. Thrasyllus' left wing had been giving a good account of itself and forcing the Syracusans back; when the latter suddenly saw their comrades appear in flight, they, too, broke and fled. In full rout, the entire Peloponnesian fleet finally sought shelter at its base in Abydos.

The above account of the battle comes from Thucydides, and most modern treatments of it have been content to stop there, ignoring Diodorus' narrative as of little or no value.[42] To be sure, Diodorus' version is full of errors and grossly inferior, but it is, in fact, a valuable supplement and helps explain important aspects of the battle taken for granted, no doubt by Thucydides, and therefore omitted. Naturally, Thucydides' description is that of an admiral, one that surveys the entire field of battle from the standpoint of the commanders, moving wings, centers, and entire fleets. What comes through Diodorus' account is something much rarer, the view from the decks of individual ships as it might be seen by individual trierarchs trying to explain in much narrower but finer detail what happened and why. The broad

---

[42]Grote (VIII, 110, n. 1) says that Diodorus' version is "not reconcilable with Thucydides. It is vain to try to blend them." Busolt (*GG* III:2, 1519 n. 1) says that "the narrative of Ephorus (Diod. 13.39–40) is worthless."

overview is missing, but the details are important, and there is no reason why we should doubt their authenticity.[43]

Diodorus tells us that the Peloponnesians had better marines, which helps us understand why they were so successful in the center, where the fighting must have been at close quarters and grappling and boarding possible. They would also have been important when the Athenians were driven to the shore, and in that part of the field, the sea battle became a land battle. On the other hand, he tells us that the steersmen of the Athenians, "who were far superior in experience, contributed greatly to the victory."[44] Andrewes has rightly pointed out that Thucydides' excellent account nonetheless has gaps: "It is not fully clear how Thrasyboulos at 105.3 was able to put to flight the ships that pressed so hard on him at 105.2 (it was the Peloponnesian centre that fell into disorder, not the left wing)."[45] Here is where Diodorus can help us. Events in the center, we may deduce from Thucydides, changed Thrasybulus' tactics. He no longer sought to escape being blocked by Mindarus. The confusion in the Peloponnesian center led him to seek battle with Mindarus quickly so that he might defeat him in time to take advantage of the disorder, without being caught between two orderly lines of the enemy. But how, as Andrewes asks, did he defeat Mindarus? We can do no better than quote Diodorus in reply:

The skill of the Athenian pilots rendered the superiority of their opponents [in number and in the quality of marines] of no effect. For whenever the Peloponnesians with their ships in a body, would charge swiftly forward to ram, the pilots would manoeuvre their own ships so skilfully that their opponents were unable to strike them at any other spot but only meet them bows on, ram against ram. Consequently Mindarus, seeing that the force of the rams was proving ineffective, gave orders for his ships to come to grips in small groups, or one at a time. But not by this manoeuvre either, as it turned out, was the skill of the Athenian pilots rendered ineffective; on the contrary, cleverly avoiding the on-coming rams of the ships, they struck them on the side and damaged many.[46]

---

[43]After a long period of being treated with contempt, Diodorus' narrative, especially of naval battles in this period, has been accorded greater respect in recent years. (See I. A. F. Bruce, *An Historical Commentary on the* Hellenica Oxyrhynchia [Cambridge, 1967], 20–22; R. J. Littman, *TAPA* XCIX [1968], 265–272; Paul Pédech, *REG* LXXXII [1969], 43–55.) The quality of the detail offered by Diodorus here, moreover, seems in itself to speak in favor of authenticity.

[44]13.39.5.

[45]*HCT* V, 354.

[46]13.40.1–2, translated by C. H. Oldfather in vol. 5 of the Loeb edition.

By use of such skills and superior speed, as well as by the brilliant and resourceful leadership of Thrasybulus, the Athenians were able to defeat their opponents. Thrasybulus' crew set up the trophy of victory on top of the Cynossema promontory and sent messengers to bring the happy news to Athens.[47] In spite of routing the enemy, however, the Athenians were able to capture only twenty-one ships while losing fifteen of their own.[48] Thucydides tells us that the Athenians received the news of the victory as "unhoped for good fortune." They had won no important victory since the Sicilian campaign and had suffered a series of losses in Ionia and the straits. Worst of all was the terrible loss of Euboea. The timing of the news was almost as important as the victory itself, for it came just after the loss of Euboea and the internal strife surrounding the overthrow of the Four Hundred. It gave a remarkable boost to the sagging spirits of the Athenians: "They were greatly encouraged, and they thought that their cause could still win out if they set to work zealously."[49] Modern historians have undervalued the importance of this victory by Thrasybulus and the Athenians, making no comment or limiting its significance to its effect on Athenian morale.[50] In fact, it was of the greatest importance to the course of the war. It may be justly said of Thrasybulus at Cynossema, as it was later said of Jellicoe at Jutland, that he could have lost the war in the space of a single afternoon. Had Mindarus succeeded in annihilating the Athenian fleet on that early October day in 411, had he merely defeated it and maintained control of the straits, the Athenians probably would have been forced to surrender before very long. They had no funds to build a new fleet and, therefore, no way to gain access to the food they needed for survival. The news of their defeat, moreover, coming on the heels of their loss of Euboea, would almost surely have caused new defections in the empire, in Ionia

[47]Diod. 13.40.6: οἱ περὶ τὸν Θρασύβουλον ἔστησαν τρόπαιον ἐπὶ τῆς ἄκρας. Oldfather says "Thrasybulus set up a trophy," but that must be shorthand. "Those around Thrasybulus," as the Greek reads, must, I presume, refer to the crew of his own trireme. The significance is the same in either case: Thrasybulus made the greatest contribution.

[48]8.106. Diodorus' list (13.40.5) is almost identical.

[49]8.106.5.

[50]For example, Grote (VIII, 112) says that "it produced no very important consequences except that of encouragement to the Athenians." Meyer (GdA, IV, 308) says nothing about its significance; Busolt (GG III:2, 1519) calls it the most important maritime victory after the Sicilian catastrophe but limits his comment to its effect on morale; Beloch (GG II:1, 393) calls it "a victory more of moral than of material significance."

and the islands, and in the enemy-occupied Hellespontine region. The victory of Cynossema prevented all that and kept Athens in the war with a chance to emerge from it intact and with honor. When we consider the disadvantages under which the Athenians fought, we cannot fail to award high praise to them and their remarkable commander.

Thrasybulus and his colleagues wasted little time in exploiting their victory. At some time before the battle, Cyzicus, in the Propontis (see Map 5), had revolted from the Athenians and had called in Pharnabazus and the Spartan commander Clearchus, who had marched to the Hellespont from Miletus during the summer.[51] Sailing from their base at Sestos, the Athenians came to Priapus and Harpagium. Anchored before these towns, they found eight ships from the squadron the Megarian Helixus had managed to get through to bring about the rebellion of Byzantium about the same time as Clearchus' march.[52] They easily defeated and captured this small force and the army defending it on land. After that they went on to the unwalled city of Cyzicus, demanded a money payment, and forced it back into the Athenian Empire.[53]

When the Athenians returned to their base, they found that Mindarus had made good use of their absence. He had made a raid on Elaeus, where the Athenians had taken the Spartan ships captured at Cynossema, and had recaptured those that the Elaeans had not already burned. He also had sent messengers to the Peloponnesian fleet at Euboea, asking Agesandridas to send reinforcements for the next battle in the Hellespont that was sure to come. Fifty ships sailed to join Mindarus, undoubtedly leaving Euboea almost entirely without a naval force.[54] Not long after the battle of Cynossema, the Athenians had a fleet of 74 triremes with which they had to face 97 under Mindarus. If all of the 50 ships from Euboea had reached him, he would have commanded a fleet of about 140 ships, an overwhelming force that would have guaranteed victory, even against the more skillful Athenians.[55] On this occasion, however, fortune favored the Athenians.

[51] 8.80.3.
[52] 8.80.4.
[53] 8.107.1.
[54] 8.107.2. Agesandridas came to Euboea with forty-two ships (8.94.1) and captured twenty-two from the Athenians (8.95.7). The number of ships sent to Mindarus is reported by Diodorus (13.41.1–2).
[55] The number is approximate but fairly accurate. After Cynossema, Mindarus had

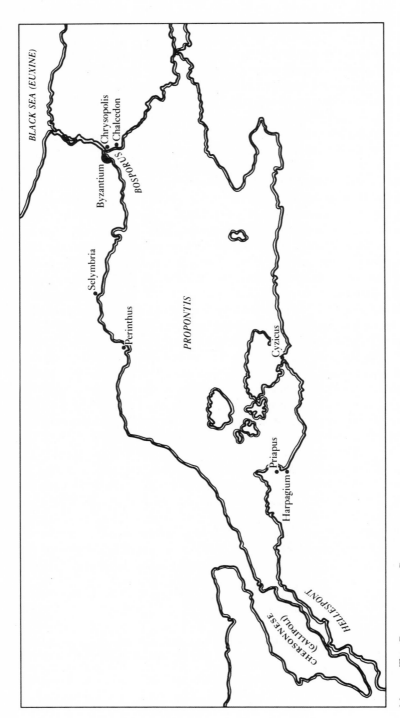

MAP 9. THE BOSPORUS AND PROPONTIS

The ships were wrecked in a storm off Mt. Athos, and only a few got through to Mindarus, one of them commanded by Agesandridas.[56] As he made his way into the Hellespont with the battered remains of his fleet, he encountered Thymochares, the Athenian commander at Euboea, who was bringing as reinforcements to Thrasybulus the 14 ships that remained after his defeat there. Another battle ensued, and once again the forces under Agesandridas defeated their Athenian opponents, but both fleets seem to have gotten some ships through to reinforce their Hellespontine commanders-in-chief.[57]

Recognizing that the next battle could be decisive, that any solid naval victory over the Athenians could bring an end to the war, Mindarus also sent word to Rhodes asking Dorieus to bring his fleet north to the Hellespont.[58] About the same time that Mindarus had moved to the Hellespont, probably late in September, he had sent the Thurian commander to prevent a rebellion in Rhodes.[59] Also about the same time, Alcibiades returned to Samos from the southern coast of Asia Minor, where he had gone after Tissaphernes had joined the Phoenician fleet at Aspendus. We cannot be sure that he even met with the satrap.[60] But when the Phoenician fleet sailed home, Alcibiades hurried

sixty-seven ships left. At Abydos a little later, according to Diodorus (13.45.6), he had eighty-four. The additional seventeen came from those ships recovered from Elaeus and whatever few escaped the storm off Mt. Athos. My estimate here places that figure at seven. Diodorus' figures are probably not completely correct, and the estimate I have made may be somewhat incorrect, but that Peloponnesian superiority was overwhelming is evident.

[56]Diod. 13.41.1–3. Neither Thucydides nor Xenophon mentions the storm and the loss of the ships, but those events fall into the gap where the two histories merge imperfectly. Diodorus cites a verse inscription set up at the temple at Coroneia in Boeotia by some survivors. We need not doubt the reality of the disaster, although Diodorus' numbers may not be accurate. See Busolt, GG III:2, 1522, n. 1.

[57]Xen. 1.1.1; Busolt, GG III:2, 1522 and nn. 1 and 2. Although we have no evidence to prove it, Agesandridas may have gained the support of some Peloponnesian ships, for he was probably outnumbered. Perhaps ten or so of his ships got through. But some of Thymochares' ships, perhaps five, must have gotten through, too, for the Athenian fleet, sixty-one after Cynossema, grew to seventy-four at Abydos. Busolt attributes the entire growth of thirteen to the arrival of Thymochares, forgetting the eight ships the Athenians captured after Cynossema (8.107.1).

[58]Xenophon (1.1.2) tells us only that Dorieus arrived with fourteen ships. Diodorus (13.45.1), however, makes it clear that Mindarus was summoning help from every quarter to his base at Abydos.

[59]Diod. 13.38.5.

[60]No ancient source says that he did. Thucydides says only that when Alcibiades learned that Tissaphernes was going to Aspendus, "he also sailed out"; he aimed not at Aspendus, however, but rather at Phaselis and Caunus nearby (8.88), and it is from Caunus and Phaselis that he returned (8.108.1). It is Thucydides' opinion that Alci-

back to the main Athenian base to claim credit for preventing its coming and for making Tissaphernes more friendly to the Athenians than before.[61] Although the greater part of the fleet had gone to the Hellespont under Thrasybulus, Alcibiades did not take his thirteen ships to join it. Instead, he added nine of the triremes guarding Samos to his own fleet and sailed in the direction of Caria. Dorieus' fleet at Rhodes posed a threat to Athenian positions in that neighborhood, and Alcibiades could use his visit to collect some badly needed funds. At Halicarnassus he collected a great deal of money. From there he sailed to Cos, where he built a fort and left an Athenian official in charge of it. The action at Cos was effective, for the Carian cities near by appear to have remained under Athenian control almost until the end of the war. When he returned to Samos "toward autumn" (late September), he shrewdly shared the money he had gathered with the troops there, adding to his popularity as well as relieving a serious shortage of funds.[62]

Full of achievements, both real and pretended, Alcibiades remained at Samos, apparently inactive, while the outnumbered forces of Thrasybulus fought for survival at Cynossema and while both sides sought reinforcements for the next round. The ancient writers neither noticed nor explained his inactivity.[63] Someone had to command the Athenian fleet at Samos and guard the Aegean, but since the departure of Mindarus to the north, that was not a major responsibility requiring the

---

biades knew that the satrap would never bring the ships into the Aegean and that Alcibiades' purposes in going after him were to gain credit for preventing their arrival, to discredit Tissaphernes thereby in the eyes of the Peloponnesians, and so to increase the likelihood of bringing him over to the Athenian side. For those purposes it would not be necessary to see or talk with the satrap but merely to be in his neighborhood and *seem* to be doing so.

[61] 8.108.1.

[62] 8.108.2; Diod. 13.42.2–3; Hatzfeld, *Alcibiade*, 262.

[63] Modern historians have done little better. Hatzfeld (*Alcibiade*, 262 and n. 2) deals with the problem by improperly diminishing it. He explains Alcibiades' decision to go back to Samos from Caria on the grounds that he heard that Dorieus was on his way to the Hellespont Alcibiades would then have followed immediately, stopping first at Samos before pursuing Dorieus to the north. But that misrepresents the chronology. Hatzfeld says that Alcibiades "seems not to have made a long stay" at Samos. In fact, he arrived at Samos "before the autumn" πρὸς τὸ μετόπωρον (8.108.2) and arrived in the Hellespont on the same day as Dorieus "at the beginning of winter," ἀρχομένου χειμῶνος, early November (Xen. 1.1.2). Dorieus could not have taken more than a month to go from Rhodes to the Hellespont, so the problem remains. Busolt recognizes the difficulty clearly: "What he did until the beginning of winter is unknown" (*GG* III:2, 1521). His own guess, that he was occupied with Dorieus' fleet, is shrewd but not precise enough.

presence of an important general. The fleet of Dorieus, on the other hand, continued to pose a possible threat to Athenian possessions. Perhaps more important, it was likely to be called to the Hellespont to reinforce Mindarus. Alcibiades might do more good by preventing Dorieus' arrival than by going to the Hellespont himself. It seems likely, therefore, that Alcibiades was ordered to stay at Samos to keep watch on Dorieus, meet any attacks he might make on Athenian allies, and, most important, prevent him from getting past Samos to the Hellespont. If indeed those were Alcibiades' responsibilities, he failed to carry out the most important one, for when he finally arrived in the Hellespont, it was on the heels of Dorieus, who had slipped by him.[64]

The Hellespont had become the center of attention for everyone, and Tissaphernes, too, was on his way there. The news that Mindarus had taken his fleet from Miletus to Abydos made the satrap quit Aspendus and travel north. He was jealous of Pharnabazus and fearful that his rival satrap, using less time and money, would succeed against the Athenians where he himself had failed.[65] But he was moved by a more tangible fear as well. The Greeks, recently under Persian sway at Cnidus and Miletus, had rebelled against Tissaphernes and had ejected his garrisons, although in the latter case the Spartan Lichas chastised the rebels and urged them to abide by Persian rule.[66] Now Tissaphernes learned that the Antandrians, on the Aegean coast opposite Lesbos (see Map 3), had collected hoplites from the Spartan base at Abydos, had marched them overland, and had driven his lieutenant Arsaces and the Persian garrison down from their acropolis and out of the city.[67] This was truly alarming. The Spartans were out of the Aegean, no longer dependent on Tissaphernes' money and promises, and very angry with him. They had already taken the first action against him at Antandrus, complaints against him were being heard in Sparta, and there was no telling what further harm his "allies" might yet do to him. His plan to keep the Athenians and Spartans roughly equal in strength, suing for his favor and under his control, so wearing them both out until he should have the final word, had gone awry

[64] I owe this understanding of Alcibiades' actions to David M. Weil, "Alcibiades' Role as a Naval General in the Peloponnesian War, 411–407 B.C." (Senior essay in History, Yale University, 1984).
[65] 8.108.3, 109.
[66] 8.109; Miletus: 8.84.
[67] 8.108.4–5.

when the fleet of Mindarus slipped by Thrasyllus to the Hellespont. Keeping the Athenian navy at Samos against such a move had been crucial not only for Athens' own interests but also for Tissaphernes' plan. He could engage in insolent deceptions and break his promises at will as long as the Athenians barred the way north. Their failure to do so changed everything. Tissaphernes hurried to complain of the assistance to Antandrus, make a defense against the charges lodged against him, and try to salvage something from the disaster that threatened his interests.[68]

At dawn on a day early in November, Dorieus sailed toward the mouth of the Hellespont with his fourteen ships from Rhodes.[69] He probably had hoped to slip by the Athenian lookouts under cover of darkness, as he may well have done to get by Alcibiades at Samos, but his timing was off, and he was seen sailing past Sigeum (see Map 8) at daybreak. The watchman signaled the news of his arrival to the Athenian generals at Sestos who swiftly sent a squadron of twenty triremes to cut him off. When Dorieus saw the Athenian ships bearing down on him, he fled to the shore and pulled his ships up on the beach near Rhoeteum. The Athenians pursued but were not prepared to prolong what amounted to a battle on land. They withdrew to Madytus, where they joined the rest of their fleet, which by this time was at sea and ready to fight. From there the whole fleet was in a better position than from Sestos to prevent the squadron of Dorieus from joining the main Peloponnesian fleet at Abydos. When Dorieus saw the Athenian squadron withdraw, he resumed his course up the Hellespont toward Abydos, but soon he was attacked again, this time by the entire Athenian force of seventy-four ships.[70] Overwhelmingly outnumbered, he had no choice but to put in to land at the first likely place, which was Dardanus. He pulled his ships onto the beach, dis-

---

[68]8.109.

[69]Xen. 1.1.2; Diod. 13.45.2. Busolt's reconstruction of the battle of Abydos (*GG* III:2, 1522–1523) is based entirely on the account of Xenophon (1.1.2–7); he regards the account of Diodorus as merely a transcription of that of Ephorus and considers it worthless (*GG* III:2, 1523, n. 1). We now have reason to believe that Diodorus may also have had the *Hellenica Oxyrhynchia* as a source—and a good one—for this period. Moreover, we cannot be sure that he had no other good sources. His account is fuller and, to my mind, more satisfactory than Xenophon's, although the latter seems to have some accurate information omitted by Diodorus. Grote (VIII, 117), without the benefit of valuable information available to us, nonetheless constructed his account from a combination of the two authors, rightly, I think.

[70]Diod. 13.45.2–3. Diodorus' numbers here are entirely plausible. After Cynossema the Athenians had sixty-one ships; they captured eight more in the Propontis, and Thymochares may well have brought them five more.

embarked the crews, and enlisted the troops guarding the city. He placed men at strategic locations on the beach and on the ships themselves, supplied them with spears and arrows, and prepared to defend the ships. The Athenians, now on hand with vastly superior forces, attacked to good effect and began to wear down the enemy.

Mindarus had been at Troy sacrificing to Athena when Dorieus put in at Rhoeteum. When he saw the battle there, he hurried to his base at Abydos and also must have sent word to Pharnabazus. By the time he prepared his fleet and sailed down the Hellespont to the rescue, it was afternoon and the Athenians had Dorieus pinned down at Dardanus.[71] Mindarus had eighty-four ships, and Pharnabazus had brought up an army to support Dorieus on land, so the Athenians were compelled to abandon their attack on land, withdraw into the straits, and place their ships into formation for a naval battle. The Peloponnesians' fleet, now joined with the squadron from Rhodes, numbered ninety-seven, and its line extended from Dardanus all the way to Abydos.[72]

Diodorus once again offers a combatant's view of the battle that, in spite of its rhetorical character, would be unwise to ignore. Mindarus this time commanded the right wing, nearest his base at Abydos, placing the Syracusans on the left. That put him opposite Thrasyllus, who commanded the Athenian left, while Thrasybulus was in charge on the right. The fighting began when the commanders on each side raised a visible signal on which trumpeters sounded the attack. This time we hear nothing of the superior skill of the Peloponnesian marines and the Athenian steersmen, although we may assume that nothing had changed in that respect. In this battle, however, Diodorus gives an account of how the marines on the decks of the triremes fared during a major battle:

Some, while they were still at a considerable distance apart, sent off a continuous rain of arrows, and the place was quickly full of missiles; others waited until each time the ships approached each other and hurled javelins, some aiming at the marines and others at the steersmen themselves. And whenever the ships came very close together they not only fought against each other with pikes but when they made contact they leaped onto the enemy's triremes and fought with swords. Each time someone was defeated the winners would

[71]For the timing, see Busolt, *GG* III:2, 1522.
[72]Diod. 13.45.6–7. Once again, the numbers given by Diodorus are very plausible. After Cynossema the Peloponnesians had sixty-seven ships. The additions from Agesandridas and from the ships recovered at Elaeus could easily have added up to seventeen. Dorieus must have lost one of his original fourteen to the Athenians to give the total of ninety-seven.

shout the war cry and the losers would cry out for help, so a mixed uproar sounded over the whole area of the battle.[73]

The battle continued fiercely and evenly for a long time. Finally, toward evening a fleet of eighteen ships appeared on the horizon.[74] At first, its allegiance was not obvious; since both sides had sent to their allies for assistance, each thought the new force was its own reinforcement and was encouraged. Then its commander, Alcibiades, ran up a red flag, a prearranged signal that told the Athenians the good news.[75] Although the ancient writers emphasize the fortuitous nature of his arrival, it was not unexpected, as the prearranged signal shows.[76] Alcibiades had been ordered to intercept Dorieus. When the Thurian and his fleet circumvented the Athenian position at Samos, Alcibiades must have set out in pursuit and sent a fast messenger ship ahead to warn Thrasybulus at Sestos. His message was probably something like this: "Dorieus has eluded me and is on his way to the Hellespont. I am following at top speed. When I arrive I will raise a red flag so you can recognize me at once." What was lucky was not the arrival of Alcibiades but its timing. He probably had little time to take part in the fighting, but his hot pursuit and good fortune made victory possible. His energy and luck retrieved a potentially serious mistake that might have had disastrous consequences and turned it into a great Athenian victory, but that was the extent of his contribution.

As soon as the Peloponnesians learned that the new arrivals were Athenian ships, they turned and fled toward Abydos. The Athenians pursued them eagerly and successfully, although they may have been hampered by a strong wind that came up and troubled the sea. The Peloponnesian ships were stretched out over a long distance, and many of them were unable to return safely to their base. Their captains were forced to beach their ships along the shore and to use them as a defensive barrier against the assault of the Athenians. In this they were aided considerably by Pharnabazus, who brought up his cavalry and infantry. He himself fought from horseback, even riding his horse into the sea to ward off the enemy. His intervention and the coming of

---

[73]Diod. 13.45.1–2.
[74]Xen. 1.1.6; Plut. *Alc.* 27.2. Diodorus (13.46.2) says the number was twenty, but I assume his source was rounding out the figure.
[75]Diod. 13.46.3.
[76]Diod. 13.46.2; Plut. *Alc.* 27.2. See also E. F. Bloedow, *Alcibiades Reexamined* (Wiesbaden, 1973), 43, n. 265.

darkness probably prevented a total disaster, but the cost of the battle was great enough. The Athenians captured thirty Peloponnesian ships and recovered the fifteen they had lost at Cynossema. Mindarus stole away to Abydos under cover of night with his remaining fleet, and the Athenians retired to Sestos. The next morning they returned at leisure to collect their damaged ships and set up another trophy of victory, not far from the first one at Cynossema.[77] Once again, the Athenians commanded the waters of the Hellespont.

For the rest of the winter, Mindarus stayed at Sestos repairing his fleet and sending to Sparta for both military and naval reinforcements. His plan was to join with Pharnabazus and attack Athenian allies on the Asian coast by land and sea.[78] The proper Athenian response would have been to maintain a superior fleet in the Hellespont, reinforce it, and try to bring on another battle to annihilate the remaining enemy force at Sestos. Failing that, and Mindarus was unlikely to oblige them by offering battle, the Athenians ought to have cut off any attempt at naval reinforcement to the enemy and moved to recover the cities that had rebelled from their empire in the region of the Hellespont, Propontis, and Bosporus.[79] The Athenians were prevented from taking these steps by their lack of money. While Pharnabazus continued to support the Spartans generously, the Athenian treasury was exhausted.[80] The Athenian crews could not sustain themselves without pay, and the treasury at Athens could not provide it. The battles at Cynossema and Abydos, moreover, had shown the importance of hoplites. The narrowness of the straits often led to the ships' being hauled up on shore, turning a sea battle into a fight on land, and the Athenian forces were short of hoplites.

The Athenian generals at Sestos, therefore, divided their fleet among themselves, along with their various responsibilities. Alcibiades and Chaereas commanded the forty ships that stayed on guard in the Hel-

---

[77]Diod. 13.47.1; Xen. 1.1.7.

[78]Diod. 13.47.2.

[79]Busolt (*GG* III:2, 1523–1524) thinks the Athenian generals intended to gather forces for an attack on Ionia, "since the enemy's main force was defeated and held fast in the Hellespont." But he takes no notice of the reinforcements that were on the way, the support of Pharnabazus, and the considerable fleet still under Mindarus' command. It would have been folly to sail out of the Hellespont with such an enemy force still intact.

[80]*ATL* III, 366; W. S. Ferguson, *The Treasurers of Athena* (Cambridge, Mass., 1932), 41; Meiggs, *Athenian Empire*, 370.

lespont at Sestos.[81] Thrasyllus, who had fought well but had not yet distinguished himself as an admiral, went to Athens to report the victory at Abydos and to ask for more hoplites and ships. He himself remained in Athens and did not reappear in the Hellespont until the autumn of 409,[82] but it may well be that the expedition of Theramenes was the Athenian response to his request, for that commander later joined the main Athenian force in time for the battle of Cyzicus.[83]

In any case, Theramenes sailed from the Piraeus to Euboea with thirty ships. His first mission was to prevent the Euboeans and the Boeotians from building a causeway between Chalcis and Aulis, connecting the island to the mainland. Eager to preserve their newly won freedom and fearful of Athenian naval power, the Euboean cities appear to have formed a league and asked the Boeotians to help them.[84] The success of such a project would make recovery of Euboea much harder for the Athenians, but Theramenes' force was too small to defeat the larger number of troops defending the workers, so he turned to other tasks. He devastated the land of the enemy, presumably along the Euboean and Boeotian coasts, collecting considerable booty. He also sailed among the islands of the Cyclades both to gather money and to put down oligarchies established in the time of the Four Hundred.[85] In this way, he gathered badly needed funds, cleared the islands of enemies of the new regime, enlisted democratic support there for the Athenian cause, and established his own and the Five Thou-

[81]Xen. 1.1.8–9; Diod. 13.49.6. Although he is mentioned only in connection with the battle of Cyzicus in the spring of 410, Chaereas must have been with the main fleet at the earlier battles as well, even though Xenophon speaks of Alcibiades as though he were sole commander. For arguments against the sole command of Alcibiades, see Bloedow, *Alcibiades*, 46–47.

[82]W. J. McCoy, *AJP* XCVIII (1977), 271 and 274, n. 41.

[83]Diod. 13.47.6–8; 49.1–3, 50.1–5. We cannot be sure that the mission of Theramenes was not approved before the arrival of Thrasyllus, but it might well have been a response to it. McCoy (*AJP* XCVIII [1977], 272, n. 37) calls attention to Xen. 1.1.34, which says that after Thrasyllus' good work in fighting off Agis' raid on Athens, the Athenians "were even more eager" to give him the forces for which he had come. We might interpret that to mean that they had been eager to help him before, but that the force under Theramenes, with its complicated mission, was the best they could do at the time.

[84]Diod. 13.47.3–5. On the union of Euboean cities and the numismatic evidence for it, see W. P. Wallace, *The Euboean League and Its Coinage*, Numismatic Notes and Monographs no. 134 (New York, 1956, 1–7; and Meiggs, *Athenian Empire*, 367.

[85]Diodorus (13.47.7–8) says he took money only from those islanders who had taken part in oligarchies or advocated them. If that is true, he and the Five Thousand were attempting to sharpen the cleavage between oligarchs and democrats and to use democratic sentiment in favor of Athens.

sand's credentials in the eyes of the Athenian democrats both in Athens and with the fleet in the Hellespont.

After establishing a democracy at Paros, Theramenes sailed north to assist the recently enthroned Macedonian king Archelaus in his siege of Pydna. The Athenians had good reason to be helpful to the king, for Macedonia was the major source of timber for shipbuilding, and Archelaus appears to have supplied their needs.[86] It is likely, however, that the Macedonian king also provided money for their services, so that Theramenes' voyage to Pydna was probably meant to raise funds for the fleet as well as to cement relations with Archelaus.[87] Theramenes could not stay to see the fall of the city, for he had urgent business to the north. He joined Thrasybulus in Thrace, where the united fleets could quickly reach the Hellespont in case of emergency.[88] Thrasybulus had been collecting what money he could at Thasos through plunder, since the island was still under oligarchic, anti-Athenian rule, and in other places in the Thraceward region.[89]

While these other generals were off gathering money, Alcibiades was still with the fleet at Sestos when Tissaphernes arrived at the Hellespont. Alcibiades had little choice but to go and greet him as a friend and benefactor. So far as the Athenians knew, the two men were still on good terms, and it had been the influence of Alcibiades that had persuaded the satrap to send the Phoenician fleet home. Alcibiades knew otherwise, but he must play out the charade. Perhaps, too, his sanguine temperament allowed him to believe that he could still make use of Tissaphernes; he might use his envy of Pharnabazus and his breach with the Spartans to obtain financial support for the Athenians. Attended by a retinue worthy of a supreme commander,

---

[86]Antiphon (2.11) reports that in 411 the king allowed him to cut and export to the Athenian fleet at Samos as many oars as he liked. If Meritt's restoration of a very fragmentary decree (*Classical Studies Presented to Edward Capps* [Princeton, N.J., 1936], 246–253) and *GHI*, 91 (277–280) are correct, the Athenians honored Archelaus in 407/6 for providing them with materials and allowing them to construct ships in his territory.

[87]Grote, VIII, 118; Busolt, *GG* III:2, 1526.

[88]Diod. 13.49.1–2.

[89]Xenophon's statement that Thrasybulus arrived from Thasos and Theramenes from Macedonia, where both were collecting money (1.1.12), seems to suggest that Thasos had been restored to Athenian rule, but the likelihood is that it had not. J. Pouilloux (*Recherches sur l'histoire et les cultes de Thasos*, vol. I [Paris, 1954], 153ff.) suggests that Xenophon's "Thasos" should be taken to mean "from Thasian waters," and Meiggs (*Athenian Empire*, 577) accepts that suggestion, but there is no need. Both plundering the enemy's country and collecting contributions from friends are ways to get money.

which he was not,[90] and bearing gifts to a guest-friend, he sailed to Tissaphernes in a single ship.[91]

Alcibiades had misjudged the situation badly. The satrap was desperate and could not even contemplate cooperation with the Athenians. His own plan had failed; the Spartans were out of his control and working with his rival, but the Athenians were once again a menace to the Great King's lands, as their recent victories proved. The Spartans blamed Tissaphernes for their misfortunes, and their complaints certainly will have reached the Great King's ears. He had permitted the satrap the use of the royal fleet, but Tissaphernes had merely kept it at Aspendus, at considerable expense, and had made no use of it before sending it back. The result of all this was not to wear down the Greeks and allow the Persians to regain their lost lands but to bring the Athenians into the Hellespont where they threatened to finish off the Spartan naval force. We need not doubt that Tissaphernes "was afraid that he would be blamed by the King."[92] He may even have been telling the truth when he said that the Great King had ordered him to make war on the Athenians.[93] He therefore seized Alcibiades and sent him off to Sardis for safekeeping. It seemed to him a wonderful and fortuitous opportunity to disprove the charges of the Spartans and to restore himself into the good graces of the Great King. Within a month, however, Alcibiades, along with another Athenian prisoner, was able to get away and make his escape at night on horseback to Clazomenae and from there sail to safety at Lesbos.[94] His ever-fertile imagination conceived still another trick: To make more trouble for the satrap, he spread the story that Tissaphernes had connived at his escape. Still, an important truth had been revealed: Alcibiades had no influence with Tissaphernes. Henceforth his authority must depend on his achievements in battle and on his ability to make the most of them.

All through the winter, ever since his defeat at Abydos, Mindarus had been gathering ships from wherever he could.[95] By the beginning

---

[90]Diodorus (13.49.1) tells us that Thrasybulus was "the leader of the entire fleet."
[91]Xen. 1.1.9; Plut. Alc. 4.
[92]Plut. Alc. 27.5.
[93]Xen. 1.1.9; Plut. Alc. 27.5.
[94]Xen. 1.1.10; Plut. Alc. 28.1.
[95] The following account of the battle of Cyzicus and its preliminaries draws evidence from Diodorus (13.49.2–51), Xenophon (1.1.11–18), and Plutarch (Alc. 28). Until the middle of this century, scholars generally used Xenophon's account, rejecting the others or using them to flesh out his version. The work of Hatzfeld (Alcibiade, 269–273), R. J. Littman (TAPA XCIX [1968], 265–272), and Bloedow (Alcibiades, 46–55) has shown

of spring, he had collected a fleet of eighty ships, and the Athenian commanders at Sestos were afraid lest he attack their own fleet of forty.[96] They therefore left Sestos by night and sailed around the Gallipoli peninsula to the port of Cardia on its northern shore (see Map 5).[97] From there they sent ships to Thrasybulus and Theramenes in Thrace and Alcibiades at Lesbos with the message that they should sail to Cardia as soon as possible. When the whole fleet was gathered in one place, it numbered eighty-six, and "its generals were eager for a decisive battle."[98] At Cardia they heard that Mindarus had taken his entire force off to Cyzicus on the southern shore of the Propontis (see Map 5). Pharnabazus marched a large army to the same place; together they besieged the city and took it by storm. The Athenian generals decided to pursue the enemy to Cyzicus, force a battle there, and recover the city. They sailed around to Elaeus and waited until nightfall before undertaking the next leg of the journey. They moved past Abydos under cover of darkness so that the enemy lookouts could not see their numbers and made their way to Parium and from there to the island of Proconnesus, just to the northwest of the peninsula on which Cyzicus was located.[99]

---

that the best account is that of Diodorus, and my own narrative follows him, making use of the others where appropriate.

My version of the battle, along with the rest of the book, was in press when I discovered A. Andrewes' excellent article discussing the battles of Cyzicus and Notium (*JHS* CII [1982], 15–25). It is gratifying that the account offered here is in substantial agreement with his.

[96]Diodorus (13.49.2) mentions Athenian "generals" at Sestos, and there may well have been at least one other, unnamed, beside Chaereas. The figure of eighty ships is his (13.50.2); Xenophon (1.1.11) gives the number as sixty, which may be right, but I have preferred to accept the figure from the account that is in general superior.

[97]Xenophon 1.1.11 provides the detail of the departure at night.

[98]Such is a cautious rendering of Diod. 13.49.3–4: σπευδόντων τῶν στρατηγῶν περὶ τῶν ὅλων διακινδυνεῶσαι. A more literal translation would be: "They were eager to run every risk for the whole thing." We cannot know just what they had in mind. The "whole thing" could have been a final victory in the war; at the very least, it must have meant control of the Hellespont. Xenophon's account, here and elsewhere, places Alcibiades at the center of everything and ignores the other generals most implausibly. It is hard to avoid the conclusion that he is following a source close to Alcibiades, perhaps even Alcibiades himself. (See Bloedow, *Alcibiades*, 55, n. 325.) For the number of Athenian ships, see Xen. 1.1.13.

[99]Diod. 13.49.3–6. Xenophon 1.1.11–13 tells the story as though Alcibiades was in full command and making all of the decisions. He alone goes overland from Cardia to Sestos and orders the fleet to sail around to meet him. From there he is on the point of sailing off to battle with only forty-six ships when Theramenes and Thrasybulus arrive with twenty ships each. Littman and Bloedow make clear how implausible that account is. Where Xenophon and Diodorus differ on details about this journey to

The Athenians spent the night at Proconnesus, and the generals planned their strategy for the next day's battle. The situation was entirely different from those facing the Athenians in the previous two battles in the narrow waters of the Hellespont. They had chosen the place to fight and the time to begin; they had a numerical advantage and enough open water in which to use their technical superiority. To maintain the element of surprise, they had seized every vessel in the harbor at Proconnesus and proclaimed the death penalty against anyone sailing out to the Cyzicene peninsula. The generals gave the task of addressing the soldiers and sailors before embarkation to the best orator among them. Alcibiades told the assembled forces that they must "fight at sea, on land, and against fortifications, for the enemy had plenty of money from the King, but [the Athenians] would have none unless they won a total victory."[100] After these preliminaries, the Athenians boarded the ships and set out for Cyzicus.

The ancient sources present very different accounts of the naval part of the battle of Cyzicus. As Xenophon tells the story, the Athenians, commanded by Alcibiades alone, set out for Cyzicus in a heavy rain. When they came near to the city, the weather suddenly cleared, and in the bright sunshine they found Mindarus giving the Peloponnesian fleet practice well out in the harbor, already cut off from the city by the Athenians. When Mindarus saw his predicament, he fled to shore where he could, away from the city. The rest of the battle was fought on land.[101] This account is brief, lacking in detail, and unsatisfactory in most respects: it says nothing about other commanders, who we know were present and played a significant part in the battle.[102] Also, it attributes the Athenians' success to the bad weather that permitted them to reach the neighborhood of Cyzicus without being seen and to the coincidence that caused Mindarus to be exercising his fleet so far from the city at just the moment when the weather cleared.

Proconnesus, I have followed the latter, except in the case of the stop at Parium, which probably occurred and was omitted by Diodorus.

[100] The details of the seizure of boats and the address to the troops are reported by Xenophon (1.1.14) and accepted by Plutarch (*Alc.* 28). My version of the speech is an amalgamation of the reports of Xenophon and Plutarch. Diodorus omits both details, but there is no reason to doubt their authenticity.

[101] Xen. 1.1.16–18.

[102] Nepos (*Alc.* 5.4, 5.6) makes it clear that Alcibiades, Theramenes, and Thrasybulus had joint command. Diodorus' account is clear and convincing in describing their specific roles in the battle at Cyzicus.

In Diodorus' version, the weather plays no part in the Athenians' success, which instead is the result of intelligent strategic planning and execution. The Athenians divide their fleet into three squadrons under Theramenes, Thrasybulus, and Alcibiades; a fourth general, Chaereas, is given command of a force on land. The victory at sea depends upon a deceptive stratagem, whereby Alcibiades takes a relatively small force toward Cyzicus and lures Mindarus out into the open waters. Alcibiades feigns flight, Mindarus pursues, and the other Athenian squadrons cut him off from the city, forcing him to flee to land at Cleri where Pharnabazus had his army. The rest of the battle is fought on land.[103] This account is plainly much better, but it is not without problems. The main difficulty is that it does not explain how the large Athenian fleet, without the cover of bad weather, caught the Peloponnesian fleet out of the Cyzicus harbor. We have seen repeatedly that no Spartan commander would risk a battle with an Athenian fleet unless it was very much smaller than his own, which was not true at Cyzicus. In clear weather, Peloponnesian or Persian lookouts would have observed the Athenian fleet sailing toward Cyzicus easily in time to avoid Mindarus' ships from being caught out at sea.[104] The account that follows depends chiefly on Diodorus' version but makes some use of Xenophon's as well.[105]

The Athenians set out for Cyzicus under cover of a heavy rainstorm.[106] The generals must have been prepared to risk taking to sea in bad weather in return for its concealment of their approach and the size of their force. Cyzicus lay on the neck of the peninsula, and their route took them down its western side, between the mainland and the island of Haloni (see Map 10).[107] On reaching the promontory of Artaki and the island of the same name not far off shore, they divided their

---

[103] 13.50.1–5.

[104] I am indebted to P. A. Rahe for making this point to me and for making a special trip to Cyzicus to compare my account and maps with its current geography as he observed it. He also criticized an earlier draft of my discussion of the battle at Cyzicus, and the present version owes much to his critique, although he would not agree with it entirely.

[105] Plutarch's very brief version (*Alc.* 27.3–4) likewise combines the two accounts, mentioning both the storm and the stratagem.

[106] Xen. 1.1.16.

[107] The accounts of the ancient writers are not precise enough to allow certainty about the locations of the encounters on land or sea or even the route taken by the Athenian fleet before the battle. The best discussion of these matters is Bloedow (*Alcibiades*, 51, n. 304), although Hatzfeld's (in *Alcibiade*, 271–273) is also helpful. For the western approach see now Andrewes, *JHS* CII (1982), 21.

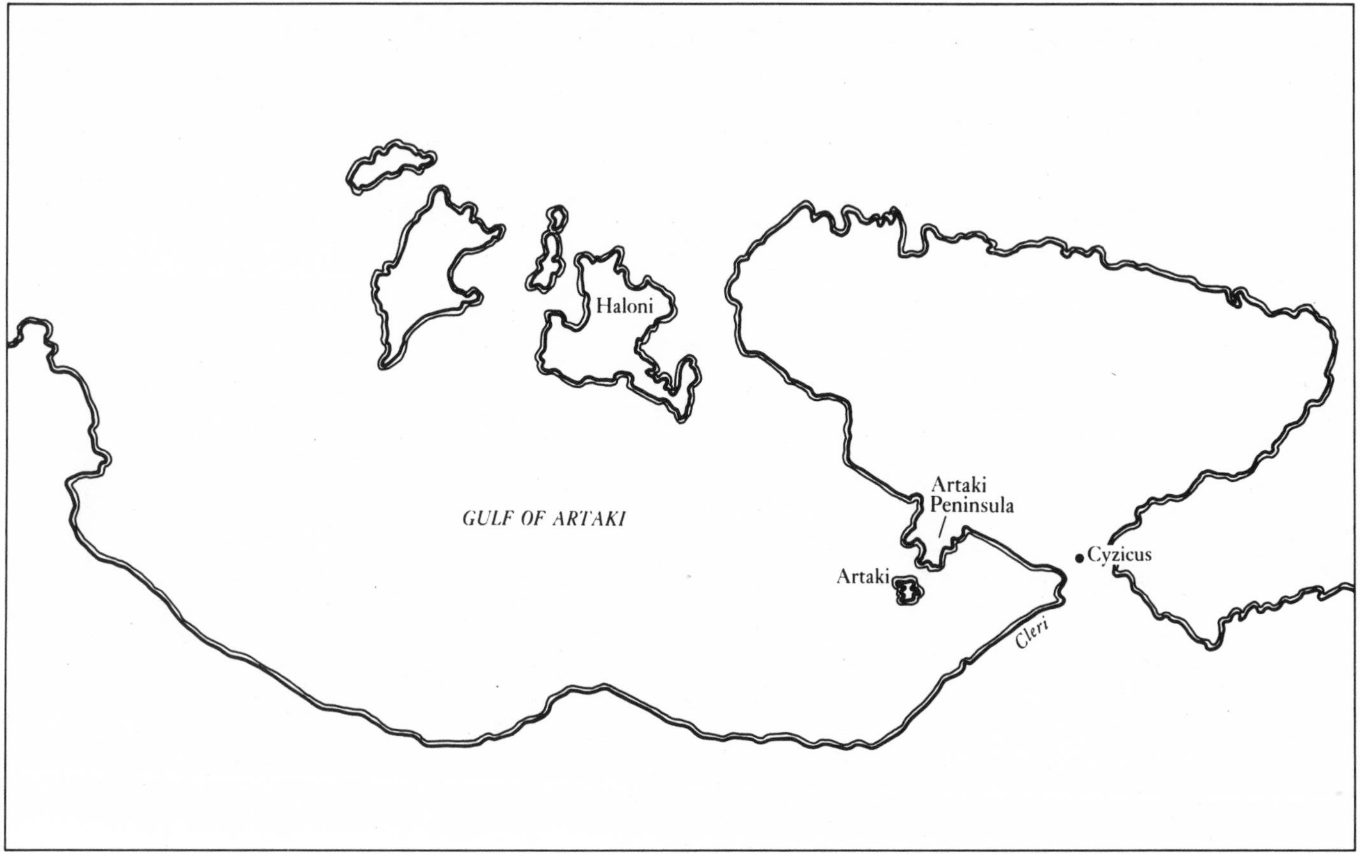

Map 10. The Battle of Cyzicus

forces. Chaereas and his hoplites were put ashore on the mainland with orders to march against the city of Cyzicus. Dividing forty-six ships between them, Theramenes and Thrasybulus each hid his fleet in the little harbor to the north of the promontory.[108] With the remaining forty ships Alcibiades sailed eastward, into Artaki Bay, directly toward Cyzicus.[109] The stratagem worked perfectly. When

[108]Frontinus (2.5.44), who seems to be using the same source as Diodorus, says that Chaereas' force landed at night. If so, it would probably have landed much further north and well before the main fleet set out. I am not persuaded that this detail is correct, for it would have required a longer march and left the troops exposed to discovery for a much greater time. Discovery would have alerted the fleet at Cyzicus and damaged the prospects of the entire plan. In the same passage, however, Frontinus tells us that the Athenians hid part of their fleet "behind a certain promontory" (*post quaedam promunturia*), surely the promontory of Artaki. See Andrewes, *JHS* CII (1982), 20–21. The ships could easily be concealed from the city of Cyzicus by the promontory, which ends in a steep hill, so that they would be hidden from the Peloponnesians at sea level at Cyzicus. Rahe points out, however, that they could be seen by lookouts posted on high ground behind the city. G. S. Kirk made the same point about possible lookouts on the heights of Arktonnesos, the large peninsula north of Cyzicus (Andrewes, *JHS* CII [1982], 21, n. 18). That is why the Athenians needed the protection of foul weather to move into position to launch their unusual strategy. In bad weather, the Peloponnesians would not have expected the enemy to come by sea. Probably no guards were even at their posts at such times, but if they were, they would not have been able to see the Athenian ships several miles away. Once the attack was launched, however, and Mindarus, taking the bait, moved out against the advancing Athenian squadron, no warning could come in time to help, even if the clouds suddenly disappeared.

Frontinus' evidence provides support for an account that is compatible with Diodorus' narrative. The first action he reports is the landing of Chaereas and his soldiers, but he does not say where they were put aground. The likeliest spot would be at the harbor of Artaki, where the entire fleet would be sheltered, as it needed to be in foul weather, and where it would be easy to land an army. That was also the closest place on the coast where it would be safe to put in. Diodorus reports that immediately thereafter the fleet divided into three squadrons: Alcibiades "sailing far ahead of the others" toward Cyzicus, "waiting to draw the Spartans out to a fight at sea," while Theramenes and Thrasybulus lay behind and "prepared the device of encirclement and of blocking the enemy's escape to the city" (13.50.1). But if Alcibiades was to move toward Cyzicus with a fleet small enough to draw the Spartans out and other squadrons were to get in behind them, those others needed to be nearby and yet out of sight. The place that best met the requirements was the harbor behind the promontory.

[109]Diodorus (13.50.2) gives no number, although Vogel conjectured that the number 20 had dropped out of the MSS. There is no reason to accept that emendation. Xenophon, though he does not give a number for this particular part of the plan, shows Alcibiades commanding 20 ships later in the same battle (1.1.18). In this instance I prefer Plutarch's figure of 40 (*Alc.* 28.4) with Littman (*TAPA* XCIX [1968]), and against Bloedow (*Alcibiades*, 49, n. 294). Before Mindarus left Abydos for Cyzicus he knew that the Athenians had at least 40 ships at Sestos. If he saw an Athenian fleet of only 20 approaching Cyzicus, he ought to have expected a trap and would have been reluctant to come out to fight. Seeing 40 ships, however, he might well believe that the entire

Mindarus saw the approach of Alcibiades, he must have assumed that the Athenians had rashly come against him with only their force in the Hellespont and that they were unaware of how large his own force had grown. With all eighty triremes he sailed out, confident of victory, and Alcibiades' response must have encouraged him further, for the Athenian ships turned and fled to the west in the direction of the island. The Peloponnesian fleet, thinking victory was at hand, pursued them eagerly. When Mindarus' ships were far enough into the harbor, Alcibiades raised a signal and turned his own force to face the pursuing enemy. Meanwhile, Theramenes moved his force from behind the promontory in the direction of Cyzicus to prevent the Peloponnesians from getting back to the city or the beaches close to it.[110] At the same time, Thrasybulus took his squadron south to cut off the escape route from the west. Mindarus responded swiftly, understanding the trap that had been set for him and turning back in time to prevent Thrasybulus and Theramenes from completing the encirclement that had been planned. Still, the soldiers and sailors on the Peloponnesian ships, seeing themselves outnumbered and cut off from the city, were terrified. Mindarus' only hope was to race for safety in the one direction available to him, toward a place called Cleri, a beach southwest of the city, where Pharnabazus had his army.[111]

Athenian fleet was challenging him to battle, perhaps in ignorance of what he believed to be his own overwhelming numerical superiority. In these circumstances the Athenians could hope to lure him out.

[110]In antiquity the area south of Cyzicus called Snipe Marsh was a waterway crossed by an artificial causeway and a bridge, and the triangular piece of land on which the city stood an island (F. W. Hasluck, Cyzicus [Cambridge, 1910], 1–4). North of the waterway and the city was a rocky coast where ships could not be beached.

It is theoretically possible that the Athenians happened to catch Mindarus' fleet training far away from its harbor at Cyzicus, as Xenophon says, but that seems most unlikely. If Xenophon's account is correct, Alcibiades first saw Mindarus' fleet and, presumably, was seen by the Spartans when the sun suddenly came out and revealed that the Spartans were already cut off from their harbor by the Athenian fleet. That could only have happened by the most remarkable of accidents, for Alcibiades, who is the only general mentioned, could hardly have planned such a meteorological miracle. In fact, Xenophon does not indicate that the Athenians had any plan at all. His version is brief, lacking in detail and in all sense of strategic planning, and inherently implausible. Diodorus, on the other hand, presents a version that is detailed, makes strategic sense, and does not require the suspension of reasonable expectations. Diodorus says plainly that when Mindarus first saw Alcibiades' fleet, he was still at Cyzicus and "boldly launched his sortie from the city" (13.50.2), because of their paltry number, and we should believe him.

[111]It is not possible to locate Cleri with certainty. I have put it at a place marked on the British military map as "landing place." Theramenes' ships cut Mindarus off from

Alcibiades pursued Mindarus to the shore, sinking some ships and capturing others. The Peloponnesians managed to pull most of their triremes up on the beach, so Alcibiades attached grappling hooks to them and tried to pull them out to sea. Then Pharnabazus came to the rescue with his army, which outnumbered the Athenians by far and had the advantage of fighting from the firm footing of the land, while the Athenians had to stand in the water. The Athenians fought courageously and caused much slaughter, but they would have been destroyed or driven off had they not received help. As Thrasybulus' fleet approached from the northwest, he quickly grasped the situation and the danger. He signaled Theramenes to join forces with the army of Chaereas, which must have been in the neighborhood of Cyzicus by then, and hurried forward to join in the battle on land. He disembarked with his marines and rushed to help Alcibiades. Athenian relief columns, therefore, were soon moving toward the embattled Alcibiades from two directions. As Mindarus struggled to prevent Alcibiades from towing away his ships, he could see Thrasybulus' approach, so he sent Clearchus with a part of his own force and a contingent of Pharnabazus' mercenaries to stop it. With only the hoplites and archers from no more than about twenty-five ships, Thrasybulus was badly outnumbered. Although they fought well, his troops began to suffer significant

---

the city and the hospitable shore near it. The spot I have designated is the only nearby place to the south not too rocky for landing. Diodorus' account fits this interpretation well. Xenophon's version is further undermined, for if the Spartan ships were really caught out at sea practicing and were surrounded by the Athenians, as he says, they would either have been destroyed at sea or compelled to fight their way through the Athenians to land. For his narrative to be consistent, it should mention some fighting at sea while the Peloponnesians break out of the encirclement, but Xenophon speaks of no fighting before the Peloponnesian ships reach land: "When the Peloponnesians saw that the Athenian triremes were much more numerous that before and near the harbor, they fled toward land; and anchoring the ships side by side they fought against the enemy who sailed down against them" (1.1.17). Diodorus, on the other hand, does mention fighting at sea in a way consistent with his version: "Finally, since the Athenians were appearing from everywhere, and had cut the Peloponnesians off from the return route to the city, Mindarus was forced to flee to the land to a spot near the place called Cleri, where Pharnabazus also had his army. Alcibiades pursued eagerly, sinking some ships and damaging and capturing others; on the greatest number, which were anchored side by side, drawn up on the land itself, he threw grappling hooks and tried to drag them from the land in this way" (13.50.2). This passage does not describe a fight between two fleets, such as would need to have taken place if the Peloponnesians were trying to break through an encirclement, but the kind of one-sided attack compatible with one fleet pursuing another that is in flight. This moment in the battle shows as clearly as any the superiority of Diodorus' account, which is detailed and consistent, over Xenophon's brief and vague version.

casualties. They were on the point of being surrounded and destroyed when Theramenes arrived in time at the head of his own troops and those of Chaereas. Thrasybulus' exhausted men were revived by the sight of reinforcements, and a long and bitter battle ensued. Finally, Pharnabazus' mercenaries turned to flight and broke the line, and the Spartans were driven from the field as well.

With Thrasybulus' men safe, Theramenes was free to go to the aid of Alcibiades, still fighting for the ships at the shore. Mindarus now found himself caught between the troops of Alcibiades and Theramenes' corps, approaching from another direction. With the boldness, courage, and leadership he had shown in the past, the Spartan commander calmy divided his army in half, sending one part to meet the approaching forces of Theramenes, while he formed a line against Alcibiades. He fought bravely and well but finally died fighting among the ships. His death deprived his men of all poise and courage, and both Peloponnesians and their allies panicked and fled. Only the arrival of Pharnabazus with his cavalry cut short the Athenian pursuit.

The Athenians went back to their ships and withdrew to Proconnesus for a night of rest and rejoicing while the Peloponnesians from within the city of Cyzicus and the survivors of the battle fled to safety at a camp of Pharnabazus'.[112] The next day the Athenians could return at leisure to find that the enemy had abandoned Cyzicus, so its citizens had no choice but to return to their former allegiance. The Athenians took many prisoners, a vast collection of booty, and all of the enemy's ships except those from Syracuse, whose crews had burned them before they could fall into Athenian hands.[113] The Athenians set up two trophies, one to commemorate the naval victory at the island of Artaki and the other where the rout began on land.[114]

The Athenians wasted no time in making good use of their great victory. Alcibiades stayed at Cyzicus for twenty days collecting a large supply of money. From there he sailed to the north shore of the Propontis in the direction of the Bosporus. At Perinthus he and his troops were admitted into the city; at Selymbria they obtained more money. Then they went to Chrysopolis, on the Asiatic side of the Bosporus, opposite Byzantium. There, they established a fort

[112]Xenophon provides the detail of the withdrawal to Proconnesus (1.1.20). Plutarch (Alc. 28.6) says the Peloponnesians in Cyzicus were abandoned and destroyed, but Diodorus' version is much to be preferred.
[113]The action of the Syracusans is reported in Xen. 1.1.18.
[114]I take Artaki to be the island called Polydorus by Diodorus (13.51.7).

guarded by thirty ships under two generals, Theramenes and Euma-
chus. It would serve as a base for attacks against the enemy but, more
important, as a customs house. Henceforth the Athenians would levy
a duty of one-tenth on all merchant ships passing through the Bosporus,
potentially a valuable source of revenue. The most important result
of the battle at Cyzicus, however, is succinctly expressed by Plutarch:
"Not only did the Athenians securely hold the Hellespont, they also
drove the Spartans from the rest of the sea in any force."[115] Perhaps
equally important, though less tangible, was the blow to Spartan morale. Some time after the battle the Athenians intercepted a letter from
Hippocrates, secretary to the fallen Spartan navarch: "The ships are
lost. Mindarus is dead. The men are starving. We know not what to
do."[116] Before long Sparta would offer peace.

   The victory at Cyzicus was of the greatest importance. It removed
the threat to Athens' food supply and to the dominance of its navy.
It permitted the Athenians to survive their most dangerous crisis and
once again to have reasonable hopes of victory. Xenophon and Plutarch
give Alcibiades exclusive credit for the triumph, but Theramenes and
Thrasybulus played at least an equal part. We do not know who was
responsible for the excellent naval strategy that worked so well at
Cyzicus, but we can be sure that Alcibiades had no hand in planning
the strategies at Cynossema or Abydos, for he was absent from the
former and arrived at the latter only when it was almost over. Since
Diodorus tells us that Thrasybulus was both the commander of the
whole fleet and the decisive commander at Cynossema, it seems likely
that he also planned the strategy at Abydos and had the leading strategic role at Cyzicus. There, Alcibiades fought splendidly and carried
out his assignment to perfection. Theramenes was also outstanding,
and his appearance with reinforcements made success possible. A careful examination of the events, however, strongly suggests that once
again Thrasybulus' role was decisive. For all of the brilliance of the
naval portion of the fighting, the outcome was determined on land.
The key moment was when Alcibiades was under attack by Mindarus
and the army of Pharnabazus. Had he been left to his own devices,
he would surely have been driven off, leaving most of the ships in
Peloponnesian hands where they could be protected by Pharnabazus'

[115]*Alc.* 28.6.
[116]Xen. 1.1.23: ἔρρει τὰ κᾶλα. Μίνδαρος ἀπεσσύα. πεινῶντι τὤνδρες. ἀπορίομες
τί χρὴ δρᾶν.

infantry and cavalry. At the decisive moment, however, Thrasybulus landed with a small force that diverted a part of the enemy's troops and saved Alcibiades. No less important was his order to Theramenes that sealed the victory. As a strategist, a tactician, and a brilliant commander in the field, Thrasybulus deserves to be regarded as the hero of Cyzicus. We would do well to remember and respect the judgment of Cornelius Nepos: "In the Peloponnesian War Thrasybulus accomplished many victories without Alcibiades; the latter accomplished nothing without the former, yet he, by some gift of his nature, gained the credit for everything."[117]

[117] *Thrasybulus* 1.3: "Primum Peloponnesio bello multa sine Alcibiade gessit, ille nullam rem sine hoc; quae ille universa naturali quodam bono fecit lucri."

10. The Restoration

The great victory at Cyzicus took place in March or April of 410, and the news of it filled the Athenians with elation.[1] The entire population came together in solemn assembly to offer sacrifices in gratitude to the gods.[2] The news of the Spartan disaster had the opposite effect on its population. In spite of unprecedented efforts at sea, reliable and consistent support from Pharnabazus, and an enemy distracted by lack of funds, they had experienced nothing but defeat since the scene of battle had shifted to the Hellespont. They had lost an astonishing number of ships, between 135 and 155, within a few months.[3] The Athenians once again controlled the seas everywhere and had free access to the vital food supply from the lands of the Black Sea. Agis remained in control of the fort at Decelea and was still free to ravage the Attic countryside, but he well understood that he could accomplish nothing significant while the grain ships sailed freely through the Bosporus and Hellespont to the Piraeus.[4] The promise of continued Persian support did not guarantee victory, certainly not in the near future. Tissaphernes was entirely discredited, and Pharnabazus, though reliable, lacked the means of his rival satrap. The help that Sparta re-

[1] Busolt (GG III:2, 1527, n. 2) places it in March, Beloch (GG II:1, 394) in May, but most scholars put it in April (e.g., G. E. Underhill, *A Commentary with Introduction and Appendix on the* Hellenica *of Xenophon* [Oxford, 1940], xl; W. S. Ferguson, *CAH* V, 343). I agree with A. Andrewes (*JHS* LXXIII [1953]) that March or April are both reasonable dates.

[2] Diod. 13.52.1.2.

[3] Busolt, *GG* III:2, 1534, n. 2. The total depends on whether we accept Xenophon's or Diodorus' figure for the Spartan fleet at Cyzicus.

[4] Xen. 1.1.35.

ceived from Italy and Sicily had been much less than expected, and the revolution in Syracuse deprived them of Hermocrates, the most fervent and ablest of the allied generals, raising questions about the quality of Syracusan support in the future.[5] The Spartans also appear to have lost enough men to the Athenians as prisoners to make them eager for a peace that would allow their exchange and return.[6]

Under these circumstances, the Spartans, in violation of their treaty with Persia, decided to negotiate for peace with Athens.[7] The chief of the mission was Endius, who had been part of the embassy that had failed to prevent the Athenian alliance with Argos in 420. As ephor for the year 413/12, he had collaborated with Alcibiades in persuading the Spartans to work with Tissaphernes in Ionia.[8] This, and his old family friendship with Alcibiades, may have been important recommendations for his role in the negotiations, but Alcibiades was in the east, and other men would influence the Athenian decision. Perhaps he was chosen because he represented the Spartan faction favoring accommodation or perhaps because he was thought to be an expert in Athenian affairs.[9] Diodorus reports Endius' statement of the Spartan proposal as follows: "We wish to make peace with you, men of Athens, and that each side should keep the cities it now controls but abandon the garrisons it holds in the other's territory, ransoming prisoners, one Athenian for one Laconian."[10]

The Athenians, no doubt, would have been glad to abandon Pylos in exchange for peace and Decelea and to return prisoners, but to accept the status quo in the empire was a different matter. Even after Cyzicus the Spartans controlled Rhodes, Miletus, Ephesus, Chios,

[5]8.2.3; Xen. 1.1.27–31.

[6]On this occasion and again in 408/7 (Androtion, *FGrH* III, 324, Fr. 44) the Spartans came to Athens with a request for the exchange of prisoners. Lewis (*Sparta and Persia*, 126) says: "It looks as if the number of Spartiates in Athenian hands may once again have risen to the point where there was strong internal pressure for an arrangement that would bring the boys home. As in the period from 425 to 421, this can have been a factor which ʃwarfed all more general considerations." That seems a stronger statement than the evidence warrants, but the desire to recover their men in Athenian hands clearly was an important concern of the Spartans.

[7]Diod. 13.52.2; Nepos, *Alc.* 5; Justin 5.4; Philochorus, *FGrH* III, 328, Fr. 139, 140.

[8]5.44; 8.6.3 and 12.

[9]Lewis, *Sparta and Persia*, 114, n. 44.

[10]Diod. 13.52.3. I agree with Lewis (*Sparta and Persia*, 114 and n. 46) that the speech of Endius reported by Diodorus is unlikely to be authentic, but there is no reason to doubt the accuracy of his account of the peace terms. The narrative, as Lewis suggests, may well derive from the *Hellenica Oxyrhynchia*, but I am less impressed by the similarity he sees between Diod.13.53.1 and *Hell. Oxy.* 6.3.

Thasos, and Euboea in the Aegean; a number of places on the Thracian coast; Abydos in the Hellespont; and Byzantium and Chalcedon on both sides of the Bosporus. From antiquity to modern times, the general opinion has been that this peace proposal was, nonetheless, an offer that the Athenians should not have refused. Diodorus tells us that "the most reasonable of the Athenians" favored accepting the Spartan offer, but the assembly rejected it, deceived by "practiced warmongers who made private profit from public troubles." With the benefit of hindsight, he calls it an error from which the Athenians were never able to recover.[11] Most modern scholars have made similar judgments. Only a half-year earlier the Athenians had been in a desperate condition, and now they ought to have been happy to recover the greater part of their empire. Every reasonable person must understand that Athenian resources were inadequate to recover the lost territories. Even if the peace should not last, every year without war should be counted an invaluable gain.[12] Athenian resources, stretched to the limit of the almost-exhausted treasury, would not be adequate against the inexhaustible wealth of Persia that could easily replace whatever ships the Athenians sank.[13] The Athenians, moreover, could expect no better offer from the Spartans, who could not restore the recently liberated cities of the Athenian alliance without violating their own honor.[14]

The leader of those opposing the offer was Cleophon, "the greatest demagogue at that time."[15] Like most popular politicians in the last quarter of the century, Cleophon was the butt of satirical attacks by the comic poets and treated with a mixture of contempt and loathing by more serious writers. He is referred to as a lyre-maker, just as Cleon was called a tanner, Lysicles a cattle dealer, Eucrates a flax merchant, and Hyperbolus a lamp-maker. His mother is alleged to have been a barbarian and he himself a rapacious foreigner, a lowly craftsman of no family background.[16] More serious writers depict him as a drunkard, a cut-throat, and a raving wild man in his public behavior.[17] Although

---

[11] 13.53.
[12] Meyer, *GdA* IV, 312.
[13] Busolt, *GG* III:2, 1537.
[14] Beloch, *GG* II:1, 395.
[15] 13.53.2.
[16] For references, see Busolt, *GG* III:2, 1537, n. 1.
[17] Diodorus (13.53.3) calls him a flatterer of the people. Aristotle (*Ath. Pol.* 34.1) tells us that he came drunk into the assembly wearing his military breastplate. Aeschines (*De Falsa Legatione* 76) says he threatened to cut the throats of his opponents in the assembly.

his manner and rhetoric may have been indecorous and his political views extreme, that picture is biased and inaccurate. Cleophon was surely an Athenian, as were both his parents. His father, Cleippides, was a general in 428/27 and was important enough to have been involved in an ostracism, perhaps as early as 444/43. Cleophon himself may have been a general and a member of the board of financial officials (*poristai*). Years after his death an orator could say that Cleophon "had managed all the affairs of the state for many years."[18] Making every allowance for exaggeration, such a man could not have been an impecunious craftsman; if he made lyres, he must have done so as the owner of a workshop or factory, a man of means, as his father must have been. Since the peace proposal came during the constitution of the Five Thousand, he must been a man of at least of hoplite status, but probably higher, in order to take part in the debate.[19] The charge that he argued against peace in search of personal profit is easily dismissed. There is no record of any charge against him for peculation or corruption at a time when such accusations against politicians were not rare, and there is evidence that he died a poor man.[20] Perhaps Busolt's characterization, although it denies Cleophon any political insight or understanding of what was possible in the circumstances, conveys some idea of his qualities: "He was honest, a democrat by true conviction, and an effective popular orator. His passionate, terroristic behavior gives the impression of a true Jacobin."[21]

Such a man would naturally have argued for fighting on until Athens had won a total victory, and Diodorus tells us that Cleophon dwelt upon the greatness of Athens' recent victories and the prospects for future success. We may well believe that he promoted this view and that the Athenians came to have great hopes that, under the leadership of Alcibiades, who had managed to gain chief credit for the victories in the Hellespont, "they would quickly recover their empire."[22] More moderate Athenians, however, and even those not dazzled by Alci-

---

[18]Lys. 19.48.

[19]Since the old democracy was not restored until June at the earliest, the debate in April or May must have taken place within the assembly of the Five Thousand.

[20]Lys. 19.48. Grote (VIII, 123–124) provides other valid arguments against the charge of corruption, and even Busolt, who accepts many of the ancient calumnies, rejects this one as unjustified (*GG* III:2, 1536, n. 2).

[21]*GG* III:2, 1536. For friendlier and, I believe, better rounded accounts, see R. Renaud, *LAC* XXXVIII (1970), 458–477, and W. R. Connor, *The New Politicians of Fifth–Century Athens* (Princeton, 1971), 83 n. 82, 139, 143, 145–147, 153, 158, 169–171.

[22]Diod. 13.53.4.

biades, could also have found respectable reasons to reject the proffered peace in the spring of 410 after the battle of Cyzicus. To ratify the territorial status quo overseas was not merely to accept half a loaf but to leave the future security of Athens in serious jeopardy. Should circumstances and the political balance in Sparta change and the peace be broken, the war would resume with Sparta again posing a major threat to Athens. If the Athenians did not exploit their advantage at once, the Spartans, still loyally supported by Pharnabazus, would have time to build another fleet and again challenge them for control of the Hellespont. The Athenians, it must be emphasized, needed to suffer only one major defeat to their fleet in order to lose the war. On the other hand, if they moved swiftly, they could deprive the enemy of its bases along the route to the Black Sea and so make the Straits secure. If they also attacked Ionia, they might recover it without too much trouble, while the glow of their victory at Cyzicus still encouraged their friends and awed their enemies. The prestige of their victories, the establishment of the customs house at the Bosporus, and the recovery of lost subject cities would allow a restoration of Athenian finances to something like their previous level.

Nor did the Athenians need to believe that the bond between Sparta and Persia was unbreakable. From the beginning these allies had been an odd couple and had faced considerable difficulty in arriving at a mutually acceptable agreement. Not long after an agreement had finally been reached, the Spartans had become disillusioned by the broken promises and duplicity of Tissaphernes and had turned against him. Pharnabazus, as we have seen, was loyal but had limited resources. A few more defeats and some attacks on his territory might convince him that he had made a mistake in supporting Sparta against the Athenian Empire. No one could be sure of the attitude of the Great King, but history showed that he could be discouraged by repeated defeats and continuing fruitless expenditures. Moreover, he ruled a vast empire and might be faced at any time with a rebellion in some other region that could compel him to abandon the war on his western boundaries. In fact, he might decide to do so at once in response to the Spartans' offer of a separate peace with Athens, a flagrant violation of their treaty with Persia. With these considerations in mind, we need be neither surprised nor censorious because the Athenians rejected the Spartan offer.[23]

[23]Busolt (*GG* III:2, 1537 and n. 1) believes that Cleophon persuaded the Athenians

The Athenians refused Sparta's proposal for peace some time in May. Within two months, probably late in June, the regime of the Five Thousand was removed and replaced by the full, untrammeled democracy that Athens had enjoyed before the introduction of the *probouloi* in 413.[24] After praising the moderate regime of the Five Thousand, Aristotle says: "The people quickly took away their control of the state."[25] This is the only direct ancient reference to the transition, but there is plenty of evidence to show that the full democracy was again in control in the summer of 410. We are not told how or why the change came about. Modern writers connect it with the new confidence felt by the people after the battle of Cyzicus, but if that were sufficient, we would expect the restoration to have occurred in May, under the first impact of the good news rather than a month or two later. In fact, if anything, the victory at Cyzicus, ought to have bolstered the prestige of the Five Thousand. The success at Cyzicus and the two preceding victories came under their auspices and under the command chiefly of Thrasybulus, Alcibiades, and Theramenes, none of them a radical democrat. It is often suggested that the transition between constitutions was gradual, but no matter how gradual it may have been, there had to be a decisive moment when the exclusive powers of the Five Thousand were abolished and full political rights were restored to the entire citizen body. We cannot be certain what event or events provided the immediate cause of the change, but the evidence permits some reasonably plausible speculation.

---

to make a counter demand requiring the Spartans to restore all of the former Athenian cities. He bases this on Aristotle (*Ath. Pol.* 34.1), who places that demand after the Athenian victory at Arginusae in 406. There seems no compelling reason to move those demands to an earlier occasion.

[24]For the date, see B. D. Meritt, *Athenian Financial Documents* (Ann Arbor, 1932), 105–7, *Proceedings of the American Philosophical Society* CXV (1971), 106, 114–115; and Rhodes, *Commentary*, 415. The first evidence we have of the change in regimes is provided by the decree of Demophantus (And. 1.96–98), which deals with punishments for those who plot against the democracy. It is dated to the first prytany of the year 410/9. An inscription recording the accounts of the treasurers of Athena for that year (*GHI*, 37, lines 5–7) shows that payments for the Great Panathenaia were made in the second prytany, leading Meritt (followed by Meiggs and Lewis [*GHI*, 258]) to infer that the conciliar year began earlier than the archontic year, perhaps about June 16. I agree with Rhodes that the payment could have been made after the festival, permitting the conciliar and archontic years to have begun at the same time, in the month of July. In either case the transition to democracy would have occurred at least a month after the rejection of the Spartan offer.

[25]*Ath. Pol.* 34.1: Τούτους μὲν οὖν ἀφείλετο τὴν πολιτείαν ὁ δῆμος διὰ τάχους. I follow the interpretation of Rhodes, *Commentary*, 414–415.

Indeed, the victory at Cyzicus must have increased the credit of the Five Thousand and provided an occasion for unity among the Athenians, but the Spartan peace offer that followed was terribly divisive. We cannot tell what Theramenes would have thought of the proposal, but his fellow moderates must have been among "the most reasonable Athenians" who favored accepting it. Even more than the majority of Athenians who were willing to accept the less-than-perfect Peace of Nicias in 421, they would have been eager to escape from the miseries of a war that had become expensive, painful, and dangerous to the survival of Athens. The leaders of the Five Thousand, we may believe, were among those arguing for peace on the proffered terms, but in 410 the majority clearly thought otherwise, and the debate over the peace, the only important event we know between the victory at Cyzicus and the restoration of democracy, may well have been the trigger that started the movement away from the Five Thousand. Having lost the crucial argument, the leaders of the moderate regime were forced on to the defensive. Their opponents could say that men who were eager for peace on unsatisfactory terms were not the men to lead a vigorous renewal of the war. In a sense, the rejection of the Spartan offer was the loss of a vote of confidence for the government in power.

The momentum toward full democracy must have grown quickly. The democrats had a considerable advantage: in the debate they had found a talented and effective leader, a spokesman who could sway the assembly in his direction. The moderates, on the other hand, were without their most skillful and effective advocate. Theramenes was on military duty at Chrysopolis; without his political and rhetorical abilities, his colleagues could not match the new democratic leader. At a deeper level, the advantage was all with the democrats. Democracy, apart from its natural appeal to the majority, was more than 100 years old at Athens. It had come to be thought of as the traditional government. Cleisthenes, Solon, and even Draco and the legendary Theseus were seen as forefathers of democracy in some way. Oligarchy, whether extreme or moderate, was seen to be an innovation, untraditional and unnatural, by most Athenians. They had only given way to it in the darkest hours of their history, when defeat seemed imminent and no other salvation seemed possible. It is not surprising, then, that when naval victories brought new hope, the democratic political leaders would seize the first favorable opportunity to return to the traditional regime. The Spartan peace offer appears to have provided that opportunity. By June someone must have proposed the abolition of the

Five Thousand and the restoration of the traditional democratic constitution. By the first prytany of the year 410/9, late June or July of
410, the old democracy was in place and passing fierce laws to defend
itself against its enemies.[26]

Since no ancient narrative has described the democratic restoration,
modern scholars have found it hard to grasp its character and even its
reality. Evidence for it comes from scattered references in the orators
and inscriptions, increasing the impression that it was an ill-organized
collection of measures without plan or purpose. The decrees bear
names otherwise unknown to us, and no famous statesman is credited
with putting forward a general plan, yet a study of the Athenians'
actions in the first year or so of the restored democracy reveals a
surprising consistency and coherence. From it emerges a comprehen-
sive program for waging a successful war under a thoroughgoing and
invigorated democratic regime. The changes introduced in 410/9 were
constitutional, legal, financial, social, and spiritual. Together, they
produced a city recovered from defeat and despair and capable of
remarkable efforts and astonishing success.

The earliest document we possess from the restored regime, the
decree of Demophantus, shows that the Five Thousand were gone and
the old assembly and Council of Five Hundred were back in power
in the old way. It begins with the old democratic formula: "Enacted
by the Council and the People."[27] The council, moreover, is not the
elected one of the moderate constitution but is specifically designated
as "the Council of Five Hundred allotted by the bean," as though to
emphasize the difference.[28] The Council of Four Hundred of the oligarchs and the elected Council of Five Hundred of the moderates,
however, had made the democrats wary of the power of councils. To
check the restored council and to guarantee its subordination to the
popular assembly, they placed unprecedented restraints on it. The
Council of Five Hundred appears to have been deprived of the power
to impose penalties beyond a stated level of severity; it could not impose
the death penalty or a fine above 500 drachmas without the consent
of the assembly or the popular courts.[29] Another new law required

[26] And. 1.96–98.
[27] And. 1.96.
[28] *Ibid.*: ἡ βουλὴ οἱ πεντακόσιοι οἱ λαχόντες τῷ κυάμῳ.
[29] The evidence comes from a badly mutilated and undated inscription, *IG* I², 114.
There is general agreement, however, that the provisions listed here were enacted by
the restored democracy in 410. See Busolt, *GG* III:2, 1539; Hignett, *HAC*, 281; Rhodes,
The Athenian Boule (Oxford, 1972), 183–184.

members of the council to sit in seats assigned them by lot, with the obvious intention of reducing the influence of factions sitting together.[30]

The shifts from democracy to the oligarchy of the Four Hundred to the rule of the Five Thousand had caused great confusion about the laws of Athens.[31] Their experience under the Four Hundred, moreover, had shown the democrats that attacks on traditional law were a threat to the survival of democracy. The Four Hundred had begun their revolution by establishing a commission of *syngrapheis* to draft new laws without the usual limitations on unconstitutional proposals.[32] Although some of them tried to disguise the radical novelty of their proposals, few could have been deceived.[33] Likewise, the Five Thousand were committed to constitutional and legal innovation. One of their first acts was to appoint a board of *nomothetai*.[34] In the short period of their existence, they do not seem to have accomplished anything, and we cannot be sure what function they were meant to perform, but some revision of traditional law was probably part of it.[35] If the draft constitution for the future reproduced by Aristotle represents their thinking, these men were prepared to institute a new constitution and laws of a highly novel and theoretical nature, casting aside traditional law and procedure.[36] Although we think of the full Athenian democracy as "radical" in its devotion to complete popular government and full political participation by all citizens, we must remember that in 410 it was a century old, the traditional government; no living Athenian had known any other form until the revolution of 411. By the late fifth century, the legislation of Draco and Solon, whatever its true nature, had become part of the democratic tradition in the popular mind, and its creators were seen as founding fathers of

[30]Philochorus, *FGrH* III, 328, Fr. 140. Jacoby (*FGrH* IIIb, 511) says that "events since the establishment of the *probouloi* must have shown the people that the sitting together of political sympathizers was not a mere formality."

[31]Dem. 24.154.

[32]8.57.1.

[33]Cleitophon's rider attached to the proposal of Pythodorus urged the examination of the laws of Cleisthenes, which he suggested were compatible with those of Solon (*Ath. Pol.* 29.3). Whatever its other purposes, it was also meant to remove the glare from the revolutionary novelty of what was happening. The establishment of the council of Four Hundred was described as *kata ta patria*, "in accordance with ancestral tradition" (*Ath. Pol.* 31.1). This must have been an attempt to link this entirely new institution with the entirely different council of Four Hundred established by Solon.

[34]8.97.2.

[35]See *HCT* V, 330.

[36]*Ath. Pol.* 30.

the Athenian democracy.[37] In these circumstances, it is not surprising that the restored democracy appointed a board of *anagrapheis* to draw up and publish in an authoritative manner the laws of Solon and Draco's law on homicide.[38] The innovative, revolutionary, sophistic, antidemocratic ideas of the most recent past were rejected as the democrats sought a return to the old days.

The old laws, however, had not been enough to defend the democracy against subversion; for that, new legislation was needed. In the first prytany of the new year, July 410, the Athenians enacted a law proposed by a certain Demophantus to safeguard the restored democratic constitution. It provided that anyone taking part in the destruction of the democracy, or even holding office in a regime after its suppression, be declared an enemy of Athens to be killed with impunity; his possessions would become public property, a tenth going to Athena. It further required that all Athenians take the following oath over an unblemished sacrifice before the next festival of Dionysus:

I shall kill by word and by deed, by vote and with my own hand, if I can, anyone who subverts the democracy at Athens, whoever holds public office after its suppression, and whoever tries to become a tyrant or helps to install one. And if anyone else kills such a person I will regard him as blameless before the gods and demons as having killed an enemy of the Athenian people. And I will sell all the property of the man who has been killed and give half to the man who has killed him and hold nothing back. And if anyone dies while killing such a person or attempting to kill him I shall treat him and his children well just as if they were Harmodius and Aristogeiton [the tyrannicides of the late sixth century who had become canonized by Athenian public opinion] and their children. I dissolve and reject all oaths for the overthrow of the Athenian democracy, whether in Athens, or in the camp of the army, or anywhere else.[39]

---

[37]M. I. Finley, referring to the moment discussed here, says: "The metaphorically ancestral constitution of the present was coalesced with the literally ancestral constitution going back two hundred years" (*The Ancestral Constitution* [Cambridge, 1971], 13).

[38]Lys.30.2; *IG* I² 115 = *GHI*, 86, 11.5–6. It is sometimes said that there also was a board of *syngrapheis*, which was given the task of revising the laws, but I agree with R. S. Stroud (*Draco's Law on Homicide* [Berkeley, Calif., 1968], 27–28) that the evidence for such a board is not adequate to prove its existence. In addition to the arguments he offers, I suggest that such a revision would have been against the spirit of a return to tradition, which seems to me an important aspect of the democratic restoration of 410.

[39]And. 1.96–98.

The law was inscribed on stone at the entrance to the council-chamber and remained in force well into the fourth century.[40]

Very much in the spirit of this decree, the Athenians, in the spring of 409, honored the men who had killed Phrynichus two years earlier with Athenian citizenship, awarding them a golden crown, and various other benefits.[41] In the next few years, this decree and the spirit it embodied gave rise to a rash of accusations and trials directed against former members of the Four Hundred, men who had held office under their rule, and any who had served them.[42] Although membership in the Four Hundred was not a crime in itself, prejudice against that group was so strong that accusers seem to have included it among the charges, even when the claim was not justified.[43] Those convicted suffered penalties including exile, fines, and loss of citizen rights, full or partial.[44] Accusers in turn were accused of abusing the situation, of venality and blackmail, and there must be at least some truth in these charges. It is further true that giving vent to this feeling of hatred and vengeance against the enemies of democracy was costly to the unity of the state at a time when harmony was badly needed. We must recognize, however, that the behavior of the restored democracy was understandable and, when compared with the actions of other peoples after revolutionary episodes, marked by restraint and moderation. Elsewhere, defeated revolutionary factions were usually slaughtered or exiled en masse for membership in the offending group. The Athenians in 410, on the other hand, did not outlaw the members of the Four Hundred as a group. Indeed, some of them served the democracy in the highest offices, even as generals. The decree of Demophantus was not retroactive, and actions had to be taken against offending individuals and for specific offenses. Nor did widespread executions take place, and penalties seem to have been assigned in proportion to the gravity of offenses. Given the circumstances, the democrats did not behave badly.[45]

The restoration of the full democracy entailed the restoration also

---

[40]Dem. 20.159; Lyc., *Against Leocrates*, 124–127. See also D. M. MacDowell, *The Law in Classical Athens* (Ithaca, N.Y., 1978), 176.

[41]*GHI*, 85.

[42]See Busolt, *GG* III:2, 1541–1543; and Hignett, *HAC*, 280–282.

[43]One of Lysias' speeches includes the assertion that if all such accusations were believed, the Four Hundred would have numbered over a thousand.

[44]And. 1.73–79.

[45]For a harsher assessment see, e.g., Busolt and Hignett in n. 42 above.

of payment for service on the council, on juries, and for other public services[46] the return of political rights to the lower classes would have had little meaning without such payment. In 410, however, payment for public service was not enough to meet the needs of poor Athenian citizens who had suffered greatly since the resumption of the war or of citizens who had not previously been needy but had fallen into poverty as a result of Spartan depredations from Decelea. Many, forced to abandon their farms and squeeze into the crowded city, were deprived of their livelihood and must have crossed the line, never very clear, into the lowest class of thetes from the zeugites (or hoplites) above them. To meet the needs of all of these people, Cleophon introduced a new public subvention called the *diobelia* because it paid each recipient a daily sum of 2 obols, or a third of a drachma. We are not told what its purpose was, who received it, or how much it cost the state. Most likely, it was paid to needy citizens not otherwise on the public payroll when funds for the purpose were available, and probably it did not involve a great expenditure.[47] In the fourth century, the introduction of the *diobelia* was denounced as a corruption of the people by means of money and as the first encouragement of the base human appetite for gain that begins with small sums but inevitably increases over time.[48] Whatever its effects in the long term, however, there can be little doubt of its necessity and appropriateness in 410. Even so harsh a critic of the Athenian democracy and its leaders as Eduard Meyer concedes that "it was a measure which, in a state of siege, was unavoidable and thoroughly justified."[49]

These actions required money, but the democracy had inherited an empty treasury.[50] How did the Athenians expect to pay for the new expenditures as well as the much larger ones they must make to wage the war? The victory of Cyzicus promised to increase the flow of revenue from the empire. States that had fallen into arrears during Athens' weakness would now pay both those arrears and current tribute because it was strong again. The Athenians appear to have believed

[46]Beloch, *GG* II:1, 397–398; Meyer, *GdA* IV, 316.
[47]*Ath. Pol.* 28.3. For useful modern discussions, see U. von Wilamowitz-Moellendorf, *Aristoteles und Athen* (Berlin, 1893), II, 212–216; Meyer, *GdA* IV, 316–317; J. J. Buchanan, *Theorika* (Locust Valley, N.Y., 1962), 35–48; *GHI*, 260; Rhodes, *Commentary*, 355–356. For a calculation of the cost, see Glotz and Cohen, *HG*, 739, n. 96.
[48]Aesch. 2.76; Arist. *Pol.* 1267b, 11–12.
[49]*GdA* IV, 317.
[50]W. S. Ferguson, *The Treasurers of Athena* (Cambridge, Mass., 1932), 38.

that the substitution of the old tribute and its quotas would bring in more money than the 5 percent tax on trade that had been introduced in 414, for they seem to have reintroduced the tribute quotas in 410.[51] The establishment of the customs-house at the Bosporus, moreover, could be expected to bring in income beyond that obtained from the subject cities. In some way, therefore, the Athenians expected to recover their empire and its revenues and to use the revenues to pay for the conduct of the war and the expenditures at home. The records of the *Hellenotamiai*, who controlled the imperial funds, show that in 410/ 9 payments were made from the treasuries of Athena on the Acropolis for military purposes and for the *diobelia*, among various other domestic expenses.[52] Finally, the democratic regime was willing to make use of a source of revenue that the Five Thousand had refused to employ, the direct war tax *(eisphora)*. In any case, we would expect that a government limited to the propertied classes would resist such an impost, and the evidence is clear that even after the fall of the moderate regime, the generals associated with the moderates wanted to avoid its imposition.[53] The democrats, however, were more ready to tap the fortunes of the upper classes, although prudence and the exhaustion of those fortunes appear to have limited their impositions to only two from 410 to 405.[54]

The restored democracy made still further demands on the Athenian treasury by resuming the building program on the Acropolis that had been abandoned at least since the Sicilian expedition. It has been usual to speak of this activity as still another way for the state to give economic aid to its needy citizens.[55] One scholar has put it most dramatically: "What once had been the manifestation of the power and wealth of the state was now a means of maintenance in the greatest need,"[56] but a purely social and economic explanation for the resumption of

---

[51]*ATL* II, A13; 3, 91–92, 363 (accepted in *GHI*, 258–259). This view is challenged by H. B. Mattingly (*BSA* LXII [1967], 14–17) and defended by Meiggs (*Athenian Empire*, 438–439).

[52]*GHI*, 63, 255–260.

[53]Diodorus (13.47.7) tells us that Theramenes collected booty from the islands he ravaged "because he wished to relieve the citizens and allies from the *eisphorai*." At 13.64.4 he says that after the victory at Cyzicus, Alcibiades gathered booty from the territory of Pharnabazus "because he wanted to spare the people from the *eisphorai*."

[54]R. Thomsen, *Eisphora* (Copenhagen, 1964), 176–177.

[55]See, for example, Busolt, *GG* III:2, 1545, and E. Will, *Le monde grec et l'orient*, vol. 1, *Le Ve siècle (510–403)* (Paris, 1972), 380.

[56]Meyer, *GdA* IV, 318.

activity is hard to believe. The scale of the new building program was small, even tiny compared to the great works undertaken before the war. The only works begun at this time were the addition of a parapet to the temple of Athena Nike and the completion of the temple to Athena Polias, the Erechtheum, as it has come to be known.[57] The parapet would have employed few men; the greater part of the Erechtheum had been done by the time work resumed in 409, so that not many would have been given employment. Not many of the workers, moreover, were citizens. Of the seventy-one contractors and workers named in the inscription for 409/8, only twenty were citizens, the rest being slaves and resident aliens.[58] That is no way for democratic politicians to organize construction projects meant to give work to the voters. It seems more likely that the citizens of the restored democracy and their leaders were trying precisely to hark back to the great days of the democracy under Pericles, to build monuments to prove their own greatness and make them "the objects of admiration both to contemporaries and to men in the future."[59] The sight of great and new buildings was meant to bring confidence, hope, and courage to the men who must gain victory over formidable foes after suffering terrible misfortunes.

It is tempting to believe, although we have no positive proof, that the parapet surrounding the temple of Athena Nike was erected to commemorate the great double victory at Cyzicus.[60] The relief carvings show *Nikai*, goddesses of victory, setting up trophies and leading sacrificial bulls to Athena for ceremonies of thanksgiving. To display this beautiful carving with the theme of victory in so prominent a place would deliver an unmistakable message to all who saw it. The Erechtheum met different, but no less important, needs of the moment. The response of the Athenians to the scandals of 415, the mutilation of the Hermae and the parody of the Eleusinian mysteries, reveal how close to the surface lay the religious feelings of the Athenian people.[61] The Periclean era had been a time of experiment, novelty, enlight-

---

[57]The date for the parapet is somewhat speculative. Among those proposing the date accepted here are Glotz and Cohen (*HG* II, 739) and Will (*Le monde grec*, 380). The date of the resumption of work on the Erechtheum is firmly fixed by an inscription (*IG* I² 372–374) in the year 409/8.

[58]M. N. Tod, *CAH* V, 5.

[59]1.41.4.

[60]I am grateful to J. J. Pollitt for calling my attention to this suggestion made by Eve Harrison in an unpublished paper.

[61]C. A. Powell, *Historia* XXVIII (1979), 15–31.

enment, and the questioning of tradition. The experience of war, pestilence, and defeat had produced a sobering response. It was the upper class that studied with and supported the sophists and scientists; the average man inclined more to a return to traditional religion, ideas, and values and, even beyond, toward irrationalism. The war years saw the introduction into Athens of mystical and orgiastic foreign deities from Thrace and the east. At the very time that the rational and scientific Hippocratic school of medicine was at its height on the island of Cos, the Athenians imported from Epidaurus the cult of Asclepius, the god represented by a serpent, who cured by miracles. "This diversion of religious feelings towards foreign forms in which could be seen the resurgence of irrational, 'primitive,' aspirations such as the archaic period had known at the time of the rise of Dionysism or of Orphism, went far beyond, in the direction of regression, the conservative reaction of civic religion."[62]

Such a movement seems to provide a plausible background for the restored democracy's decision to complete the construction, begun after the Peace of Nicias, of the temple to Athena Polias. In that form, as the patron goddess of the city, protectress of the Acropolis itself, which was the earliest location of Athens, she was the oldest representation of the state cult. Her statue, which received the sacred garment at each Panathenaic festival, had sat in the earliest temple on the Acropolis, which was destroyed by the Persians and never rebuilt. The architects who planned the new structure were given a most difficult assignment.

The area which the Erechtheion eventually occupied includes the most ancient shrines of the Acropolis, sites connected with fertility cults, chthonic deities, and hero cults whose origins stretched into the remote Bronze Age. Here were the tombs of Kekrops, Erechtheus, and Bootes, early kings of Athens; the miraculous olive tree of Athena; the trident mark and saline springs left by Poseidon; the crevice in which the child god Erechthonios guarded the Acropolis in serpent form; a sanctuary of Pandrosus, the "moistener of all," one of the three daughters of Kekrops who went mad and jumped from the Acropolis when they beheld Erechthonios in the form of a snake-legged child; and other shrines as well.[63]

The completion of the Erechtheum, therefore, was an act of civic piety, traditional in its intention, like the publication of the ancient laws of

[62]Will, *Le monde grec*, 615–616.
[63]J. J. Pollitt, *Art and Experience in Classical Greece* (Cambridge, 1972), 132–133.

Draco and Solon, meant to win the favor of the gods and to lend confidence and courage to the Athenian people as they faced the efforts and dangers that lay ahead of them.

Although Cleophon is the best-known democratic politician of the day, we cannot know what part he may have played in carrying through this new program of activity. The most dynamic and imaginative Athenians—men such as Theramenes, Thrasybulus, and Alcibiades—seem to have been with the fleet in the Hellespont. Probably no single man planned the entire undertaking; instead, it seems to have represented a broad consensus of ordinary Athenians without the leadership of extraordinary men. Yet the entire program had an inherent logic and made considerable sense, given its premises. If the terms of peace offered by Sparta were unacceptable, the war must continue. That would require financial reorganization. The oligarchs and moderates had approached the financial problem by tightening the collective Athenian belt, chiefly at the expense of the poor, but that plan could work only in the short run. If a quick peace could not be achieved, the only answer was to expand the sources of revenue. The victory at Cyzicus opened the possibility of doing so in the empire, and the resort to the *eisphora* tapped domestic resources. The increase of public expenditure to assist the hard-pressed Athenian poor has been criticized but unjustly. The costs were not so great as to ruin Athens' prospects. If the recovery of the empire and its revenues continued, they could be easily sustained; if not, the war was lost anyway. In any case, there was no way to continue fighting without attention to the plight of Athens' poorer citizens. Finally, the building program, modest as it was, represented an important and intelligent attempt to restore the Athenians' moral and spiritual vitality.

In the end, however, the outcome of the entire program depended on the military success of Athenian forces, and the newly restored democracy got off to a good start in that respect. It was probably in the month of July that Agis once again launched a raid from Decelea that sent his troops right up to the walls of Athens.[64] No doubt he thought that another change in regime might have caused internal division and increased the chances of confusion, chaos, and perhaps even treason, but once again his hopes were disappointed. Thrasyllus,

[64]Xen. 1.1.33. Busolt (*GG* III:2, 1528–1529 and n. 2 on 1528) places this event in mid-March, but W. J. McCoy (*AJP* XCVIII [1977], 276, n. 49) makes a powerful case for a date shortly after mid-summer.

back from the straits, led a force of Athenians and allies, who happened to be in the city, to the Lyceum outside the walls and put them in fighting array. The sight of the organized Athenian force was enough for Agis, who quickly fled. The Athenians pursued and were able to pick off some of the enemy laggards. It was only a skirmish, but it further raised Athenian spirits and considerably helped the prestige of Thrasyllus.[65] At some time during the same summer, no doubt as a result of the Athenian victory at Cyzicus, an anti-Spartan faction on Chios gained control of the island and exiled its opponents.[66] It was probably during the same summer that the city of Neapolis on the Thracian coast was attacked by the Thasians aided by Peloponnesian forces. The Neapolitans resisted successfully, remaining loyal to Athens and continuing to assist the Athenians in their attempts to regain control of Thasos.[67] The Athenians will also have taken comfort in a reverse suffered by the Spartans late in the winter of 410/9. Their colony at Heraclea in Trachis was defeated in battle by the neighboring peoples; 700 colonists died and with them the Spartan governor.[68]

The Athenians derived the greatest material benefit from the Carthaginian invasion of Sicily, launched in the summer of 409. Ironically, they gained this advantage as a result of the disaster they had suffered there in 413. The Athenian ally Segesta had been left at the mercy of its enemies by the Athenian defeat. Fearing attack, the Segestans called in Carthage as an ally. The resulting major invasion forced the Syracusans to withdraw their fleet from eastern waters and the war against Athens to use it in defense of the homeland. The departure of the Syracusans deprived the Spartans of their ablest, most daring, and most determined naval allies at a time when they could not easily be spared.[69]

The year 410/9, nevertheless, brought more losses than gains to the Athenians. Even before the democratic restoration, probably late in the winter of 411/10, Athens lost the prospect of gaining assistance from its Corcyraean allies. The oligarchs there, who had been almost

[65]Xenophon (1.1.34) says that the Athenians then voted Thrasyllus the forces he had come to request, but we shall see that the resources needed were not available until the next year. It is possible that, in their enthusiasm, the Athenians voted the forces in the summer of 410 but did not produce them until the following year. More likely, Xenophon has misplaced the decision.

[66]Diod. 13.65.3–4; Busolt, GG III:2, 1552.

[67]GHI, 89; Busolt, GG III:2, 1552.

[68]Xen. 1.2.18.

[69]Diod. 13.43–44, 54–63; Busolt, GG III:2, 1555.

annihilated in the civil strife of earlier years, once again tried to bring their state over to the Spartans. In response, the democrats called on Conon, the Athenian general at Naupactus, for help. With his assistance the democrats killed many of their opponents and drove most of them, more than a thousand, into exile. Fearing that the oligarchs might return, they took the extreme step of freeing their slaves and giving citizenship to their resident aliens to strengthen their forces. In fact, after Conon had withdrawn, a group of oligarchic supporters still in the city seized control of the marketplace and called back the exiles from their camp on the mainland. The resulting battle lasted all day, but the fall of night prevented a clear decision. Instead of resuming the slaughter, however, the opponents came to an agreement and put an end to civil strife. For the rest of the war, Corcyra remained neutral; the Athenians had lost an important ally.[70] Soon even more serious misfortunes struck the restored democracy. In the winter of 410/9, the Spartans attacked the Athenian fort at Pylos, which had been left in the hands of a Messenian garrison. The Athenians sent a relief force under the command of Anytus, but winter storms drove him back as he tried to round Cape Malea. On the point of starvation, the Messenians left Pylos under truce. The Athenians had lost an important base for operations against the Peloponnesus and a valuable bargaining counter for future peace negotiations.[71]

In the following summer, the Athenians suffered still another blow. The Megarians captured Nisaea, their port on the Saronic Gulf, which the Athenians had held since 424. The Athenians responded by sending 1,000 hoplites and 400 cavalry to get it back. Their generals, Leotrophides and Timarchus, led them into battle against a much larger force of all of the Megarians and some of their allies at the heights called "The Horns" (ta kerata) near the frontier between the two states. The Athenians routed the enemy and killed many Megarians, but they could not recover Nisaea.[72] The loss of Nisaea was

[70]Diod. 13.48; Busolt, GG III:2, 1530–1533 and n. 1 on 1533.

[71]Diod. 13.64. Diodorus tells us that the Athenians brought Anytus to trial on a charge of treason, but he got off by bribing the jury, the first bribery of this kind in Athenian history (Diod. 13.64.6; Ath. Pol. 27.5). Anytus had been a lover of the young Alcibiades (Plut. Alc. 4). After the war he was one of the moderates associated with Theramenes (Ath. Pol. 34.3) and went into exile with Thrasybulus in opposition to the Thirty (Xen. 2.3.42, 44). In 399 he was one of the three accusers of Socrates (Plato, Apology 18b). We may assume that he was a moderate in 410/9 as well, and the charge against him may have been part of the democratic assault against political opponents.

[72]Diod. 13.65.1–2. For the date, see Busolt, GG III:2, 1554, n. 1.

annoying but of no great strategic importance. The fate of Athens would be decided in the Aegean and the straits, but the year 409 also brought a reversal to the Athenians in this area. The Spartans sent a fleet of twenty-five ships to Ionia under their new admiral, Cratesippidas. The Chian exiles persuaded him to restore them and drive out their opponents, and in this way Chios returned to Spartan control. The newly exiled anti-Spartan Chians then established a base at Atarneus on the opposite mainland from which they launched attacks on their homeland.[73]

These losses were troubling, but much more serious was Athens' failure to provide its generals in the straits the resources with which to exploit the great victory at Cyzicus. That victory had driven the enemy fleet from Hellespontine waters, but vital cities such as Sestos, Byzantium, and Chalcedon remained in hostile hands. Immediately after the battle at Cyzicus, Pharnabazus had given the Spartans encouragement and money to build another fleet as great as the one destroyed.[74] Unless the Athenians recaptured the ports, they would be compelled to fight more naval battles to win control of the narrow seas once again. Without more resources, moreover, they could not attempt to regain the lost cities of the Aegean and with them the lost imperial income. Yet between December of 411 and April or May of 409 Thrasyllus remained in Athens, and between the spring of 410 and the winter of 409/8 the generals in the Hellespont did nothing of note.[75] Why did the Athenians fail to supply Thrasyllus with the forces he requested and send him out to reinforce the generals in the summer of 410?

One explanation that has been offered involves political motives.[76] It assumes a major split between the generals in the Hellespont—Theramenes, Alcibiades, and Thrasybulus—with supporters of the departed Five Thousand on the one side against the restored democrats and their favorite general, Thrasyllus, on the other side. In this view, the very greatness of the victory at Cyzicus worked against the vic-

[73]Diod. 13.65.3–4.
[74]Xen. 1.1.24–26.
[75]See Andrewes' brief statement of Ferguson's chronology, also accepted here: "The battle of Kyzikos in March or April 410, Thrasyllos' expedition to Ionia in summer 409, the recovery of Byzantium and Kalchedon in 408, Alkibiades' return to Athens in 407, the battle of Notion late in 407 or early in 406" (*JHS* LXXIII [1953], 2).
[76]Andrewes, *JHS* LXXIII (1953), 2–9. Bloedow (*Alcibiades*, 57, n. 332) accepts the general interpretation while rejecting its belief in Alcibiades' leading position after Cyzicus.

torious generals, for it freed the democrats from their fear of the enemy
that alone made them tolerate the Five Thousand. "The first thought
of the restored democrats was to safeguard themselves against another
revolution, and they were in no mood to be fair to the men of the
5000."[77] As part of the plan they held new elections for generals,
choosing ten loyal democrats and "passing over Alkibiades and Theramenes, probably Thrasybulus also."[78] They did not recall the generals
in the Hellespont but allowed them to continue to operate in that
region for the next few years with an "irregular" command. The second
part of the democratic political scheme was to send out Thrasyllus at
the head of an armed force in 409 not to the Hellespont but to Ionia.
"The expedition to Ionia was their solution to the problem, and had
an ideological as well as a purely military purpose: no doubt Thrasyllos
honestly hoped to damage the Spartans and recover a rich area for
Athens, but he also wanted to improve the city's position against the
victors of Kyzikos, to show that loyal democratic generals could win
their victories, too."[79]

This explanation is ingenious but mistaken. We have little reason
to believe that there was a significant political division between the
city of Athens and its generals in the Hellespont from 410 to 407.
Although the argument from silence cannot be decisive here, we must
notice that none of our ancient sources speaks of such a rift. On the
contrary, both Xenophon and Diodorus show all three of the generals
in question leading Athenian forces on land and sea in each of the
years between 410/9 and 408/7 without suggesting any change in their
status.[80] Apart from the facts, it hardly seems likely that the democrats
in Athens would have been at odds with the thoroughly democratic
fleet and its generals. One of those generals was Thrasybulus, the
leader, in collaboration with Thrasyllus, of the defense of democracy
on Samos: he had sworn his troops on that island to an oath in defense
of democracy even before democracy returned to Athens. Why should
the Athenian democrats trust him less than Thrasyllus?[81] Alcibiades
was different, but he, too, like Thrasybulus and Thrasyllus, had been
elected general by the fleet at Samos.[82] The speaker in Lysias' speech

[77]Andrewes, *JHS* LXXIII (1953), 4.
[78]Ibid.
[79]Ibid., 4–5.
[80]Xen. 1.3.3, 1.4.8–9; Diod. 13.64.2–3, 66.1, 68.1. See Fornara, *Generals*, 68–69.
[81]See above, 169–173.
[82]See above, 178.

On the Property of Aristophanes tells his audience: "I think you know that Alcibiades was general for four or five years in a row," a statement that could only refer to the period we are considering and one that is not tendentious.[83] Neither he nor his audience appear to know that Alcibiades' office was in any way irregular. How, indeed, could the Athenians remove him from his position, confirmed by formal election in Athens, without insulting and alienating the democratic sailors and soldiers in the Hellespont? Like Alcibiades, Theramenes, too, was different but in another way: he had been elected only by the Five Thousand, not by the democratic fleet, but that disability would easily have been eased by the loyal and effective exercise of his command under the restored democracy and thoroughly obliterated by his magnificent performance at Cyzicus. He was one of the generals who independently negotiated an agreement with Pharnabazus on behalf of Athens in 408. Thrasyllus, presumably, was on the scene, yet no one appears to have objected to an "irregular" general participating in so formal an act, one that was not later repudiated.[84] What, moreover, would be gained by declaring the generals "irregular" while leaving them in command of troops who might be turned against the offending democratic politicians in Athens? There was no reason in the world for the Athenians to estrange their successful generals and their loyal men at this time.[85] There is no reason, therefore, to believe in new

[83]Lys. 19.52.

[84]Diod. 13.66.3; Xen. 1.3.8; Plut. *Alc.* 31.1. Only Diodorus mentions Theramenes by name, but he is obviously one of the generals included by the other sources. See the valuable article by M. Amit in *LAC* XLII (1973), 436–457.

[85]Andrewes recognizes this difficulty and answers it as follows: "A new board of generals was elected, passing over Alkibiades and Theramenes, probably Thrasyboulos also. But it was a more tricky matter actually to replace these men in their command, for the fleet itself had chosen Alkibiades and Thrasyboulos, and under them and Theramenes had just won an exhilarating victory, so that it was not clear that the fleet would be willing to obey the democrats' commanders and send Alkibiades and Theramenes home to face Kleophon. Their prospects in Athens would be at least uncertain, a matter of balancing the prestige of Kyzikos, some months past, against the immediate hostility of the democrats to the 5000. But this fleet, possibly loyal to its victorious generals, was in possession of the sea passage through the Hellespont, without which Athens would starve. So the democrats, prudently, did not try to recall the generals— but neither did they send them reinforcements" (*JHS* LXXIII [1953], 4).

This seems a very forced interpretation of events. It implies that the democrats at Athens were both foolish and unpatriotic: foolish because they would have risked offending the generals and their men by declaring them "irregular" without depriving them of their power; unpatriotic because they would have failed to exploit the victory at Cyzicus, thereby endangering the safety of Athens, merely for their own political benefit. There is no hint of any such attitudes in the sources and no reason to believe in it except for Andrewes' hypothesis.

elections of generals after the regular ones that were held under the Five Thousand in the spring of 410.[86] Finally, there is no reason to think that domestic political considerations governed Athenian military policy in the summer of 410.

Moreover, such an assumption about the influence of domestic politics is unnecessary, for the Athenians had good and sufficient reasons to wait until 409 to send out a new force and to send it to Ionia before going to the Hellespont. A body of fifty triremes, 5,000 of its rowers equipped as peltasts and light-armed, mobile infantrymen; 1,000 hoplites; and 100 cavalry—the forces actually sent in 409—all together would be composed of 11,100 men.[87] Even if all were paid at the low, post-Sicily rate of 3 obols daily, the cost would be almost 30 talents a month, and the fleet could not set sail without several months' salary in hand. There would also be troop- and horse-carriers for the hoplites and cavalry, and the state would have to provide the peltasts with weapons. In mid-summer of 410, however, the treasury was almost empty.[88] But during the year, money became available from various

---

[86]Andrewes' belief in a new election is not supported by the evidence he adduces but depends on accepting his general view of the situation. Of Theramenes he says: "He could hardly feel friendly towards the radical democrats or they towards him, and it is most unlikely that he was elected general in these years" (*JHS* LXXIII [1953], 4). (1) Against this is the undoubted fact that Theramenes held commands in each year in question. If they were "irregular," only modern theorists say so. Alcibiades, as we have seen, also held commands every one of those years, but Andrewes excludes him from the board of generals for 410/9 on the grounds that another general for that year, Pasiphon, came from his tribe. (2) But the evidence is clear that the presence of two men from the same tribe on the board of generals was more frequent than infrequent in the years between 441/40 and 412/11. In that stretch we know of eight or nine doublets. There are three years in which we find two sets of doublets and one in which there was a doublet and a triplet (Fornara, *Generals*, 71). Nothing, therefore, can be concluded from the fact adduced, much less the following statement: "It is to be presumed that the restored democracy held fresh elections, cancelling or passing over any appointments the 5000 made for 410/9" (Andrewes, *JHS* LXXIII [1953], 6). (3) Andrewes' other evidence against Alcibiades' generalship is that he was nervous about returning to Athens in 407 and that Xenophon refers to him as being an exile (*pheugonta*) while away from Athens. As we have seen, these matters can both be explained as the result of Alcibiades' legal situation and his legitimate fear of prejudice against him by some Athenians. They need say nothing about his generalship. As to Thrasybulus, Andrewes proposes no evidence against his legitimate command in these years, saying only that he was no extreme democrat and may be presumed to share the equivocal position of his two colleagues. None of the evidence adduced proves what it intends to prove.

[87]Xen. 1.1.34, 1.2.1; Diodorus (13.64.1) gives the number of ships as only thirty, but Xenophon appears to be better informed about this expedition.

[88]Ferguson, *Treasurers*, 38, cited by McCoy, *AJP* XCVIII (1977), 277.

sources and allowed the treasurers to disburse funds for military and other purposes.[89] There is also considerable reason to doubt that the Athenians had as many as fifty triremes available for the campaign in 410.[90] Practical considerations, therefore, required the Athenians to delay the reinforcements.

In the summer of 409, Thrasyllus finally set out with his force but not to the Hellespont. Instead, he sailed for Samos before launching an attack on the Ionian mainland.[91] The decision to go there has raised questions among modern scholars,[92] but it should not be surprising. Thrasyllus had been sent to Athens from the Hellespont in the winter of 411/10 after the battle at Sestos to ask for reinforcements.[93] Then there would have been good reason to send a force to the Hellespont immediately, had the Athenians been able to do so. In the spring of 410, after Cyzicus, it still would have been important to send a force directly to that theater of warfare before the Spartans could restore their navy, but as we have seen, Athenian resources were not yet up to the challenge. By the summer of 409, however, the strategic situation had changed. The Athenians in the Hellespont no longer faced immediate danger, as they had after Sestos, nor did they confront an extraordinary opportunity, for the Spartans once again had a fleet. A delay of a month or so in beginning the campaign in the Hellespont was not crucial. On the other hand, there were attractive prospects in Ionia. Tissaphernes' satrapy must have appeared very vulnerable; he had thoroughly alienated the Spartans on whose forces he had previously relied, and in any case, they were off in the straits where they had other concerns. Three Greek cities in his province—Miletus, Cnidus, and Antandros—had ejected his garrisons.[94] Moreover, in most cities there were Atticizers waiting to reverse policy if the Athenians gained even temporary successes.[95] Victories in Ionia would restore Athenian control, bring money into Athenian coffers, and build a

[89]McCoy, *AJP* XCVIII (1977), 277–278.

[90]Ibid., 273, n. 39.

[91]Xen. 1.2.1; Diodorus (13.64.1) omits the early stages of the expedition and begins his account with the attack on Ephesus.

[92]It is a central point in Andrewes' argument (*JHS* LXXIII [1953], 2–9). See also McCoy (*AJP* XCVIII [1977], 279–281), who follows Andrewes in accepting a political explanation for the choice of Ionia.

[93]Xen. 1.1.8.

[94]8.84; 108.4–5; 109.1.

[95]Meiggs, *Athenian Empire*, 371. For a good discussion of the situation, see McCoy, *AJP* XCVIII (1977), 281–282.

victorious momentum. All of these results would be useful in preparation for what could then be a final confrontation with the enemy in the straits.

Even so, there is no reason to believe that the Athenians neglected the needs of their forces in the Hellespont when they sent Thrasyllus to Ionia in 409. His forces were precisely those needed by Alcibiades and Theramenes, and Thrasyllus' actions are consistent with the view that his orders required him to move on to the straits after his activities in Ionia. Such a double mission was in no way unusual for Athenian commanders. In the winter of 433/32, Archestratus was sent to Macedonia with orders to secure Potidaea along the way; in 429 an Athenian fleet was ordered to bring help to Phormio at Naupactus and to set matters right in Crete along the way; in 425 Sophocles and Eurymedon were sent with a fleet to Sicily with orders to perform services on the Peloponnesian coast and at Corcyra before they arrived.[96] We need not doubt, therefore, that Thrasyllus' orders covered both Ionia and the Hellespont.

Thrasyllus set out at the beginning of summer, perhaps early in June of 409.[97] His first stop was Samos, where he spent three days. From there he sailed against Pygela, on the coast just to the south of Ephesus (see Map 3). He devastated the countryside before attacking the town wall. But the ravaging provided warning and time for the Milesians to send a relief force. The Athenians were caught unaware, and the Milesian column found the Athenians scattered, not in battle order, and pursued the exposed peltasts. The remaining Athenians, hoplites and peltasts, rallied and came to the rescue, killing most of the Milesians and capturing 200 enemy shields abandoned in flight. They set up a trophy to celebrate their triumph, but it was a hollow victory. The walls of Pygela stood, and the city remained in enemy hands.[98] The next day the Athenians sailed to Notium, on the coast to the northwest of Ephesus. From there they marched inland to Colophon and brought that city back under Athenian control. They were in a good position to attack Ephesus, the main target in the area, and would have been in even a better position had they taken Pygela,

---

[96] 1.57.6; 2.85.4–6; 4.2.3.

[97] Xen. 1.2.1. Busolt (*GG* III:2, 1549) places the start of the campaign at the beginning of June, but Meyer (*GdA* IV, 323) puts it in May. "The beginning of summer" (ἀρχομένου τοῦ θέρους) suits June better. Both place the events in 410, which is a year too early.

[98] Xen. 1.2.2–3.

which would have allowed them to threaten the city from two directions. Instead of making an immediate assault, however, they continued inland to Lydia, where they did much damage and collected a great deal of booty, but once again the failure of the commander to impose strict discipline proved costly. Stages, the Persian commander in the area, caught the Athenians scattered and in disarray, killed some, and would have done even more damage had not the Athenian cavalry come to the rescue. Thrasyllus turned back to the coast, intending to sail against Ephesus.

Once again the ravaging and delay gave the enemy warning and time to rally its troops. It was not until the seventeenth day after the raid that Thrasyllus set sail for Ephesus. By that time Tissaphernes was on the scene with a large army, swelled by the crews of twenty-five Syracusan ships and two from Selinus, for the Carthaginian attack on Sicily had not yet begun. Tissaphernes used the time well, sending horsemen into the countryside, urging the people of the neighborhood "to come to the aid of Artemis."[99] We should not forget that the last event reported by Thucydides is Tissaphernes' sacrifice to Artemis at Ephesus.[100] We may be sure that it was public and well advertised. The satrap must have carefully nourished a reputation for piety toward the Greek gods and especially Artemis of the Ephesians. His appeal, therefore, will have been both plausible and effective. Thrasyllus landed at daybreak and split his forces: he landed his hoplites on one side of the city, at the foot of Mt. Coressus, and the other troops near a marsh on the opposite side. This may have seemed a clever strategy to Thrasyllus, but it turned out to be disastrous. The enemy concentrated its forces and attacked the hoplites first, routing them, killing about a hundred, and driving the rest to the sea. Then they turned their full force against the troops by the marsh, once again routing the Athenians and killing another 300. The Ephesians set up two trophies, one at each battle site, and gave prizes for valor to the Sicilians, who had especially distinguished themselves, and to individuals among them for particularly conspicuous bravery.[101]

[99]Ibid., 4–6.
[100]8.109.
[101]Xen. 1.2.10. All of the Sicilians were invited to settle in Ephesus as resident aliens freed from the taxes other such metics paid. Later, when the Carthaginians destroyed Selinus, its people were offered Ephesian citizenship. See now the new papyrus fragment of P. published by L. Koenen in *Studia Papyrologica* XV (1976), 55–76. It agrees with the account of the other sources and adds some details.

The Athenians had to to ask for a truce to recover and bury their dead. They sailed back to Notium and from there northward to Lesbos and the Hellespont. They seem to have stayed at Lesbos throughout the rest of the summer and into the fall, for they did not reach the Hellespont until shortly before winter.[102] What kept them there so long?[103] The likeliest answer is that after his performance in Ionia, Thrasyllus was in no hurry to get to the Hellespont. Even more important, he must have been influenced by the memory of his failure to prevent an enemy fleet from getting into the Hellespont in 411.[104] After withdrawing from Ephesus, Thrasyllus probably took up a station at Lesbos to wait for the Syracusan fleet and to be sure to cut it off on its way north. He must have waited until fall before they appeared, and when they did, he was ready. From his anchorage in Methymna he spied the twenty-five Syracusan ships trying to make their way from Ephesus to the Hellespont. He attacked, capturing four ships and their full crews and driving the others back from where they came.[105] At least Thrasyllus had not made the same mistake twice.

His expedition had regained Colophon for Athens and had collected some booty, but it had plainly failed in its main purpose: to regain Ephesus and its neighboring cities and thereby start a major movement toward the restoration of full Athenian control of Ionia. The campaign once again revealed the inexperience and inadequacy of Thrasyllus as a general. On two occasions, he had wasted time by ravaging the country and had allowed the enemy to prepare for his attack. Had he moved against Ephesus at once, before Tissaphernes could rally his forces and before the Sicilians could arrive, the Athenians might have taken the city as easily as they had recaptured Colophon. When he

[102]Ibid. 2.13–14.
[103]Busolt (*GG* III:2, 1551) has seen the problem: "The trip of Thrasyllus to the Hellespont must not have been delayed merely by the pursuit [of enemy ships], but also by other expeditions and whatever other troubles, for he joined Alcibiades at Sestos in the late fall of 410 [409 in our chronology]."
[104]See above, 216–217.
[105]Xen. 1.2.12–13. Thrasyllus sent the prisoners back to Athens, all except Alcibiades' cousin of the same name, who was in exile because of his involvement in the scandals of 415 (Kagan, *Peace of Nicias*, 201). The text of Xenophon in all the manuscripts says that Thrasyllus had this man stoned to death (κατέλευσεν). The reading ἀπέλυσεν has been suggested which would mean that Thrasyllus singled Alcibiades' cousin out for especially favorable treatment and let him go. It is not possible to feel confident on this point; perhaps Alcibiades was on bad terms with his cousin, but it certainly seems unlikely that Thrasyllus would have deliberately angered the general in the Hellespont at this moment.

finally did attack against a fully prepared enemy, he chose a bad strategy that allowed the enemy to attack his divided forces with their own concentrated army, with dire and predictable results. The first major campaign launched by the restored democracy had failed in its first goal. It had lost 400 valuable hoplites of the 1,000 who had started out; nonetheless, it arrived in the Hellespont otherwise intact. Together with the Athenians already there, Thrasyllus' corps was a formidable force that might still accomplish great things under more experienced and abler leaders.

11. The Return of Alcibiades

The battle of Cyzicus took place in April or May of 410. In the next month or two, the generals in the Straits exploited their victory, chiefly by establishing a customs-house at Chrysopolis (see Map 9).[1] For about eighteen months thereafter they appear to have done little of note. With the Spartans swept from the sea, future tasks of importance would require more hoplites than they had and cavalry to protect them against the able horsemen of Pharnabazus.[2] They could, therefore, do little until reinforcements arrived. The Spartans used the lull in action as best they could. Over the winter of 410/9, they built new ships at Antandrus with Pharnabazus' money and timber from Mt. Ida, and their Syracusan allies helped fortify the city against attack.[3] Pasippidas, the admiral who succeeded Mindarus, also gathered ships from Sparta's allies, before being sent into exile for intriguing with Tissaphernes.[4] In the summer of 410, after Agis' abortive raid on Athens, the Spartans decided to strengthen their control of the Bosporus. They sent Clearchus, the Spartan who was Byzantium's *proxenos*, the representative of

---

[1]See above, 244–245.

[2]Andrewes (*JHS* LXXIII [1953], 2) rightly emphasizes the importance of hoplites for the campaigns the Athenians needed to fight after Cyzicus, but he says nothing of the cavalry, which was also necessary. Pharnabazus' cavalry had helped save the Peloponnesian army fleeing from the Athenians, who had no cavalry, at Abydos in the winter of 411/10 (Xen. 1.1.6–7). At Lampsacus in the winter of 409/8, Pharnabazus commanded a large cavalry force, but the Athenian cavalry brought by Thrasyllus allowed them to fight if off (Xen. 1.2.16).

[3]Xen. 1.1.24–6. Early in 408 they also built some new ships at Byzantium (Xen. 1.3.17).

[4]Xen. 1.1.32; 1.3.17.

that city's interests at Sparta, through the Hellespont to improve the defense of Chalcedon and Byzantium on either side of the entrance to the Black Sea. He took a force of Megarians and other allies on fifteen ships that were "troopships rather than warships." Three of them were destroyed by the Athenian patrol guarding the Hellespont, but the others got through to Byzantium.[5]

The arrival of Thrasyllus in November or December of 409 finally gave the Athenians the opportunity to resume the initiative, but co-ordination of the two forces was not easily accomplished. Alcibiades and Thrasyllus seem to have worked together well enough,[6] but their troops had more difficulty. When Alcibiades tried to integrate them into a single unit, the veterans of the battles in the straits refused to allow Thrasyllus' men within their ranks. This has been seen as the result of political rivalry between the generals,[7] but there is no reason to take this position. The ancient writers give an explanation that is perfectly understandable; Xenophon tells us that the old soldiers, who were undefeated, refused to mingle with the newcomers, who came fresh from defeat, and Plutarch fills in the details: The men of the Hellespont had heard about the defeat at Ephesus and about the Ephesians erecting a bronze trophy of victory "to the shame of the Athenians." These were the things with which the troops of Alcibiades reproached the men of Thrasyllus, and "exalting themselves and their general, they refused to share physical exercises with them or to allow them into their part of the camp."[8] If we add to these feelings the resentment at Thrasyllus' long delay in arriving, we need no further explanation of what took place. In spite of this rift, the two generals moved the Athenian forces to Lampsacus on the Asiatic side of the Hellespont. It was a good location from which to launch raids into the province of Pharnabazus and a good place from which to attack the main Spartan base at Abydos. With their newly acquired land forces added to their unchallenged navy, they could move down the coast and threaten the enemy from land and sea (see Map 5). During the

---

[5]Xen. 1.1.35–36.

[6]Diodorus (13.64.4) shows them cooperating smoothly.

[7]W. J. McCoy (*AJP* XCVIII [1977], 284), for instance, says "there can be little doubt (especially in light of the events of 407 and 406) that Alcibiades continued to view Thrasyllus with suspicion and contempt — and perhaps the feeling was mutual." In fact, we have no reason to believe there was friction between the generals in 408, whatever might have happened later. Such evidence as there is points to their collaboration.

[8]Xen. 1.2.15; Plut. *Alc.* 29.1–2.

winter of 409/8, the two contingents worked together to fortify Lampsacus and turn it into a secure center for operations.

When all was ready, the Athenians attacked Abydos. Success would deprive the Spartans of their only base on the Hellespont and give Athens full control of that waterway. The battle seems to have unfolded as follows: Thrasyllus made the first assault, having been sent ahead by sea with thirty ships. Pharnabazus discovered what was happening and came to the rescue of Abydos with a large force of both infantry and cavalry. He arrived after Thrasyllus' force had landed and launched an attack against him. Alcibiades appears to have traveled over land at the head of the Athenian cavalry, accompanied by 120 hoplites under the command of an officer named Menander. The Athenians seem to have timed his arrival to catch Pharnabazus unaware, while the satrap was engaged with Thrasyllus' force. He defeated the Persian and drove his army to flight, pursuing the enemy until the fall of darkness. The Athenians set up a trophy and exploited the victory by raiding the territory of Pharnabazus and collecting a considerable quantity of booty. Perhaps the plan had been to take the city by a double assault from land and sea before the Persian force could arrive, and Pharnabazus' quick appearance saved the city, in spite of his defeat; our sources do not say. However that may be, the Athenians did not achieve the main purpose of the expedition: Abydos remained in Spartan hands. One happy outcome of the affair, however, was that the rift in the Athenian army was healed: "The two factions were united and returned to camp together with mutual good will and joy."[9]

In the spring of 408, the Athenians, united and confident, set out to drive the enemy from the Bosporus and gain free passage to the Black Sea. Byzantium, on the European shore, had revolted from the Athenians in the summer of 411.[10] Chalcedon, on the opposite shore, had defected at some unspecified time before the Athenian assault. The Spartans had occupied it and had posted a garrison to defend it under the harmost, or governor, Hippocrates.[11] From his base nearby at Chrysopolis, Theramenes began laying waste to Chalcedonian ter-

---

[9]No single source tells the full story of the battle. The account offered here is constructed from the versions of Xenophon (1.2.15–17), Plutarch (*Alc.* 29.2–3), and Diodorus (13.64.4), who regularly confuses Thrasybulus with Thrasyllus. All three seem to have accurate information about the battle, but none of them has all of the facts or even all of those available to us. The final quotation is from Plut. *Alc.* 29.2.

[10]8.80.2–3.

[11]Xen. 1.3.5; Plut. *Alc.* 29.6.

ritory even before the arrival of the main Athenian force. Alcibiades and Thrasyllus left an adequate garrison to guard Lampsacus and sailed for the Bosporus. When they joined forces and made camp before Chalcedon, the combined fleet may have reached a total of almost 190 ships.[12] On learning of the vast armada sailing against them, the Chalcedonians turned over what remained of their portable property to their friendly neighbors, the Thracians of Bithynia, for safekeeping. Alcibiades took a force of infantry and cavalry, marching them along the shore protected by the fleet, into Bithynian territory. The frightened Bithynians surrendered the booty on demand, agreed to a treaty, and were not heard from again.[13]

The entire army then turned to the siege of Chalcedon. The Athenians constructed a wooden wall running from the Bosporus to the Sea of Marmora. This enclosed the Chalcedonians within a triangle of land, with the Athenian army and the wooden palisade between them and the Persians. The Athenians were free to throw most of their force against the city, since the wall, manned by only a few men, could hold off Pharnabazus. Since the Athenian fleet controlled the seas, the encirclement was complete. Hippocrates, the Spartan harmost of the city, chose to march his hoplites out and offer battle, and Thrasyllus led the main force of Athenian hoplites against him. The battle was hard-fought and, for a long time, confined to the two hoplite phalanxes. Pharnabazus had a large force of infantry and cavalry, but the wall kept him from using them to good effect. Alcibiades was once again in command of the cavalry and a small body of hoplites and joined the battle only after it had been long in progress; whether or not he waited intentionally, we cannot tell. In any case, his intervention was valuable; Hippocrates was killed and his army forced to flee. The battle, however, was not decisive, for the defending army made good its escape to the city, closed its gates, and continued the siege. Alcibiades did not stay to see it through to the end but went off instead to seek money on the Hellespontine shores, leaving the last chapter to Theramenes and Thrasyllus.[14]

[12]Xen. 1.3.1–2; Diod. 13.66.1; Plut. *Alc.* 29.3. For the calculation of Athenian numbers, see Hatzfeld, *Alcibiade*, 281, n. 4.

[13]Xen. 1.3.2–4; Plut. *Alc.* 29.3. Busolt (*GG* III:2, 1556 n. 2) doubts Diodorus' story that Theramenes wasted the territory of Chalcedon before the arrival of the main force, but E. F. Bloedow (*Alcibiades Reexamined* [Wiesbaden, 1973], 60, n. 350) shows there is no reason for disbelief.

[14]This account is based mainly on Xenophon (1.3.4–8). Diodorus (13.66.1–3) and Plutarch (*Alc.* 30.1) offer brief descriptions that add nothing of value.

Scholars have thought that at this point the fate of Chalcedon was sealed, that it was only a matter of time before it fell,[15] but Pharnabazus and his large army of infantry and cavalry, strong and frustrated, was only a short distance away at the sanctuary of Heracles in Chalcedonian territory. There could be no certainty that they would not find a way to get through the fence and present the besieging Athenians with a challenge from two directions. Perhaps these circumstances help explain the action the remaining Athenian generals took after the departure of Alcibiades. They negotiated a treaty with Pharnabazus on behalf of Chalcedon containing the following terms: the Chalcedonians would pay the tribute they had been accustomed to paying before their defection as well as the arrears that had accumulated; Pharnabazus himself would pay the Athenians 20 talents and would conduct Athenian ambassadors to the Great King; in return the Athenians swore not to attack the Chalcedonians or the territory of Pharnabazus until those ambassadors returned. The generals and Pharnabazus swore the required oaths to approve the treaty, but the satrap insisted that Alcibiades must swear too. When the latter returned, he refused merely to add his oath to the ones sworn by his colleagues and insisted that he would swear to Pharnabazus only if the satrap did the same to him. Each finally swore the oath in the presence of representatives of the other, and the deed was done.[16]

The Athenian negotiations with Pharnabazus reveal much about the situation in 408 and also raise important questions. They show that the Athenian generals in the Hellespont were cooperating and acting without any distinction of status, for the sources say nothing of any disagreement among them in undertaking such important and novel actions. Diodorus attributes the agreement to Theramenes, but Thrasyllus was also present and must have approved of and taken part in

---

[15]E.g., Hatzfeld, *Alcibiade*, 282; and Amit, *LAC* XLII (1973), 440.

[16]Xenophon (1.3.8–12), Diodorus (13.66.3), and Plutarch (*Alc.* 31.1–2) all tell the story somewhat differently. Xenophon's account is the fullest and most satisfactory, and I follow it, with one addition. Xenophon says the Athenians swore "not to make war on the Chalcedonians." Plutarch, however, says nothing about Chalcedonians, reporting that the Athenians promised "not to harm the territory of Pharnabazus." Scholars, without any manuscript support, have suggested that a scribal error is responsible for the reading we have and propose to substitute Pharnabazus for the Chalcedonians to make the account agree with Plutarch (see Grote, VIII, 132 with n. 3; Hatzfeld, *Alcibiade*, 285, n. 2; M. Amit, *LAC* XLII [1973], 456). I see no good reason to do so. Instead, I suggest that the Athenians promised to refrain from attacking either party, which in fact they did, going off at once to the siege of Byzantium. Xenophon and Plutarch simply reported different clauses of the treaty.

the negotiations.[17] The events also show that Alcibiades was not the supreme commander of the Athenian forces in the Hellespont and the other generals his subordinates. They clearly undertook an important action without his knowledge or participation.[18] On the other hand, Alcibiades obviously had a special, if informal, position, especially in the eyes of the Persians. Pharnabazus clearly did not think the treaty would be binding without his approval, and Alcibiades took full advantage of the opportunity to display his own importance both to the Persians and his own forces.

The agreement itself, however, is the most interesting development. Its novel and surprising character has confused modern scholars about the events themselves as well as their significance.[19] Normally, when the Athenians reconquered a rebellious ally, they required it to return to their control, often under a new constitution supported by Athenian officials and sometimes a garrison. If they did not regain physical control, they did collect tribute. The arrangement with Chalcedon kept the Athenians out of the city but gave them the tribute, arrears, and what amounted to an indemnity paid by Pharnabazus on behalf of the city. The Athenians were glad to accept the arrangement because it gave them at once the money they badly needed and promised them more in the future; it spared them the necessity of a difficult and costly siege and freed them to move against Byzantium, crucial for control of the Bosporus; finally, the arrangement was only temporary, until negotiations with the Great King could be completed. Pharnabazus agreed because it spared him a siege and a battle he was not eager to undertake, without losing control of a city that neither he nor the Great King wanted to lose. No one could be sure how long the Athenian discussions with the Great King might take or how they would

[17]Diodorus says that οἱ δὲ περὶ τὸν Θεραμένην made the treaty (13.66.3). He has a tendency to magnify the role of Theramenes, and his words may mean that Theramenes alone was involved. However, they may mean "Theramenes and the other Athenian generals." I take it in the latter sense, but even if Diodorus intended the former, we must believe that Thrasyllus was also involved.

[18]Bloedow (Alcibiades, 62, n. 364) makes the excellent point that "the fact that Alcibiades went for money shows that he cannot have anticipated the agreement with Pharnabazus, for the latter agreed to pay the Athenians 20 talents . . . a sum that would have offset the need to go in search of more funds."

[19]Most scholars, for instance, have said that Chalcedon fell into Athenian hands at this time. Amit, however (LAC XLII [1973], 445–446), who provides a list of scholarly opinion on the subject, has shown that it remained free under the protection of Pharnabazus. My own understanding of the events discussed here owes much to his important article.

work out, but meanwhile the satrap could hold onto Chalcedon and hope that the delay would turn events in his favor. That prospect was easily worth 20 talents.

Even more interesting is the Athenian decision to negotiate with the Great King. After the Athenians had rejected the Spartan peace offer, why were their generals willing to talk peace with the Persians? What made them think that the Great King would be interested, and what terms could they have had in mind? The Athenians, as we have seen, rejected the peace with Sparta because they did not trust the Spartans, because they had hopes of winning a better and more secure peace by further fighting, and because they hoped to persuade the Persians to abandon their allies by victories yet to come.[20] Peace with Sparta, moreover, need not bring peace with Persia. If, on the other hand, the Athenians could make peace with the Persians, "the King would cease to furnish money to the Spartans, the Athenians had every reason to believe that Sparta would be forced to renounce the war at sea, and in Greece itself the Athenians could obtain very much more favorable terms."[21] Their unbroken successes since Cynossema must have persuaded the Athenians that the time had come to see whether the Persians were ready to come to terms, and they determined to do so by negotiating with the Great King himself, not through untrustworthy or impotent satraps serving as intermediaries. They might hope for success not only because their recent victories had shown the vanity of counting on the Spartans to win at sea, regardless of Persian financial support, but also because of recent Spartan behavior. By now the Persians must have known of the Spartans' offer of a separate peace with Athens, a clear violation of their treaty with Persia. That action showed them to be not only incompetent but also unreliable allies and might be considered reason enough for the Great King to desist from supporting them further and to seek an accommodation with Athens.

It is harder to see what terms might be acceptable to both sides. The suggestion has been made that the temporary arrangement in respect to Chalcedon was meant to serve as a model for a general settlement between Athens and Persia that would see the Athenians abandon the Greek cities of Asia Minor by letting them come under Persian rule again but, at the same time, would allow the Athenians to collect the money they needed and maintain free access to the Black

[20]See above, 250–251.
[21]Amit, *LAC* XLII (1973), 453.

Sea.[22] Even without the benefit of hindsight, however, which tells us that the negotiations failed, we would find it hard to believe that the two sides could reach agreement. The cities of Asia Minor were not of much profit to the Great King if they did not pay him tribute. The model, moreover, of cities nominally under Persian rule but paying tribute to a foreign power would be glaring evidence of Persian weakness and a bad example for other subjects of the Great King. The Athenians, therefore, could hardly expect the Great King to continue to allow his subject cities to pay Athens for very long after the war was over. The Athenians may have been moved to seek out the Great King because they had heard of a Spartan mission to Susa led by Boeotius.[23] Perhaps they wanted to forestall closer cooperation between the Spartans and Persians. On perhaps they were unduly elated by their victories and overestimated the Great King's eagerness for peace. Possibly, they were more realistic and were willing to make an unsatisfactory peace with Persia that would free them to defeat the Spartans. After that they could return to recover the Greek cities of Asia, as they had done after the Persian War. In any case, they had little to lose by the attempt.

After the agreement Chalcedon was in no position to interfere with the Athenians' movement through the Bosporus, and their fort at Chrysopolis further secured the Asiatic side of the passage for the Athenians. Meanwhile, Alcibiades had been gathering money and troops from among the Thracians of the Gallipoli Peninsula. On the way back he stopped to attack Selymbria, a city from which he extracted money after the battle of Cyzicus but which had not admitted him within its walls.[24] The Athenian strategy called for the recovery of all coastal cities in the straits, so Alcibiades moved his whole force against Selymbria. Instead of imposing a lengthy and costly siege or attempting an assault that would almost surely be vain, Alcibiades used a combination of guile and generosity to gain control of Selymbria. In collusion with a pro-Athenian party within the city, he had the gates opened to him at night; rather than risk a fight with the terrified

[22]Ibid., 454–456. Amit does not make entirely clear the details of the settlement. Would the Athenians abandon the cities of Ionia completely and not collect revenue from them? Would they retain control of the cities in the Hellespont? Did they expect to continue indefinitely to collect revenue from cities that they did not physically control?

[23]Xen. 1.4.2.

[24]Xen. 1.1.21.

inhabitants, he offered reasonable terms and imposed strict discipline on his Thracian troops to see that they were observed. No harm was done to the city or its citizens; the Athenians received more money, placed a garrison in the city, and swiftly moved on toward Byzantium.[25] It was a skillful performance that saved time, money, and lives and also fully achieved its goal. This was the kind of warfare in which Alcibiades was most comfortable and in which he excelled.

The next target was Byzantium, the remaining key needed to unlock the Bosporus and the route to the Black Sea. Theramenes and Thrasyllus had already brought their forces to its territory after concluding the treaty with Pharnabazus, and Alcibiades joined them from Selymbria.[26] The Athenians disposed of considerable forces by the standards of the time: a massive fleet, unchallenged by the enemy; a hoplite force greatly enlarged by Alcibiades' Thracians; a cavalry; and more money than they had enjoyed for some time.[27] Even so, to take a fortified city willing to resist was neither easy nor certain. The Athenians once again, as at Chalcedon, built a wall to cut off the city on the landward side while their fleet prevented access by sea, but once again, neither siege nor assault promised quick success. Byzantium was an important city with a large population. It was defended by Clearchus, a tough Spartan harmost who had been sent to take command in the summer of 411.[28] As usual, the commander was the only Spartiate sent so far from home, but he was accompanied by a corps of *perioikoi* and a few *neodamodeis;* a Megarian contingent under Helixus, the man who had brought Byzantium into rebellion; a force of Boeotians under Coeratadas; and a body of mercenaries.[29] The Athenians spent some time assaulting the city but with so little success that Clearchus felt secure enough to leave Byzantium in the hands of his subordinates and cross over to the Asiatic shore to meet Pharnabazus. His first purpose was to get money to pay his troops, but he also intended to put together a fleet from the few ships left behind by the deposed admiral Pasippidas, the new ships recently constructed at Antandrus, and the fleet

[25]I have followed the fullest account, that of Plutarch (*Alc.* 30.2–5), whose details seem worthy of credit. See also Xen. 1.3.10; and Diod. 13.66.3–4.

[26]Xen. 1.3.14; Diod. 13.66.4; Plut. *Alc.* 31.2. Plutarch mentions only Alcibiades at Byzantium. Xenophon speaks of "the Athenians." Diodorus places Theramenes at Byzantium first, where Alcibiades joins him. No one names Thrasyllus, but Xenophon (1.4.10) makes it plain that he was on the scene until the end of the campaign.

[27]See Bloedow, *Alcibiades*, 63.

[28]8.80.3; Diod. 13.40.6.

[29]Xen. 1.3.15–16; Diod. 13.66.5.

under Agesandridas on the Thracian coast. With such a force he meant to draw the Athenians away from Byzantium by attacking their allies in the straits.[30]

Clearchus, however, had misjudged the situation in Byzantium. The siege was already having its effect on the civilians, who were suffering from hunger. The harmost, moreover, appears to have behaved with the harshness and arrogance typical of Spartans abroad and so to have alienated important Byzantines.[31] These men were able to communicate with Alcibiades, and together they devised a clever plan. He promised Byzantium the same gentle treatment he had given Selymbria, and the Byzantines agreed to let the Athenians enter the city on a fixed night. Then he circulated the story that new developments in Ionia required the Athenian forces to go there. On the afternoon of the agreed-upon day, the entire Athenian fleet sailed off, and the army marched a considerable distance from the city, presumably out of sight. After night fell the army stole back to within striking distance of the walls of Byzantium; meanwhile, the fleet sailed back into the harbor and began attacking the Peloponnesian boats moored there. The defenders rushed to the shore to bring help, leaving the walls unattended and most of the city without defense. Now the Byzantine plotters gave the signal to the waiting army of Alcibiades and Theramenes and let them into the city by placing ladders at the undefended walls. Even so, the enemy put up a stiff fight, aided as they were by most of the Byzantines who knew nothing of the plotters' agreement with the Athenians. Seeing that the struggle was going to be difficult, at the very least, Alcibiades saw to it that an announcement was made promising that the Byzantines would not be harmed. That turned the tide of battle; the citizens changed sides and turned against the Peloponnesian army, most of whom died fighting, although about 500 took refuge as suppliants in the temples. The victorious Athenians behaved with the same honor and restraint they had shown at Selymbria. No Byzantines were killed or exiled. The city was restored to its status as an ally of Athens and presumably resumed paying its old tribute, but its autonomy was restored; that is, the Peloponnesian garrison and governor were removed, and no Athenians took their place. Even the Peloponnesian prisoners were treated correctly: they were disarmed

[30]Xen. 1.3.17.
[31]Xen. 1.3.18–19; Diod. 13.66.6.

and sent to Athens for judgment.[32] The Athenians appear to have been consciously following a new policy of correctness and conciliation as they tried to restore control over their empire. The evidence suggests that at least Alcibiades and Theramenes and probably Thrasyllus shared in the formulation and execution of these strategies and policies. Probably, Alcibiades played the leading role in intriguing with the factions in the cities, and certainly, he came away with the lion's share of the credit.

As part of the agreement at Chalcedon, Pharnabazus had promised to conduct Athenian ambassadors to the Great King at Susa, and after the exchange of oaths with Alcibiades, he sent word that they should meet him at Cyzicus. The Athenians sent an embassy of five men accompanied by two Argives, no doubt because of the old ties of friendship between Argos and Persia.[33] During the siege of Byzantium, Pharnabazus was conducting this motley delegation into the interior but not very swiftly. At the onset of winter, they had reached only Gordium in Phrygia, where they received the news of the fall of Byzantium and waited until spring.[34] Perhaps they were delayed by bad weather, but it may be that Pharnabazus was aware of the Spartan mission to Susa—possibly he may even have inspired it[35]—and was procrastinating until its goal was accomplished.[36] Finally, after the beginning of spring, the journey toward Susa continued but not far, for the ambassadors from Athens soon encountered the Spartan embassy led by Boeotius. He was returning from a successful meeting with the Great King carrying the message that the Spartans had gotten everything they wanted from him. If proof of that assertion was

[32] The foregoing account takes elements from Xenophon (1.3.14–22), Diodorus (13.66.4–67), and Plutarch (Alc. 31.2–6) but is closest to Diodorus' detailed and persuasive narrative. Plutarch tells much the same story, differing in some details. Xenophon omits the Athenian trick of mock withdrawal but gives a fuller account of the Peloponnesian side than do the others.

[33] Xen. 1.3.13. Xenophon also says that Pasippidas, the condemned and exiled Spartan admiral, and Hermocrates, the Syracusan exile, and his brother went along on the journey. Amit (LAC XLII [1973], 454) may well be right in thinking that these exiles were on a private mission meant to secure privileges for themselves for previous services rendered, but the text of Xenophon speaks of them as "ambassadors of the Lacedaemonians": Λακεδαιμονιῶν πρέσβεις. The problem would be alleviated if we accept the suggestion of deleting πρέσβεις. Otherwise, their presence on this mission is most puzzling.

[34] Xen. 1.4.10.

[35] That is the suggestion of Hatzfeld, Alcibiade, 289.

[36] Amit, LAC XLII (1973), 455.

needed, it was provided by Cyrus, the king's son, who accompanied the Spartans and had come "to rule all the people on the coast and to fight alongside the Spartans."[37] Athenian hopes of an accommodation were dead. In retrospect, we know that the war had reached a decisive turning point. From here on the Persians would make a serious and continuing effort to support the Spartans and defeat the Athenians.

The bad news, however, will not have reached Athens for some time. It had surely not reached the generals in the straits by the time they sailed out of the Hellespont, ultimately on their way to Athens in the spring of 407.[38] The men under Alcibiades and Theramenes had not seen their homes since 411, and Thrasyllus' crews had left Athens in the summer of 409. The conquest of Byzantium had freed the generals and their men to leave the straits, for they were now safely under Athenian control, except for Abydos, which was no threat without a Spartan fleet. All were eager to return, but for none was the need greater or the moment more opportune than for Alcibiades. He had last seen Athens in the summer of 413. His adventures had placed him in a situation in which neither Sparta and the cities of its alliance nor the Persian Empire were safe for him. His future hopes must rest on a return to Athens and the resumption of a public career in war and politics.

Even after his arrival in the Athenian camp on Samos in 411, however, his situation was precarious. He had been recalled by the efforts of a faction and especially by the efforts of one man, Thrasybulus, amidst widespread suspicion and annoyance. His election to the generalship was irregular, since it came from the fleet at Samos, not in a regular election in Athens. Although his status was confirmed and he and other exiles were permitted to return, that action was taken by the short-lived government of the Five Thousand and might not be considered entirely valid by the restored democracy. The city still contained many of his enemies of various political opinions: democrats who distrusted his commitment to the Athenian democracy and who

[37]Xen. 1.4.1–3.
[38]Xenophon (1.4.5–7) tells us that Cyrus asked Pharnabazus to turn the Athenian ambassadors over to him, or at least to detain them, so that the Athenians would not know what was going on. He also says that Pharnabazus held them for three years. Amit (*LAC* XLII [1973], 452, n. 16) is right to find so long a period of captivity implausible. He suggests an emendation of the text to replace "three years" with "three months." Even if that is accepted, the Athenians will not have heard of the arrival of Cyrus and its significance until mid-summer of 407 at the earliest.

might have heard of his characterization of its form of government as "acknowledged foolishness";[39] the priestly colleges of the Eumolpidai and Kerykes, who had formally cursed him for mocking the sacred mysteries; individual competitors for political leadership and their supporters; and ordinary Athenians alienated by his defection and treason at Sparta and the harm he had done Athens. Alcibiades could never be sure that when he returned he would not be accused and brought to trial on some serious charge, real or invented, and condemned once again. Everything depended on the esteem in which he was held by influential Athenians and the masses and on the value for Athens he was thought to have.

Winning victories was obviously not enough, for even after the key role he had played in the victory at Abydos and his brilliant performance at Cyzicus, he did not return home, although he could have done so. No doubt he was concerned about the risk of allowing others to gain the glory of further victories and putting his own in the shade, but there were risks in staying on as well. A long, unsuccessful siege or a military defeat at Chalcedon or Byzantium would have undone his accomplishments and left him in an unenviable position. No doubt his good work at Selymbria and Byzantium added to his reputation and confidence, but it may well be that the most important element in his decision to return came from an action in which he was not involved, the treaty of Chalcedon. When Pharnabazus refused to consider that treaty valid without the oath of Alcibiades, he gave the Athenian commander a unique opportunity that he used to full advantage. By requiring the satrap to swear the oath again on equal terms with himself, Alcibiades dramatized the special stature he had in the eyes of the Persians at the very time when the Athenians had undertaken negotiations with the Great King, relying on the good offices of Pharnabazus to help them succeed. Alcibiades, therefore, was returning to Athens in the spring of 407 not only as a spectacularly successful general but also, once again, as the one man most likely to deprive the Spartans of Persian help. It appears to have been that combination of advantages that finally gave him the courage to set out for Athens.

The Athenian commanders made careful provision to leave the northern theater of operations in good order. Thrasybulus went to the coast of Thrace with thirty ships. There he brought back under Athenian control the places that had gone over to the enemy, chief among

[39]6.89.6.

them the great island of Thasos. War, civil strife, and hunger had reduced the strength of the oligarchic, pro-Spartan, regime there and forced it to yield to the Athenians, assisted by their loyal allies, the Neapolitans of Thrace. The Thasians were compelled to restore the pro-Athenian exiles, accept a garrison, and return to the Athenian alliance. Thrasybulus also recovered Abdera, the most powerful city in Thrace, for the Athenians.[40] In the straits they left a force, adequate to hold what had been regained, under the command of Diodorus and Mantitheus.[41] This freed Thrasyllus and Theramenes to return to Athens with most of the fleet.[42] Before all the others Alcibiades had left the Hellespont with twenty ships, sailing straight for Samos. From there he did not go directly to Athens but sailed far to the south and east to Caria. There, he collected 100 talents and sailed back to Samos. The money, no doubt, would increase the warmth of his welcome in Athens, but still he delayed his return. From Samos he went to Paros and from there to Gytheum, the main Spartan naval base in Laconia. He observed the thirty ships he had heard the Spartans were building there but took no action against them. By now it was probably May— why the delay?[43]

Xenophon's explanation for the visit to Gytheum is probably correct, not only for Alcibiades' hesitation there but also for his rambling route since his first arrival at Samos: he waited at Gytheum to see "how the city felt about him and his homecoming."[44] The key indication for which he was waiting was the outcome of the elections to the generalship. These elections took place "on the first meeting after the sixth prytany when the omens are favorable," normally in March.[45] Alcibiades, therefore, could well have expected to learn the results when he arrived at Samos, perhaps in late March or early April. The elections of 407, however, appear to have taken place later than usual, perhaps as late as May.[46] When the results finally reached Alcibiades, they

[40]Xen. 1.4.9; Diod. 13.72.1. On the Neapolitans, see *GHI* no. 89, 271–275.
[41]Diod. 13.68.2.
[42]Xen. 1.4.10. Xenophon names only Thrasyllus, but since Theramenes is not mentioned as being given another assignment and his term as general was coming to an end, we should assume that he, too, went home.
[43]Xen. 1.4.8, 11. For the date, see Hatzfeld, *Alcibiade*, 292, n. 5.
[44]Xen. 1.4.11: τοῦ οἴκαδε κατάπλου ὅπως ἡ πόλις πρὸς αὐτὸν ἔχοι.
[45]*Ath. Pol.* 44.4.
[46]For the date of the elections, see Hatzfeld, *Alcibiade*, 292, n. 5. We do not know why they were delayed, but late elections were not unique to this year. See Hatzfeld, *Alcibiade*, 94, for the late elections in the year 420.

must have been comforting. The new board of generals included Alcibiades, his friend and supporter Thrasybulus, and Adeimantus, his fellow demesman who, like him, had been condemned and exiled for his role in the affair of the Mysteries. The three others whose names we know—Phanosthenes, Aristocrates, and Conon—seem not yet to have played any prominent role in political life but were probably chosen for their military and naval expertise.[47] Neither Theramenes nor Thrasyllus was reelected. Theramenes had performed superbly as a general in the straits, and his omission may well be the result of political considerations. The father of the regime of the Five Thousand was clearly not at the height of popularity at a time when the jubilant democracy was rejoicing over its achievements and those of its rediscovered hero, Alcibiades. The failure of Thrasyllus to be chosen, on the other hand, needs no political explanation. His failure at Ephesus had not been redeemed by extraordinary achievements in the campaigns in the straits, where he played a secondary role. There was good reason to pass him by in 407. The new board of generals included some of Alcibiades' friends and none of his enemies.

This encouraging news was accompanied and followed by personal notes from his supporters urging him to return to Athens, but even they did not entirely allay his fears. He could not forget that he was still legally a condemned man, an exile who had fled judgment, and a man accursed by the most solemn religious ceremonies or that a stele bearing his condemnation and the curse against him still stood on the Acropolis.[48] He therefore approached the Piraeus cautiously and modestly, with only his small force of twenty triremes.[49] Even after drop-

---

[47] Hatzfeld, *Alcibiade*, 293–294. Meritt (*Athenian Financial Documents*, 113) has supplied the name of Pericles the younger, son of the great Pericles, as a general mentioned in an inscription honoring Archelaus of Macedon, which he dates to 407/6 (*GHI* no. 91, 277, 11.5–6). That reading is accepted by Meiggs and Lewis, and on the basis of it, Fornara (*Generals*, 69) includes Pericles among the generals for that year. The stone in its present condition contains only the initial letter P, which seems to me insufficient to make any suggestion. I think it more prudent not to include the young Pericles.

[48] Hatzfeld, *Alcibiade*, 294–295.

[49] Such is the account of Xenophon (1.4.11–12). Diodorus (13.68.2–3) and Nepos (*Alc.* 6.3) have all the generals arriving together with a vast fleet leading captive ships, soldiers, and booty. Plutarch (*Alc.* 32.1–3) also portrays Alcibiades arriving with hundreds of captured ships, men, and booty, but he rejects the excesses of Duris of Samos, who claimed to be a descendant of Alcibiades and described his entry into the Piraeus in an implausibly gorgeous setting. He points out that the accounts of Xenophon, Theopompus, and Ephorus omit such details and concludes that this was an unlikely occasion for Alcibiades to display his magnificence to the Athenians. It is very

ping anchor he did not disembark immediately, "in fear of his enemies." Xenophon describes the landing and arrival: "Climbing onto the deck of his ship, he looked to see if his friends were there. When he saw his cousin Euryptolemus, son of Peisianax, and his other relatives and his friends with them, then he landed and went up to the city, accompanied by a party of bodyguards ready to defend him against any attack that might come."[50] It soon became evident, however, that the crowds who came rushing down to the shore to see his arrival meant him no harm. Instead, he was welcomed with shouts of congratulation and with wreaths in honor of his achievements.[51] Although his election to the generalship and the warmth of the people's reception indicated that his flight from judgment and condemnation were erased from the public consciousness, he wasted no time in going before meetings of the council and assembly to defend himself formally against the charges of which he had been accused eight years earlier: those brought by Thessalus before the council and those brought by Pythonicus before the assembly.[52] He denied that he had committed the sacrilege of which he had been accused and asserted that he had been treated unjustly. Then he repeated the tactic he had used so successfully on his return to Samos in 411, complaining of his own bad fortune but blaming neither individuals nor the people at large. Instead, he blamed his own bad luck and a kind of personal evil demon that haunted him.[53] Then, as he had done on the former occasion, he turned away from the past to focus on the great prospects for the future: the enemy's hopes were vain; the Athenians had reason to take courage.

The performance was masterful and the results everything Alcibiades could wish. He entirely captured the hearts of his listeners. No one raised the awkward questions of treasonous cooperation with the Spartans and Persians; in fact, no one spoke against anything he or his supporters said. He was cleared of all charges; the property that had been confiscated from him as a result of his condemnation was ordered restored; the priests who had placed a curse on him, the Eumolpidai and Kerykes, were commanded to revoke those curses; the stelae bearing his sentence and other actions taken against him were

---

likely that Xenophon was an eyewitness to the arrival of Alcibiades, and we should prefer his account.

[50]1.4.18–19.
[51]Diod. 13.69.1; Plut. *Alc.* 32.4.
[52]See Kagan, *Peace of Nicias*, 195, 203; and Hatzfeld, *Alcibiade*, 296.
[53]8.81.2.

thrown into the sea. The people voted him golden crowns and made him general-in-chief (strategos autokrator) with command on land and sea.[54] Alcibiades' military success, the respect shown him by Pharnabazus, his magnificent talents as a propagandist, and the skill he had demonstrated on his return had brought him to the pinnacle of influence and power, but even this brilliant moment was not without some clouds. A certain Theodorus, the hierophant, or high priest of the Mysteries, when ordered to revoke the curse responded: "But I invoked no evil on him if he does no wrong to the city."[55] It was a sign that at least some Athenians had not been carried away by recent events and retained the memory of past enmities. As long as Alcibiades was successful he was safe but only so long.

Another uncertainty was the evil portent that some saw in the fact that he had returned to Athens on the day when the ceremony of the Plynteria was being celebrated (the twenty-fifth day of the Attic month Thargelion, perhaps about June 16).[56] On that day the robes on the ancient wooden statue of Athena Polias were removed and washed, and her statue was concealed from view. It was regarded as the unluckiest day of the year to undertake anything of importance. Plutarch tells us that it seemed as if the goddess did not wish to welcome Alcibiades in a friendly manner but concealed herself from him and rejected him. Xenophon says that his arrival on that day seemed to some Athenians an evil omen both for him and the state.[57] But it was an oversight and one ignored by most Athenians on that day. His enemies, however, took note of it and kept it in mind for a future occasion. Alcibiades himself had already paid a heavy price for the religious fears and beliefs of the Athenian people. For a man widely suspected of the scorn of the gods, it was most inopportune to be seen on the wrong side of the deities, however inadvertently. To the ancient Greeks it was not less bad for a public figure to be out of favor with the divine through misfortune than for other reasons. In either case he was sure to be unlucky, and his bad luck might rub off on his state. It is ironic that after taking such pains about his safe arrival, Alcibiades had forgotten about the holy day. His old rival Nicias would never have made such a mistake.

Perhaps in recognition of this problem, Alcibiades made his first

[54]Xen. 1.4.20; Diod. 13.69.1–3; Plut. Alc. 33.2–3.
[55]Plut. Alc. 33.3.
[56]For the date, see Plut. Alc. 34.1; and Busolt, GG III:2, 1562.
[57]Xen. 1.4.12; Plut. Alc. 34.2.

important action after his restoration one with deep religious significance. The festival connected with the Eleusinian mysteries was perhaps the most solemn and impressive event in the Athenian religious
calendar.[58] Each year, in the middle of the month Boedromion (early
September), a sacred procession made its way by foot along a fixed
route that traversed the fourteen miles between the city and Eleusis
near Attica's northwestern frontier. The climax of the festival occurred
on the fifth day, when the Sacred Objects of Demeter were brought
from the Eleusinion near the Athenian Acropolis escorted by *mystai*
about to be initiated. They were also accompanied by the image of
Iacchus, represented as a young male deity bearing a torch and attending the goddesses Demeter and Persephone. The initiates wore
wreaths of myrtle, the priests wore impressive and distinctive robes,
and the vast procession was accompanied by bands of flute and lyre
players as well as choruses singing hymns. It must have been an impressive and awe-inspiring occasion, but ever since the Spartans had
established their fort at Decelea it had not taken place. Instead, the
initiates and their conductors had been compelled to make the trip by
sea without the splendor and ceremony that were so important to it.

Alcibiades saw the chance to remove his religious problems with a
bold stroke. Revealing his plans in advance to the Eumolpidai and
Kerykes, some of whose members had been reluctant to accept his
restoration to grace, he prepared to celebrate the procession of Iacchus
in the traditional manner. He placed sentries where they could give
notice of an enemy attack and accompanied the procession along its
sacred route with an armed guard. The procession reached Eleusis in
safety and returned the same way.[59] Agis made no attempt to interfere,
whether because he was taken by surprise or because he did not want
to be accused of sacrilege or simply because an attack did not seem
worth the trouble.[60] The procession to Eleusis benefited its planner in
several ways. From a religious point of view, it was a demonstration
of his piety that helped undermine the old attacks against him and the
suspicions that still clung to him. As a military demonstration, it
seemed to justify the extraordinary powers recently voted to him and
raised the spirit and confidence of the Athenian army.[61] Politically, it

[58]For a discussion of the festival, see H. W. Parke, *Festivals of the Athenians* (Ithaca,
N.Y. and London, 1977), 55–72.
[59]Xen. 1.4.20; Plut. *Alc.* 34.
[60]Hatzfeld, *Alcibiade*, 299.
[61]Plut. *Alc.* 34.6.

provided Alcibiades with an aura of invincibility that won the passionate support of many Athenians. In conception and execution it
was a spectacular gesture worthy of the late Nicias, whom his major
opponent may have consciously imitated. On the other hand, it may
have raised expectations that would be difficult to fulfill.

12. Cyrus, Lysander, and the Fall of Alcibiades

The great procession to Eleusis took place in September, but Alcibiades had been in Athens since June without undertaking any serious military action. The delay was understandable; his ships needed attention and repair, and even more, their crews needed rest and recreation after years at sea. Alcibiades himself needed time to restore his political base before moving on, but the time had come to fulfill the high hopes the Athenians had for him. Not long after the triumphant return from Eleusis, the assembly had voted to place a force of 1,500 hoplites, 150 cavalrymen, and 100 triremes under his command. He was accompanied by Aristocrates and Adeimantus, skilled as infantry commanders, and Conon, an experienced admiral, all designated in accordance with his wishes.[1] In October, some four months after his arrival in Athens, Alcibiades sailed out of the Piraeus at the head of his powerful force.[2] The target of the expedition was Ionia and the goals obvious. The Spartans had been effectively driven from the straits, but important parts of the Anatolian coast and some significant islands in the Aegean remained under their control. Major cities such

---

[1] Xen. 1.4.21. Diodorus (13.69.3) says the Athenians chose the generals Alcibiades wanted, naming Adeimantus and Thrasybulus. Plutarch (*Alc.* 35.1) tells us merely that they chose the generals he wanted. Since Conon seems to have been with Alcibiades at Andros, the first stop on his campaign, and stayed behind for the siege (Xen. 1.5.18; Hatzfeld, *Alcibiade*, 306), he may have been one of those designated by Alcibiades as well.

[2] Xenophon (1.4.21) tells us that Alcibiades sailed in the fourth month after his arrival at Athens. The expedition is generally placed in October. See, e.g., Hatzfeld, *Alcibiade*, 305; D. Lotze, *Lysander und der Peloponnesische Krieg* (Berlin, 1965), 19; J.-F. Bommelaer, *Lysandre de Sparte* (Paris, 1981), 71.

as Miletus and Ephesus, the key island of Chios, and important step-ping-stones between Athens and Ionia such as Andros and Tenos were still in enemy hands. The Athenians hoped to drive the Spartans from all of these places and from the sea altogether, to recover their empire, and to persuade the Persians to abandon the war.

The Athenians' long delay before taking action, however, had given the enemy a valuable respite. Immediately after the Spartans' crushing defeat at Cyzicus in the spring of 410, they had begun to rebuild their fleet, and by the summer of 407 they had gathered a navy of seventy ships.[3] Even more ominous for the Athenians were the changes that had taken place in the leadership of their two opponents in Asia Minor. The Athenian ambassadors who had gone with Pharnabazus in the year 408/7 to seek out the Great King had met the new commander of the satrapy of western Asia Minor somewhere between Gordium and the royal capital at Susa: Cyrus, a younger son of Darius, with his queen, Parysatis.[4] Tissaphernes, the former satrap, had been dis-credited by the apparent failure of his policy, the discontent and com-plaints of the Spartans, and, perhaps, by the defection of Alcibiades to Athens. Later events would show that his plan of not allowing either of the major Greek cities to win the war was not bad, but in 408/7 his tricky policy seemed to have brought Athens to the brink of victory and endangered Persian recovery of the Anatolian coast. It is not surprising, therefore, that he was replaced. There were, however, more likely candidates for the position than Cyrus, who had no command experience in Asia Minor or anywhere else, was only a younger son, and was not yet seventeen years old.[5] Arsaces, Darius' oldest son, may have served in Asia Minor as a lieutenant to Tissaphernes as late as 411; in any case, he was a man in his thirties;[6] Hieramenes, brother-in-law to Darius, had sworn to the third Persian treaty with Sparta in the same year.[7] Yet it was the untried adolescent whom the Great King sent to Sardis with the title of *karanos* (lord, or ruler) "of those

[3]Xen. 1.5.1.

[4]Xen. 1.4.3. I have learned much about Cyrus and Persian politics at this time, as well as about the career of Lysander, from P. A. Rahe, "Lysander and the Spartan Settlement 407–403 B.C." (Ph.D. diss., Yale University, 1977).

[5]Lotze, *Lysander*, 11, n. 2. Rahe ("Lysander," 2, n. 4) argues that Cyrus may have been as young as fifteen.

[6]8.108.4. The Arsaces mentioned here, however, may have been a different man (see Lewis, *Sparta and Persia*, 80, n. 198). For the age of the royal Arsaces, see J. M. Cook, *The Persian Empire* (New York, 1983), 222.

[7]8.58.1; Xen. 2.1.8–9.

who gather in Castolus."⁸ This appointment gave him control of Lydia, Greater Phrygia, and Cappadocia, in addition to his command in Ionia—enormous power and responsibility for any official and even more so for an untested stripling.⁹ Why did Darius entrust so much to this adolescent?

The answer must be sought in the politics of the royal palace at Susa. Parysatis was hostile to her oldest son, Arsaces, and favored Cyrus, her second-born.¹⁰ She worked to secure the succession for her favorite and had good reason to hope to achieve her goal. Although Cyrus was not the first-born, he was the first to have been born after his father's succession to the throne, and his claim was supported by some precedent. The wives of Persian kings, moreover, had exercised great influence in the past. The first Xerxes had been the oldest of the sons of the first Darius born after his succession, and Herodotus tells us that he had gained the throne at the expense of his older brothers because his mother, Atossa, "had full power."¹¹ Cyrus' father had been one of seventeen bastard sons, and he had come to power after the murder of the legitimate heir and was advised and powerfully assisted by his wife and half-sister Parysatis.¹² Parysatis came to hate her daughter-in-law Stateira, the wife of Arsaces, who was another woman of strong will and powerful connections. The rivalry increased her determination to secure the succession of her favorite, Cyrus, at the expense of Arsaces and his detested wife. When Darius sent his young son to Sardis as *karanos* in 407, Cyrus replaced the powerful Tissaphernes, who was relegated to the lesser command of the province of Caria.¹³ Thereby, the young prince got an opportunity to exercise great power, achieve greater influence, and win support for his succession.

That Cyrus had designs on the throne we know from his attempt

---

⁸Xen. 1.4.3–4, where Xenophon tells us that Cyrus had come "to rule" ἄρξων all the people along the coast and equates the Persian word *karanos* with the Greek *kyrios*. For further discussion of the word's meaning, see Lotze, *Lysander*, 10, n. 8.

⁹For the extent of Cyrus' command, see Rahe, "Lysander," 2, n. 5.

¹⁰Plut. *Artax.* 2.2–3; Ctesias *FGrH* 688 Fr. 15, 51. For the story of the family quarrels, see A. T. Olmstead, *A History of the Persian Empire* (Chicago, 1948), 356–376. See also Lewis, *Sparta and Persia*, 134–135. For a recent study of ancient Persia, see Cook, *Persian Empire*.

¹¹Hdt. 7.2:

¹²See Rahe, "Lysander," 1–5.

¹³Lewis, *Sparta and Persia*, 119, n. 78.

to take it from his brother after the death of Darius.[14] But his ambitions were made clear even earlier. In 406 he put to death two of his royal cousins, nephews of the Great King, because they refused to put their hands into their long sleeves in his presence, an honor reserved only for the Great King.[15] The act itself was terrible, and the parents of the victims, Darius' sister and her husband, Hieramenes, demanded that Cyrus be called to account. They called the murder an act of *hybris*.[16] But it was more than that. For the young prince, still in his teens, to demand the ceremonial deference owed to the Great King was a form of treason in a land where absolute monarchy rested so heavily on ceremony. Cyrus, however, was not called to account, perhaps because his father was already afflicted with the illness that would soon take his life or perhaps because his mother's power shielded him.[17]

The young man's problems were nevertheless formidable: he must cope with his still powerful domestic enemies, carry out his father's orders to assist the Spartans and win the war against the Athenians, and find a way to gain effective support for an eventual attempt at the throne. His enemies included Tissaphernes, whose influence had declined but was still considerable;[18] his sister-in-law Stateira, who nursed a bitter hatred until finally she was poisoned by Parysatis;[19] the parents of his murdered cousins; and his older brother, Arsaces. Defeating the Athenians would not be an easy task. Their victories in the straits had left them in command of the seas, powerful, and confident. The Spartans had consistently shown themselves unable to defeat the Athenians in naval battles, and unless they could find a way to do so, no amount of Persian financial support could put an end to the Athenian Empire. Cyrus must find a Spartan naval commander

---

[14]Xen. *Anab.* 1.1.3 and passim.

[15]Xen. 2.1.8–9. This passage is widely thought to be an interpolation. If it is, Lewis' suggestion that Ctesias is its ultimate source (*Sparta and Persia*, 104, n. 83) is very likely. There is no compelling reason to doubt the authenticity of the story.

[16]Xen. 2.1.8–9.

[17]Ibid.; *Anab.* 1.1.3.

[18]Plutarch (*Lys.* 4.2) reports the pleasure Cyrus took in hearing the Spartans speak ill of Tissaphernes, and Xenophon says (1.5.8–9) that he rejected his predecessor's advice and even refused to receive the Athenian ambassadors sponsored by him. After the death of Darius it was Tissaphernes who denounced Cyrus as a plotter against his brother, now King Artaxerxes, which led to his arrest and almost to his death (*Anab.* 1.1.2). Finally, Tissaphernes was a valuable ally to Artaxerxes in his war against his brother and was rewarded with Cyrus' provinces (Xen. 3.1.3).

[19]Plut. *Artax.* 6.4–6, 19; Ctesias *FGrH* 688, Fr. 27, 70.

who could win. Finally, Cyrus was unlikely to gain the Persian throne without fighting for it, for Arsaces was young, vigorous, and competent enough to defend his claim to the succession when the time came. Ever since the battle of Marathon, repeated conflicts between Greeks and the armies of the Persian Empire had shown the superiority of the Greek hoplite phalanx. Collaboration with the Spartans and their Peloponnesian allies, by and large the best of Greek hoplites, offered the chance to acquire the army he needed.

His mother's power and influence could protect him against his Persian enemies, but to satisfy his other needs, he must find unusual Spartans, men who could win at sea and men who would have the power and the will to use the soldiers of the Peloponnesus for Cyrus' purposes. Although it would not be easy to find a successful Spartan admiral, men possessing all of the required qualities would be even rarer. After all, Spartan and Persian interests were far from identical. Spartans might differ in their plans for the Greek cities of Asia Minor, some wanting to restore their freedom and others to replace Athens as their masters, but none had any interest in turning them over to Persia as the treaties required. The Spartan state, however, had even less interest in supporting an effort by a younger son to usurp the Persian throne. There was little chance that Cyrus could persuade the Spartan kings, ephors, gerousia, and assembly to use their power in his behalf, even if they could find a way to win the war. To succeed, he must discover a faction or an individual with a reason to cooperate with him and the power to bring Sparta along with him. By a re-markable stroke of luck such a man was waiting for him as he made his way to Sardis in the summer of 407.[20]

Some months before, in the spring of 407, the new Spartan navarch, Lysander, had entered the Aegean to take up his command at the expiration of the term of his predecessor, Cratesippidas.[21] Like Gylip-

---

[20]Xen. 1.5.1.

[21]Ibid. The date of Lysander's assumption of the navarchy has been much debated. Xenophon says that the Spartans had sent Lysander out "not long before these things": πρότερον τούτων οὐ πολλῷ χρόνῳ. If τούτων refers to the events described in the pre-vious passage, Alcibiades' attack on Andros and his arrival on Samos, which took place in late October or early November, Lysander will have taken office in the autumn of 407. But Xenophon's chronological transitions are sometimes imprecise: at 3.2.21, for in-stance, having related events of the year 399, he makes a transition with the words "while these things were being done in Asia" to events in Greece of the year 402 (Lotze, *Lysander*, 14, n. 1). Beloch, therefore, has suggested (*GG*² II:2, 273–274) that the reference is to Alcibiades' decision to return to Athens in 1.4.8, perhaps in mid-May, and places Lys-

pus, the Spartan hero at Syracuse, he was a *mothax*, the son of a Spartiate father and a helot mother or possibly of an impoverished Spartan who had lost his status because of his poverty.[22] In either case he will have been raised as the companion for his son by some Spartiate of adequate means, educated in the Spartan manner, and made eligible for full citizenship by the very unusual grant of an allotment of land.[23] Although poor, his father, Aristocritus, boasted distinguished lineage, claiming descent from the hero and god Heracles and maintaining the honorable status of guest-friend *(xenos)* with the Cyrenaic king Libys, after whom he named Lysander's brother.[24] The assignment to important commands late in the Peloponnesian War of men such as Gylippus, Lysander, and his successor as navarch, Callicratidas, all *mothakes*, shows that his elevation was not unique.[25] But it is unusual enough to raise the question of how a man of marginal status could have risen to eminence in a society as caste-ridden as Sparta's.

The long war had put the talents of Sparta's ruling class to a severe test, and many of its members had been found wanting, especially at

---

ander's arrival not later than the beginning of that month. That sequence has the advantage of eliminating the delay of three or four months between his meeting with Pharnabazus and the ambassadors in the spring (1.4.2) and his arrival at Sardis in midsummer, a delay out of character for this active and ambitious young man.

Beloch's chronology has been widely accepted (e.g., by A. Andrewes, *JHS* LXXIII [1953], 2, n. 1; Lotze, *Lysander*, 14; Sealey, *Klio* 58 [1976], 347; Bommelaer, *Lysandre*, 73–74), but it has raised difficulties of its own. Those who believe that Sparta's navarchs were always elected for a fixed term of one year must cope with the fact that previous navarchs seem to have taken office in the fall or late summer and must account for Lysander's succession in the spring. Lotze is driven to suggest that Lysander was elected at the usual time, in late summer of 408, but waited to take office until the ships being built at Gytheum (Xen. 1.4.11) were completed. Sealey has argued that annual navarchies were instituted for the first time late in the war, probably in 409, after the defeat at Cyzicus convinced the Spartans that the naval war would be a long one, and that the term began in the spring (348–349). Bommelaer, who seems not to know about Sealey's article, tries to solve the problem by suggesting a change in the date when the navarch took office from late summer or autumn to spring, to correspond better with the military year, a change that took place just before Lysander's navarchy (75–79). The evidence will not permit certainty, but what seems clear is that from at least 407 to the end of the war the Spartan navarchy was an annual office that began in the spring.

[22]Phylarchus *FGrH* 81, Fr. 43; Aelian 12.43. See also Kagan, *Peace of Nicias*, 258, n. 73; and P. Oliva, *Sparta and Her Social Problems* (Amsterdam and Prague, 1971), 173–177. Although the sources attributing low status to Lysander are late, there is no reason to doubt their accuracy. See Meyer, *GdA* IV, 331, n. 2.

[23]Oliva, *Sparta*, 174.

[24]Diod. 14.13.6.

[25]Aelian 12.43.

sea. The performance of the three navarchs whose work we know during the Archidamian War ranged from unsuccessful to disastrous. After the Sicilian campaign Melanchridas, Astyochus, Mindarus, Pasippidas, and Cratesippidas served as navarchs before the appointment of Lysander. The first one never had an opportunity to serve; the second one served so poorly that he was suspected of corruption and treason; the third one was the only one to show some talent, but he suffered a series of defeats ending with the disaster at Cyzicus and his own death; the fourth one was believed to be intriguing with Tissaphernes against Spartan interests and was banished; and the last one accomplished nothing at all. In those circumstances, it is tempting to believe that, in their desperation, the Spartans were finally ready to promote men of proven talent, regardless of their doubtful status. They appear to have done so with Gylippus in Sicily with splendid results. Their appointment of two *mothakes*, Lysander and Callicratidas, in the successive years 407/6 and 406/5 suggests that events led them to repeat the experiment. Unfortunately, we do not know anything of Lysander's military career before his navarchy, but it seems likely that he had distinguished himself in some way.

Even so, few men reach eminence in any society or political system without some supporting influence or patronage, and Lysander seems not to have been an exception. Plutarch tells us that Lysander was the lover *(erastes)* of the young Agesilaus, half-brother to King Agis.[26] It was normal for a young Spartiate who reached the age of twelve, as part of his education, to take an older young man, between the ages of twenty and thirty, as his lover.[27] Plutarch and Xenophon emphasize the moral and spiritual aspects of the relationship, but we need not doubt that it had its physical aspects as well. Beyond that, it could have political significance too. The relationship between adult lover and adolescent beloved was bound to be close and over the years would create a strong bond between them and, probably, their families. In Sparta's intensely competitive society, success in gaining the half-brother of a king as one's *paidika* would surely increase the acknowledged lover's status and his influence in the royal family. As one scholar has put it: "There were few bigger fish in the Spartan sea than the adolescent Agesilaos, and there can be little doubt that it was because

---

[26]*Ages.* 2.1; *Lys.* 22.3.
[27]Plut. *Lyc.* 16.6, 17.1–2; Xen. *Lac. Pol.* 2.12–14; P. Cartledge, *PCPS* XXVII (1981), 17–36.

he was such an outstanding catch that Lysander courted him."[28] Lysander's relations with Agesilaus remained close almost to the end of his life. He played a crucial role in helping him succeed to the throne and persuaded him to undertake his great campaign against Persia in 396.[29]

The facts about his association with King Agis are less abundant and clear, but they strongly suggest that the lover of Agesilaus had the political support of his royal brother. They clearly shared a general policy aimed at overthrowing the Athenian Empire, as did most Spartans, but sought to erect a Spartan hegemony in its place, as many Spartans did not.[30] The two men collaborated in shaping strategy toward the end of the war and presented a common proposal on the fate of the defeated Athens;[31] there is good reason to support the usual view that sees Lysander and Agis as political associates once the former had achieved eminence.[32] We need not doubt that this association went back to an earlier time and that Lysander benefited from it greatly.

If Plutarch is right, Lysander assiduously cultivated these, and perhaps other, personal relationships with influential Spartans in the service of his political ambitions, "for he seems by nature to have been attentive to the men of power, beyond what was customary for a Spartiate, and to have put up pleasantly with the excesses of authority for the sake of advantage." He was a man outstanding even among the Spartans for his competitive spirit and ambition.[33] When he reached the heights of achievement at the end of the Peloponnesian War, this boundless ambition revealed itself clearly. He allowed the Samians to change the name of their great festival to the goddess Hera to the "Lysandreia" in his honor, to erect an altar, to sing victory songs to him, and to sacrifice to him as to a god.[34] Memorials to his victory at Aegospotami were placed in the sanctuary at Delphi. Pausanias describes the most striking of them, the "navarch's monument" paid for

[28]Cartledge, *PCPS* XXVII (1981), 28.
[29]Xen. 3.3.3; 3.4.2; Plut. *Lys.* 22.3–6, 23.1–3; *Ages.* 3.3–5, 6.1–3.
[30]Rahe, "Lysander," 9, n. 36; C. D. Hamilton, *Sparta's Bitter Victories* (Ithaca, N.Y., and London, 1979), 84–86.
[31]For strategic collaboration, see Plut. *Lys.* 9.2–5; Diod. 13.104.8 with E. Will, *Le monde grec et l'orient*, vol. 1, *le Ve siècle (510–403)* (Paris, 1972), 388; Bommelaer, *Lysandre*, 102; and Lotze, *Lysander*, 40. For the terms for Athens, see Paus. 3.8.6.
[32]Among those holding such a view are Busolt, *GG* III: 2, 1627; Meyer, *GdA* V, 31 and n. 1, 40; and Glotz and Cohen, *HG* II, 756.
[33]Plut. *Lys.* 2.1–3.
[34]Hamilton, *Sparta's Bitter Victories*, 70.

by the booty taken from the Athenians; it was made up of "statues of the Dioscuri, Zeus, Apollo, Artemis and, in addition to these, Poseidon, Lysander, son of Aristocritus, being crowned by Poseidon, Agias, Lysander's soothsayer, and Hermon, who steered his flagship."[35] Lysander's ambition, however, was not satisfied by glory; he also wanted power. A strong and credible ancient tradition shows him trying to alter the Spartan constitution to allow himself to become king.[36] There is every reason to believe that such powerful ambitions, which dominated the first part of his life during his years in Sparta and his later career after he had achieved eminence and greatness, also guided his behavior when he took up his naval command in 407. The needs of his state and of his own political future called for success in the war, but his personal ambitions required that he demonstrate his unique qualities, establish a firm base of political support, allow no other Spartan to make an important contribution to victory, and show himself to be essential and irreplaceable. If his own interests conflicted with those of the state, the former would not be allowed to suffer. He was just the sort of man Cyrus needed.

Setting out in the spring, Lysander's first task was to gather as large a fleet as he could with which to face the Athenians. Presumably, at one time or another, he had the use of the thirty ships that Alcibiades had seen in preparation at Gytheum in May.[37] On the way to his destination, he stopped at Rhodes, where he collected some more ships, and at Cos, where he may have done the same.[38] Then he went to Miletus, until then Sparta's main base in the Aegean, but he did not stay long. Instead, he sailed to Ephesus and from there sent to Chios for the fleet commanded by his predecessor, perhaps another twenty-five ships. When he mustered his full force at his base, he was in command of seventy triremes.[39]

That base, however, was no longer Miletus but Ephesus, and the change was significant. From a geographical point of view alone, Miletus had already shown its inferiority as the Spartan fleet's headquar-

[35]Paus. 10.9.7.
[36]Diod. 14.13.2–8; Plut. Lys. 24–26; Nepos, Lys. 3; Arist. Pol. 1306b 31–33. Ephorus is the main but not the only source for this tradition, which is believed by most modern scholars. See, e.g., Oliva, Sparta, 185–186; Hamilton, Sparta's Bitter Victories, 92–94; and Bommelaer, Lysandre, 223–225.
[37]Xen. 1.4.11; above, n. 23.
[38]Xen. 1.5.1.
[39]Ibid.; Diod. 13.70.1–2; Lotze, Lysander, 15.

ters in the Aegean. Because it lay well to the south of the Athenian headquarters on Samos, movement between the Spartan base at Miletus and Chios and the straits could always be cut off, if the Athenians were vigilant. Ephesus, being north of Samos, was much better suited to Sparta's strategic needs. From the diplomatic point of view, too, Ephesus had important advantages, being closer than Miletus to the Persian satrap's capital at Sardis. Ephesus had for many years been under strong Persian influence and was a favorite resort for high Persian officials, so communication and cooperation between the allies would be easier.[40] Politically, too, the new base had advantages. Plutarch tells us that Lysander found the city "both friendly to him and zealous in the Spartan cause."[41] Ephesus appears to have been dominated by its aristocracy, having avoided the imposition of a democracy under Athenian rule. That would help explain why it was friendly to Sparta, the bulwark of oligarchic and aristocratic government.[42] For Lysander, there were political advantages in being the man who established the Spartan base at Ephesus, where it had not been before. He would benefit from the gratitude that setting up the base might produce, from the opportunity to select those citizens with whom he would work, and from the chance to establish conditions to his liking.[43]

When Lysander arrived, Ephesus was not in good economic condition, but his activities soon changed that. He turned it into a major commercial center and an important naval shipyard. His efforts turned Ephesus into "a port comparable to the Piraeus for providing equipment and services" and one securely connected with a hinterland capable of supplying the needs of the city and of large numbers of soldiers and sailors staying there.[44] It gave Lysander what the Spartans needed, although previous navarchs seem not to have understood the need: a place to gather and maintain large numbers of ships and men in safety and sufficiency until they chose to fight at a time and place advantageous to them. The Athenians' delay in launching their campaign of 407 gave Lysander something else he badly needed: time to train his

[40]Plut. *Lys.* 3.2; Lotze, *Lysander*, 15.
[41]Plut. *Lys.* 3.2. It is hard to know whether we are meant to think that the Ephesians had a special inclination toward Lysander as an individual rather than as a Spartan commander. If they did, their goodwill was probably based more on his decision to make their city his base than for any prior knowledge of his abilities.
[42]Lotze, *Lysander*, 15.
[43]Bommelaer, *Lysandre*, 88.
[44]Ibid., 85.

forces and shape them into a disciplined and effective navy. The Athenian navy, besides being more numerous than the Spartans' in 407, had repeatedly shown itself to be superior in technique and morale. We need not wonder that the new navarch did not seek battle with the enemy or attack Athenian allies in the months between his arrival in the spring and the following winter. He needed time to build his fleet and base and to train and to encourage his men. If he could succeed in acquiring adequate and reliable financial support, he could wait.

The opportunity to solve that problem came in the summer, when Cyrus arrived at Sardis. Lysander went to meet the Persian prince in the company of the Spartan ambassadors who had traveled with him from Susa by way of Gordium.[45] Their meeting was one of those conjunctures in history where the individuals involved play a decisive role in determining the course of momentous events. To be sure, the Spartan decision to send a mission to Susa in 408 was evidence of a resolve to pursue the war against Athens vigorously, and any new navarch would have tried to do so. Yet the behavior of Lysander's successor would show that some Spartan commanders, and perhaps most, would be unwilling or unable to cooperate with the Persians effectively and gain from them the regular and sufficient support that no Spartan had yet been able to acquire. Some, with the interests and reputation of their state their chief concern, might create friction, as Lichas had, by objecting to the terms of the treaty with Persia that promised the restoration of Greek cities to Persian rule.[46] They might also annoy the Persians with the straightforward, brusque, superior, and arrogant manner and behavior they used toward foreigners and which often angered their fellow Greeks. Lysander, however, ran none of these risks. He pursued not only the interests of Sparta but also his own, and the latter required that he win the favor of the Persian who controlled the purse, thereby making himself indispensable to the Spartan cause. If it troubled him to surrender Greeks to the Persians, and it may have, for he seemed to have in mind the establishment of a Spartan empire to replace the Athenian empire, he would not find it difficult to dissimulate. He was accustomed, so it was said, "to deceive

---

[45]Xenophon (1.5.1) says merely that he went "with the ambassadors from Sparta," which would seem to mean that new ambassadors had come from Sparta, perhaps to instruct Lysander and to oversee his negotiations with Cyrus. I have adopted Lotze's suggestion (*Lysander*, 16, n. 1) that the ambassadors mentioned here without any explanation are the same men mentioned twice before.

[46]8.43.3.

boys with knuckle-bones and men with oaths."[47] Spartan training produced men so stiff and proud as to make ordinary friendly discourse
with foreigners difficult and the kind of courtesy and flattery to which
a Persian prince was accustomed impossible, but Lysander was a man
in his late forties in 407.[48] He had reached his current position by
paying assiduous court throughout his life to one of Sparta's royal
families, gaining a reputation for natural subservience to men of
power.[49] It is entirely possible that Lysander was the only Spartan of
his time who could work so well with Cyrus as to gain the support
needed for victory.

The Persians were also committed to defeating the Athenians. The
Spartans' disastrous defeat at Cyzicus had not produced the result the
Athenians desired. Instead of persuading the Persians to change sides
or, at least, to stop aiding the Spartans, it led them to undertake an
even stronger effort against Athens. We cannot know what role Cyrus,
or rather his mother, may have played in helping Darius to make that
decision. The fact, however, that he appointed her favorite son, still
in his adolescence, to the chief command with unprecedented powers
in place of other, more likely, candidates may suggest that she influenced the policy decision as well. Any satrap appointed in 407 would
have made an effort to work with the Spartans, but it is most unlikely
that others would have been given as much power and money; none
would have had the same freedom of action or have had so strong a
motive for working closely with the Spartans and gaining their friendship. As one scholar suggests, we should not "neglect the possibility
that this large command for Cyrus was in part created at her [Parysatis']
suggestion as a move in the forthcoming succession struggle. . . . Al-
ternatively, she is simply getting Cyrus the possibility of winning the
gratitude and support of the Spartans, the best professional soldiers
in the world."[50]

Lysander and the Spartan ambassadors began the interview at Sardis
by complaining of the duplicity of Tissaphernes, of his collaboration
with Alcibiades, and of his failure to keep his promises, deliver payment adequately and regularly, and carry out the Great King's orders

[47]Plut. *Lys.* 8.4.
[48]Lotze (*Lysander*, 13) places his birth about 454, which would make him forty-seven
during his navarchy.
[49]Plut. *Lys.* 2.3.
[50]Lewis, *Sparta and Persia*, 134–135.

to help the Spartans and drive the Athenians from the sea.[51] It was the obvious and tactful line to take, for it set forth Sparta's grievances but blamed them on the new satrap's discredited predecessor. It had the further advantage of especially pleasing Cyrus, who enjoyed hearing his and his mother's enemy blamed and condemned.[52] In response to the Spartans' plea that he, unlike Tissaphernes, should carry on the war with full dedication, Cyrus replied that those were his father's orders and that he himself intended to do everything possible. He announced that he had brought along 500 talents and that if they were inadequate, he would spend his own money and if that were not enough, he would break up the very throne on which he sat, which was made of gold and silver.[53] The response, no doubt, was gratifying but hyperbolic, as further discussion revealed. The Spartans thanked him and asked him to raise the daily pay of each sailor to an Attic drachma, twice the rate specified in the treaty with Persia and twice what the Athenians were paying. They argued that such a rate would make the sailors rowing for Athens desert to their side, thus bringing a quick end to the war and thereby saving the Persians money. Cyrus conceded that the idea was good but was forced to admit that his rhetoric had gone beyond his instructions. He was authorized to pay the 3 obols, half a drachma, specified in the treaty, for however many ships the Spartans might bring but no more.[54]

For the moment, the Spartans had no response and let the matter drop, but Lysander put his talents as a courtier to work. By various devices, but especially, Plutarch tells us, "by his submissive deference in conversation," he won the heart of the young prince.[55] When the visit was over and it was time for the Spartans to return to Ephesus, Cyrus had been thoroughly flattered by such treatment from a man three times his age and the commander of the best fighters in the world. At the farewell banquet, Cyrus asked how he could please Lysander most, and the Spartan answered: "if you add one obol to the pay of each sailor." Cyrus granted the request. He also paid the arrears in salary and gave Lysander a month's pay in advance. As a

---

[51]Xen. 1.5.2; Plut. *Lys.* 4.1.
[52]Plut. *Lys.* 4.2. If Lysander had not already known of the quarrels within the Persian ruling circles, the ambassadors, who had been to Susa and traveled with Cyrus, would have informed him.
[53]Xen. 1.5.3.
[54]Xen. 1.5.3–5.
[55]Plut. *Lys.* 4.2.

result, the Spartan force became "much more enthusiastic."[56] We should not forget that Cyrus was hardly more than a boy; no doubt he was moved by generous feelings of friendship and admiration for the courteous Spartan commander. At the same time, his interests required that he win the confidence and friendship of the Spartans and reverse the negative trend the naval war had taken. Moreover, only a royal prince, and the queen's favorite at that, could have raised the Spartans' pay on the spot without consulting Susa.

When Lysander returned to Ephesus, he brought enough money to raise the spirits of his men and promises of more, but he had received only enough to carry on for a month. However sincere Cyrus' rhetoric and intentions may have been, Lysander remained on a leash to the prince; to get more money he would need to stay in Cyrus' good graces and account to him.[57] That may have been one reason that Lysander took steps to gain the support of the aristocrats of Ionia when he returned from his trip to Sardis. He called the most powerful men from the various cities to a meeting at Ephesus. There he urged them to form political organizations (hetairiai) and promised that if he succeeded and overthrew the Athenian Empire he would put down the democracies and give each of their groups control of its city. The immediate result was gratifying: he aroused great enthusiasm and collected impressive contributions toward his conduct of the war.[58] If Plutarch is right, he also used the occasion to build a political base for his own ambitions, doing favors for, encouraging, and collaborating with these men and "planting in them the seeds of the revolutionary decarchies he would later bring into being."[59] Although Plutarch may

---

[56]Xen. 1.5.6–7.

[57]Bommelaer, *Lysandre*, 86. With 200 men per ship, each trireme cost about 133 drachmas each day at the new rate of 4 obols. Lysander's fleet of seventy ships, therefore, cost 9,210 drachmas a day and 276,300 drachmas, or about 46 talents, each month. At that rate, the royal money would last almost eleven months. Lysander, however, planned to increase his fleet and did, so the money would run out even sooner. No doubt Cyrus could also have used the revenues from his province, as well, before turning to his own money. In any case, we should not credit the assertion by Diodorus (13.70.3) that Cyrus had instructions from his father to give the Spartans whatever they might want. Diodorus and Plutarch (*Lys.* 4.6) say that Cyrus gave Lysander 10,000 darics on the spot. We cannot be sure of the value of the daric at this time, although it seems to have been worth 20 drachmas. Lewis (*Sparta and Persia*, 131, n. 136) says "it certainly is less than the arrears plus a month's pay."

[58]Diod. 13.70.4. Plutarch (*Lys.* 6.3) places this assembly after the battle of Notium, but as Lotze (*Lysander*, 18, n. 1) points out, he does so chiefly for artistic reasons. Diodorus' placement of the event is preferable.

[59]Plut. *Lys.* 6.3–4.

be too readily projecting into an earlier time things that would happen only later, we need not doubt that Lysander began to build a personal clientele among these ambitious Ionian enemies of democracy. But the Spartans had renounced all claim to the Greek cities of Asia in their treaties, and it is not clear how or if Lysander meant to keep his promises.[60] What is important, however, is that the men he appealed to believed him and became enthusiastic about his cause. He could count on them to support Sparta and, even more fervently, himself.

It did not take long for the news of the meeting at Sardis and its consequences to reach the Athenians. When they heard that Cyrus had arrived with lots of money and orders to support the Spartans vigorously and that he had agreed to raise the wages of the Spartan rowers, they were discouraged. They decided to send ambassadors to discuss the situation with Cyrus, using Tissaphernes as an intermediary.[61] It has been suggested that the idea was inspired by Alcibiades, who was characteristically employing diplomatic means before resorting to war.[62] Since Alcibiades was at the height of his power, it seems unlikely that the Athenians would have taken any diplomatic action at that time without his agreement. His recent ill treatment by the former satrap notwithstanding, Alcibiades was sufficiently dedicated to *realpolitik* to make use of Tissaphernes if he could be helpful, and the former satrap could be counted on to pursue his own interests, whatever he might think about Alcibiades. Still, whoever recommended this approach revealed a serious ignorance of Persian politics. Although it may have suited their purposes to conceal the fact, Cyrus and Tissaphernes were deadly enemies, and the former satrap at Sardis was not the man to persuade the prince to change his policy. Tissaphernes, nonetheless, tried to introduce the Athenian ambassadors and urged Cyrus to adopt the old policy: to prevent any Greek state from winning, thereby allowing them all to wear themselves out. Cyrus ignored Tissaphernes' advice, perhaps pleased to have a chance to do so and thereby display his independence and the impotence of the former satrap; he refused to see the Athenians. The Athenians' attempts to end the war by diplomacy had failed both with Darius and with Cyrus. Only fighting could now bring peace.

The main target of the Athenian expedition was Lysander's fleet at

[60]For an interesting discussion, see Lotze, *Lysander*, 18–19.
[61]Xen. 1.5.8.
[62]M. Amit, *Grazer Beiträge* III (1975), 7. Cf. Lewis, *Sparta and Persia*, 131, n. 134.

Ephesus, and the obvious strategy was to lure it out for a battle at sea and destroy it. If this could be achieved, the advantages would be great. The Athenian fleet would be free to move about the Aegean and the straits without hindrance and to attack, besiege, or blockade defenders and thereby recover all of the islands in their empire, probably also some states on the mainland, and, with them, revenues for Athens' hungry treasury. The annihilation of still another fleet might again persuade the Spartans to offer peace, perhaps this time on terms acceptable to Athens. Failing that happy outcome, the Athenians might still hope to negotiate with a Persian monarch chastened by still another defeat of his ally and another fruitless expenditure of his money. Even if such negotiations failed, the impact of a great Athenian victory in Ionian waters would surely have a powerful effect on the Greek cities of Asia Minor that had defected from the Athenians. Those that did not come over of their own volition could be attacked at a time of Spartan despair and helplessness. It might be possible to drive Sparta from her most essential bases, Chios and even Miletus and Ephesus. Should the Athenians have succeeded in such efforts, it is hard to see how the Spartans could have continued the war.[63]

Alcibiades had every reason to sail at once against Lysander's fleet at Ephesus, for the news that Cyrus was providing strong and reliable financial support to Lysander that allowed him to raise the rowers' pay meant that every passing day helped increase the size of the Spartan armada.[64] Yet his first action was against Andros, where he seized and fortified a strong point called Gaurium from which they could attack the city. When the Andrians and the Peloponnesian garrison guarding the island came out to fight, the Athenians routed them. Alcibiades set up a trophy to mark the minor victory, but he was unable to take the island's main city. He stayed a few days, launching a series of unsuccessful assaults; then he sailed on, leaving a garrison, apparently under Conon, sufficient to man the fort and keep pressure on the Andrians.[65] The attack made good sense, for Andros lay on the route

---

[63] The ancient writers say nothing about Alcibiades' intentions or general strategy in this campaign. The best discussion of this and the other military issues of the Notium campaign is by Eugenia C. Kiesling, "The Battle of Notium" (Senior essay, Yale University, 1978). It has influenced my account of the campaign throughout. See also Amit, *Grazer Beiträge* III (1975), 1–13.

[64] The Athenians' mission to Cyrus under the aegis of Tissaphernes (Xen. 1.5.8) proves that the Athenians knew what had happened at Sardis.

[65] Xen. 1.4.22–23; Diod. 13.69.4–5. The account of Diodorus here is fuller and more satisfactory. There are two separate traditions that discuss the campaign leading to the

that the grain ships from the Hellespont to Athens were likely to take now that Euboea and the Euripus were under enemy control. Alcibiades, no doubt, had hoped to take the island by surprise and conquer it swiftly and easily. Although he did not succeed, the effort cost him only a few days, and the garrison subtracted only slightly from his forces. It was clearly worth the trouble from a strategic point of view,[66] but Alcibiades' failure to win a swift and complete success in his first new undertaking had serious political consequences. His inability to capture Andros would later be one of the complaints his enemies would raise against his conduct of the entire expedition.[67] In fact, we may be sure that the grumbling started as soon as the news of the incomplete victory reached Athens.

After leaving Andros, Alcibiades still did not go immediately toward Ephesus but sailed to the southeast to ravage Cos and Rhodes and to collect booty with which to support his men.[68] That he should delay further when he clearly knew that the enemy's power was waxing calls for explanation. The most obvious one is the continuing Athenian shortage of money. The cost of his expedition was about 50 talents each month, That would be no small sum for the Athens of 407/6, and we do not know how much money he was given. It was probably not enough to support the expedition for long if Lysander stayed in port and refused to fight, as was entirely possible.[69] In that case, he

---

battle of Notium, that of Xenophon, which is followed by Plutarch, and the one in Diodorus. As was common in the last century and the first part of this one, most scholars preferred the former on general and unsatisfactory grounds. G. de Sanctis (*Riv. Fil.* IX [1931], 222–229) was the first to suggest that Diodorus' account might derive from P, the author of the *Hellenica Oxyrhynchia*, probably via Ephorus. His opinion was confirmed by the discovery of the Florentine Papyrus of that work in 1934 (see I. A. F. Bruce, *An Historical Commentary on the* Hellenica Oxyrhynchia [Cambridge, 1967], 35–45). Section four of that papyrus gives an account of events that is clearly in the same tradition as Diodorus. It is therefore necessary to treat that tradition with respect and try to use all our sources to discover what happened. (In addition to Bruce, see H. Breitenbach, *Historia* XX [1971], 152–171.) Diodorus says that Thrasybulus was commander of the Athenian garrison at Andros; which is an obvious mistake, for the same Diodorus places Thrasybulus at Thasos at the very same time (13.72.1). Although no source explicitly names Conon as garrison commander at Andros, it is from there that he goes to Samos to replace Alcibiades a few weeks later, after the battle at Notium. See Hatzfeld, *Alcibiade*, 306, n. 3.

[66] E. F. Bloedow (*Alcibiades Reexamined* [Wiesbaden, 1973], 73) suggests that the attack on Andros was "a strategical blunder." For a more just assessment, see Hatzfeld, *Alcibiade*, 306.

[67] Plut. *Lys.* 35.1.

[68] Diod. 13.69.5.

[69] Plutarch (*Lys.* 35.3) emphasizes Alcibiades' lack of money in explaining why the

would have to abandon the campaign, having accomplished nothing, for he could not maintain his forces without money. It was far better to collect funds first and so be able to sustain the effort until some significant success could be achieved.

His collections completed, Alcibiades sailed north to Samos and from there to Notium, the port of Colophon, on the coast to the northwest of Ephesus (see Map 3).[70] Colophon and its port were the only cities in the neighborhood still under Athenian control. Notium was not a major naval base like Samos, Miletus, or, now, Ephesus, but it was well situated for sailing out against Ephesus, cutting off Spartan ships going between Ephesus and Chios and preventing the Spartans from sailing north to the Hellespont. Under the circumstances, it was the obvious place to go and the one from which the Athenians had the best chance of bringing Lysander to battle.[71] At Notium, Alcibiades commanded eighty ships, having left twenty to conduct the siege at Andros.[72] Lysander's force had meanwhile grown to ninety.[73] This size gave the Spartans a numerical advantage, but Lysander did not offer to fight. As part of his preparations, he had pulled his triremes out of the water to dry them and effect repairs, and they may very well have remained on the beach when the Athenians took up their station at Notium.[74] Lysander clearly believed that time was very much on his side. After the experience of Cynossema, Sestos, and Cyzicus, no Spartan admiral should have been eager to encounter an Athenian

---

Athenians' expectations were excessive. "They did not reckon with his lack of money. Since he was fighting men who had the Great King as their provider, he was forced to sail off, leaving his camp behind, in order to obtain wages and provisions." Bloedow (*Alcibiades*, 76, n. 448) dismisses Plutarch's views about the shortage of money as "melodramatic" and "improbable" and asks where were the 100 talents Alcibiades had collected in Caria (Xen. 1.4.8)? However much money Alcibiades may have collected in Caria the previous May, it will have been delivered to the Athenian treasury upon his arrival in June. There is no good reason to believe that all of it had been given to him when he set out in October. It is highly unlikely, moreover, that 100 talents is a plausible figure for what anyone might hope to collect in Caria in 407. The Athenians had collected nothing like that from the region in more prosperous times (see Meiggs, *Athenian Empire*, 254). Either the figure in the manuscript or Xenophon's information is badly wrong. Even if Alcibiades had received as many as 100 talents at Athens, moreover, that would pay for only two months of campaigning.

[70]Xen. 1.4.23; Diod. 13.71.1.
[71]Amit, *Grazer Beiträge*, III (1975), 8.
[72]Xen. 1.5.18.
[73]Xen. 1.5.10.
[74]Ibid. See 8.44.4 for an occasion when the Spartans pulled their ships onto the Rhodian shore, although they outnumbered the enemy, and were inactive for eighty days.

fleet in a straightforward naval battle, even with favorable odds of nine to eight. But the passage of time allowed Lysander to increase the quantity of his ships and improve their quality.

Plutarch suggests yet another reason why Lysander might have been glad to wait: the higher wage permitted by Cyrus' bounty "emptied the ships of the enemy. For most of the sailors came over to those paying more, while those who stayed were dispirited and rebellious and made trouble for their commanders every day."[75] Although Plutarch exaggerates considerably, the evidence shows that there is much to what he says. After the battle of Notium, the Athenian fleet should have consisted of 108 ships,[76] yet when Conon came to relieve Alcibiades, he was able to man only "seventy triremes instead of the former number of more than one hundred" with which Alcibiades outnumbered Lysander after the battle of Notium.[77] The loss of sailors in the battle cannot explain this diminution, for most of them survived.[78] When Callicratidas took over the fleet from Lysander in the spring of 406, some months after the battle, the Spartan fleet had grown to 140 ships.[79] It is inconceivable that the Spartan fleet could have grown by 50 ships at the same time that the Athenians' decreased by 38 if many rowers had not changed sides. Plutarch has wrongly placed most of the defections before Notium rather than after it, but he is right about the phenomenon in general. Defections began, however, even before the battle,[80] so Lysander will have been able to expect more and to plan accordingly. We should not think, moreover, that Lysander could or would have remained inactive indefinitely. He would be keenly aware of the suspicion and dissatisfaction aroused by the long inactivity of Astyochus. Neither Cyrus nor the Spartans would be satisfied with a navarch who remained in port and allowed the Athenians to roam freely about the Aegean doing as they liked. No doubt he hoped to achieve overwhelming numerical superiority before offering battle, but if a really attractive opportunity appeared before then, he was ready to take advantage of it.

[75]*Lys.* 4.4.
[76]At Notium the Athenians lost 22 of their original 80 ships, leaving 58. To these ships should be added the 30 that were with Thrasybulus at Phocaea and the 20 that came with Conon from Andros, for a total of 108. I owe this point and the calculations to E. Kiesling, "Notium," 12.
[77]Xen. 1.5.15, 20.
[78]Xen. 1.5.14.
[79]Xen. 1.6.3.
[80]Diod. 13.71.3.

The same reasons that made delay attractive to Lysander compelled Alcibiades to seek quick action. Any Athenian admiral would have been pressed by the objective circumstances of a shortage of money and the threat of desertion to force the pace of events, but Alcibiades had additional reasons of his own. Plutarch is persuasive in describing the Athenians' opinion of him: "It seems that if any one was ever destroyed by his own reputation it was Alcibiades. For he was thought to be so full of daring and intelligence, from which his successes derived, that they suspected him of not trying when he failed and would not believe there was anything he could not do. If he tried, nothing could escape him."[81] He had been given extraordinary power, had been allowed to name his associates, and had been given a large force tailored to his desires, all because the Athenians expected him to perform wonders. Yet his attempt at Andros had failed, and when he got to Ionia, Lysander refused to fight. Alcibiades had little choice but to seek victories elsewhere. He probably reached Notium some time in November and stayed for a month, or even more, but certainly no later than February of 406 he left his fleet in the hands of a subordinate and went in search of action.[82]

The ancient writers do not agree on where he went, Cyme, Clazomenae, and Phocaea being the more plausible destinations mentioned by one or more of them.[83] Although he might have stopped at all of them, the main target must have been Phocaea, where Thrasybulus had already arrived and was laying siege to the city.[84] That Thrasybulus had timed his arrival at Phocaea to coincide with Alcibiades' appearance at Ephesus strongly suggests that the plan had been con-

[81] *Alc.* 35.2.

[82] The date of the battle of Notium cannot be fixed with precision. The evidence would indicate a date as early as December and as late as April (see Hatzfeld, *Alcibiade*, 312, n. 1; Lotze, *Lysander*, 19–20, 73; Bommelaer, *Lysandre*, 70–72). My own view is that the pressures working on Alcibiades would have led him to move earlier rather than later, so I vould place the battle in late December or early January. Naval battles during the inclement weather of the winter months were most unusual, but the pressures working on the Athenians, and especially Alcibiades, led them to force the pace and risk a fight even outside the normal campaigning season.

[83] Xenophon (1.5.11) and Plutarch (*Lys.* 5.1) name Phocaea. Diodorus (13.71.1) names Clazomenae but also speaks of an attack by Alcibiades on Cyme (13.74.3–5). In his account of the life of Alcibiades (35.8), Plutarch says he went to Caria to gather money, but that is surely a reference to his earlier depredations, before his arrival at Notium.

[84] Thrasybulus at Phocaea: Xen. 1.5.11; Hatzfeld, *Alcibiade*, 309, n. 6. Busolt (*GG* III:2, 1574–1575) believes Alcibiades went to Clazomenae and Cyme as well, but sees Phocaea as the main target.

certed well in advance. There is good reason to believe that attacks on Ionian cities had been part of Alcibiades' original plan, for he had taken along significant numbers of infantry and cavalry at considerable expense and trouble. Although some of the hoplites could have served as marines, there was little chance that they would be needed in a fight at sea, and the cavalry could be of no value except on land, but both forces would be needed for assaults and sieges.[85] Any Athenian commander would have had to reckon with the possibility that Lysander would stay in port and refuse to fight. How, then, could he be forced out to battle? One way would be to attack and conquer cities in northern Ionia while the Spartans remained helplessly in Ephesus. If the Athenians succeeded, Lysander could hardly stand by idly but would be forced to risk a fight and the destruction of still another Spartan fleet. If he insisted on remaining quiet, Athens would be allowed to recover lost allies and revenues, Spartan prestige would sink still further, and the Persians might think again about their commitment.[86] Phocaea was an excellent place to begin such a campaign. It was a prosperous city that was well situated as a base for further assaults on Cyme on the Gulf of Elaea to the north, as well as on Clazomenae across the Gulf of Smyrna to the south, while a dash to the west would bring a fleet opposite the northern shore of Chios (see Map 3).

Alcibiades sailed to join Thrasybulus at Phocaea, taking only the troopships and no triremes. Lysander's fleet was bottled up at Ephesus and was no threat, and Thrasybulus had thirty triremes with him. More ships and their contingents of marines might still have been helpful, but the need to leave twenty ships at the siege of Andros and

---

[85] If the Sicilian campaign had not been enough to instruct him in the need for cavalry to defend infantry in battle and in laying down a siege (Kagan, *Peace of Nicias*, 239–240), the work done by Pharnabazus' horsemen in the battles of 411/10 should have done so.

[86] This, in somewhat elaborated detail, is essentially the suggestion put forth by Busolt (above, n. 84). Bloedow (*Alcibiades*, 75, n. 447) is skeptical: "This, however, sounds more like Busolt's than Alcibiades' strategy. There is no specific evidence to support it." If by "specific evidence" he means the statements of ancient writers he is correct, but the ancient writers say nothing of any strategy. Are we then to believe that the Athenians set out without any plan, that they could not see problems and opportunities obvious even to us? The narratives, however, as will be seen, do present us with valuable evidence, if we care to use it. Even Bloedow concedes that this is an "admittedly ingenious strategy" that "can be deduced from the situation as plausible enough." He then wonders why, if this was Alcibiades' strategy, he left his fleet in the hands that he did. That is a very good but different question.

the growth of Lysander's forces made it too dangerous to reduce the size of the main Athenian fleet further. As it was, the Athenians were outnumbered ninety to eighty, but that ratio had existed from the time of the fleet's arrival, and in all that time Lysander had refused to venture out. The Athenians as yet had not succeeded in recovering any Ionian cities, so it was too early to expect that any pressure would force Lysander to fight while Alcibiades was away from the fleet. His main concern was to avoid having the Athenians instigate a battle while he was gone, and he gave his surrogate commander strict orders to avoid doing so.[87] He had good reason to be confident that nothing untoward would happen in his absence.

The man to whom he left the command was not a general or even a trierarch but Antiochus, a *kybernetes*—a helmsman or pilot of Alcibiades' own ship.[88] The appointment has been criticized from antiquity to modern times. As far as we know, it was unique in the entire history of the Athenian navy, and it requires explanation. The obvious choice would have been a general experienced in naval warfare. Of the generals who sailed with Alcibiades from Athens, Conon was just such a man, but he had been left behind to conduct the blockade and siege of Andros. The other two generals with the expedition were Aristocrates and Adeimantus, but they must have gone on the troopships to Phocaea, for they had been designated specifically as generals for fighting on the land.[89] Since no general was available, the conventional choice would have been a trierarch. Although many of them would have been merely men rich enough to outfit a trireme, without naval skill or experience, some among the eighty ship-captains at Notium would surely have been at sea and had fought in battles before. Leading a single ship into battle under the orders of a fleet-commander, however, was very different from organizing an entire fleet, planning a battle, making specific assignments, and deciding on and ordering particular maneuvers during the fighting. Unless a trierarch had previously served as general, there is no reason to believe he could do

---

[87]Xen. 1.5.11; Diod. 13.71.1; Plut. *Alc.* 35.5. I believe that Xenophon's version of the instructions is most accurate: "don't attack Lysander's ships": μὴ ἐπιπλεῖν ἐπὶ τὰς Λυσάνδρου ναῦς; Plutarch's version, "don't fight a battle even if the enemy attacks": μηδ᾽ ἂν ἐπιπλέωσιν οἱ πολέμιοι διαναυμαχεῖν, and Diodorus' "Don't fight a battle until I am present": μὴ ναυμαχεῖν ἕως ἂν αὐτὸς παραγένηται, are either vague or impossible to carry out.
[88]Xen. 1.5.11; Diod. 13.71.1; Plut. *Alc.* 35.4.
[89]Xen. 1.4.21.

these things better than the *kybernetai*. They were men of great experience and ability in the tactics of naval warfare and had participated in many battles. As we have seen, they played a crucial role in Athens' victories at sea.[90] Apart from these generalizations, however, we must consider the specific situation: *Alcibiades did not expect his replacement to fight in his absence.* In that case a subordinate officer might be a better choice since he would be less likely to act on his own and more obedient. What Alcibiades needed was a man he could trust, and Antiochus, his personal helmsman and associate for many years, must have seemed the perfect choice.[91] No other Athenian would have dared to make so unusual an appointment, but Alcibiades was *strategos autokrator*, at the height of his power and influence and free to act as he thought best.

Alcibiades, however, had made a serious mistake. Either he had badly misjudged Antiochus' character or the exaltation of the sudden and unprecedented promotion had produced qualities of independence and ambition not seen before. Instead of standing on the defensive in obedience to his orders, the newly appointed commander deliberately provoked a battle.[92] Diodorus calls him an impetuous man "eager to accomplish something glorious on his own,"[93] and his behavior on this occasion justifies the characterization. It would be wrong, however, to accept the picture that emerges from the accounts of Xenophon and Plutarch of a man challenging the enemy fleet, sailing close by, and insulting the Spartans by word and gesture with no apparent plan of battle. Both Diodorus and the Hellenica Oxyrhynchia make it clear that Antiochus had a strategy that involved the entire fleet,[94] but it is not obvious what his plan was. It has been suggested that his model

---

[90]For a good discussion of the role of the *kybernetai*, see Amit, *Grazer Beiträge* III (1975), 9–10.

[91]Plutarch (*Alc.* 10.1) relates an anecdote connecting Antiochus with Alcibiades' entry into public life.

[92]The four ancient sources—Xenophon (1.5.12–15), Diodorus (13.71), Plutarch (*Alc.* 35.5–6; *Lys.* 5.1–2), and P (*Hell. Oxy.* 4)—all agree on the general course of the battle while differing in detail. Xenophon and Plutarch form one tradition; Diodorus and P are part of another. As is so often true in descriptions of naval battles in this period, the second tradition is far superior both in detail and in providing some understanding of the plans and intentions of the commanders. The following account rests chiefly on the versions of Diodorus and P. For useful discussions of the problems presented by the sources, see Bruce, *Commentary*, 35–45; and Breitenbach, *Historia* XX (1971), 152–171.

[93]Diod. 13.71.2.

[94]Ibid.; *Hell. Oxy.* 4.1.

was the battle of Cyzicus, and it would not be surprising if that were so.[95] The Athenian strategy there had been brilliant and magnificently successful; it may have been the greatest naval achievement of the trireme era, if conception, execution, and results are all considered. Moreover, it was fresh in everyone's memory and may have exercised the same hold over naval thinking at the end of the fifth century that the idea of "crossing the T" had over modern admirals from Trafalgar, to Tsushima, to Leyte Gulf.

If the battle of Cyzicus was in Antiochus' mind, however, the waters between Notium and Ephesus were not the place to try a reenactment. The batte of Cyzicus had succeeded because the Athenians could arrive without warning, the Spartans were unaware of their numbers, and there were convenient places where they could hide part of their fleet. In these circumstances, deception and surprise could be expected to succeed, but none of these advantages existed at Notium. There were no islands or promontories that could conceal triremes between the two bases. The Athenians and Spartans had been looking at one another for at least a month, and neither could have failed to know just how many ships the other had. If any doubt remained, deserters will have brought Lysander fully up to date. The Spartans, moreover, had been at Cyzicus too. Lysander will have been no less aware of the strategy and tactics used there and would be wary of similar tricks. Yet Antiochus' scheme clearly involved an attempt at deception that resembled Alcibiades' opening maneuver at Cyzicus.[96] He took the ten best ships in the fleet and, placing his own trireme in the lead, sailed toward Ephesus. He told the rest of the fleet to remain in readiness at Notium "until the enemy was far away from the land."[97] The implication seems obvious that the idea was for Antiochus' ten ships to lure the enemy out of harbor and entice him in the direction of Notium.[98] Once the Spartans were in open water far enough from land,

---

[95]Hatzfeld, *Alcibiade*, 312.

[96]See above, 239–242.

[97]*Hell. Oxy.* 4.1: τὰς μὲν ἐτ [έρας ἐκέλευσε ναυ] λοχεῖν ἕως ἄν ἀπαρῶ[σιν αἰ τῶν πολεμί] ων πόρρω τῆς γῆς.

[98]Diodorus says that Antiochus "sailed toward the enemy to provoke the enemy into fighting at sea": ἐπέπλευσε τοῖς πολεμίοις προκαλεσόμενος εἰς ναυμαχίαν (13.71.2–3). In P there is a lacuna before προσαξόμενος αὐτά[ς (4.1). Several suggestions have been made to fill the gap. Maas suggests εἰς τὸ ναυμαχῆσαι, which would give just the same sense as Diodorus. Wade-Gery proposes εἰς τὴν εὐρυχωρίαν before the gap, which would give the passage the meaning "to induce them [the Spartan ships] out into the open sea" (Bruce, *Commentary*, 40; Bruce himself makes it clear that αὐτά[ς

the Athenians would either cut them off from their base and force a battle or overtake them before they could escape. It must have seemed to Antiochus that there was little risk; either Lysander would take the bait and give the Athenians an opportunity for a major victory, or more probably, he would refuse to fight, as he had steadfastly done in the past.

Lysander, as we have seen, could not have intended to avoid fighting for the rest of his term of command. Normally, he probably would have waited longer to move, until the odds were even greater in his favor, but Alcibiades' departure presented him with a special opportunity and a new urgency. Deserters had brought him the news that Alcibiades had taken his land troops to join Thrasybulus in the attack on Phocaea. This told him that his delaying tactics would be more costly from then on and that the Athenian fleet was without an experienced general and in the hands of a man who had never before held a command. It was an opportunity not to be missed, and Lysander decided "to do something worthy of Sparta."[99] He was ready when the moment came, and his careful preparation paid dividends. It may well be that overconfidence, encouraged by previous Spartan inertia, led Antiochus to be careless as he sailed toward Ephesus. Perhaps he forged ahead too fast and allowed too great a gap between his ship and the second one in the column, or perhaps he came too close to shore; in any case, he was not prepared for what happened. Lysander launched a lightning attack against the lead ship of Antiochus with three triremes of his own.[100] He quickly sank it, killing Antiochus.[101] The trailing Athenian triremes were stunned. They panicked, turning to flee toward Notium, and the entire Spartan fleet set out in pursuit. Lysander did not need his entire fleet to chase nine ships. He must have understood that things had not gone according to the Athenian plan, whatever that might be. He had reason to expect that the remainder of the Athenian fleet would be confused and disorganized

---

refers to the enemy ships). Bommelaer (*Lysandre*, 92) proposes [ὡς ἐκ τοῦ λιμένος] προσαξόμενος, which would mean "to induce them to leave the harbor." The meaning is clear in any case: Antiochus' maneuver was meant to draw the enemy out to sea in the direction of Notium. His instructions to the rest of the fleet make it clear that he intended to draw the Spartans so far out as to allow the main Athenian fleet to attack.

[99] Diod. 13.71.3.

[100] *Hell. Oxy.* 4.2. Xenophon (1.5.13) and Plutarch (*Alc.* 35.6) speak of "a few" ships. Diodorus (13.71.3), omitting the detail, has the entire Spartan navy launching at once.

[101] *Hell. Oxy.* 4.2, with note in Bruce, *Commentary*, 40–41; Plut. *Lys.* 35.6.

with their commander dead and their plans awry. What better moment
to risk the battle that must come soon in any case?

In fact, the Athenians were not ready. They had received orders to
wait until the enemy was well out to sea before moving themselves.
They must have expected to see their advance guard fleeing, well ahead
of the enemy, in no danger, as Alcibiades' group had done at Cyzicus.
Perhaps they were to wait for a signal from the admiral, such as
Thrasybulus had sent to Theramenes in that same battle.[102] That would
give them plenty of time to get into battle order as the enemy was
drawn deeper into the trap, but they received no signal, for the admiral
was dead. First, they saw their advance force fleeing from an overwhelming enemy force, which threatened to destroy them. There was
no time to get into good battle order. Without a directing hand to
restrain them, each trierarch must have launched his ship as soon as
he saw what was happening. As a result, the Athenians came to the
rescue "in no order whatever."[103] The ensuing battle, therefore, was
one-sided; the Athenians were routed, losing twenty-two ships.[104] Lysander collected the enemy ships still afloat, set up a trophy to mark
the victory at Notium, and sailed back to Ephesus. The Athenians
stayed at Notium for three days to repair damaged ships, and there
they were joined by Alcibiades who had hurried back from Phocaea
after hearing the bad news. He must have taken Thrasybulus' thirty
triremes with him to bring the total of Athenian ships at Notium to
eighty-eight, for he would not otherwise have ventured out to Ephesus
to challenge Lysander to battle again. We do not know how many
ships the Spartans had lost in the battle; the course of the fighting
suggests there were few losses, if any. Still, the two navies were about
even in number, and Lysander had no wish to lose the fruits of his
victory by fighting at a time and place of the Athenians' choosing,
without numerical superiority. When he refused to come out and fight,
Alcibiades had no choice but to return to Samos.[105]

---

[102]See above, 243.

[103]Diod. 13.71.4: ἐν οὐδεμιᾷ τάξει. Xenophon (1.5.14) says the Spartan fleet was
"in order" (ἐν τάξει), but the Athenians ships were "scattered" (διεσπαρμέναις). For
the Athenian confusion, see Hell. Oxy. 4.3 with Bruce, Commentary, 42–43.

[104]The figure is from Diodorus (13.71.4) and P (4.3). Xenophon gives the figure as
fifteen, whereas Plutarch just says "many."

[105]For the trophy, see Xen. 1.5.14; Plut. Alc. 35.6; Hell. Oxy. 4.4. Only P mentions
the three days at Notium, but Diodorus (13.71.4) reports that Alcibiades sailed there
to unite the fleet before challenging Lysander at Ephesus again. Xenophon (1.5.15)
and Plutarch (Alc. 35.6) have the defeated fleet sailing to Samos after the battle, being

Lysander deserves great credit for this victory, which vindicated his policy of watchful waiting, of refusing to fight until circumstances made success probable. The performance of his fleet also demonstrates the high quality of the training he had given his crews, for they responded to his orders swiftly and maintained excellent discipline throughout the battle. He himself demonstrated talent of a high order; he was quick to see an opportunity and seize it and was decisive and shrewd in using it to the full when greater prospects beckoned. The key decision was to order his main fleet out in pursuit after he had sunk Antiochus' vessel and seen the panic and confusion of the nine remaining Athenian ships. Although they must have been ready to come on signal, timing was everything; they must move quickly to catch the main Athenian fleet at Notium unaware. The swiftness of Lysander's appreciation of the situation and the alacrity of his fleet's response speak very well for his ability as an admiral. Still, Lysander could not have done anything without the mistakes made by Antiochus, whose strategy was misconceived and whose execution was disastrous. Such failures are not surprising in a man who had not previously exercised command, and they raise questions about his appointment. We have seen that Alcibiades had plausible reasons for choosing Antiochus as his substitute, but even if these reasons are accepted, it is impossible to free him from blame. To leave the main Athenian fleet in the hands of an inexperienced man within a few miles of the main enemy force was a gamble, and considering how serious the defeat and possible destruction of that fleet would be, it was a reckless and unjustifiable gamble.

In material terms, the Athenians' defeat at Notium was not very serious, for they suffered few casualties, and they still had 108 ships in the Aegean, more than the enemy.[106] It did, however, cancel Athenian plans for recovering the lost allied cities in Ionia. The withdrawal of the fleet from Phocaea put an end to the campaign there, and before long Conon would have to abandon the siege of Andros.[107] In fact, soon after the battle the Spartans seized Delphinium on the island of Chios and Teos not far from Notium.[108] The Athenian soldiers and

---

joined there by Alcibiades, and the whole force coming back to Ephesus to challenge Lysander in vain.

[106]Alcibiades' 88 and Conon's 20.

[107]Xen. 1.5.18.

[108]Xen. 1.5.15. The text reads Eion, but editors have suggested an emendation to Teos on the basis of Diod. 13.76.4. See Underhill, *Commentary*, 22.

sailors on Samos had lost the confidence and high spirits they had enjoyed since 410, and their morale was low.[109] The momentum of Athenian success that had started at Cyzicus was stopped and even reversed at Notium, but even more important than that was the battle's effect on the political scene at Athens.

Alcibiades was eager to reverse this trend as soon as possible, to achieve something tangible and restore the morale of his troops by giving them something to do that would yield an easy success. By this time, moreover, he must have been short of money again. He therefore took his entire force to Cyme, an Athenian ally of considerable prosperity.[110] As a pretext, he used false accusations of disloyalty and, perhaps, the voluntary enrollment of fifty Cymaean hoplites in an anti-Athenian movement on Lesbos.[111] Then he began ravaging the territory around the city. The attack was a complete surprise and caught many citizens outside the walls. Alcibiades had expected no trouble and had left his infantry at Mytilene. As he was leading his captives to the ships, however, the entire Cymaean army attacked him from the city, freeing the prisoners and driving the Athenians to their ships. This was a dreadful embarrassment for Alcibiades. He tried to recover by sending to Mytilene for his hoplites and marching them to Cyme in

[109]Xen. 1.5.20.

[110]Before the war Cyme was assessed at as many as 12 talents of tribute, twice as much as Ephesus and the most of any city in the Ionian District (see Meiggs, *Athenian Empire*, 540–542). The historicity of this affair has been doubted because Diodorus' account (13.73.3–5) is thought to derive from Ephorus, himself a citizen of Cyme, who apparently enjoyed intruding information about his native city, whether or not true (see G. L. Barber, *The Historian Ephorus* [London, 1935], 86). Nepos (*Alc.* 7.1–2), however, also tells of Alcibiades' attack on Cyme but with important differences that suggest there was more than one source attesting to its reality. (The point is made by J. T. Roberts, *Accountability in Athenian Government* [Madison, Wisc., 1982], 224, n. 67.) Diodorus' story, moreover, contains such detail and is inherently so plausible as to deserve credit.

There is dispute, too, about his assertion that Cyme was still an Athenian ally at this time. Thucydides (8.100.3) is cited as evidence that in 411 the city had defected. Even if it had, it could well have been recovered in the interim without finding a place in the sparse narratives of the extant sources, all full of lacunae. The Thucydidean passage, however, does not prove there was a defection. It says only that a group of anti-Athenian exiles took into their political clubs fifty hoplites from Cyme. These men could easily have been volunteers from a minority faction who joined the anti-Athenian cause in hopes of bringing on a general rebellion in the region. It may well be their action of which Alcibiades complained when he sought an excuse to attack Ephesus in 406 (Diod. 13.73.3). There is no good reason to reject the reality of the event, the accuracy of Diodorus' account, or its chronological placement between Notium and the political attacks against Alcibiades in Athens.

[111]See above, n. 110.

battle order. But the Cymaeans refused the challenge, the Alcibiades had to content himself with some further pillaging of the neighborhood before sailing to Mytilene. This fiasco not only compounded the defeat at Notium but also provided additional charges for his enemies to use against him.[112]

Meanwhile, events in Attica had undermined the confident and hopeful mood that had raised Alcibiades to the heights of popularity. Some time after Alcibiades' departure in October, Agis had learned that the best Athenian soldiers had gone to Asia with him and had decided to attack Athens in their absence. He may have been moved by the fear that another Athenian naval victory might bring the faction in Sparta favoring peace to power and that this time they might offer terms that would give Athens victory. Perhaps he thought only of taking advantage of the opportunity to attack the city when a significant force of hoplites and cavalrymen were away. In any case, he gathered a large force of Peloponnesian and Boeotian hoplites, light-armed troops, and cavalry at Decelea and marched from there to the walls of Athens on a dark night.[113] The Athenians repelled the attack and forced the large enemy force to be satisfied with ravaging Attica before dispersing,[114] but it must have caused some nervousness.

In this mood the Athenians received the news of the defeat at Notium and the complaints of an embassy from Cyme. The time had come for Alcibiades' enemies to have their day. One of the most notorious of them was Thrasybulus, the son of Thraso.[115] He came from the camp on Samos, where, as we have seen, morale was low. The trierarchs must have been outraged at being passed over in favor of a *kybernetes* who had brought disaster, and they bitterly blamed the man responsible. No doubt their anger spread to the men, and we need not think that Thrasybulus spoke only for himself when he attacked Alcibiades. In the Athenian assembly, he blamed the disaster at Notium on the supreme commander of the expedition. Alcibiades, he claimed,

---

[112]Diod. 13.73.3–6.

[113]Diod. 13.72.3–4. Neither Xenophon nor any other ancient writer mentions this attack. Since it failed and had no material effect on the course of the war, its omission is not surprising. As Hatzfeld (*Alcibiade*, 316, n. 1) says, there is no reason to confound this large undertaking with the small raid Agis undertook in 410, which is mentioned only by Xenophon (1.1.33–34).

[114]Diod. 13.72.4–73.2.

[115]Plut. *Alc.* 36.1. This man is not to be confused with the famous Thrasybulus of Steiria, the son of Lycus, general at Cynossema, Abydos, and Cyzicus, and supporter of Alcibiades.

322 THE FALL OF THE ATHENIAN EMPIRE

had conducted the campaign like a luxury cruise. He had handed over the command of the fleet to a man whose only talents were drinking and telling tall sailor's tales, "so that he himself might be free to sail around collecting money and engaging in debauchery by getting drunk and visiting whores in Abydos and Ionia, even while the enemy fleet was close by."[116] The ambassadors from Cyme accused him of attacking "an allied city that had done no wrong."[117] At the same time, some Athenians blamed him for not trying to capture that city, claiming that he had been bribed by the Great King.[118] Other Athenian soldiers came from Samos to accuse him of favoring the Spartans; after all it was inevitable that his dalliance with the enemy between 415 and 411 would not be forgotten and would come back to haunt him as soon as misfortune destroyed his invulnerability. His friendship with Tissaphernes and Persia were also not forgotten. It would not be plausible to accuse him of plotting with Tissaphernes after that satrap had thrown Alcibiades into prison, so instead, he was accused of friendship with Pharnabazus, who, it was alleged, would make him tyrant at Athens after the war.[119] The old prejudices came forth and worked powerfully against him; by this time emotion was high enough that it was safe to take action against him. A successful proposal to remove him from office was made in the assembly, possibly by Cleophon and probably not long before the regular elections in early March.[120]

[116]Plut. Alc. 36.1–2.
[117]Diod. 13.73.6.
[118]Nepos 7.7.2.
[119]Ibid.
[120]There is a dispute about whether Alcibiades was removed from office by a formal vote of ἀποχειροτονία or was simply not reelected in 406. Xenophon (1.5.16–17); Plutarch (Alc. 36.3), who seems here, as often elsewhere, merely to be echoing Xenophon; and Diodorus (13.74.1) tell the story as though he was merely not reelected. In his account of the life of Lysander, however, Plutarch (5.2) says that Alcibiades was "deposed from his command," using the technical term for removal from office, ἀπεχειροτόνησεν. Lysias (21.7) says the Athenians "put an end to his office" (ἐπαύσατε τῆς ἀρχῆς), which is somewhat ambiguous, but Nepos (7.7.3) says flatly that "they took away his office while he was absent and substituted another in his place" (absenti magistratum abrogarent et alium in eius locum sustituerent). Busolt (GG III:2, 1578, n. 2) argues that his replacement as commander on Samos by Conon, who was sent from Andros immediately, shows that the official year had not yet run out. The strongest evidence that he was removed from office, however, comes from the fact that Phanosthenes, who replaced Conon at Andros, was not general in 406/5, so the official year cannot have expired when Alcibiades was relieved (Fornara, Generals, 69–70). This critical point seems to have been noticed only by Roberts (Accountability, 224, n. 62). The part played by Cleophon is attested only in a late source (Himerius 36.16 [Photius Bibl. 377]) whose evidence does not, in fact, fit the circumstances here. The brief notice

The Athenians voted to send Conon from Andros to take over command of the fleet at Samos. It is not clear whether he waited to hand over his responsibilities to his replacement or departed beforehand.[121] In either case, he had no intention of returning to Athens, where many private lawsuits had been brought against him and his enemies were many and strong.[122] Nor could he stay on Samos, for the army there had turned against him.[123] Also, the escape hatches to Sparta and Persia had been closed. However, he had foreseen the danger and prepared a retreat for himself in a fortified castle he had built on the Gallipoli Peninsula during his years in service in the Hellespont, and to it he went in voluntary exile.[124] The removal of Alcibiades from Athens and from the command of her forces is generally thought to have been disastrous for Athens. Plutarch represents the Athenians after their defeat in the war as bemoaning their mistakes, of which the greatest was their second rejection of Alcibiades, their "ablest and most skilled general," and even the restrained and judicious Thucydides endorses his military talents.[125] Most modern scholars have agreed and regarded his final removal as the turning point in the last phase of the war.[126] The record, however, does not support such judgments. Alcibiades accomplished nothing of note as a military or naval commander until his service in the straits between 411 and 408. There, he showed himself to be a good commander, especially of cavalry, and a capable naval officer, but he did not demonstrate any extraordinary ability as a strategist or tactician. The ablest commander in the campaigns in

---

reads "Cleophon indicted Alcibiades," without mentioning the charge, date, or occasion. Gilbert (*Beiträge*, 366) suggests that the charge was treason (προδοσία) and that it was brought immediately after the deposition of Alcibiades, as was not unusual. Busolt (*GG* III:2, 1578, n. 2) points out that if Alcibiades had been indicted at this time, he would surely have been convicted, in which case he would have had his property confiscated, which did not occur. He concludes, therefore, that neither Cleophon nor anyone else brought such a charge. Himerius or his source might have misunderstood the fifth-century Athenian constitution and imagined that it was a form of indictment, which it was not (see Roberts, *Accountability*, 15). In any case, the evidence connecting Cleophon with this occasion is not strong.

[121]Diodorus (13.74.2) says he waited; Xenophon (1.5.17) says, but not clearly, that he left before Conon's arrival; Plutarch (*Alc.* 35.3) and Nepos (7.7.4) say that he fled on learning of his deposition.

[122]Diod. 13.74.2–4.

[123]Xen. 1.5.17.

[124]Busolt, *GG* III:2, 1580, n. 1; Hatzfeld, *Alcibiade*, 318–323.

[125]Plut. *Alc.* 38.2; Thuc. 6.15.4.

[126]See, e.g., Busolt, *GG* III:2, 1579; Glotz and Cohen, *HG* II, 745; Ferguson, *CAH* V (1940), 354.

the straits was not Alcibiades but Thrasybulus. Athens could certainly
have used another military leader of Alcibiades' ability in the last years
of the war, if he could have subordinated his own needs and interests
to those of the state. But whatever Alcibiades' personal inclinations
might have been in 406, the burden of his past was too great. Even
apart from his personality and ambitions, the number of his enemies,
the intensity of their hatred, and the eagerness with which they waited
to attack him compelled him to seek extraordinary achievements and
make promises that could not be fulfilled in order to acquire and
maintain a popularity that was his only security. This drove him to
take risks that another general would have avoided and that were bound
to bring disaster to Athens.

From a political point of view, moreover, Alcibiades was a burden
to his native city. What Athens needed more than anything in its time
of crisis was unity of the kind Pericles had provided at the start of the
war. Alcibiades, however, was preeminently a divisive figure who
evoked powerful feelings of admiration or dislike but not steady support from a large portion of the citizenry. He could not win a reliable
majority to support his own policies, but he could prevent anyone else
from doing so, for when things went badly, the Athenians often looked
to the glamor and promise of Alcibiades for salvation. As a character
in Aristophanes' *Frogs* said less than a year after Notium: "They yearn
for him, they hate him, but they want to have him back."[127] It is
interesting, if vain, to speculate about what would have happened if
Alcibiades had departed and Thrasybulus, who would later prove
himself an able political leader as well as a great general, had been
allowed to emerge in his place, but the disgrace of Alcibiades discredited his friends as well as himself. In the new elections of the spring
of 406, neither Thrasybulus nor Theramenes were chosen. Perhaps
that was the most serious result of the Spartan victory at Notium.

[127] 1425.

13. The Battle of Arginusae

The new board of generals elected in March of 406 excluded both Thrasybulus and Theramenes as well as any other close associates of Alcibiades. Its members were Conon, Diomedon, Leon, Pericles, Erasinides, Aristocrates, Archestratus, Protomachus, Thrasyllus, and Aristogenes.[1] It has been common to analyze these elections in regard to the competition between political factions. The generals are said to belong to "the moderate democracy."[2] In other words, they belong to "that democratic middle party that once saw its leader in Nicias and was as far removed from oligarchic aspirations as from the demagogy of the gutter."[3] These descriptions, however, are not very helpful. They would describe Thrasybulus as well as any of the new generals. If they do not apply to Theramenes, moreover, they should not apply

[1]For the date of the elections, see Busolt, *GG* III:2, 1580, n. 3; and Beloch, *GG²* II:2, 252. The list comes from Xen. 1.6.16–17. Diodorus (13.74.1) gives the same list, except for his usual mistake in writing "Thrasybulus" in place of "Thrasyllus" and for his substitution of "Lysias" for "Leon." It is possible that Xenophon has simply made a mistake in listing Leon (Fornara, *Generals*, 70, n. 124), for Leon is not mentioned at Arginusae or thereafter whereas Lysias is. On the other hand, Xenophon mentions Leon not only in his list but also as one of the generals blockaded at Mytilene with Conon (1.6.16). He is also mentioned by the scholiast on Aristid. *Pan.* 162.19. Beloch (*GG²* II:2, 268) suggests that Lysias may have been elected to replace Archestratus, who died at Mytilene (Lys. 21.8). It is also possible that Leon was on board the ship that was captured trying to escape from Mytilene (Xen. 1.6.21 and G. E. Underhill, *A Commentary with an Introduction and Appendix on the* Hellenica *of Xenophon* [Oxford, 1900], 26) and that Lysias was chosen to replace him. Although certainty is impossible, Leon was probably among the generals elected in March.

[2]Busolt, *GG* III:2, 1581.

[3]Beloch, *AP*, 85.

to Aristocrates, who worked closely with Theramenes when both were members of the Four Hundred.[4] In fact, mainly two considerations guided the voters: that as many as possible of the new generals should be experienced naval commanders and that none of them should be close associates of Alcibiades.[5] Only in the latter sense does factional politics appear to have played any important part in the choice.

Conon took command of the Athenian fleet at Samos no later than February of 406, after the deposition of Alcibiades, and he appears to have exercised full control of it until the new generals arrived in July, at the start of the new official year in the archonship of Callias (406/ 5).[6] There were still at least four months in which he could have attempted to recover lost ground, but the condition of the fleet made it impossible to undertake any significant action. Morale was low, and the number of men under his command had shrunk. Although he had

[4]6.89.2; 8.92.2.
[5]Busolt, GG III:2, 1581.
[6]Xenophon (1.5.18–20) gives Conon the leading position in the activities of the Athenian fleet at Samos. Diodorus (13.74.1) is more direct and emphatic, saying that the Athenian assembly "selected him for a superior command" (προκρίνας) before sending him out to replace Alcibiades. His chronology, however, is typically confused. He pictures Conon as being selected for the superior command from among the ten newly elected generals, but we know from Xenophon that he was sent to Samos from Andros before the elections. Diodorus may be speaking of a superior command that was in effect for the new year, 406/5, which Conon may well have exercised before Arginusae, but he does not seem to have done so afterward. However that may be, he clearly seems to have been in full control for the last months of 407/6. Busolt (GG III:2, 1578), among others, believes that Thrasybulus and Adeimantus were removed from office along with Alcibiades, apparently on the basis of a passage in Lysias (21.7). It says: "When you put an end to the office of those men and selected the ten of whom Thrasyllus was one, they all wanted to sail on my ship": ἐπειδὴ δὲ ἐκείνους μὲν ὑμεῖς ἐπαύσατε τῆς ἀρχῆς, τοὺς δὲ μετὰ Θρασύλλου δέκα εἵλεσθε, οὗτοι πάντες ἐβούλοντο ἐπὶ τῆς ἐμῆς νεὼς πλεῖν, κ.τ.λ.
ἐπαύσατε is taken to be the equivalent of ἀποχειροτονήσατε (which would mean "you removed them from office by formal vote"), but it need not mean that. It can easily mean nothing more than that the generals of Alcibiades' year (407/6) had their term of office ended when they were not reelected for the next year. Certainly, the speaker could not be taken to mean that all ten generals for 407/6 were removed before the election of 406, because we know that Conon was not. The assumption that only three were so removed has no support in the evidence. We need not believe that anyone but Alcibiades was deposed. The old generals, therefore, except for Alcibiades, will have retained their commands until the end of the official year. The name of the eponymous archon is provided by Xen. 1.6.1. B. D. Meritt (Proceedings of the American Philosophical Society CXV [1971], 114) proposes July 1 as the date of the first day of the official year 406/5.

more than 100 ships, he had crews to fill only 70 of them.[7] The loss
of so many men cannot be explained by casualties at Notium; it must
have been the result, in large part, of the extra obol per day that
Lysander offered, although the Spartan victory at Notium will have
been important as well. To many non-Athenian rowers in the fleet, it
must have seemed that the tide had turned, that Sparta would win the
war and probably soon. The combination of that expectation with the
lure of money must have made possible large-scale changes of allegiance
after the battle that money alone could not achieve before it. Conon,
therefore, had to limit himself to plundering raids on enemy territories
for the rest of the official year.[8] These actions served several purposes:
they kept the men busy, which is a good way to help morale, and gave
Conon a chance to improve the training and cohesion of the newly
formed crews; they provided some money and provisions, both of
which must have been much needed; finally, the discipline on the
campaign made it more difficult to desert. For now, the Athenian
commander could do no more as he awaited reinforcements from home
and the enemy's next move.

In the Spartan camp at Ephesus, the scene was entirely different.
There was plenty of money and high morale. The fleet had been
increasing steadily, and the number of available ships and rowers continued to grow. The Spartans had found a successful admiral, and in
most states he would have been encouraged to complete the work he
had started so well. The Spartan constitution, however, prevented
that, for it required that the navarch retire after the completion of his
annual term.[9] The new navarch was Callicratidas, who was, like Lysander, a *mothax*, a man of marginal status, but there the resemblance
ends. Lysander was a mature man of middle years, cautious in spite
of his great ambition, skilled in the political arts of flattery and deception, and always alert to his own interests, even at the expense of
his city's. Callicratidas was an "extremely young man."[10] He was aggressive and daring, but his brief career yields no evidence of personal
ambition beyond giving glorious service to his city. He had the reputation of being "without guile and straightforward in character," to

[7]Xen. 1.5.20.
[8]Ibid.
[9]Xen. 1.6.1.
[10]Diod. 13.76.2: νέος μὲν ἦν παντελῶς. His exact age is not known, but if these
words are justified, he could hardly have been much over thirty.

the point of naivete, for "he was not yet experienced in the ways of foreigners." He was thought to be "the justest of the Spartans."[11]

As we have seen in the case of Lysander, no *mothax*, whatever his personal qualities, could rise to the important office of navarch without powerful friends in the highest Spartan circles. We have no direct testimony about Callicratidas' sponsors and supporters, but the evidence strongly suggests that he represented the views of the faction surrounding the Agiad kings, the late Pleistoanax, who had died in 408, and his son Pausanias.[12] The father, throughout his long reign, had been a supporter of peace and friendship with Athens and was one of the keenest advocates of the Peace of Nicias.[13] The son would show himself to be a deadly enemy of Lysander and the leader of a political faction in Sparta that has been characterized as a "moderate, traditionalist group which objected to the erection of the Spartan Empire." They wanted to limit Sparta's activities to the Peloponnesus, "stressing diplomacy rather than force." At home, "they feared the corrupting influence of the introduction of wealth and luxury which imperialism would bring, and they wanted a return to the austere principles of the Lycurgan constitution."[14] Pausanias' conservatism is underscored by a saying attributed to him in which he explained why the Spartans did not allow any laws to be changed: "Because the laws ought to be the masters over men, not men over the laws."[15] The natural and usual rivalry between Sparta's two royal houses made it likely that Pausanias would not favor the protégé of the Eurypontids. In addition, however, men who held such views could not fail to fear and oppose Lysander's policies and the man himself, whose sudden success had made him more powerful than any previous navarch. Since Callicratidas would soon show himself to be against the entire direction of Lysander's policy, it is easy to believe that he had risen to office with the support of the Agiads and the faction surrounding them. The election of Callicratidas shows that the behavior of Lysander in Asia, his close relationship with Cyrus, and his organization of political clubs

[11]Ibid. Plut. *Lys.* 5.5 offers a similar encomium, which he attributes to the friends of Lysander, Callicratidas' opponents.
[12]For the death of Pleistoanax and the succession of Pausanias, see Diod. 13.75.
[13]5.17.1; Kagan, *Archidamian War*, 335–336.
[14]C. D. Hamilton, *Sparta's Bitter Victories* (Ithaca, N.Y., and London, 1979), 82–83.
[15]Plut. *Mor.* 230F. If the attribution is not authentic, the sentiment, at least, must have been thought characteristic.

loyal to him personally had raised more fears in Sparta than his victory at Notium had won support for him.[16]

Since the battle of Notium in December or January, Lysander had undertaken no significant actions. Although the Athenian fleet had been sharply reduced in numbers and quality and the more numerous Spartan fleet had proved its mettle, Lysander made no attempt to interfere with Conon's raids and was content to remain in port. Another victory over the Athenians, this time under Conon's command, might have been decisive, but Lysander did not try to force a battle. Callicratidas arrived at Ephesus to assume his command, probably in April of 406.[17] At once the hostility between the retiring navarch and his successor came to the surface. As Lysander turned over the fleet to the new commander, he told him that he "handed it over as ruler of the sea and as one who had conquered in a battle at sea."[18] It was a boast not fully justified, as Callicratidas was quick to point out. He told Lysander to take his fleet southward from Ephesus, past the Athenian fleet at Samos, and deliver it at Miletus; then he would agree that he was ruler of the sea. That was a jibe at Lysander's overblown pretensions and at his failure to exploit the victory at Notium; it was also a declaration of rivalry and ill will. The former navarch merely pointed out that he was no longer in command and set out for home.[19]

Before leaving, however, Lysander had taken steps to see that his successor would not have an easy time. His friends and partisans began to work against Callicratidas at once. They not only failed to serve him with enthusiasm but also spread the word throughout the Greek cities that the Spartans had made a grave and dangerous mistake by replacing Lysander with a new, ignorant, and inexperienced commander. It is inconceivable that they acted without the approval, and perhaps even the instigation, of Lysander.[20] These were the men Lysander had called together and promised a brilliant future to if they supported him and his policy.[21] They were dismayed at the loss of their leader at a time when victory seemed imminent and were determined that his successor, who was unfriendly to Lysander and sup-

---

[16]Busolt, *GG* III:2, 1584.
[17]Beloch, *GG*² II: 2, 275; J.-F. Bommelaer, *Lysandre de Sparte* (Paris, 1981), 72–73.
[18]Xen. 1.6.2.
[19]Ibid., 1.6.2–3.
[20]Ibid., 1.6.4. Plutarch (*Lys.* 6.1) says flatly that "he made these men even more hostile to Callicratidas."
[21]See above, 306.

ported policies inimical to their own interests, should not gain the success that belonged to their patron and would deprive them of victory.

Callicratidas met the challenge swiftly, courageously, and shrewdly. He called together the entire Spartan fleet, which had grown to 140 ships by then, and addressed the men. This, in itself, was a clever maneuver, for the faction of Lysander would have formed only a very small group in the gathering of 28,000 or so. Xenophon's report of his brief, laconic speech deserves quotation: "I, for my part, am satisfied to stay at home, and if Lysander or anyone else believes he is more expert in naval matters I certainly will not stand in his way. But I have been sent by the state to command the fleet, and I can do nothing else than what I have been ordered to do to the best of my ability. Your task is to consider the ambitions I am striving to achieve and the criticisms made against our state, for you know them as well as I do, and give me your best advice as to whether I should stay or sail home and report the state of affairs here."[22] The speech was entirely effective, for Callicratidas had called the bluff of Lysander's men. No one dared suggest that he disobey the orders he had received; still less could they permit him to report their mutinous behavior to the authorities in Sparta.

Lysander, however, had done something else to sabotage his successor that presented an obstacle far more difficult to overcome. He had not spent all of the money Cyrus had given him. Although it would have been natural for a retiring commander to give the remainder to a new commander when he turned over the fleet, Lysander instead returned the money to Cyrus.[23] This was a truly shocking act. It did harm to the Spartan cause by depriving the new commander, who had brought no money from home, of the resources he needed to act against the enemy. Beyond that, it showed that Lysander regarded the money Cyrus had provided not as given to him as the Spartan commander but as given to him personally; "the act implied that Lysander considered himself . . . as an agent of the Prince."[24] It was intended, no doubt, both to ingratiate himself with Cyrus by compelling the new navarch to ask for the money and so make himself responsible to the

[22]Xen. 1.6.4.
[23]Ibid., 1.6.10; Plut. *Lys.* 6.1.
[24]Bommelaer, *Lysandre*, 96.

prince and to reduce his chances of success. Both results would serve Lysander's own purposes at the expense of Sparta's interests.

Callicratidas was compelled to go to Sardis and ask Cyrus for money with which to pay his men. The young prince would not receive him at once but made him wait for two days. It was a deliberate insult, but its purpose is not clear. Perhaps Cyrus meant only to humble the new man and make him understand his dependence on and subordination to the Persian paymaster. Perhaps he deliberately intended to anger him and produce a breach, which might open the way for the restoration to power of Cyrus' friend and collaborator. In any case, the result was that Callicratidas became angry and left without the money. Xenophon reports his parting words: "He said that the Greeks were in a most miserable condition because they flattered barbarians for the sake of money and, if he got home safely, he would try his best to reconcile the Athenians and the Spartans."[25] Here, Callicratidas was the spokesman for the faction in Sparta that had favored peace and collaboration with Athens over the years and that was unhappy with the arrangement that had placed Sparta, the liberator of the Greeks, as they liked to think of it, in the position of working with the barbarians to put the Greeks of Asia Minor under Persian rule. The words had a powerful appeal to traditional Spartan sentiment, and they amounted to a declaration of independence from Persian control and a determination to pursue a different policy without reliance on Persian money.[26] If carried to completion, this program would amount to a breach of the spirit, if not the letter, of the treaty with Persia, but the Spartans, no doubt led by the same faction as the one supporting Callicratidas, had already violated the treaty blatantly by offering Athens a separate peace after the battle of Cyzicus.[27] Calli-

[25]Xen. 1.6.6–7; Plut. *Lys.* 6.5–7: *Mor.* 222D.

[26]It is still valuable to read Grote's stirring, if somewhat excessive, encomium (VIII, 161–166) to Callicratidas as champion of Panhellenism.

[27]The last treaty with Persia required that any peace must provide the same terms for both Sparta and Persia (8.58.7), so the Spartan negotiations, which made no reference to Persia, were a clear violation. The same treaty provided that "the ships of the allies and those of the King should make war on the enemy in common," but that clause referred to the Great King's own fleet, whose arrival was promised but never occurred. De facto, the Spartans had accepted the situation, and Lysander's negotiations with Cyrus and his acceptance of money from the Persian prince could be thought to affirm the alliance without reference to the Great King's fleet, but those who favored independent action could argue that the failure of the Persian ships to appear nullified the treaty.

cratidas' rejection of Persian aid and cooperation, therefore, represented an important change in policy.[28]

His first step was to move the Spartan base from Ephesus to Miletus, and from there he sent to Sparta for money.[29] The shift of base was not the result of strategic considerations, since Ephesus was better located for the attacks on Chios and Lesbos that Callicratidas was about to undertake.[30] Callicratidas knew that Ephesus was a major center of Persian influence, and he must have perceived that it had become strongly attached to Lysander and would not be a comfortable base of operations for his rival. Moreover, it was not a place where he could readily raise the money he needed for his campaigns. Miletus, on the other hand, had vigorously resisted the Persian presence and might be better disposed toward an independent effort.[31] There, he called an assembly where he asked for contributions in a speech that openly called for a policy of winning the war without Persian support. "With the help of the gods," he concluded, "let us show the barbarians that without paying homage to them we can punish our enemies."[32] The appeal was successful; even Lysander's supporters contributed, for it would be dangerous to offend this bold and forceful young navarch who might turn out to be the winner in the struggle for power.[33]

With the money he obtained at Miletus, and more that he collected from Sparta's supporters at Chios, he began his campaign. There was good reason to act quickly and to attack the Athenians even before funds arrived from Sparta. For the moment, Callicratidas' fleet of 140

[28]Lewis (*Sparta and Persia*, 124–125) has made the interesting argument that a fourth treaty between Sparta and Persia, not specifically mentioned by the ancient writers, was negotiated by Boeotius in the winter of 408/7. He suggests that the new treaty contained a clause that "provided for the autonomy of the Greek cities of Asia Minor . . . on condition that they paid the ancient tribute to the King. . . . At a further guess, there may have been a provision for the withdrawal of Spartan forces at the end of the war. Whatever precisely was in the Treaty, it will have been enough to relieve the worst fears of the Ionian cities and to calm the Spartan conscience." If there was such a treaty, the actions of Callicratidas could be seen as a rejection of it as leaving Sparta still too dependent on Persia and not providing true freedom for the Greeks. However, I am unable to accept the reality of a fourth treaty. The omission of such an important and debatable event, one that would surely have been known publicly, is too hard to accept. The positive evidence for it, moreover, is slim.

[29]Xen. 1.6.7.

[30]Bommelaer, *Lysandre*, 88–89.

[31]8.84.

[32]Xen. 1.6.11.

[33]Ibid., 1.6.12. The best understanding of Callicratidas' actions is that of P. A. Rahe ("Lysander and the Spartan Settlement" [Ph.D. diss., Yale University, 1970], 28–29).

ships was twice as large as Conon's force, and its quality was better. The Athenians were making a major effort to put a large reinforcement out to sea, and its arrival would change the balance of power to Sparta's disadvantage. By attacking places under Athenian control, Callicratidas, at the very least, could hope to gain easy victories while a cowed Athenian fleet stayed in port. If he were more fortunate, he might lure Conon out to sea and destroy the only Athenian naval force in being. Any commander would have been attracted by these prospects, but for Callicratidas they were irresistible. He was young and bold. His rebuke to Lysander, moreover, blamed him for inactivity while the Athenian fleet served as a barrier and stood as a challenge to Spartan control of the sea. His own rhetoric called for action, and financial necessity demanded that it be quick. Even if funds came from Sparta, they would not be enough to compensate for the loss of Persian support. If he won swift victories, on the other hand, he might raise funds more easily among the Greek cities; besides, he might hope to destroy the Athenian navy and win the war at a stroke. Even if that did not happen, it would be better to eliminate Conon before the Athenian reinforcements arrived. For all of these reasons Callicratidas set out at once.

His first target was Delphinium, a fort on the island of Chios held by the Athenians (see Map 3). His overwhelming force persuaded the mere 500 Athenians who held it to give it up without a fight and leave under a truce. After destroying the fort, he sailed to Teos, where he took that city by assault at night.[34] These actions quickly demonstrated the young navarch's willingness to challenge the Athenian fleet at Samos, for both places were north of the Athenian base, and the Spartans were required to sail past Samos to reach them. The badly outnumbered Conon, however, chose to stay in port. Next, the Spartans sailed against the island of Lesbos, itself important to the Athenians but critical in preventing the Spartans from returning to the Hellespont. The first target was Methymna, a city on the northern coast of Lesbos controlled by a faction friendly to Athens and by an Athenian garrison of 500 men. Callicratidas took the city by assault, with the help of traitors within the city, and allowed his troops to plunder the place. He did not allow them to do as they liked with the

[34]Diod. 13.76.3–4. Xenophon (1.5.15) reports the capture of Delphinium and Eion (emended to Teos by most editors) just after Notium. He does not provide a precise date, and his words "a little later" may refer to the actions of Callicratidas described by Diodorus. If not, we should prefer Diodorus' fuller account with its persuasive details.

prisoners but had them assembled in the marketplace. His allies urged him to sell them all as slaves to acquire further booty, but he refused. There was no question of freeing the Athenians from the garrison; these men, along with the captives who were already slaves, were sold. But he released the Methymnaeans and restored the autonomy of the city, no doubt turning it over to the faction friendly to Sparta. He underscored his generosity with a ringing proclamation that brought to mind the noble slogan of freedom for the Greeks with which the Spartans had undertaken the war. He said that "while I am in command, so far as is in my power, no Greek will be enslaved."[35] The proclamation announced Callicratidas' policy; it was aimed both at the Greeks who were free from Athenian control and those who were still allied to Athens. To the former, it was a call to Panhellenism, a second step, after the rejection of Persian aid, toward a campaign conducted by Greeks to achieve freedom both from Persia and Athens. To the latter, it offered gentle and generous treatment to those who broke away from Athenian control. Both action and statement were excellent propaganda in a campaign to win the war quickly without Persian help.

After the victory on Lesbos, he sent a message to Conon in which he expressed his intention to put an end to the Athenian admiral's "adulterous affair with the sea." We may well believe that this was more than youthful bluster and was part of the psychological warfare the young navarch had been using since his arrival. It appears to have had a double purpose, implying that control of the sea legitimately belonged to Sparta and that Conon had been free to conduct an affair with it until his arrival because of the failures of his predecessor and rival, Lysander, and also offering a challenge meant to draw Conon's fleet into battle against overwhelming odds. Conon was too clever to take the bait, but the threat to Athenian interests posed by Callicratidas' attack on Lesbos was too great for him to ignore. He had made the best possible use of his brief time as commander on Samos. After consolidating his forces, he had trained and equipped them and "prepared them for battle as no previous general had done."[36] News of the attack on Methymna had led him to take his full force of seventy ships from port and move them toward Lesbos. He arrived too late to prevent

[35]Xen. 1.6.12–14; Diod. 13.76.4–5.
[36]Diod. 13.77.1.

its capture and withdrew to the Hekatonnesoi Islands to the east of Methymna (see Map 11).

Callicratidas must have received information of the location of the Athenian fleet. With characteristic boldness he set out before dawn to cut off Conon's retreat to Samos, but the excellence of the carefully selected and well-trained Athenian crews overcame the effects of surprise. The Athenians escaped the trap and made their way to sea. By now the Spartan fleet numbered 170, so Conon could do nothing but flee and try to reach safety in the harbor of Mytilene. The Spartans and their allies had been in service with regular pay for a year, and Lysander had given them excellent training during that period. Also, their numbers had been increased by the arrival of many skilled and experienced rowers deserting from the Athenian fleet, so their quality had become comparable to that of Conon's men. As a result, the Athenian ships were not able to put distance between themselves and their pursuers as they ran for port and safety. Callicratidas' ships arrived at Mytilene about the same time as Conon's. The narrowness of the entrance to the harbor and its defenses allowed 40 of the Athenian ships to reach the safety of land, but 30 were lost in the fighting at the mouth of the port, although their crews escaped. Callicratidas appears to have planned an attack on Mytilene even before these events, for after the victory at Methymna, he had placed the Spartan Thorax at the head of a body of hoplites, ordering him to march overland to Mytilene.[37] Now he ordered his newly acquired allies at Methymna to bring their entire force, and he also brought over his army from Chios, as he completely blockaded Mytilene by land and by sea.[38]

Conon's situation was extremely perilous. He was cut off from obtaining supplies, and he found himself in a large city containing many people who had revealed themselves to be hostile to Athens in the past. Recent events at Methymna had shown the danger of betrayal, even in a town that was much more friendly to Athens. All of his

[37] Diod. 13.76.6.
[38] The foregoing account derives almost entirely from Xenophon (1.6.15–18). Although Diodorus (13.77.2–79.7) gives a very different account, with the usual greater fullness of detail, on this occasion I find it hard to believe. According to Diodorus, Conon fled with with the intention of giving battle off Mytilene. In my view, he could not have meant to fight at all with only 70 ships against 170. He fled from the Hekatonnesoi because he could not withstand an assault or a siege there and was in danger of losing his entire fleet. If he could get to Mytilene, he might be able to hold out until relief came from Athens. The rest of Diodorus' account contains details that are also difficult to accept.

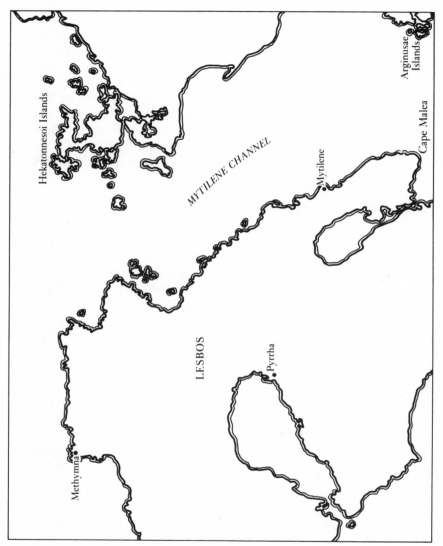

Hekatonnesoi Islands

Arginusae Islands

MYTILENE CHANNEL

Cape Malea

Mytilene

LESBOS

Pyrrha

Methymna

MAP 11. LESBOS AND ARGINUSAE

ships, moreover, had either been lost or shut into the harbor; none had escaped to get word of the situation to Athens. Unless a message got through, Mytilene might fall because of treason before help could arrive. The fall of the city would surely cause the loss of the whole island and, no less important, of the rest of the fleet. Conon devised a scheme for getting word to Athens. After four days of waiting for an opportunity, he sent two of his fastest ships manned by his best rowers to slip through the blockade, one sailing to the north and the other to the south. The enemy was caught napping, and both ships made their way out of the harbor about midday. The Spartans pursued the ship heading south, caught it at sunset, and brought it back to Mytilene. The ship sailing north, however, escaped and got to Athens with the news of Conon's peril.[39]

Callicratidas had won a victory but not such a decisive one as he might have hoped. He had not destroyed the entire Athenian fleet and conquered Lesbos, achievements that might have allowed him to capture the last major Athenian base at undefended Samos, close off the grain route, and bring a swift end to the war.[40] Unless treason put Mytilene into his hands, he was faced with a lengthy siege and, he had reason to expect, a confrontation with another Athenian naval force. He no longer had money to maintain his forces, but his achievements had made a powerful impression on Cyrus. The Persian prince had cause to believe that the Spartans would soon triumph without his help and under a commander he had alienated. That would be disastrous for his personal plans for the future, so regardless of his affection for Lysander, he tried to win the goodwill of Callicratidas. He sent money for the troops' pay and more as a present of friendship for the navarch himself. Callicratidas had no choice but to accept the money for his men, but he rejected the gift for himself saying "there

[39]Xen. 1.6.19–22. It seems likely that Leon was on the captured ship and Erasinides on the one that escaped, for we know that both generals were with Conon at Mytilene (1.6.16), but whereas Erasinides fought at Arginusae about a month later, Leon had been replaced by Lysias. See Busolt, GG III:2, 1589 n. 1.

[40]Such a total defeat might have discouraged the Athenians and led them to make peace. Even if they had chosen to fight on, they would have been compelled to send to sea the same force they sent to Arginusae, 110 ships that were no match for the enemy in quality. After losing Lesbos and Samos, they would not have been able to raise the additional 40 ships that they then got from their allies. The Spartans, on the other hand, would not have been compelled to detach 50 ships to guard Conon at Mytilene. The ensuing battle, therefore, would have matched 110 Athenian ships, manned by inferior, inexperienced crews, against 170 Spartan ships of high quality. The decision would not have been in doubt.

was no need for a private friendship between himself and Cyrus, but the agreement that had been made with all the Spartans was enough for him."[41] The rebuff could not have pleased Cyrus and must have impressed upon him the uniqueness of Lysander and his own dependence on the former navarch. Callicratidas, on the other hand, once again was separating himself and his policies from those of Lysander. Still, he, too, had suffered a rebuff to his hopes of ending the war without Persian assistance. The only way to achieve everything he wanted was to defeat Athens swiftly, before Persian money became decisive. Both his character and his policy led him to seek a decisive battle as soon as possible.

The ship escaping from Mytilene with the news of Conon's defeat and the Spartan blockade reached Athens about the middle of June.[42] The Athenians recognized the gravity of their situation and determined to make the fullest possible effort. There were probably about 40 or so triremes already on hand, Conon having sent 30 back from Samos after consolidating his force.[43] The Athenian shipwrights set feverishly to work, and at the end of thirty days, they had raised the number of ships available to 110.[44] The cost of building such a fleet and, even more, of paying the crews for the campaign ahead was too great for the depleted Athenian treasury. To meet the expense they were compelled to melt down the statues of the goddess Nike from the Acropolis and strike them as gold coins.[45] These coins and other gold and silver bullion still available in the temples on the Acropolis seem to have produced a sum worth something over 200 silver talents.[46] This was enough to build the ships and keep them at sea for the fighting ahead.

Providing manpower for the expedition was an even more difficult problem. The elite crews of the Athenian navy, some 14,000 men carefully selected by Conon for their superior ability, were locked up

[41]The story of the exchange, including the quotation, is from Plutarch (*Mor.* 222E). Xenophon (1.6.18) says only "the money came to him from Cyrus." There is, however, no reason to doubt Plutarch's version.

[42]Busolt, *GG* III:2, 1590, n. 2.

[43]Ibid., 1590, n. 1.

[44]Xen. 1.6.24. Diodorus (13.97.1) says the Athenians brought only sixty ships to Samos, where they were joined by eighty from the islands. As Busolt points out (*GG* III:2, 1590, n. 1), the figure is impossibly large. We must prefer Xenophon's account here.

[45]Aristoph. *Frogs* 720 with scholion. The scholiast's sources are Hellanicus (*FGrH* III, 323a, Fr. 26) and Philochorus (*FGrH* III, 328f, Fr. 144). See Jacoby, *FGrH* 3b, Suppl. 1.54, 511.

[46]The calculations are those of W. E. Thompson, *Numismatic Chronicle* X (1970), 1–6.

in Mytilene. The relief fleet would require 22,000 more men. The best of them would be those rejected by Conon as below his standard for the fleet in the Aegean, in normal times the scrapings from the bottom of the barrel, but they would have filled no more than thirty ships or so. For the rest, the Athenians had to enroll men from every class in society—the unpropertied who usually served as rowers, the farmers who normally fought in the phalanx as hoplites, and even the wealthy and aristocratic cavalrymen. Final evidence of the desperation of the situation is that the Athenians even enrolled slaves, offering them freedom as a reward and Athenian citizenship on the same terms that they had given the Plataeans: "They embarked all those who were of military age, both slave annd free."[47] Obviously, crews made up of such men lacked experience, discipline, and cohesion. Many of them, moreover, will have been commanded by inexperienced and unskilled captains and served by unskilled steersmen, who must have been in short supply. For the first time in the war, the Athenians entered a naval battle tactically inferior.[48] This rag-tag Athenian fleet, thrown together in the space of a month, must face a Spartan force that was well paid and well drilled, confident after its recent victories, and led by a bold young commander who had just defeated the Athenians' best admiral, Conon.

Around the middle of July the new Athenian fleet set out for its base on Samos under the command of no fewer than eight generals.[49] They were joined there by 10 Samian warships and perhaps 35 more collected from various allies, bringing their total to 155 triremes.[50] The mobilization had left the city walls to be defended by a small force of those men left behind, those who were under the age of twenty and over fifty, as well as any others unfit or excused from service on the ships.[51] This would have been a fine opportunity for Agis to launch an assault on Athens with his army from Decelea, but unaccountably, he did not move. Thucydides might have had this moment, among

[47]Xen. 1.6.24. For the enfranchisement of slaves, see Aristoph. *Frogs* 693–694 with scholion. The scholiast cites Hellanicus, *FGrH* III, 323a, Fr. 25.

[48]Xenophon (1.6.31) tells us that the Athenians at Arginusae chose their alignment "because they were inferior in seamanship" (χεῖρον γὰρ ἔπλεον), and the Spartans chose theirs "because they had superior seamanship" (διὰ τὸ βέλτιον πλεῖν).

[49]Busolt, *GG* III:2, 1591–1592.

[50]Xen. 1.6.25. Xenophon gives the number of ships coming from allies other than Samos as "more than 30" and the total as "more than 150." I have taken these numbers as 35 and 155, which should not be far wrong.

[51]Busolt, *GG* III:2, 1592–1593; *HCT* 1.308.

others, in mind when, criticizing the Spartans' failure to attack Athens in 411, he wrote: "It was not only at this time that the Spartans were the most convenient of all enemies for the Athenians but on many other occasions as well."[52]

At Mytilene, Callicratidas received word of the approaching Athenian fleet. Rather than wait to encounter the enemy with Conon's blockaded fleet at his back he sailed out to cut off the Athenians as they came north from Samos, stopping at Cape Malea on the southeastern tip of Lesbos. He was compelled to leave 50 ships at Mytilene under Eteonicus to maintain the blockade of Conon, reducing his own force to 120 triremes. He probably did not know the exact number of the enemy's ships, but he had reason to be confident in the technical superiority of his own fleet, even if it should be somewhat outnumbered. He arrived in time to have dinner at Cape Malea, and it happened that at the same time the Athenians were having their dinner at the Arginusae Islands, just off the coast of the mainland, about two miles due east of the cape (see Map 11).[53] Characteristically, Callicratidas took the initiative at once. When he saw the Athenian fires after sunset and learned where the Athenians were, he formed the plan of launching his ships during the the night, as he had done against Conon, in the hope of taking the enemy by surprise. A heavy thunderstorm intervened, however, and forced him to wait until dawn.[54]

The battle that followed takes its name from the Arginusae Islands, off whose western shores it was fought. In the number of ships engaged, it was the greatest battle of the war and, indeed, the greatest fought until then among the Greek navies.[55] Because of events in Athens to which it gave rise, more than because of its outcome, it was one of the most memorable of naval battles. Although Xenophon's description of it is relatively clear and plausible, it is incomplete, taking no note of the geography, which played an important part in the

---

[52]8.96.5.

[53]Xen. 1.6.26–27. Diodorus (13.97.3) numbers the Spartan fleet at 140, but in this battle Xenophon's account is much more plausible and his figures more reliable. The following interpretation is based chiefly on his account but makes use of Diodorus when it seems appropriate to do so.

[54]Xen. 1.6.28. Diodorus (13.97.4) at this point tells the story from the Athenian point of view. He says nothing of Callicratidas' plans or of any rain. Instead, he mentions strong winds that led both sides to delay battle until the day after they became known to each other.

[55]Diod. 13.98.5.

Athenian strategy, and saying little about the course of the fighting once the battle began. Diodorus' narrative, although taking better account of the geography and containing a few useful details, is generally implausible and full of rhetorical flourishes that contribute nothing to our understanding of the fighting. On this occasion, he seems to be following Ephorus at his rhetorical worst rather than the sober and judicious anonymous historian whose work has come to us on a papyrus from Oxyrhynchus.[56] Modern accounts have attempted to deal with the problems, to fill in the gaps, and to make sense of the battle, with greater or lesser degrees of success.[57] None of them, however, has fully accounted for the precision of some of the details provided by Xenophon, for the role played by the islands themselves in the Athenian strategy, for the clues available about the course of the battle, and for the direction it took. The following description tries to give a fuller account.

As the sun rose on the day of battle, Callicratidas' fleet began to row toward the east across the two miles of water that separated Cape Malea from the Athenian ships at the Arginusae Islands (see Map 11).

[56]The main problem of Xenophon's account is that it offers no explanation of why the Athenians were not outflanked and defeated by the Spartans, who were arrayed in a single line of 120 ships, while the Athenians were arranged in a formation in which their wings were formed in double lines, offering a front line of only 30 ships on each wing joined by a center in single line of about 30, giving a front of only 90 ships. Since the Spartans are described as superior tactically, such an overlap ought to have given them the victory, but Xenophon does not notice the problem. Diodorus recognizes the Athenians' difficulty and says that they used the islands as a means of extending their line. His explanation of the Spartans' response to the Athenian formation, however, is implausible, as we shall see, nor does he make clear the Athenian strategy. Once the fighting starts, his story is of even less value, containing statements that range from some contradicting his earlier ones, to others that are highly implausible, to still others that seem impossible. He calls most of the participants in the battle "experienced" and "the best" fighters (13.99.2), even though he has spoken of the emergency muster in which the Athenians were forced to enroll anyone able to serve (13.97.1). He has Thrasyllus name the trierarch Theramenes a command, although there were already eight Athenian generals at hand, and it is unclear where he would have found the authority to do this. He has Callicratidas sink the ship of the Athenian general Lysias, although the former led the right wing of his fleet and the latter served at the opposite end of the battle, on the right wing of his fleet. His account of the preliminaries to the battle is full of portents, dreams, and rhetoric. His narrative of Callicratidas' deeds in battle reads more like an epic *aristeia* than a historical description.

[57]The first thorough discussion was Grote's (VIII, 170–173). L. F. Herbst (*Die Schlacht bei den Arginusen* [Hamburg, 1855]) made some useful contributions, although in several respects the work is inferior to Grote's. Probably the best discussion is Busolt's (*GG* III:2, 1593–1596), although it contains a fundamental error about the Athenian order of battle.

Diodorus tells wonderful tales of dire and remarkably accurate portents that led the seers on both sides vainly to advise against fighting on the appointed day. On the Spartan side, waves are said to have covered the head of the sacrificial victim, portending the death of the Spartan admiral. Thrasyllus (wrongly called Thrasybulus, as usual), whom Diodorus designates as the chief commander of the Athenian forces on the fatal day, is said to have had a dream in which he and his seven fellow generals were performing Euripides' *Phoenissae* while their opponents were doing the same poet's *Suppliants*, both plays about the legend of the seven against Thebes. Thrasyllus and his comrades won a "Cadmeian victory" in which they were all killed. It did not take a very imaginative seer to see this as a portent of Athenian victory at the expense of the lives of its generals. Callicratidas, we are told, believed the Spartan prophecy but was not deterred. He was willing to die to achieve a Spartan victory. He was prudent enough, however, to name the experienced commander Clearchus to take his place in case he died in battle.[58] Through all of the romantic invention here, we probably can discern a fact. It did not take portents or seers to suggest the desirability of establishing a clear chain of command in a naval battle but only a memory of what had happened at Notium. The death of Antiochus early in the fighting and the disastrous confusion it caused were certainly known to both sides, and Callicratidas acted with prudence to avoid such an outcome.

The Spartan fleet entered the battle in standard array, moving forward line abreast, the 120 ships side by side, spanning a distance of about 2,400 yards, or a mile and a third.[59] It was an order that would

---

[58]Diod. 13.97.4–98.1.

[59]I know of no ancient testimony on or modern discussion of the normal space between triremes when rowing abreast. My estimate is based on two calculations: the greatest space between ships compatible with preventing an enemy from making the maneuver called the *diekplous* (breaking through the line) and the space needed to permit a quick half-turn to either side, allowing a change to the line ahead; or columnar formation. (For a good discussion of these tactics, see J. S. Morrison and R. T. Williams, *Greek Oared Ships, 900–322* B.C. [Cambridge, 1968], 314.) The first distance may be calculated by adding the maximum breadth of the top deck of the trireme attempting the *diekplous* from outrigger to outrigger (16 feet), doubling the distance between the outrigger on one side and the place where the oars amidships strike the water, plus 2 feet on each side for the distance between the outrigger and the top of the gunwale amidships, and the same distance to account for the distance between gunwale and the place where the oar strikes the water on the inboard side of each of the defending ships. (The dimensions of triremes and oars are given in Morrison and Williams, *Greek Oared Ships*, 285, 289; and L. Casson, *Ships and Seamanship in the Ancient World* [Princeton, N.J., 1971], 77.) The distance between the outrigger and the place where the oar strikes the

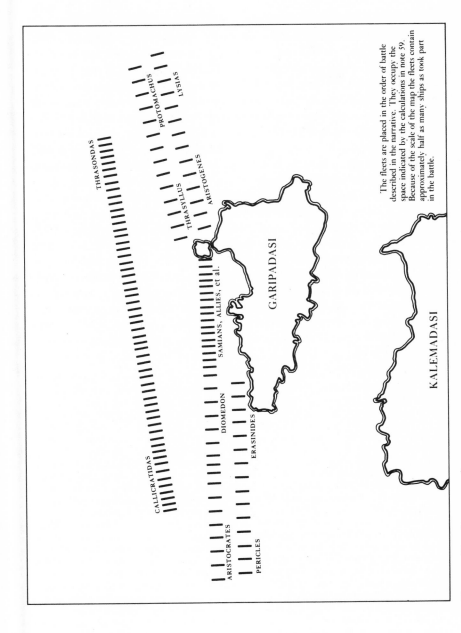

The fleets are placed in the order of battle described in the narrative. They occupy the space indicated by the calculations in note 59. Because of the scale of the map the fleets contain approximately half as many ships as took part in the battle.

CALLICRATIDAS

THRASONDAS

PROTOMACHUS

LYSIAS

ARISTOGENES

THRASYLLUS

SAMIANS, ALLIES, et al.

GARIPADASI

KALEMADASI

DIOMEDON

ERASINIDES

ARISTOCRATES

PERICLES

MAP 12. THE BATTLE OF ARGINUSAE

allow them to employ the tactics perfected by the Athenians in the many decades of their naval supremacy: the *periplous*, employing superior speed to row around the enemy formation and strike from its side or rear, and the *diekplous*, in which a ship sailed into the gap between two enemy ships and did the same. If the Spartans knew that they were outnumbered, they were unconcerned, for they counted on their tactical superiority to carry the day.[60] "All the Spartan ships were aligned in a single line abreast so as to be in position for the *diekplous* and the *periplous*, for they were the better seamen."[61] Recent events had given the Spartans the skill to try such maneuvers while the Athenians had lost the ability to use them but must fear them instead.

The Athenians, therefore, received the enemy in a formation that was arranged in an unusual way, was commanded in an unprecedented manner, and, as far as we know, was unique in Greek naval history.[62] Each wing consisted of sixty ships, arranged in a double line and divided into units of fifteen triremes, each under its own general (see Map 12). Aristocrates and Diomedon commanded the forward units on the left, with Pericles and Erasinides behind them. Protomachus and Thrasyllus led the forward units on the right wing, with Lysias and Aristogenes behind them.[63] In the center, next to Diomedon's unit, were ten Samian ships under their own commander, Hippeus,

---

water amidships is calculated by applying the Pythagorean theorem: side *a* is the height of the trireme from outrigger to water line (8.5 feet) and the hypotenuse, side *c*, is the length of the oar between oarlock on the outrigger and tip. (The oar used amidships was 14 feet, 4 inches. If we allow about 3 feet for the distance inboard from outrigger to rower's hands, we get a distance of about 11 feet.) The result is about 9 feet from the gunwale to the tip of the oar in the water. (72.25 feet + X^2 = 121 feet; X = 6.98 feet, rounded to 7 feet plus 2 feet for distance from outrigger to gunwale = 9 feet.) The ship trying the *diekplous*, therefore, requires a minimum of 34 feet (16 + 9 + 9). To that must be added 9 feet for the extended oars of each defending ship, giving a total of 52 feet, or 17.3 yards. In fact, the defending ships will prefer a bit of leeway, which they can safely allow, yielding a space between triremes abreast of roughly 18 to 20 yards. Since the length of a trireme was between 115 and 120 feet, a half-turn would require a space of about 60 feet, or 20 yards. Again, some leeway would be desirable; perhaps the interval may have been as great as 25 yards, but 20 yards seems roughly correct for the normal interval between Greek triremes aligned abreast.

[60]Apparently, they did not know it before they set out, for Hermon, the *kybernetes* on Callicratidas' flagship, warned his admiral to turn back because they were outnumbered only when they came in sight of the Athenian fleet (Xen. 1.6.32).

[61]Xen. 1.6.31.

[62]See below, n. 67.

[63]Xen. 1.6.29–30. Diodorus (13.98.2–3) has only a limited and confused idea of the Athenian alignment, saying nothing about a single or double line or about separate units and certainly getting the assignments of the commanders wrong.

and ten Athenian ships under the taxiarchs, normally important officers in the hoplite army and now serving with the fleet.[64] In addition, there were three ships of subordinate Athenian naval officers called "navarchs" and some twelve ships from allied states.[65] These triremes, unlike those on the wings, were arranged in a single line.[66] Xenophon also tells us why the Athenians chose this arrangement: "They were arrayed in this way so that they might not permit the *diekplous*, for their seamanship was inferior."[67] This account presents a problem: we can imagine that the double line of ships could hope to thwart the *diekplous*, but the single line in the center would not, and if the Spartans broke through the center they could wreak havoc on the wings from the rear. Here, Diodorus provides us with a vital clue, telling us that the Athenians "included the Arginusae Islands in their battle-order."[68] The thirty-five ships in the Athenian center, about 20 yards apart, extended some 660 yards in front of the more western of the two significant Arginusae Islands, today called Garipadasi. With that island close at their backs, the ships of the Athenian center were safe from the maneuver they feared.[69]

[64] For the taxiarchs, see Jordan, *Athenian Navy*, 130–134.

[65] Xen. 1.6.29.

[66] Xenophon (1.6.29) makes it clear that these central ships were "drawn up in a single line" (ἐπὶ μιᾶς τεταγμένοι). Each wing consisted of a double line with two units of fifteen in front and two behind.

[67] Xen. 1.6.31. The use of a double line of triremes to thwart the *diekplous* was not new. We have a papyrus fragment of a work by Sosylus of Sparta describing a naval campaign by Hannibal (*FGrH* 176, Fr. 1) that tells of such a tactic employed by the Greeks of Marseilles in emulation of a certain Heracleides of Mylasa who first used it at the battle of Artemisium in 480. They "had read in history about the battle of Artemisium fought by Heracleides of Mylasa, one of the most resourceful captains of his time, and accordingly they gave orders for a first line abreast to be followed by a second at appropriate intervals, the ships of which, as soon as the enemy passed through the line in front, should attack them while still passing. This was what Heracleides had done long before, and been the architect of victory" (quoted and trans. by Morrison in Morrison and Williams, *Greek Oared Ships*, 138). At least one of the Athenian generals at Arginusae appears to have been a keen student of naval history. The innovation added to this tactic was to divide the fleet into independent commands under several generals.

[68] Diod. 13.98.3.

[69] Grote (VIII, 171) has correctly understood the order of the Athenian center and its relationship to the islands. Herbst (*Arginusen*, 30) knows that the center was arranged in a single line between the doubled wings and that it stood in a significant relationship with the islands but is wrong, I believe, on two small details. He believes that the Athenian center stood in front of the same island I have designated but believes it stretched all the way to the tiny speck in the sea that is the island to its north (see Map 12). Leaving a stretch of open sea behind a part of the single line would defeat its

The double lines on the wings were meant to achieve the same effect there, where there were no islands to provide protection.[70] But it is worth considering how they were arranged to achieve the best results. The most obvious alignment would place the rear line of ships behind the gaps separating the ships in the front line, serving as a clear deterrent to the *diekplous*. Closer study of the evidence, however, suggests that the Athenians employed a refinement that had extraordinary advantages. They appear to have separated their ships on the wings by about twice the usual distance, with the ships in the rear line filling the gaps behind the front.[71] The greater gap might lure the Spartans into attempting the *diekplous*; the Athenian ships behind the gap could come forward to stop an intruding ship's progress, leaving it vulnerable to a ram from either side. The element of surprise so achieved could have devastating results. The double gap between Athenian ships on the wings, however, had another crucial result: it lengthened the Athenian line and enabled it to outflank the enemy rather than being outflanked. Keeping the usual separations, the Athenians would have presented a front of about 95 ships, 30 on each wing and about 35 in the center, against a Spartan front of 120; the Spartans would have extended beyond each end of the Athenian by 12 or 13 ships. In that

purpose. Herbst fell into this error because he failed to consider the spacing between ships or the length of the main island, although he took the trouble of discovering the depth of the sea around it (80, n. 29). He also believed that the three ships of the navarchs stood behind the others in the center. Although the dative in ἐπὶ δὲ ταύταις may mean "after" or "behind" these ships, and is often so translated, it need not be and in this context cannot be, because the passage goes on to place the twelve or so allied ships next to these three, which would make for a double line in the center, flatly contradicting Xenophon's assertion at the beginning that the Samians and the taxiarchs were in a single line. I prefer to render the dative "in addition to" these ships, and thus to see them next in line after the taxiarchs and before the allies.

[70] The west coast of the island from its southern tip to the little islet near the northern end, which would protect the center's right flank and beyond which it need not extend, is about 900 yards long (see Map 12). If the center of the Athenian fleet placed its right wing next to the islet, there would have been some 240 yards of coast beyond its left wing. The right wing probably took up a position entirely north of the island; the left wing might have taken a position immediately next to the center, in which case some forty-eight of their ships would have extended beyond the island's southern tip. In fact, there was no need to line up close to the center, for it was rendered safe against encirclement by the proximity of the island. It seems likely that the wings allowed the center to stand alone, placed their double lines in the open water at either end of the island, and thereby lengthened their line well beyond that of the enemy.

[71] Busolt alone (*GG* III:2, 1594–1595) has seen that the second line of ships must have stood behind the gaps and that the separation between ships must have been greater than usual.

case, they could have ignored the *diekplous* and, with their superior skill, easily could have attacked the Athenians in the flank and rear. With such an advantage, it is hard to see how they could have lost the battle, much less suffer the terrible disaster they encountered.

With the double gap, however, the Athenian line covered the space normally occupied by 155 ships in line abreast, overlapping the enemy by at least 16 or 17 ships at each end.[72] In such a position, with the double lines protecting their wings and the island their center against the *diekplous*, and the length of their own line preventing the enemy's *periplous*, the Athenians were in good order to avoid undue harm to themselves and to do great damage to their enemies.[73] The Athenians' division of their wings into eight independent units, moreover, each under its own commander and able to act separately from the rest, allowed them to take the offensive with safety. Xenophon gives us the clue that shows how they proceeded. As Callicratidas came toward them, "the Athenians came out against him, extending their left wing out towards the open sea."[74] Since the wings already outflanked the Spartan fleet, the looping movement to the left was even more threatening to the Spartan right, for unless it were met, it might circle behind

---

[72] If they lined up away from the center, using the entire island as a way of extending their line, as suggested in n. 70, above, their advantage would have been even greater.

[73] Apart from the argument just given, there are three pieces of evidence that tend to support the suggested alignment. Diodorus (13.98.4) tells us that the Athenians included the islands in their battle order, "being eager to extend their line of ships as far as possible" (σπεύδων ὅτι πλεῖστον παρεκτεῖναι τὰς ναῦς). The arrangement suggested here seems to suit that purpose well, while others do not. The second evidence comes from Xenophon's report of Hermon's warning to Callicratidas, when the Spartans came close enough to see the Athenians' numerical superiority (1.6.32). If the Athenians were separated by the usual distance, they would have been outflanked, as we have seen. It is hard to see how Hermon could have determined that the Athenians were superior in numbers in that formation. Nothing, however, could have been easier than to see that the Spartans were numerically inferior when they were outflanked. The most direct and powerful evidence in favor of this reconstruction is another passage in Diodorus (13.98.4), which tells us that Callicratidas "was unable to make his line equal to the enemy's because the islands took up too much space" (οὐ δυνάμενος δὲ τὴν τάξιν ἐξισῶσαι τοῖς πολεμίοις διὰ τὸ τὰς νήσους πολὺν ἐπέχειν τόπον). Diodorus' lack of precision in writing of islands instead of a single island and his failure to make clear exactly how the Athenians were aligned and how their line was related to the island do not deprive his account of value. His source may or may not have had these details right, but he clearly understood the Athenian strategy and the place the islands had in it.

[74] 1.6.29: οἱ δὲ Ἀθηναῖοι ἀντανήγοντο εἰς τὸ πέλαγος τῷ εὐωνόμῳ. The words "out toward the open sea" (εἰς τὸ πέλαγος) mean that the Athenian left moved not straight at the Spartans, across the narrows, but made an arc the south, where the sea is open, as part of a flanking movement.

it and attack from the rear. In the normal single alignment, however, such a maneuver would open a gap in the Athenian line or leave a gap on its left that the Spartans could exploit. The alignment at Arginusae allowed Pericles to take his detachment on a wide swing to the left, leaving Aristocrates in a position that still outflanked the enemy. Any Spartan assault on a weakened position could be met by moving the second rear detachment of Erasinides to meet the challenge. In fact, it seems likely that the Athenian maneuver deprived the Spartans of the initiative; the threat to their flank and rear would have been so great and so obvious as to raise no thought of moving forward and being encircled entirely. The Athenian right may have performed the same maneuver, although we are not so informed. Even if it did not, it was nevertheless in a position to outflank the enemy without a wide sweeping movement, and it had the advantage of the same tactical flexibility. We have no reason to think that the Athenian center moved away from the safety of the island behind it; it simply waited to see what the Spartans would do.

Callicratidas commanded the Spartan right, while Thrasonidas of Thebes was in charge of the Boeotian contingent on the left.[75] As the Athenian fleet came clearly into view, Hermon of Megara, Callicratidas' *kybernetes*, urged his admiral not to engage but to avoid battle, "for the triremes of the Athenians were more numerous by far."[76] The length of the Athenian line, which outflanked the Spartans at both ends, gave the unmistakable evidence of the correctness of this judgment and the danger it presented, but Callicratidas refused to draw back. Xenophon attributes to the admiral a brave and patriotic response: "Sparta would not be the worse if he died, but to flee would be shameful."[77] These are the words of an old-fashioned Spartan, schooled in the tradition of Lycurgus, and they are perfectly in character for this bold, aggressive, and fearless commander. These character traits may seem enough to explain the young admiral's decision: "The answer is the whole man; for that reason he could not retreat even now. Noble, bold, and grand, always direct, without a care for difficulties or pushing them aside, he pursued his goal with speed and drive and hoped to reach it even now, since his determined uprightness had always brought him through successfully up to now."[78] Even

[75]Xen. 1.6.31; Diod. 13.98.4.
[76]Xen. 1.6.32.
[77]Ibid.
[78]Herbst, *Arginusen*, 33.

without the benefit of hindsight, however, we can see that Hermon's advice was worth taking seriously. Until the battle of Arginusae, Callicratidas had always enjoyed the advantages of superior numbers, as well as superior tactical ability, so his bold and aggressive style were fully justified. This time, however, he was heavily outnumbered and the Athenians had been able to select the place of battle much to their own advantage. It would seem to behoove a prudent Spartan admiral to break off the attack and choose to fight another day. Time, after all, was on Sparta's side; the Athenians had scarcely enough money in their treasury to pay for the current expedition, and when that money was spent, they would find it hard, perhaps impossible, to keep their fleet at sea. Since Cyrus had resumed payments, on the other hand, Sparta could afford to wait. Moreover, the passage of time promised further desertions from the Athenian fleet to the Spartans, who could wait to fight with better numerical odds and at a more favorable location. The Athenians, it has been suggested, must be the aggressors "and seek battle even under unfavorable conditions." It was Sparta's misfortune to have its fate in the hands of a man who insisted on a quick decision and who, "along with the nobility of his nature, did not possess the careful prudence of his predecessor."[79]

Not only did Callicratidas' character argue against delay, but also his policy and his political position counseled against it. Every day that passed made Sparta more dependent on Cyrus and Persia, something that might not trouble another commander but was unacceptable to Callicratidas. Moreover, it was always possible that for some unforeseeable reason the Athenians might not offer another opportunity for battle. In that case, the navarch's term would come to an end without a decisive battle. The glory of victory and the power to determine the settlement would then fall to another, perhaps to someone with the views and goals of Lysander. If the Athenians did seek battle, as was more probable, where were they likely to do so? Let us imagine that Callicratidas took the advice of Hermon and aborted the battle at the Arginusae Islands. He would then need to withdraw to Mytilene, where the Athenians were bound to go to relieve the blockade of Conon. There he would rejoin the 50 ships of Eteonicus, bringing his numbers to 170 ships. The Athenians would confront him with their 155 ships outside the harbor, while Conon's 40 ships would threaten him from the rear. The Athenian advantage in numbers would be

[79]Ibid., 34.

reduced from 35 to 25, not an overwhelmingly significant change. The Athenians would have given up the advantage afforded them by the islands, but they would present him with a threat from the front and rear. Conon's force, to be sure, was shut up in the harbor, but the Spartan situation would still be unusual and uncomfortable. In any case, the prospect was not remarkably attractive. On balance, it might still have been better to fight at Mytilene than at Arginusae, but the difference was not so great as to be obvious and decisive. But we do not know whether any of these thoughts went through Callicratidas' mind when he saw the Athenian array and heard the warning of Hermon. It is enough to say that his words need not have been merely the thoughtless response of a rash young man.

Having decided to fight, Callicratidas chose the best tactics he could. The threat on the flanks was primary, and he had no choice but to meet it. Diodorus tells us that since he could not make his line equal to the length of the enemy's, "he divided his force, forming it into two fleets, fighting a double battle, one on each wing. For this reason he aroused great astonishment in the spectators, who were looking on from many sides, since there were four fleets fighting the naval battle."[80] The fighting, then, took place on the two wings, with half of the Spartan fleet against four Athenian detachments on each wing. Callicratidas' maneuver left the Spartan fleet without a center with which to face the Athenian single line in front of the island. This movement created a risk of attack by the Athenian center against the inner flanks of the two Spartan fleets, but there was no way to meet the unorthodox Athenian strategy without running some risk, and the danger on the outer flanks from the massed Athenian wings was both more imminent and more dangerous. Perhaps Callicratidas made his decision after seeing that the Athenian center was a single line and would probably stand on the defensive; perhaps he ignored the threat from the center only because of the need to respond to the danger on the wings. In either case, he was forced to gamble, and his choice seems to have been the best he could make in the circumstances.

Since the Athenians had the advantage of numbers and position and had seized the initiative as well, we might expect them to have achieved a quick and easy victory, but they did not. The battle was long and hard. "First the fighting was in close order, and later it was scattered."[81]

[80] 13.98.4–5.
[81] Xen. 1.6.33.

The Athenian flanking movements must have succeeded in forcing the enemy into a tightly packed formation where superior seamanship was less important. In the first part of the battle, the Athenian center must have stayed out of the fighting, for it is inconceivable that none of the ships of the Samians, taxiarchs, or navarchs, all arrayed in the center, would have been lost if they had engaged in any serious fighting.[82] The center, nevertheless, played an important part in the battle, even while it remained stationary before the island, for the ships of the Athenian center acted as guards for the inner ends of the two wings. Any Spartan ship attempting a *periplous* around these inner ends, or even venturing in to engage a single ship, would soon find itself exposed broadside to the rams of the Athenian center, inactive for the time being. As the battle progressed, the psychological usefulness of the immobile Athenian center must have increased, for the presence of a fresh and undamaged enemy contingent so near at hand must have begun to unnerve the Spartans as the long fight wore on. Toward the end of the fighting, with their formation broken, the Spartan ships will have found themselves scattered about the sea singly or in small groups, where Athenian numbers will have been more effective. Finally, Callicratidas was killed, falling overboard as his ship rammed an enemy.[83] Soon afterward, the left wing of the Spartans gave way and turned to flight. When the Spartans began to flee, the Samian and Athenian ships in the center were released to pursue the routed enemy. Their fresh crews were able to overtake and destroy the weary Spartans in a manner unprecedented in the annals of trireme warfare, which contributed greatly to the extraordinarily high percentage of losses suffered by the Spartan fleet. The same circumstance of their engagement helps explain why they themselves suffered no losses, for pursuers in a rout are almost entirely free from risk.[84]

The fighting on the right must have continued fiercely until the very end, for of the ten Laconian ships that served with the navarch, all but one were lost, but after a while all of the survivors were forced to flee. The Athenian right wing must have cut off the natural escape route to the north, toward the remaining Spartan fleet at Mytilene

[82]Xenophon (1.7.30) tells us that all these ships survived the battle. Busolt (*GG* III:2, 1595, n. 6) is the only one to notice the significance of this fact.
[83]Ibid.
[84]I am indebted to John R. Hale for showing me that Diodorus was right in telling us that the Spartans divided their ships into two fleets without a center between them and for making clear to me the role played by the Athenian center.

under Eteonicus, for all the ships that got away made their escape to the south, landing at Chios, Phocaea, and Cyme.[85] The Spartans lost seventy-seven ships, some 64 percent of their force, a truly astonishing number.[86] By comparison, the average of the losses of the defeated side at the battles of Cynossema, Abydos, and Notium was only about 28 percent.[87] In all of these battles the losing side was able to break off and escape to safety on land that was not far away. The battle of Cyzicus, where the Spartans lost their entire fleet, was an amazing exception to most naval battles; yet it may help us understand what happened at Arginusae. At Cyzicus the Athenians used deception, surprise, and independently commanded units to draw the enemy away from the safety of land and encircle it. That guaranteed victory at sea. Their subsequent victory on land allowed them the unprecedented achievement of capturing all of the surviving ships. At Arginusae the Athenians, once again, employed deception and surprise, as well as units under independent command, to achieve a great victory. The double rows on the wings with units free to swing wide to outflank and encircle their opponents shocked the Spartans and deprived them of whatever battle plan they may have had. The right wing of the Athenians was able to close off the two-mile channel between Arginusae and Lesbos and thereby prevent easy escape to the north. The left wing, however, was unable to complete the double envelopment, allowing forty-three Spartan ships to escape.

The Athenians lost twenty-five ships.[88] But they had won a magnificent victory in the largest battle ever fought between Greek navies.[89] The chief goal of their campaign, the liberation of Conon and his fleet, was quickly accomplished, for Eteonicus got word of the outcome of the battle and quickly sailed to Chios, leaving Conon free to rejoin the

---

[85]Xen. 1.6.33. Diodorus (13.99.5) reports that the right wing of the Spartan line gave way first, but Xenophon's version is more likely. If the ships around Callicratidas had fled early, they would have found it relatively easy to escape, since they were located at the southern end of the battle. The Laconian contingent, in that case, would not have lost nine out of ten of its ships.

[86]Diodorus (13.100.4) provides the precise number of losses on the Spartan side. Xenophon (1.6.34) says that the Spartans lost nine of ten Laconian ships and the allies lost more than sixty. The figures are compatible.

[87]At Cynossema the Spartans lost twenty-one of eighty-six, or 24 percent; at Abydos, thirty of ninety-seven, or 31 percent; at Notium, the Athenians lost twenty-two of eighty, or 28 percent.

[88]Xen. 1.6.34; Diod. 13.100.3.

[89]Diod. 13.98.5.

main Athenian fleet.[90] Beyond that, they had crushed the excellent Spartan fleet so carefully prepared and trained by Lysander and killed his brilliant and daring young successor, who had threatened to win the war in a few months. An Athenian defeat at Arginusae would have won the war for the Spartans. Instead, the successful outcome restored Athenian control of the sea and brought another Spartan peace offer.[91] Although Diodorus says Thrasyllus was in command on the day of the battle, we need not believe he was the architect of the winning strategy.[92] The battle at Arginusae appears to have been planned and fought under a joint command, and the Athenians owed much to the generals who fought at Arginusae for the original and brilliant scheme that brought them victory and survival.

[90]Xen. 1.6.36–38; Diod. 13.100.5–6.

[91]*Ath. Pol.* 34.1.

[92]Diodorus' account (13.98.3) of the Athenian battle line and the placement of its leaders is sparse and implausible. He tells us that Thrasyllus was on the right wing, which agrees with Xenophon's complete and reasonable version (1.6.29–30), but he also places Pericles on the right when Xenophon has him on the left. He also produces the entirely implausible tale of Thrasyllus giving Theramenes a command alongside him, although Theramenes was only a trierarch and eight other generals were present. He presents the generals as having been spread out along the line, whereas Xenophon has them only on the wings. Although his account contains valuable information about the Athenian strategy, he is not well informed on the details of command. It is entirely possible that Thrasyllus was not in command, even on a rotating basis, on the day of battle.

14. The Trial of the Generals

The victory at Arginusae ought to have brought relief, joy, and unity to the Athenians. Instead, it became the source of acrimony, division, and a public outrage that may have been the most shameful in Athenian history. Soon after their great triumph, six of the generals who commanded at Arginusae were condemned and executed by the Athenian people for whom they had fought so successfully; the other two escaped only because they had rejected the summons ordering them to return to Athens for scrutiny, going into voluntary exile instead. The charge against them was failing to rescue survivors of the battle and to recover the bodies of the dead. Controversy surrounding the legitimacy of the complaint, the procedures employed in the investigation and trial, the verdict, and the penalty has been heated from the start. Neither of the major ancient sources is full, dispassionate, or satisfactory, and these sources cannot be perfectly blended to construct a complete and thoroughly reliable account. The narrative presented here, therefore, is very much an interpretation.[1]

---

[1] The two ancient narratives are in Xenophon (1.6.33–7.35) and Diodorus (13.100–103.2). Although they differ on many points, the main and most obvious disagreement between their versions concerns the activities of Theramenes. For Xenophon, he is the villain of the piece; for Diodorus, it is not he but the Athenian mob that is to blame. Busolt, as was his usual practice and like most scholars of his time, followed Xenophon, rejecting Diodorus as rhetorically inventive and unreliable (for typical strictures, see *GG* III:2, 1596, n. 4, and 1598, n. 1). Even Grote (VIII, 175–210)—whose brilliant and moving account rejects Theramenes' culpability, softens and explains the behavior of the people, and places the chief blame on the generals—stays close to Xenophon while accepting some evidence from Diodorus on occasion. P. Cloché's most thorough and very useful discussion (*Revue Historique* CXXX [1919], 5–68) treats the two accounts

The last phase of the battle found the Athenian fleet stretched over a large area of the sea. The original line of battle had been long, and the opening maneuvers in which the ships on the wings had made flanking movements had stretched it further. Later, the right wing must have advanced the two miles to the west to Cape Malea on Lesbos to close off escape to the north. Afterward, some of the Athenian ships will have gone south in pursuit of the routed enemy. The ships on the Athenian left also will have pursued the defeated enemy ships to the south when they turned to flee. On both wings the pursuit was fierce and extended, for it was important to destroy as much of the enemy fleet as possible.[2] Thirteen of the twenty-five lost Athenian ships had disappeared beneath the waves, but the wrecks of twelve ships,[3] with well over a thousand men clinging to them, and the bodies of many dead Athenian sailors bobbed on the choppy sea over a space of at least four square miles.[4] Breaking off their pursuit, the scattered Athenian ships made no effort to rescue the survivors or pick up the bodies but hurried back to the Arginusae Islands to regroup and confer about their next step.[5]

In his passionate defense of the Athenian people for their ultimate condemnation of the generals, Grote denounced the latter for their

---

with an open mind, using each when it seems appropriate. Influenced by the discovery of the *Hellenica Oxyrhynchia* and the unmistakable evidence that Diodorus often used it, A. Andrewes (*Phoenix* XXVIII [1974], 112–122) has argued that he used it, in part, for his account of the trial as well. He says, "we need not hesitate to prefer the Diodoran version, at least down to that point towards the end of 101 where he begins to abbreviate so heavily that we lose any flavour of his ultimate original" (120). His argument is persuasive, and I think we should be ready to believe Diodorus when there seems good reason to do so. At the same time, we need to be willing to accept Xenophon when his version is better. My own practice resembles Cloché's, although my conclusions are different.

[2]Diodorus (13.100.1) tells us that the Athenians pursued for a considerable distance: ἐφ' ἱκανὸν.

[3]Xen. 1.6.35; 7.30; Busolt, *GG* III:2, 1596, n. 1.

[4]Diod. 13.100.1. I calculate the area by assuming that pursuit to the south went as far as the distance between the islands and Lesbos, two miles. It seems likely that this is a low estimate. The number of survivors is likewise conservative. L. Herbst (*Die Schlacht bei den Arginusen* [Hamburg, 1855], 37, n. 51) places the number at 1,200, Busolt (*GG* III:2, 1596) at 2,000. It is noteworthy that Diodorus consistently refers to corpses only throughout the affair, whereas Xenophon speaks of the survivors.

[5]Xenophon (1.6.33; 7.29) makes it clear that the Athenians returned to the islands and held a conference there before making any attempt at rescue. Diodorus (13.100.1–3) tells of the conference before the return to Arginusae, but Xenophon is surely correct. As Cloché points out (*RH* CXXX [1919]), it is entirely unclear how the scattered Athenian ships could have met for a discussion anywhere but Arginusae.

failure to rescue the survivors at once, even before the return to Arginusae:

Neither with an English, nor French, nor American fleet, could such events have taken place as those which followed the victory of Arginusae. Neither admiral nor seaman, after gaining a victory and driving off the enemy, could have endured the thoughts of going back to their anchorage, leaving their own disabled wrecks unmanageable on the waters, with many living comrades aboard, helpless, and depending upon extraneous succor for all their chance of escape.. . . .

If these generals, after their victory, instead of sailing back to land, had employed themselves first of all in visiting the crippled ships, there would have been ample time to perform this duty, and to save all the living men aboard . . . this is what any English, French, or American naval commander would have thought it an imperative duty to do.[6]

If we are to understand the depth of the distress of the Athenian people caused by the aftermath of the battle, we must add to this concern for the survivors the immense significance to the Greeks of proper burial of the dead, a religious duty of the greatest importance. To many Athenians, the failure to recover the corpses would have seemed almost as shocking as the failure to rescue the living. How can we explain the apparent callousness with which the Athenian generals and ship captains ignored their comrades in the water and sailed past them to rendezvous at Arginusae?

We may gain some understanding by taking note of the differences between the battle of Arginusae and the other naval battles that the Athenians had fought since 411. The battles of Cynossema and Abydos had been fought in the narrow confines of the Hellespont, Cyzicus in the limited space of Artaki Bay, and Notium in the short distance between the Spartan base at Ephesus and the Athenian base at Notium. In each battle, the losing navy could quickly escape to the land, so there was no long pursuit, no scattering of fleets. The winning ships could rendezvous at a convenient place after the battle, decide on the most efficient manner of picking up survivors and corpses, and execute their plan in plenty of time to achieve the desired results. After none of these battles was the victor pressed to resume fighting elsewhere, for there was no other enemy fleet in the vicinity. The generals at Arginusae have been blamed for failing to formulate in advance a plan

[6]VIII, 208–209.

for rescuing survivors of the battle.[7] But that criticism seems unjust. They must have assumed that the same procedure used in previous battles would be appropriate again. If we believe that their original battle plan aimed at a double envelopment in which the enemy fleet would be trapped between the islands and a closed circle of Athenian ships, as seems likely, the usual procedure would have worked. There would have been no long pursuit and no dispersion of ships. All of the fighting would have been close to the islands, and rescue would have been simple.

The actual course of the battle made the usual plan impossible. The enemy fled far, and the Athenians were bound to press the pursuit. It might have been possible to improvise a rescue plan, but that would have required a confident, experienced leader with a personal authority recognized by trierarchs and fellow generals. Such a man might have produced a new plan on the spur of the moment and communicated with other ships by flag signal or semaphore of some kind, as Thrasybulus had done at the battle of Cyzicus.[8] But Thrasybulus was only a trierarch at Arginusae, and none of the generals had his experience or the authority, either personal or official, to take charge. With a collective leadership that lacked a proven and authoritative figure, the Athenians cannot be blamed for behaving in a conventional way in the confusion after the battle, although the situation called for an unconventional response.

When the generals convened at Arginusae after the ships had returned to the islands, there was probably still time to organize a program of rescue and recovery that might have had some degree of success, but the unusual strategic situation interfered. Unlike previous battles in which the enemy had fled safely to the land or had been swept from the sea or had been victorious—that is, where there was no further action that the Athenians needed to take or could undertake—the battle at Arginusae left an important task undone. No more than twelve miles northwest of the islands lay a Spartan fleet of fifty ships blockading Conon at Mytilene. As soon as the Spartan commander, Eteonicus, learned that the main Spartan force had been defeated, he was certain to try to escape. If he fled to Chios to join those ships that had escaped from the battle, the Spartan fleet at Chios would number over ninety triremes, a force the size of Lysander's victorious

[7]Cloché, *RH* CXXX (1919), 12–13.
[8]See above, 243.

fleet at Notium and one that could quickly grow large enough to undo the results of Arginusae. The Athenian generals had reason to be eager to sail to Mytilene as quickly as possible to cut off and destroy the fleet of Eteonicus. They had two important but competing goals, and the conflict soon emerged in their discussion. Diomedon urged that the entire fleet should turn to rescue and recovery. Erasinides had been with Conon at Mytilene and had slipped through the blockade to get word to Athens.[9] It is not surprising, therefore, that he was especially conscious of the Spartan fleet at Mytilene, and he proposed that the entire force should hurry to meet the enemy there. Thrasyllus proposed a compromise that won consent: part of the fleet would remain to pick up survivors and corpses, while the rest would go to Mytilene. Each of the eight generals would provide four ships from his squadron, and twenty-three ships that had formed most of the center, the ten from Samos and the thirteen carrying the Athenian taxiarchs and navarchs, would join them to form a rescue group of forty-seven triremes, almost four for each of the twelve wrecks still at sea. Theramenes and Thrasybulus, although only trierarchs, were among those placed in command of this mission, while all eight generals, including Diomedon, were to lead the remaining two-thirds of the fleet to Mytilene.[10]

Modern scholars have criticized the generals for sailing away and leaving the rescue mission in the hands of subordinates, and they have suggested motives such as a desire to seek glory in further battle rather than undertake a more prosaic task that offered none, an unwillingness to undertake what was becoming an increasingly dangerous task as the weather grew worse, and a wish to leave so dangerous a task, which also carried a high risk of failure and of the blame attached to it, to political opponents.[11] The charge of political motives is not well founded. Only four of the eight generals—Diomedon, Erasinides, Pericles, and Thrasyllus—can be designated as "democrats,"[12] but they

[9]See above, 337, n. 39.
[10]Xenophon tells the story of the conference most fully in the speech in defense of the generals by Euryptolemus (1.7.31) and in less detail in his own voice at 1.6.35. Diodorus (13.100.1) reports an abbreviated version that mentions no names and omits the compromise that was in fact adopted. He also erroneously places it before the return to the islands. It should be noticed that Theramenes and Thrasybulus are not designated as having any command superior to the other captains (Xen. 1.7.5–6).
[11]The harshest judge of the generals' decision is Grote, although he suggests no motive (VIII, 186). Beloch (AP, 87) emphasizes political motives. Busolt (GG III:2, 1608, n. 4) speaks of their desire to get to Mytilene.
[12]See Beloch, AP, 65; and Busolt, GG III:2, 1581.

should be considered democrats no more than Thrasybulus, their alleged opponent, who collaborated with Thrasyllus to save the democracy on Samos in 411.[13] Among the generals, moreover, was Aristocrates, Theramenes' close collaborator in bringing the government of the Five Thousand into being.[14] If collaboration with Alcibiades is judged the factional touchstone, we must remember that the original unfriendliness between Thrasyllus' troops and those of Alcibiades was quickly ended, and that Thrasyllus worked with both Alcibiades and Theramenes without any untoward incident as they cleared the straits of the enemy between 409 and 407. Nor should we forget that other trierarchs, as well as taxiarchs and navarchs, shared the risks and the fate of Theramenes and Thrasybulus. We do not know their names, but we have no reason to assume that they shared the political opinions or associations of their more famous colleagues. What little we know of the political situation at this time does not permit us to assume that factional considerations influenced the decision of the generals.

We cannot know what part an excessive desire for glory or the reluctance to undertake a difficult and dangerous task played, but the generals' decision can be perfectly understood without such motives. If the Athenians were going to sail against the enemy, it was natural to employ the ships and generals who had proved their excellence in the battle just finished. On the other hand, if we have understood that battle correctly, most of the ships left for the rescue mission had served in the center, where they had taken part in little or no combat. If it is argued that the difficult task of rescue and recovery required leadership of the highest order, the generals could answer that they had assigned it to men who had previously held the highest command, among them Theramenes and Thrasybulus, who had proven their excellence on more than one occasion.[15]

Having made their decisions and assignments, the generals left for Mytilene, leaving the rescue mission to the designated officers.[16] The

[13]See above, 173.

[14]See above, 184–198.

[15]The generals made precisely this point in their own defense in Athens (Xen. 1.7.5–6).

[16]There should be no doubt that the generals actually left Arginusae and tried to sail against the enemy at Mytilene. The generals said so plainly in their own defense before the assembly (Xen. 1.7.5), and Euryptolemus repeated the statement in his speech at a later meeting (1.7.31): ἔπλεον ἐπὶ τὰς πολεμίας. The imperfect is conative and implies that the fleet set out but was unable to meet the enemy. See Cloché, *RH*

captains gave orders to their crews to begin the operation but encountered resistance. The men, Diodorus tells us, "because of their suffering in the battle and because of the great size of the waves, argued against picking up the corpses."[17] It is tempting to believe that here his source has preserved the words spoken, for it would be natural for men, worn out after a lengthy battle and frightened by a storm growing stronger by the minute, to put the best face on their reluctance by speaking as if there were no survivors any longer but only corpses for which no lives should be risked. Perhaps this is what led Diodorus to write only of corpses throughout his account. However that may be, the captains were unable to get the men to move before the storm grew so violent as to prevent any attempt to go to sea. The early appearance and severity of the storm would be a key element in later discussions of who was responsible for the failure of rescue and recovery, and Grote has doubted both: "There exists here strong presumptive proof that the storm on this occasion was not such as would have deterred any Grecian seamen animated by an earnest and courageous sense of duty."[18]

The proof that Grote adduces is that when Eteonicus got word of the Athenian victory, he sailed safely from Mytilene to Chios with the help of a "fair wind."[19] If the weather was good between Mytilene and Chios, a route bringing his ships close by Arginusae, how could there have been a storm near Arginusae violent enough to prevent the rescue? There is, however, no contradiction; in fact, the evidence supports the idea that a storm arose near Arginusae at a time and with such a violence that it prevented attempts to recover men and corpses. Both ancient accounts describe a storm gradually increasing in severity. Xenophon reports heavy rain and a thunderstorm that prevented Callicratidas from launching an attack the night before the battle and a wind and "a great storm" that prevented the Athenians from rescuing their men and from attacking Eteonicus at Mytilene. According to Xenophon, Conon made his way from Mytilene to meet the forces at Arginusae

---

CXXX (1919), 21, n. 1. Since there were thousands of men who knew the truth, the generals could not have misrepresented it.

[17] 13.100.2. Diodorus places this before the return to Arginusae, which is impossible. We should not, however, reject his evidence on that account. He might well have confused, as he often does, the time that the events really took place. I accept the historicity of his narrative here but put it in what seems to be its proper context.

[18] VIII, 189.

[19] Xen. 1.6.37: ἦν δὲ τὸ πνεῦμα οὔριον.

only after "the enemy had sneaked away and the wind was quieter."[20] Diodorus tells us of strong winds on the day before the battle, saying that a storm arose that led the Athenian sailors to argue against the rescue mission; that it became so violent as to prevent both the rescue mission and the expedition to Mytilene, forcing the latter to return to Arginusae; and finally, that the wind was so strong that it carried bodies and wreckage as far to the south and southeast as Phocaea and Cyme.[21] From these clues we can readily reconstruct the events. The season was a stormy one in which tempests of considerable severity come and go. Some of these storms can be local, having very different effects within a few miles. Soon after the battle, a wind sprang up with increasing intensity from the north-northwest. Before it had become very strong, while the Athenians were still pursuing the enemy, a dispatch boat got through to Eteonicus at Mytilene. He quickly set out for Chios and, assisted by an increasingly fresh wind, got through the narrows off Cape Malea, probably while the Athenians were convening at the islands. By the time the Athenians set out for Mytilene, the storm had grown so strong as to force them back to Arginusae. At the same time, on the islands, the crews were dismayed by the lowering storm, whose waves were already frighteningly high for the not-very-seaworthy triremes. Before long the storm had grown so violent as to make further discussion moot and rescue and recovery impossible. Passing from north to south, the storm abated first at Mytilene, allowing Conon to set out for Arginusae, not far from which he met the main fleet, which had just been able to leave shore as the force of the storm lessened. Such an account is entirely in accord with the evidence. Moreover, there can be no doubt that the storm came in such force and at such a time as to be relevant to the failure to execute both missions after the battle and that the captains made a legitimate effort to carry out their orders but were frustrated, first by the reluctance of their men and then by the violence of the storm.

A calm, disinterested, well-informed analysis of the facts leads to the conclusion that neither the generals nor the captains deserve condemnation for failing to rescue the living and to recover the dead, but few of the men involved could have been calm or disinterested, and fewer still would have been sufficiently well informed. The generals were not present when the crews commanded by the captains balked.

---

[20]Xen. 1.6.28, 35, 37–38.
[21]13.97.4; 100.2–4.

It would be easy for some of them to believe that the fault lay with the captains for not imposing better discipline. Captains such as Theramenes and Thrasybulus, who had been generals and performed remarkable deeds and improvised plans in the midst of battles, might find fault with the eight generals' lengthy pursuit of the enemy and the failure to rescue the survivors before returning to Arginusae. They might well resent the assignment that had been given them; it had turned out to be impossible, as they might have thought could have been foreseen; yet they might well be blamed for failing to accomplish it. When the two divisions of the Athenian navy reunited after the storm, we can imagine that the generals expressed surprise, dismay, and even anger that the rescue mission had not been carried out. We should not forget that the officers and men on the ships would have been no less distressed by the loss of their comrades' lives than were other Athenians. All would have been angry, convinced of their own innocence, and ready to lay the blame on others. It is hard to believe that there were no scenes of angry recrimination between generals and captains after the reunion of forces.

However that may be, the entire Athenian fleet set out again for Mytilene after the weather had cleared. Before they had gone far, they met Conon coming from there to report that Eteonicus had escaped to the south with his fleet of fifty ships. This was bad news, but the generals were not yet ready to accept their failure to clear the seas of the enemy's navy. They continued to Mytilene for a brief stop and then followed the Spartans' trail to Chios. But the Spartans were safely in port and wisely refused to come out and fight. The Athenians were compelled to be satisfied with the victory they had already won and sailed back to their base on Samos.[22] The generals had reason to be proud of their work at Arginusae, but their joy should have been tempered not only by the failure of the mission of rescue and recovery but also of their inability to deliver a devastating blow like the one delivered at Cyzicus. They had not cleared the seas of the enemy but had left it with a powerful nucleus of a fleet that must soon be fought again.

From Samos the generals launched a series of pillaging raids on enemy territory,[23] but their first task was to compose their report to the Athenian people. The failure of rescue and recovery could not be

[22]Xen. 1.6.38.
[23]Diod. 13.100.6.

concealed, so the problem was not simple. Their first inclination was to tell the full story, including the assignment of the mission to Theramenes and Thrasybulus and the other captains and their failure to carry it out.[24] Pericles and Diomedon, however, persuaded them not to mention the rescue mission but simply to blame the storm for the failure to rescue the living and recover the dead.[25] It is not hard to understand why the generals accepted that advice. A report, pointing the finger of guilt at Theramenes and Thrasybulus, would spark a controversy in which the accused were sure to defend themselves by turning the accusation against the generals. Both men were formidable speakers, potent political leaders, and had many friends and supporters. They would be the most dangerous of enemies.[26] It was far better to present a united front, blaming no one but only the forces of nature. No doubt there would be questions and complaints, but if the generals and captains told the same story, and no other, all would be well.

The Athenians greeted the news of the victory with joy, voting a decree in praise of the generals, but they were also angry to learn of the men not rescued and the bodies not recovered.[27] Theramenes and Thrasybulus had hurried home after their return to Samos.[28] No doubt they realized that theirs was the most vulnerable position and were eager to defend themselves if necessary. There is no evidence that they were accused, for no one in Athens knew of their assignment or their failure to accomplish it, nor is there reason to believe that they blamed the generals or spoke out at all.[29] Still, discontent grew, and accusations were made against the generals. When word of the turmoil and the

---

[24]Xen. 1.7.17–18. This information comes from Euryptolemus' speech in defense of the generals, not in a consecutive narrative, where we might expect to find it. Andrewes (*Phoenix* XXVIII [1974], 112–122) has called attention to the remarkable gap in Xenophon's account between the end of the battle and the recall of the generals, which seems unmotivated as a result. The effect is to make the action of the Athenian people seem entirely mindless. The gap can be filled by using evidence provided by Diodorus and by information that comes elsewhere in Xenophon's narrative. Although Euryptolemus' account is tendentious and meant to support the cause of the generals against Theramenes, we have no reason to doubt his account of the discussion among the generals. The content of the general's letter is verified by Theramenes' reading of it to the assembly (1.7.4–5).
[25]Xen. 1.7.17–18.
[26]Diod. 13.101.3.
[27]Diod. 13.101.1.
[28]Diod. 13.101.2.
[29]Cloché shows clearly (*RH* CXXX [1919], 37–39) that the first breach in the agreement to maintain solidarity and to conceal the role of the captains came from the generals.

charges reached Samos, the generals were convinced that Theramenes and Thrasybulus must be their source. Believing that they had been betrayed, they wrote new letters to the assembly in which they revealed that the mission of picking up survivors and corpses had been delegated to the captains.[30]

Diodorus tells us that this action "was especially the cause of the evils that befell them," for it turned the powerful figures of Theramenes and Thrasybulus from associates to enemies and "bitter accusers."[31] The trouble might have come in any case. After all, there were thousands of Athenians who knew the basic facts and could reveal them. Many, no doubt, could not understand why the rescue mission had not been undertaken, sooner or later, and blamed the generals, the captains, or all of them. They would have muttered and complained, and formal charges might have been brought, however the generals behaved. Nevertheless, it is hard to disagree with Diodorus on the importance of the generals' alteration of their original strategy. The new letters angered Theramenes and his associates and compelled them to defend themselves. Since the simple defense that the storm alone had been responsible was no longer adequate, they were forced to place the responsibility on the generals. They did not deny the importance of the storm.[32] On the contrary, they probably claimed that by the time they received their orders, the severity of the storm made it impossible to carry them out. Diodorus tells us that their defense turned the anger of the assembly against the generals.[33] So they must have blamed them for the long delay before giving their orders to the captains. They could point to the long and fruitless pursuit of the enemy, the failure to make an effort at rescue before returning to Arginusae, and the time wasted in debate before making a decision. Such complaints, no doubt, would have the effect of protecting the captains by blaming the generals, but we need not believe they would be insincere. Theramenes and Thrasybulus were former generals of an eminence not reached by any of those at Arginusae. What could

---

[30]Diod. 13.101.2. Grote (VIII, 187) and Busolt (GG III:2, 1598) say that the generals wrote private letters home inculpating Theramenes and Thrasybulus, but the ancient writers do not say so, and Andrewes (*Phoenix* XXVIII [1974], 116) is right to emphasize the official character of their communications.

[31]13.101.3.

[32]Grote (VIII, 185, n. 2) argues that they did, but Cloché (*RH* CXXX [1919], 22–23) persuasively shows that they accepted the reality, ferocity, and relevance of the storm.

[33]13.101.4–5.

be more natural than for such men, forced by political considerations to a subordinate role after an unbroken series of magnificent naval successes, to be annoyed by the shortcomings of their superiors, irritated by any of their failures, and convinced that all would have gone well had capable men like themselves been in charge?

Their defense of themselves and indictment of the generals were effective. The assembly voted to depose the eight generals of Arginusae and ordered them to return and face the charges against them.[34] Aristogenes and Protomachus chose to flee into voluntary exile, "fearing the anger of the people."[35] Their flight does not prove their guilt but suggests only that they had weaker nerves than their colleagues or less confidence in the Athenian people, but it could not fail to prejudice the case against those who returned to face trial. The procedure to which the returning generals appear to have submitted was the *euthynai*, the review undergone by every Athenian magistrate at the end of his term of office. It consisted of an examination of his financial accounts, if any, as well as a scrutiny of his conduct in all other respects.[36]

The first general to submit his accounts was Erasinides, and they were found unsatisfactory. Archedemus, at that moment the leading democratic politician and the man in charge of the *diobelia*, brought Erasinides before a popular court and charged him with misappropriation of public funds and with misconduct as a general. The court found him guilty and imprisoned him.[37] Some scholars have seen political motives behind the singling out of this one general for condemnation before the others were heard, suggesting that the attack on Erasinides was a tactic of the democratic faction to place the blame on

[34]Xen. 1.7.1; Diod. 13.101.5. The procedure used was probably ἀποχειροτονία. Officials removed by this process had not been convicted of a crime but stood accused and must make a defense before the appropriate body. See J. T. Roberts, *Accountability in Athenian Government* (Madison, Wisc., 1982), 15. Since Conon, at Mytilene during the entire affair, was innocent, he was given command of the fleet, and Adeimantus and Philocles were sent to assist him.

[35]Xen. 1.7.1. The quotation is from Diod. 13.101.5.

[36]On the *euthynai*, see Hignett, *HAC* 203–205; D. M. MacDowell, *The Law in Classical Athens* (Ithaca, N.Y., and London, 1978), 170–172; and Roberts, *Accountability*, 17–18. The sources do not directly say that the procedure employed was the *euthynai*, but the evidence is consistent with it. As we shall see, Erasinides was charged first with mismanagement of funds and then of misconduct as general, the two parts of the *euthynai* investigation. That he was then placed before a popular court (Xen. 1.7.2) is a normal consequence. The other generals made their first statement to the *boule*, and both the *logistai* and the *euthynai*, the men who conducted the two parts of the review, were boards chosen from the *boule* (Arist. *Ath. Pol.* 48.4–5).

[37]Xen. 1.7.2.

him alone, thus sparing the others.[38] It is hard to see, however, why a member of the democratic faction should want to condemn Erasinides, one of the generals most plausibly identified as a democrat himself.[39] Why would he do this to save, among others, a man like Aristocrates, a member of the Four Hundred and a leading figure in the Five Thousand? The most likely motive for attacking Erasinides first was his unique vulnerability. Not long after the return of the generals, the story of the conference and Erasinides' recommendation that the whole fleet sail to Mytilene and abandon the survivors will have become known. Archedemus may have accused him because he believed that he was uniquely guilty or, at least, more guilty than the others. Perhaps he wanted to be sure that someone was punished; perhaps he hoped that if Erasinides was singled out he might give evidence against his colleagues. Whatever the value of these speculations, we need not invent political motives to understand Archedemus' actions.

Next, the five remaining generals came before the Council of 500. At this point they appear to have returned to their original defense, that the violence of the storm was to blame.[40] Assessing the situation in Athens after their return, they may have discovered that Theramenes and Thrasybulus had not been the source of the accusations against them and that it had been a mistake to antagonize them. If so, the reversion to the earlier strategy was of no avail. On the motion of a certain Timocrates, the council voted to imprison the generals and remand them to the assembly for trial.[41] At that assembly several men, chief among them Theramenes, accused the generals of being responsible for the loss of the survivors. Theramenes and the others argued that the generals should be made to explain their failure to rescue the shipwrecked men. As evidence that the generals alone should be held responsible, Theramenes read their first letter in which they blamed only the storm.[42]

In light of the generals' restraint, why did Theramenes and his associates take the offensive instead of renewing the common front and claiming that no one was to blame? There are the usual attempts to find motives in factional politics, but as we have seen, they are un-

[38]Cloché, *RH* CXXX (1919), 41.
[39]See above, n. 12.
[40]Xen. 1.7.3.
[41]Xen. 1.7.3.
[42]Xen. 1.7.4.

persuasive.[43] More basic and universal human motives are at hand. Theramenes, Thrasybulus, and their associates were angry and frightened. The second series of letters sent to Athens by the generals shifted the burden of responsibility from themselves to the captains and put them in great danger. In the minds of the captains, the implications of those letters were false and the letters themselves a breach of an agreement that was at least tacit and possibly overt. Anger, the determination to clear their own names and place guilt where it belonged, and a desire for revenge for betrayal all come to mind as motives for the captains' actions. Beyond that, there was reason to fear that merely blaming the storm would not work as a defense. As long as no details of the events after the battle were known, it might be possible to blame the storm alone. By now, however, the Athenians had been told of the assignment given to the captains, the conference, the positions taken in it, and the final decision. Having heard these things, and probably more, an Athenian court had convicted one general and the Council of 500 had indicted the others. Theramenes and his colleagues, on the other hand, had averted the wrath of the Athenians by turning it against the generals. They could hardly be expected to change their story at this point, for to do so would destroy their own credibility. The likely outcome might well be their own condemnation along with the generals'.

The charges made by Theramenes and his associates had a strong effect. Defenders of the generals were interrupted and shouted down, and the generals themselves were not given the full time prescribed by law to defend themselves.[44] The assaults of Theramenes forced the generals to alter their original line of defense. It was no longer possible to omit details and talk only of the storm. Since the captains had held them responsible, they had no choice but to point out that the assignment to rescue the survivors and pick up the bodies had been the captains'. The generals had sailed off to seek out the enemy, leaving the task of rescue and recovery to competent officers who had been generals, to Theramenes and Thrasybulus and men like them: "If it were necessary to blame any one in respect to the recovery, there was no one else to blame than those to whom the task had been assigned." Still, the generals refused to place the blame on the captains, although they had been accused by them, and insisted that "the violence of the

[43]Beloch, AP, 85–89; Cloché, RH CXXX (1919), 39–40.
[44]Diod. 13.101.6; Xen. 1.7.5.

storm prevented the recovery."[45] In support of their assertions, they offered the testimony of pilots and other sailors who had been part of the fleet. This admirably moderate defense was persuasive and moving. Sympathetic and neutral listeners could believe that the generals had always told the same fundamental story and that it was plausible. They had concealed the role of the captains out of a conviction that such details were irrelevant, since the storm alone made rescue impossible. Many Athenians were so convinced that they offered to stand bail for the generals, and the assembly as a whole was well on the way to being persuaded.[46] At that point fate, in the form of darkness, intervened. It was too late in the day for the counting of votes to be possible. The decision was made to postpone action until the next assembly. Meanwhile, the Council of 500 was to draft a proposal to determine the procedure of the trial.[47]

Evening's interruption of the assembly was not the last of fate's interventions. The Athenians' celebration of the festival Apaturia fell on a day soon after that assembly, some time in mid-October in 406.[48] The feast was celebrated by the *phratriai*, or brotherhoods, ancestral organizations of great antiquity and reverence. The celebration went on for three days and brought together families from all over Attica. Boys born since the previous year were registered, as were young men coming of age, and the marriages that had taken place in the interval were noted and celebrated. "Much of the festival, then, was occupied with these family occasions—birth, manhood, marriage."[49] Normally, these feasts were joyous, even riotous, occasions, but the Apaturia of 406 was not. As the families and the clans gathered, the gaps caused by the recent deaths at Arginusae became painfully apparent. These were not deaths caused by wounds at the hands of the enemy, many must have thought, but by the neglect and cowardice of Athenians. When the Athenian assembly met to resume its consideration of the fate of the generals, it found in its number many relatives of the dead wearing the garments and shaved heads of mourners who asked for

[45]Xen. 1.7.6.

[46]Xenophon (1.7.7) says: "By saying these things they were on the point of persuading people" τοιαῦτα λέγοντες ἔπειθον τὸν δῆμον. ἔπειθον is imperfect, indicating that the process of persuasion was still under way but had not been completed.

[47]Xen. 1.7.7. Xenophon's language makes it clear that the darkness was real and not merely a pretext. We should not, therefore, impute the postponement to machinations by the enemies of the generals. See Cloché, *RH* CXXX (1919), 46–47.

[48]Xen. 1.7.8. For the date, see Busolt, *GG* III:2, 1603.

[49]H. W. Parke, *Festivals of the Athenians* (Ithaca, N.Y., and London, 1977), 88–92.

vengeance against those who had failed to rescue the survivors of the battle and "begged the people to punish those who had allowed men who had gladly died in defense of their country to go unburied."[50]

Xenophon accuses Theramenes and his associates of hiring people to pretend that they were relatives of the dead, of a trick, that is, to stir up feeling against the generals.[51] Some scholars have accepted this charge.[52] But we have good reasons to reject it. That Diodorus accepts the authenticity of the mourners and says nothing of any part played by Theramenes in their activities does not count for much, for his account is brief and his attitude toward Theramenes friendly throughout. More telling is the fact that Lysias, whose speeches contain much denunciation of Theramenes, never accuses him of this deception or mentions him in connection with Arginusae.[53] Finally, suspicions of such maneuvers could not have been widespread in the year 406/5, for Theramenes was not one of those prosecuted when Athenian opinion turned against the accusers of the generals, and he was sufficiently popular to be elected general in the spring of 405.[54] It would have been foolish and dangerous to organize such a fraud. The real mourners, and, in any case, there would have been some, would easily recognize the false ones. Besides it would have been reckless for Theramenes to arouse public opinion in so general a way at a time when no one could be sure which way sentiment would go or against whom the angry mob might turn.[55] Long ago Grote presented arguments that should have settled the matter: "The case was one in which no artifice was needed. The universal and self-acting stimulus of intense human sympathy stand here so prominently marked, that it is not simply superfluous but even misleading, to look behind for the gold and machinations of a political instigator."[56]

The intervention of the Apaturia clearly caused a great change in the public mood. Grief and anger replaced the sympathy and understanding with which many Athenians had received the generals' defense at the first assembly. A member of the Council of 500

[50]Diod. 13.101.6.
[51]1.7.8.
[52]E.g., Busolt, GG III: 2, 1603. Cloché (RH CXXX [1919], 48–49) does not go so far as to believe in fraud and bribery but suggests that Theramenes merely urged the truly bereaved to come to the assembly and remonstrate.
[53]Especially 12.62–78, but see also 12.36.
[54]Xen. 1.7.35; Lys. 13.10.
[55]Andrewes, Phoenix XXVIII (1974), 118.
[56]VIII, 193–194.

Callixeinus, took advantage of the new atmosphere to propose a procedure for dealing with the generals that was most prejudicial to them. It assumed that the cases for both accusers and defense had been fully made at the first assembly, so there would be no further discussion at the second. That would guarantee that the vote on guilt or innocence would take place in the current hostile atmosphere, so that the generals and their defenders would have no chance to change minds with argument. The vote would be taken by tribe and would ask whether or not the generals were guilty "for not rescuing the men who had won the victory in the naval battle," a way of putting the question most damaging to the defendants. If they were judged guilty, they were to be put to death and their property confiscated, a tenth of it to be given to Athena. These penalties were almost as severe as those imposed on Phrynichus, Antiphon, and Archeptolemus for treason, but those men had been given individual trials with full time to defend themselves before regular courts, enjoying due process. Callixeinus' proposal required that the generals be tried in common and that the inadequate time they had been given to speak in the first assembly suffice for their entire defense. In spite of the prejudicial character of his proposals, the council, nonetheless, voted for them, and their terms governed the procedure at the second assembly.[57]

The discussion in the second assembly obviously began in the emotional atmosphere created by the Apaturia and was reflected in the Council of 500's choice of procedure. Xenophon reports that a man claimed he had been at Arginusae and had been saved by clinging to a tub and that he had heard drowning men near by ask him to tell the people that "the generals had not rescued the men who had shown themselves the best in the service of their country."[58] In the heated atmosphere created by such talk, it took courage to resist the tide of passion, but Euryptolemus the son of Peisianax rose to do so. Euryptolemus was a cousin of Alcibiades and had been one of his closest associates. He had been one of his representatives in his dealings with Pharnabazus, and it had been the sight of Euryptolemus that had given Alcibiades the courage to land at the Piraeus after his return from the

[57]Xen. 1.7.9–10. Xenophon alleges that Theramenes bribed Callixeinus to make his proposal in the Council of 500, but this accusation, like that concerning the mourners, is implausible and unnecessary. Callixeinus' proposal would have been of no value if more than half of the 500 members of the council had not approved it. If so many men liked the idea, why was there any need to bribe someone to put it forth?
[58]1.7.11.

Hellespont in 407.[59] His actions in defense of the generals is an important refutation of the claim that factional politics played a significant part in the trial of the generals, for a common version of that claim is that the attack by Theramenes and Thrasybulus against the generals was really an attack of the faction of Alcibiades against the democratic forces hostile to him.[60] It is true that one of the accused generals, Pericles, was his relative and another, Diomedon, was his friend, but that someone so close to Alcibiades as Euryptolemus was the generals' chief defender should dispose of the theory that the attack against them was plot by the faction of Alcibiades.

Euryptolemus and others accused Callixeinus of making an illegal proposal, thereby invoking the *graphe paranomon*. Under its terms, his proposal could not be acted upon until he had been tried and acquitted on the charge.[61] Some applauded this action, but many more cried out against it on the grounds that it would be terrible to prevent the people from doing what they wished. A certain Lysiscus then rose to move that those who had proposed the *graphe* should themselves be judged by the same vote as the generals unless they withdrew their charge. That suggestion was greeted with so much enthusiasm that the charge was withdrawn. Next, some of the prytanies, the presiding officials at the assembly, refused to put the original question to the vote on the grounds that it was illegal. Callixeinus thereupon suggested that the same charge be brought against them, and he was supported by such an uproar that the officials were terrified and agreed to put the question. It happened that the philosopher Socrates was one of the prytanies on that day, and he alone had the courage to persist in his refusal but to no avail. His refusal was ignored, and the process went forward.[62]

In the face of the assembly's passion and in spite of the threats and dangers, Euryptolemus rose again to try another line in defense of the generals, proposing a procedure different from the one put forward by the council. He suggested that the accused be tried in accordance with the decree of Cannonus, which provided that defendants accused of "wronging the People" must appear before the assembly in chains; if convicted, they were killed by being thrown into a pit, and their

[59]Xen. 1.3.12–13; 4.19.
[60]Beloch, *AP*, 86; B. W. Henderson, *The Great War between Athens and Sparta* (London, 1927), 472; Andrewes, *Phoenix* XXVIII (1974), 116; W. J. McCoy, *AJP* XCVIII (1977), 287–289; Roberts, *Accountability*, 66.
[61]MacDowell, *The Law in Classical Athens*, 188.
[62]Xen. 1.7.11–16.

property was confiscated, with a tenth of it going to Athens. If the assembly did not like that proposal, he offered them still another choice. They could use the procedure employed against those accused of robbing temples or of treason: they were tried before a popular court, and if convicted, they were killed, their bodies buried outside Attica, and their property confiscated with a tenth going to Athena. Any of these severe procedures he urged the assembly to choose, as long as the defendants were tried separately and each given a full day to make his defense.[63] Euryptolemus clearly believed that the passion of the Athenian assembly was momentary, having been fanned by the emotional experience of the Apaturia. Given time to recover and to listen to reasoned argument, they would not condemn the generals. His eloquent defense of the generals' actions; his refusal to blame the captains, even as he pointed out the responsibility they had borne; his warnings against illegal procedures; and his reminder that the accused had just won a great victory for Athens almost swayed the angry and excited Athenians. His motion to try the generals under the provisions of the decree of Cannonus at first won approval as indicated by the show of hands. A certain Menecles, however, raised some technical objection, whose nature we are not told. On a second vote the motion of the council prevailed. The assembly condemned all eight generals, including the two who had fled, Erasinides, and the five others, and the six in Athens were put to death.[64]

Diodorus attributes the decision to the relatives of the dead and their many friends and to Theramenes and his associates.[65] Others were required to achieve the majority against the generals, but we may well believe that these two groups played the greatest part in the decision, one because of its numbers and the other because of its role in the debate and its effective organization. The behavior of the friends and relatives of the dead need no explanation, but the actions of Theramenes, Thrasybulus, and their associates deserves further examination. If we reject factional politics as an important motive, as the evidence demands, we must ask why they were so insistent on the condemnation of the generals. The evidence permits no more than conjecture, but the analysis we have made suggests that the events after the battle, not planned or arranged by any individual or group,

[63]Xen. 1.7.16–23.
[64]Xen. 1.7.24–34.
[65]13.101.6–7.

created a situation in which passion required that someone be punished; the only question was who.

Under those circumstances, Theramenes could well believe that he and his fellow captains had been placed in jeopardy by the second series of letters from the generals. He must have seen himself and his associates as unjustly accused and their action in making counteraccusations as self-defense.[66] Once anger and recrimination reached a certain pitch, compromise and mutual restraint were no longer possible, and fear and anger took control. We must not fail to notice that in the speech of Euryptolemus, although it finally took a conciliatory tone and blamed the failure on the storm alone, the following passage appeared: "It is just, therefore, that those who were assigned to go against the enemy give an account of their failure to carry out their assignment against the enemy, while those who were assigned to the rescue mission should be tried for not carrying out what the generals had ordered, because they did not pick up the survivors."[67] The captains could not be sure that if the generals were acquitted, the anger of the citizenry would not turn against them. A long string of trials, moreover, in which each of the generals fought to defend his own innocence, was bound to raise, over and over again, the role of the captains, and as the generals tried to save their own lives they might well place the blame on the captains. Feelings of unassuaged grief and anger would be kept alive for weeks, and the result was both unpredictable and frightening. Finally, as we have seen, Theramenes, Thrasybulus, and their associates probably honestly found fault with the generals' performance after the battle, held them at least partially responsible for the failure to rescue the living and recover the dead, and resented the delegation to them of so unpleasant, difficult, and dangerous a task so late in the day. Such, perhaps, were the thoughts and feelings that made Theramenes and his colleagues press for the trial of the generals en masse and their condemnation, which must certainly follow.

Athens had no written constitution, and it is not perfectly clear whether the trial and condemnation of the generals were illegal.[68] The Athenians, however, soon regretted their action. Callixeinus and four

---

[66] That is precisely the line he took in defending himself against Critias' charges under the reign of the Thirty Tyrants after the war (Xen. 2.3.35).

[67] Xen. 1.7.31.

[68] MacDowell, *The Law in Classical Athens*, 189.

others were convicted of deceiving the people.[69] From ancient times critics have denounced the treatment of the generals. Diodorus drew a moral lesson from it, saying that the outcome was like an expression of divine anger and that the imposition of the despotism of the Thirty Tyrants after the war was the punishment for their error.[70] Grote, the great champion of Athenian democracy, defended the Athenians by declaring the generals guilty as charged, but even he was forced to admit the impropriety of the trial, referring to it as "the guilty proceedings" to which the passionate grief the Athenians felt for their drowned men drove them.[71] Excesses and illegalities are all too common in the history of peoples and governments roused to anger by sorrow, tension, and passion. In despotisms they rouse little attention and are not long remembered, for arbitrary and excessive behavior is their normal pattern of life. In constitutional, moderate, lawful states, however, they are seized upon as outrages and never forgotten, precisely because they stand out so sharply as contrary to what is usual. So Englishmen remember with shame Titus Oates and the Popish plot, the bloody assizes of Judge Jeffries, the execution of Admiral Byng, "pour encourager les autres," as Voltaire put it; Frenchmen are embarrassed by the judicial butchery carried out by Robespierre and the revolutionary tribunals; Americans painfully recall the witch trials in Salem, Massachusetts, and the unjustified internment of Japanese-Americans in the Second World War. So, too, did the Athenians regret the trial and execution of the Arginusae generals, so shocking because it was so sharp a departure from the respect for law, fairness, and due process that normally characterized the Athenian democracy.

For this lapse the Athenians paid a high price. The eight generals killed or exiled as a result of the trial were not available for service in 405/4, which turned out to be the last year of the war. The ill will and suspicion raised by the affair also deprived the Athenians of Theramenes' experienced services, for although he was elected general for that year, he was rejected at the regular scrutiny of the qualifications of the newly elected officials *(dokimasia)*.[72] Thrasybulus, likewise, suffered from the same animus and was not even elected. The skill and

---

[69]Xen. 1.7.35; Diod. 13.103.1–2. The date of the Athenians' change of heart is unclear, but Andrewes (*Phoenix* XXVIII [1974], 121) is probably right in saying that "an immediate revulsion seems intrinsically the most likely."

[70]13.103.1–2.

[71]VIII, 209.

[72]Lys. 13.10.

experience of all of these men would be badly missed. The treatment of the Athenian generals, moreover, must have had a bad effect on the new board elected for 405/4. No Athenian general had ever before been executed. Apart from these military considerations, the trial and executions divided the Athenian people when they most needed unity and mutual confidence. These divisions made it harder to find steady, reasoned leadership in very perilous times and easier for politicians to counterpose passion to reason.

15. The Fall of Athens

The Athenian victory at Arginusae did not annihilate the Spartan fleet, but the more than ninety ships that survived it and gathered at Chios were in a bad way. All of the money supplied by Cyrus was gone, and none had arrived from home. The soldiers and sailors were reduced to working as hired laborers on the island as long as summer provided them with work and food. When the cold weather came, however, they found themselves without food, clothing, or shoes. Some of them became so desperate that they planned a mutiny and an attack on the main city of Chios. The Spartan commander Eteonicus discovered the plot and was able to disarm it before it got very far. Faced by the danger of the mutiny, the Chians agreed to contribute their own money to support the troops. By paying each man a month's wages Eteonicus was able to return the men to loyalty and order, but without Persian money, Sparta's future in the Aegean was grim.[1]

The defeat at Arginusae, combined with the desperate condition of their forces at Chios, persuaded the Spartans once again to offer peace to Athens.[2] As usual, we are not informed of the discussion in Sparta or how groups or individuals divided on the question. The events, however, suggest that the Spartans who led the way had supported Callicratidas out of dislike for Persia's role in the war and Sparta's part as a junior partner in the restoration of the lost provinces of the Persian Empire and the consequent subjugation of Greeks and out of distrust

[1]Xen. 1.2.1–5.
[2]Arist. *Ath. Pol.* 34.1.

of Lysander's growing power. They could argue that collaboration with Persia, even when funds were provided according to the agreement, had led to one great defeat after another, to the useless loss of Spartan and Peloponnesian lives, and to the decline of Spartan prestige. The one important Spartan victory at Notium had resulted from a peculiar Athenian error, and the enemy was not likely to leave its fleet under the command of a *kybernetes* again. At Arginusae, the Athenians had won even when using inexperienced crews that included liberated slaves. The prospects for future Spartan victories at sea must have seemed bleak. These arguments would have carried weight with many, perhaps most, Spartans, but those worried about Lysander had even stronger reasons to want peace. Requests for the return of the hero of Notium may have been already making their way to Sparta; if the war continued, the Spartans would need Persian money from Cyrus, and he would probably insist on his friend as commander. In the depression that must have followed the defeat at Arginusae, Spartans holding such views were able to gain support for another attempt at peace.

The Spartans offered to withdraw from their fortress at Decelea and otherwise to make peace on the basis of the status quo.[3] These terms were similar to those offered after the battle of Cyzicus, but under the circumstances, they were more generous. In 410 the Athenians still held Pylos, which they were to give up in exchange for Decelea, but in 406 they had no such fortress to trade. After the battle of Cyzicus the Spartans still held Byzantium and Chalcedon and had control of the Bosporus, the entrance to the Black Sea, and a grip on the Athenian lifeline. By 406 Athens had recovered control of the straits. On the

---

[3] Ibid. There is no reason to question the historicity of this report, as some have done. (See the list of doubters in Rhodes, *Commentary*, 424.) Doubts arise from the similarity between the terms offered after the battle of Cyzicus and those reported by Aristotle after the battle of Arginusae and from the fact that Cleophon is said to have played the chief role in rejecting each peace. Aristotle, however, is unmistakably clear in connecting this proposal for peace with the battle of Arginusae. Moreover, the terms after the battle of Cyzicus as reported by Diodorus (13.52.3) are not identical with those described by Aristotle after the battle of Arginusae. The former speak of mutual withdrawal of garrisons, whereas the latter speak only of a Spartan evacuation of Decelea, as the real circumstances require. The former speak of a mutual ransoming of prisoners, whereas the latter do not, as is appropriate since an arrangement for such exchanges had been agreed upon in 408/7 (Androtion, *FGrH* III 324, Fr. 44). Moreover, there is no reason why Cleophon should not have argued against peace proposals on every occasion they were made between 410 and 405, just as Cato the Censor repeatedly demanded the destruction of Carthage and Winston Churchill continually demanded rearmament and resistance to Hitler during the decade before the Second World War.

other hand, Athens had been forced to desperate measures to win at Arginusae and was still badly short of money. A renewal of Persian support for Sparta and the extension of the fighting it would entail would exhaust the Athenian treasury and perhaps eventually even Athenian manpower. In these circumstances, the Spartans' offer ought to have been most appealing; yet the Athenians rejected it. To be sure, the Spartans still held Abydos in the Hellespont, the important island of Chios, and significant cities such as Ephesus, Phocaea, and Cyme. The loss of these places would not be pleasant, but none was vital to the economic, financial, or military security of Athens. The loss of all would have been well worth a true and lasting peace and even a cessation of hostilities that lasted long enough to give Athens a chance to put her empire back in order, fill her treasury, and restore her agricultural activity.

In the face of such tempting advantages, how can the Athenian rejection be explained? It is both easy and traditional to blame the foolish Athenian masses and the reckless demagogues who misled them. That is the line Aristotle takes, saying: "Some were eager to make peace, but the mob did not listen to them, for they were deceived by Cleophon. He prevented the peace from coming into being; entering the assembly drunk and dressed in his military breastplate, he said that he would not permit a peace agreement unless the Spartans surrendered all the cities."[4] Even if we accept what seems very much like a hostile version of the facts, the question remains as to why the majority of the assembly voted with the allegedly drunken and bellicose demagogue. They were fully aware of the state of their treasury and the drain on their manpower. They, most of all, must have been tempted by an end to the fighting, the withdrawal of the Spartans, and a return to their farms; yet they voted against peace. However foolish they may have been, they must have had some reasons. Once again, we may find a clue in their suspicion of the good faith of the enemy. We would be mistaken to neglect the great impact made on the Athenians by the failure of the Peace of Nicias. No sooner had the peace been sworn than the Spartans failed to carry out its main provision, the return of Amphipolis. The Athenians had extended themselves and made a treaty of alliance with the erstwhile enemy only to find that Amphipolis was still unredeemed and that the Spartans allowed the Boeotians to demolish the Athenian fort of Panactum

[4]Arist. *Ath. Pol.* 34.1.

contrary to the original treaty.[5] Those events had left the Athenians with a sense that the Spartans could not be trusted, a feeling that had never disappeared.

After the battle of Arginusae, they may have had the fear that the Spartans, defeated and impoverished, might use a truce to restore their relations with Persia, build a new fleet, and attack before the Athenians were ready. The alternative was to take advantage of the moment, seek out what remained of the Spartan fleet and destroy it, and hope that Cyrus would be put out of play, as Tissaphernes and Pharnabazus had been before him. The time must come, they might have thought, when the Great King would tire of an investment that was repeatedly lost. If such was the thinking of the Athenians, we must judge them mistaken not merely because we know of the unhappy outcome of their policy but because they should have seen its folly. The Athenians could not be sure of forcing a battle at a time and place to their liking. Cyrus was still satrap, and there was no sign of any change of policy on his part. He had relented and granted support even to the unfriendly Callicratidas; how much more readily would he give it to a friendly Spartan commander such as Lysander? With Persian money in hand, the Spartans could revert to the waiting game, allow Athenian resources to run down even further, win over rowers by means of higher pay, and fight at a time and place of their choosing. One more Athenian defeat would certainly be the end; yet the Athenians could not refuse to fight for long. These considerations, it appears, made a peace treaty on the terms offered in 406 well worth the gamble, but the Athenian assembly thought otherwise, and the war went on.

Not long after the Athenian rejection of peace, the Spartans received a delegation from their allies in the Aegean asking that Lysander be restored to command of the fleet.[6] During the winter of 406/5, the suffering of the Spartan forces had required the Chians to make a significant contribution of money to preserve their safety. The victorious Athenian fleet at Samos was free to raid and plunder the islands

---

[5] See 5.21–46; and Kagan, *Peace of Nicias*, 19–59.

[6] Xen. 2.1.6; Diod. 13.100.7; Plut. *Lys.* 7.1. Since neither of the narrative historians mentions the Spartan offer of peace and Aristotle does not place it in relation to any event except the battle of Arginusae, we cannot establish the sequence of events with certainty. The sequence accepted here—the peace offer about the same time as the conference of Sparta's allies at Ephesus, Athenian rejection of the peace, arrival of the delegation at Sparta, and the decision to send Lysander to the Aegean again—is obvious and generally accepted. See, e.g., Busolt, *GG* III:2, 1610–1612; J.-F. Bommelaer, *Lysandre de Sparte* (Paris, 1981), 96–98.

and the mainland cities friendly to Sparta without opposition.[7] The allies, therefore, had met at Ephesus to take concerted action. Their ambassadors reported the situation and asked the Spartans to restore Lysander to the navarchy, and they were joined in their mission by representatives of Cyrus who made the same request.[8] Since the war must continue and the support of the allies and the Persians was necessary, the Spartans could not refuse. Athens' rejection of the peace probably discredited the opponents of Lysander and his policy in any case, so most Spartans would have supported his restoration. A constitutional difficulty, however, stood in the way. The law forbade anyone to hold the powerful navarchy twice, but the Spartans got around it easily enough by appointing Aracus navarch and Lysander as his *epistoleus*. Normally, the *epistoleus* was the navarch's secretary, as the word implies, and vice-admiral, taking command in case of the death of the admiral. On this occasion, the appointments were a legal fiction and reality the reverse of appearances. There was no doubt that Lysander was in command of the fleet.[9]

Lysander set out toward the end of the winter of 406/5 with a force of thirty-five ships collected from the Peloponnesus. He landed not at Miletus but at his old headquarters on Ephesus, ordered Eteonicus to bring his fleet there from Chios, and sent word to collect any other allied ships that might be available. At the same time, he ordered new ships to be built at Antandrus and set to work repairing and improving his fleet at Ephesus.[10] The shift of bases had the same significance as in his previous command: Ephesus was better located in respect to access to the Hellespont, it provided easier communication with Cyrus, and it was friendly both to Sparta and Lysander.[11] At this moment, however, it had still a further meaning, marking the first of a series of departures from the policy of Callicratidas. Lysander's first need was money, and he wasted little time before going to Sardis to see Cyrus. The prince was compelled to report that all of the money provided by the Great King had been spent. In fact, Cyrus had spent

---

[7]Diod. 13.100.

[8]Xen. 2.1.6–7; Diod. 13.100.7–8; Plut. *Lys.* 7.1.

[9]Xen. 2.1.7; Diod. 13.100.8; Plut. *Lys.* 7.2. Xenophon says "nevertheless they gave the ships over to Lysander"; Plutarch says "in reality he was in command of everything"; Diodorus says the Spartans "ordered Aracus to obey Lysander in everything." Diodorus makes a mistake in saying that Lysander went along as a private citizen.

[10]Xen. 2.1.10; Diod. 13.104.3.

[11]See above, 301–302.

a good deal of his own, and he showed Lysander the accounts of his payments to the Spartan admirals to prove it.[12] Plutarch says that he made him gifts and promises to win his favor, saying that if his father refused support, he would supply it from his own resources and would even cut up his gold and silver throne if necessary.[13]

We need not doubt Cyrus' sincerity, in spite of his inflated rhetoric, for he immediately gave Lysander a large sum of money with which the Spartan commander was able to pay the arrears in his men's salary.[14] Cyrus' commitment and loyalty were real. He was delighted to see Lysander not only because of their friendship and previous association but also because of his need of reliable support from a Greek army. He had plans for the future that would probably need such an armed force, and his current entanglement in Persian court politics made him eager to have a reliable and competent friend. During the winter of 406/7, Cyrus had put to death two of his cousins, sons of Darius' sister and her husband, Hieramenes, because they had refused to thrust their hands into their sleeves in the presence of Cyrus, a gesture of respect normally reserved for the Great King. The root of the quarrel was probably political; no doubt the cousins had challenged the pretensions of the very young satrap, and his demand may have been an attempt to assert his authority. In any case, news of the executions and the story of their cause reached the parents of the victims at the Persian court. Naturally, they complained, and Darius could not avoid investigating. Pleading illness, he sent word to Sardis recalling Cyrus to his side.[15] Before leaving, Cyrus took steps to protect himself. There was no Persian at Sardis he could trust; indeed, supporters of his rivals might be anywhere. He therefore called Lysander back to Sardis and made him his surrogate satrap, turning over to him all the money he had on hand and granting him the collection of the tribute from his provinces. That guaranteed him against Persian machinations, but Cyrus knew of Lysander's goals and ambitions, which might threaten the security of his possessions in a different way during his absence with his father in Media. An unsuccessful attack on the Athenians might destroy the force on which he relied and might bring the Athenians into his province. He therefore reminded Lysander that the abundance of Persian money and resources put time on his side

---

[12]Xen. 2.1.11.
[13]*Lys.* 9.1.
[14]Xen. 2.1.12; Diod. 13.104.3.
[15]Xen. 2.1.8–9.

and urged him not to offer battle against the Athenians until he outnumbered them by many ships. This amounted to a request not to
fight until Cyrus returned, for the Spartans could not reach numerical
superiority for many months. With a warm embrace and reminders
of his personal friendship, Cyrus left for Media, having entrusted his
power to his Spartan friend.[16]

Lysander, with all of the money he needed, did not tarry long at
Ephesus but sailed southward to Miletus. To get there he probably
sailed through the narrow waters between Samos and the mainland,
but we hear nothing of any efforts on his part to avoid detection or of
any Athenian attempt to cut him off. The Spartan fleet will have
numbered something over 125 ships, perhaps as many as 150.[17] However, the fleet probably was not at the peak of its form, for Lysander
had not yet had time to train it for long. The Athenian fleet at Samos
reached 180 later in the summer.[18] It probably was not much smaller
in the previous spring. The Athenian strategy should have been to
search out the enemy and force a battle as soon as possible, before
money ran low, men began to desert, and Lysander had a chance to
improve and increase his navy and to threaten the Hellespont. The
Athenians may have been away on one of their plundering raids, but
that would not be an adequate excuse for failing to keep a close watch
on Lysander's fleet at Ephesus and for letting it safely out into the
open sea. Divided command, a number of inexperienced admirals, and
timidity and suspicion caused by the trial of the generals may all have
played a part in this serious failure.

Miletus had been a vigorous Spartan ally since its rebellion from
Athens in 413. The Spartan cause did not require action there, but
Lysander's did. Miletus had been Callicratidas' base, and the young
navarch had succeeded in undermining Lysander's political support
there. His eloquence and political skill had persuaded Lysander's
friends to contribute money to his treasury and to become reconciled

---

[16]Xen. 2.1.13–14; Diod. 13.104.4; Plut. *Lys.* 9.2. Xenophon does not specifically say
that Cyrus turned his command of the satrapy over to Lysander, but his statement
that he turned its revenues over to him clearly supports the more specific statements
of the other writers. Plutarch says that Cyrus promised Lysander to bring back ships
from Phoenicia and Cilicia, but it is not likely that Lysander would have enjoyed
sharing the command and the credit for any victory with a Persian fleet, and I believe
that this unique reference to it is mistaken.

[17]That would include the ninety or so ships under Eteonicus from Chios, the thirty-
five ships brought from the Peloponnesus, and twenty or more from elsewhere.

[18]Xen. 2.1.20.

with the democratic government they had been hoping to overthrow with Lysander's help.[19] That was not to Lysander's liking; what he wanted was not a unified city, loyal to Sparta, but one capable of looking to its own interests. Lysander needed cities ruled by small groups, threatened by the opposition of the mass of citizens, and dependent upon him for rewards and security. He therefore incited a revolution to achieve his purposes. It is in connection with this affair that Plutarch records two well-known sayings attributed to Lysander. To those who criticized the use of deceit by a Spartan, he is reported to have said: "Where the lion's skin will not reach, it must be patched with the fox's." Another ancient authority claims that he boasted of cheating "boys with knuckle-bones and men with oaths."[20] No man beginning where Lysander had started could reach the goal he set for himself by adhering to the ordinary rules of aristocratic Spartan behavior. He publicly praised the reconciliation of factions in Miletus, but in private he chastised his associates and urged them on to rebellion. During the festival of Dionysus, when people were gathered in a single place and off guard, Lysander's friends attacked their political opponents. They killed 40 in their homes and 300 of Miletus' richest men in the marketplace. A thousand of "the most respectable citizens" who were friendly to the democratic cause fled in fear for their lives. The murderous and rebellious faction destroyed the Milesian democracy and placed itself in control of the oligarchy that had replaced it.[21] Lysander had shown his power and the value of his support for men willing to form factions in his service.

The fugitive Milesians found asylum with the Persian satrap Pharnabazus, who received them kindly, gave them some money, and settled them at Blauda, a fortress in Lydia.[22] This was obviously a

[19]Xen. 1.6.12; Plut. *Lys.* 8.1.

[20]*Lys.* 7.4; 8.4.

[21]Diod. 13.104.5–6; Plut. *Lys.* 8; Polyaenus 1.45.1. Xenophon makes no mention of the affair. Plutarch mentions the events at Miletus before Lysander's second visit to Sardis, but his structure here is typically literary and moralistic rather than historical. Diodorus' sequence is preferable. For useful discussions of the chronological problem, see F. Bilabel, *Philologus*, suppl. (1920), 95; and P. A. Rahe, "Lysander and the Spartan Settlement, 407–403 B.C." (Ph.D. diss., Yale University, 1977), 76, n. 1.

[22]Diod. 13.104.6. For the location of Blauda, see Strabo 12.587; and Busolt, *GG* III:2, 1614, n. 2. Since Diodorus frequently confuses Tissaphernes with Pharnabazus in Book 13, many scholars credit the former with this action too. This time, however, it really was Pharnabazus who received the refugees, for Tissaphernes accompanied Cyrus on his trip to see his father (Xen. *Anab.* 1.1.1–2) and must have been in Media at the time. See Rahe, "Lysander," 78, n. 5.

step taken to undermine the influence of Lysander by supporting his opponents. Later, Tissaphernes would restore these anti-Lysandrian Milesians to their city, which then became a center of hostility to Cyrus and Lysander.[23] At the same time that Pharnabazus was preparing to check the influence of Lysander, Tissaphernes had gone with Cyrus to Media under the guise of friendship.[24] In fact, he was keeping close watch on the prince, as his father's illness made a succession crisis seem imminent. The two Persian magnates were alert to the danger presented by the alliance of the ambitious Persian prince and his Spartan associate.

From Miletus, Lysander continued on his way south to Caria. There he attacked Iasus, which had returned to the Athenian side after its conquest by the Spartans in 412.[25] He stormed the walls, killed the men, sold the women and children as slaves, and leveled the city. From there he sailed to Cedreiae on the Ceramic Gulf, another Athenian ally, which he also took by storm, enslaving its population.[26] These acts of terror against Greek cities were in sharp contrast to the Panhellenic policies of Callicratidas, no doubt deliberately so. All of Lysander's actions since his return demonstrated the advantages of collaboration with him and the danger of opposition. The significant distinction was not between Greek and barbarian but between friend and foe. From Caria, Lysander sailed west across the Aegean. He gained control of some islands along the way and overran Aegina and Salamis before landing in Attica itself, where Agis came from Decelea to meet him.[27] The ancient writers do not explain the purpose of this voyage, and some modern scholars have denied that it happened.[28] No doubt, Lysander was glad of a chance to display his power and daring, to terrify the Athenians, and to plan a coordinated strategy with his political ally Agis.[29] But he may have had a more pressing strategic motive as well. Lysander's ultimate target was the Hellespont. Al-

[23]Xen. Anab. 1.1.6; 9.9; 7.18.2; Polyaenus 7.18.2.
[24]Xen. Anab. 1.1.2.
[25]Diod. 13.104.7. Conquest by Spartans: Thuc. 8.28.3. I accept the emendation Iasos for the Thassos or Thasos of the MSS.
[26]Xen. 2.1.15.
[27]Rhodes: Xen. 2.1.16; Attica: Diod. 13.104.8; the islands and Attica: Plut. Lys. 9.2.3.
[28]Xenophon omits everything west of Rhodes, and Diodorus gives it only a sentence. Plutarch alone gives it any substance. Beloch (GG² II:2, 1423–1424) and Busolt (GG III:2, 1617) reject the voyage across the Aegean.
[29]These are among the motives suggested by Rahe, "Lysander," 80–82.

though he had slipped by the Athenian base on Samos on his way to Miletus, he could not be certain of passing it safely again on his way north. The unexpected burst into the Aegean, to the very shore of Attica, would surely lure the Athenians from Samos and the Asian coast and allow him to get safely to the straits. Plutarch says that "when he learned that the Athenians were pursuing him, he fled to Asia by a different route through the islands."[30] It is likely that such an outcome was what he intended when he set out. He seems to have made his way safely to Rhodes and from there sailed up the Ionian coast to the Hellespont, "to prevent the merchant-ships from sailing out and against the cities that had rebelled against the Spartans."[31] It would have been difficult to get by Samos again had the Athenians not been drawn across the Aegean by Lysander's circuitous maneuver.

In the Hellespont he landed at Abydos, the only remaining Spartan base. His arrival was apparently met enthusiastically by many people in the region, for he was able to raise an army from Abydos and other cities nearby. Under the Spartan commander Thorax, they marched overland to Lampsacus while Lysander took his fleet to attack it from the sea. The combined assault took the city by storm; the soldiers were permitted to plunder the wealthy town, but its free citizens were allowed to leave without hindrance.[32] This treatment of the captured was in sharp contrast with the harshness shown to the people of Iasus and Cedreiae. Perhaps Lysander was changing his tactics. Having displayed his willingness to employ terror in the south, he may have thought it wise to display moderation in the north in the hope that the combination of moderation and force would lead the cities in the straits to yield more readily. The conquest of Lampsacus put the Spartans at the edge of the Propontis, a position from which they could strike the many cities on both its coasts and threaten the great prizes of Byzantium and Chalcedon on either side of the Bosporus.

News that Lysander had eluded them and had made his way into the Hellespont with a large fleet must have been most alarming to the Athenians. His excursion undid the gains they had made with such difficulty and danger in 411/10 at Cynossema, Abydos, and Cyzicus. Once more the very existence of their city was at risk, and the threat could be met only by pursuing the enemy, forcing him to fight, de-

[30]*Lys.* 9.3.
[31]Xen. 2.1.16, 18.
[32]Xen. 2.1.18–19.

stroying his fleet, and driving him from the straits. The Athenians appear to have pursued Lysander by way of Chios.[33] But they were at least a day or two behind, for they were only at Elaeus, at the mouth of the Hellespont, when they heard of the fall of Lampsacus. They hurried to their base at Sestos and then made camp at Aegospotami, on the beach just across the Hellespont, about three miles away (see Map 13).[34] A key to understanding the course of events is that Aegospotami was *only* a beach, a place without a proper harbor, a little to the east of the modern Turkish town called Sütlüce, or Galata in its Greek form, the ancient town of Aegospotami.[35] The Athenian fleet consisted of 180 ships.[36] This included about 36,000 men, so the small town of Aegospotami was unable to supply the food, water, and other things that so vast a force required.

The nearest place to get adequate supplies was Sestos, about twelve miles away, so the Athenians would often need to divide their forces to obtain supplies, and the men would often be scattered in search of food and water. Why did they establish their base in so inconvenient a location? The answer lies in strategic requirements that seemed to outweigh logistical difficulties. The Athenians were eager to engage the enemy in a great battle as soon as possible, before their own money

[33]Xen. 2.1.18.

[34]Xen. 2.1.20–21. For the location of Aegospotami, see Bommelaer, *Lysandre*, 111–113; and map at end. The ancient sources for the battle of Aegospotami are Xen. 2.1.22–30; Diod. 13.105–6; Plut. *Lys.* 10–11 and *Alc.* 36–37; Frontinus 2.1.18; Polyaenus 1.45.2; Paus. 9.32.9; and Nepos, *Alc.* 8. The most helpful modern accounts are: D. Lotze, *Lysander und der Peloponnesische Krieg* (Berlin, 1965), 32–37; C. Ehrhart, *Phoenix* XXIV (1970), 225–228; B. S. Strauss, *AJP* CIV (1983), 24–35; and Bommelaer, *Lysandre*, 101–115.

[35]Plut. *Alc.* 36.5. For the location of the Athenian base and the town of Aegospotami, see Strabo 7.331, fr. 55. Bommelaer (*Lysandre*, 111–113) has a useful discussion, placing the site to the east of the modern Turkish town of Sütlüce, at the mouth of the stream called Büyük Dere, located just south of the point, the Sütlüce Burnu (see Map 13). B. S. Strauss, in a forthcoming article ("A Note on the Topography and Tactics of the Battle of Aegospotami" to be published in *AJP*), which he has been kind enough to show me, points out the advantages of such a location: "It has two streams (hence potam*i*), a beach for triremes, and it is indeed directly opposite Lampsacus." In addition, a site farther to the southwest would require the Athenians rowing to Lampsacus to fight a strong current and an unfavorable wind. "The wind is a strong northeasterly; the surface current flows southward at an average rate of about 1 knot along the coast . . . and even faster in the center of the straits." These facts, coupled with the greater distance between Lampsacus and any other suggested site, make it clear that an Athenian fleet sailing up the strait from any other site would have run the risk of exhausting itself by the time it came to grips with the enemy.

[36]Diod. 13.105.1.

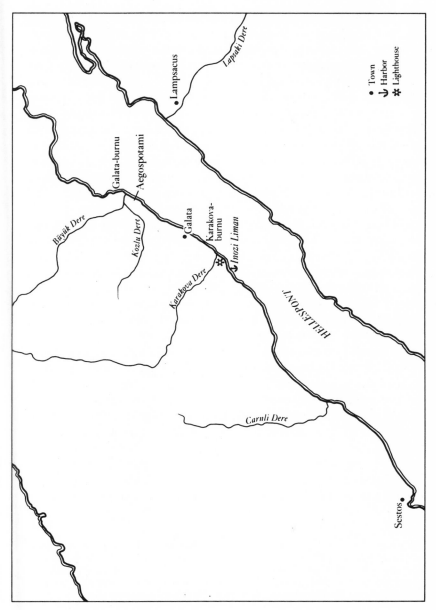

MAP 13. THE BATTLE OF AEGOSPOTAMI. Adapted from map drawn by Marcia Mogelonsky to accompany "A Note on the Topography and Tactics of the Battle of Aegospotami," forthcoming in *AJP*.

387

ran out and before their wily opponent found an opportunity to slip away. A withdrawal to Sestos, which could have provided a good harbor and adequate supplies, would have had two serious disadvantages. It would have forced the Athenians to row some twelve miles to be in position to challenge the enemy, and thus they would arrive tired and vulnerable.[37] It would also have prevented them from keeping close watch on the Spartan fleet. The Athenians had already been embarrassed on more than one occasion by allowing the Spartans to slip by or away from them. If Lysander sailed into the Propontis, as the Athenians could not prevent him from doing from Sestos, he could bring over other cities as easily as he had done with Lampsacus before the Athenians could prevent it, perhaps even Byzantium and Chalcedon. The Athenian generals could not afford the risk. For all of its shortcomings, the beach at Aegospotami allowed them to challenge the Spartans from short range and to prevent Lysander from slipping by them.[38]

As at the battle of Arginusae, here the Athenians appear not to have had a supreme commander but to have made decisions by conference and consensus. The six generals whom we know to have been present— Adeimantus, Cephisodorus, Conon, Menander, Philocles, and Tydeus—rotated the command on a daily basis.[39] Their first strategy was obvious: to sail into the mouth of the harbor at Lampsacus each morning and challenge the Spartans to come out and fight. We do not know the size of the Spartan fleet, but it may have been reasonably close to the numbers of the Athenians' force.[40] Lysander, however, chose not to take the bait, putting his ships in battle order but keeping them close to shore.[41] The same routine continued for four days, no doubt frustrating and annoying the Athenian generals. During that period, the tension was increased by the appearance of Alcibiades, ready to offer advice and assistance.

The Athenian exile had seen the situation from one of his castles

---

[37]See above, n. 35.

[38]Strauss (*AJP* CIV [1983], 28) emphasizes the importance of close access, and Bommelaer (*Lysandre*, 112) places great weight on close surveillance.

[39]Strauss, *AJP* CIV (1983), 29, n. 19.

[40]After the battle, Lysander was able to put out to sea with 200 ships (Xen. 2.2.5), but some of them will have been among those captured intact from the Athenians at the battle of Aegospotami. On the other hand, if the Spartan fleet was decidedly smaller than the Athenian fleet, Lysander hardly could have been expected to accept the challenge to battle.

[41]Xen. 2.1.22–23.

near by and had come down to the camp at Aegospotami on horse-back.[42] He pointed out the inadequacies of the place as a base and advised the generals to move to Sestos, where they would have a city, a harbor, adequate supplies, and a place from which they could fight whenever they liked. He also claimed to have the friendship of the Thracian kings Medocus and Seuthes, who, he alleged, had agreed to give him a large army with which he could finish off the war with the Spartans.[43] The offer seems promising, and we should not be surprised that Alcibiades thought of it. Athens' greatest naval victory at the battle of Cyzicus, in which Alcibiades had played such an important part, had been won by the skillful use of combined operations on land and sea. The fighting in the Hellespont between 411 and 407 had shown the need for land troops to support the fleets. If the Athenians could employ a superior land army against Lampsacus, they could force Lysander's hand. If the city were taken, the Spartan fleet would be deprived of supplies and could be starved out. The Spartans would then be forced either to fight their way out or surrender. If they fought, locked in the harbor, they would almost surely be defeated and, shut in by the Athenian fleet and with the land in hostile hands, the Spartan fleet would be annihilated, as it was at the battle of Cyzicus.

The Athenian generals, however, rejected both the advice and the offer. The advice was not as good as Alcibiades thought, for in spite of the disadvantages of Aegospotami as a base, the Athenians needed to stay close to Lysander's fleet. The offer, on the other hand, presented an important opportunity, but there were adequate reasons for the generals' refusal. One of them must have been simple disbelief in Alcibiades' ability to deliver on his promise. He had made many promises in the past that he had not carried out, most notably to bring Tissaphernes over to the Athenian side. He was fully capable of promising a vast army, regaining a position of influence in the Athenian army, and then delivering only a fraction of what he had promised.

---

[42]Plut. *Alc.* 36.5; Xen. 2.1.25; Diod. 13.105.3; Nepos 7.8.2.

[43]Xenophon (2.1.25) speaks only of the advice to move the base. Diodorus (13.105.3) mentions only the offer to supply Thracian troops. Nepos (7.8) mentions both, presenting Alcibiades as giving the advice to move after his offer of military aid was rejected. Plutarch (*Alc.* 36.5–37.2) also mentions both, although in a different way. After his advice to move is rejected, Alcibiades leaves, telling his friends that if he had not been insulted by the generals, he would have forced the Spartans to fight or lose their ships because his Thracian troops could attack the enemy camp. Whatever the order of these events and the details, there is no reason why he should not have made both the suggestion and the offer.

A second reason, closely connected to the first, was suspicion of his motives. Diodorus tells us that Alcibiades made his offer on condition that he be given a share of the command.[44] Although this demand has been doubted, it is entirely plausible.[45] Diodorus tells us that he acted "because of a desire to accomplish some great deed for his country through his own efforts and through his accomplishments restore the people to their old affection for him."[46] Had the generals agreed, they would have been doing no more than the Athenian force on Samos in 411, which had taken in Alcibiades and elected him general without consulting Athens.

The situation that Alcibiades faced at Aegospotami in 405 was very different. The camp was not dominated by his friends and supporters, whereas the Samian camp had been controlled by Thrasybulus and Theramenes; instead, most of the generals seem to have been hostile. Adeimantus was an old friend and associate of Alcibiades.[47] But Conon was the man sent to replace Alcibiades after the battle of Notium, when he and his associates were in the greatest disfavor. Also, Tydeus and Menander would soon display their unfriendliness to Alcibiades, as would Philocles, who had already shown his opposition to Adeimantus.[48] Whatever their previous feelings and commitments, the generals must have known that with Alcibiades on the scene they would all be diminished to secondary significance.[49] With the exception of Adeimantus, perhaps, they would have been afraid to become involved with such a controversial figure; if they collaborated with him and things went wrong, they were sure to suffer. As Diodorus puts it, "the Athenian generals thought that if they were defeated they themselves would get the blame but that the credit for any success would go to Alcibiades."[50] The generals, therefore, Tydeus and Menander taking the lead, rejected his advice and refused his offer brusquely. "They were the generals now, and not he," they said and ordered him from the camp.[51]

As the days passed and Lysander continued to refuse battle, the

[44]13.105.3.
[45]Hatzfeld, *Alcibiade*, 337.
[46]13.105.4.
[47]Strauss, *AJP* CIV (1983), 30 and n. 23.
[48]Ibid. 29–31.
[49]Nepos (7.8.4) specifically attributes such a thought to Philocles.
[50]13.105.4.
[51]Xen. 2.1.26; Diod. 13.105.4; Plut. *Alc.* 37.1–2.

Athenians became contemptuous and careless. They became accustomed to going off in search of provisions as soon as their ships returned to Aegospotami. Their forces were in a most inconvenient base; supplies were short and laborious to obtain. The enemy, who had time on his side, refused to fight, and the generals had no plan that could change the situation. Instead, they continued with their original strategy, which now seemed to have no chance of success, and the men must have thought they were engaged in a useless and meaningless routine. It would have been difficult for any general to maintain morale and discipline under the prevailing conditions, and with a divided command and the mutual suspicion inevitable in the year after the trial of the Arginusae generals, their problems were intensified. On the fifth day, when the rotating command fell to Philocles, the stalemate came to an end. He set out from shore with a squadron of thirty ships, having given orders to the other trierarchs to man their ships and follow him.[52] We are not told his intentions, but there are three possibilities: he may have been planning the usual cruise to Lampsacus, carelessly setting out with his own squadron in advance of the rest of the fleet in contempt of the enemy; he may have belatedly accepted the advice of Alcibiades and begun a withdrawal to Sestos;[53] he may have been trying to lure Lysander into a trap, as the Athenians had done at the battle of Cyzicus and had tried to do at the battle of Notium.[54] Although we cannot know what plan he had in mind, we must try to understand the situation and assess the possibilities. There was no advantage in setting out with only thirty ships without waiting for the others if Philocles intended the usual voyage to Lampsacus. If that was what he meant to do, he and his colleagues were truly reckless and incompetent. The second plan also seems unlikely, for nothing had changed to make it wise to move to Sestos. The third scheme, if we understand it as a simple device to draw

---

[52]Diod. 13.106.1. For the details of the battle I follow Diodorus, as do Ehrhart, Strauss, and Bommelaer (see above, n. 34). Xenophon (2.1.27–29) gives an entirely different account that has rightly gone out of favor. He says nothing of an Athenian initiative but tells of the usual sailing from Aegospotami and back. This time, however, he has Lysander take advantage of the Athenians' lack of discipline to attack the scattered and careless enemy. Lysander then captures almost the entire fleet on the beach without a battle. For the most concise demonstration of the unlikelihood of that account, see Ehrhart, *Phoenix* XXIV (1970).

[53]That is the suggestion of Lotze (*Lysander*, 34).

[54]That is the opinion of Ehrhart (*Phoenix* XXIV (1970), 227) and Bommelaer (*Lysandre*, 110).

Lysander out to attack thirty ships and then to launch the rest of the fleet against him, appears entirely foolish. Lysander knew perfectly well the size of the Athenian fleet and could not have been deceived by such a maneuver.[55]

Perhaps we can make more sense of events by combining the second and third suggestions. In that case, the plan would be to lure Lysander from Lampsacus by feinting a withdrawal to Sestos. The Spartans might be emboldened to attack a detachment of thirty ships in the process of withdrawal and then to turn on the rest of the fleet, which, they might believe, would not be expecting to fight. If that were the plan it was not a bad one, for Lysander had done almost exactly that at the battle of Notium, where he had attacked the Athenian commander Antiochus, who was at the head of a small squadron; had sunk his ship; and had defeated the rest of his fleet before it was ready.[56] Philocles may have hoped to lure Lysander into an attempt to repeat his triumph at Notium and then to take him by surprise with an attack from the main Athenian fleet, this time ready for battle.

Such a plan required secrecy, discipline, and careful coordination between the divisions of the fleet if it were to succeed, but none of these elements was present on the day of the fight. After the battle there was much talk of treason.[57] Lysander, who was prepared to use the skills of the fox and to cheat men with oaths, was certainly willing to bribe an enemy to reveal his plans. Diodorus tells us that Lysander had learned of Philocles' plan from deserters from the Athenian fleet.[58] This is possible since desertion across the narrow strait would not have been difficult. Knowledge in advance of Athenian intentions would have been helpful but not essential. After all, the Athenians could not stay at Aegospotami forever. Either they would withdraw in one direction or another with their entire force, leaving Lysander free to recover control of the cities on the coasts, or they would try some stratagem. All Lysander needed to do was to wait patiently until the time came, to keep a close watch on the enemy, and to maintain his own forces in a condition of discipline and readiness to take advantage of any opportunity. The fact is that knowledge in advance would not

---

[55]Strauss, *AJP* CIV (1983), 25, n. 5.

[56]See above, 316–317.

[57]Adeimantus, Alcibiades, and Tydeus were accused of treason at one time or another. We hear of no such charge against Conon, but he was careful not to return to Athens after the battle. See Busolt, *GG* III:2, 1623, n. 1.

[58]13.106.2.

have helped Lysander if the Athenians had performed as they should. Had they been ready to move as soon as Lysander attacked Philocles' squadron, their stratagem could have worked. It was not a breach of security that decided the battle of Aegospotami but the training, discipline, and execution made possible by a unified command under a talented leader.

There is every reason to think that Lysander had hoped to be presented with an opportunity like the one he had been given at Notium, and when it arose, he was quick to seize it. He set out quickly to cut off Philocles' route to Sestos, so that when he attacked and routed Philocles' squadron, the pursuit was toward the rest of the Athenian fleet at Aegospotami (see Map 13). The Athenians there were taken by surprise; they had not expected to see the Spartan fleet bearing down on their base, chasing the squadron of Philocles before it. Confusion struck the Athenian camp, and many ships were still on the beach without men or only partially manned. Lysander, quickly grasping the situation, put ashore a corps of soldiers under the command of Eteonicus, and they were able to gain control of part of the Athenian camp. Meanwhile, Lysander had defeated whatever Athenian ships had come out against him and had begun to drag away the beached Athenian ships with grappling hooks. Since the Athenians had no organized land force with which to resist Eteonicus, and most of their fleet could not get out to sea, they had no chance. After a brief resistance, they ran from the camp and the ships, fleeing to safety in every direction, most of them ultimately getting away to Sestos. Ten Athenian ships managed to escape. Conon commanded one of them; remembering the generals of Arginusae and "fearing the anger of the people," he did not return to Athens but sought asylum at Cyprus with his personal friend, the tyrant Evagoras. The remaining 170 Athenian triremes were destroyed or captured.[59] Lysander had won a "Cyzicus" in reverse, but the Athenians, unlike the Spartans in 410, had no ally to whom they could turn for help in restoring their fortunes. The Athenians' resources were exhausted; they could not again build a fleet to replace the one lost at Aegospotami. Athens had lost the war; the only questions that remained were how long it would hold out before surrendering and what terms the Athenians could obtain.

After the battle, Lysander returned to Lampsacus with his captured

---

[59]Diod. 13.106.1–6.

ships, between 3,000 and 4,000 prisoners, and the rest of the booty.[60] The first order of business was to send the great news back home to Sparta. Lysander loaded his swiftest ship, a privateer under the command of the Milesian pirate Theopompus, with the most impressive captured arms and the most expensive booty and sent it off at once. Speed was more important than the status of the captain, and Theopompus arrived in Sparta to announce the victory on the third day after his departure.[61] Next came the question of what to do with the prisoners, fully a tenth of the entire Athenian force at Aegospotami. To make the decision Lysander called an assembly of all of the allies gathered at Lampsacus. His recent actions foreshadowed harsh treatment; he might kill all of the men, as he had done at Iasus, or sell them into slavery, as he had done at Cedreiae. Lysander's cruelty, however, seems to have been of a cold, pragmatic kind, aimed at producing a desired result. The massacre of his political opponents at Miletus was meant to place his own men securely in power and to terrify potential opponents in other cities.[62] Likewise, his acts of terror at Iasus and Cedreiae were meant to discourage other small cities in Asia from resisting him. To kill or enslave the Athenian prisoners, however, would have no such advantage. After the battle of Aegospotami, Lysander's next goal was the surrender of Athens. The murder or enslavement of thousands of Athenians captured in battle was not likely to encourage their fellow citizens to yield. On the contrary, it was bound to increase resistance. Lysander would soon show that he was ready to spare many Athenian lives in order to increase hunger in Athens and thereby hasten the city's surrender.[63]

We may guess that had the decision been left to Lysander, he would have released the prisoners and sent them home. Their fate, however, was decided by the allies, and they made their decision in an atmosphere of anger and vengeance. After all, the war was far into its third decade, and many allies had suffered irreparable harm and the loss of many lives. States like Corinth, Megara, and Aegina, once proud and prosperous places, had suffered repeated devastation of their land,

---

[60]Xen. 2.1.30. Neither Xenophon nor Diodorus gives a figure for the Athenian prisoners taken. Plutarch (*Alc.* 37.3) sets it at 3,000, Pausanias (9.32.9) at 4,000. It may be that the true figure was something in between and that one author, or his source, rounded the figure up and the other down. See Strauss, *AJP* CIV (1983), 34.

[61]Xen. 2.1.30; Diod. 13.106.7.

[62]See above, 382–383.

[63]See below, 396.

destruction of their trade, civil strife, and even removal from their native soil. They emerged from the war permanently diminished. If these complaints were not enough, recent events had entirely removed the possibility of prudence in place of revenge. Atrocities had begun early in the war and had became more horrible as it proceeded. Although both sides were guilty, the Athenian massacres and enslavements of the populations of cities like Scione and Melos were well known, and it is not uncommon for victors to excuse or forget their own excesses even as they are infuriated by those they have suffered. Only lately, moreover, the Athenians had taken some especially unpleasant actions. They had voted to cut off the right hand of every captive, apparently on the motion of the general Philocles.[64] That cruel proposal no doubt was made in anger at the deserters from the Athenian fleet who were swelling the ranks of the enemy. In the same mood, Philocles, after capturing a Corinthian and an Andrian trireme, went beyond his own cruel law and ordered the full crews of both ships thrown overboard.[65] With such actions fresh in their minds, the Spartans and their allies voted to kill all of their Athenian prisoners, Philocles among them. Adeimantus, another of the generals captured alive, was the only Athenian spared. Xenophon tells us that this was because Adeimantus alone had opposed Philocles' proposal in the assembly, but he also informs us that Adeimantus was accused of having betrayed the Athenian fleet.[66] The rest of the Athenians, perhaps some 3,500, were killed.[67]

We are not told how the news of the victory was received at Sparta, although it is easy to imagine with what joy its people received word that meant the long war would soon be brought to a thoroughly successful conclusion. Xenophon, however, who was almost certainly an eyewitness, reports how the Athenians received the news of their disaster:

The *Paralus* arrived at Athens at night and announced the disaster, and a wailing came from the Piraeus, through the long walls, to the city, one man

[64]Xen. 2.1.32; Plut. *Lys.* 13.1–2.

[65]Xen. 2.1.31.

[66]Xen. 2.1.32.

[67]Since Diodorus says nothing of any executions except for that of Philocles, scholars who prefer his account to that of Xenophon have doubted that they occurred; see Ehrhart, *Phoenix* XXIV (1970), 228; and E. Will, *Le monde grec et l'orient*, vol. 1, *Le V*^e *siecle (510–403)* (Paris, 1972), 389. Strauss (*AJP* CIV [1983], 132–134), however, makes a convincing argument in defense of Xenophon on this point.

passing the word to another, so that on that night no one slept. They wept not only for the men who had been killed but even far more for themselves, thinking that they would suffer the kind of fate they had imposed on the Melians, colonists of the Spartans, after they had conquered them by siege, and on the Histiaeans and Scionaeans and Toronaeans and Aeginetans and many others among the Hellenes.[68]

In light not only of the atrocities they had committed but also of Lysander's treatment of his Athenian prisoners, we can easily understand their fears. Bitterly hostile neighbors such as Megara, Corinth, Aegina, and Thebes were likely to urge the destruction of the entire city and the killing or enslavement of all of its people, and the experience after the battle of Aegospotami suggested that Lysander and the Spartans would agree. On the next day, therefore, the Athenians met in assembly and voted to block all of the harbors except one, repair their walls, and place guards to defend them. The Athenians were determined to fight on and resist the siege that was certain to come.[69]

Lysander, meanwhile, was busy in the straits. After settling affairs at Lampsacus, he sailed to the Bosporus to cut off any further shipments of grain to Athens. The people of those cities quickly made terms with Lysander and admitted him within their walls. The Spartans encountered no opposition from dissenters wanting to resist, for Lysander now employed a policy of practical advantage rather than of vengeance. Perhaps the allies' lust for revenge had been satisfied by the death of the prisoners, perhaps they were swayed by the desire to avoid a long and difficult siege of the cities, perhaps Lysander was more prepared to assert his authority while on campaign than after a battle. In any case, the peace terms allowed the Athenian garrisons, and any Athenians in the vicinity, to withdraw safely on condition that they return to Athens and nowhere else. This became his general policy, applied to all of the cities containing Athenians. Lysander knew that the Athenian walls could withstand assault and that the city could be forced to surrender only by siege and the famine it caused. He therefore wanted to fill Athens, the Piraeus, and the area between the long walls with as many mouths to feed as possible, thereby shortening the time the Athenians could hold out.[70]

Before sailing back toward the Aegean, Lysander appointed Sthe-

[68]2.2.3.
[69]Xen. 2.2.4.
[70]Xen. 2.2.2.

nelaus as harmost in command of garrisons at Byzantium and Chalcedon. The strategic importance of these places and the need to be sure that no ships got through to Athens are enough to explain these establishments. In fact, Lysander promulgated a decree imposing the death penalty on anyone bringing grain into Athens, although a few Athenians were able to intercept grain ships headed for the Peloponnesus and bring them to the Piraeus.[71] Lysander placed harmosts and garrisons in control of the cities of the Bosporus, the first of many identical arrangements Lysander imposed on the Greek cities, both those that had been hostile to Sparta and those that had been allies.[72] Harmosts and garrisons were nothing new for the Spartans in 405. They had been used for various purposes since the 420s but always in connection with the conduct of the war. After the battle of Aegospotami they could no longer be justified in the same way; yet Lysander kept them in place where he found them and installed them where they had not been before. At the same time, he pursued a policy of removing democratic regimes and replacing them with oligarchies of his own supporters, as he had done at Miletus. Frequently, the form of government was a very tight oligarchy, called a "decarchy," of only ten men chosen from among his personal supporters.[73] His choice of rulers was not based on ideology or consideration of class; as Plutarch tells us, "he did not appoint the rulers on the basis of aristocratic birth or of wealth, but he put control of affairs into the hands of members of his political faction and those connected to him by personal ties, and he put them in charge of rewards and punishments."[74] Before long the Spartans would impose a tribute on the cities they occupied, thereby completing the transition from Athenian imperial rule to the establishment of a new Spartan empire founded by Lysander. These developments took time and were surely not accomplished immediately. It was certainly not until sometime in 404, after the surrender of Athens, that the ephors on behalf of the Spartan government gave official sanction to the new arrangement, but Lysander began to lay its foundations immediately after the battle of Aegospotami.[75]

[71]Isoc. 18.61.
[72]Plut. *Lys.* 13.4.
[73]For the establishment of decarchies, see Diod. 14.10.1–2, 13.1; Plut. *Lys.* 13.3–5; E. Cavaignac, *Revue des études historiques* XC (1924), 285–316.
[74]Plut. *Lys.* 13.4.
[75]For a fine discussion of the foundation of the Spartan empire see C. D. Hamilton, *Sparta's Bitter Victories* (Ithaca, N.Y., and London, 1979), 56–62.

After completing his arrangements at Byzantium and Chalcedon, Lysander set out for the Aegean. Probably on the way he stopped to capture the Athenian base on Sestos, where once again he spared the men of the garrison and sent them to Athens.[76] With a fleet of 200 ships he left the Hellespont and came to Lesbos, where he settled things to his liking at Mytilene and the other cities. From there he sent Eteonicus with 10 ships to the coast of Thrace. This must have been one of the few areas still loyal to Athens, but before long all of the cities went over to the Spartan commander.[77] By this time, almost the entire Athenian Empire had collapsed, with all of the cities opening their gates to Lysander except for the island of Samos. There, the strength of factional feeling and the strong loyalty of the Samian democrats to Athens produced a unique resistance. The democrats slaughtered their aristocratic opponents and refused to yield to the Spartans. The Athenians were so grateful that they passed a remarkable decree granting the Samians Athenian citizenship even while they retained their autonomy.[78] Before going farther, Lysander left a fleet of 40 ships to reduce the island by siege.[79] On his way to Athens, he stopped at Melos and Aegina and began the process of restoring the populations to their native islands from which the Athenians had removed them.[80] At least these actions were in accord with the high-minded goals of freedom and autonomy with which the Spartans had entered the war. Since the goals did not conflict with Lysander's interests and were sure to do him good politically, he did not hesitate to carry them out.

As Lysander sailed toward Athens early in October, with his fleet now numbering 150 ships, the Spartans were sending a great army over land to join him in overawing the Athenians and persuading them to surrender without a long siege. The entire army, not the usual contingent of two-thirds, of all Peloponnesian states with the exception of Argos marched into Attica under the command of King Pausanias. At the Academy just outside the city, they joined the force from

---

[76]Diod. 13.106.8. Later, after the surrender of Athens, he went so far as to drive out the native Sestians and turn the city over to his own junior officers, but this was too much for the Spartan government, which restored Sestos to its own people. See Plut. *Lys.* 14.2; Lotze, *Lysander*, 38; and Hamilton, *Sparta's Bitter Victories*, 44.

[77]Xen. 2.2.5.

[78]*GHI*, 94, 283.

[79]Xen. 2.2.5–6; Diod. 13.106.8. For the division of the Spartan fleet and the date of the Samian blockade, see Lotze, *Lysander*, 40–41; and P. Krentz, *The Thirty at Athens* (Ithaca, N.Y., and London, 1982), 30, n. 2.

[80]Xen. 2.2.9.

Decelea under Agis and made camp. It was the first time since the sixth century that both Spartan kings had appeared in the field at the same time.[81] In spite of the unprecedented and imposing forces arrayed against them, the Athenians refused to yield and prepared to defend their city. Xenophon says: "The Athenians, besieged by land and sea, were at a loss as to what they should do, for they had no ships, no money, no food." He was no friend of the Athenian imperial democracy, and he explains its decision to hold out against all odds by moralizing that the Athenians saw no way out but to suffer the same atrocities they had perpetrated on so many others.[82] Probably, a better explanation is that they held out in fear that capitulation would bring them the terrible fate Xenophon had in mind, and they were right to be afraid. The execution of the Athenian prisoners after the battle of Aegospotami was a clue, if one were needed, to the anger of the allies. In the months after that battle, the Thebans, Corinthians, and other allies of Sparta made clear their desire to destroy the city of Athens, turning Attica into one great pasture, and to kill its people or sell them into slavery.[83]

With such a fate in prospect the Athenians had nothing to lose by holding out, but in fact, the Athenians may have been moved by hope as well as fear. The goals and interests of the allies were not necessarily the same as those of the Spartans. In particular, the Thebans had demonstrated ambitions of their own, sometimes in conflict with Spartan interests.[84] They might be glad to see Athens destroyed and Attica depopulated, for they, as powerful neighbors, could exploit the opportunity, expand into the deserted territory, and increase their own power. Perhaps, as time passed, the Spartans might see that they would not be well served by such an outcome and offer terms more to the liking of the Athenians. The Athenians also had reason to know that Sparta itself was rarely unified in its policies. Lysander and others might aim at an ambitious extra-Peloponnesian policy, but King Pausanias, like his father Pleistoanax, might prefer the more traditional one of withdrawal within the Peloponnesus and a policy of collaboration with a friendly and reliable Athens. In any case, the Athenians had little to lose by waiting to see if a better opportunity might come

[81]Xen. 2.2.8; Diod. 13.107.2; Plut. *Lys.* 14.1. The observation about the Spartan kings is made by Krentz (*Thirty*, 30).
[82]Xen. 2.2.10.
[83]Xen. 2.2.19; Plut. *Lys.* 15.2; And. 1.142, 3.21; Isoc. 14.31, 18.29; Justin 5.8.4.
[84]See below, 405–406.

their way. They tried to regain internal harmony by restoring civil
and political rights to those who had been deprived of them in previous
political conflicts, especially during the time of the Four Hundred.[85]
They also resolved not to surrender.

When the Spartans saw that the Athenians were determined to resist,
they withdrew the large Peloponnesian army under Pausanias, leaving
Agis' force to conduct the siege by land.[86] At the same time, Lysander
sailed off to carry on the siege of Samos, leaving enough ships to
maintain the blockade he had decreed.[87] For some weeks the Athenians
held firm and did not communicate with the enemy, but by November
food had begun to run low.[88] Perhaps the Athenians were also encouraged by the withdrawal of the main Spartan army and fleet to
believe that the Spartans would be ready to grant an acceptable peace,
since their hopes of a quick capitulation had faded.[89] Probably about
this time, shortly before the withdrawal of the great Peloponnesian
army under Pausanias and the departure of Lysander to Samos, the
Spartans called a congress of its allies to discuss the fate of Athens,
whenever it should fall.[90] This must have been the first time when
Thebes, Corinth, and other vengeful states proposed the total destruction of Athens.[91] On this occasion, if Pausanias is right, they were
supported by both Agis and Lysander, who, "on their own initiative
and without the approval of the Spartan assembly, brought a proposal
before the allies to destroy Athens root and branch."[92] Whether or not
they knew of the mood of the congress, the Athenians sent an embassy
to Agis at Decelea offering to make peace and to join the Spartan
alliance on condition that they keep their walls and the Piraeus.[93] By
implication they abandoned their empire, which was already lost, but

[85]Xen. 2.2.11; And. 1.73–79; Lys. 25.27.
[86]Diod. 13.107.3.
[87]Hamilton, *Sparta's Bitter Victories*, 45.
[88]Xenophon (2.2.11) says that the food had given out entirely and that people were
starving to death, but he must be mistaken, for the Athenians did not surrender for
another three months. For the chronology, see Lotze, *Lysander*, 42.
[89]I take this to be the import of Hamilton's suggestion (*Sparta's Bitter Victories*, 45),
endorsed by Krentz (*Thirty*, 30).
[90]This time for the discussion is proposed by Hamilton (*Sparta's Bitter Victories*, 52),
and it seems entirely likely that the allies will have wanted to discuss this question
with the Spartans before disbanding.
[91]See above, n. 24.
[92]3.8.6. For a defense of the historicity of Pausanias' report and also of the apparently
contradictory one in Polyaenus 1.45.5, see Hamilton, *Sparta's Bitter Victories*, 50–52.
[93]Xen. 2.2.11.

such terms, which left Athens autonomous and defensible, were too mild to suit the enemy's mood of the moment. Agis' reply was technically correct, that he himself had no authority to negotiate a peace and that the Athenians must go to Sparta for that purpose.[94] But we may well believe that his answer was meant to indicate his own disapproval of the terms. The Athenians surely knew that Agis could not negotiate a peace without reference to the government in Sparta. They approached him to sound out a powerful individual and to enlist him, if possible, in support of their proposal.

His cold refusal could not have encouraged them, but they sent the ambassadors on to Sparta to discover what peace terms might be acceptable. They were not even permitted to enter the city. Instead, the ephors came out to meet them at Sellasia, at the border of Laconia, and asked them what proposals they had brought. On hearing the same terms that had been mentioned to Agis, the ephors gave a brutally menacing response, ordering them "to go back from that very spot and, if they wanted a peace of any kind, to return with a better proposal."[95] They made it clear, however, that a minimum condition was the destruction of the long walls for a distance of ten stadia (about 6,000 feet) each.[96] The Athenians found the answer chilling, for they were afraid that accepting the terms would mean their own destruction or enslavement. In any case, the delay for further negotiations would mean the death of many by starvation.[97] A certain Archestratus arose in the council and proposed that the Athenians accept the Spartan terms, but the people were not ready to do so. We can understand their behavior only in terms of fear; no matter what the Spartans said, the Athenians believed that if they had free access to the city, the Piraeus, and the long walls, they would use the opportunity to kill or enslave them. Accordingly, they threw Archestratus into prison for making the proposal and passed Cleophon's motion forbidding anyone from making a similar one.[98]

[94] Xen. 2.2.12.
[95] Xen. 2.2.13.
[96] Xen. 2.2.15; Lys. 13.8.
[97] Xen. 2.2.14. Aeschines (2.76) mentions a peace offer by the Spartans that would have given the Athenians autonomy and allowed them to keep their democratic constitution, as well as the islands of Lemnos, Imbros, and Scyros. Since he also connects it with Cleophon's resistance to any peace offer, it must refer to discussions in 405. Krentz (*Thirty*, 33, n. 11) considers such an offer plausible at this time, but it seems to me entirely unlikely in the mood of the moment.
[98] Xen. 2.2.15; Lys. 13.8. Aeschines (2.76) goes so far as to claim that Cleophon threatened to cut the throat of any who mentioned making peace.

No one, therefore, dared to discuss asking for peace, but the passage of time brought the Athenians closer to starvation. The stalemate could not last, and Theramenes came forward to break it. As Xenophon tells the story, Theramenes proposed to go to Lysander to discover whether the Spartans insisted on the breach of the walls in order to enslave the Athenians or merely as a demonstration of good faith.[99] Lysias has a different version. He reports that Theramenes promised that if he were given full powers to negotiate, he would bring back peace without giving up hostages or ships and without breaching the walls, asserting that he had discovered either "some other good thing for the city" or, more likely, "something of great value." When pressed to say what it was, he refused, simply asking the Athenians to trust him.[100] Lysias was bitterly hostile to Theramenes, and the context of his speeches required that the reputation of the man who had been a member of the Four Hundred and of the terrible Thirty be as reprehensible as possible. His evidence, therefore, must be regarded with suspicion, but the "Theramenes Papyrus," first published in 1968, lends his account some support. It depicts Theramenes as explaining his refusal to reveal his secret as a way of not committing the Athenians to excessive concessions in advance, and it confirms that the assembly chose him as ambassador with full powers to negotiate a peace.[101] It seems likely, then, that even if Theramenes did not make the specific and implausible promises Lysias attributes to him, he was sent to do more than discover Lysander's and the Spartans' intentions, to which Xenophon limits him, since for that purpose he would not have needed the full negotiating powers he asked for and received. He really must have thought that he knew something that would allow him to bring back an acceptable peace.

Theramenes sailed off to Samos, where he spent more than three

---

[99] 2.2.16.

[100] Lys. 13.9, 14, 12.68; Krentz, *Thirty*, 34, n. 16. My discussion of Theramenes' mission to Lysander depends on Krentz's fascinating suggestion and discussion (34–43).

[101] The document is Michigan papyrus no. 5982. The publication is by R. Merkelbach and H. C. Youtie, *ZPE* II (1968), 161–169. The reliability of the document has been questioned (see A. Andrewes, *ZPE* VI [1970], 35–38, who thinks it is part of a pro-Theramenean pamphlet, and A. Henrichs, *ZPE* III [1969], 101–108, who thinks it the work of a second-rate historian dependent on Lysias), but I agree with R. Sealey (*ZPE* XI [1975], 279–288) and Krentz (*Thirty*, 34, n. 17) that the fragment most likely comes from some reliable fourth-century history.

months with Lysander.[102] When he returned toward the beginning of March, he explained his long absence by saying that Lysander had kept him against his will and had told him only what Agis had: that he himself had no authority to discuss peace terms; if Theramenes wanted the answers to his questions, he must go to Sparta and ask the ephors.[103] If Lysander wanted the Athenians to surrender as soon as possible, he could only lose by detaining Theramenes, for the Athenians were less likely to accept Spartan terms while their ambassador was still negotiating better ones than if he had returned immediately and without hope. Neither Xenophon nor Lysias believed Theramenes' story, nor should we. Both the ancient writers thought that Theramenes had stayed away so long of his own free will so that the Athenians would grow so hungry that they would accept whatever terms the Spartans might offer.[104] That explanation has been widely accepted.[105] Moreover, it often has been accepted with the understanding that Theramenes employed part of his time plotting with Lysander to install an oligarchic regime to the liking of them both.[106] Such an explanation, however, presents very real problems. The first is that the delay was more likely to put off surrender than to hasten it. The quickest way for Theramenes to have brought Athens to terms, had that been his only purpose, would have been to come back within a couple of weeks and report that the Spartans had no wish to destroy Athens or its people but were adamant about peace terms.

A second difficulty is presented by the fact that when Theramenes returned from Lysander after an extraordinarily long and painful delay only to announce what Xenophon and Lysias, even more, represent as a totally unsuccessful mission, the Athenians at once chose him again as ambassador with full powers and sent him to Sparta at the head of a mission of ten men to continue the negotiations.[107] To believe all of that strains credulity beyond reasonable limits. At the very least, we must reject Lysias' assertions that Theramenes made specific promises impossible to carry out, for had he done so and had returned

[102]Xen. 2.2.16. Lysias (13.11) says that he went to Sparta and stayed there "a long time." The "Theramenes Papyrus" (1.41) shows that he is wrong and that Lysander was on Samos.

[103]Xen. 2.2.17.

[104]Xen. 2.2.16; Lys. 13.11.

[105]For references, see Krentz, *Thirty*, 36, n. 21.

[106]See, e.g., Busolt, *GG* III:2, 1631.

[107]Xen. 2.2.

empty-handed, having left the Athenians to starve for three months
in his absence, we may be sure that the Athenian assembly would
have treated him roughly. Beyond that, it is hard to see why the hungry
and presumably disappointed Athenians should have believed a story
that he had been detained by Lysander against his will any more than
Xenophon or Lysias did. Even if they did, however, it is still harder
to believe that they would then have sent a man who had returned
without a single concession as the head of a new delegation to negotiate
an agreement at Sparta.

Both ancient accounts are tendentious, incomplete, and inherently
implausible; to understand the situation, we must try to see beyond
them. Probably, Theramenes came before the Athenians in December
and asked to be sent to Lysander with full powers to negotiate a peace,
promising only to see what were Lysander's and the Spartans' intentions and telling the Athenians that he had discovered "something of
great value" that would help him achieve an acceptable agreement.
The Athenians would have accepted the secrecy involved on the obvious grounds that public revelation would undermine Theramenes'
ability to use whatever opportunity or advantage he might have. In
any case, we should remember that in spite of Theramenes' full power
to negotiate, the assembly retained the right to ratify or reject any
agreement he might bring back. We do not know whether Theramenes
stayed away for more than three months or some shorter period.[108]
But we should not be surprised by a very long interval. There was
plenty to talk about, and many differences of opinion needed to be
overcome. Theramenes would have had a difficult time persuading
Lysander to accept his views, and the Spartan commander will not
have been quick to give in, knowing that every passing day reduced
Athens' food supply and its people's capacity to resist. Only in that
sense should we believe the allegation that Lysander had detained
Theramenes against his will.

What did the two men discuss? What were Theramenes' intentions?
What was the "something of great value" he hoped to make use of in
obtaining acceptable peace terms? Once again, the evidence does not
admit certainty, but some plausible answers are available. Theramenes'
goals are not difficult to discern; the first three would have been common to any Athenian except a determined and extreme oligarch: the
physical survival of the city and its people, freedom for its citizens,

[108]As Krentz, *Thirty*, 36, suggests.

and internal autonomy for the state. It would not have been possible for anyone to save the empire, the walls, the fleet, or Athens' freedom of action in foreign policy, and we may believe that Theramenes spent little time on those questions. All of the others, however, required argument. Hostile allies like Thebes and Corinth opposed the first two points, and Lysander himself would prefer an Athens ruled by a clique of his own supporters and firmly under his own control. Theramenes' task was to convince him that it was in his own interest to grant what the Athenians asked.

The most important goal was to save the city and its people. The Thebans, Corinthians, and others had asked for the destruction of both, and we have suggested that Lysander agreed with them at first. It was not difficult, however, to make the case that the destruction of Athens would be advantageous not to Sparta but to Thebes and that Thebes was becoming a rival more than an ally. Theban power had grown significantly during the Archidamian War as a result of the destruction of Plataea, the annexation of several Boeotian towns, and the consequent Theban domination of the Boeotian League.[109] Their victory at the battle of Delium had given the Thebans new confidence in their military power and in their capacity to pursue an independent policy. In 419 they had gone so far as to take control of the Spartan colony at Heraclea in Central Greece and evict its Spartan governor, to the great anger of the Spartans.[110] At the time of the Peace of Nicias, they had defied the Spartans and pursued an independent policy by refusing to accept the peace. Even worse, they had destroyed Sparta's hopes of recovering Pylos by dismantling the fort of Panactum rather than returning it to the Athenians.[111] For whatever reason, they had failed to appear at the Battle of Mantinea in 418, when the very safety of Sparta was at stake.[112] During the Decelean War they gained the lion's share of the material benefits of ravaging the Attic countryside.[113] At the end they were bold enough to demand a tenth of the booty taken at Decelea for Apollo at Delphi. The Thebans, however, were bitterly dissatisfied with Sparta's failure to share the greater spoils of war.[114]

[109]Kagan, *Peace of Nicias*, 23.
[110]Ibid., 76–77.
[111]Ibid., 23–24, 56–58.
[112]Ibid., 107–108.
[113]*Hell. Oxy.* 12.4–5.
[114]Hamilton, *Sparta's Bitter Victories*, 149.

Within their city two political factions vied for control of policy, and one of them was powerfully hostile to Sparta.[115] Within the next two years the Thebans would oppose and even flatly defy Spartan policy on several occasions. They gave shelter and support to Athenians fleeing from the government the Spartans imposed on Athens. When the Spartans issued an order demanding the return of the Athenian exiles, the Thebans issued a decree commanding their citizens to give asylum to the exiles and defend them against arrest.[116] The Athenian rebels who later overthrew the Spartan puppets ruling their city used Thebes as their base, and when the Spartans massed an army to put down the rebellion, the Thebans and their fellow Boeotians refused to take part.[117] These acts of defiance and hostility had not yet occurred when Theramenes met with Lysander, but the anti-Spartan faction in Thebes was in place and strong enough to be on the point of controlling policy. It is not too much to believe that Theramenes was aware of their influence and pointed out the dangers they presented to Sparta and to Lysander's policy. When added to the growth of Theban power and the many grievances Sparta had accumulated during the war, the prospect of such a faction gaining control of Thebes helped make a powerful case for not destroying Athens, as the Thebans desired, but for retaining it under a regime the Spartans could trust as a barrier to Theban ambitions. In any case, that was the advice Lysander ultimately gave at the conference that decided Athens' fate.[118] We may well believe that Theramenes helped him come to that opinion.[119]

[115]For a good discussion of Theban politics at this time, see ibid., 145–160.

[116]Diod. 14.6.1–3; Plut. *Lys.* 27.2. For the authenticity of these accounts, see Hamilton, *Sparta's Bitter Victories*, 149–150.

[117]Athens as base: Xen. 2.4.2; Diod. 14.32.1; [Lys.] frg. 120; Justin 5.9.8. Theban refusal to march: Xen. 2.4.30.

[118]Polyaenus 1.45.5.

[119]At some point in their consideration of what to do about Athens, the Spartans sought divine advice from the oracle of Apollo at Delphi. They received a reply warning them "not to destroy the common hearth of Hellas." (The sources of the response are a scholiast to Aristeides 341 and Aelian, *Varia Historia* 4.6, collected in H. W. Parke and D. E. W. Wormell, *The Delphic Oracle* [Oxford, 1956], II, 74, no. 171.) Hamilton (*Sparta's Bitter Victories*, 53) suggests that it was Lysander who sent to the oracle with the intention of obtaining the response actually received, "well in advance of the actual peace congress." That suggestion is plausible in view of Lysander's widespread reputation for influencing various oracles in different ways (ibid., 92–95, especially 94, n. 95). I suggest the likeliest time for such an effort in connection with the fate of Athens was when Theramenes was with him on Samos. If that is correct, the delay in Theramenes' return to Athens may have been caused, in part, by the need to wait for the reponse of the oracle.

Whatever trouble Theramenes may have had in persuading Lysander to spare Athens and its people, he probably found it even harder to convince him to allow the Athenians a significant degree of autonomy in arranging their own constitution. As part of his ambition to gain power in Sparta, Lysander wanted and needed to impose governments loyal to him everywhere he could, and Athens was particularly important. He preferred narrow oligarchies made up entirely of his own supporters for this purpose. Theramenes, on the other hand, continued to seek a moderate regime that was not the old extreme democracy and that limited active participation in the state to men of property but was very far from the decarchies and tight oligarchies Lysander desired.[120] How could the Athenian negotiator persuade the Spartan commander, at the height of his power and reputation, to yield any concessions in this matter?

One answer may lie in the potential weakness of Lysander's political situation in Sparta. Although he was more powerful and highly regarded than any other Spartan, that very fact created danger. The young King Pausanias' entire career would show him to be an enemy of Spartan imperialism and a champion of traditional Spartan values and policies.[121] He was certain to oppose Lysander's policies and also to be jealous of the power and fearful of the ambition of so powerful a subject. Even Agis, who had collaborated with Lysander and favored a more aggressive policy, was bound to be jealous and resentful. The ancient writers testify to these feelings of envy on the part of both kings and to their fear of Lysander's power and ambition. In fact, in 403, the two kings joined forces to deprive Lysander of the command of the Spartan army sent to restore order in Athens, an act that led to the fall of Lysander's friends and the restoration of the democracy.[122] That happened more than a year after Theramenes' conversations with Lysander, but the feelings that lay behind it must have been obvious already. Theramenes could argue that Lysander's political opponents in Sparta might not agree to the establishment of a narrow oligarchy

---

[120]W. J. McCoy, *YCS* XXIV (1975), 131–145, especially 137; Krentz, *Thirty*, 36–37. Those who insist on seeing Theramenes as plotting an oligarchy and collaborating with extremists such as Critias to establish one must face the fact that he took many personal risks to bring down the oligarchy of the Four Hundred, establishing a moderate regime as soon as he could, and that he lost his life when he was a member of the Thirty by resisting the attempts of the extremists to establish a true oligarchy in Athens.

[121]Hamilton, *Sparta's Bitter Victories*, 82–83.

[122]Xen. 2.4.29.

in Athens that would be as subservient to him as the decarchies were throughout the empire. Insistence on that point might bring on a political struggle in which Lysander would drive the two kings together against him. Instead, Theramenes could offer to accept the return of the political exiles friendly to Lysander and to include them in a government that was moderate, docile, and friendly to Sparta and to Lysander and was broadly based and popular enough not to cause an immediate and embarrassing resistance, perhaps even a civil war among the Athenians.[123]

The outcome of the discussion was probably an agreement to include in the peace treaty a provision for the return of exiles and a clause specifying that Athens could retain the *patrios politeia*, the ancestral constitution. The term was imprecise and deliberately so. Its meaning lay in the ears of each listener. To most, it would denote the full democracy that had existed with only brief interruptions since the reforms of Ephialtes in 462. To others, it would bring to mind still older and more moderate forms of democracy between the reforms of Cleisthenes in 508 and those of Ephialtes. Some would think of the Solonian constitution of the sixth century, and a few might even think of the dimly remembered days of Draco's laws in the seventh century.[124] Theramenes, no doubt, believed that the term would be defined by those who held political power immediately after the peace and expected himself and his friends to be the leaders of that group. Lysander, on the other hand, must have thought that since real power remained in his hands, he could define the term as he liked after the conclusion of peace.[125]

It is possible that Theramenes had still another argument to help persuade Lysander to support concessions. In part, the Spartan commander's strength lay in his support within Sparta but even more, perhaps, on the financial and military support given him by Cyrus and the promise of future support from him based on their close personal association. After Aegospotami, however, Cyrus' current influence and future prospects came into serious question. Even before the battle he had been recalled from his command in Asia Minor in response to the complaints of his enemies.[126] When he reached his father's

[123]Krentz, *Thirty*, 40.
[124]McCoy, *YCS* XXIV (1975), 139–141; A. Fuks, *The Ancestral Constitution* (London, 1953); M. I. Finley, *The Ancestral Constitution* (Cambridge, 1971).
[125]McCoy, *YCS* XXIV (1975), 139.
[126]Xen. *Hell.* 1.8–9.

side in Media, he found the Great King gravely ill. We know that he would die in March of 404.[127] So the seriousness of the illness must have been apparent, and news of it must have reached the Greeks by the winter of 405/4. The death of Darius II would bring to the Persian throne Artaxerxes II, the older brother and bitter rival of Cyrus. That would mean an end to Cyrus' command in Asia Minor, as we know it did, and his power to aid Lysander. The new Persian monarch might revert to the policy of playing Sparta off against Athens or might even support Athens against Sparta, which was rapidly becoming the new imperial power in the Aegean. Such developments would hardly bring Athens victory, but they could help Athens hold out until it secured even better terms. They would also undercut Lysander's importance. His own interests lay in obtaining an Athenian surrender while he was still in command, at the height of his influence. The glory of defeating Athens must be his, and a compromise on the terms proposed by Theramenes would not be too much to ask to achieve it.

Perhaps the knowledge of the state of affairs in Persia was the "something of great value" to which Theramenes had referred.[128] Perhaps it was that as well as his knowledge of Lysander's precarious position in Spartan politics. In any case, when Theramenes finally returned to Athens about the beginning of March, he brought news of important, indeed vital, concessions he had won. To be sure, Athens must give up its empire, walls, and fleet, and it must receive its exiles. However, the city and its people would be spared and would enjoy autonomy under the ancestral constitution. We need not be surprised that this report persuaded the Athenians to place Theramenes at the head of the delegation that must go to Sparta to make the formal peace with Sparta and its allies.

At Sparta the Corinthians, Thebans, and many others urged the destruction of Athens. Erianthus, the Theban commander at Aegospotami, is said on this occasion to have proposed the enslavement of the Athenians, the leveling of the city, and the conversion of Attica

---

[127] Krentz, *Thirty*, 32, n. 8.

[128] That is the view of Krentz (*Thirty*, 36–41), whose interesting ideas about the significance of the imminent death of Darius I have followed here. He also suggests that Theramenes may have stayed with Lysander for so long not to make the Athenians surrender but for precisely the opposite reason: to prevent them from surrendering in hopes that Darius would die and change the situation. My own view is that the delay was needed for the difficult negotiations and, perhaps, to allow time for the question to be put to the oracle at Delphi and the response to arrive at Sparta.

into pastureland.[129] Before the congress ever met, however, Lysander had sent a message to the ephors, telling them of his discussion with Theramenes.[130] It will have said that he had changed his mind and no longer favored the destruction of Athens, which would only strengthen Thebes at Spartan expense. We may assume that the ephors and both kings agreed with his judgment or at least did not oppose it, for we hear of no dispute among the Spartans. On the contrary, they seem to have vied with each other to produce fair-sounding reasons for sparing Athens. Xenophon reports that they made a gallant reference to Athens' service in the Persian Wars, refusing to enslave "a Greek city that had done great good when the greatest dangers threatened Greece."[131] Justin tells us that they refused "to pluck out one of Greece's two eyes."[132] After the rhetoric had subsided, the Spartans proposed a peace on these terms: the long walls and the walls protecting the Piraeus were to be destroyed; Lysander, as the Spartan commander on the spot, would determine how many ships Athens could keep; the exiles were to return; the Athenians were to leave all of the cities but keep their own land; Athens would be governed by its ancestral constitution; the Athenians were to have the same friends and enemies as the Spartans and follow them wherever they might lead on land or sea.[133]

Theramenes and his colleagues brought this peace back to an Athens anxiously awaiting their news. By now many were starving, and a great crowd gathered around the ambassadors in fear that the Spartans had refused to make an agreement and would insist on surrender without condition. Only a few years later some Athenians, forgetting the circumstances, or choosing to forget them, condemned the peace as part of a plot to subvert the democracy, insisting that a better peace could have been made.[134] At the time, however, the chief concern of most Athenians was not for their constitution but for their city and their lives. They worried not about a better peace treaty but about no peace treaty at all and the starvation, slavery, or exile that absence of

[129]Xen. 2.2.19; Plut. *Lys.* 15.2; Paus. 10.9.9.
[130]Xen. 2.2.16.
[131]Xen. 2.2.20.
[132]5.8.4.
[133]Xen. 2.2.20; Diod. 13.107.4, 14.3.2; Plut. *Lys.* 14.4.; Lys. 13.14; *Ath. Pol.* 34.3. I do not accept the clause (reported only by Andocides [3.12]) that mentions Lemnos, Imbros, and Scyros, chiefly because no one else mentions it.
[134]Lys. 13.15–16.

a treaty would mean. Even so, some Athenians resisted the kind of peace the ambassadors had brought from Sparta. During the months that Theramenes had been negotiating with the Spartans, at first alone and then with the other ambassadors, a fierce struggle had been going forward in Athens between those prepared to make peace and those who still wanted to resist. The chief resisters were passionate adherents of the full democracy like Cleophon, who knew that any peace agreed to at that time was certain to put an end to a thoroughly democratic constitution and bring back exiles bitterly hostile to it. Such men were certain to turn against the leading politicians of the extreme democratic faction. Without in any way casting doubt on the sincerity of the democratic leaders' devotion to their cause, we may, nonetheless, believe that the vehemence and tenacity of their resistance was increased by the knowledge of their likely fate after the peace.

Their opponents in Athens found it necessary not only to argue in favor of peace but also to remove its most able opponents, and during one of Theramenes' absences, they trumped up a charge against Cleophon, brought him to trial, and had him executed.[135] Even with the boldest resister gone, however, the opponents of peace did not give up. Some of the generals and taxiarchs and other citizens—Strombichides, Dionysodorus, and Eucrates among them—went to Theramenes to complain about the peace terms. The supporters of the peace, in fear that the assembly might be swayed, brought charges of plotting against the people against all of the resisters they could identify and had them imprisoned.[136] These actions were carried through with remarkable and, perhaps, unconstitutional swiftness, for on the day after the arrival of Theramenes and his colleagues, the Athenian assembly met to consider Sparta's terms of peace.[137] Theramenes spoke on behalf of the ambassadors in favor of accepting the offer. Even at this last moment, when the outcome was inevitable, some Athenians voted against the proposal. The great majority, however, voted in favor. On that day in March 404, just twenty-seven years "and a few days over," as Thucydides says, the great war between the Athenian Empire and the Spartan Alliance came to an end.[138] Not long afterward, on the sixteenth day of the Athenian month Munychion, toward the end of

[135]Xen. 1.7.35; Lys. 13.12, 30.10–14. Krentz, *Thirty*, 36, n. 23.
[136]Lys. 13.13–20, 47–48, 84; 18.5.
[137]For a defense of this very crowded account of events, which derives from combining Lysias with Xenophon, see Krentz, *Thirty*, 43, n. 35.
[138]5.26.1–3.

March, Lysander sailed into the harbor at the Piraeus to carry out the terms of the peace, and the exiles returned to begin what they thought would be a new era in Athenian history. Soon the Peloponnesians set to work destroying the defenses that the Athenians had thrown up so hurriedly three-quarters of a century earlier to give them security and independence and allowed them to organize their naval empire with or without Spartan approval. Their allies crowned themselves with garlands, danced, and rejoiced.[139] "With great zeal," Xenophon tells us, "they set about tearing down the walls to the music of flute-girls, thinking that this day was the beginning of freedom for Hellas."[140]

[139]Plut. *Lys.* 15.4.
[140]2.2.23.

16. Conclusions

The irony of Xenophon's words would have been evident to many who observed Athens' surrender. Many Greek cities in Asia Minor were back in the hands of the Persians, soon to become pawns in the conflict for power between Tissaphernes and Cyrus.[1] Others were already under Lysander's domination. Not long after the Athenian surrender, the Spartan government established a naval empire in the Aegean, imposing narrow oligarchies, Spartan garrisons and governors, and tribute on the former subjects of the Athenian Empire.[2] So ended Sparta's crusade to bring freedom and autonomy to the Greeks.

There were other ironies as well. The defeat of Athens threatened at one time to destroy it and its people entirely and was certainly expected to end its democratic constitution, its power, its ability to dominate others, and even its capacity to conduct an independent foreign policy, but it failed to do any of those things for long. Within a year the Athenians had regained their democracy, complete and untrammeled. Within a decade the Athenians had recovered their fleet, walls, and independence, and Athens was a central member in a coalition of states fighting to prevent Sparta from interfering in the rest of Greece. Within a quarter-century they had regained many of their former allies and had restored their power to the point where it is possible to speak of a "Second Athenian Empire."

The Spartans, on the other hand, did not find victory an unmixed

---

[1] Xen. *Anab.* 1.1.6–7.
[2] C. D. Hamilton, *Sparta's Bitter Victories* (Ithaca, N.Y., and London, 1979), 57; Diod. 14.3.4, 10.1–2, 13.1; Plut. *Lys.* 14.1.

blessing. Within a few years they were compelled to abandon their empire and its tribute but not before enough money had made its way into their state to help undermine its traditional discipline and institutions. Instead of achieving triumphant unity and greater safety for themselves, the Spartiates were quickly faced with plots that threatened their constitution and their very existence. Instead of winning the gratitude and respect of their allies, they soon had to fight a major war against a combination of former allies and former enemies that held them in check within the Peloponnesus and from which they were able to emerge intact only through the intervention of Persia. For a short time they clung to a kind of hegemony over their fellow Greeks but only as long as the Persian king wanted them to do so. Within three decades of their great victory, the Spartans were defeated by the Thebans in a major land battle, and their power was destroyed forever.

The costs of so long a war involving so many states was immense. The loss of life from a collection of causes related to the war varied from one city to another, but in some places it was devastating. Population figures barely exist outside of Athens,[3] but loss of life was clearly heavy and surely unprecedented in the Greek experience. Some states, such as Melos and Scione, had their entire male populations wiped out. Others, like Plataea, lost a great many of their men. A decade after the end of the war, the population of Athenian male adults may have been about half its size at the start of the war.[4] The Athenians probably suffered higher casualties in proportion to their population than other states; they alone suffered from the plague that took away perhaps a third of their population. Still, the consequences of a long war—that is, poverty, malnutrition, and diseases other than the great plague, accompanied by devastation of the land and interference with trade—must have contributed to Athens' suffering, and other states suffered from these things as well. Megara saw its fields devastated year after year and its commerce cut off almost entirely for many years. "The war had left Megara decimated and impoverished." Her diminished population required an increase in the reliance on slave labor to restore the city's prosperity.[5] Corinth, a city that likewise depended on trade for a considerable portion of its prosperity, was

[3]For an excellent discussion of Athenian population figures and their meaning, see B. S. Strauss, "Division and Conquest: Athens, 403–386 B.C." (Ph.D. diss., Yale University, 1979), 71–91.

[4]Ibid., 89.

[5]R. P. Legon, *Megara* (Ithaca, N.Y., and London, 1981), 256, 258–259, 279–282.

able to send 5,000 hoplites to Plataea in 479 but could provide only 3,000 to Nemea to defend its own territory in 394.[6] Some of the decline, but surely not all, can be explained by social and economic changes that deprived men of the wealth they needed to serve as hoplites. If only half of the decline was caused by a fall in the population, that would imply a decline in the number of adult males of some 20 percent in less than a century. Sparta's population also declined during the war, although this was not caused by great losses in battle or extensive economic damage but appears to be part of a continuing decline related to its peculiar social and economic institutions.[7] The hardships of war, however, direct or indirect, took a toll in human life throughout the Greek world from Sicily to the Bosporus.

Economic damage, too, was severe in many places. The loss of its empire put an end to Athens' great public wealth and with it the extraordinary building programs of the fifth century. Agricultural damage took many years to repair. Megara suffered severely from repeated destruction of its fields, and so, too, did the Aegean islands that were subjected to frequent ravaging. Corinth, Megara, and Sicyon, Isthmian states for whom commerce was important, were shut off from trade with the Aegean for almost three decades, and during most of the same time their trade with the West was at least severely curtailed. The ready availability of Greeks as mercenary soldiers after the war, especially from the Peloponnesus, also shows that poverty was widespread.

The dangers and hardships of war heightened factional strife. Thucydides' chilling accounts of the terrible effects of civil war, at first in Corcyra and then in the rest of Greece, need no comment, and those of Xenophon and Diodorus show that such horrors became more commonplace as the war proceeded until "almost all Greece was moved"

---

[6]Plataea: Hdt. 9.28; Nemea: Xen. 4.2.17. J. B. Salmon (*Wealthy Corinth* [Oxford, 1984], 165–169) argues that Corinthian population did not decline during the war. He explains the decline of the number of hoplites to 3,000 at Nemea, where the battle was fought almost within sight of the city of Corinth, by assuming that the young and old men stayed in Corinth "to defend the city in case of defeat" (166) and that some pro-Spartan Corinthians "who were called up for the Nemea may have declined to turn out" (167). Those are rather desperate attempts at an argument, for the sources say nothing of either assumption; yet both actions would be unusual, if not unprecedented.

[7]For a useful discussion of Spartan population decline see P. Cartledge, *Sparta and Lakonia* (London, 1979), 307–318.

by violent and vicious conflicts between democrats and oligarchs.[8] Anger, frustration, and the desire for vengeance were passions that increased as the war dragged on, and they produced a progression of atrocities that reached the point of maiming and killing captured opponents, throwing them into pits to die of thirst, starvation, and exposure, hurling them into the sea to drown, enslaving and killing women and children, and destroying cities with their entire populations. This war, more than most, was "a violent teacher."[9]

The collapse of ethical standards in war and politics was accompanied by the breakdown even of the powerful ties of family and of the most sacred religious observances. There can be no doubt that the war and its effects deepened, broadened, and hastened the questioning of the traditional values on which classical Greek society rested and in the process further divided society. Some responded by rejecting all faith in favor of a skeptical or even cynical rationality, whereas others tried to return to a more archaic and less rational piety. The defeat of Athens in the war was a blow to the prospects for democracy in the Greek cities. The influence of political systems on people outside them is closely connected with their success in foreign relations and especially in war. When Athens was powerful and successful, its democratic constitution had a magnetic effect on other states, providing a model for others even in the heart of the Peloponnesus. Its defeat in the war against Sparta was taken as proof of its inadequacy; Athenian errors were seized upon as democratic errors; ordinary human mistakes and misfortunes were seen as peculiar consequences of democracy. It is probably correct to see the Spartan victory over the democratic coalition in Mantinea in 418 "as the turning point in the political development of Greece" that sent it in the direction of oligarchy rather than democracy, but the final defeat of Athens guaranteed the result.[10]

In spite of its apparently decisive outcome, the war did not establish a stable balance of power to replace the uneasy one that had evolved after the end of the Persian War. The great Peloponnesian War was not the type of war that, for all of its costs, creates a new order that permits general peace for a generation or more. The peace treaty of 404 reflected a temporary growth of Spartan influence far beyond its normal strength. The Spartans' resources—human, material, and po-

[8]3.81.1.
[9]3.82.2.
[10]Busolt, *GG* III:2, 1251.

litical—were not adequate to maintain the empire they had acquired or even to control events outside the Peloponnesus for long. Their attempts brought division and weakness to their own state and to the rest of Greece. Athens, on the other hand, was potentially much stronger than the position assigned her by the peace. Once Athens had been spared, it was natural that Athenian power would once again become considerable.

The settlement of 404 was neither a "Punic Peace" that permanently destroyed Athenian power nor a moderate, negotiated settlement that softened hard feelings. No sooner was Athens free than its people and leaders began to plan for the return of the empire, with associated power, glory, and resistance to Spartan domination of the Greek states. Like Germany after the First World War, Athens in 404 was disarmed but unappeased. Keeping it disarmed would require strength, commitment, cooperation, and unity of purpose not possessed by the victorious powers. Theban ambition had already grown to the point of demanding parity with the leading states and, after a while, hegemony. Sparta's vain attempts at domination brought only division and weakness that soon put an end to Greek power and subjected the Greeks to the control of outsiders, first to the interventions of Persia and then to conquest by Macedonia. It is both legitimate and instructive to think of what we call the Peloponnesian War as "the great war between Athens and Sparta," as one scholar has designated it.[11] Like the European war from 1914 to 1918 to which the title the "Great War" was applied by an earlier generation that knew only one, it was a tragic event; a great turning point in history; the end of an era of progress, prosperity, confidence, and hope; and the beginning of a darker time.

The vast and bleak consequences of the war lead us to look back upon it and wonder whether its course and outcome might have been different. The answers to such questions are not available to the historian in his professional role, but the search for them is irresistible to anyone who has a normal curiosity and hopes that history may reward its devoted students with a degree of understanding and even wisdom. In earlier volumes we have asked whether the war might have been avoided entirely and whether different strategies or changes in leadership might have produced different results. It remains here to ask why the last phase of the war, after the Sicilian campaign, produced a total victory for the Spartans and whether another outcome was

[11]B. W. Henderson, *The Great War between Athens and Sparta* (London, 1927).

possible. Thucydides' answers to these questions seem to arise very clearly from his general remarks on the war: the fact that the Athenians held out for so long after the Sicilian affair is extraordinary; the Athenians "destroyed themselves" by means of internal disharmony.[12] The evidence we have examined, both in Thucydides' account and in that of those who continued the narrative, supports those opinions in general. Thucydides' language, however, is terse, and his precise meaning is far from clear, so we need to examine it more closely.

The Athenians' ability to hold out so long after the destruction of their forces in Sicily and the damage that it did to their prestige are truly remarkable. Thucydides makes the point to demonstrate the correctness of Pericles' predictions and the rightness of his strategy. We have argued, however, that Pericles' strategy was a failure and that Athenian resources would not have been adequate to last even through the Archidamian War had not his successors departed from that strategy.[13] Moreover, in another passage Thucydides tells us that the Athenians would have lost as early as 411 had not the Spartans shown themselves to be "the most convenient of all opponents."[14] Here, Thucydides seems on more solid ground, for after the campaign in Sicily, the prolongation of the war depended less on the excellent fighting qualities of the Athenians, although they were very important, than on the failure of their opponents. If the Spartans could persuade the Persians to make the commitment needed to provide a navy capable of defeating the Athenians and to maintain it as long as necessary, the Athenians would lose, for Athens lacked the financial resources to match the Persian treasury, and money was the essential element. Athenian hopes rested on dividing their opponents and defeating the enemy's fleets until the Persians became discouraged and lost interest. That they could do this for so long was a tribute to their naval skill, their courage, and their determination but, even more, to the Spartans' difficulties in gaining adequate and reliable Persian support.

In light of those difficulties and the shifting political situation that made Persian assistance unreliable, Thucydides was entirely right to suggest that the Athenians might have emerged from the war with a Periclean victory, that is, with their walls, their fleet, and their empire intact and with the Spartans in no position to challenge their continued

[12]2.65.12–13.
[13]Kagan, *Archidamian War*, 350–362.
[14]8.96.5.

possession of those things. It was only necessary to continue to inflict naval defeats on the Spartans until the political situation in Persia changed decisively. Had the Athenians defeated Lysander in the Hellespont in 405, or even averted defeat at that time, the decisive moment might have come in the spring of 404 with the death of Darius. That would have removed Cyrus from power and very probably put an end to adequate and reliable Persian support for Sparta. The new king might have been inclined to reject the policies and associates of his brother and rival; he might have reverted to his friend Tissaphernes' old policy of supporting the weaker against the stronger power while giving neither enough help for victory, or he might have lost interest in the Aegean entirely, as the Persians had largely done between the battle at the Eurymedon in the 460s and their intervention a half-century later.

Thucydides was also right to see internal strife as a major cause of the Athenian defeat, but here again, we must examine more precisely what this means. It does not mean that factional quarrels led to betrayals that cost Athens the war. We have no reason to believe that Thucydides accepted the allegations that blamed defeat at the battle of Aegospotami on treason. Moreover, it is worth noticing that the democratic regime that emerged from the most striking examples of factional strife—the oligarchic coup of 411, the moderate countercoup in the same year, and the reversion to complete democracy in 410—carried on the war more effectively than any since the Sicilian disaster. Those "private quarrels" certainly did not lead to the defeat of Athens.

Perhaps we may approach Thucydides' intentions by assuming that he refers to the factional and personal conflicts that led to the two expulsions of Alcibiades. It is certainly hard to believe that events could have gone as badly for the Athenians in Sicily had Alcibiades remained as one of the commanders, and if there had been no Sicilian disaster, it is not likely that the allies would have dared rebel or the Persians intervene. Without these developments, the Athenians would not have lost the war. If that is what Thucydides means, we must agree with his judgment. His words, however, seem to refer to the period after the calamity in Sicily, to the Decelean or Ionian phase of the war. In that case, he would mean that the exile of Alcibiades after the battle of Notium was crucial for Athenian fortunes. If the implication is that Alcibiades' gifts as a military leader were vital to Athenian success, we cannot agree. The evidence is that Alcibiades was a commander of considerable ability, particularly in certain special areas such as the use of cavalry and combined operations on land and sea. He was also a skillful diplomat, adept at combining statecraft with military operations. He was, however, capable of important errors and serious miscalculations. In Italy and Sicily he failed to recognize that the large size to which the Athenian expedition had grown undermined the diplomatic scheme on which his strategy rested. There is no evidence that he had conceived of a practical substitute plan before he fled into exile or that he would have done so had he remained. His finest moment was at Cyzicus, but as we have argued, the key figure there was not Alcibiades but Thrasybulus. At Notium he made a serious error in leaving his fleet in the hands of an inexperienced commander facing the main enemy force, and the Athenians were right to be angry with him. Alcibiades was no military genius but a talented soldier of the second rank whose confidence and ambitions went far beyond his ability. Moreover, whatever contribution he might make as a soldier was undermined by the divisive part he played in Athenian politics. In itself, then, the removal of Alcibiades did not contribute decisively to the Athenian defeat.

The personal rivalries, factional disputes, and general distrust that swirled around this unique figure in Athenian life did cause his city great harm and had much to do with Athens' loss of the war. The most serious consequence of Alcibiades' disgrace was that it removed his friends and associates from influence and command when their military and political skills were most needed. Theramenes and Thrasybulus were not among the generals during the last two years of the war and so were not in command at the battle of Arginusae or Aegospotami. Theramenes had commanded his ships with skill and success from 411 to 407; Thrasybulus had been responsible for Athens' greatest naval victories in the war. By 407 Thrasybulus, especially, had gained the success and experience that would allow him to command the largest fleets with confidence and authority. It is hard to believe, had he and Theramenes been generals at the battle of Arginusae instead of only trierarchs, that the Athenians would have suffered from the indecisiveness resulting from inexperienced and divided command. It is inconceivable, had they served as commanders at Aegospotami, that they would have permitted the discipline of the Athenian fleet to deteriorate or have made the tactical and strategic errors that contributed to the final defeat. Had the political influence of the two men not been destroyed by their association with the disgraced Alcibiades, they might have contributed a stability and moderation that Athens desperately needed. Theramenes was the leader of the Athenian moderates. Thrasybulus had the confidence of the democratic sailors and, no doubt, many of their friends. Under normal circumstances, they could have worked together to help produce unity in Athens. Instead, the events surrounding the fiasco after Arginusae embroiled them in a bitter controversy that further divided Athens and undermined their influence. We do not know what their views were in 406, but it is at least possible that they were among those who favored accepting the Spartan peace offer. If so, they lacked the political strength to win the argument, and the opportunity passed. Our investigations have led us to conclude that Athens' hope for victory or survival lay in the cooperative leadership of Theramenes and Thrasybulus, but the disgrace of Alcibiades removed them from the leading positions. In that very important sense, but in no other, the "private quarrels" that produced the disgrace of Alcibiades led to the defeat of Athens.

It is by no means clear whether Thucydides had in mind the removal of Theramenes and Thrasybulus, and one of the many reasons we have for regretting his failure to complete his account of the war is that we will never know. In any case, the modern student of the Peloponnesian War, with the full advantage of hindsight and the experience of twenty-five centuries of history, may suggest still other reasons for the Athenian failure. One, we have argued, was the solitary, but effective, decision of Phrynichus to refuse to engage the Spartan navy off Miletus in 412. At that place and time, the Athenians had the chance to stamp out the rebellion in the Aegean before it had spread too far and reached the Hellespont, before the Persians had become deeply involved, and before the Spartans had found an effective leader like Lysander. The opportunity was great enough to justify considerable risk, but in fact, the risk was not unduly great.[15] We should not be surprised that the Athenians later blamed Phrynichus for this decision and removed him from office as a result. What does cause surprise is Thucydides' rare and vehement defense of Phrynichus against his critics.[16]

The failure to fight a potentially decisive naval battle at Miletus, however, was not the only lost opportunity for Athens. We have seen that during the last phase of the war the Spartans offered peace on

[15]See above, 65–68.
[16]8.27.5–6.

two occasions, and we have suggested that on at least one occasion, after the battle of Arginusae, the Athenians would have been well advised to accept. Had they done so, they would certainly have averted defeat in 405, and the death of Darius in the next year might well have removed the threat to the Athenian Empire for a very long time. Why, then, did the Athenians reject the opportunity? It is easy enough to point to the influence of demagogues and to denounce the foolishness and volatility of the Athenian democracy, but there were skillful demagogues like Hyperbolus in Athens in 421, and the city was no less democratic then; yet the Athenians made peace, swiftly followed by a treaty of alliance with Sparta. Moreover, if we have judged the situations rightly, there was a much better argument for peace in 406 than in 421. It was precisely the failure of that peace and the disappointment and suspicion it caused that may help explain the Athenians' refusal to accept a negotiated peace when it might have been much more advantageous.

In 421 the Athenians abandoned the war just when circumstances were about to give them great advantages and opportunities.[17] When the Spartans failed to carry out the terms of the peace, the Athenians tried to save it by making an alliance with the Spartans and returning their prisoners, one of Athens' most valuable assets. They did these things because they were tired of war and so eager to maintain the peace that they were persuaded to run some risks and give up tangible advantages for a chance to preserve it. The results were disappointing and infuriating. Sparta did not return Amphipolis, and the Boeotians did not restore Panactum intact.[18] The Athenians were convinced that they had been deliberately deceived by the Spartans and soon made alliances that kept hostilities alive. The memory of these events was burnt into the minds of the Athenians, most of whom were thereafter certain that the Spartans were not to be trusted. That memory played a vital part in leading them to reject Spartan offers of peace later, when acceptance would have been advantageous. The advocates of peace in 421 allowed their eagerness to achieve it stand in the way of objective assessments of reality and sound policy. Had they insisted on the fulfillment of commitments and on actions rather than words, they might have compelled the Spartans to meet their obligations, thereby establishing the basis for a lasting peace. Failing that, at least they

---

[17]See Kagan, *Archidamian War*, 333–349.
[18]Kagan, *Peace of Nicias*, 17–32.

would not have sacrificed Athenian interests for no return and destroyed the basis for negotiations in the future. At the time, their desperate longing for peace at almost any price disastrously undermined later prospects for peace by negotiation and, still more, for a victorious peace.

Also, it seems possible that the Athenians, at one point at least during the long course of the war, had the opportunity to achieve a complete victory that would have made their empire secure by ridding them of the perpetual threat posed by Sparta's suspicion and envy. That point was in 418, in the campaign that concluded with the battle of Mantinea. A Spartan defeat on that occasion was a very real possibility although their army numbered about a thousand hoplites more than the enemy. The Athenians might have made an appropriate effort, and sent the 4,000 hoplites they used against Epidaurus in 430 instead of the 1,000 who fought at Mantinea, and perhaps, they might have distracted the enemy and forced it to keep greater forces at home by launching simultaneous raids against the Laconian coast with their navy and using their Messenian allies on a raid from Pylos. It seems more than likely, then, that the Spartans would have been beaten and the results of Leuctra anticipated by almost half a century. But they failed to do these things in part because the culmination of the policy of alliance against Sparta came at a time when power was in the hands of its opponents. It is fair to say, however, that a policy of engagement on land and confrontation with the Spartans in a battle of hoplites was not one with which most Athenians felt comfortable.

The Peloponnesian War was one of those classic confrontations between a great land power and a great naval power. Each entered the war hoping and expecting to keep to its own element and to win a victory in a way that conformed to its strength at a relatively low cost. Within a few years events showed that victory would not be possible in that way for either side. To win, each had to acquire the capacity to fight and succeed on the other's favorite domain. The Athenian defeat in Sicily gave the Spartans the opportunity to succeed by making an alliance with Persia. After many failures, they won the war by defeating the Athenian fleet. There was no other way to win. To win a true victory rather than a Periclean stand-off, the Athenians would have had to find a way to defeat the Spartans on land. Their own army could never have done that alone, but divisions in the Spartan alliance and the expiration of the Argive treaty in 421 offered them the forces that could bring victory. Nicias and the other advocates of peace and alliance with Sparta, however, rejected the opportunity. The Athenian response to Spartan behavior drove them from power and set Athens on the path that could end the war by defeating Sparta on land in the Peloponnesus, but the policy designed by Pericles and continued by Nicias had become Athens' natural policy. A more aggressive one that meant fighting on land but did not bring a quick victory could not be sustained for long by a democratic Athens that had grown accustomed to war at low risk and small cost in lives. By the time the new policy urged by Alcibiades came to a crisis, the old forces under Nicias were again dominant; men who shared his view were the generals, and they carried out the more aggressive strategy without boldness and conviction, glad to escape disaster as the new policy was destroyed. After the defeat at Mantinea, Nicias and his associates were pleased to return to the simulacrum of peace, although real peace remained an illusion, for Athens and Sparta continued to view each other with suspicion and hostility.

The destruction of the Sicilian expedition was a crucial turning point in the war and made a powerful and lasting impression on all Athenians. A terrible mistake in the form it finally took, it convinced Thucydides of the folly of any offensive action and led him to endorse the defensive and naval strategy with which Pericles began the war as the only reasonable one. His own account, however, reveals that such a strategy was unable to achieve even the limited victory that Pericles envisioned, much less a victory that would deprive the enemy of the capacity to fight made necessary by Spartan determination. For that, the Athenians would have to take the offensive, face the need for a major battle on land, and find a way and a time to win it. The way was provided by the alliance with Argos, Elis, and Mantinea and the time was 418, but the Athenians shrank from the commitment needed to win. Such a response is entirely understandable in a state that had come to think of itself as an invulnerable island since its acquisition of a fleet, a vast treasury, and defensible walls. It had developed a unique and enviable way of fighting that used these advantages and avoided much of the danger and unpleasantness of ordinary warfare. It allowed the Athenians to concentrate their forces quickly and attack the enemy before it was prepared; it permitted them to strike others without danger to their own city and population. Success in this style of warfare—in which offensive actions were taken only at sea or launched from the sea, costing little in lives or damage to their own property—made it seem the only one necessary, and defeats with great losses on land made the Athenians reluctant to risk other land battles.[19] Offensive actions should be taken only at sea or launched from the sea. The great Cimon had fought on those principles, winning victory after victory without great loss and without defeat. Pericles, therefore, simply carried previous trends to their logical conclusion when he committed the Athenians strictly to what we may call "the Athenian way of warfare."[20]

Cimon, however, pursued a policy that complemented his strategy. He maintained friendly relations with powers that were superior in hoplites and not vulnerable to defeat by sea power. Pericles would have liked to do the same, but when his attempts to deter war failed, he reverted to the traditional strategy, taking it even one step further by refusing to use a land army even in defense. That left him with no hope of disabling the enemy but only of punishing the Spartans and their allies to a greater or lesser degree and discouraging them from continuing the fight. The nature of the enemy made "the Athenian way of warfare" inadequate, and Pericles' strategy was a form of wishful thinking that failed.

For a state like Periclean Athens in 431, satisfied with its situation, not wishing to expand but merely to protect what it has and capable of keeping an enemy at bay, the temptation to stand on the defensive and avoid the risks of offensive actions is great. Such a plan has much to recommend it, but it also has important dangers. It tends to create a rigid way of thinking that we might call "the cult of the defensive."[21] Such a cast of mind leads men to apply a previously successful strategy to a situation in which it is not adequate, but it may have other disadvantages as well. Its capacity to deter potential enemies from provoking a war is severely limited. Deterrence by standing behind a strong defensive position and thereby depriving an enemy of the prospect of victory assumes a high degree of rationality and a strong imagination on his part. When the Spartans invaded Attica in 431, they must have thought that they were risking little. Even if the Athenians refused to fight, even if they persisted in that refusal for a long time, both of which seemed unlikely and unnatural, the Spartans would risk

[19]Such as those at Coronea in 446 (see Kagan, *Outbreak*, 123–124) and Delium in 424 (see Kagan, *Archidamian War*, 280–286).
[20]I adapt the term from B. Liddell Hart, *The British Way of Warfare* (London, 1932).
[21]I adapt the term from what some modern students have called "the cult of the offensive," which dominated European military circles in the years before the First World War.

little more than time and effort. In any case, their own city and lands would be safe. Had the Athenians possessed the capacity to strike the Spartans where they were most vulnerable, and had that capacity been obvious to all, Pericles' strategy of deterrence might have been more effective.

Once the war started, the "cult of the defensive" dissuaded the Athenians from doing what was necessary for victory. Years of success at little cost to human life had made them reluctant to accept the risk and the cost demanded by a new situation in which the traditional strategy was not appropriate. They lost their best opportunity in 418, only to make a much greater investment and undertake greater risks in the Sicilian expedition three years later. It is tempting to see a connection between the two events. Perhaps the outcome of the battle of Mantinea discredited the cautious traditional policy, encouraging a bolder, more aggressive spirit that was then inappropriately and disastrously applied to a campaign of only marginal importance. After the affair in Sicily the Athenians could only try to hold out until the Spartans' incapacities and internal divisions led them to offer some kind of acceptable peace. Even then, distrust of the Spartans and confidence in their own naval superiority led the Athenians to reject their only remaining hope of avoiding defeat. But the treasury on which Athenian naval power relied was exhausted, and political quarrels had deprived the Athenians of their best commanders. The Spartans, on the other hand, with the support of Persian money and led by the shrewd Lysander, had learned how to fight at sea well enough to win. The greatest irony of all may be that the swift, aggressive, innovative Athenians described by the Corinthians before the war proved less able to adjust to a different way of fighting than the slow, traditional, unimaginative Spartans they also described. Perhaps the Corinthians' evaluation was not entirely right. At any rate, the Athenian experience in the Peloponnesian War suggests that in warfare democracies, where everything must be debated in the open and relatively uninformed majorities persuaded, may find it harder to adjust to the necessities of war than other, less open societies. Perhaps that is what Thucydides had in mind when he connected the Athenian defeat with the death of Pericles, who alone among Athenian politicians could persuade the people to fight in a way contrary to their prejudices and experiences.

Bibliography

Adeleye, G. "Critias: Member of the Four Hundred?" *TAPA* CIV (1974), 1–9.

Amit, M. *Athens and the Sea.* Brussels, 1965.

———. "Le traité de Chalcedoine entre Pharnabaze et les stratèges athéniens." *LAC* XLII (1973), 436–457.

———. "The Disintegration of the Athenian Empire in Asia Minor (412–405 B.C.E.)." *SCI* II (1975), 38–71.

———. "La campagne d'Ionie de 407/6 et la bataille de Notion." *Grazer Beiträge* III (1975), 1–13.

Andrewes, A. "The Generals in the Hellespont, 410–407 B.C." *JHS* LXXIII (1953), 2–9.

———. "Lysias and the Theramenes Papyrus." *ZPE* VI (1970), 35–38.

———. "Thucydides and the Persians." *Historia* X (1971), 1–18.

———. "Androtion and the Four Hundred." *PCPS* XXII (1976), 14–25.

———. "Notion and Kyzikos: The Sources Compared." *JHS* CII (1982), 15–25.

Avery, H. C. "Critias and the Four Hundred." *CP* LVIII (1963), 165–167.

Barber, G. L. *The Historian Ephorus.* London, 1935.

———. "Oxyrhynchus, The Historian from." *Oxford Classical Dictionary.* 2d ed. Oxford, 1970.

Barron, J. P. *The Silver Coins of Samos.* London, 1966.

Beloch, K. J. *Die Attische Politik seit Perikles.* Leipzig, 1884.

———. *Die Bevölkerung der griechisch-römischen Welt.* Leipzig, 1885.

———. *Griechische Geschichte.* 2d ed. Strassburg, Berlin, and Leipzig, 1912–1927.

Bilabel, F. "Die Ionische Kolonisation." *Philologus* suppl. 14 (1920).

Blamire, A. "Epilycus' Negotiations with Persia." *Phoenix* XXIX (1975), 21–26.

Bloedow, E. F. *Alcibiades Reexamined.* Wiesbaden, 1973.

Bokisch, G. "*Harmostai.*" *Klio* XLVI (1965), 129–239.

Bommelaer, J.-F. *Lysandre de Sparte.* Paris, 1981.

Bradeen, D. W. "The Popularity of the Athenian Empire." *Historia* IX (1960), 257–269.
Breitenbach, H. R. "Die Seeschlacht bei Notion (407/6)." *Historia* XX (1971), 152–171.
Bruce, I. A. F. *An Historical Commentary on the* Hellenica Oxyrhynchia. Cambridge, 1967.
Brunt, P. A. "Thucydides and Alcibiades." *REG* LXV (1952), 59–96.
Buchanan, J. J. *Theorika*. Locust Valley, N.Y., 1962.
Busolt, G. *Griechische Geschichte*. 3 vols. Gotha, 1893–1904.
Cartledge, P. *Sparta and Lakonia*. London, 1979.
———. "The Politics of Spartan Pederasty." *PCPS* XXVII (1981), 17–38.
Casson, L. *Ships and Seamanship in the Ancient World*. Princeton, N.J., 1971.
Cavaignac, E. "Les dekarchies de Lysandre." *Revue des études historiques* XC (1924), 285–316.
Cloché, P. "L'affaire des Arginuses (406 avant J.C.)." *Revue historique* CXXX (1919), 5–68.
———. "Le Conseil athénien des Cinq Cents et les partis." *REG* XXXV (1922), 269–295.
Connor, W. R. *The New Politicians of Fifth-Century Athens*. Princeton, N.J., 1971.
Cook, J. M. *The Persian Empire*. New York, 1983.
Davies, J. K. *Athenian Propertied Families*. Oxford, 1971.
De Laix, R. A. *Probouleusis at Athens*. Berkeley, Calif., 1973.
Delebecque, E. *Thucydide et Alcibiade*. Aix-en-Provence, 1965.
———. "Une fable d'Alcibiade sur le mythe d'une flotte." *Études classiques* II (1967): Ann. Fac. Lettres Aix-en-Provence, XLIII, 13–31.
De Sanctis, G. "La battaglia di Notion." *Riv. fil.* IX (1931), 222–229.
———. *Studi di storia della storiografia greca*. Florence, 1951.
Donini, G. *La posizione di Tucidide verso il governo dei cinquemila*. Turin, 1969.
Eddy, S. K. "The Cold War between Athens and Persia, Ca. 448–412 B.C." *CP* LXVIII (1973), 241–258.
Ehrenberg, V. *Sophocles and Pericles*. Oxford, 1954.
Ehrhart, C. "Xenophon and Diodorus on Aegospotami." *Phoenix* XXIV (1970), 225–228.
Ferguson, W. S. "The Constitution of Theramenes." *CP* XXI (1926), 72–75.
———. *The Treasurers of Athena*. Cambridge, Mass., 1932.
———. "The Oligarchical Movement in Athens." *CAH* V (1940), 312–347.
———. "The Fall of the Athenian Empire." *CAH* V (1940), 348–375.
Finley, M. I. *The World of Odysseus*. 2d ed. New York, 1964.
———. *The Ancestral Constitution*. Cambridge, 1971.
Fornara, C. *The Athenian Board of Generals*. Wiesbaden, 1971.
Forrest, W. G. "The Tribal Organization of Chios." *BSA* LV (1960), 172–189.
———. "The Date of the Pseudo-Xenophontic Athenaion Politeia." *Klio* LII (1970), 107–116.
———. "An Athenian Generation Gap." *YCS* XXIV (1973), 37–52.
Frisch, H. *The Constitution of the Athenians*. Copenhagen, 1942, rpt. New York, 1976.

Fuks, A. *The Ancestral Constitution*. London, 1953.

Gilbert, G. *Beiträge zur innern geschichte Athens im zeitalter des peloponnesischen Krieges*. Leipzig, 1877.

Glotz, G., and R. Cohen. *Histoire grecque*, vol. II. Paris, 1929.

Gomme, A. W. "Aristophanes and Politics." *CR* LII (1938), 97–109.

———. *The Population of Athens in the Fifth and Fourth Centuries* B.C. Chicago, 1967.

Gomme, A. W., A. Andrewes, and K. J. Dover. *A Historical Commentary on Thucydides*. 5 vols. Oxford, 1950–1981.

Grote, G. *A History of Greece*. 12 vols. New York, 1855.

Hamburger, J. *Macaulay and the Whig Tradition*. Chicago, 1976.

Hamilton, C. D. *Sparta's Bitter Victories*. Ithaca, N.Y., and London, 1979.

Harding, P. E. "The Theramenes Myth." *Phoenix* XXVIII (1974), 101–111.

Hasluck, F. W. *Cyzicus*. Cambridge, 1910.

Hatzfeld, J. "Notes sur la chronologie des Helléniques." *REA* XXV (1933), 387–395.

———. *Alcibiade: Etude sur l'histoire d'Athènes à la fin du Ve siècle*. 2d ed. Paris, 1951.

Henderson, B. W. *The Great War between Athens and Sparta*. London, 1927.

Henrichs, A. "Zur Interpretation des Michigan-Papyrus über Theramenes." *ZPE* III (1969), 101–108.

Herbst, L. *Die Schlacht bei den Arginusen*. Hamburg, 1855.

Hignett, C. *A History of the Athenian Constitution*. Oxford, 1952.

Hiller von Gaertringen, F. *Inscriptiones Graecae*, I: *Editio minor, Inscriptiones Atticae Euclidis anno anteriores*. Berlin, 1924.

Jacoby, F. *Die Fragmente der griechischen Historiker*. 3 vols. I–II, Berlin, 1923–1930; III, Leiden, 1940.

Jameson, M. "Sophocles and the Four Hundred." *Historia* XX (1971), 541–568.

Jones, A. H. M. *Athenian Democracy*. Oxford, 1969.

Jordan, B. *The Athenian Navy in the Classical Period*. Berkeley, Calif., 1975.

Kagan, Donald. *The Outbreak of the Peloponnesian War*. Ithaca, N.Y., and London, 1969.

———. *The Archidamian War*. Ithaca, N.Y., and London, 1974.

———. *The Peace of Nicias and the Sicilian Expedition*. Ithaca, N.Y., and London, 1981.

Kahrstedt, U. *Griechisches Staatsrecht*. Göttingen, 1922.

Koenen, L. "A New Fragment of the Oxyrhynchia Historian." *Studia Papyrologica* XV (1976), 55–76.

Krentz, P., *The Thirty at Athens*. Ithaca, N.Y., and London, 1982.

Lateiner, D. "Tissaphernes and the Phoenician Fleet (Thucydides 8.87)." *TAPA* CVI (1976), 281–288.

Legon, R. P. "Samos in the Delian League." *Historia* XXI (1972), 145–158.

———. *Megara*. Ithaca, N.Y., and London, 1981.

Lévy, E. *Athènes devant la défaite de 404, histoire d'une crise idéologique*. Paris, 1976.

Lewis, D. M. "Notes on Attic Inscriptions." *BSA* XLIX (1954), 29–31.

———. "The Phoenician Fleet in 411." *Historia* VII (1958), 392–397.
———. *Sparta and Persia*. Leiden, 1977.
Liddell Hart, B. *The British Way of Warfare*. London, 1932.
Littman, R. J. "The Strategy of the Battle of Cyzicus." *TAPA* XCIX (1968), 265–272.
Lotze, D. "Mothakes." *Historia* XI (1962), 427–435.
———. *Lysander und der Peloponnesische Krieg*. Berlin, 1964.
Luria, M. "Zum politischen Kampf in Sparta gegen Ende des 5 Jahrhunderts." *Klio* XXI (1927), 404–419.
McCoy, W. J. "Theramenes, Thrasybulus and the Athenian Moderates." Ph.D. diss. Yale University, 1970.
———. "Aristotle's *Athenaion Politeia* and the Establishment of the Thirty Tyrants." *YCS* XXIII (1975), 131–145.
———. "Thrasyllus." *AJP* XCVIII (1977), 264–289.
MacDowell, D. M. *The Law in Classical Athens*. Ithaca, N.Y., and London, 1978.
McGregor, M. F. "The Politics of the Historian Thucydides." *Phoenix* X (1956), 93–102.
———. "The Genius of Alcibiades." *Phoenix* XIX (1965), 27–46.
Meiggs, R. *The Athenian Empire*. Oxford, 1972.
Meiggs, R., and D. M. Lewis. *A Selection of Greek Historical Inscriptions to the End of the Fifth Century* B.C. Oxford, 1969.
Meritt, B. D. "Archelaos and the Decelean War." *Classical Studies Presented to Edward Capps*. Princeton, N.J., 1936, 246–253.
———. "The Chronology of the Peloponnesian War." *Proceedings of the American Philosophical Society* CXV (1971), 97–124.
Meritt, B. D., H. T. Wade-Gery, and M. F. McGregor. *The Athenian Tribute Lists*. 4 vols. I, Cambridge, Mass., 1939; II–IV, Princeton, 1949–1953.
Merkelbach, R., and H. C. Youtie. "Ein Michigan-Papyrus über Theramenes." *ZPE* II (1968), 161–169.
Meyer, E. *Forschungen zur alten Geschichte*, II. Halle, 1899.
———. *Geschichte des Altertums*. 5th ed. rpt. Basel, 1954 and 1956.
Morrison, J. S., and R. T. Williams. *Greek Oared Ships, 900–322* B.C. Cambridge, 1968.
Murray, O. 'Ο 'ΑΡΧΑΙΟΣ ΔΑΣΜΟΣ." *Historia* XV (1966), 142–156.
Oliva, P. *Sparta and Her Social Problems*. Amsterdam and Prague, 1971.
Olmstead, A. T. *A History of the Persian Empire*. Chicago, 1948.
Parke, H. W. "The Development of the Second Spartan Empire (405–371 B.C." *JHS* L (1930), 37–79.
———. *Festivals of the Athenians*. Ithaca, N.Y., and London, 1977.
Parke, H. W., and D. E. W. Wormell. *The Delphic Oracle*. 2 vols. Oxford, 1956.
Pédech, P. "Batailles navales dans les historiens grecs." *REG* LXXXII (1969), 43–55.
Pleket, H. W. "Thasos and the Popularity of the Athenian Empire." *Historia* XII (1963), 70–77.
Plutarch. *Lives*. Vols. 2–4. Text and trans. by Bernadotte Perrin. Loeb ed. London and Cambridge, Mass., 1914–1916.

Pöhlig, C. "Der Athener Theramenes." *Jahrbücher für Klassische Philologie* suppl. IX (1877–1878), 227–320.
Pollitt, J. J. *Art and Experience in Classical Greece.* Cambridge, 1972.
Pouilloux, J. *Recherches sur l'histoire et les cultes de Thasos*, I. Paris, 1954.
Powell, C. A. "Religion and the Sicilian Expedition." *Historia* XXVIII (1979), 15–31.
Quinn, T. J. "Political Groups at Chios: 412." *Historia* XVIII (1969), 22–30.
———. *Athens and Samos, Lesbos and Chios.* Manchester, 1981.
Rahe, P. A. "Lysander and the Spartan Settlement, 407–403 B.C." Ph.D. diss. Yale University, 1977.
———. "The Selection of Ephors at Sparta." *Historia* XXIX (1980), 385–401.
Renaud, R. "Cléophon et la guerre du Péloponnèse." *LAC* XXXVIII (1970), 458–477.
Rhodes, P. J. *The Athenian Boule.* Oxford, 1972.
———. "The Five Thousand in the Athenian Revolution of 411 B.C." *JHS* XCII (1972), 115–127.
———. *A Commentary on the Aristotelian* Athenaion Politeia. Oxford, 1981.
———. "The Selection of Ephors at Sparta." *Historia* XXX (1981), 498–502.
Roberts, J. T. *Accountability in Athenian Government.* Madison, Wisc., 1982.
Ste. Croix, G. E. M. de. "The Character of the Athenian Empire." *Historia* III (1954–1955), 1–41.
———. "The Constitution of the Five Thousand." *Historia* V (1956), 1–23.
———. "Notes on Jurisdiction in the Athenian Empire." *CQ* LV - N. S. II (1961), 94–112, 268–280.
———. *The Origins of the Peloponnesian War.* Ithaca, N.Y., and London, 1972.
Salmon, J. B. *Wealthy Corinth.* Oxford, 1984.
Schaefer, H. "Probouloi." *PW* XLV (1957), 1222–1231.
Sealey, R. *Essays in Greek Politics.* New York, 1967.
———. "Pap. Mich. Inv. 5982: Theramenes." *ZPE* XVI (1975), 279–288.
———. "Die Spartanische Navarchie." *Klio* LVIII (1976), 335–358.
Smith, F. D. *Athenian Political Commissions.* Chicago, 1920.
Sommerstein, A. H. "Aristophanes and the Events of 411." *JHS* XCVII (1977), 112–126.
Stockton, D. L. "The Peace of Callias." *Historia* VIII (1959), 61–79.
Strauss, Barry S. "Division and Conquest: Athens, 403–386 B.C." Ph.D. diss., Yale University, 1979.
———. "Aegospotami Reexamined." *AJP* CIV (1983), 24–35.
Stroud, R. S. *Draco's Law on Homicide.* Berkeley, Calif., 1968.
Thomsen, R. *Eisphora.* Copenhagen, 1964.
Thucydide, La guerre du Péloponnèse, II. Text and trans. by J. de Romilly (Budé). Paris, 1962. VIII. Text and by R. Weil and J. de Romilly. Paris, 1972.
Thucydides. Text and trans. by Charles Forster Smith. Loeb ed., I–IV, London and Cambridge, Mass., 1919–1923.
Toynbee, A. *Some Problems of Greek History.* London, 1969.
Underhill, G. E. *A Commentary with Introduction and Appendix on the* Hellenica *of Xenophon.* Oxford, 1900.
Van de Maele, S. "Livre VIII de Thucydide et la politique de Sparte en Asie Mineure (412–411 av. J.C.)." *Phoenix* XXV (1971), 32–50.

Vlastos, G. "The Constitution of the Five Thousand." *AJP* LXXIII (1952), 189–198.

———. *"Isonomia politikē."* in J. May and E. G. Schmidt, eds., *Isonomia*. Berlin, 1964.

Wade-Gery, H. T. *Essays in Greek History*. Oxford, 1958.

Wallace, W. P. *The Euboean League and its Coinage*. Numismatic Notes and Monographs no. 134. New York, 1956.

Westlake, H. D. "Alcibiades, Agis and Spartan Policy." *JHS* LVIII (1938), 31–40.

———. "Phrynichus and Astyochus." *JHS* LXXVI (1956), 99–104.

———. *Individuals in Thucydides*. Cambridge, 1968.

———. "Athens and Amorges." *Phoenix* XXXI (1977), 319–329.

———. "Ionians in the Ionian War." *CQ* N. S. XXIX (1979), 9–44.

Wilamowitz-Moellendorf, U. von. *Aristoteles und Athen*. Berlin, 1893.

Will, E. "Notes sur les régimes politiques de Samos au Vᵉ siècle." *REA* LXXI (1969), 305–319.

———. *Le monde grec et l'orient, 1: Le Vᵉ siècle (510–403)*. Paris, 1972.

Woodhead, A. G. "Peisander." *AJP* LXXV (1954), 132–146.

———. *Thucydides on the Nature of Power*. Cambridge, Mass., 1970.

General Index

Abdera, 287
Abydos, 101, 102, 217, 218, 220, 227,
229–234, 237, 245, 249, 275, 276,
286, 287, 302, 352, 356, 378,
385; battle of, 231–233; chief
Spartan base in Hellespont, 218
Achaea Phthiotis, 27
Adeimantus, 28, 293, 314, 388, 390,.
392, 395
Aegean Sea, 13–16, 19, 27, 39, 41, 60,
62, 92, 112, 122, 138, 157, 166,
193, 212–228, 229, 249, 265,
293, 297, 300, 302, 308, 311,
319, 339, 376, 379, 384, 385,
396, 398, 419, 421
Aegina, 384, 394, 396
Aegospotami, battle of, 386–394, 396,
397, 399, 408, 409, 419, 420
Aeniania, 27
Agesandridas, 192, 198–201, 225, 227,
231, 283
Agesilaus, King of Sparta, 42, 299, 300
Agis, son of Archidamus, King of
Sparta, 14, 24, 32, 41, 54, 74, 86,
168, 181, 234, 291, 299, 300,
403; and Alcibiades, 42, 49, 71,
72; and Astyochus, 79; and the
Athenian Four Hundred, 165; attacks Athens, 167, 262–263, 321;
besieges Athens, 400; in Central
Greece, 25, 27; and Corinthians,
38; at Decelea, 13, 25, 28, 33, 39,
167, 247, 339; and Euboea, 28; at
Isthmus of Corinth, 36; and Lysan-

der, 300, 407; at Mantinea, 25;
meets Lysander in Attica, 384; rejects Athenian peace offer, 401; rejects peace terms from the Four
Hundred, 166
Alcamenes, 28, 36, 38, 39, 87
Alcibiades, 78, 86, 87, 91, 110, 117,
119–121, 131–134, 146, 150, 155,
163–165, 169, 170, 180, 183,
187, 188, 201, 210, 214, 234, 250,
252, 259, 262, 288, 301, 304, 307,
325, 326, 359, 371; abandoned by
Athenian oligarchs, 139; accused
of treason, 392; at Aegospotami,
388–390; and Agis, 42; at Andros,
308, 309; and Athenian politics,
324; at battle of Abydos, 232–233,
276; at battle of Cyzicus, 236–
246; and battle of Notium, 310–
320; at Bosporus, 277; at Byzantium, 282–284; and Chalcideus,
49, 54; at Chios, 45; cousin of Euryptolemus, 370; at Cyme, 320;
deposed as general, 322–323; and
Dorieus, 224; elected general at Samos, 178; and Endius, 33, 34, 41,
79, 248; at Ephesus, 312; evaluated as general 323–324; exiled in
Sparta, 4; and the Four Hundred
at Athens, 204; as general, 267; in
Hellespont, 265, 266, 285; and
Ionia, 35, 46, 47; judgment of,
419–420; at Miletus, 61, 63; and
Oligarchy, 112, 113; and Pharna-

433

Index of Ancient Authors

Aelian
    4.6: 406
    12.43: 298
Aeschines
  De Falsa Legatione
    (2).76: 249, 258, 401
Andocides
  Against Alcibiades
    (4).30: 35
  On the Mysteries
    (1).27: 118
    36: 118
    43: 118
    73–79: 400
    96: 204, 252, 254
    97–98: 252, 254
    142: 399
    (2).11: 7
  On the Peace
    (3).11: 163
    12: 410
    21: 399
    29: 20, 29, 30
    30–31: 30
Androtion
  frg.38 (*FGrH*): 6
    43: 43
    44: 248, 377
Antiphon
    2.11: 235
Aristides
    162.19: 325
    341: 406

Aristophanes
  Frogs
    404: 4
    534–541: 152
    693–694: 339
    720: 338
    967–970: 152
    1425: 324
  Lysistrata
    313: 208
    421: 147
    410–610: 5
    490–491: 132
    573–586: 9
    980–1012: 5
    1169–1170: 27
  Thesmophoriazusae
    804: 89
Aristotle
  Athenaion Politeia
    27: 264
    28: 153, 188, 258
    29: 144, 145, 148–150, 255
    30: 158, 160, 255
    31: 158, 159, 162, 255
    32: 157, 166
    33: 161, 202–204
    34: 153, 163, 202, 249, 252, 264, 353, 376, 378, 410
    44: 287
    48: 365

GHI (cont.)

70:	8
77:	30
85:	257
86:	256
89:	263, 287
91:	7, 235, 288
94:	398

Hellanicus

frg.25 (FGrH):	339
26:	338

Hellenica Oxyrhynchia

4:	315
4.1:	316
4.2:	317
4.3–4:	318
6.3:	248
7.4:	141, 164
12.4–5:	405

Herodotus

7.2:	295
9.28:	415

Himerius

36.16:	322

Homer

Iliad 2.188–278:	106

IG

i^2

71:	7
100:	57
105:	7
114:	254
115:	256
372–374:	260

ii^2

8:	20

Isocrates

14.31:	399
18.29:	399
18.61:	397

Justin

5.2:	73
5.4:	248
5.8:	399
5.9:	406

Lycurgus
Against Leocrates

113:	208

115:	208
124–127:	257

Lysias

12.36:	369
12.62–78:	152
12.65:	6
12.67:	207
12.68:	402
13.8:	401
13.9:	402
13.10:	369
13.11:	403
13.12–20:	411
13.13–16:	410
13.14:	402
13.47–48:	411
13.73:	207
13.84:	411
18.5:	411
19.42–48:	111
19.48:	250
19.52:	267
20.6:	198
20.11–12:	53, 123
20.13:	110, 158, 203
20.14:	198, 209
21.1–5:	111
21.7:	326
25.9:	53, 118
25.27:	400
30.2:	256
30.10–14:	411
32.24:	4
frg.120:	406

Marmor Parium

54.6
56.6

Nepos
Alcibiades (7)

1–2:	320
3:	119
5:	155, 206, 238, 248
6:	286
7:	322, 323
8:	386, 389, 390

Thrasybulus (8)

1:	246

Pausanias

3.8:	400

Index of Modern Authors

Library of Congress Cataloging-in-Publication Data

Kagan, Donald.
    The fall of the Athenian Empire.

    Bibliography: p.
    Includes index.
    1. Greece—History—Peloponnesian War, 431–404 B.C.
2. Athens (Greece)—History. I. Title.
DF229.37.K34 1987   938'.05   86-32946
ISBN 0-8014-1935-2 (alk. paper)